JE 2 0

ALSO BY THOMAS PENN

Winter King: Henry VII and the Dawn of Tudor England

THOMAS PENN

The Brothers York

A Royal Tragedy

Simon & Schuster
New York   London   Toronto   Sydney   New Delhi

SIMON & SCHUSTER
1230 Avenue of the Americas
New York, NY 10020

First Simon & Schuster hardcover edition June 2020

SIMON & SCHUSTER and colophon are registered trademarks of Simon & Schuster, Inc.

For information about special discounts for bulk purchases, please contact
Simon & Schuster Special Sales at 1-866-506-1949 or business@simonandschuster.com.

The Simon & Schuster Speakers Bureau can bring authors to your live event.
For more information or to book an event contact the Simon & Schuster Speakers Bureau
at 1-866-248-3049 or visit our website at www.simonspeakers.com.

Manufactured in the United States of America

1   3   5   7   9   10   8   6   4   2

Library of Congress Cataloging-in-Publication Data

Names: Penn, Thomas, author.
Title: The brothers York : a royal tragedy / Thomas Penn.
Description: First Simon & Schuster hardcover edition. | New York : Simon &
Schuster, 2020. | "Originally published in Great Britain in 2019 by
Penguin Random House UK." | Includes bibliographical references and
index.
Identifiers: LCCN 2019045050 | ISBN 9781451694178 | ISBN 9781451694192
(ebook)
Subjects: LCSH: Great Britain—History—Wars of the Roses, 1455-1485. |
York, House of. | Edward IV, King of England, 1442-1483. | Richard III,
King of England, 1452-1485. | Clarence, George, Duke of, 1449-1478.
Classification: LCC DA250 .P46 2020 | DDC 942.04—dc23
LC record available at https://lccn.loc.gov/2019045050

ISBN 978-1-4516-9417-8
ISBN 978-1-4516-9419-2 (ebook)

For my parents, Alan and Jessica

Three glorious suns, each one a perfect sun;
Not separated with the racking clouds,
But sever'd in a pale clear-shining sky.
See, see! they join, embrace, and seem to kiss,
As if they vow'd some league inviolable:
Now are they but one lamp, one light, one sun.
In this the heaven figures some event.

William Shakespeare, *Henry VI*, Part 3

These three brothers possessed such surpassing talent that, if they had been able to avoid conflict, their triple bond could have been broken only with the utmost difficulty.

Crowland Chronicle Continuations, c. 1486

Herein may be seen noble chivalry, courtesy, humanity, friendliness, hardiness, love, friendship, cowardice, murder, hate, virtue and sin.

William Caxton, Preface to Malory, *Morte d'Arthur,* 1485

Contents

1. England, 1455–85

areas of high land
battle site with dates

N

SCOTLAND

Berwick-upon-Tweed
Bamburgh
Hedgeley Dunstanburgh
Moot 1464 Alnwick

Anglo-Scottish
Marches

Newcastle

Carlisle 1464 Hexham
Durham

Richmond Scarborough
Middleham Sheriff Hutton
Lancaster York
Towton 1461 Hull Humber
Wakefield 1460 Pontefract Ravenspur
Doncaster

North
Sea

Isle of Man

Irish
Sea

Isle of Anglesey
Chester Lincoln

Nottingham The Wash

Harlech Blore Heath Losecote Field 1470 Lynn Walsingham
1459 Bosworth Stamford Norwich
Shrewsbury 1485 Leicester Fotheringhay East
Mortimer's Cross Coventry Midlands Cambridge Ely Anglia
1461 Ludlow Warwick Northampton Bury St Edmunds
Hereford 1460 Edgecote 1469 Ipswich
Carmarthen Tewkesbury 1471 Oxford
Milford Haven Gloucester St Albans 1455, 1462
Chepstow Barnet 1471
Pembroke Bristol Windsor LONDON
Bath Thames Canterbury
Salisbury Winchester Weald Sandwich
Southampton Dover
Exeter Poole
Weymouth Isle of Wight
Plymouth Dartmouth

Welsh Marches
Severn
Cotswolds

English Channel

Channel Islands

FRANCE

0   50   100 miles
0 50 100 150 km

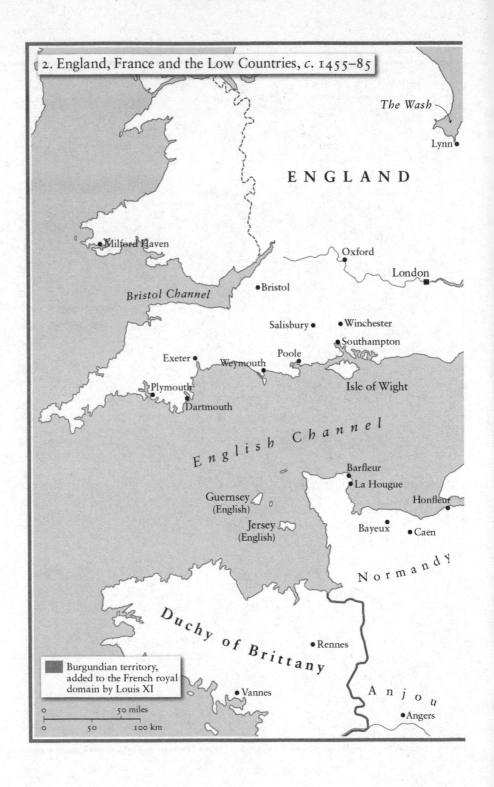

2. England, France and the Low Countries, *c.* 1455–85

The Wash

Lynn

ENGLAND

Milford Haven

Oxford

London

Bristol Channel

Bristol

Salisbury
Winchester
Southampton

Exeter
Weymouth
Poole

Plymouth
Dartmouth

Isle of Wight

English Channel

Barfleur
La Hougue

Honfleur

Guernsey
(English)

Jersey
(English)

Bayeux
Caen

Normandy

Duchy of Brittany

Rennes

Burgundian territory,
added to the French royal
domain by Louis XI

Vannes

Anjou

Angers

0   50 miles

0   50   100 km

N

North Sea

Frisian Islands

Texel

East
Anglia

Norwich

Alkmaar

H
o
l
l
a
n
d

Utrecht

Utrecht

Ipswich

The Hague

Z e e l a n d

Walcheren

Veere

Vlissingen   Middelburg

Rhine

Neuss

Canterbury

Sandwich

Sluis

Bruges

Antwerp

F l a n d e r s

Dover

Gravelines

Ghent

B
u
r
g
u
n
d
i
a
n

N
e
t
h
e
r
l
a
n
d
s

Aachen

Strait of Dover

Calais
(English)

Hammes

Guisnes

Scheldt

L
i
è
g
e

St Omer

Lille

Boulogne

A
r
t
o
i
s

Maas

Hesdin

St Pol

Arras

P
i
c
a
r
d
y

Peronne

Picquigny

Somme

Amiens

St Quentin

Rouen

Reims

Metz

Seine

Koeur

Nancy

Paris

Montlhéry

F R A N C E

Orléans

Loire

Duchy of
Burgundy

EDWARD III (*r.* 1327–77)
m. Philippa of Hainault

House of Lancaster

Edward Prince of Wales
a.k.a. the Black Prince
(*d.* 1376)

Lionel duke of Clarence *m.*
Elizabeth de Burgh

John of Gaunt, duke of Lancaster (*d.* 1399)
m. (1) Blanche of Lancaster *m.* (2) Constance, daughter of
Peter, King of Castile

RICHARD II (*r.* 1377–99)

Philippa *m.*
Edmund Mortimer
3rd earl of March

HENRY IV(*r.* 1399–1413)

Catherine *m.* Henry
III King of Castile

Roger Mortimer
4th earl of March (*d.* 1398)
m. Eleanor Holland

HENRY V (*r.* 1413–22) *m.* (1) Catherine, daughter of
Charles VI, King of France
m. (2) Owen Tudor
(executed 1461)

Edmund Mortimer
5th earl of March
(*d.* 1425)

Anne
Mortimer
(*d.* 1411)

= Richard earl
of Cambridge

HENRY VI (*r.* 1422–61, 1470–71)
m. Margaret of Anjou

HOUSE OF YORK
Richard Plantagenet
3rd duke of York (killed 1460)
m. Cecily Neville (*d.* 1495)

Edward
Prince of Wales
(killed 1471)

Jasper Tudor
earl of Pembroke
(*d.* 1495)

The Woodvilles
Richard Woodville *m.* Jacquetta of Luxembourg
1st earl Rivers
(executed 1469)

EDWARD IV *m.* Elizabeth *m.* Sir John Grey
(*r.* 1461–70,   (*d.* 1492)   (killed 1461)
1471–83)

Edmund
Earl of Rutland
(killed 1460)

Thomas Grey
marquis of Dorset
(*d.* 1501)

Sir Richard
Grey
(killed 1483)

House of Tudor

HENRY VII *m.* Elizabeth
(*r.* 1485–1509)   (*d.* 1503)

Edward V
(disappeared 1483)

Richard of Shrewsbury
duke of York
(disappeared 1483)

Cecily
m. John viscount
Welles

Princes in the Tower

Arthur Prince of Wales *m.* (1) Catherine of Aragon *m.* (2) Henry duke of York
(*d.* 1502)   (from 1509 HENRY VIII)

Margaret
m. JAMES IV King of Scotland

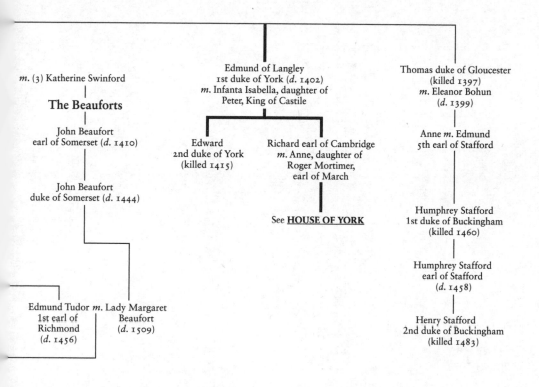

m. (3) Katherine Swinford

The Beauforts

John Beaufort
earl of Somerset (d. 1410)

John Beaufort
duke of Somerset (d. 1444)

Edmund Tudor m. Lady Margaret
1st earl of   Beaufort
Richmond   (d. 1509)
(d. 1456)

Edmund of Langley
1st duke of York (d. 1402)
m. Infanta Isabella, daughter of
Peter, King of Castile

Edward   Richard earl of Cambridge
2nd duke of York   m. Anne, daughter of
(killed 1415)   Roger Mortimer,
                      earl of March

See **HOUSE OF YORK**

Thomas duke of Gloucester
(killed 1397)
m. Eleanor Bohun
(d. 1399)

Anne m. Edmund
5th earl of Stafford

Humphrey Stafford
1st duke of Buckingham
(killed 1460)

Humphrey Stafford
earl of Stafford
(d. 1458)

Henry Stafford
2nd duke of Buckingham
(killed 1483)

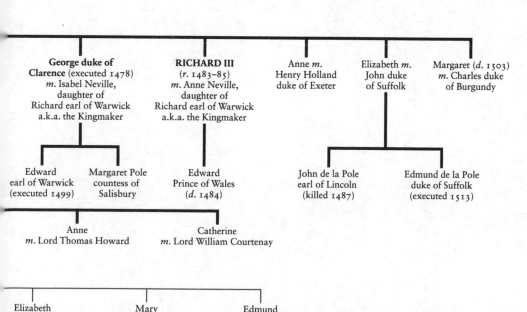

**George duke of
Clarence** (executed 1478)
m. Isabel Neville,
daughter of
Richard earl of Warwick
a.k.a. the Kingmaker

RICHARD III
(r. 1483–85)
m. Anne Neville,
daughter of
Richard earl of Warwick
a.k.a. the Kingmaker

Anne m.
Henry Holland
duke of Exeter

Elizabeth m.
John duke
of Suffolk

Margaret (d. 1503)
m. Charles duke
of Burgundy

Edward   Margaret Pole
earl of Warwick   countess of
(executed 1499)   Salisbury

Edward
Prince of Wales
(d. 1484)

John de la Pole
earl of Lincoln
(killed 1487)

Edmund de la Pole
duke of Suffolk
(executed 1513)

Anne
m. Lord Thomas Howard

Catherine
m. Lord William Courtenay

Elizabeth   Mary   Edmund
(d. 1495)   (d. 1500)

Note on the Text

I have modernized spellings throughout, including surnames: the family of Edward IV's queen is 'Woodville' rather than the variant 'Wydeville'. All quotations have likewise been silently modernised.

The medieval year started on 25 March; notwithstanding this, people celebrated New Year on 1 January. Dating here is in New Style, with the beginning of the year silently adjusted to 1 January.

Then, as now, the English system of money was based on pounds and pence. There, the similarities end. One pound (*liber*, abbreviated to *l.*) comprised 240 pennies (*denarii*, or *d.*). Other common values were the shilling (*solidus*, or *s.*), worth twelve pence, and the mark, worth two thirds of a pound or 160 pence. Edward IV's recoinage in 1465 introduced two new coins: the rose-noble or ryal (10s.); and the noble-angel, valued at 6s 8d.

The average yearly income for a knight was around £200; the minimum qualification for gentry status roughly £10 per annum. A skilled labourer could expect to receive anywhere between £6 and £9 per year; the day rate of an agricultural labourer was 4d. The website measuringworth provides a detailed approach to the knotty issue of ascribing modern monetary worth to historical currency values.

Introduction

During the mid-fifteenth century, England was crippled by civil war. The conflict dragged on for three decades and more, successive waves of violence engulfing the country before subsiding again, leaving behind a wreckage of mutual mistrust, suspicion and profound instability. This sequence of vendettas and turf wars became known as the Wars of the Roses: a struggle between the two royal houses of York and Lancaster, red rose against white, for the English crown. This was the story told by the Tudors, the leviathan of a dynasty that professed to unite these two warring houses. It was neater that way.

Yet for most of this period only one of these families dominated England: the house of York. The Yorkist kings – Edward IV, followed by his youngest brother Richard III – ruled the country for just under a quarter of a century, between 1461 and 1485. These years saw the civil wars change in nature. In 1461, the conflict was indisputably between two rival families, the usurping eighteen-year-old Edward taking the crown from the tremulous grasp of the Lancastrian king Henry VI. In the years that followed it began to turn inwards: a destructive chain of rebellion, deposition, vendetta, fratricide, usurpation and regicide, all originating within the house of York itself. The dynasty's end was brutal. It came on 22 August 1485 at Bosworth, with the killing of Richard III, the ritual humiliation of his battered body and his burial in an unmarked grave in a Leicester priory. But whatever the victorious Tudors later liked to say about Bosworth being the victory of the red rose over the white, the battle was also a settling of scores between two factions of the house of York: white on white.

At the heart of this was the relationship between three royal brothers: Edward IV; Richard duke of Gloucester, later Richard III; and, sandwiched between them, the middle brother George duke of Clarence, who wanted to be king but never was. Contemporaries acknowledged that these were three men of unusual gifts: shoulder to shoulder, they were practically invincible. Yet as one Yorkist insider put it in the aftermath of Bosworth, the three brothers could not avoid conflict with each other. This, he implied, was the tragic flaw in the Yorkist dynasty.

The rise and fall of the house of York remains one of the most seductive and contested stories in English history. By the usual dynastic standards, it was over in the blink of an eye, the Yorkists' twenty-four-year period in power lasting as long as their successor Henry VII's reign on its own. The three brothers themselves burned fiercely and died young: Edward at forty; Clarence at twenty-eight; and Richard still only thirty-two when he was killed at Bosworth. Yet the house of York did shake off its usurper origins to establish itself as England's undisputed ruling dynasty. In the process, it achieved a kind of greatness, restoring the monarchy's authority and reforming its finances, creating conditions for renewed peace and prosperity. This all happened under Edward IV's rule. A king of flawed, compulsive magnificence, his manifold excesses and contradictions provoked both admiration and disgust in contemporaries, and have often left historians struggling to reconcile them.

When Edward seized the throne, Clarence was eleven; Richard was eight. The civil turmoil in which the brothers grew up shaped the way they saw the world and their place in it. It was a time of acute insecurity, when political, social and legal norms were bent out of shape by warring protagonists for whom the system had long since ceased to work and who sensed, in its weaknesses, an opportunity to remould the world according to their desires. At times, the centre seemed unable to hold. Politicians urging unity and moderation watched aghast as factions tore at each other, all restraint set aside. This was a landscape littered by murders and executions enacted through fearful self-defence and hungry ambition, and justified with the merest skim of legal process. Speaking the language of populism and clamouring for reform, squabbling elites raised private armies and manipulated widespread public discontent to their own advantage, sparking insurgency and revolt against a battered political establishment. The system of hereditary monarchy itself seemed to teeter on the brink.

These outbreaks of bloody score-settling appalled contemporaries. In trying to make sense of the disorder people reached for the language of sickness, both in terms of explaining what had happened to politics and how it made them feel. Trying to survive in this failing, uncertain system was a matter of political agility, timing and luck – and, in the tangle of extended families and networks of affinity that bound England together, it was all too easy to make the wrong choices. Existing attachments and loyalties became more contingent, quickly dropped in favour of new friendships, only to be abandoned in turn.

All this was especially pronounced for the conflict's leading protagonists. Circumstances had thrust Edward, Clarence and Richard into a place of exceptional power and wealth. For all three brothers, the sense that they could lose it all at an instant was rarely absent. This sense of precariousness and possibility was, at times, overwhelming. It distorted their behaviour and decision-making, their views of the world and of each other.

This is a story that stretches across England and Wales: from London and Westminster, the country's financial and political heart, and the luxurious royal houses of the Thames valley to the north of the country, which it suited some to portray as a very different land – wilder, remote, pricklingly independent, heavily militarized. It moves beyond national boundaries: further north, to Scotland; across the English Channel, to the courts of France and its antagonistic ducal satellites Burgundy and Brittany; to the great entrepôts of Flanders, in whose counting houses, warehouses and ateliers the shockwaves of England's civil conflict made themselves felt; and to the offices of the Medici bank in Florence and the lobbies of the papal curia in Rome.

For if the Wars of the Roses were a domestic concern, fought on English soil, they were inextricably entangled with European affairs. The country's very relationship and attitude to northern Europe were slowly being reshaped. The doubtful glories of the Hundred Years War, with English kings seeking the crown of France, were fading from view; after centuries England was becoming once more an island nation. This was a state of affairs that the Yorkist kings were reluctant to acknowledge, as their entangled, often aggressive, constantly shifting relationships with their northern European neighbours – themselves in a state of flux – made all too clear. These relationships were to play an instrumental role in the house of York's downfall.

Other key players, of course, drove and defined this evolving conflict, among them Richard earl of Warwick, 'the kingmaker', the powerful, manipulative mentor to all three brothers; and Elizabeth Woodville, Edward IV's divisive queen, and her upwardly mobile family. Around them was an equally compelling supporting cast, from men like Edward's loyal friend William Hastings and his legal enforcer John Tiptoft, a man of cultured savagery, to the influential servants and officials, fixers and hangers-on who were the connective tissue of the Yorkist regime and who, ultimately, were involved in ripping it apart. This book portrays a world of household and court that, in its claustrophobic politicking, perhaps resembles the stifling world of the Yorkists' successor Henry Tudor more closely than historians have hitherto allowed.

In putting the three Yorkist brothers centre stage, this book casts the Wars of the Roses in a fresh light: as a conflict between two royal houses that, apparently resolved, in fact re-emerged as a sickness within the Yorkist family. It reassesses the brothers themselves: Edward IV, whose slow transformation from virile teenaged war-leader to bloated, avaricious tyrant – traits that, skipping a generation, found new form in his grandson Henry VIII – remains obscure in the public imagination; the simmering stew of self-entitlement and personal inadequacy that was George duke of Clarence; and Richard III. Richard's notorious reign, of course, needs no introduction. Yet by placing it in the context of his fraternal relationships, we can perhaps arrive at a sharper understanding of why Richard behaved and acted as he did; and to find, if not definitive answers to the controversial questions that hang around him, then at least a hint of smoke.

Appropriately for this disruptive, disrupted age, this is a story reconstructed from fragments. In the surviving written record – itself exceptionally uneven – these extraordinary historical characters are elusive, flickering presences. They are glimpsed in chronicle accounts and diplomats' reports; in the administrative and financial records of government and household; in letters and manifestos. Their ways of thinking are traced, too, through the books and political tracts that people read or absorbed second hand as they sought paths through these crisis-ridden years, clutching hold of ideas and ideals that, all too often, evaporated on their first contact with reality.

In exploring the brothers York and their mutually destructive relationship we can form a clearer sense of why such an ostensibly successful ruling house – and one that, unlike its successors the Tudors, produced in abundance that prerequisite for dynastic succession, legitimate male heirs – should have so suddenly and completely collapsed in on itself. In a consummate historical irony, it was an unlikely offshoot of the Lancastrian dynasty – the house the Yorkists had long since exterminated – that profited from its demise: Henry Tudor.

Surveying the corpse-strewn battlefield at Bosworth, Shakespeare's Tudor pronounces ruefully on the state of his new kingdom. 'England', he declares, 'hath long been mad, and scarr'd herself; The brother blindly shed the brother's blood.' The tragedy of the brothers York was that they destroyed themselves. This book explores how and why they did so.

PART ONE

Blood Royal

Winter 1461 – Summer 1464

'The king has had false counsel, for his lands are lost, his merchandise is lost, his commons destroyed, the sea is lost, France is lost ... He owes more than ever did king in England, and yet daily his traitors that be about him wait wherever thing should come to him by his law, and they ask it from him.'

Cade's manifesto, 1450

'I warn you everyone,
    for you should understand,
There sprang a rose in Rouen
    and spread into England.'

Yorkist verse on the Battle of Towton,
29 March 1461

'Necessity knows no law.'

Yorkist verses on the Battle of Northampton,
10 July 1460

I

Three Suns

On 2 February 1461, dawn broke clear and freezing over the Welsh Marches. At an obscure Herefordshire crossroads in the valley of the River Lugg an army was deploying in battle formation. Its commanders, whose land this was, had chosen their position well, their flanks protected by an escarpment on the right and, on their left, the river. Behind them, the valley narrowed. Ahead, it broadened into meadow, the Roman road slicing through the frost-encrusted plain. Along that road, from the south, their enemies were coming.

As scouts rode in with updates on the advancing forces, the troops went deliberately through their preparations: knights and infantrymen buckled on armour, swords and daggers; archers in their padded, steel-reinforced jackets strung longbows, staking out arrows in the ground ready for rapid fire. Then, at around ten in the morning, unease swept through the ranks. Either side of the low sun two illusory suns appeared: men looked skywards, aghast. The three suns – an effect of light refracting on drifting ice crystals – climbed higher, drawing closer, their light blinding; finally they resolved, merging into one. As captains tried to restore focus and discipline among the frantic soldiers, their leader, a giant eighteen-year-old, knelt and thanked God; then, getting to his feet, he addressed his men.

If Edward earl of March was scared, he hid it well. Some three months before, at a parliament in Westminster, his father Richard duke of York had been named heir to the throne of England, governing in the name of the incapable Lancastrian king Henry VI. But by Christmas Richard was dead, ambushed near Wakefield on his south Yorkshire estates by vengeful Lancastrian noblemen. The news of his father's killing had reached Edward as he recruited soldiers in the Welsh Marches, too late, too distant to go to his aid. Now, marching towards Edward was an army of Welshmen, bolstered by French and Breton mercenaries, led by a diehard Lancastrian: Henry VI's half-brother Jasper Tudor, earl of Pembroke.

The two royal houses of Lancaster and York were at war. With his father's death, Edward became heir to the house of York; still, his situation was bleak. He was a teenager who had never led an army. Nonetheless there was something about him that was irresistible; his certainty that cold winter morning, faced by his own frightened troops, was total.

The Marches, the patchwork of fiefdoms that bordered England and Wales, was Edward's land. Intimately familiar with the surrounding country, the fortress-studded hills of his youth, he had grown up among the men whose loyalties he now commanded, their affinity to the house of York hardened in the turf wars of recent years – many of which had been fought against Henry VI's relatives. A few miles to the north of Edward's army was Wigmore Castle, the eagles' nest from which his forebears, the Mortimer earls of March, had ruled the surrounding lands since time out of mind.

Royal blood ran in the Mortimers' veins: blood which, if their family tree was to be believed, flowed from Cadwaladr, the great king of British prehistory, through the peerless Edward III to Richard of York and his heirs. But sixty years previously, that line had been usurped. When Henry IV deposed Richard II in 1399, he became the first king of the house of Lancaster. Henry IV's claim to the crown – stemming from Edward III's third son through the male line of descent – appeared robust enough; and, indeed, served to establish the Lancastrian dynasty. But his was not the only claim nor, as some believed, the best. If you traced another line, from Edward III's second son – through the women, this time, rather than the men – you came to Anne Mortimer and her son Richard duke of York. This claim made the Lancastrian kings uneasy. They tried both to explain it away – the presence of women in the direct line of succession, Lancastrian lawyers argued, invalidated it – and to airbrush it from history, omitting the line from their genealogies. Despite their efforts, the idea of Mortimer had lingered: an ancient, imperishable right.[1] The Yorkist Edward was the family's latest hope and, on that unbearably bright winter morning, even the name of the muddy crossroads at which he now awaited Jasper Tudor's army seemed freighted with significance: Mortimer's Cross.[2]

Once the fighting started, Edward's Marcher men – hard, experienced, in familiar territory, led by the eighteen-year-old who tore with terrifying aggression into the enemy ranks – massacred Jasper Tudor's forces. The battle gave birth to a new myth: of a young noble warrior who, asking for a sign from God, received it in the form of three suns symbolizing the Holy Trinity, and whose God-given victory transformed him into England's king-in-waiting, his inevitable succession long foretold by prophecy. In its aftermath, Edward adopted a new emblem. Taking his father's badge, the white rose, and an emblem of his illustrious forebear Edward III, a sun bursting through cloud, he combined them. From that point on, the badge that his men wore – pinned or sewn into their jackets, on armbands round their biceps – was a sun in splendour, golden sunbeams streaming out from the white rose of York.[3]

Myth-making aside, the fact remained that the incumbent king, Henry VI, was still very much alive. In pressing his claim, Edward looked to many like a young nobleman simply chancing his arm. In the previous months, moreover, any pretence that England's warring factions might somehow be brought together by an appeal to national unity had evaporated. On the other side of England, the main Lancastrian army, having massacred Richard of York and his men, was moving south at speed, pillaging and plundering, towards an exposed London. In the city were Edward's mother, three sisters and two younger brothers, George and Richard, both still children. If Edward were to prevail, he would need all the fortune that had accompanied him at Mortimer's Cross and more. He would also have to prove to England that he was rather different from his father.

Edward was eight years old and living in Ludlow when in September 1450 his father, returning from a tour of duty as the king's lieutenant in the restive province of Ireland, made landfall on the north coast of Wales. It had been a terrible year for England. During the preceding few decades the bankrupt, broken regime of Henry VI had lurched from one disaster to another. War had proved a massive drain on royal resources, exacerbated by a deepening Europe-wide recession, and Henry had proved an appalling monarch, his vague extravagance a gift to the grasping courtiers that clustered around him. The king's bloated, chaotic, fiscally incompetent household had become a symbol of all that was rotten about the regime, his servants lining their pockets even as trade dried up and revenues dwindled. Throughout the country, civil unrest started to spread.

Across the Channel, things were even worse. Thirty years previously the king's warrior father, Henry V, had conquered swathes of northern France, including Paris, and had claimed the French crown that English kings believed was rightfully theirs. It was a remarkable but fleeting achievement. Soon after, dysentery had killed Henry V. In the following decades a resurgent France regained much of its lost territory, leaving only Normandy in English hands, a colony that provided rich pickings for the country's elites. Nobody was prepared for its capitulation. But in 1449, in the face of a new French offensive, the response of Henry VI's government was incoherent and disastrous. English rule in Normandy collapsed, demoralized garrisons falling like dominoes. Still only twenty-eight years old, Henry VI was proving not just a shadow of his father, but his negation.

Across the country, people struggling to make a living – from the propertied gentry to smallholders and labourers – were sick of a ruling class that had become a byword for venality and corruption: frittering away taxpayers' money; incapable of dealing with the slow collapse in public order; indifferent to even the most modest proposals for reform; ineffective and disunited in every respect – except, apparently, when it came to preserving their own vested interests. The 'common voice' of this increasingly literate and politically conscious public was growing louder. In manifestos and the darkly allusive language of prophecy, it called in the name of the king's 'true liege men' for the removal and punishment of the 'untrue' councillors who had led their sovereign astray, and for financial and political reform. It was a message that England's great noblemen, officers of state and royal household – men in whom 'the might of the land' rested, their own economic and political privileges enmeshed in this dysfunctional system – chose to ignore. In the spring of 1450, as French privateers raided England's coasts, the discontent exploded.[4]

Led by a man named Jack Cade, southeast England rose in revolt. The Kentish commons surged towards London and, as the king and his court fled into the midlands, trashed the city. The insurgency had barely been suppressed and Cade executed when, in August, a ragged English army returned from France, marching through London's gates. Days later, refugees started to arrive from England's lost territories in Normandy: a stream of men, women and children, carts heaped with armour, bedding, household goods and whatever families had been able to seize as they fled their homes ahead of the marauding French – 'piteous to see', noted one onlooker grimly. During these long, disastrous months, Richard of York had been absent from England but not, it seemed, from people's minds.

News of York's sudden return from Ireland in September 1450 panicked the government. During the recent troubles, royal agents had heard 'much strange language' about him, and the insurgents' list of demands had included a call for Henry to put York, a great nobleman unjustly shouldered aside by the king's evil councillors, in charge of his government. York would put things straight, they argued, because he was 'the true blood of the realm': untainted both by association with Henry VI's disastrous government, or – so the implication went – by Lancastrian blood.[5]

For the first thirty-nine years of his life, York had proved a dutiful subject to the Lancastrian kings. He was orphaned by the age of four – his mother dead through illness; his father executed for a plot to seize power – and was brought up a royal ward in a securely Lancastrian environment. The marriage arranged for him bound him even more tightly to the regime: his wife Cecily's family, the Nevilles, were a powerful northern clan with solid Lancastrian connections.[6] He was appointed regent of France, where his vast hereditary power and wealth were directed to shoring up England's crumbling overseas dominions and to carrying the fight to the resurgent French.

Richard and Cecily had endured 'long barrenness' early in their marriage, but their move to France proved fruitful. Though Richard spent long stretches at the front on campaign, much of the time he was within a day's ride of the great Norman city of Rouen, the capital of England's French territories, and the couple found enough opportunity to be together. There, Cecily gave birth to three children, two boys and a daughter, in quick succession. The first arrived in the early hours of 28 April 1442 and was named Edward, like his illustrious ancestor Edward III. Edward's christening was apparently low-key, yet there was no doubting his parents' relief, pride and ambition for their son and heir. By the time Edward was three years old, his father was in talks to marry him to one of the king of France's daughters. By the end of the year, however, Richard had been recalled to England.[7]

Back home, though he continued to receive a steady trickle of royal favour, he wasn't especially close to Henry VI. Despite Henry's marriage in 1445 to the fifteen-year-old French aristocrat Margaret of Anjou, the king, who had a saintly horror of sex, remained childless. As time went on, the extended Lancastrian family pressed ever more tightly around the hapless monarch. Foremost among them were his Beaufort relatives, descendants of the dynasty's founder, John of Gaunt, and his mistress Katherine Swynford; although subsequently legitimated, the family had, as its detractors liked to point out, been barred from the throne. The Beauforts gobbled up the fruits of royal favour and, in 1447, destroyed the king's de facto heir, his uncle Humphrey duke of Gloucester. Gloucester's death marked a shift in the political landscape. The role of royal heir now passed, unofficially but tangibly, to England's greatest nobleman of royal – though not of Lancastrian – blood, Richard of York. Richard, though, kept his head down, and in July 1449 took up the post of lieutenant of Ireland. In Dublin on 21 October, Cecily gave birth to another son, George.[8]

Like the rest of England, York had been aghast at the loss of Normandy. He had maintained extensive interests and responsibilities there and had grown deeply sceptical of his successor as regent, the king's cousin Edmund Beaufort, duke of Somerset. York himself had an unbending sense of duty and honour: as he wrote fiercely to his brother-in-law that summer, he 'dreaded shame' and would rather die than lose control of a precarious Ireland. Somerset's behaviour in Normandy, York felt, had been unchivalrous, bordering on treasonable, particularly in his ignominious surrender of York's beloved Rouen. Yet following Somerset's inglorious return home – it had been Somerset's dishevelled troops that straggled into London that summer – he had, to York's horror, been instantly rewarded for his failure with a place at the heart of the political establishment, as the king's chief minister.[9]

All York would say, that September of 1450, was that his return from Ireland had been prompted by 'very necessity': with disturbances escalating there, the government had failed to respond to his increasingly urgent demands for military aid and York was anxious about being held accountable for the disorder. He was, though, concerned about his own place in Somerset's new administration, wanting to be at the centre of things as the regime teetered on the brink, to see what happened. Landing in north Wales and dodging an attempt to arrest him, he headed south to London.[10]

The prevailing language of political reform gave shape to York's ambitions, and his alignment with the cause of the people that summer allowed him to believe his own rhetoric. In London, he issued a succession of public manifestos demanding 'due reformation' of government, at the same time stressing his loyalty to Henry VI's regime: his concern was purely for the 'surety and prosperity' of the king and the 'welfare' of England. Like a character from a book in his own library, the Roman general Stilicho, York convinced himself of his destiny as a reforming hero, moulding the people's calls for change into his own political programme. By sweeping away the 'traitors' who had led England astray – foremost among them Somerset, the man he loathed – York could take up that position at the head of government to which the rightness of his cause and the purity of his royal blood entitled him. Soon, he had harnessed the people's bitter discontent. York, reported one correspondent, 'desired much thing, which is much after the commons' desire'. And, he added, 'all the king's household was, and is, afeared right sore'.[11]

An anxious government expected violence. That November, as Westminster's streets and lanes crawled with royal troops, a restive Parliament took up York's demands. As Somerset's apartments at Blackfriars were looted – York's supporters, it was said, urged on an enraged crowd – Somerset himself was hustled to the safety of the Tower and locked up. But in the face of the Commons' attempts to push through wide-ranging reforms, the regime closed ranks, swamping proposed legislation in amendments and obfuscation. While England's establishment might have accepted the odd policy gesture,

9

sweeping and destabilizing change was not what they had in mind. Besides which, there was something about Richard – the sense of high-minded public morality, perhaps, in which he cloaked his personal ambitions – that made them bristle. Their suspicions over York's ultimate aims only intensified when Thomas Younge, an MP in the duke's pay, tried to push a bill through Parliament formally recognizing York as the king's heir presumptive. It didn't succeed. The government closed ranks and, as the popular protests ran out of steam, wrestled back the initiative. Henry VI released Somerset from the Tower.[12]

In the months that followed, York found himself out in the cold. At the king's shoulder, a vengeful Somerset enforced royal authority, made a tentative stab at financial reform, and went after York's key followers. Early in 1452 York made another, more desperate, bid to prise Somerset away from the king. Issuing manifestos and raising men, he was confronted at the Kentish town of Dartford by the combined armies of the lords, then brought to London and forced to make a humiliatingly public pledge of allegiance to Henry in St Paul's Cathedral before being set at liberty. York's release was apparently hastened by the fleeting news that, at barely ten years old, his son and heir Edward earl of March was marching to his aid with a 'great posse' of ten thousand Welshmen. In fact, Edward had not moved from Ludlow in the Marches where, at seven years old – the age when noble children left the female world of the nursery and started their formal education – he had been set up with his own household and council, along with his brother Edmund, just a year younger.[13]

For York, there now seemed little way back into favour. His predicament was exacerbated by his growing family, a further cause for alarm in a Lancastrian regime without an heir. On 2 October 1452, at his family's Northamptonshire home of Fotheringhay, his fourth son was born, named Richard after his father. York himself was not with Cecily at the birth; rather, the picture of a newly dutiful subject, he was slogging round the legal circuit, handing down the king's justice at the Oxfordshire town of Thame.

The following January, he carefully sent the customary New Year's gifts to the royal family which, finally, was also in the process of expanding. Early in 1453, Margaret of Anjou announced that she was pregnant, to general surprise. That spring, Cecily wrote to Queen Margaret; expressing joy at Margaret's pregnancy, she then described her husband's 'infinite sorrow' and 'unrest of heart' at being 'estranged' from the king. She begged Margaret to talk with Henry about York's possible restoration to favour.[14] His prospects, though, looked more remote than ever. Summer came, and little changed.

Then, on Tuesday, 17 July 1453, in southwest France, thirty miles east of Bordeaux at the town of Castillon, English forces were anni-hilated by an advancing French army. The English kings had held Gascony for almost three hundred years, and suddenly it was gone. With the exception of the prized enclave of Calais, England was solely an island nation – and a vulnerable one at that. It was all too much for Henry VI.

That August the king suffered a 'sudden and unexpected fright' and fell into a catatonic stupor, unresponsive to all external stimuli. Throughout history, English kings had had their physical and mental weaknesses, but never before had a monarch, as it was now said, been so bereft of 'natural sense or intelligence' that he was unable to rule.[15]

With the king's mental crisis came renewed insecurity. Noblemen throughout England, wary of what was to come, recruited armed men, distributing their badges and liveries and handing out cash payments. In the north, the mutual and long-standing hatred between the two great regional families of Neville and Percy threatened open war. Unity among England's lords was vital to maintaining order and some semblance of effective government. As the greatest of those lords, Richard of York seized his opportunity.[16]

Dusting off his reforming agenda, in the winter of 1453 he seized control of the royal council, had Somerset locked in the Tower, and prepared to make his pre-eminence permanent. Alongside him in London – no rumour now but a solid presence – was the twelve-year-old Edward earl of March and two noblemen whose support had transformed York's prospects: his brother-in-law Richard earl of Salisbury, head of the powerful Neville family, and Salisbury's oldest son, the twenty-five-year-old Richard Neville, earl of Warwick. An exceptionally wealthy man of ruthless political instincts, Warwick had clashed violently with Somerset over some Welsh estates that formed part of his vast inheritance. He didn't like Somerset. Backing York made sense.

With Neville support, Richard of York acquired a new potency as the leader of a power bloc. Still, that January, as Parliament gathered to decide how England should be ruled, he faced a formidable new opponent: Henry's queen and Somerset's ally, Margaret of Anjou. Margaret had given birth to a baby boy. Now, as queen and mother to the Lancastrian heir, she issued a manifesto of her own, demanding 'the whole rule of the land', a parliamentary mandate to wield power on behalf of her insensate husband and their young son.[17]

But while there were French precedents for a regency of the kind Margaret sought, England – as political theorists never ceased to point out – was not France. In England, when the king was for whatever reason unable to rule in person, the tried-and-tested model of government was the one that had been used during the minority of Henry VI himself: a unified council of lords, acting collectively on behalf of the king and country, headed by a 'chief councillor and protector'. The obvious candidate was Richard of York.

Behind the closed doors of the council chamber, the atmosphere was palpably hesitant. The council's most urgent task was to balance the differing interests and demands of its two most vocal factions – one led by York, one clustering around Somerset and Queen Margaret – and to make sure their mutual hostility was kept in check. Handing a great nobleman the powers of a protector was always a dangerous move, especially so given the existence of an adult king and a queen who had made her antipathy to York all too clear. So, while York's appointment was made, it was done reluctantly and hedged about with conditions to limit his power. When York and his allies came to form a governing council, many noblemen, unwilling to appear partisan, were suddenly reluctant to get involved. Some remembered pressing business elsewhere; others reported sudden and incapacitating illness. There was no getting away from the fact that few were enthusiastic about the solution, and about York himself – but, given the state of emergency that now gripped England, he was the least-worst option.[18]

*

Throughout 1454, York worked hard to get a grip on the twin problems of national security and internal disorder. His supporters felt he
governed England 'nobly and in the best way'; his detractors saw
government by a faction for a faction, a stitching-up of vested interests. As he tackled what was by now open conflict in the north
between the Neville and Percy clans – favouring, naturally, his Neville partners in government – York kept his two eldest sons in Ludlow
up to date with news. In Easter Week, Edward and Edmund wrote
thanking him for his latest dispatch. Amid demands for some 'fine
bonnets' to go with the green gowns their father had sent them,
and complaints about bullying by a pair of older boys being brought
up in their household, they offered their heartfelt hopes and prayers
that York would prevail against 'the malice of your evilwillers'.[19]

Yet by the end of the year, York's official role was redundant. After
sixteen vacant months, Henry VI woke from his trance on Christmas
Day, apparently fully recovered. York and the Nevilles were stripped
of their authority. In their place Somerset, released from his incarceration, took up where he had left off at the head of government, the
political clocks reset to the time before the king's illness. As an Italian
merchant writing from London remarked, matter-of-factly, Somerset
'ruled as usual'. Quite what part the supposedly functioning Henry
played was unclear: not much, was the merchant's implication.[20]

In mid-April 1455 Somerset's restored government summoned a
great council, a meeting of all England's nobility, to Leicester; its
purpose, ostensibly, was to make arrangements for the 'surety of the
king's person'. To York and his allies, the agenda looked more like a
menacing settling of scores. Heading first into Yorkshire to gather
troops, they returned south at speed, stressing in a letter how – for
the avoidance of 'doubts and ambiguities' – the three thousand armed
men at their backs were a purely defensive measure, insurance against
Somerset's aggression. Making their leisurely preparations for the
journey to Leicester, the king and his advisers were caught out.

Up to this point, the simmering hostility between the two factions
had just about been contained. Now, with no political resolution
forthcoming, conflict seemed inevitable. Scrambling to mobilize troops,
Somerset and his allies, the king in their midst, advanced cautiously
out of London. York was marching through Hertfordshire when his

outriders spotted the royal army near the abbey town of St Albans. He changed direction to meet it.[21]

Early on the morning of 22 May, the king's forces moved into St Albans and secured the town, barricading and fortifying its approach roads. A stream of heralds and envoys shuttled between the two sides. The king himself – his authority desperately needed to calm an explosive situation – was nowhere to be seen. In fact, York and his allies got the impression that Henry wasn't being shown their letters at all. In response to a peremptory order to disperse, the Yorkists were blunt. They would 'redress the mischief that now reigneth', or they would die trying.[22]

The two armies that now faced each other across the heavily defended streets and lanes of St Albans bore the signs of their recent and hasty recruitment. Groups of armed men wore badges and colours indicating their allegiance, 'so that every man might know his own fellowship by his livery'.[23] At about 10 a.m. Yorkist archers, deployed to the northeast of St Albans, started to advance cautiously along the narrow, barricaded lanes into the town. Encountering resistance, they were forced back. It was at this point that Richard Neville, earl of Warwick, made an audacious move. Skirting the town's perimeter, he led his troops across an undefended part of the city ditch and, scrambling through gardens, closes, houses and inns, attacked the densely packed royal forces at the southern end of the marketplace, a cacophony of blaring trumpets and war cries adding to the confusion. As the royal ranks disintegrated, the Yorkists hunted down their enemies. Henry Percy, earl of Northumberland, the Nevilles' great rival in the northeast, was killed as he tried to make his way to a nearby inn where Somerset was holed up. Deciding to take his chances, Somerset tried to hack his way out before being butchered himself with axe blows. Henry VI was found sheltering in a nearby tanner's, bewildered, his neck bleeding from an arrow wound.

With the king in their hands, and their opponents either dead or captured, York and the Nevilles followed up their victory with a display of conspicuous loyalty to the monarch they now controlled. Back in London, Henry's authority was dramatized in a ceremonial crown-wearing at St Paul's, York himself placing the crown on the king's head.[24] That summer of 1455, the loose ends were swept up. In

Westminster, the streets thick with Yorkist troops, a compliant Parliament extended sweeping pardons to York and his backers for their actions at St Albans – which, seen in another light, had been tantamount to treason, an attack on the king – and placed their loyalty on parliamentary record. With blame for the conflict dumped emphatically at the door of the dead Somerset, the issue of St Albans was firmly closed: 'nothing done there never after this time to be spoken of'.[25]

As York and the Nevilles resumed control of government, Henry was reportedly 'sick again'. He seemed to inhabit a sort of mental twilight: *compos mentis* for stretches but listless, the business of ruling apparently well beyond his capacities. York was once more made protector.[26]

This time, his ambitions were more fully evident. The central plank of his planned fiscal reforms was a far-reaching parliamentary act of resumption. This was the process by which the king clawed back, or 'resumed', royal grants of land and office from their recipients, thereby providing him with an income-generating property portfolio: lands which, judiciously managed by his disinterested councillors, would allow him to fund the royal household without making excessive financial demands of his resentful subjects. A move constantly advocated by political theorists, it was far more difficult in practice than on paper. Great landowners were alarmed by a move that threatened their own fortunes and interests. Their consternation was given a further edge by a new Yorkist genealogy doing the rounds in which the superior descent of the family's Mortimer forebears was conspicuously reinstated, underscoring York's royal bloodline.[27]

Establishment anxieties over the act of resumption gave York's opponents a new window of opportunity. In the months following St Albans, Queen Margaret who was 'strong laboured', constantly lobbied, by the alarmed elites became the focus of resistance to both York's reforms and his efforts to consolidate his power and authority. In February 1456 Henry VI was brought into Parliament and, surrounded by 'almost all the lords', set about obstructing the act of resumption. Isolated, York resigned his protectorate on the spot.[28]

With Henry VI manipulated by both sides, England's political community looked on appalled. York and Margaret were apparently irreconcilable, the reciprocal loathing of their two factions infused with spilt blood. Opposing York and the Nevilles, and clustering round the queen, were the sons of those who had been slaughtered at St Albans. Chief among these was the new duke of Somerset, Henry Beaufort, who had seen his father killed and, an aggressive and charismatic twenty-year-old, had scores to settle.

During the months that followed, both sides settled into a phoney war. In mid-1456 Margaret of Anjou and her toddler son left a volatile London for her powerbase, the great duchy of Lancaster estates in the midlands, where she was joined soon after by her feeble husband and increasing numbers of England's nobles. York stayed in his Yorkshire heartlands, watching for her next move. As their proxies fought a vicious turf war in southwest Wales, the Yorkist Sir William Herbert detained the king's half-brother Edmund Tudor, earl of Richmond, who then died soon after his release, leaving his thirteen-year-old wife, Lady Margaret Beaufort, six months pregnant and frantic with worry.[29]

Margaret of Anjou's influence, meanwhile, was growing. When she attended a great council meeting in Coventry in the spring of 1457, one observer noted, surprised, how the civic authorities attended on her 'like as they before time did before the king'. But she was also high-handed and dismissive and, as she built a new regime in the midlands, existing governmental structures began to collapse. Sensing anarchy at the regime's heart, England's traditional enemies – the Scots and the French – probed the country's flimsy defences. No community felt more anxious, more disillusioned about the lack of national security than England's financial elites, who had extended credit hand over fist to the regime. London's oligarchs, shaken by a succession of riots in the capital, were concerned about the 'great navies' of France that menaced England's export trade; so too were the wool merchants of Calais, whose wealth underwrote the security of this precious English enclave on the north-eastern French coast.

The Yorkists subtly recalibrated. Now, their message of populism and unity was shot through with another kind of appeal. Where Margaret had been deaf to the concerns of big business, the Yorkists lent a sympathetic ear, providing quiet assurances on security and on trade. Nobody was more receptive, more smoothly reassuring, than the man whose appointment as captain of Calais York had managed to push through during his second protectorate, and who now remained in charge of the garrison there – Richard Neville, earl of Warwick. The Calais merchants threw their support behind him.[30]

Early on the morning of 28 August 1457, national anxieties were catalysed. A French fleet materialized off the Kentish port of Sandwich and disgorged a large raiding force, which overwhelmed the town's defences and went on the rampage, killing, burning and looting. Even to a region inured to French raids, the sack of Sandwich was shocking. The French 'went again unpunished', noted one commentator through gritted teeth. The regime appeared unable to protect its merchants, its own people, England itself.

This was a turning point. In March 1458, amid renewed calls for unity and for the two feuding factions to come together and 'be friends to each other and obedient to the king', London played host to a loveday, a negotiated arbitration that, so it was hoped, would 'eradicate the roots of rancour' and achieve a final peace. As the lords arrived in the capital with their private armies, thousands strong, the authorities tried desperately to prevent an armed standoff in the city's streets. The two groups were kept apart: walls and gates under heavy guard, curfews imposed, squads of urban militiamen on patrol.

Yet the talks, held at Westminster Palace in the wavering presence of the king, progressed with relatively little incident, and after a week, on the morning of Friday the 25th, church bells rang across the city. Crowds crammed into the cavernous interior of St Paul's to give thanks and to watch the reconciliation being acted out. The date was no accident; it was Lady Day, the Feast of the Annunciation of the Virgin Mary, and the first day of the new year, pregnant with associations of renewal and rebirth after the winter darkness. Behind a crowned Henry VI came Richard and Margaret of Anjou, hands clasped and 'lovely countenance' between them – even if, to those who looked closely, the smiles were fixed, the 'great familiarity' forced. In the margin alongside his account of events, one chronicler wrote tersely, 'Concordia ficta': 'False friendship'.

Almost three years had passed since the bloodshed at St Albans. Yet the arbitration was based on an inbuilt assumption of Yorkist guilt and

Lancastrian innocence, the Yorkists bound to future obedience. More-over, in treating the problem as a series of private quarrels, the settlement ignored the wider issue of great public concern that had cast a long shadow over the country: of how to hold government together when the king was clearly incapable of ruling. Despite desperate attempts to bring together the two warring sides, no solution had been found, and this weakness ran through the loveday like a stress fracture. Rather than an incontestable display of impartial royal authority, it was a settlement made by a king squarely in the control of Queen Margaret and her attendant noblemen; obedience to the king, the aggrieved Yorkists felt, meant bending the knee to the faction who controlled him. Rather than addressing the 'roots of rancour', the accord was a fudge. As one com-mentator put it, 'it endured not long'.[31]

The signs of fresh Yorkist self-assertion were soon evident. From his base in Calais, the earl of Warwick started to establish closer rela-tions with the ruler of the surrounding lands, Philip duke of Burgundy, whose dominions encompassed the Low Countries, northern Europe's industrial and financial powerhouse.[32] If such unilateral diplomacy irritated Queen Margaret, who was close to Burgundy's antagonistic neighbour and overlord, the French king Charles VII, so too did Warwick's other initiative. That summer, he addressed the piracy that plagued the eastern reaches of the Channel – by joining in. From May to September, his ships attacked and overwhelmed fleets irre-spective of nationality, provoking international incidents with England's key trading partners, from Genoa to the powerful Hanseatic League of Baltic states, and – inevitably – with France. If the government could not defend England and its interests, it seemed the Yorkists would do so. Warwick's privateering made his reputation – a 'famous knight', people said – and made him and the Calais garrison, their wages perpetually in arrears, a tidy and morale-boosting profit into the bargain.[33]

Meanwhile, there were growing whispers about Margaret herself: the corruption of her household, her plans to depose her husband and install her son – who, people speculated, was not even the king's – in his place. The source of these venomous rumours, Margaret suspected, was Warwick who, even more than York, was rapidly becoming the

regime's biggest headache. That autumn, years of sporadic harass-
ment against the Yorkist lords came to a head. In the latest of a string
of assassination attempts, a pack of household servants, knives
drawn, tried to corner Warwick as he left a council meeting in Westminster Palace. His men pressed around him, hustling him out across
the Palace Yard and onto his waiting barge on the Thames. He left
for Calais immediately. Once there, he sat tight.[34]

In June 1459, at a meeting of the great council in Coventry, everything finally reached crisis point. With the leading Yorkists and a
number of their supporters absent – uninvited, or failing to turn up –
Margaret accused them of treason. The council accepted the charges.
News of the meeting soon reached York and Salisbury, hunkered down
on their estates in the Welsh Marches and Yorkshire, and Warwick,
away in Calais. As they had done four years previously prior to St
Albans, the Yorkist lords sought a meeting with Henry VI to clarify
their position. And, just as before, they brought their combined 'fellowship' of armed retinues – for their own security, naturally.[35]

Late in September, they managed to rendezvous at Worcester. While
Warwick, crossing the Channel with the Calais garrison, dodged a
Lancastrian ambush, his father Salisbury almost ran straight into
one. As he marched across Blore Heath in Staffordshire his scouts,
scouring the countryside, glimpsed banners badly concealed behind a
'great hedge'. Abruptly taking up a defensive position, the earl watched
as the waiting Lancastrian army emerged, at some ten thousand men
it was twice as large as his own. Pretending to retreat, the experienced Salisbury suckered the Lancastrians into charging across the
steep-banked brook that separated the two forces, then mowed them
down in a hail of arrowfire.

In Worcester Cathedral, the three lords signed a letter to the king,
protesting their loyalty and asking for dialogue. It was met with a
counter-offer of a royal pardon – excluding Salisbury, whose fighting
against royal forces at Blore Heath automatically triggered charges of
treason – provided the lords submitted to Henry VI in person, within
six days. They refused.

Pursued by the royal army, the Yorkists reached Ludlow on 10
October. As they put it in a defiant letter to Henry VI, those around
the king had, 'out of extreme malice' and in order to get their

hands on 'our lands, offices and goods', done everything to try and proclaim them traitors. They had done everything to try and avoid confrontation. At this point, though, it seemed inevitable.[36]

On the afternoon of 12 October, below Ludlow, the bridge of the River Teme at their backs and the natural defence of the river curling around their left flank, the Yorkist forces drew up in battle order, embedded behind a deep ditch and a barricade of stakes and wagon-mounted guns. Alongside York were his two oldest sons, Edward earl of March, now seventeen, and the sixteen-year-old Edmund earl of Rutland. They watched as Henry VI's massive army, marching in battle formation under its heavy canvas standards, came to a halt a few hundred yards away from their lines. They saw a herald step forward from the Lancastrian ranks, his voice carrying on the air, stating that the king was prepared to give royal pardons to anybody who now joined him.

Enticed by the offer, men soon began to slip away from the Yorkist lines and through the evening, the trickle of deserters became a flood. Hopelessly outnumbered, the Yorkist lords realized there was only one thing for it. Around midnight, they announced that they were going back across the bridge into Ludlow 'to refresh themselves awhile'. Reasoning that Henry's offer of a pardon was hardly likely to apply to them, they fled under cover of darkness, abandoning not only their remaining troops but also York's wife Cecily and their younger children, cooped up in Ludlow Castle.[37]

The fleeing lords split up. Richard and his second son Edmund, with a small group of retainers, made their way west through Wales, destroying bridges in their wake; reaching the coast, they commandeered a ship and sailed for York's old stronghold of Dublin. Edward earl of March, with Warwick and Salisbury, headed southwest to Devon, where they were given a boat and supplies by a sympathetic local knight named John Dinham. They sailed up the English Channel, hugging the French coast, to Calais. There, they were greeted by the reassuring, diminutive figure of Warwick's uncle, William 'little' Lord Fauconberg, a veteran of the French wars who had held the town and its garrison for Warwick in his absence. Back in England the Yorkist cause was being ripped apart.[38]

*

In the aftermath of Ludford Bridge, Lancastrian troops rampaged through Ludlow, drinking the local taverns dry, pillaging and raping. Among those detained were Cecily duchess of York and her two youngest boys: George, nearly eleven years old, and the seven-year-old Richard. Cecily, so one partisan commentator alleged, was badly treated and 'spoiled'.[39]

In Coventry that December, Parliament assembled in the chapter house of St Mary's Priory, in front of an enthroned Henry VI. The royal case against the absent Yorkists was uncompromising: they were guilty of treason, their titles and lands permanently forfeit, their noble titles erased, their heirs forbidden ever from inheriting.

Orchestrating proceedings were sharp legal and political minds among Henry's councillors, persuasive men committed to the Lancastrian regime. Prominent among them were Sir John Fortescue, a Lincoln's Inn-educated Devonian who had become Henry's chief justice, and another west-countryman whose forensic brilliance and political acuity had led to his appointment as chancellor to the little Edward of Lancaster, Henry and Margaret's son and heir. In his late thirties, John Morton had already come a long way. He would go much further.

During the parliament a piece of Lancastrian propaganda circulated, aiming to harden any wavering consciences. The *Somnium Vigilantis*, 'Dream of the Vigilant', depicted a courtroom where, in front of a king and his lords, two men were locked in debate. One was a boorish Yorkist lout claiming to represent the 'common weal'; the other a royal orator who, after listening patiently, dissected and refuted his arguments. The Yorkists, the orator retorted, had it the wrong way round. The true 'common good' lay not in taking up the cause of the people – who were in any case irrational, fickle and stupid – but in loyalty to the king, whose supreme authority enabled the rule of law and the functioning of society. Anybody who failed in such loyalty was acting for their 'singular will', in their own self-interest. And anybody, the orator stressed, who claimed for themselves some kind of supreme authority as 'protector of the commonwealth' could not do so 'without lying'. The Yorkists wanted to subvert royal authority. Their very existence presented a threat to the security of the king and the 'universal quiet' of the country as a whole. The time for mercy was over.

In Parliament, Henry reminded people of his 'prerogative to show such mercy and grace as shall please his highness'. But it was little more than window dressing. The Yorkist lords were found guilty of treason, their fate enacted in statute. Richard of York, the Nevilles and their heirs were now legally dead – or, as the royal orator in the *Somnium* sneered, 'lords of time past'.[40]

Matters had acquired a new and terrible clarity. In the 'parliament of devils', as the Yorkists termed it bitterly, all hope of reconciliation between the warring parties had effectively been destroyed. Cast out into the political wilderness with no route back, they now had no option but to fight against the regime that had put them there. From now on, they would do so not as reformers of that regime, but as its alternative.

That winter, besieging Lancastrian troops ringed the borders of the Calais Pale, trying to get a stranglehold on the Yorkist lords. The earl of Warwick, unruffled, had taken things in hand, securing the town and port with practised efficiency, and smoothing the anxieties of Calais' merchants. Hit hard in recent years, the wool trade was further menaced by war and crippled by the trade embargo that Queen Margaret, suspicious of the merchants' Yorkist tendencies, had slapped on Calais. Warwick did his best to keep trade routes open. But under constant, wearing attack, the Calais garrison's morale began to slump, and deserters trickled away. Something spectacular was needed.

Hours before dawn on Tuesday, 19 January 1460, a seaborne detachment of seven hundred Yorkists landed quietly at Sandwich. Overwhelming the Lancastrian defences, they bundled the commander, Richard Woodville, Lord Rivers, and his son Sir Anthony Woodville, onto a ship and took them back across the Dover Strait. The government's point man in the region, Rivers had been assembling a navy to deal with the Yorkist lords in their enclave across the Channel. Warwick had got in a pre-emptive strike.

Awaiting the captive Lancastrians in Calais harbour, weapons and armour glinting in the light of 160 blazing torches, was a detachment of the garrison and the three Yorkist lords: Salisbury, Warwick and Edward earl of March. Edward was emerging from his absent father's shadow. In his older cousin Warwick he found much to emulate: a man cool under fire but with a nose for the disruptive. As persuasive in front of a crowd as he was negotiating loans with merchants or diplomatic settlements with foreign princes, Warwick was becoming as notorious for his savagery – capturing Lancastrian ships, he had singled out and summarily executed the crewmen who had previously been in his service – as for his freebooting in the Channel's eastern approaches. That winter, there was in the relationship between Warwick, now thirty-one, and York's energetic, charismatic eldest son, something of a partnership – or at least, that was how Edward later remembered the 'tender zeal, love and affection that he bore to our person and our security'. It was a mentoring role that Warwick played with accomplished skill.[41]

In the raid on Sandwich, Warwick had shown at a stroke what the English people, angry and humiliated at the loss of their 'power of the sea' under Henry VI's hopeless government, were missing. Realizing this, on Sunday 1 March the king put in one of his rare and aimless appearances in the capital. By this time, with the Yorkist position in Calais increasingly secure, Warwick had left to head west with a small fleet of ships to Ireland, to rendezvous with Richard of York.

Landing at Waterford on 17 March, St Patrick's Day, Warwick spent the following weeks with York, the pair chewing over their course of action. The plan that Warwick brought back to Edward in Calais that spring was not recorded – or, perhaps, was quite deliberately kept secret. Whatever the case, it made a strong impression on Richard's heir: it was, Edward would later recall, 'our greatest joy and consolation earthly'.[42] It would not be long before the Yorkist plans, guided by Warwick's unerring instincts, started to reveal themselves.

Short, busy and eloquent, the papal envoy Francesco Coppini viewed his mission to England as the chance to put his claim for the red cardinal's hat he craved. The previous year Pope Pius II, seeking to belie his reputation as an accomplished writer of erotica, had announced a crusade against the Ottoman Turks who threatened Europe's southeastern border and its trading interests throughout the Mediterranean. It was an ambitious aim. Not only were Christendom's cash-strapped princes reluctant to let the pope collect crusading revenues from their churches, but they showed rather more interest in fighting each other than the Turks – England being a case in point. Arriving in the country in 1459 to knock heads together, Coppini had at first met with an 'agreeable' reception but, as the months passed, the wining, dining and fine promises came to nothing. Increasingly desperate, he left England for Calais at the invitation of the earl of Warwick; there, the pair had a full and frank conversation.[43]

Outlining to Coppini their plans for regime change, Warwick stated that the Yorkist lords would govern the kingdom themselves. Henry VI, 'a dolt and a fool', would be kept on as a figurehead with only the 'bare name of sovereign'. Warwick went further. He told Coppini that Richard of York should by rights be 'reigning' – or, to put it another way, York, with his superior blood claim, was the true king of England.

Dynastic change was a cataclysmic solution to the country's political morass. But it also promised a clean break, a fresh start. Over almost ten years, as York had struggled unsuccessfully to assert himself and his populist cause and to reform the system from within, he had constantly stressed his loyalty to Henry VI, the anointed king of England. And here lay the problem. Henry may have been hopeless, but he was also blameless. Back in 1399, Henry's grandfather, Henry Bolingbroke, had confronted Richard II with his many crimes and had forced him to abdicate. Henry VI, though, had done nothing wrong. Indeed, he had barely done anything at all, but while his inaction had provoked a constitutional crisis, it was hardly a crime. There were no grounds for removing him from the throne. If, however, there turned out to have been a genealogical error – that Richard of York, by virtue of his finer lineage, was actually England's rightful king and that the house of Lancaster had been reigning for sixty years by mistake – that was another matter entirely.

The problem was that dynastic change was hardly a solution destined to attract the widespread backing the Yorkists so desperately needed; rather, it was more inclined to make potential supporters run the other way. Deposing a crowned king was incomprehensible to most. Besides which, Lancastrian rule was well over two generations old: by 1460, it was all England's people had ever known. Unsurprisingly, in his talks with Coppini Warwick played down the idea of revolution. Rather, he stressed the Yorkists' reforming programme and their allegiance to Henry VI, and pledged to send a fleet to participate in the pope's crusade – just as soon as the Yorkists had, with papal help, restored peace and order in England.

By mid-June, Warwick had constructed an international coalition of support for the Yorkist cause, foremost among which was the legitimating spiritual might of the Curia. Calais, meanwhile, supplied finance and the military heft of its permanent garrison. With this establishment backing in the bag, the Yorkist lords were, as ever, assiduous in their cultivation of the 'true hearts of the people'.[44]

Late that spring, various anonymous manifestos, seeming to bubble up from a deep wellspring of popular sentiment and speaking in their various ways of Lancastrian betrayal, were circulating through Kent: copied, passed from hand to hand, read out in taverns and marketplaces, pinned up on gates and doors. Echoing through them were the usual complaints. England was ruled by venal, base-born councillors; Henry VI himself was incapable; his marriage and his son were both 'false'. Rightful king he may have been, the implication went, but his wife and son were illegitimate and could not possibly be included in any political settlement. The Yorkists, on the other hand, were the true-blooded representatives of the people. As one manifesto spelled out, redemption was at hand in the shape of both Richard of York and his son and heir, Edward earl of March. A boy of 'blood royal', conceived 'in wedlock' – unlike the rumoured bastardy of his Lancastrian namesake, Henry VI's heir – Edward would 'save England' and lead it into a bright new future: 'his fame the earth shall spread'.

Whatever the manifestos implied, and whatever the Yorkist lords said in private, their official pronouncements remained the bland expressions of loyalty that they had always been. Henry, they stated, remained 'our most sovereign and Christian king'. All Warwick and Edward wanted was to 'amend defaults' to the benefit of all England, with Richard of York at the head of a reforming council. Through all the conciliatory language, however, ran an uncompromising tone. Whoever stood in their way, the Yorkists promised, 'we shall mark him'.[45]

On 26 June 1460 the Yorkist lords, with Coppini in tow, crossed the Channel to Sandwich. Their arrival, smoothed by fair winds and weather, was 'gracious', more like a state arrival than an invasion. With the Kentish commons at their backs, and a swelling number of local big men disillusioned with the regime – at Canterbury, the city's commanders, Sir John Fogge and Sir John Scott, ordered to defend the city against the Yorkists, opened the gates to them instead – they advanced on London.[46]

The first impulse of the city's mayor and aldermen was to bar the gates. But the mood of resistance was weakened by political divisions among the civic elites and eroded still further by the mood of ordinary Londoners, who had chuckled admiringly over Warwick's anti-establishment exploits and were, by and large, belligerently pro-Yorkist. The pressure told. On 2 July, impressed by the size of the Yorkist lords' support, and after receiving assurances of their loyalty to Henry VI, London's authorities opened the gates. The Lancastrian garrison still occupying the Tower, the great royal fortress on the city's eastern edge, was told to stay put – and to stay out of trouble.[47] After raising loans from city businessmen, Warwick and Edward then led their forces out of London and rode north.

Days later, advancing up the Great North Road in torrential summer rain, the Yorkists approached Northampton. They were confronted by a formidable sight. South of the town, the River Nene at their backs, dug in behind earthworks and ditches fortified by massive amounts of artillery, Henry's army was waiting for them.

Playing their spiritual trump card, Warwick and Edward dispatched a cluster of clergymen, headed by the pliable Coppini and Thomas Bourchier, archbishop of Canterbury, to talk with Henry VI. Their efforts fell on stony ground. The Lancastrian commander Humphrey Stafford, duke of Buckingham, a veteran of St Albans, sent a blunt message back to the Yorkist commanders. If they tried to approach the king, they would die.[48]

In the early afternoon of 10 July, as the deluge continued, the Yorkist army advanced through meadows turning rapidly to mud. With the saturated Lancastrian artillery out of action, the commander of Henry's vanguard, Lord Grey of Ruthin – to whom, before the battle, Warwick had given a nod and a wink regarding the security of his precariously held family estates under a future Yorkist administration – decided that, rather than preventing the Yorkists reaching the Lancastrian fortifications, he would be better off helping them over.

It was all done in half an hour. As the Lancastrian lines collapsed, Warwick and Edward, shouting to their troops to spare the commons and kill the nobles, hunted down the Lancastrian commanders. Buckingham was slaughtered making a last stand outside the king's tent. Inside it, the scene from St Albans was re-enacted: the Yorkist lords falling to their knees at the feet of their witless king, his agitation quickly turned to 'great recomfort' by their protestations of loyalty.[49]

Back in London, the Lancastrian defenders in the Tower traded fire with the Yorkist besiegers. There was collateral damage, men, women and children injured and killed in the surrounding streets. When news arrived of the Yorkist victory at Northampton, the Lancastrians tried to escape. Their commander, Lord Scales, was murdered by the boatman who was supposedly rowing him across the Thames to safety, his naked corpse dumped in the Southwark churchyard of St Mary Overy. On 16 July, as the remaining defenders surrendered, Warwick and Edward re-entered London with Henry VI, a relieved city offering 'great laud and thanking' to God.

With Henry securely installed at the bishop of London's palace on the north side of St Paul's, the Yorkist reprisals started. Members of the Tower garrison were tried by a panel headed by Warwick: seven, found guilty of treason, were hanged, drawn and quartered. The legality of Warwick's actions, for which he had received no royal sanction, was highly dubious – after all, the Lancastrians had been fighting in the king's name. But, as one commentator remarked meaningfully, 'necessity knows no law'.[50]

That summer, Lancastrians were removed from key positions in the king's household and government, their property and assets seized. Yorkists were installed in their place. If the dispatches of dazzled European diplomats were to be believed, Warwick was at the heart of everything, his energy inexhaustible. Almost singlehandedly, one Milanese observer recounted, he had brought an end to war in England and, in control of government, was doing 'marvellous things' as he awaited York's return from Ireland. Amid the superlatives, the

Milanese reported another piece of speculation: 'It is thought they will make a son of the duke of York king.'[51]

Like most foreign envoys struggling to make sense of England's fast-changing political landscape, the letter-writer was probably fed most of his information by Warwick. Not long before, Warwick had told the papal legate Coppini that it was his belief that by rights Richard of York should be on the throne.[52] Yet if the Milanese was to be believed, the thinking now emanating from Warwick's camp was that Henry VI should be replaced, not by York but by his son and heir Edward earl of March. It was perhaps an indication of the way Warwick and Edward had grown together in the past months of exile and battle; an indication, too, of the promise that the earl saw in his young protégé.

Approaching his full adult height of six feet four inches, Edward was the physical antithesis of his short, dark father. His good looks were striking, wide cheekbones throwing into relief a roman nose and cupid's-bow mouth. His demeanour was intensified by an effortless expansiveness, though something in his eyes – narrow, hard – offset all this beauty, almost as if he was perfectly conscious of the effect he created and how to use it.[53] In Yorkist propaganda, Edward was the embodiment of England's future, untainted by the years of destructive factional deadlock. Besides which, as one Yorkist poem on the recent battle of Northampton noted, Edward and Warwick seemed to understand each other instinctively. Warwick, in an allusion to the earl's bear-and-ragged-staff badge, was the savage bear, Edward his 'bearward', the only man capable of controlling this fearsome instrument of his will. Edward, the poet remarked, had a disposition for 'solace', for enjoying himself: while he relaxed, Warwick did the dirty work. Or, looked at another way, the young bearward's authority gave Warwick the freedom to act as he liked.

The Yorkists now needed to make their seizure of power legitimate, and to repeal the damning acts of attainder passed against them the previous winter. Summoning parliament, Edward and Warwick settled down to wait for the return from Dublin of Richard of York – who was, after all, 'the master of this game'.[54]

Edward, meanwhile, took the opportunity to catch up with his three sisters and two younger brothers: George, now rising eleven, and

Richard, almost eight years old. In his father's absence Edward was the head of the family, and his attentiveness towards his younger siblings was noted: he 'cometh every day to see them'. And, like all great noblemen – or noblemen who aspired to be thought of as great – he kept a magnificent household. Magnificence invariably involved an inexhaustible supply of alcohol: of the £39 9s 11d-worth of credit he ran up with one merchant on necessaries 'for the use of our household', £33 went on five tuns, 252-gallon barrels, of red wine.[55]

On 9 September 1460, Richard of York came ashore on the heavily wooded Wirral peninsula. There, he joined forces with Sir William Stanley and made his way south, recruiting men as he went. On his return from Ireland a decade previously, he had made vocal protestations of loyalty to Henry VI. This time, such declarations were conspicuous by their absence. As men committed their service to York, the indentures they signed omitted the king's regnal year; missing too was the customary, overriding, pledge of loyalty to the crown. Signatories were simply to 'promise and bind themselves' to Richard and his son and heir Edward earl of March.[56] As York rode through the Welsh Marches, his retainers wearing his falcon-and-fetterlock badge, his sword carried before him and banners displaying the full royal arms of England, people turned out in force to acclaim him.

A month later, on Friday 10 October, York rode into Westminster Palace Yard, accompanied by eight hundred armed men on horseback. His arrival announced by the blaring of trumpets, he strode through Westminster Hall and into the Painted Chamber, where Parliament was in session. Making for the king's throne, empty under its cloth of estate, York laid a hand on it 'like a man taking possession' and stated flatly that he had come to 'challenge his right': to claim the crown of England. He was met, not with a ringing acclamation, but with a sea of faces frozen with shock.

The first to break the silence was Archbishop Thomas Bourchier, who asked mildly if York wanted to see the king. York's retort was inflammatory: 'I can think of nobody in the kingdom who should not come to see me, rather than I him.'[57]

Only weeks before, as York journeyed south, Warwick had met him at Shrewsbury and the pair had reviewed the possible courses of action open to them. One, which they had discussed months before in Ireland, was the possibility of York laying claim to the throne. Whether they had argued about it, whether Warwick had advised against it and York had ignored him, or whether Warwick, assessing the mood in London, had got cold feet at the last minute, the reality was that York's claim would never have worked. All the Yorkists' carefully cultivated support had been achieved by portraying themselves as loyal reformers of Henry VI's regime. Parliament was not prepared for anything else – and neither was it prepared to depose an anointed, crowned king of England. At a stroke, York's precipitate claim had validated all the Lancastrian accusations of Yorkist treachery and ambition. That Friday morning, nobody seemed more horrified than Warwick himself.[58]

As York sulked in the king's apartments – kicking the doors in, he had turfed a bewildered Henry out – the lords, chief among them Warwick and Edward, reconvened around the curve of the Thames at Blackfriars in an atmosphere of studied avoidance. Not wanting to find against York's claim, they passed the buck to the judges, the government's senior legal advisers. Declaring the issue beyond their competence, the judges passed it back. A week later, as York threatened to proceed with his own coronation come what may, the lords reconvened at Westminster and proposed a radical compromise.[59]

Henry VI would remain king for life. On his death, the crown would pass not to his young son and heir Edward of Lancaster, who was debarred from the succession, but to Richard of York and his sons. It was an astonishing settlement. Nevertheless, for not quite the last time, York had found himself blindsided. Given that, at forty-nine, he was a full decade older than the Lancastrian king, there was every chance he would die first. Not even York's closest supporters, it seemed, wanted him as king. He reacted with savage petulance, riding torchlit through Westminster Palace as though he owned it, repeating insistently that the crown was his 'by very right'. There was talk that he didn't intend to wait for Henry to die of natural causes. But if even York's closest allies had been unconvinced about the prospect of him as king, there were others who hated it.[60]

*

North of the Trent, news of Richard of York's 'untrue pretensed claim' was greeted with fury by Queen Margaret and her supporters, chief among them the powerful northern lord Henry Percy, earl of Northumberland. Since the summer, Percy's men had been raiding the Yorkshire estates of York and the Nevilles, the earl's bitter rivals; now, they went on the rampage, wrecking property, slaughtering and driving off livestock, killing anybody who resisted and leaving a trail of destruction in their wake. Meanwhile, Lancastrian forces were massing across the country, their mobilization co-ordinated 'full privily' by Margaret from her base in the port town of Hull. It was said that Margaret had raised fifteen thousand troops in a matter of weeks – figures so excessive that in London, anybody who mentioned them was accused of spreading Lancastrian propaganda.[61] Nevertheless, the disorder in Yorkshire was real enough. Early that December, Richard of York, his second son Edmund earl of Rutland, and Warwick's father the earl of Salisbury marched north to reassert control over their devastated estates.

The weather late that autumn had been terrible. Harvests had failed; the roads were flooded and impassable. As York rode north, he found food and billeting harder to come by than usual; supply lines were difficult to maintain. Then, as his scouts rode into the Nottinghamshire town of Worksop, they were ambushed and killed. Unnervingly, the attackers wore the distinctive portcullis badge of the young Lancastrian nobleman Henry Beaufort, duke of Somerset, whom York had believed to be two hundred miles away in Dorset. Just before Christmas Richard finally arrived at his castle of Sandal, a couple of miles south of the market town of Wakefield. He did so to bad news. Somerset and Northumberland were at Pontefract Castle, barely ten miles east, and their army had already stripped the region bare of supplies.

Probably it came as a relief to Richard when Somerset agreed a seasonal truce, which would hold until after Epiphany, the sixth day of January.[62] But, that Christmas, York's foraging parties were attacked by Somerset's troops and the truce was broken. Acutely aware of the greater Lancastrian numbers, York's commanders urged him to sit tight within the castle walls and wait for the arrival of Edward and his Marcher men, now believed to be on the move. Richard, itching for combat, 'would not be counselled'.

As he led his men out of Sandal Castle and down into the fields below, his miscalculation soon became clear. The Lancastrian army waiting for him, partly concealed in nearby woods, was vast. At its heart were the retinues of no fewer than nine lords, some of whom, armed with Richard's royal commissions of array, had recruited forces in his name before defecting to Lancaster. With disciplined fury, Somerset allowed York to move onto the level terrain between Sandal and Wakefield until he was, as one report had it, 'surrounded on every side, like fish in a net'.[63]

Some two thousand Yorkists were slaughtered. York himself was hunted down and butchered; his son Edmund, trying desperately to flee the fighting, was ridden down at the bridge into Wakefield. Salisbury was captured and led back to Pontefract Castle, where a group of locals who 'loved him not' frogmarched the earl outside the castle walls, then hacked off his head: an extra-judicial score-settling on Somerset's part, so one chronicler felt, masquerading as rough popular justice. Stuck on spiked poles, the heads of the dead Yorkists were paraded the thirty miles to the city of York. For Richard's head, Somerset had added a special, malevolent touch: a paper crown.[64]

Weeks later, on that brilliant, bitter day in the Welsh Marches, as Edward led his men into battle, he carried with him the devastating news from Wakefield, still raw. If it gave his fighting an added rage, so too did the knowledge that he had come into his inheritance. Head of the house of York, Edward was also heir to the throne of England.

2

The Rose Stands Alone

In the early weeks of 1461, Londoners tried to digest the news of the massacre at Wakefield. There were reports of Margaret of Anjou's Lancastrian army now marching inexorably south, and rumours of the threatening storm: an all-consuming 'plague of locusts', wrote one trembling chronicler; worse than Attila the Hun, surmised another, apprehensively.[1] It was true, there had been some destruction. As they made their way through the east midlands, the Lancastrians had pillaged the Yorkist towns of Grantham and Stamford, though talk of a belt of devastation some thirty miles wide, and of the ransacking of churches and abbeys, seemed exaggerated.

In London the earl of Warwick, pulling the strings of Henry VI's puppet government, was expertly fanning the fears of southern England into a white heat. As sermons were preached at Paul's Cross, the open-air pulpit in the cathedral's churchyard, and ballads and verses circulated, the struggle between the two rival claims to the crown was coloured by another, more atavistic narrative. 'All the lords of the north', went one verse, 'wrought by one assent/ To destroy the south country'. This vision of a divided country suited Warwick down to the ground: in Norfolk, one report stated, anxieties about northern robbing and pillaging were so intense that 'every man' was 'well willing' to follow the Yorkist lords.[2]

Warwick strode through the chaos with reassuring authority – 'like another Caesar', noted one impressed Italian diplomat – mobilizing troops, securing more loans from a terrified London, and raising spiritual, financial and military support from the house of York's international backers, among them the compliant papal legate Francesco Coppini and, in Flanders, Philip duke of Burgundy. 'All will end well', he told them breezily. But, as Warwick waited for news from

Edward in the Welsh Marches, and as his messengers fanned out across England's southern counties with urgent orders for troops to mobilize and join him in 'all possible haste', he knew it wasn't quite as straightforward as that.[3]

In an emergency session of Parliament, Warwick and his advisers had tried to get a grip on the constantly shifting loyalties of England's nobility. Attempting to map the results of their lobbying – the bargaining and appeals to loyalty that took place in quiet corridors or private rooms, the terse exchanges and delicate, evasive replies or, perhaps, a glance and barely perceptible incline of the head – somebody had scribbled down names on a scrap of paper, in two speculative lists. One was a core group of twenty-one nobles believed to be committed to the Yorkist cause; the other, sixteen names above which had been written the word 'newtri': neutrals. As the lists were worked over again, their author, his initial certainty clouding, covered them in jottings, crossings-out and duplications, switching names between columns as he tried to work out precisely whether certain nobles meant what they said. After all, as familiar allegiances and connections had been abraded by anxiety, wariness and opportunism, people had said one thing and done another, swapped sides on the battlefield, done nothing at all – or even, as in the case of the great north-western nobleman Thomas, Lord Stanley, whose name had been optimistically jotted down among the Yorkist lords, all of these things at once.[4]

Then there was the question of precisely what these lords were supposed to be supporting. Ostensibly, the Yorkist cause remained that of a reformed government under the sovereign authority of Henry VI, and indeed, in these hastily drawn-up lists, the idea of an alternative Yorkist monarchy had been played down. While the list of neutrals had been clearly labelled, the list of Yorkists had been left untitled. What was more, the name of Edward – head of the house of York and now, by act of Parliament, heir to the crown – appeared not first in the list, but fifth; nor was he called by his new style of duke of York. While the error might have stemmed from long familiarity with his title of earl of March, it was odd, given how thoroughly the list had been gone over in other respects, that it hadn't been corrected.[5] Perhaps, in order to attract neutrals worried that in backing the Yorkists they might be betraying a reigning king, Warwick had decided to play down Edward's claim. Or it simply showed quite how fast events were moving.

This assessment of noble hearts and minds revealed something else. Despite the list of presumed neutrals, it was clear that the allegiances of England's lords were polarizing. Conspicuous by their absence were the names of eighteen irreconcilable Lancastrian lords, most of whom were now marching rapidly towards London with Margaret of Anjou. England's political classes were headed for an overwhelming showdown. As Warwick put it to an English envoy to Rome, unless some sort of papal-brokered intervention could happen quickly – in favour of the Yorkist cause, naturally – England would tear itself apart. The violence, Warwick intimated, would be terrible, worse than anything for a thousand years.[6]

On 12 February, Warwick and his forces rode out of London to confront Margaret's northmen. Receiving reports that the Lancastrians had diverted west, he moved slowly, barely more than a few miles a day. The last thing he needed was to be bypassed and to leave the city, with its reservoir of cash and supplies, exposed. On the 16th, four days into this game of cat-and-mouse, he halted at the Hertfordshire town of St Albans.

Warwick had every reason to be confident. Six years previously, in the same place, he had routed the Lancastrian army. His forces this time were several thousand strong, bolstered by the retinues of several Yorkist lords; they also included a detachment of crack Burgundian hand-gunners sent by Philip of Burgundy. He also had with him Henry VI, whose presence in his ranks gave him royal legitimacy. In fighting Warwick, Margaret's troops would be bearing arms against their king, the very definition of treason.

Hearing that the Lancastrians were some nine miles away to the north, Warwick redeployed his forces in the customary three 'battles' or divisions in open ground, strung out along the Wheathampstead road down which he expected them to appear. His rear division, bristling with firepower, was dug in along the great Iron Age earthwork of Beech Bottom just to the north of the town. He was prepared. But as Shrove Tuesday dawned, as one observer put it, 'all thing was sick and out of order'.[7]

Warwick's intelligence had been terrible. His network of scouts had all failed to report back – except one, who had brought bad information. The previous day, the Lancastrians had surprised and massacred a Yorkist outpost of two hundred men in nearby Dunstable. Led by Somerset, fresh from his savage triumph at Wakefield, they then turned Warwick's outflanking manoeuvre, so decisive six years before, back on himself. Somerset made his way round the outskirts of St Albans, headed at speed across the open heathland and attacked the entrenched Yorkist ordnance, which was expecting an attack from the other direction.

Assaulted 'before they could level their guns', Warwick's new recruits from the Low Countries proved useless: as they tried desperately to deploy a mortar firing explosive shells, it erupted in their faces, the 'fire turned back upon them'. Even so, the Yorkist rearguard – now, effectively, the vanguard – fought until the short winter day began to wane. In the fading light, as its remnants were pursued through the countryside, the rest of the Yorkist army, which had remained detached from the fighting, began to slip away. In the mayhem Warwick, along with the other Yorkist generals, escaped and went to ground. Although Yorkist sources – probably emanating from Warwick himself – later blamed the defeat on a deserting detachment of Kentishmen, it looked rather more like a comprehensive failure of leadership and organization.[8]

This time, it was the victorious Lancastrians who found Henry VI. The king had been left behind by the fleeing Yorkists, as useless as he had been during the first battle of St Albans, but in a rather better mood. He was discovered sitting under an oak tree, where, as the fighting progressed, he had passed the time laughing and singing to himself. That evening, he was reunited with his queen and son, now seven years old. After the boy's status as heir to the house of Lancaster was ceremonially reaffirmed by his chancellor, John Morton, the little prince sat in his capacity as Constable of England, passing sentence 'his own self' on Yorkist prisoners, looking on as they were executed.[9]

The next day, Ash Wednesday, London awoke hungover after the carnival of Shrovetide. Citizens trooped to church, where priests marked their foreheads with dabs of wet ash murmuring *pulvis es et in pulverem reverteris*: 'thou art dust and to dust thou shalt return'. Sometime that same morning, riders galloped into the city and, reining in their sweating horses, announced the news that twenty-five miles away at St Albans, the Yorkist army had been destroyed and Warwick had disappeared.

The city was shocked. Over the past weeks and months Warwick had talked an excellent game, and London had backed his leadership. Suddenly, it lay at Margaret of Anjou's mercy. If the rumours were to be believed, she lacked the cash to pay her troops and, to compensate, had promised them they could instead ransack the city. As the reality of the situation sank in, the hangovers deepened. 'Ash Wednesday', wrote one Londoner, was a day on which 'we lived in much dread'.[10]

The city gates were locked and barred; guards patrolled the walls. Shops were shuttered. Few ventured outside their neighbourhoods. Groups of civic militiamen passed watchfully through the deserted streets. London's oligarchs, rarely in accord, were all agreed on one thing: a Lancastrian sacking had to be avoided at all costs.

They also thought that Margaret would be open to talks. Far from home, her supply lines were overextended and her apparently solid bastions of support no longer so reliable: the city of Coventry, its loyalties split, had refused Margaret aid on her way south, angering her so much that she had reportedly given her soldiers licence to 'spoil and rob' it on their way back through the midlands. Furious as she may have been at London's support of the Yorkists, Margaret badly needed the capital's goodwill, supplies and finances. Ordering her army to sit tight, she assured the city that rumours about her army's viciousness were 'untrue and feigned', guaranteeing that 'none of you shall be robbed, despoiled or wronged'. Perhaps, London's leading citizens felt, they could negotiate the Lancastrians' peaceful entrance – and, in doing so, play for time. Nobody knew for sure where Edward was but, people heard, he was in the Cotswolds, a few days' march away. The corporation acted fast.[11]

An official deputation left for St Albans. Along with the various 'clerks and curates' sent to plead the city's cause were three high-born noblewomen with exceptional Lancastrian credentials: the widows of the duke of Buckingham and Lord Scales, who had both been slaughtered the previous summer; and, the senior of the three, Jacquetta of St Pol, wife to the Lancastrian nobleman Richard Woodville, Lord Rivers. Elegant, aristocratic, from one of northern France's most ancient noble families, Jacquetta had been close to Margaret since the queen's arrival in England fifteen years before.[12] The noblewomen proved convincing, returning with Lancastrian assurances that the army would keep its distance; in return, London was to send food and cash to the Lancastrian troops. Margaret also handed the deputation a list of wanted Yorkist associates, demanding that the city authorities admit a detachment of four hundred soldiers to hunt them down. The city's oligarchs agreed to everything and – anticipating the response of ordinary Londoners – who had absorbed Warwick's dire warnings of the northerners' ferocity, proclaimed a general curfew.

Within an hour of the proclamation, the city was in uproar. Carlo Gigli, a Lucchese businessman who had settled in London, via Bruges, had seen a fair amount of rioting in his adoptive home over the years but, as he put it, 'I was never more afraid'. Some panicked citizens daubed Somerset's portcullis badge on their front doors in the hope of warding off his troops' attentions; others seized weapons and, appointing captains, prepared to resist the Lancastrian advance force.[13] At the port of London, hastily laden ships cast off and headed down the Thames towards the open sea, carrying Yorkist adherents for whom staying behind meant certain punishment.

On board one Antwerp-bound vessel were a number of men on Margaret's wanted list, together with their treasure and moveable goods. Among them were high-profile London merchants such as the notorious, rich and unpopular draper Philip Malpas, who clearly didn't fancy his chances of explaining himself to the Lancastrian queen, though he had in fact financed both sides. He had already had his property looted once, by Jack Cade's rebels a decade before, and was keen to avoid a repeat. On board the same ship were Thomas Vaughan, an administrator and ordnance specialist, as comfortable handling gunpowder as he was a high-level diplomatic mission, and a physician named William Hatteclyffe. After years at Cambridge and Padua, Europe's finest medical university, Hatteclyffe had helped nurse Henry VI through his first bout of catatonia; Margaret, who clearly rated his skills and discreet urbanity, had appointed him her doctor. Both Vaughan and Hatteclyffe had been the queen's trusted, confidential servants – until their defection to the house of York, when they were embraced with equal wholeheartedness by Richard of York and his wife, now widow, Cecily. It was probably Cecily who, in the face of Margaret of Anjou's wrath, advised the pair to flee, entrusting them with the family gold that they now attempted to carry to safety.[14] Another ship carried Cecily's two younger sons, Edward's brothers George and Richard.

As she came to terms with the loss of her husband and second son, Cecily had remained resolute in fighting the Yorkist corner. Even in adversity Cecily, who had been known to spend a baron's yearly income in a single shopping spree, maintained a magnificent household in the family's London home of Baynard's Castle, whose turreted bulk, arranged round two great courtyards, rose sheer from the Thames on the city's western edge. She also knew Margaret well. The two women had once been close, their friendship persisting deep into the faction-ridden 1450s. Cecily's support of Margaret's difficult pregnancy had been empathic, since by that point Cecily herself had borne twelve children, losing five. It was also shrewd, providing a crucial back-channel of influence as her husband became increasingly sidelined.[15] But those days were long past and Margaret had since proved uncompromising. There was, Cecily clearly felt, no way that their friendship could be revived in the current frenzy of bloodletting.

Cecily's instincts were sound. Her sons' very existence was an obstacle to the dynastic pretensions of the house of Lancaster. Thanks to the parliamentary legislation of the previous autumn, both the eleven-year-old George, and Richard, three years his junior, were now prominent in the line of succession: indeed, should anything happen to their oldest brother Edward, George would be next in line to inherit the throne. After the disaster at Wakefield, Cecily had sent the boys into hiding to keep them out of 'danger and peril', in the unobtrusive household of a London widow named Alice Martyn. Now, even that had become unsafe. As London prepared to admit the Lancastrian troops, Cecily bundled her boys on board a ship that took them across the North Sea to the Low Countries and the court of Philip of Burgundy, who was happy enough to take them into his protection. Amid the panic Cecily herself stayed in the city, unswerving. Her overwhelming priority was to hold things together for her eldest son, Edward.[16]

On Sunday, 22 February, the promised cartloads of provisions rumbled through London's streets for delivery to the waiting Lancastrians.

But at Cripplegate, in the north of the city, the carts were stopped by armed citizens who barred the gates and distributed the food among themselves; the money destined for the soldiers' wages also disappeared. When a Lancastrian advance guard tried to enter London from the east, through Aldgate, it was ambushed by city militiamen, who killed and wounded several troops; the rest fled. Around the same time, news spread through the streets, a rumour that gave an edge to the city's resistance, and which forced Margaret's weary, hungry army to give up the idea of entering London and to start the long retreat north. Edward was coming.[17]

After his victory at Mortimer's Cross, Edward had regrouped in the Marches, recruiting fresh men, resupplying and rearming before marching across England. On 19 February, as news reached him of Warwick's defeat at St Albans, he set off east through the Cotswolds; three days later, the two men met at Warwick's town of Burford, in the rolling Oxfordshire hills.

Since the cousins had last seen each other, over three months previously, much had changed, and mostly for the worse. Despite his recent victory, Edward was jumpy: still swinging between a state of adrenalin-fuelled exhilaration and an acute sense of vulnerability and uncertainty. If Mortimer's Cross had electrified him with a sense of his manifest royal destiny, the fact was that the house of York had endured two swift and catastrophic defeats, at Wakefield and now St Albans, and two shattering family losses: his father and his brother Edmund. Given the deafening silence that had greeted his father's own attempt the previous autumn, the question was: could Edward convincingly claim the throne?

Warwick, as ever, had a plan. As he explained with his customary coolness, there had been nothing disastrous about his own fiasco at St Albans. Indeed, it had clarified matters wonderfully. There was, he suggested, no longer any need for the Yorkists' carefully modulated expressions of loyalty and devotion to Henry VI, because at St Albans Henry – who, in Warwick's mind, was morphing from an imbecile in need of Yorkist guidance to a double-dealing king with his own malign agency – had deserted them; in doing so, he had broken the binding parliamentary oath that he had made to the house of York the previous autumn. And, having broken his own oath, Henry had released Edward from his. The way was now clear for Edward to claim the crown of England – a crown that was his and his family's 'by right'. Besides which, the people loved him.[18]

Warwick had a clear idea of what made his younger cousin tick. In resolving the confused shades of grey into distinct black and white, the scenario he now unfolded was of a struggle that the extrovert Edward could fully understand: a war of good against evil for the highest of stakes, with Edward, England's redeeming hero, at its centre. Just like the prophecies had said.

Edward was instantly energized. He wanted to be in the right; and he wanted to be adored. There was also, presumably, some satisfaction in the fact that Warwick was unequivocally prepared to back his claim to the throne, in a way that he had never backed that of Edward's father.

The reality was that with Henry VI no longer in their grasp, this was more or less the only move that the Yorkists, their government deprived of the legitimacy conferred by their control of the king, could now make. Warwick was also reasserting his own credibility. London had been distinctly underwhelmed by his generalship at St Albans, but if he returned to liberate the city alongside a new, young and victorious heir to the throne, the story of his earlier inability to defend it from Margaret's armies would look rather different. For his part, Edward didn't let his own chivalric fantasies cloud the practicalities of the situation. As he told his cousin, he 'had no money'. Most of his troops had come at their own cost – and a kingdom, as both men knew all too well, could hardly run on loyalty alone.

On Thursday, 26 February, almost a week after the curfew had been imposed, crowds crammed into London's streets to welcome Edward, Warwick and their army into the city. It was a reception marked by stunned and disbelieving joy – not least because, as one chronicler put it, the Lancastrians could have taken London at any time they wanted in the preceding days. Yorkist supporters had been hard at work whipping up enthusiasm for the young pretender, a king in whose person England would be both saved and renewed. 'Let us walk in a new vineyard', went one saying, 'and let us make a gay garden in the month of March with this fair white rose and herb, the earl of March.'[19]

Still, notwithstanding Warwick's assurances and the Yorkists' insistence that they were the true champions of the commons and the unifiers of the nobility, Edward's claim to the throne was flimsy. Whatever his personal inadequacies, Henry VI was God's anointed; Edward was merely a young nobleman, albeit an impressive one. Neither did he appear to have much in the way of noble backing. As one onlooker remarked, watching Edward's troops marching into London, there were 'few of note' among his commanders. If Edward were to make good on his claim to be England's rightful king, it was a transformation that would have to happen convincingly and – with Margaret's armies already regrouping in the north – fast. Edward had neither time nor money for a coronation. Luckily for him, he had men around him who knew precisely what to do.

Warwick's youngest brother, George Neville, bishop of Exeter, was a man to whom everything in life seemed to come easily. Intellectual, epicurean, he shared with Warwick a protean eloquence, equally at home addressing kings and charming diplomats as stirring up crowds with incendiary sermons. The previous summer, his precociousness and his brother's influence had landed him the chancellorship of England at the age of twenty-nine. It was a post that Edward now unhesitatingly confirmed. Over the next days, George Neville would start to prove his worth.[20]

On Sunday, 1 March, between three and four thousand people gathered north of the city walls at St John's Fields, a place synonymous with popular protest. The assembly consisted, more or less, of Edward's troops – the Welsh accents were a giveaway – 'mustered', as one observer put it, with military precision. Choreographing the display of popular acclamation that followed was George Neville, who demanded of the crowd whether, having 'wickedly forsworn' his 'true lords' the Yorkists at St Albans, Henry VI was any longer a worthy king. After the obliging roar of 'No' had subsided on the air, he asked them if they wanted Edward as king, to which they shouted 'with one voice, Yes Yes'.

A delegation of representative 'captains' – the significance of the term, with its resonances of popular leadership, was lost on no one – then headed through the city to Baynard's Castle, where Edward, reunited with his mother Cecily, was now in residence. Surrounded by his councillors, Edward gravely received the news that the people, in truth represented by a few detachments of his army, 'had chosen him king'.

Over the following days, this acting-out of Edward's right to the throne continued, with his title proclaimed throughout London's streets and ratified by a 'great council' which, even padded out by the hasty ennoblement of some of his key supporters, looked less like a representative gathering of the 'natural governors' of the kingdom than the partisan group it was. After listing nine names, one chronicler ran out of steam: 'and many more', he ended, lamely.[21]

Early on Wednesday, 4 March, a large crowd, primed by a rousing sermon from George Neville, pressed into Westminster Hall to witness England's new king take possession of his realm.[22] A head taller than most, imposing in his royal robes and cap of estate, Edward processed through the crowd to the King's Bench, the great marble seat of royal justice, where he sat, the lawgiver facing his people. Swearing his coronation oath, to rule justly and maintain the rule of law, Edward announced that, from that moment onward, he would begin to reign.

It had been a rickety set of ceremonies, with manufactured popular assent, rubber-stamping by a small cabal of nobles masquerading as a great council, and an enthronement in place of a coronation. The master of ceremonies, George Neville, thought things had turned out rather well. Shortly after, he wrote with an air of satisfied certainty to the papal envoy Francesco Coppini that Edward had practically been compelled 'by force' to take the crown. Though Neville was overstating the case, on that morning in Westminster Hall, with the Lords and Commons hailing him king, Edward had nevertheless undergone that profound, imperceptible transformation that elevated him above the ranks of the lords from which he had emerged. What was more, there was a sense that the eighteen-year-old Edward IV showed rather more signs of delivering on his oaths to bring peace and justice to a conflict-ridden country than Henry VI had ever done.[23]

Edward now had to move quickly. Entrenched in the north, with Henry in her possession, Margaret of Anjou was happy to play a waiting game: to sit tight, repel Yorkist attacks and cause havoc until Edward's newfound popularity began to wear off. It was up to Edward to go and find her, and to validate his right to the crown in what was the supreme expression of God's will – battle.

As the ceremonies unfolded, the new king and his councillors were working feverishly, mobilizing troops, stockpiling supplies and raising funds. Edward seemed to have an unusual ability to make people feel good about parting with their money. The city contributed another hefty corporate loan of over £4,000: four times the sum it had extended to Warwick before St Albans. Others – institutions and individuals – also expressed their allegiance in cash. Edward insisted on receiving the contributions in person, 'with our own hands', giving his creditors the opportunity to bask in the glow of his vigorous charm. He also demonstrated a new seriousness towards creditors. Although loans were funnelled into the coffers of his household for immediate disbursement, Edward gave assurances that they would be properly recorded in the Exchequer and a sense that – one day – lenders would receive their rewards. It was rather different from the practices of the house of Lancaster, where credit seemed simply to disappear into a bottomless pit.[24]

Other Londoners showed their loyalty in different ways. John Orwell, a goldsmith, was hard at work engraving Edward's seals, the symbols of the regime's authority, which allowed government to function and for Edward to raise troops on his own account. He made a new great seal, handed to the chancellor, George Neville; a privy seal, whose office acted as a formal clearing-house for the business done by the king and his officers; and a golden signet ring, with which the king's secretariat authenticated Edward's personal decisions. Meanwhile a grocer, John Nicholl, supplied the new king with a large consignment of gunpowder.[25]

Edward issued his first proclamations, loaded with denunciations of the northern lords, 'moved and steered by the spirit of the devil', and their 'ungodly' king Henry, whose acts of violence were condemned as 'treasons and rebellions' against England's rightful king, Edward IV. By contrast, Edward, modest and God-fearing, was a paragon of moral virtue who would rule on behalf of the whole country, a statement underscored by his offer of a pardon to any follower of Henry VI who submitted to him within ten days and – balancing conciliation with rigour – the offer of £100 to anybody who killed any of the Lancastrians on a list circulating with the proclamation. Anyone disobeying his injunctions to public order, Edward assured his new subjects, would be met with the full coercive force of his sovereign laws.[26]

After presiding over an exemplary beheading in Smithfield – it wasn't clear whether the executed man, a grocer named Walter Walker, had been tried for any offence, but the point was made – and announcing to the city's elites that his mother Cecily would deputize for him in his absence, 'our new king Edward' rode out of London through Bishopsgate 'with great triumph' at the head of his army of Welshmen and Kentishmen and headed north, collecting more cash loans as he went.[27] Away in their own regions, armed with royal commissions of array fixed with the heavy wax cake of Edward's new great seal, were the Yorkist general John Mowbray, duke of Norfolk, recruiting his willing East Anglian men, and Warwick himself, distributing his badges throughout his midlands estates. As Edward progressed, his army was swelled by supporters ordered to assemble with as many armed men as they could bring, 'in all haste possible', at pre-arranged muster stations along the line of march. Edward was all too mindful of his father's recent, disastrous journey. As well as a baggage train stretching several miles behind him, a fleet shadowed his progress up the east coast, resupplying his troops at regular intervals. Ahead of his growing army, the Lancastrians, instead of confronting him, melted away.[28]

As he crossed the Trent river, the traditional dividing line between north and south, Edward was heading deep into what had become enemy territory. At the south Yorkshire town of Doncaster, he linked up with Warwick and his forces. With the duke of Norfolk's East Anglians not yet arrived, he pressed on through his family's ravaged estates towards Pontefract Castle, scene of the killing of his father and brother the previous December. He found the castle abandoned, the Lancastrians having retreated across the nearby Aire river, now in spate, a natural barrier to the Yorkist line of march. After an advance Yorkist force, trying to secure a crossing to the east at Ferrybridge, was ambushed, Edward decided to move forward himself.

Although Easter week was approaching, it still felt like winter. On the morning of 28 March, as the Yorkist army advanced towards Ferrybridge, snow and sleet were in the air. Around the bridge, half-destroyed by Lancastrian sappers, arrowfire gave way to vicious, hand-to-hand fighting on the riverbanks and in the shallows. Then, as the weather set in, a detachment under Warwick's uncle Lord Fauconberg forded the fast-moving river a few miles upstream at Castleford and surprised the Lancastrians. When their commander, Lord Clifford, was shot in the throat, they broke and fled towards the main Lancastrian army, drawn up outside the nearby village of Towton.[29]

That night, after crossing the Aire, Edward's army bivouacked in the freezing open fields, acutely aware of the presence of the enemy forces a few miles to the north. Both sides had mustered huge numbers of troops, but the Lancastrian army, commanded by the duke of Somerset, was considerably bigger. Confronting Edward's twenty thousand were perhaps thirty thousand men, mostly northerners, as well as the majority of England's lords – or, as one commentator put it, 'the substance of the noble blood of this land'. Warwick had been overly bullish in his assessment of crucial loyalties. Five of the lords on his 'neutrals' list were now fighting for Lancaster, among them Richard Woodville, Lord Rivers and his twenty-one-year-old son Anthony.

Warwick's sense of an imminent reckoning, after the paralysing uncertainty of recent years, had been correct – unsurprisingly, given how much he had done to bring it about. Most of England's noblemen and their retinues were now ranged against each other across a few bleak miles of north Yorkshire. But Warwick himself was not there. Shot in the leg during the crossing at Ferrybridge, he had been forced to stay in the rear nursing his wound and, doubtless, cursing his bad luck.[30]

The following morning, Palm Sunday, the weather worsened, and the armies faced each other in driving sleet and snow. The Lancastrians, a large dark mass discernible through the blizzard, were drawn up on higher ground, their flanks protected on the left by boggy terrain and, on their right, by a sheer slope down to the river below. Through the whiteness could be glimpsed the brightly painted standards of Lancaster, among them Margaret's banner, which bore a verse from Psalm 43: '*Judica me, Deus, discerne causam meum de gente non sancta*', 'Judge me, O lord, and favour my cause from that of unholy people'.[31] But with Margaret and Henry both sheltering behind the walls at York, twelve miles away, there was only one royal claimant present on the battlefield.

When the Yorkist battle lines had deployed early that morning, Edward addressed his commanders. They had all wanted to make him their king, he shouted above the wind, and here he was: heir to a crown that had been usurped by Lancaster long ago. So help me reclaim my right, he cried. The yell went up: they would follow him until death. Edward, surrounded by his phalanx of heavily armoured household men, took up position beside his standards: his father's falcon-and-fetterlock, the black bull of his Clarence ancestors and the white lion of Mortimer, and, newest of all, his rose-en-soleil, a sunburst's rays streaming from a white rose.

The Yorkist archers, several thousand strong, marched forward and, having made the sign of the cross on the ground and kissed it, prepared to fire. As they did so, their commander Fauconberg had a hunch. If the Lancastrians' position, numbers and nobility were all to their advantage, one thing was not: the blizzard, which was blowing straight into their faces. Fauconberg ordered his archers to shoot an opening volley then, as the dense cloud of the arrowstorm hissed through the air, 'made them stand still', listening for the tell-tale screams in the enemy ranks.[32] As their arrows hit the Lancastrian vanguard, it began to return fire rapidly: fire which fell well short, thudding into the ground in front of the Yorkist ranks. Blinded by the snowstorm, shooting into the wind, the Lancastrian archers were neutered. Somerset had only one option: to advance. As the Lancastrian footmen moved slowly and relentlessly forward, the Yorkist archers loosed off their last arrows before running for the safety of their own ranks. Then the two sides engaged.[33]

In the treacherous conditions, the close fighting took on an even greater intensity than usual. For hours the tightly packed troops, the weather further hampering the view through their visor slits, fought viciously, stabbing and slashing, maces and flails crushing armour and bone, stumbling over the bodies of the injured and dying.[34] The Yorkist lines were held in place by the massive steel-armoured figure of Edward, fighting like a madman at the heart of his phalanx of household men. Though both armies comprised thousands of hastily enlisted commoners – 'naked', poorly equipped recruits who wore their commitment and discipline as scantily as their armour – it was this core of drilled, disciplined, loyal fighters who counted most. Nevertheless, as the day wore on, the weight of superior Lancastrian numbers began to tell, the Yorkist lines wavering under pressure.

Then, for the Yorkists, relief arrived. The duke of Norfolk's long-awaited East Anglian recruits finally materialized, fresh troops surging into the Lancastrian ranks. For a while, the Lancastrians withstood the pressure. Then, they buckled. Suddenly, men in their thousands were turning and running in panic, flinging off weapons, shields, helmets, anything that would weigh them down. Somerset and his commanders wheeled their horses about, spurring up the York road, away from the battlefield. Those on foot had no such recourse. Later, Edward reminisced that he had urged his troops to spare the common soldiers and kill the lords. He lied. His men killed everybody.[35]

The Lancastrians scattered over the open ground. Rode down by Yorkist horsemen, they fell, heads and faces sliced open by blades, smashed in by maces and hammers, poleaxe spikes driven into their skulls. The steep snow-covered slopes down to the nearby beck, which had previously protected the Lancastrian right flank, turned into a slippery death-trap; corpses piled up in the river, forming bridges of flesh over which survivors tried to scramble. On the York road, men were slaughtered as they bottlenecked around a partly destroyed bridge over the River Wharfe; more were drowned as they desperately tried to cross. The river's waters ran with blood.[36]

Darkness brought an end to the carnage. The following day, the blizzard had blown itself out. Edward rode slowly towards York through a landscape carpeted with bodies: corpses, it was said, littered an area six miles by three. Blood and gore mixed with snowmelt, trickling into furrows and ditches. Looters moved about the field, relieving the dead of money and clothes, severing rings from swollen and stiffening hands, ransacking tents and baggage carts; heralds counted the bodies and gravediggers began their work. Many of the Lancastrian dead were to be denied rest in the afterlife. Before burial, noses and ears were sliced off and faces gouged at, to prevent their identification at the Resurrection; then corpses were packed tightly in pits. In a final indignity, they were laid with heads facing west. When they awoke and sat up on the Day of Resurrection, their scarred, sightless eyes would be looking away from the sun and the risen Christ.[37]

As Edward was received into York with 'great solemnity and processions', the Yorkist reprisals began. The Lancastrian earl of Devon and forty-two knights captured during the battle were declared guilty of treason and beheaded. Five days later, on Easter Saturday, riders reached London around mid-morning, carrying a letter from Edward to his mother. A clutch of eager courtiers, waiting at Baynard's Castle for news, gathered round the dispatch, its seal broken, its message exultantly declaimed: 'it was seen and read by me', confirmed the jubilant Norfolk esquire William Paston. Heralds had counted twenty thousand Lancastrian dead, and eight thousand Yorkists. Heading the list of dead Lancastrian noblemen was Northumberland, hunted down by the Neville brothers in the latest act of vengeance between the two great northeastern families. But the people Edward most wanted had given him the slip. Riding north, Henry VI, Margaret and their son, together with Somerset, had evaded their Yorkist pursuers and, reaching Newcastle, then Berwick, disappeared over the Scottish border.[38] Over the following weeks, as Edward headed into the northeast, mopping up pockets of resistance and dispensing summary justice, more fleeing Lancastrians joined the fugitive royal family in Scotland. There they were given political asylum by Mary of Guelders, ruling on behalf of her young son James III.[39]

Later that spring, Edward turned south again. He stopped off for a few days in early May, just after his nineteenth birthday, at the earl of Warwick's castle of Middleham, deep in the dales of north Yorkshire. With him were a number of Lancastrian prisoners, men who, in their different ways, were of far more value alive than dead to a precarious new regime. Among them were skilled and experienced administrators like John Morton, arrested at the town of Cockermouth as he tried to escape by boat; an ageing clerk in Margaret of Anjou's secretariat named George Ashby; and other Lancastrian nobles and gentry who, rapidly evaluating their options, decided that their cause was now hopeless. Foremost among them were the Woodvilles, Lord Rivers and his son Anthony, who had ridden as far north as Bamburgh on the Northumbrian coast before second thoughts prompted them to throw themselves on Edward's mercy. Along with the others, they were taken to London and locked in the Tower.[40]

To those who had backed Edward, his success at Towton had proved God's clear endorsement of his royal credentials. Edward was, wrote the abbot of St Albans John Whethamstede, reaching for typically overblown classical analogies, an all-conquering warrior, Hector and Achilles rolled into one. As a Yorkist versifier put it, he was the rose that 'stands alone': the country's 'chief flower', who had come to save 'all England' – and had triumphed. In the same breath, though, the poet revealed that it was a victory, not for all England, but for the south. Now the property-owning southerner could live, without fear of northerners, 'in his own place/ His wife, and also his fair daughter, and all the goods that he has.' In enumerating Edward's support at Towton – Calais and London, Edward's main financial backers, were first on the list – the poet also inadvertently showed how geographically limited, how patchy it was.[41] Which was why, as Whethamstede noted, as well as being a dread dispenser of justice, Edward was going out of his way to embody another quality expected in kings: mercy. Fresh from his astonishing triumphs as war-leader, he now embraced the role of peacemaker.

Conciliation made sense, for a variety of reasons. The loyalties of many had been fluid, their commitment to either York or Lancaster the result of a tangle of family connections and interests, as well as a decision taken hastily in the face of unpredictable, fast-moving events. At Towton, as one appalled commentator noted, the fabric of English society had been torn apart. Families had found themselves pitted against each other, 'the son against the father, the brother against brother, the nephew against nephew'. Now, perhaps, those ties of blood and kinship could help to heal England; the sprawling extended families that knitted together England's political classes could enable Lancastrians to integrate with the new regime, if given the chance to do so. But genuine rehabilitation depended on people being convinced by their new king.

Already, Edward's ease in his own skin was surprising people. Here was a young monarch who, though inclined to opulence and able to work a sensational wardrobe, could cut through the glittering formality at a stroke: summoning stunned commoners into his presence; lifting kneeling diplomats up with a handshake or an enveloping embrace. The contrast with Henry VI, a king with whom familiarity only bred contempt, was marked. Tactile, with an appetite for physical contact, Edward was happy for people to get up close – and the closer you got, said contemporaries, the better it was: his face 'lovely', his body 'mighty, strong and clean made'. Here was a heady presence who could inspire a warband and melt resistance, in both men and women. Perhaps justly, given the staggering victories he had achieved at such a young age, nobody seemed more intoxicated by his charisma than Edward himself.

Indeed, there was something calculated about his insouciance. Edward, people remarked – astonished to find themselves in the presence of a king who remembered anything at all – never forgot a face, or a name. Whoever you were, noted one chronicler, once you were fixed in his memory, for good or bad, you stayed there.[42]

In the first week of April, news of Towton began to reach Flanders and northern France, first in a trickle then, 'hour by hour', in a flood, carried by heralds, in diplomatic letter-bags, by merchants as they travelled their regular routes between London and the cities of the Burgundian Low Countries. In Bruges, the papal legate Francesco Coppini, having stuck his neck out for the Yorkist cause, was in excellent good humour as he related how Warwick had 'made a new king of the son of the duke of York', a teenage king who was already proving 'prudent and magnanimous'. And, said Coppini's secretary, as he relayed the news to Pigello Portinari, head of the Bruges branch of the powerful Medici bank of Florence, it was a result that was both good for England and – with Edward intending to 'amend and organize matters' – good for 'future well-being'. After the last ruinous years of Henry VI's reign, Yorkist England would soon be open for business.[43]

When the news reached Philip of Burgundy, custodian of Edward's younger brothers George and Richard, he acted fast. Previously, he had packed the boys off to Utrecht, an independent city 140 miles away outside Burgundian jurisdiction, keeping his association with the house of York at arm's length, just in case. Now, he transferred them hurriedly to his glittering household in Bruges, where they were put up in lavish apartments staffed by Philip's own servants. The duke himself paid the princes a personal visit, showed them off at court, threw a banquet on their behalf and, in general, paid them 'the highest honour'. Laden with gifts and under tight security, they were transferred the seventy or so miles west to Calais, where a ship was waiting to ferry them across the Channel. They made the journey to London in slow, triumphant stages, proclaimed as 'the brothers of King Edward of England and France'. On 12 June, the three brothers were reunited west of London at the Thames-side manor of Sheen, formerly a favoured Lancastrian house. As craftsmen set about eradicating the Lancastrian devices that were everywhere moulded, painted and glazed into the house's fabric – the antelopes, swans, ostrich feathers and, for Henry VI and Margaret, the crowned initials 'H and M' – and replacing them with Edward's sunburst and white rose, the new king prepared for his coronation.[44]

Two weeks later, surrounded by his household men and preceded by a mounted escort of London's red-robed mayor and aldermen and four hundred citizens dressed in green, Edward rode over London Bridge and east through the city's narrow streets to the Tower, where he overnighted. There, as tradition demanded, he created a number of knights of the Bath, their loyalties bound to him as the fount of chivalric honour. Foremost among them were his 'dearest beloved brethren', George and Richard. The next day, as the royal procession wound through London's crowds and out, through Ludgate, to Westminster, the two boys were in the pack of newly dubbed knights who, wearing their blue gowns and white hoods, tokens of white silk lace adorning their left shoulders, rode directly in front of Edward himself.[45]

In Westminster Abbey on the morning of Sunday, 28 June 1461, in front of the high altar – and rather more lords spiritual and temporal than had been present at his inauguration as king some three months previously – Edward was anointed and crowned by the ever-reliable Thomas Bourchier, archbishop of Canterbury, with Edward the Confessor's 'rich crown' of solid, jewel-encrusted gold.[46]

Even though Edward had, in the words of one poet, come to 'love

London', the love wasn't universally reciprocated. One citizen bluntly turned down his neighbours' invitation to join them in cheering Edward along his coronation route: 'Twat and turd for him,' he retorted, adding that he would rather watch a duck-hunt. The neighbours, failing to see the funny side, reported him to the authorities. In the city, never mind the rest of the country, Edward still had plenty of convincing to do.[47]

In the following days, Edward's natural right to the crown of England was driven home. On Monday 29th he returned to the Abbey, where he sat enthroned and crowned, a figure of regal authority. His lineage was traced in a profusion of brightly coloured illuminated rolls, visual masterpieces that, unfurled and pinned to boards in the Abbey, helped spectators understand the magnitude of what they had seen. One, prefaced by an image of an armoured, crowned Edward riding into battle, bordered by the heraldic banners and badges of his predecessors alternating with his white rose-en-soleil, and sprinkled with white roses and sunbursts, revealed his lineage through the arcana of British myth-history.[48] In another, depicted with a cartoonist's eye, the tangled descent of Lancaster and the pure line of York twisted upwards in the thorned branches of a rose briar, each member of the house of Plantagenet springing from a rosebud. At the top, Henry VI, barely seeming to know one end of his sword from the other, was confronted by a martial Edward IV. Above them, Edward's deeds unfolded in a storyboard: five dramatic panels, each paralleled by an image from the Old Testament. The defining, transformative battle of Mortimer's Cross – signified by three crowned suns and, in case anybody missed the point, the words 'sol in forma triplia' – was Edward's Damascene moment: 'Lord, what would you have me do?', he said, a speech bubble scrolling from his lips. Later, he was Moses in front of the burning bush, taking his commandments from God. Other genealogies underscored Edward's Welsh Mortimer ancestry: lines of red and gold arrowing their way across the parchment to his Mortimer ancestors and, through them, to the mythical king of Britain, Cadwaladr. Here, Edward's crowning was the inevitable fulfilment of a prophecy made by the archangel Michael to the despairing Cadwaladr as his people were driven out of their devastated country: in time future, the angel told him, his heir would conquer all before him. Uniting England, Wales and Scotland, the 'three portions' of Britain, this descendant would bear the ancient name of Britain, 'rubius draco', the red dragon, and he and his heirs would reign to the world's end.[49]

Edward's immediate heir was – until such time as he married and had sons of his own – his brother, the eleven-year-old George. Later that same Monday at a great feast in George's honour, in the bishop of London's palace, Edward created him duke of Clarence. A title that had originally belonged to the second son of the great Plantagenet king Edward III, from whom the Yorkists were descended, it resonated with York's superior claim to the throne. It also underscored George's own significance as heir presumptive.[50]

The glittering ceremonial continued. Edward 'went crowned' twice, processing around Westminster Abbey and then St Paul's Cathedral. In St Paul's, a packed congregation watched as a figure dressed as an angel was lowered dramatically through the great vaulted interior, swinging a censer, bathing Edward in wafts of incense: Cadwaladr's prophecy re-enacted and fulfilled. Some onlookers, even those sympathetic to the regime, were unimpressed. In wanting 'to heap glory on glory' the crown-wearings, with their overcooked symbolism and expensive populist stunts, were, one observer thought, striving for effect. Surely the coronation, the supreme moment of legitimation, was enough.[51] It looked, he implied, a bit desperate.

This was hardly surprising. While Edward's charismatic leadership promised much to those who had witnessed it in action, his claim to the throne still needed a great deal of explaining to the vast majority. What was more, Edward had been brought up a nobleman, not a king-in-waiting. Now, as he began to reign, he had to undergo a rapid education in kingship to learn how to rule the whole country 'indifferently' or impartially, and how to command the undivided loyalties of all – not simply the hungry, expectant faction that had brought him to power and now clustered round to receive its rewards. Although government clerks were busy churning out the formulas of the new regime – the warrants, patents and proclamations that briskly dismissed Henry VI as king of England 'in fact but not of right' – the truth was that not until Henry's cause was eliminated could Edward be sovereign in his own land.[52]

For many, throughout both England and Europe, Edward was the usurper; Henry VI remained the rightful king. Conflict had not ended with the carnage of Towton. Rather, with the existence of two crowned kings of England, it had mutated. As spring turned into summer, disorder continued unabated across huge swathes of the country. Much of the violence, from the southwest, through Wales and the midlands to the northeast, was explicitly connected with the house of Lancaster. Meanwhile, at both ends of the country, the new Yorkist regime was under stress. Across the English Channel, Henry VI's uncle Charles VII of France, his sympathies squarely with the Lancastrian regime, was believed to be assembling an armada. That same May, a French force had taken control of Jersey: rumours abounded that the French would take control of the other Channel Islands and use them as a springboard to invade England.[53] Where the French led, the Scots, their junior partners in the 'auld alliance', tended to follow. At the Scottish court the exiled Lancastrians had quickly cut a deal with their hosts, receiving military aid in exchange for the valuable, perpetually contested border stronghold of Berwick. Soon, packs of Scottish and Lancastrian raiders were pouring back across England's northern border.

The opulence of Edward's coronation ceremonies, meanwhile, barely masked the new regime's insolvency. Since his accession, Edward had been living on individual and corporate loans from well-wishers. The coronation had been paid for with the last scrapings of cash from a near-empty Exchequer or, as Edward commanded with some desperation, 'the first and most ready money that is come or by any means may come to your hands'.[54]

Nevertheless, the sudden materializing on England's throne of this fresh-faced giant gave force to all the redemptive Yorkist propaganda. Edward's coming marked a clean break from the tired, squalid struggles of the past decade. In order to make good on the Yorkist promise to 'save all England', he would have to deliver on the pledges that he, and his father before him, had made: to bring security to England's borders and the surrounding seas; to stamp out the violence in England's provinces, which had fuelled and been exacerbated by civil war; and to deliver justice, peace, prosperity and fiscal reform, starting with the crown's own rickety finances. If Edward were to reset the crown's battered sovereignty on new foundations, those of the house of York, he would have to show that royal authority lay in him, and him alone.

3

The World is Right Wild

In July 1461 two envoys from the duke of Milan, Francesco Sforza, rode up through Kent towards London. Previously one of northern Italy's most brutal mercenary commanders, Sforza had proved himself as deft a diplomat as he was a military tactician. With Charles VII of France maintaining a predatory interest in the Italian peninsula, Sforza grew closer to those princes who feared French expansion, among them Philip of Burgundy. In recent years, relations between France and its most powerful vassal state, always tense, had deteriorated further when the man Charles loathed most of all – his own estranged son and heir, Louis – fled France for the Burgundian court. There, sheltered by Philip, Louis spent much of his time fervently praying for his father's death. Sforza, meanwhile, had followed developments with interest – an outbreak of war on France's north-eastern frontier would, after all, be just the way to distract the French king from further meddling in Italy – and had been further encouraged by events in England. Close to Burgundy, hostile to France and in desperate need of international recognition, the fledgling Yorkist regime was, Sforza felt, a government with which he could do business.[1]

Earlier that summer Sforza's agent in Bruges had complained that it was impossible to get any clear picture of the situation in England: 'every day and every hour, conditions change'. As the envoys entered London, however, any impression that they might have formed of Edward IV's impermanence was quickly dispelled. Awaiting them, fresh from his coronation and surrounded by a pack of lords and gentlemen, was the king himself. Edward lavished attention on his Milanese visitors: never, members of London's Italian merchant community assured them, had so much honour been shown to an embassy.[2]

Edward had his priorities clear. As king, it was his duty to dazzle, to

lift himself above even the greatest of his nobles – which, in the sumptuary arms race of the time, nobles turning up at court in ever more
'excessive and inordinate arrays', was no mean challenge – and to project his 'royal majesty' through conspicuous wealth. The royal household
was a reflection of both the king's authority and power and, in microcosm, the condition of his kingdom. It was, contemporary theorists
stressed, an urgent political necessity that the king stuff his houses with
costly tapestries and other fine furnishings; that he fill his wardrobes
and jewelhouse with 'rich clothes, rich furs, rich stones, and other jewels and ornaments'. With his love of clothes, his awareness of exactly
how good he looked in them, and his compulsive magpie eye for fine
things, Edward didn't need a second invitation. From the moment he
ascended the throne, George Darell, the newly appointed keeper of his
Great Wardrobe – which, from its sprawling complex at Blackfriars on
London's western edge, supplied the king's personal wardrobes, as well
as those of his family, with all the fine textiles they needed – was working overtime buying furs, velvets, satins, silks, cloth-of-gold and delicate
linens and, with his army of craftsmen, transforming them into sensational outfits for his fashion-conscious young king. In the process, he
was quickly running up a substantial deficit, outstripping his income by
hundreds, then thousands of pounds.[3]

Magnificence didn't lie simply in soft furnishings, knick-knacks
and an impressive wardrobe. Kings were supposed to overwhelm
subjects, guests and adversaries alike through every aspect of their
household: its smooth, well-drilled functioning; its polished, courtly,
intimidating servants; and the endless stream of fragrant, exquisite
dishes that emerged from its kitchens, washed down by a lavish supply of wine from its well-stocked cellars. Ostentatious hospitality was
called for. That July, the only thing preoccupying an intensely relaxed
Edward, it appeared, was making sure that he and his guests had as
much fun as possible.

The ensuing days and weeks passed in a blur of royal hospitality.
As the envoys made their way slowly west up the Thames valley to
Windsor, they remarked on how Edward was constantly immersed in
'some sort of pleasure', showering on the ambassadors 'every gratifi-
cation'. Daily hunting parties, lubricated by the tuns of 'good Gascon
wine' that a perpetually thirsty Edward demanded be stationed at

convenient intervals 'ready there for our drinking', grew increasingly sodden. By night, the ambassadors were treated to 'festivities of ladies', as they put it with diplomatic vagueness; where once a horrified Henry VI, confronted with a troupe of bare-breasted dancing girls laid on to 'entice' him, had quickly left the room, Edward could not get enough of such enticement.[4]

Keeping pace with the appetites of England's prodigious eighteen-year-old king proved a challenge – one of the ambassadors, Count Ludovico Dallugo, had a recurrence of gout – and in fact the envoys had tried repeatedly to leave. But Edward, all 'fair words' and court-eous conviviality, refused to let them, plunging them instead into yet another round of entertainment. Not only did Edward push his own hedonism to the limit, he expected his guests, as well as his closest servants, to keep up.

Amid the relentless partying, Dallugo managed to glean some information about the state of England. Things were improving for the new regime with each day that passed. In the north, the earl of Warwick and his uncompromising brother John Neville had pushed the bands of Scottish and Lancastrian raiders back over the border. In Wales, too, Edward's loyal point man William, Lord Herbert, sent by the king to 'cleanse' the principality, was proving effective, so much so that Edward, who had plans to lead an army into Wales, kept putting them off. There was, he felt, no need to go until later in the summer, after harvest, when there would be plenty of food for his men. Run-ning through this strategic decision, however, was the sense that Edward was having rather too much fun where he was.

Dallugo had managed to get close to one nobleman in particular, with whom he had several conversations, and who had told him bluntly that, with all Henry VI's lords coming over to Edward, the Lancastrian cause was irretrievably lost. Dallugo was impressed: the nobleman in question had formerly been one of Henry's foremost lords. Indeed, he and his son – both men of 'very great valour' – had been released from the Tower only weeks before; now, pardoned and rehabilitated, they were working their way into Edward's good graces. The nobleman's name, Dallugo remembered, was Richard Wood-ville, Lord Rivers.[5]

Although Dallugo was inclined to take everything he was told at face value, late in July events did indeed seem to be sliding decisively in Edward's favour. The French king, ill for years, succumbed to the infections that had left his face and intestines so swollen that he was unable to take liquid. Nobody was more delighted than his son, the thirty-eight-year-old Louis, who had been assiduously following astrologers' predictions of his father's death and was agreeably surprised to find that it had come even sooner than they had forecast. Crowned Louis XI at the great cathedral of Notre-Dame in Reims, he carried out a wholesale purge of his father's ministers. Among the people he locked up were the two key commanders of the planned Lancastrian reinvasion of England: the French general Pierre de Brézé and Henry Beaufort, duke of Somerset. Whether Louis had absorbed Duke Philip's pro-Yorkist tendencies during his Burgundian exile – at Towton, a detachment of Burgundian troops had fought for Edward under Louis' banner – or whether his behaviour was a last vindictive spasm against his hated father, was unclear. Either way, French backing for the Lancastrian cause was, at least for the time being, off.[6]

Finally, early in August, the ambassadors, taking with them nine 'very handsome' white horses and some English hunting dogs that Sforza had asked them to pick up, departed London and, accompanied by Edward and the royal household, rode back through Kent to the port of Sandwich. As they passed through towns and cities, they were astonished by Edward's reception: the people, Dallugo wrote, 'adore him like a God'.

The Milanese ambassadors left with the impression of a monarch whose sprawling insouciance conveyed his ease in his own kingdom, confident in the loyalties of his subjects and only too happy to embrace the Lancastrian opponents who were now flocking to offer him their 'tender obedience', and whose total victory was only a matter of time. Their visit, in other words, had gone precisely as Edward would have wanted. There had, though, been something obsessive about the king's constant attentiveness towards his guests. From the moment he had met them, to his insistence on personally escorting them to the ship that would take them out of England, he barely let them out of his sight.

Edward threw himself into the government of his new realm with the same intensity with which he partied. As he sat, an imposing presence in the council chamber, chewing over with his councillors the challenges faced by his regime; as he processed business, receiving petitioners, authorizing warrants, letters and bills with a regal 'word of mouth', a capacious flourish of his sign manual 'R. E.', or the wax stamp of his signet, Edward's dominance was striking.[7] If some foreign observers speculated that the king was putty in the hands of his family – one got the impression that Warwick was 'everything in this kingdom'; his mother Cecily, noted another, could 'rule the king as she pleases' – anybody who mistook his affability for inattention was rapidly put straight.[8] Over the past decade, with Henry VI's government impotent in the face of endemic disorder, the king's laws had gradually become a dead letter. Edward was determined to be obeyed. When, perhaps in the habit of ignoring royal summons, the Norfolk gentleman John Paston failed to respond to two privy seals from the king, his brother wrote from London late one night, reporting how a raging Edward had sworn to kill Paston if he again 'disobeys our writing', adding insistently that 'the king will keep his promise'.[9] Paston duly turned up.

Long-standing kinsmen and associates of the house of York settled comfortably into positions of power and influence in the new regime. Now, they were indisputably Edward's men, bound to him in a slew of ennoblements and knightings after Towton. Among them were his ever-reliable uncle Henry Bourchier, older brother of the archbishop of Canterbury, who was made earl of Essex and treasurer; Sir John Howard, a Norfolk soldier of explosive violence who was as 'mad as a wild bullock' when things didn't go his way, and the uncompromising William Herbert, busy restoring order in Wales. But there was one man who, more than any other, defined Edward's rise.[10]

The emergence of William Hastings had been almost as sudden as Edward's own. A bluff Leicestershire esquire, he had followed his father into Richard duke of York's service, but rather than fleeing into exile with the Yorkist lords after the fiasco of Ludford Bridge, had kept his head down. He resurfaced as Edward surged to the throne, becoming a key member of his warband; the bloodbath at Towton, in which Hastings fought shoulder-to-shoulder alongside his teenage king, transformed his fortunes. Knighting him amid the battlefield carnage, Edward deluged him with grants and rewards. Then, towards the end of July, he made Hastings, now in his early thirties, chamberlain of his household: an appointment that showed just how close, how quickly, the two men had become.

Tough, of unswerving and proven loyalty, Hastings also seemed to get on with everybody – 'a loving man, and passing well beloved', as Thomas More later put it. As chamberlain he headed the king's 'chamber', the sequence of royal apartments that constituted the above-stairs of the king's household and the team of personal servants that ran them. Here, the king slept, ate, processed business and entertained, displaying his wealth and power to awed petitioners and diplomats alike. In the space of four months, this obscure Leicestershire esquire had become a friend whom Edward not only relied upon to help project his regime's image, but whom he trusted with his security and his life. Whatever it was that Edward first found in Hastings – his relaxed conviviality, his 'pliancy', his constant readiness to anticipate his king's needs and desires – he had an added attraction for the king: the sense that Hastings was entirely his own creation. With no lineage and little land to speak of, Hastings owed everything he had to his monarch, his fortunes inextricably linked with Edward's own.[11]

As Edward's travelling household rumbled through southern England that summer, Hastings was at his side. Heading unhurriedly towards Wales to link up with Herbert's counter-insurgency campaign, Edward showed himself to his admiring people: meeting and greeting, hearing complaints and delivering justice, graciously accepting gifts of cash and plate from civic dignitaries and enjoying their lavish hospitality. Welcomed into Bristol by elaborate pageants figuring forth his royal heritage, Edward stayed for a week. He oversaw the provision of seaborne supplies, sent round the coast to Herbert as he besieged Jasper Tudor's stronghold of Pembroke Castle on the tip of southwest Wales, and presided over the treason trial and execution of the troublemaking Devon knight Sir Baldwin Fulford, who had been stirring up Lancastrian resistance across his native southwest. (Fulford's head, stuck on a spike in Exeter marketplace to discourage Lancastrian tendencies among the locals, stayed there for some eighteen months until his son, noting that bits of it 'daily falleth down', pleadingly petitioned to remove it.[12])

At Bristol, Edward changed his plans. With Herbert's mopping-up operation still proving effective, the king left him to get on with it. Standing down the forces that had been due to muster at Hereford and taking their wages – two thousand marks, sent in eight pairs of saddlebags – he carried on through the Welsh Marches, through the scene of his triumph at Mortimer's Cross, to his childhood home of Ludlow, before returning to London by equally comfortable stages. Ahead of him, news reached the capital that Herbert had taken Pembroke Castle and, after pursuing Jasper Tudor's forces up the Welsh coast, had caught up with them and crushed them at Twt Hill outside Caernarfon. Lancastrian resistance in Wales had collapsed, with only a few isolated groups still holding out.[13]

Although Jasper Tudor himself remained on the run in the mountains of Snowdonia, Herbert could console himself with the capture of his four-year-old nephew Henry, earl of Richmond. The boy's patrimony had been confiscated, but things could always change; besides which, his mother, the great Lancastrian heiress Lady Margaret Beaufort, had managed to hold on to her inheritance. Henry Tudor had exceptional value in the wardship and marriage market. Herbert paid Edward £1,000 for his custody, bringing him up alongside his own daughters at his great Monmouthshire castle of Raglan. He probably thought he had got a bargain.[14]

That October, Edward spent a fortnight downstream of London at his manor of Greenwich, on a bend in the Thames as it broadened towards the sea. There, to his delight, two of his father's former servants reappeared. Earlier in the year, as Margaret of Anjou's army had approached London, Thomas Vaughan and William Hatteclyffe had left London by ship with the family treasure, hoping to courier it to the safety of the Low Countries. Promptly captured by French privateers, they had spent the intervening months kicking their heels in a French gaol, until Edward paid their ransoms. Both were experienced, highly capable, valuable men and Edward was quick to find them influential posts in his household. As an esquire for the body, Vaughan became one of the most intimate of Edward's chamber servants. On hand to fulfil the king's desires, should 'anything lack for his person or his pleasure', he was also entrusted with the most confidential information, the keeping of 'many secrets'. As well as dressing and undressing the king, Vaughan formed part of his first line of security, watching over him 'day and night'. Hatteclyffe, meanwhile, was appointed king's physician. Having formerly looked after the abstemious, listless Henry VI, he now had a rather different challenge on his hands.[15]

Given Edward's tendency to compulsive self-gratification, it would take all Hatteclyffe's skill and tact to keep in balance the four bodily humours that, following the Greek medical authority Galen, were held to derive from the consumption of food and drink: to point out, as he stood 'in the presence of the king's meals', that it might be an idea to slow down, or not eat or drink quite so much of this or that; and to have rather more robust private discussions with the king's chief household officers about trying to rein in his compulsive consumption of 'meat and drinks'. As he counselled Edward on his lifestyle and attempted to encourage him to follow the regimen they had drawn up together, Hatteclyffe became one of his most intimate advisers, dispensing judicious advice about the state of the kingdom of England, incarnate in the body of its new, young king.[16]

Late in the month, Edward was rowed upstream in the royal barge through London to Westminster. Before the opening of Parliament, he had some fraternal business to settle. On All Saints' Day, crowned and in rich purple velvet robes, he processed around a Westminster Abbey filled with nobles and city dignitaries as the feast-day responses were sung: five boys of the chapel royal clustered on the altar steps, one holding a lighted candle, their interweaving voices fragile in the incensed air. The same day, Edward created his youngest brother Richard duke of Gloucester, the great royal dukedom previously held by Henry VI's uncle Humphrey, whose populist cause had been taken up by the Yorkists. It had taken Edward a while to get round to it, some four months after Clarence had received his title and lands – but then Clarence was heir to the throne. To the nine-year-old Richard, the ceremony must have seemed worth the wait; less so the ragbag of grants with which Edward endowed him. Edward had a lot of people to reward and for now his young brother was well down the pecking order. Besides, Richard was scarcely in a position to object.[17]

On Thursday 12 November, in Westminster, the new speaker of Parliament Sir James Strangways, a Yorkshireman with close connections to the Neville family, rose to set out for the assembled Lords and Commons Edward's right and title to the English crown. He launched into an official version of the recent convulsions, enshrining in parliamentary record the accounts that had been evolving in Yorkist verses, prophecies and genealogies: a story of foul, unnatural Lancastrian rule swept away, and true order restored by Edward's 'knightly courage' and 'mighty power'. Following Strangways' peroration, Parliament proceeded to turn this narrative into legal reality, passing a comprehensive act of attainder that declared the house of Lancaster and its descendants legally dead and perpetually disinherited. Eliminating them from the political map, the act also formalized the comprehensive land grab that Edward had carried out the previous summer, which had turned the poverty-stricken nobleman of Mortimer's Cross into one of the greatest royal landowners since William the Conqueror. Now, he possessed a vast portfolio of property stretching across England, his own landed inheritance swelled by the royal duchy of Cornwall, the great private estates of the duchy of Lancaster – which, in a neat legal move, were now made the permanent possessions of the kings of England – and the confiscated lands of great Lancastrian noblemen.[18] All of which looked good on paper. The problem was that Edward had already given much of it away. Unsurprisingly, the man who had gained most was the earl of Warwick, who was handed a massive swathe of lands and grants, from the captaincy of Calais and control of the Cinque Ports on the Kent coast to wardenship of the Anglo-Scottish Marches, as well as estates across the north of England and the midlands.

Still, Edward and his advisers were mindful that patronage was a balancing act: kings were meant to retain enough land to provide them with an income that enabled them to live in royal style. Henry VI, who had granted everything away, had got this catastrophically wrong. And having used Henry's incontinent generosity as a stick to beat him with, the new Yorkist regime had to start as it meant to go on.

At the heart of royal finance was the Exchequer, whose old-fashioned processes ground slowly, subject to its 'ancient course', and with maddening inefficiency in terms of providing the king with ready money. But there was another method that Edward knew, having grown up with it as earl of March: the flexible, direct process of land management used by noblemen up and down the country to extract the value of their estates in cash. Months into his new reign, Edward started to impose the same system. Instead of time-serving rent collectors entrenched in the Exchequer offices in Westminster, a group of professional financial officials – appointed by and directly answerable to the king and his closest chamber servants – fanned out across the crown estates, surveying lands, receiving income and noting meticulously everything that 'might be most for the king's profit'. Their cash receipts were 'delivered to the coffers of the lord king', wherever in the kingdom he happened to be, for his immediate disbursement. The Exchequer was given a copy of the accounting for record; that was all. The real business was going on in the king's own chamber. Flexible and efficient, it was a system subject to the control of Edward and his close personal servants, one which was actioned with a scrawl of the king's signature or, as Edward regally put it when directing financial transactions, 'by our commandment given by our own mouth'.[19] In autumn 1461, he launched the new system on a portfolio of crown lands in the Welsh Marches. In time, it would spread to whatever sources of income he could get his hands on.

It was not the whole answer, however. Efficient though this new system might be, it took time to implement. More to the point, the question of whether the crown lands could provide an adequate source of royal revenue, however rigorously they were managed, remained moot. Though Edward also made the habitual claim to customs revenues on all exports and imports flowing through England's ports, this income stream had been badly dented by the disorder of recent years. And even in stable times, the kingdom's running costs, from the maintenance of the Calais garrison and the security of the country's northern borders, from diplomacy to the glittering magnificence of the royal household, were constantly in excess of its revenues.[20] These times were not stable. Edward urgently needed other sources of credit.

Apart from tackling the mountain of debt he had accumulated – both inherited from the previous regime, and which he owed to his own supporters and financial backers – Edward had to deal with the ongoing security situation. As autumn turned into winter, the relative calm of recent months began to prove illusory. Yorkist spies, sent across the border into Scotland, reported how the faction-ridden government of its young king James III was now being driven by the pro-Lancastrian bishop of St Andrews, James Kennedy, working closely and busily with Margaret of Anjou and the exiled Lancastrians there. The news from France was worse. Louis XI's kneejerk reaction against his late father's administration seemed to have got something out of his system. Calming down, he started to release all the people he had locked up, including the vengeful Somerset. Across England, meanwhile, disorder was renewed and intensified. As Edward tried to crack down on local unrest, his agents, the household men who were also the king's eyes and ears in the regions – men by whom 'may be known the disposition of the counties' – tried to sift these acts of violent criminality, looking for signs of political agitation and 'suspicious congregations', picking at networks of affinity to see what and who might, possibly, lead to the house of Lancaster.[21]

As Parliament adjourned for Christmas, Edward, massive in his robes of state, addressed the Commons, thanking them for their 'tender and true hearts' and promising to reward them with 'my body', which would 'always be ready for your defence'. Then his tone hardened. If any of his enemies who had already been pardoned for bearing arms against him should backslide, they would 'never again' be accepted into the king's grace, whatever their rank. Instead, they would be 'thoroughly punished'. There would be no more chances.[22]

Throughout the first months of 1462, reports of suspicious activity flooded in. An agent of the Norfolk gentleman John Paston wrote to him breathlessly with 'right secret' information. An army of 120,000 men, led by Somerset and backed by an international coalition of kingdoms, would make co-ordinated landings on the Kentish, Yorkshire and Welsh coasts; simultaneously, a combined Lancastrian–Scottish army would cross England's northern border. However wild the rumours, Edward and his advisers took them seriously. Along England's southern coastline, towns were put on high alert and defences strengthened. Warwick, handed the admiralty of England – a logical move, given how heavily the country's dilapidated navy relied on his own private fleet – dispatched patrols along the Channel and the vulnerable East Anglian coast.[23] Edward's slender resources were badly stretched. In Norfolk, vendettas, gang violence and shifting allegiances had combined in a toxic brew. 'For love of God, take good await to your person', one panicked correspondent advised John Paston, 'for the world is right wild.' Much to his irritation, Edward had been forced to send one of his key advisers, Thomas Montgomery, to 'set a rule' in the region: there was, he snapped, nobody whose absence from his side 'might worse have been forborne, at that time'. Newly appointed sheriff of Norfolk and Suffolk, Montgomery materialized in the area late that December and started sniffing around, armed with some names that the king had given him.[24] Whether or not his activities had anything to do with the events of the following weeks, things moved fast.

On the morning of Saturday 13 February, a group of men were brought to the Tower of London under heavy guard. They included two big fish: the great East Anglian nobleman John de Vere, earl of Oxford, and his son and heir Aubrey, together with a number of their 'feed men' or paid retainers. All were charged with plotting to kill Edward.

On the face of it, Oxford's involvement in the conspiracy was surprising. A half-hearted Lancastrian at best, he was in persistent ill-health; before Towton he had been unhesitatingly identified by the Yorkists as 'neutral', guaranteed to stay at home, since when he had apparently adapted to the new regime with ease. His oldest son Aubrey, however, was different. One of Margaret of Anjou's most charismatic courtiers, he still apparently held a flame for her; so too did retainers of Oxford's like Sir Thomas Tuddenham, once Henry VI's treasurer, whose notorious gang was responsible for recent disturbances in East Anglia, and on whom Montgomery had been keeping tabs. Nevertheless, it was Oxford's own seal that had been stamped on a set of incriminating letters addressed to Henry and Margaret, which one of his messengers, in a fit of conscience, had brought to Edward.

Opening the letters, gently warming the wax and sliding a horsehair under it to preserve the seal unbroken, Edward's agents found details of an elaborate plot. Either Oxford would link up with Somerset's seaborne invasion, using a site on the isolated east Essex coast as a beachhead, or, he would march north as part of a Yorkist army to combat Scottish and Lancastrian forces, before turning on Edward and murdering him and his men.[25] Edward's response was deliberate. The letters, copied and resealed, were handed back to the messenger, who in turn delivered them to the exiled Lancastrian court in Scotland, before returning to Edward with Henry's incriminating reply. The man Edward entrusted with the operation – who was, probably, a hawk-like presence in the room when Oxford's letters were unsealed; who was dispatched to Oxford's Essex headquarters of Hedingham Castle to round up the conspirators; and who presided over their trial – was John Tiptoft, earl of Worcester.

Sent to Rome by Henry VI on papal business some three years previously, Tiptoft had deliberately failed to fulfil his mission. A Yorkist by temperament and marriage – he had married Warwick's sister Cecily – Tiptoft had remained in Italy, staying out of the escalating civil conflict in England and indulging his scholarly interests. A cosmopolitan student of the *humanae litterae*, the reinvigorated study of classical letters, he browsed bookshops, attended lectures by some of the finest scholars of the age and moved in rarefied intellectual circles, all the time keeping up with the disturbing developments in England through his agents. Finally arriving in Rome, he set about representing not the Lancastrian government, but Edward IV's fledgling regime. After delivering an oration in front of the papal Curia, his Latin so beautifully turned that it reportedly moved Pope Pius II to tears, he was called home in the summer of 1461 by Edward, eager to take advantage of Tiptoft's abilities.

If Tiptoft's learning had instilled anything in him, it was not the vaguely progressive, reforming spirit that often animated the writings of *humanistae*, but humanism's related focus on strong, ordered government. As his secretary John Free put it, trying to explain away his master's prolonged stay in Italy, his learning would help the state regain its former strength. Immediately admitted into Edward's inner circle, Tiptoft showed a pathological interest in putting theory into practice. On 7 February 1462, precisely in order to prosecute Oxford and his accomplices, he was appointed constable of England.[26]

The constable presided over all aspects of military behaviour. His appointment was not permanent, but took place during exceptional moments: royal marriages, for instance, when he acted as a martial master of ceremonies, organizing tournaments and wargames; and in states of emergency – such as civil war – when security was prioritized over normal legal procedures and when the constable's tribunal, the court of chivalry, was called on to judge acts of treason against the king.

If the conditions for this court's operation were exceptional, so too was its process. In ruling on crimes that contravened the 'law of arms' – the laws of chivalry, of which the king was the ultimate arbiter – it followed its own guidelines and customs rather than those of common law. Although legally constituted, with powers defined by statute, many found its workings disturbing. With no due process, no formal indictments or juries, the constable's court was the supreme expression of the royal will, handing down a verdict 'ordained' in advance by the king. Given that the king needed no other information to reach a verdict than his own definition of what constituted a treasonable act, in disturbed times this glorified kangaroo court was a godsend to the monarch.[27]

In the prevailing climate, the conviction for treason of Oxford, his heir and their co-conspirators was inevitable. Their beheadings at the Tower were spaced out over three days, for the benefit of a fascinated, horrified crowd. In a concession to his infirmity, Oxford was led slowly to his execution by two clerics.

There was something particularly shocking about these killings. In part this was down to the spectacle itself, with father and son beheaded together – a 'piteous sight', murmured one onlooker. But what caused the most widespread disgust was the apparently unnatural, un-English nature of Tiptoft's verdict: one based not on English law but foreign legislation, 'the law of Padua'. In fact, Tiptoft had stuck rigidly to the letter of the 'law of arms', which was based on the international civil law that he had, indeed, studied extensively at Padua, one of Christendom's pre-eminent seats of legal learning. In the retelling, this became garbled. It was, perhaps, an understandable mistake, especially given that Tiptoft, with his Italianate ways, didn't perhaps seem entirely English himself.[28]

Edward rapidly disposed of the earl of Oxford's lands, now forfeit to the crown: the lion's share was granted to his youngest brother Richard, to bolster his underwhelming property portfolio. Of Oxford's four surviving sons, Edward handed control of the oldest, the nineteen-year-old John, to Warwick. Always on the lookout for attractive marriages for his family, Warwick soon set Oxford's heir up with his youngest sister Margaret. After all, in the fullness of time, an opportunity would almost inevitably arise to claw back the earl's forfeited title and estates.

Meanwhile, in what seemed a particularly callous act on Edward's part, he handed control of two of Oxford's younger sons to their father's executioner. Maybe it was just a question of convenience. Tiptoft, as constable of the Tower, was already the boys' gaoler; indeed, he also had custody of another prisoner there, the Lancastrian heir to the earl of Northumberland, Henry Percy. Quite how Tiptoft benefited from the arrangement was unclear. As younger sons they would hardly have inherited much; nor did Tiptoft have any children of his own for them to marry. Perhaps he just relished the chance to give the boys a rigorous classical education.[29]

That spring, the game of cat-and-mouse continued. With Scotland still backing the Lancastrians, Edward put pressure on the kingdom, funding dissident Scottish nobles to stir up unrest, while Warwick sent bands of English raiders across the border. When in April Margaret of Anjou sailed to France, attempting to secure the backing of Louis XI, an increasingly beleaguered Scottish government shouldered aside the pro-Lancastrian Bishop Kennedy and reached out to the Yorkist regime. A three-month truce was brokered: breathing space, of sorts.

Meanwhile, Edward energetically continued to fulfil his promise to restore law and order, making a judicial progress through eastern England. At Leicester that Easter, he dispatched a series of fundraising letters, outlining the dangers of Lancastrian invasion in lurid detail. Money was not as instantly forthcoming as it had been in the seismic early months of 1461, when London's panicked corporation had extended credit to Edward and Warwick hand over fist. Though sympathetic, the city's collective finances were hardly unlimited. So Edward cast his net more widely, focusing on the people at the top of London's financial food chain – the merchants of high net worth who, individually and in syndicates, might be persuaded to invest in the crown in return for trading privileges and access to the heart of royal power. He was also establishing warm relations with the community that, isolated and threatened in recent years, had been heartened by

Edward's willingness to throw England open to foreign investment: Italy's merchant bankers. On 17 March, Edward agreed a substantial loan of £2,000 with the Bruges and London branches of Christendom's greatest bank, the house of Medici. The funds went to plug the vast deficit owed to the Calais garrison – but they didn't go very far. At Edward's accession, the garrison's backdated wages stood at a colossal £37,000. While this was hardly Edward's fault, the restive garrison's commitment to the Yorkist regime was already fraying at the edges.[30]

With its immense economic, strategic and military value to England, Calais had long been coveted by the kings of France. That June, following talks with Margaret of Anjou, Louis XI publicly announced his backing for the Lancastrians. At the heart of his commitment was a secret agreement that, should Margaret fail to repay his loans within a year of Henry VI regaining the throne, Louis would receive Calais. As French troops raided deep into the enclave, the Calais garrison's loyalties began to unravel in the face of Margaret's promises of 'much silver' in return for opening the gates to her. Over the summer the Yorkist regime scrabbled for control, negotiating emergency loans from the city of London and ordering a general mobilization; in London's port, forty ships commandeered by John Tiptoft rode at anchor, ready to transport a relief force across the Channel. In mid-September the disaster was averted. A deal to pay off the garrison's debts was thrashed out with the help of the Staple, the powerful syndicate of Calais wool merchants. The Staple would fulfil the garrison's backdated wages; in return, Edward handed them a raft of trading privileges, including the right to collect customs revenues, until the debts were paid off.[31] It was a price worth paying. Edward could now focus on the Lancastrian invasion that everybody said was coming.

On Saturday, 30 October, news arrived in London from the northeast: Margaret of Anjou, her general Henry Beaufort, duke of Somerset and their forces had made landfall. It was a modest army. Louis XI's enthusiasm had quickly dissipated when a Yorkist fleet burned and looted its way along the north-western French coast in retaliation for his proclaimed support for Lancaster, and he hadn't even paid for the eight hundred French mercenaries Margaret had recruited.[32]

The Lancastrians, though, were relying on local loyalties. Yorkist control of the northeast was barely skin deep and, as Lancastrian banners were raised, people quickly rediscovered their former allegiances. The commanders of the great fortresses of Alnwick, Dunstanburgh and Bamburgh, who had pledged loyalty to Edward, declared for Margaret. From these formidable bases, the Lancastrians started raising support across the region.[33]

Edward's response was decisive. Four days later, amid a frenzy of mobilization and fundraising – with memories of Margaret's advance on London the previous year still fresh, the city now stumped up with alacrity – he was on his way north.[34]

The army that streamed up the Great North Road early that November, banners and standards flying, was a massive demonstration of the authority of Edward's rule. At Towton, some eighteen months before, his army had included the retinues of perhaps eleven lords. Now there were thirty-eight – the vast majority of England's nobility – and hundreds of knights and gentlemen. From lords Hastings and Herbert to the young Lancastrian-turned-Yorkist nobleman Anthony Woodville and seasoned fighters like Sir John Astley – a veteran jouster on whom an admiring Edward had conferred the Order of the Garter earlier in the year – it was a formidable expression of chivalric loyalty to the house of York. Indeed, this was a campaign that no self-respecting knight would want to miss. With rumours that a Scottish army was on the march to support Lancaster, the coming encounter would very possibly play out the endgame of Yorkist prophecy, one that would see the final destruction of Lancaster and the ultimate victory of York, under whose rule England, Wales and Scotland would be united.[35]

Hovering on the margins of this charmed circle was a man whose reputation for unpredictable brutality went before him. After fighting in France, Sir Thomas Malory had served as MP for his native Warwickshire before the increasingly unstable political situation had brought a latent psychopathy bubbling to the surface. After an eighteen-month rampage, much of it directed against the great Lancastrian nobleman the duke of Buckingham, Malory had been locked up on multiple charges, including extortion, criminal damage, cattle rustling, rape and attempted murder. Spending the next few years in and out of prison – some of his escapes involved armed breakouts, in another he swam a moat – Malory got drawn into the dynastic conflict, his fortunes attached to York and Warwick. Barely a week before Edward's army marched north, he had walked into the Chancery offices in Westminster Palace to receive the official paperwork for his general pardon, which he then presented at the court of King's Bench in the adjacent Westminster Hall; there, all pending charges against him were dropped.[36] There was no doubting the timing of his pardon.

Perhaps more than most, Malory saw the squalid savagery of recent times through rose-tinted lenses: in his eyes, vendettas, turf wars and atrocities, informed by the world of chivalric romance, acquired an epic grandeur. In years to come, his spectacular retelling of the Arthurian myths, the *Morte d'Arthur*, would be inflected by his own experiences of civil conflict. As he wrote about the death of Sir Lancelot, he made the dying knight insist on being buried at his great stronghold of Joyous Gard – at which point Malory paused, apparently trying to recollect a half-forgotten memory. 'Some men', he added, said that Joyous Gard 'was Alnwick,' – where Malory was deployed alongside his commander, Anthony Woodville – 'and some men say it was Bamburgh.'[37]

In times of cross-border tension and war with Scotland, the city of Newcastle, the coal- and wool-exporting port on the River Tyne, doubled as an operational headquarters, supply and munitions dump. North of there, England gave way to a more nebulous zone: the Anglo-Scottish Marches. To a stranger, the first impression was of remoteness; a bare, treeless landscape through which feuding clans moved and in which the king's writ had only the most tenuous purchase. In his memoirs Pope Pius II recalled how, journeying through the region as a young man, he had spent a traumatic night abandoned by his hosts, who slept in a fortified tower for fear of Scottish raiders, and who left him only with two, apparently eager, ladies for company. Although the women of the region were 'fair, charming' and, Pius twinkled, 'easily won', he rebuffed their advances. Around midnight, there was uproar outside: Pius feared the worst. One of the ladies explained that nothing was wrong and that some friends had just popped round – a happy outcome which, he felt, was 'the reward for his continence'. The following day Pius reached Newcastle, 'a familiar world and a habitable country', where he was able to exhale.[38] To anybody planning a military campaign, Northumberland was a similarly daunting prospect.

Late that November, with promised Scottish reinforcements failing to materialize, and their chances of success against Edward's army looking vanishingly small, Margaret's troops retreated. Re-embarking for Scotland, they ran into storms. Four hundred French mercenaries took refuge on the tidal island of Lindisfarne, where they were slaughtered by Warwick's men. Margaret's ship went down with 'much of her riches', she and Henry managed to scramble onto a fishing boat and made it to Scottish-controlled Berwick.[39]

Edward's men now found themselves with a rather different proposition to the short, victorious war that they had envisaged. Hunkered down in the string of fortresses stretching north along Northumberland's coastline, the remnants of the Lancastrian forces, under the command of Somerset and his captains, were prepared to hold out until relief arrived. The Yorkists now had to deal with the prospect of lengthy sieges and the possibility of a rampaging Scottish army turning up; meanwhile, a harsh Northumbrian winter was setting in. Edward himself was absent. Reaching Durham on 30 November, he had come down with measles and was confined to bed, feverish and covered in spots.[40]

As the sieges got under way under Warwick's energetic command, it was instantly apparent that the Yorkist army was hopelessly under-resourced. With little artillery, Warwick's only option was to starve the castle's occupants into submission – a reasonable strategy but for the fact that the besiegers themselves were low on food. Even on the march north, Edward had run short of cash to pay for wages and supplies; further loans from London, extracted by the ever-persuasive George Neville, were little more than sticking plasters.[41] As December deepened, visions of chivalric glory dissipated; the morale of the Yorkist soldiers, 'grieved by cold and rain', plummeted. Based at the supply depot in Newcastle, John Paston wrote home to Norfolk asking his brother for money to cover his men's wages. All Christmas leave, he reported, had been cancelled and all demobilization forbidden:

anybody who tried to desert or 'steal away' could expect to be 'sharply punished'. Paston signed off, with a wistful sense of missing Christmas at home, 'make as merry as you can'.[42]

Then, on Christmas Eve, a tremendous gift arrived. An envoy came to Warwick's camp from the Lancastrian general Somerset, proposing terms of surrender. Warwick and a convalescent Edward jumped at the offer.[43] It wasn't entirely unexpected, as rumours of Somerset's disaffection with Lancaster's cause had been circulating for some months. He had made contact back in September about the possibility of 'coming to grace' with Edward, but the Lancastrian invasion had strengthened his resolve; now, with Margaret and Henry VI long gone and the promised Scottish army failing to materialize, disenchantment had set in. On 29 December, along with his fellow commander Sir Ralph Percy, Somerset surrendered the castles of Dunstanburgh and Bamburgh, and gave himself up.

The defection of Somerset, who had more cause than most to hate the house of York and all it stood for, was an instant and shattering blow to the Lancastrian cause. Eager to display his newfound loyalties, he immediately turned against his former comrades-in-arms and joined forces with Warwick to besiege Alnwick, the one remaining castle in Lancastrian hands.

In pitch dark, early on the morning of 6 January 1463, a Scottish army finally reached Alnwick. Rather than risking a pitched battle, Warwick had broken his siege, withdrawing his forces a safe distance. Fearing a trap, the Scots halted. With both sides holding off, each scared of the other – the English 'had no courage to fight', the Scots were similarly 'affeared' – the besieged Lancastrian garrison saw its chance and ran for it. Having inadvertently lifted the siege, the Scottish army withdrew. Warwick, advancing cautiously, found the doors to a deserted Alnwick wide open. It wasn't the chivalric endgame that Edward and his nobles had in mind when they set out the previous October. But it was a victory nonetheless.[44]

At Durham Edward, fully recovered from the measles, eagerly received the formal submission of Somerset, the man who had slaughtered his father and brother at Wakefield and whose own father had been killed by Warwick at St Albans. Edward, though, had made conciliation his watchword. Besides, Somerset's defection had turned his Northumbrian fiasco into a triumph.

Not only had Lancastrian resistance in the north lost its leader, but Somerset's pledge of loyalty to Edward was the kind of news that gave potential backers of Lancaster, like Louis XI of France, pause for thought. With questions being asked about what precisely Edward's expensive northern campaign had achieved – as one disgruntled chronicler demanded rhetorically, despite mobilizing 'almost all the armed force of England', what had the king actually done except capture three castles? – it was a coup that Edward was keen to play up.[45]

In a letter to his London creditors Edward stressed that, contrary to rumours, he had made the Lancastrian duke no guarantees: he would spare Somerset's life, and nothing else. Besides, had every confidence in both Somerset and Sir Ralph Percy, who had assured him of their allegiance 'to the uttermost article of their honour'. So bullish was Edward that he returned to Percy's command two of the recaptured fortresses, Dunstanburgh and Bamburgh, which he had previously held for the Lancastrians. As a chronicler put it, Edward now controlled all England except a castle in North Wales, Harlech, still stuffed full of Lancastrian insurgents.[46]

Over the following weeks, Edward progressed easily south, Somerset conspicuously by his side. His expansive mood persisted. In a warm letter to Warwick, Edward put on record his 'tender respect' for his cousin, who had marshalled Yorkist forces in the northeast that December with such resolve. He recalled the formative winter they had spent together in Calais, besieged by Henry VI's troops, and the extraordinary risk and expense to which Warwick had gone in sailing to Ireland and back, to rendezvous with Edward's exiled father – a journey for which Edward now belatedly reimbursed him, ordering repayment of £3,580, in cash, from the revenues of the duchy of Lancaster.[47] As he arrived back in London on 24 February, his barge escorted triumphantly down the Thames by a civic flotilla, Edward's mind was already drifting to his next great campaign: an invasion of Scotland, where Henry VI remained out of reach in exile. He summoned Parliament to vote him a tax for the purpose.

By the time Parliament sat at Westminster two months later,

however, Edward's confidence in his ability to command the Lancastrian allegiances was looking questionable. Away in Northumberland, Sir Ralph Percy's newfound Yorkist loyalties had already evaporated. When an army of Scots and French made their way across England's northeastern border that spring, Percy opened the gates of Dunstanburgh and Bamburgh to welcome them and declared again for Henry VI and Lancaster.[48]

On 29 April, Chancellor George Neville opened Parliament with the customary sermon, a typically well-turned oration on the importance of justice. The mood was one of constructive collaboration. Appreciating the job Edward had on his hands, and the commitment he had already shown in tackling the country's ills, the Commons were willing to give him both time and money, and they quickly granted a tax for his Scottish campaign. Nonetheless, mindful of kings' regrettable habit of frittering away taxpayers' hard-earned cash on everything but the purpose for which it was raised, the Commons also insisted on minuting that it was to be spent in the way taxes were meant to be used: on the defence of the kingdom.[49] In return, as was customary, they wanted Edward to do something about their own, mostly economic problems.

While the reasons for England's economic slump were many, the Commons had a habit of blaming everything – from the moribund cloth trade to the 'vices and inconveniences of idleness' that came with mass unemployment – on 'aliens', foreigners.[50] In the minds of most English merchants, foreigners were parasites. Flemings, or Dutch, were regular targets of opprobrium. So too were the German merchants of the Hanse, the powerful trading league that, to the chagrin of England's Merchant Adventurers, had all but squeezed them out of the Scandinavian and Baltic markets, and whose fortified trading compound in London, the Steelyard, was a persistent reminder of the trading privileges they nevertheless continued to enjoy in England.[51] But there was one community that, more than most, provoked English xenophobia and envy in equal measure – the Italians.

Italian merchant banks dominated the international finance of north-western Europe, which in turn gave them access to the kind of credit of which English businessmen could only dream. In

England, Italian brokers bought up wool, cloth and tin, in return importing luxuries like spices, silks and fine textiles into the country – the kinds of goods that Englishmen secretly craved while publicly scorning them as 'nifles and trifles'. Meanwhile the massive Venetian, Florentine and Genoese galleys, dwarfing northern European vessels, were able to export on a scale that only served to drive home their dominance. Shipping English goods to the Mediterranean and beyond, they manipulated foreign currency exchanges in the process, making huge profits before they had even paid their English suppliers. As one vocal English critic put it, they 'wipe our nose with our own sleeve'. The fact was that Italians did profit while English merchants suffered – though this didn't stop English merchants trading with them, borrowing from them, or even going into business with them.[52]

The solution to these problems, as England's merchants saw it, was protectionism. Free markets only worked to the advantage of foreigners. Edward had to get tough: to impose tariffs, and preferably bans, on foreign traders and to put the English first. Such a move wouldn't just benefit the mercantile community but the country as a whole, which would be 'enriched again'.[53]

Such demands left Edward with a circle to square. England's businessmen, both London's Merchant Adventurers and the powerful syndicate of Calais wool merchants, had bankrolled his regime, and his debts to them were astronomical. On the other hand, foreigners were big business, their trade contributing hugely to royal customs revenues. Italians were a prime source of credit and luxury goods, and Edward was hungry for both; nevertheless, with his creditors watching closely and with Parliament dangling tax money in front of him, he had to do something.

On the face of it, the package of measures that he waved through Parliament was impressively protectionist. Foreign traders were prohibited from buying English wool, and a sweeping ban was imposed on foreign imports into England, from silkware to gloves, tennis balls to playing cards. But Edward retained a loophole: the royal import and export licences that allowed the holder to ship toll-free, which kings granted in reward to creditors and supporters alike. At the same time, he presumably offered quiet reassurance to the horrified

Italian merchants, who had convinced themselves that Edward was a king with whom they could work.

Meanwhile, in an eye-catching piece of legislation Edward reinforced the Calais wool monopoly. Now, all foreign buyers of English wool had to pay at least half the cost upfront, in English coin or bullion. This was a measure that would benefit the flow of money into a cash-strapped England, but it was bound to damage the economy of Flanders, which bought the bulk of its wool through Calais, and was guaranteed to put the Low Countries' overlord Philip of Burgundy's nose firmly out of joint. Not that anybody in England cared. One versifier summed up English exceptionalism with pithy truculence: 'there is no realm in no manner degree/ But they have need to our English commodity'. Other countries needed England more than England needed them.[54]

Late that spring, news arrived from Northumberland. At Alnwick Castle the former commander, Sir Ralph Grey, resentful at his demotion for Edward's favourite Sir John Astley, had locked up the new captain and declared again for Lancaster. With all three Northumbrian strongholds back in Lancastrian control, Edward was back where he had started the previous autumn.

In fact, things were worse. With a full-scale Lancastrian–Scottish offensive surging across the border, resupplied by French ships waiting unopposed off the English coast – Louis XI's flipflopping support of the Lancastrians was back on again – the forces of the Neville brothers, on whom Edward had leaned heavily since the start of the reign, were entirely inadequate to the situation. Warwick dispatched a rider to London, requesting urgent military support.[55] Edward wasted no time. Proroguing Parliament on 17 June, he was in the saddle days later, raising men as he went.

As the royal household again rumbled north, through the Hertfordshire towns of Barnet and St Albans and into the east midlands, people began to notice something odd. In place of Edward's usual bodyguard, drawn from his household and chamber staff, were the duke of Somerset and two hundred of his men, 'well harnessed': armed to the teeth. It was, said one shocked chronicler, as though a lamb had entrusted himself to wolves.[56]

*

Although Edward had stressed the strictly limited nature of Somerset's pardon, the drip-feed of royal favour – conditional upon the duke's continued loyalty – had since turned into a flood. Edward had restored to him his title and lands, accompanied by a shower of cash gifts. Nor was that all. Edward made 'full much' of Somerset, for whom he had 'great love'. Earlier that summer he had put on a tournament in Westminster, in the duke's honour. On hunting trips, he allowed Somerset to ride immediately behind him: a signal mark of favour, as was the king's pointedly lax security. Edward's eager search for intimacy continued in the royal bed, which Somerset shared 'many nights'. The king, of course, exulted in his role as healer and unifier, and there was every reason to encourage this great Lancastrian war-hero to luxuriate in the heat of his favour, former loyalties now tempered and welded to the house of York. But the compulsion with which Edward sought Somerset's friendship was, some felt, too much.

On 18 July, as the king's household stopped at Northampton, an enraged mob tried to barge its way into the royal lodgings in order to kill 'that false traitor Somerset'. Edward, turning on the charm, defused the situation with 'great difficulty'. A tun of wine was tapped in Northampton's marketplace with a royal order to 'drink and make merry', and the mollified townsfolk queued with basins and cauldrons, bowls, pans and dishes to carry away the king's claret.[57]

Quite how the fracas had ignited was unclear, though one account put it down to local anger at Somerset being 'so nigh the king's presence' and having been 'made his guard'. If the townspeople were furious, so too – more quietly – were the men Somerset's guards had displaced. These were Edward's knights and squires of the body, their loyalties forged in long service and stress-tested in war; men who doubled as the king's personal security and as his closest servants, watching out for him even as they dressed him, made his bed, fed his pet dog. Edward's relationship with Somerset threatened to destabilize the delicate ecosystem of the royal household. Arguably, nobody was more threatened than the king's closest friend, his chamberlain William Hastings.

Northamptonshire was Hastings' domain. Since the start of the reign he had accumulated royal grants and offices across the region, including the constableship of Northampton castle, which he shared with his brother Ralph. Another key figure in local law enforcement was Thomas Wake, sheriff of Northamptonshire and an usher in the king's household, who had close ties to both Hastings and his brother-in-law the earl of Warwick. Given that Hastings and Warwick had much to lose by Somerset's meteoric rise in the king's favour, it would hardly have been surprising if those responsible for law and order in the town had stood by while the violence escalated. They might even have given it a nudge. Then, when Edward had got the point, they calmed things down; indeed, the tun of wine that placated the rioters had been supplied by Thomas Wake himself.[58]

Edward's close advisers now had the excuse they needed. Somerset was secretly – and, it was explained to him, for his own security – sent to his castle of Chirk, several days' ride away in the Welsh Marches. His men, their wages fully paid up, were detached from him and dispatched to Newcastle, on the other side of the country, to bolster the garrison there.[59] If Edward was disgruntled, he soon perked up. Some days later, a messenger from the Neville brothers rode into Northampton with euphoric news: in the northeast, the vast Lancastrian-led army pouring across England's borders had been stopped in its tracks.

In the past weeks, Warwick and his brother John Neville had been mobilizing frantically to assemble a force capable of stemming the Lancastrian tide. As the Lancastrian army, confident in its vast numerical superiority, battered the frontier fortress of Norham Castle with an array of 'great ordnance', an envoy was sent to Warwick, telling him either to submit to Henry VI or be annihilated in battle. But what the Nevilles lacked in numbers, they made up for in audacity. Three hours later, advancing fast along the River Tweed, they overwhelmed the unprepared Lancastrians who fled, abandoning arms and armour, artillery and ammunition. The Nevilles pursued them deep into Scotland, sacking and burning, a *chevauchée* in which, reported an awestruck Italian, 'not a castle, nor a city, nor a town, nor a house' was left intact. The destruction only stopped when their frenzied soldiers realized they had run out of food and had to retrace their steps.

Margaret of Anjou had staked everything on this latest invasion, and it had failed spectacularly. With further help from a devastated Scotland out of the question, she was running out of options. Retreating to Bamburgh Castle, she took ship once again, along with her nine-year-old son and a coterie of around fifty close advisers and servants, foremost among them the chancellors of her household and that of her son, Sir John Fortescue and John Morton. They were headed, it was rumoured, not for France – where Louis XI, hearing news of the Neville brothers' devastating raid, had once again dropped the Lancastrian cause like a hot potato – but to the port of Sluis, in Burgundian Flanders. They did so without Henry VI, who was on board another ship that had started taking on water. Turning back, he was evacuated to the safety of the Scottish court in Edinburgh.[60]

Two hundred miles south, in Northampton, Edward mulled over his grand scheme to march north and destroy Scotland. As he did so, he went out hunting.

4

Two Kings of England

A few miles west of the Great North Road, on a bend in the River Nene, Fotheringhay was the house of York's spiritual heart. Late in the fourteenth century the first duke of York, Edmund of Langley, gifted the crumbling old castle by his father Edward III, had turned it into an expression of family ambition. Re-planning the site, he spent lavishly on two new gatehouses, a chapel and spacious new domestic apartments, along with orchards and gardens. Even the stone keep was rebuilt in the shape of a fetterlock, articulating Langley's fetterlock-and-falcon badge. Langley's foundation of a small religious college was taken up enthusiastically by succeeding dukes and by the early 1440s, under the supervision of Richard of York and Cecily Neville, it was complete. The glorious centrepiece of the cloistered college was a new church, its perpendicular lines visible for miles across the surrounding meadows. An emphatic declaration of dynastic intent, the church would also become the family mausoleum. For Edward – and his brothers – especially Richard, who had been born there – Fotheringhay had fond associations.

In early August 1463, with Warwick having so spectacularly secured the Scottish border, Edward was no longer in a rush to head north. Instead, making the leisurely thirty-mile journey up the Great North Road from Northampton, he relaxed into Fotheringhay life, hunting, hawking and directing some renovations and improvements to the castle. Unlike Warwick, who earlier that year had reinterred his own father at the Neville family mausoleum at Bisham, Edward hadn't yet got round to bringing to Fotheringhay the bodies of his father and brother Edmund, which remained where they had been hastily buried at Wakefield three years before. While he naturally continued to commemorate his father's *Obiit*, the mass held on the anniversary of his death, a reburial was costly; and Edward had other things to spend his money on.[1]

From Fotheringhay, Edward set in motion the mobilization of men and materiel for his forthcoming campaign into Scotland. Artillery, bows, ammunition and supplies were stockpiled; away in the Channel ports a fleet was fitted out. The Neville brothers' lightning raid into Scotland had completely changed the international picture. A month previously, Edward and Warwick's negotiating team had tried to attend a planned summit brokered by Philip of Burgundy, who was eager to conclude a tripartite peace with England and France, but the French king had been hostile, making it impossible for them even to cross the Channel. Now, Louis XI's decision to back the Lancastrians was looking more unwise by the day, something Edward's advisers wasted no time in pointing out. On an August Sunday at Fotheringhay, William, Lord Hastings wrote to one of the summit's brokers, a Burgundian diplomat called Jean de Lannoy, updating him on events with relish.[2]

Warwick's deeds, Hastings declared, had been a feat of chivalry achieved against all odds, and the Scots would repent their support of the Lancastrian 'traitors and rebels' until Judgment Day. In Edward, England had a king at ease in his own kingdom, confident in the loyalties of his great subjects, and 'without any doubt or fear' about their ability to suppress the violence on its peripheries. Without a care in the world, the king was currently absorbed in nothing more taxing than his 'sports and pleasures of the hunt'. Hunting, as Hastings well knew, was a word freighted with innuendo – and, as the man who controlled access to the king's chamber, he helped facilitate the ins and outs of Edward's bachelor lifestyle.

For all its apparent flippancy, the contrast that Hastings had drawn between Warwick's perpetual motion and Edward's insouciance was sharp. It played up the self-image that Edward was deliberately cultivating: the sense of sprawling, capacious authority betokened by his motto *'confort et liesse'*, 'comfort and joy' – a choice that contrasted deliberately with the aggressive mottoes of many of his leading noblemen. Edward was the sun in whose warmth his subjects basked, and around which even his greatest lords revolved.[3]

In the event, the French needed no persuading. Soon, the talks with

Louis XI were back on. They presented a chance to freeze the house of Lancaster out of international politics for good.

Later that month Edward's chancellor George Neville and his fellow ambassadors were riding to Dover, to take ship for France. They broke their journey in Canterbury. The Benedictine monks of St Augustine's Abbey were accustomed to noteworthy visitors – in recent years they had become as used to armies, passing from London to Dover and back, as they had pilgrims – but what Neville did during his short stopover shocked them. Monday 15 August, the great feast of the Assumption of the Virgin Mary, was an important date in the liturgical calendar and Neville, in the absence of Archbishop Thomas Bourchier, led the celebrations in the great Gothic splendour of Canterbury Cathedral. He did so in the red robes of a cardinal. Neville's hankering after a cardinal's hat was an open secret; but dusting off the robes that had belonged to the most recent English cardinal, Bourchier's predecessor as archbishop, John Kemp, was for the attendant clergy a strange and provocative move, not least because Bourchier had his eye on a cardinalate himself.

Unsurprisingly, Neville and his party were long gone – seen off at Dover by Edward, who had made the trip down through Kent to discuss policy objectives with him and his colleagues – when, at the end of the month, Archbishop Bourchier himself arrived in Canterbury with Edward's two brothers, George and Richard, whose education and upbringing the king had entrusted to his care.[4]

George duke of Clarence was growing up fast. Nearly fourteen, he was sharply sensitive to his role as heir presumptive and hungry for power. It was an attitude Edward understood perfectly and was quick to encourage. While he subscribed to the traditional view that the 'might of the land' rested in the 'great lords', he stressed that power should most of all be concentrated in the hands of his family, the 'king's blood'. The quantity of royal blood in people's veins correlated directly with the extent that they should 'of right' be 'honoured and enhanced of right and power'. In this vision, nobody was more deserving of such power than his brother and heir.[5]

Clarence, still in his 'tender youth', was Edward's project. In his mind's eye, as he later put it, Edward saw his brother as his right-hand man: exceeding all other noblemen in his 'might and puissance', alive to all the king's 'good pleasures and commandments' and aiding him in 'all that might be to the politic weal of this land'. But in order for this to happen, Edward had to build Clarence up. As one of Richard of York's younger sons, Clarence had had little by way of inheritance: not enough, at any rate, to support his exalted status as a royal duke and heir to the throne. He had to be endowed with lands sufficient to support this great rank, and Edward had every intention of providing such 'livelihood'. There was another motive behind his heaping of possessions and riches on Clarence. With every grant, Edward would bind his brother more tightly to him. Clarence, he later emphasized, would be tied not only by 'the bonds of nature' or blood, but by 'the bonds of so great benefit' that he received from the king. For Edward, it was a way of underscoring their familial closeness, and the servitude that lay at the heart of their fraternal relationship. Clarence would be enveloped in Edward's smothering love; in return he would give the king his unconditional obedience.[6]

Clarence, indeed, was reliant on the king for everything, right down to his daily essentials. Even the sensational wardrobe with which Edward supplied him – 'all manner stuff', textiles of every imaginable variety, from Venetian cloth-of-gold and damascene silks, to fine Flemish linens, German hats, piles of furs and seven and a half stones of feathers for beds – was a reminder of that dependence, each parcel supplied direct from the king's Great Wardrobe. A nagging sense of this reliance accentuated what was becoming evident in Clarence: a quick-eyed petulance, aggressively resentful of any perceived slight done him, and of favour shown to others. Back in August 1462, as Edward had cast around for lands with which to endow his youngest brother Richard, he had granted him the Yorkshire lordship of Richmond, recently confiscated from the young Lancastrian nobleman Henry Tudor. When Clarence kicked up a fuss, Edward, wanting only to make the problem go away, shrugged and regranted it to his middle brother instead.[7]

Pushy as Clarence was, Edward was happy enough to see him taking responsibility for the offices and lands with which he had been loaded. On 22 April 1463, St George's Eve, Clarence had attended a chapter of the Order of the Garter, a boy among great lords and hard-bitten knights. If Edward imagined his brother might be awed by the experience, it seemed to produce the opposite effect: to swell an already inflated sense of entitlement.[8]

That last Sunday in August, as Clarence and Richard processed into Canterbury Cathedral for mass, Clarence did so with an attendant in front of him bearing his sword, point uppermost, representing the king. The boy's behaviour might have jogged in Archbishop Bourchier an uneasy memory of a moment three years before, when Richard of York had marched into Parliament to claim the crown and, hesitatingly contradicted by Bourchier, had shown his bewildered rage at being denied. Now, Bourchier let Clarence have his pre-eminence and, as an onlooking monk noticed with a hint of weariness, the boy milked it for all he was worth, insisting on having his sword borne in front of him wherever he went, not just that morning for mass, but in 'other places'. There was a certain desperation in Clarence's arrogance. After all, when Edward married and produced children, his exalted status as heir to the throne would evaporate.[9]

That August, after her failed invasion and flight from northeast England, Margaret of Anjou had docked at Sluis, seeking aid from Philip of Burgundy, who was appalled at news of her arrival. At that moment Philip, self-styled honest broker between France and the house of York, was directing preparations for the upcoming summit at St Omer where George Neville and his ambassadorial team – given expansive assurances over their personal security by both Philip and a newly obliging Louis XI – were arriving under heavy escort from the enclave of Calais. The disruptive presence of the Lancastrian queen was the last thing any of them needed. Philip warned Margaret not to follow him to St Omer: the area around Calais, he said, was crawling with Yorkists. Margaret ignored him. Disguising herself as a 'poor lady' to evade capture, she commandeered a peasant cart and headed after him in pursuit. At Lille, Margaret found the welcome she craved. It came not from Duke Philip, but from his estranged son, Charles of Charolais.[10]

Thirty-two years old, Charles was everything his father was not. Stocky, with a mop of black hair and pale grey eyes, he gave an impression of fury barely contained by an exaggerated chivalric courtesy. Charles and Philip disagreed on everything, including the future of Burgundy. Charles detested his father's pro-French appeasement and viewed his complaisant relationship with Louis XI – whom Charles didn't trust an inch – as hopelessly naïve. Charles believed that Burgundy's only hope lay in the assertion of its own sovereignty, of becoming an independent state. Given that Louis was hardly likely to wave goodbye to his prized vassal state, this ultimately meant war with France. Hostile to everything his father stood for, Charles chose to identify with everything and everybody Philip did not. This included his cultured mother, Isabella of Portugal, who had left the increasingly faction-ridden Burgundian court, her husband and his clutch of mistresses and set up her own establishment. And, given that Isabella was descended (through her English mother) from the founder of the Lancastrian dynasty, John of Gaunt, Charles's causes also included the house of Lancaster.[11]

With Philip of Burgundy enduring regular bouts of ill-health, the Yorkists were becoming increasingly worried about the growing influence of his pro-Lancastrian son. In a bibulous encounter in Paris with one of Charles's agents, an envoy of the earl of Warwick blurted out their anxieties. The envoy was 'neither secret or sober', the Burgundian agent reported back to Charles with relish, and had made perfectly plain 'the fear that they' – the Yorkist regime – 'have of you', especially if Philip were to die any time soon.[12]

In his warm reception of Margaret of Anjou, Charles played up to those fears. Publicly recognizing her as queen of England, he lent her five hundred crowns and egged her on in her mission to bring Edward's rapprochement with Louis XI crashing to a halt. A move calculated to provoke his father, Louis and Edward, it was also fuelled by a deep sense of affinity, of shared Lancastrian blood.[13]

With Margaret absent in Lille, the talks at St Omer went smoothly. While the French were put out at Warwick's non-appearance – he had written to Louis personally to express his regret at having been detained in the north of England – George Neville and his delegates managed to wrap up two deals. The first was a new trade treaty with Burgundy; the second, having extracted a promise from Louis XI not to give any further 'help, aid or favour' to Henry VI, Margaret or their son, was a truce with France.[14]

Publicly, at least, Margaret was now a pariah. Philip of Burgundy was quick to hustle her off his lands to her designated place of exile:

her father's run-down castle of Koeur, in Lorraine in eastern France. As far as Louis XI was concerned, Koeur was perfect. Far enough away for Margaret not to bother him, its remoteness also gave Margaret security against possible Yorkist attack. While he had no intention of giving her any support, financial or otherwise, Louis knew it was useful to keep the exiled Lancastrians up his sleeve. Just in case.[15]

Early in September 1463, Edward left the comforts of Fotheringhay and marched north on the first leg of his Scottish campaign. Tracking him up the coast was a fleet commanded by John Tiptoft, which had taken most of the summer – and the large sum of £4,580 – to fit out. Reaching York on the 13th, the king fired off a dispatch to Warwick in Newcastle with news of his imminent arrival in the northeast. The earl's reply, within a couple of days, let Edward down gently but firmly: Warwick and his allies had everything under control. Edward should stay put.[16]

As he wrote in his 'simple hand', Warwick had been overjoyed to learn that Edward, together with his 'mighty power' of men, was intending to invade Scotland, and had no doubt whatsoever of his sovereign's ultimate success. But, he continued briskly, forward planning was essential. Edward needed to ensure he could provision his army by sea, and that those supply lines stayed open; he also needed sufficient stocks of weaponry and ammunition, and to be prepared for different kinds of warfare, including 'great guns' for sieges and pitched battles. Until he 'could be sure of the said provision', it was the general consensus of 'the lords and men of reputation of these parts' – in other words, the Neville brothers and their supporters – that Edward should 'in no way' come north now.

Although Warwick knew of Edward's plans – indeed, he had supplied six ships to Tiptoft's fleet – his letter conveyed a note of surprise, almost as though, for all Edward's warlike noises and preparation throughout the summer, he had failed to consult with his senior commander in the north before setting off. Was there just the trace of a rebuke in Warwick's reply? Edward, it seemed to say, had not sought his advice. Now, he was getting it. The Nevilles were in charge of the north – on the king's behalf, naturally – and they would be the best judges of what the king should do, and when.[17]

Running through Warwick's letter was the sense that an invasion of Scotland was neither desirable nor necessary. As he took a grip on the security of England's north, so Warwick had come to dominate diplomatic contact with Scotland, which, shorn of its powerful French ally, was now scrambling to the negotiating table. Over the past years, Bishop James Kennedy had led the Scottish government's support for the exiled Lancastrians. But as he ruefully acknowledged, now that Louis XI had abandoned the Lancastrian cause, Scotland, isolated and facing 'perdition' from Yorkist England, was now in a corner. There was no option but to open talks with Edward – or rather with the man who, from where Kennedy was standing, 'ran the kingdom' for him: Warwick.[18]

Looked at one way, the mothballing of Edward's Scottish expedition made sense. Merely the threat of war had brought Scotland to the table, and however much it might have cost to assemble an army, following through on that threat would have cost a great deal more. And while Edward's expensively assembled display of naval power was patrolling England's eastern seaboard and keeping crucial trade routes open, he had also managed to settle some of his long-standing debts to the Calais garrison with the taxes raised to cover his now-aborted invasion.

Pragmatic as it was, however, Edward's abandonment of the Scottish campaign was deeply unpopular among the taxpayers who had funded it, and among the thousands of men who had marched so far from their own regions, only to sit around doing nothing. Across the country, people 'grudged sore'. One Londoner grumbled about the squandering of resources 'in vain'; another chronicler declared it 'shame and confusion', a 'wretched outcome'. The city's authorities were particularly alarmed by one agitator, a hosier called John Peysaunt, who made several incendiary speeches at Paul's Cross.[19] That November Edward, aware of the increasing unrest, agreed to remit £6,000 of the tax granted him, and also agreed to a phased collection of the balance that remained, so that the commons could check that he was indeed spending it, as agreed, on defence.[20]

On 9 December, at York, Edward's representatives signed a truce with Scotland, the Scots promising to withdraw all support for the Lancastrian royal family. To make the point, Bishop Kennedy had Henry VI brought south into England – albeit not into Yorkist hands.

Rather, he was delivered to Bamburgh Castle, which was still in Lancastrian control. And whatever the Scots' publicly expressed intentions about peace with the house of York, Henry's reappearance south of the border coincided with a disturbing upsurge in Lancastrian activity.[21]

As a bitter winter set in, the whole country gripped by a 'fervent frost and snow', Yorkist forces in the north were on high alert. About a week before the Anglo-Scottish agreement was signed, news came from the Welsh Marches. During the past months, the duke of Somerset had done some thinking. Whether his tense experience in Edward's household earlier in the year had made him realize that genuine reconciliation with the Yorkist regime was impossible; whether he was resentful at being denied the few grants that Edward had failed to restore to him; or whether he was, simply, less enthusiastic about Edward than Edward was about him, the duke had rediscovered his Lancastrian loyalties. In early December, with a small group of men, he had left Chirk Castle and disappeared.[22]

Weeks later, Somerset was spotted some two hundred miles away in Durham, heading northeast to link up with his men who now formed a detachment of Newcastle's garrison. Yorkist forces were tipped off. Breaking into his lodgings, they detained two of his men and seized his armour and a casket of correspondence; Somerset himself escaped into the freezing night, 'in his shirt and barefoot'. As his troops in Newcastle were rounded up – those who didn't manage to escape were arrested and beheaded – he managed to make his way north to Bamburgh, where Henry VI had now arrived.

Throughout the summer and autumn, Somerset told Henry, he had been busy re-establishing links with pockets of resistance across the country. There remained, he declared, huge popular support for the house of Lancaster. No fewer than seventeen Welsh lords had sworn allegiance to him in the name of Henry VI; he had also obtained the oaths of many more in southwest England. Somerset had also been in communication with Margaret of Anjou, who, from her new place of exile at Koeur, was sending a stream of dispatches to Bamburgh. Other agents slipped through the Yorkist naval patrols on England's eastern seaboard, including one who carried 'gracious and comforting' letters from Somerset's friend Charles of Charolais, who was working with

Margaret to get supplies, guns and money to Bamburgh. Margaret was also apparently in discussions with the duke of Brittany, at the other end of the northern French coast, about sending an army into Wales under the command of the exiled Lancastrian Jasper Tudor, 'to keep Edward busy at both ends of the country'.[23]

Edward was beside himself with rage at the news of Somerset's defection. In seeking to wash away the bad blood between the house of York and the Beauforts, he had shown Somerset every conceivable expression of love. Somerset had violated his trust and had betrayed the oath of loyalty he had sworn to Edward as his sovereign, going against chivalry and 'gentleness' itself.[24] Now, Edward's love turned to hate.

Ordering the immediate confiscation of Somerset's lands and offices, the king regranted them all to his youngest brother Richard. This still didn't solve the problem of Richard's meagre endowment – the Beauforts had relatively little land, and much of it was already spoken for. Edward wanted to avenge himself on the Beaufort family by any means he could, and that winter Somerset's sick, ageing mother, Eleanor, bore the brunt of the king's malice. Arrested and imprisoned, she was subjected to months of systematic intimidation and abuse: deliberately starved, 'spoiled', with no way of accessing any income or credit, and deprived of the constant medical attention she needed due to 'bodily infirmities not likely to be recovered'. She was, as she wrote pleadingly to Edward, 'guiltless, God knoweth'.

Edward had kept by him Somerset's jousting armour, which he had presented to the duke the previous spring for a tournament held in his honour. Almost as if he couldn't bear the sight of it, he now gave it to Clarence: a stunningly grown-up gift for his precocious fourteen-year-old sibling.[25]

But Edward was shutting the stable door after the horse had bolted. Indeed, having previously convinced himself of Somerset's loyalties, he had even released Somerset's younger brother Edmund Beaufort from the Tower, where he had been kept as surety against Somerset's continued good behaviour. At the turn of 1464, as insurgency flared across England – revolts against Edward's taxes fuelling latent Lancastrian allegiances – Edward's confidence in his own personal qualities had been exposed for the hubris it was.[26]

*

During the first months of 1464, Edward rode through the southern half of his kingdom with a demented energy. In January, as the scale of the disturbances became clear, he and a number of his lords had rendezvoused with the earl of Warwick at Northampton, in the centre of the country; there, he ordered judicial commissions to be held from the west country to the midlands. Sent to the city of Gloucester, where ongoing troubles were believed to have been infected by Lancastrian sympathies, Warwick's 'smooth words' had had little effect there. Edward, by contrast, had no time for local sensitivities. Arriving with a massive armed force and his two chief justices, he restored order in a slew of hangings and beheadings; then, postponing the latest session of Parliament, he rode across the country into East Anglia to tackle more armed uprisings, mobilizing men as he went.[27]

From south Wales through to Lancashire and Cheshire, where as many as ten thousand people were rioting, Edward's lieutenants had their hands full. Deployed far from their homelands the forces of John Mowbray, duke of Norfolk, who had spent the previous winter besieging the Northumbrian castles, were now hunkered down behind the walls of Holt Castle in Denbighshire, from where they conducted long and dangerous counter-insurgency operations in the hostile countryside, trying to hunt down the ringleaders who had helped 'the duke of Somerset's going'. Among Norfolk's men was the young esquire John Paston. In a letter home he wrote how, like everybody, he was out of cash: could his father send funds?[28]

While by mid-March the situation in Wales was under some semblance of control, and Edward's swift, savage action had restored order in the southwest, Yorkist problems in the northeast had deepened. Lancastrian appeals for international aid, co-ordinated by a French agent, had borne fruit: despite his new-found enthusiasm for the house of York, Louis XI had been typically unable to pass up such a promising opportunity for skulduggery. Breaking out of their stronghold at Bamburgh and boosted by support among disaffected locals, Somerset and his troops had retaken swathes of the surrounding country, from the Scottish border to the Tyne valley, and were preparing to strike further south. Edward, it was clear, was going to have to tackle them himself. He would have to raise yet another army. More to the point, having already run through the previous taxes granted him, he would have to find more funds from his increasingly hostile subjects. Resentful at the best of times about royal demands on their scarce finances, people were becoming sceptical about how Edward was spending their money – and indeed, whether he was capable of bringing peace to England at all.

The unremitting winter cold had subsided, giving way to an unseasonal spring heat. Drought soon took hold; pasture dried up and crops started to fail. In London, the plague was about. To one chronicler in the city, the lack of rain and the pestilence exacerbated the prevailing sense of economic crisis. The price of wheat had slumped, to 4d a bushel – in fact, so had the price of all foodstuffs, while wine could also be had 'great cheap'. There was a 'great scarcity of money'. Prices were at rock bottom because there was no cash with which to buy anything.[29]

The bullion crisis had been brewing for decades. In recent years it had seen mints close across northern Europe and in Calais, and had been behind Edward's aggressive insistence that foreign exporters of English wool and cloth pay half on the nail, in cash or bullion. In 1464 the crisis came to a head. While gold was used on the international markets and by princes, silver was what ordinary people used to buy goods and to trade. Now, there was barely any silver bullion left in Europe. Brokers reported that Venice's regular galley convoys to Syria had sailed off with the last of its silver stocks, leaving the great city-state temporarily without liquid currency. Months later, Florence would endure what one appalled politician described as the city's 'greatest calamity' since the famine of 1339: a wave of bankruptcies in which one overexposed bank after another – already under the strain of prolonged economic downturn and with the outbreak of war between Venice and the Ottoman Turks disrupting lucrative trade routes in the eastern Mediterranean – collapsed. With England in the grip of a deflationary spiral, and desperate to avoid antagonizing public opinion further, Edward had to explore more creative solutions to fundraising. As ever, when Edward brought his massive energies to bear on a task, he proved rather good at it. And while he had a habit of ignoring advice when it suited him to do so, he tended to prick up his ears when his financial advisers spoke to him about money-making opportunities.[30]

On 27 March, proclaiming his latest campaign to suppress Lancastrian resistance in the north, Edward ordered a new income tax with
a difference. It was a levy on his supporters, formulated, as Edward
was at pains to point out, on the advice of his council. All recipients
of royal grants worth 10 marks (£6 13s 4d) or more since Edward had
come to power were to hand over a quarter of their annual value,
payable in cash by 5 May. Non-payment would result in instant forfeiture. If it was unpopular – the last time such a tax had been levied
was back in 1312 – it was also shrewd. By definition, anyone holding
such assets had a vested interest in keeping Edward on the throne.[31]

There were other sources of income to be tapped. With the Yorkists positioning themselves as the champions of big business, London
merchants were regularly to be seen in Edward's chamber, their presence enhancing the commercial atmosphere of the Yorkist court
where financial talk was common: tips and business contacts swapped,
and likely investments recommended. Leading noblemen and women,
among them the earl of Warwick, John Howard, and Edward's mother
Cecily, were heavily involved in international trade on their own
account; so too were the likes of Hastings, Montgomery and Hatteclyffe, close royal servants with their own intimate links to London
commerce. At the centre of such talk was Edward, his eyes gleaming
at the various money-making schemes that councillors, advisers and
merchants alike put his way.

Already, Edward was a dominant presence in England's two main
export industries, wool and cloth. He siphoned off the proceeds of
his recently voted parliamentary taxes, handing £20,000 to the Calais treasurer, William Blount, to trade in wool on the crown's behalf.
For Edward, this trade was a win–win. English wool, purchased by
royal factors, was to be shipped to Calais – John Tiptoft's fleet, which
had failed to carry out a single raid on Scotland, was on hand to
escort shipping across the Channel – for onward sale to the Low
Countries. The profits would go to meeting the vast debts owed to the
Calais garrison; Edward, meanwhile, would get back his original
investment.[32]

Hungrily alert to the possibilities of international trade and the
profits to be made, Edward was drawn closer to the one group who,
more than any other, understood its complexities. If, in the summer

of 1463, London's community of Italian merchant-bankers had been alarmed at the protectionist legislation passed by England's Parliament, their worries soon subsided. Not only did Edward facilitate their trade, he went fully into business with them.

Edward's factors, the men who travelled England, from the Welsh Marches to the Cotswolds to Kent, buying up the best English wool on his behalf and arranging its onward shipment, were Italians. As well as exporting the king's wool to Calais, they also drew other business 'aventures' to Edward's attention; opportunities of which Edward took full advantage. Holding the precious royal export licences that allowed them to ship goods toll-free, Italian galleys carried their cargoes of wool and cloth to 'diverse foreign parts', mostly through the Straits of Gibraltar to Italian ports – which, in the efficient, experienced hands of his Italian agents, offered decent rates of return. Not only were these deals done in Edward's name but, as one of his administrators later remarked with a faint air of disgust, he was negotiating them 'in person', as though he himself were 'a man living by merchandise', through his factors.[33]

Through such deals, Edward fuelled his counter-insurgency campaign against the Lancastrian rebels. That spring, as he mustered his forces for the march north to confront Somerset, the king and his councillors ordered the stockpiling of eight thousand woolcloths, to be shipped by his factor Giacomo de Sanderico for, as Edward put it, the raising of funds 'towards our great charges borne and to be borne at this time'.[34] And, convinced that they had Edward's ear, Italian merchants responded with alacrity to the king's demands for credit.

Early in April, in a timely reminder to both English and foreign merchants of the regime's pro-business stance, Warwick and his deputy, John, Lord Wenlock, hosted talks with the French ambassador over a maritime Anglo-French truce, to complement the truce by land that had been concluded the previous autumn. Helping to bring peace and security to England's key trading routes, it was an agreement that would benefit the mercantile communities who had invested so much in the house of York – though, clearly, nobody would benefit more from the rapprochement than their increasingly trade-minded king. The talks, moreover, were proving more wide-ranging.

*

In the months following Louis XI's promise to withdraw his backing from the Lancastrians, official contact between England and France had intensified, with envoys shuttling between Calais and the French court. By and large, English agents operating out of the Calais Pale reported directly to its commander, Warwick. They included men like Warwick's agent Richard Whetehill, lieutenant of Guisnes Castle on the Calais frontier, who in early 1464 played a significant role in the growing Anglo-French détente by forwarding Warwick's letters to Louis XI, sending French correspondence in the other direction, and meeting regularly with his French counterparts.

None of this was particularly unusual. Leading noblemen were expected to maintain an international profile, and Warwick had long been acknowledged as the house of York's leading diplomat. From the outset, Edward had given him free rein: after all, just as Warwick was his subject, so Warwick's servants were the king's men too. In high-level international negotiations, the pair sent double sets of letters, showing that they were working together and that Warwick knew Edward's mind. As far as routine diplomacy was concerned – the low-level processes of letter-writing, maintaining and developing contacts with foreign envoys and advisers – Warwick was, more or less, in charge: his perpetual motion and obsession for detail thrown into relief by Edward's expansive kingship.[35] It was a system that worked, so long as Edward and Warwick were on the same page – which, by and large, they appeared to be.

However, from the start of Edward's reign, many who had dealings with Warwick and his men came away with the impression that the earl was in fact dictating policy. When attending talks with the English, it was crucial for foreign diplomats to be briefed on 'the will of my lord of Warwick'; his non-appearance at negotiations, meanwhile, left people profoundly disappointed.[36] Edward may have tried to create the impression of a monarch resplendent at the centre of his own solar system; but on the international stage, at any rate, he was being eclipsed by the energy and power of his greatest subject. It was an impression that Warwick – perhaps inadvertently, perhaps not – cultivated. In fact, in certain diplomatic circles, it had become something of a joke.

At the end of March 1464, one of Louis XI's envoys reported back on a recent meeting with Richard Whetehill at which various issues had been discussed, including Edward's plans to lead an army north against the Lancastrian resistance in the northeast. Knowing what played well with Louis, who had an overdeveloped sense of the ridiculous, the envoy repeated a joke that he had apparently picked up from Warwick's men. 'They say that there are two chiefs in England', he wrote. 'One of them is the earl of Warwick and', he sniggered, 'I have forgotten the name of the other.'[37] Louis undoubtedly found it funny. He also took notice.

That April, at the Loire city of Chartres, Louis talked expansively about having received an 'excellent' letter from Warwick, informing him of the successful talks between England and France, and opining that a permanent peace would surely follow. The previous autumn there had been tentative noises about a marriage alliance between the two countries. The idea had taken root in Louis' mind, and Warwick's letter had clearly encouraged his ambitions. Parading his two sisters-in-law – one of whom was intended for Edward – in front of Warwick's herald, who made strongly appreciative noises, Louis even promised to pay the dowry.[38]

As the Yorkist regime gained credibility abroad, so the bids for Edward's hand in marriage started to come in. Talk of a high-profile European match was ongoing. Earlier in 1464, Castilian envoys had been in London to offer the hand of Isabella, heir to the throne of Castile. Edward, unenthusiastic, had turned down the offer, a rejection about which Isabella remained bitter long after her subsequent marriage to Ferdinand of Aragon. That a king should reject a marriage proposal was hardly news, but people had begun to talk about Edward's lack of interest in potential brides: 'men marvelled', one chronicler noted, that the king was 'so long without any wife' – and, he added with delicate understatement, 'were ever feared that he had not been chaste of his living'.[39]

For kings and princes, of course, marriage and extra-marital sex were hardly mutually exclusive. Still, there were contemporary medical concerns about promiscuity. As far as physicians were concerned, sex, like most things, was good in moderation: part of a lifestyle that kept the four humours in balance. But 'immoderate frequency of the work of Venus', in the words of the distinguished Oxford physician Gilbert Kymer (an associate of Edward's own doctor William

Hatteclyffe), came with a catalogue of health warnings, including corruption of the humours, increased risk of illness, 'forgetfulness, fatness, neglectfulness and foolishness'. It also, Kymer concluded, 'shortens the life'.[40] And, as his close servants and advisers were all too aware, Edward did nothing in moderation.

As William Hastings had hinted the previous summer, Edward enjoyed the hunt, and rumours of various liaisons followed him around. Unable to control himself, he moved in on whoever caught his eye: 'the married and unmarried, the noble and lowly'. When staying with Warwick on one occasion, he had abused the earl's hospitality by seducing one of the women in his household. Warwick, apparently, was furious. Indeed, while on progress around the country, Edward seemed to make a habit of lodging with obliging hostesses whenever he could: as he returned to London to meet the Castilian envoys late in February 1464, he was put up at the Hertfordshire town of Ware by a lady named Alice Farwell.[41]

That spring, whatever Edward thought of Louis XI's offer of a marriage treaty, Warwick was enthusiastic. After all, it made sense. Peace with France was the objective towards which Edward and Warwick had been working together over the previous years. What was more, the Yorkist government – or at any rate, Warwick – shared Louis' concerns about the potentially destabilizing belligerence of the Burgundian heir, Charles of Charolais. In seeking a French marriage for Edward, Warwick was pursuing this direction of travel to its logical conclusion. That, and the fact that he relished his dealings with Louis, a king who was perfectly happy to go out of his way to inflate the earl's unmistakeable sense of his own importance.

What Edward thought about the idea went unrecorded, but he let Warwick get on with it. Soon, reports were circulating through northern Europe that a fresh round of Anglo-French peace talks were to be held, once again under the benign aegis of Philip of Burgundy. This time, reported an Italian merchant-banker writing home from Bruges, talk was that Warwick himself planned to attend. 'We shall see what happens', he added.[42]

In late April, Warwick's brother John Neville rode with an army through England's northern borderlands to the frontier, to escort a Scottish delegation south for talks on a lasting peace with the Yorkist government. Neville knew Northumberland like the back of his hand. As warden of the East March, he was responsible for security in this most disaffected of regions, and had fought across it almost constantly in recent times. He knew that the Lancastrian insurgents, for whom Scottish support remained vital, were determined to stop the talks going ahead. North of Morpeth, at Hedgeley Moor, an army blocked his route: five thousand men under Somerset's command.

In the fighting that followed, Neville's men killed one of Somerset's captains, Sir Ralph Percy, who, with Somerset, had sworn loyalty to the house of York the previous winter before defecting again to Lancaster. The last surviving adult male of the Percy family, the Nevilles' bitter rivals for control of England's northeast, Sir Ralph had been a focus for local loyalties. The effect of his death on the Lancastrian troops was instantaneous: 'discomfited', they broke and fled. Somerset himself managed to get away. Having brought the Scottish embassy unscathed to Newcastle, Neville then packed them off to the safety of York, ninety miles further south. He and his men stayed in Newcastle, watchful.[43]

With Edward and Warwick finally on their way north at the head of an army, the Lancastrian options were dwindling. Edward, though, was progressing by slow stages up the Great North Road. At the end of April, apparently in no particular hurry, he spent a few days at the Northamptonshire town of Stony Stratford: hunting, or so it was said. Somerset had a fast-closing window of opportunity to strike against John Neville's forces before the main Yorkist army arrived in the region.[44]

Early that May at Somerset's base of Hexham on the River Tyne, recruits streamed in to join the Lancastrian army. It was a turnout boosted by the presence of a crowned Henry VI who, decked out in his war armour, was paraded through the region propped up on a horse. As news of the mobilization reached John Neville some twenty miles east at Newcastle, he realized he couldn't wait for Edward and Warwick to arrive. On Sunday 13 May, he assembled his men and moved fast towards Hexham. His instincts were good.[45]

While Somerset had recruited substantial numbers of troops, the majority were commons: occasional, possibly reluctant soldiers, ill-equipped and inexperienced. There was also another problem, one that affected the detachments of battle-hardened mercenaries, gunners and foot soldiers on whose solidity Somerset's otherwise ragtag army depended. A Lancastrian knight, Sir William Tailboys, had failed to appear with the Lancastrian war chest, some £2,000 in silver. Unpaid, the mercenaries refused to move: they 'would not go one foot' with Somerset 'till they had money'. By dawn on the 15th, the cash still hadn't turned up.

Camped south of Hexham, in meadowland around Devil's Water, a twisting, steep-banked tributary of the Tyne, Somerset's men were caught in the open. The battle, such as it was, quickly turned into a rout. As the Lancastrians, scattering into the surrounding woodlands, were hunted down, Somerset's charmed existence came to an end. Acting on Edward's orders, and in any case disinclined to spare the man who had slaughtered his father at Wakefield back in the winter of 1460, John Neville had him pushed to his knees and beheaded on the spot.[46]

Ten days later, his victorious journey south punctuated by rounds of executions, John Neville marched into York, where he was greeted by a beaming Edward IV and, flanking the king, Warwick and chancellor George Neville. Amid further beheadings, another detachment of Yorkist soldiers arrived with the man whose failure to turn up at Hexham had robbed the Lancastrian army of any chance it might have had. In the valley of Redesdale, some twenty miles north of Hexham, Sir William Tailboys had been found hiding down a coalmine with the missing war chest. Tailboys was summarily beheaded and the money disbursed among John Neville's troops: a 'wholesome salve' for their wounds, as one chronicler put it, as were the ministrations of Edward's surgeon, a Master Gerard, to whom the king paid £10 for his treatment of those 'late hurt in our wars in the north country'.

A few key figures had escaped the Neville dragnet, among them not only Somerset's younger brothers, Edmund and John Beaufort, but also Henry VI himself. At York, John Neville presented Edward with Henry's 'bycocket': the jewel-encrusted coronet that the Lancastrian king had worn as he went through Northumberland encouraging people to flock to his cause, and which he discarded as he fled.

With this furious bloodletting, the war in the north, which had almost brought Edward's regime to its knees during the past years, was over. A king without a crown, Henry VI was on the run somewhere in the north of the country, passed from safe house to safe house by committed partisans. Margaret of Anjou, in exile with her ten-year-old son, deserted by her former allies France and Scotland, was surrounded by a small group of courtiers and advisers whose subsistence she barely had funds to cover. In England, it seemed, the Lancastrian cause was all but eradicated. It was a triumph delivered to Edward by his cousins, the three Neville brothers.

On Sunday 27 May, Trinity Sunday, in the archbishop's palace at York, John Neville received his reward from a grateful king. Edward bestowed on him the earldom of Northumberland, which had belonged to the Nevilles' great Lancastrian rivals, the Percies, along with swathes of their ancestral lands in the northeast. One of Neville's achievements meant more to Edward than anything else. The title was granted, he said, 'for having executed the duke of Somerset'.[47]

There was still an endgame to be played out: the recapture of the three great, troublesome Northumbrian castles, still in Lancastrian hands and now utterly isolated. On Saturday 23 June, in the midsummer heat, Alnwick promptly capitulated to the Neville forces; it was followed, the next day, by Dunstanburgh, some eight miles north along the coast. The third castle, Bamburgh, proved more problematic.

With their forces and artillery deployed, including three massive, wall-breaking guns, Warwick and John Neville sent a herald to deliver their ultimatum to the garrison's renegade commander, Sir Ralph Grey. Edward, they said, wanted his anti-Scottish defences kept intact and would be exceptionally vexed if he was forced to destroy his 'jewel' of Bamburgh. Given this, he was willing to pardon all the castle's defenders if they surrendered immediately, except Grey and his deputy. But if the Yorkist besiegers were forced to fire guns at the castle walls, each shot would cost the head of a member of the garrison until there was nobody left. Grey turned his back on the herald and walked off.

The bombardment that followed was intense. Bamburgh's walls exploded in showers of splintering stone; chunks of masonry flew into the sea. One of the siege guns, the 'Dijon', trained on Grey's chamber, pounded it ferociously. Before long, Neville's troops were surging over the wrecked walls. Finding Grey still alive amid the rubble, they took him 150 miles south to the Yorkshire town of Doncaster, where Edward was in residence.

Edward's instant response was to hand Grey over to his constable of England, John Tiptoft, to be tried for treason. The trial, as all parties knew, was a formality. Sitting in judgment, invoking the full force of the laws of chivalry, Tiptoft detailed to Grey precisely why it was that he had to die.

Before Grey was killed, Tiptoft told him, he would undergo the full ritual degradation of knighthood. First, his spurs would be hacked off – here, Tiptoft gestured to Edward's master cook, standing aproned and clutching a knife in readiness – then, the royal heralds would cluster round and rip his coat-of-arms from his body, before dressing him in a paper replacement painted with his coat-of-arms reversed that he would wear as he went to his execution. Here, Edward saw fit to intervene, graciously commuting the humiliation in memory of Grey's loyal grandfather Sir Thomas, who, half a century before, had been convicted for his part in a plot to kill the Lancastrian king Henry V, and executed alongside Edward's grandfather. Without further ceremony, Grey was drawn on a hurdle to a makeshift scaffold and beheaded.[48]

Edward was in no hurry to return south. Apart from wanting to give his plague-ridden capital a wide berth, business kept him in Doncaster. The timing of his arrival in the town, the day after England's clergy had assembled there to discuss a papal request for a subsidy towards a planned crusade against the Ottoman Turks, was no coincidence. Surprisingly, given how reluctant England's kings were at the best of times to indulge the pope's demands for cash, Edward was suddenly anxious that the subsidy be raised.[49]

The previous autumn Pope Pius II, approaching Christendom's princes for a new round of funding to revive his moribund crusade, had written to Edward seeking a return on the spiritual capital that he had invested in the house of York. At the time Edward, facing a funding crisis of his own, had refused point blank. In the intervening months, however, the idea had grown on him.[50] Edward informed the pope that he was keen to help. While a papal tax on England's subjects – a 'novelty' that would set an uncomfortable precedent – was out of the question, he proposed instead a voluntary subsidy on the clergy, to be levied by Thomas Bourchier, archbishop of Canterbury.

Writing to his bishops, Bourchier instructed them to hand in their receipts not to the Exchequer in the usual way, but directly to the king or his financial representatives, who would then pass the money on to designated papal officers. Shortly after, Bourchier wrote again to say that Edward was unhappy at the proposed rate of 4d in the pound. As the pope was relying on England's support for the crusade, Bourchier, 'as tenderly as possible', required his bishops to increase their contribution to 6d. That July, Edward's presence at the Doncaster synod made it clear that there was nothing remotely discretionary about the subsidy.

Although Pius II died of a fever a month afterwards, the subsidy continued to be gathered. But when, with the help of a papal collector who seemed only too happy to look the other way, the money found its way into the king's chamber, it stayed there – either by accident or design.[51]

Later that summer, Edward embarked on a more ambitious venture. It was a project that revealed how, in his desire for ready cash, he was formalizing an ad hoc process used since the beginning of the reign, in which he bypassed the administrative red tape of the Exchequer whenever he could, funnelling finance directly into his household.

Edward made his way slowly southwards. In early August, he reached the Lincolnshire market town of Stamford where, after discussions with 'experienced men and merchants', he made an announcement. He was going to carry out a recoinage, the first for half a century.[52]

This, Edward stressed, was a measure taken 'for the common good'. It was designed to tackle the extraordinary 'scarcity of money' in the country – one made more acute, the king explained, by the high precious-metal content of English coin, meaning that people got less spending power for their bullion than in 'other princes' mints' elsewhere in Europe. But for all the public-spiritedness of his proclamation, the people who stood to benefit most were precisely those 'experienced men and merchants' who had advised him, not to mention the king himself.

The recoinage would be co-ordinated by Edward's close friend William Hastings, newly reconfirmed in his post of master of the king's mints and handed control of all the financial exchanges in England,

Ireland and Calais into the bargain. Hastings would oversee the recall of all the 'unclean' silver and gold coinage in circulation, and the minting of new, revalued coins. Now, one pound of silver bullion would yield not 360 but 450 lighter, finer silver pennies; the worth of a gold 'noble', meanwhile, would increase from 6s 8d to 8s 4d. In other words, money would go further: people's spending power would be increased by 20 per cent. At a stroke, English exports would become cheaper, to the considerable advantage of anybody involved in the country's wool and cloth export trades. This of course included the merchants who had bankrolled the regime through its first unsteady years, and Edward, one of the export trade's biggest players. Even so, the biggest profits to the king lay elsewhere. Announced at the same time were jaw-dropping hikes in seigniorage, a tax due the king from all bullion brought to the royal mint for recoining. For each pound of gold minted into coins, seigniorage was increased from 3s 6d to a staggering 47s 8d; for silver, from 3d to 3s 4d. Hastings' role was to make sure these increased takings were siphoned through to the king's chamber.

Two more of Edward's closest servants were appointed to key positions in the process. Thomas Montgomery and the king's esquire Thomas St Leger, a familiar presence at Edward's side, took up posts in the Tower Mint as, respectively, warden and assay master (who assessed the weight and purity of bullion brought to the Mint, and the new currency coined from it). Like Hastings, neither man was involved in the day-to-day running of the Mint: this was carried out by the usual combination of goldsmiths, smiths and alchemists, now under the watchful eye of Hastings' deputy, Hugh Bryce, a London goldsmith who was proving a generous creditor to Edward's regime.[53]

This extension of the royal household's reach over the Mint's financial workings was deliberate and unprecedented. Montgomery had held the same role under Henry VI, but where before he had delivered the profits from seigniorage and minting charges into the Exchequer, now he was ordered to pay them directly to the king's household treasurer, Sir John Fogge, and his cofferer John Kendal.[54] The Mint had effectively become a sub-department of the king's household, which was also consuming its profits: a closed loop.

The impact of the recoinage was astonishing. In the first three years of Edward's reign, the profits from the Mint in seigniorage and minting charges had been some £100 per year. Over the next two years, the trickle would turn into a torrent, with over £20,000 flooding into Edward's coffers, a major boost to the king's annual income. It seemed a win–win situation. Edward had gone some way to alleviating England's liquidity crisis and stood to make a fortune into the bargain. But for many throughout the country, the process was difficult to comprehend and negotiate. There was something uncanny about it, the new coins difficult to 'reckon': as though the Tower's assayers, in determining the metal content of the new coins, had somehow magicked value out of them.[55]

Nevertheless, Edward's new coins were the expression of a prophecy fulfilled. His gold rose noble eclipsed that of his illustrious Plantagenet forebear Edward III, now withdrawn from circulation. Some months later the king introduced another gold coin, an 'angel'. Its obverse showed the ship of state, its mast the cross of St George, flanked by suns in splendour; on the reverse was an image of the winged angel that gave the coin its name, St Michael, slaying Satan in the form of a dragon. In the Yorkist prophecies, it was St Michael who had appeared to the legendary Cadwaladr, to tell him of the great prince who would eventually defeat the kingdom's enemies and bring peace, unity and prosperity. Now, Edward's new gold angel proclaimed, that era had arrived.[56]

Towards the end of summer, as a sense of Edward's uncontested sovereignty settled on England, a great council was convened at Reading. With widespread talk about Edward's extended bachelorhood, it was time, people felt, that he consolidated his crushing of the Lancastrians into something more durable: dynastic stability. Marriage was an indication of kingly maturity and, at twenty-two years old, it was high time Edward made a dazzling foreign match, settled down and procreated, legitimately, for the good of his kingdom. If his advisers wanted precedents to set before him, there could be no better example than that of the mythical King Arthur, whose first action after uniting Britain through a series of bitterly fought wars was to marry the breathtakingly beautiful Guinevere. Arriving at Reading in mid-September, braced for the days of tactful persuasion that lay ahead, they were unprepared for the bombshell Edward now dropped. He was in fact already married.[57]

PART TWO

Blind Affection

Summer 1464 – Spring 1468

'I say only for spousal and wedlock
In the face of the church it oweth to be had
And not in dark corners behind thy back
Such blind bargains beith oft full bad . . .'
*Peter Idley's Instructions to
his Son*, c. 1474

'The king was wedded to Elizabeth Grey, widow . . . and the wedding was privily in a secret place.'
Warkworth's Chronicle

'In England, things are upside down and in the air.'
Giovanni Pietro Panigarola,
Milanese ambassador to France

5

Now Take Heed
What Love May Do

On Wednesday, 3 October 1464, at Reading Abbey, the veteran diplomat John, Lord Wenlock sat down to write a delicate letter. That summer, at the latest round of peace talks with France, hosted by Philip of Burgundy at his opulent castle of Hesdin, Wenlock had had the tricky task of deputizing for the earl of Warwick, away mopping up the final Lancastrian resistance in England's northeast. Irritated by Warwick's failure to turn up, the French king Louis XI had been further vexed when it became clear that Wenlock had no power to progress the issue on which Louis had become fixated – the marriage of his sister-in-law Bona of Savoy to Edward IV. In the circumstances, things had gone quite well. Presented to Edward's prospective bride, Wenlock had made enthusiastic but non-committal noises before agreeing to another round of marriage negotiations early that autumn and leaving loaded with gifts. Now, however, Wenlock wrote to the Franco-Burgundian diplomat Jean de Lannoy that the wedding was off. Edward had already taken a wife 'at his pleasure'.[1]

Nobody, Wenlock insisted, had known anything about the marriage: Edward had managed to keep it 'very secret', even from his closest advisers. Finally, backed into a corner over the impending negotiations with France, the king had broken the news to the great council that had gathered at Reading Abbey. Here and there, Wenlock's carefully modulated sentences betrayed the councillors' efforts to keep composed in front of their wilful twenty-two-year-old monarch, until they got back to the privacy of their lodgings. 'We must be patient', he exhaled, 'despite ourselves.'

Although Wenlock glossed over the bride's identity, her details were already circulating through northern Europe. In Bruges, Venetian merchants travelling from London reported what everybody was saying. Edward had married impulsively, for love. His chosen bride was no great foreign princess but an Englishwoman, the daughter of Richard Woodville, Lord Rivers and Jacquetta of St Pol, formerly brilliant ornaments of the Lancastrian court who had successfully transferred their loyalties to Edward. What was more, she was no virgin, but a widow with two children. The 'great part of the lords and the people in general', the merchants added, thought it was a very bad idea.[2]

For Elizabeth Woodville, life in recent years had been trying. Her husband, the Lancastrian knight Sir John Grey, had been killed early in 1461 at St Albans, and, with two small sons to bring up, she faced the widow's usual problem of trying to claim her jointure while fending off other interested parties. The trouble had come in the form of her mother-in-law, who was trying to get her hands on Elizabeth's land and goods. In property disputes like these, it was normal to petition the king and those around him to intervene. Although Elizabeth's own parents had grown close to Edward, her mother-in-law's Bourchier relatives – prominent among them Edward's uncle Henry Bourchier, earl of Essex – were a Yorkist family, and more influential still with the king.[3] Perhaps, her parents felt, Elizabeth stood more of a chance of getting the king's backing if she petitioned him in person.

Elizabeth, all were agreed, had something about her. She seemed to breathe new life into the platitudes that, in the pages of chivalric romance, writers habitually reached for when describing queens: the beauty and wisdom that left otherwise impervious kings delirious with desire. It wasn't just Elizabeth's dark-blonde hair and almond eyes, but also the coolness that they enhanced, a quality that radiates from a contemporary portrait of her. Dressed with understated extravagance in a fitted, low-cut black gown and costly gold jewellery, hair drawn back in the fashion of the age under a cloth-of-gold cap over which a veil was suspended, her brown eyes gaze detachedly past the artist, high cheekbones tapering to a neat chin, the trace of some secret amusement in her cupid's-bow mouth.[4] Later, it was this poise and, predictably enough, her way with words that set Thomas More's pulse racing as he wrote about her qualities. They seemed to have less effect on Edward's chamberlain William Hastings who, sometime in early 1464, the twenty-eight-year-old Elizabeth approached to see if he would put in a word with the king on her behalf.

In the first years of the reign, a number of vulnerable widows in need of a little royal intercession had found their way into the king's presence; if talk was to be believed, Edward had already bedded at least two of them.[5] Hastings knew what kind of company Edward enjoyed. He also knew what his influence with the king was worth, and he drove a hard bargain. On 13 April 1464 Hastings and Elizabeth signed a contract stipulating that, should she regain her disputed lands, she would marry one of her sons to a female relative of Hastings', or pay him 250 marks should the marriage not take place.[6] It was a high price, and Elizabeth filed the episode away in the back of her mind. Nevertheless, it was about a fortnight after the contract was signed that things started to happen – or so the story went.

At the end of April, on his way north to suppress Somerset's Lancastrian uprising, Edward had made one of his customary stopovers at the town of Stony Stratford, a communications and billeting hub in Northamptonshire. As dawn rose on May Day, he rode out with a few companions, ostensibly to go hunting. Instead, he made for the nearby Woodville home of Grafton where, in front of a huddle of witnesses that included Elizabeth's mother Jacquetta, he and Elizabeth were married by a dumbstruck priest from the nearby village of Paulerspury. Edward and Elizabeth then went to bed for 'three or four hours', following which the exhausted groom rode back to Stony Stratford, fell asleep and slept like a baby.[7]

If this romance-tinged story of their wedding seemed too perfect to be true, perhaps it was; after all, literary heroes almost invariably awoke on May Day morning to quest in search of their beloveds. But of all the accounts of Edward and Elizabeth's betrothal – some of which had a besotted king wooing Elizabeth for years, pardoning her father and brother their Lancastrian allegiance, and dining with her regularly at Grafton as he led his armies to the north and back again – this was the one that stuck. Generally, especially for the nobility, love was placed fairly low down the list of prerequisites for marriage: it was nice if it blossomed, but hardly essential. In tales of courtly love, though, it was what mattered. When, in Thomas Malory's retelling of the *Morte d'Arthur*, King Arthur asked Merlin for matrimonial advice, he was told that love was all he needed. One way of framing Edward's moment of madness in a way that people understood was to couch it in the language of pure, virtuous love. Some, at least, got it: 'Now take heed what love may do', sighed one chronicler dreamily on recounting the secret marriage, 'for love will not, nor may not, cast no fault nor peril in no thing.'[8]

If Edward was wild with desire for Elizabeth, he was also used to getting what he wanted. When his eye settled on somebody he was, it was said, happy to promise anything in order to get her into bed. It was all about the thrill of the hunt, for 'having conquered them, he dismissed them'. After a successful seduction he would get bored, passing his victim on to his close circle of friends, his eyes locking onto his next target. But in Elizabeth, Edward met his match. When he had tried to force himself on her, so it was later said, she fought him off: opinion varied as to who was holding a dagger at the time. While this particular story owed much to the lurid fantasies of courtly romance, it contained a kernel of truth.[9]

At a time when women's reputations were closely bound up with their chastity, false promises of marriage made by men to get women into bed were the subject of many cautionary tales. One man, Peter Idley, warned his eldest son Thomas how, all too often, a man 'speaketh of wedlock but thinketh it not/ But he would his sin were wrought'. Idley, though, was as concerned with litigation as morality: this making of 'blind bargains' in 'dark corners', he said, could and did land people in court.[10] Edward, who 'overcame all with money and promises', apparently made such 'bargains' on a regular basis. But then, Edward was the king of England rather than the impressionable young son of an Oxfordshire gentleman.

Still, if as a woman you had enough strength and presence of mind to resist the king's advances – a big if – such a situation might be turned to your advantage. Some five years older than Edward, a noble widow with children, Elizabeth knew her own value – or, if she didn't, she had parents vastly experienced in the ways of the court who were able to make that value emphatically clear to the king. Either way, it was brought home to Edward that if he wanted to sleep with Elizabeth, he needed to marry her first. Edward was at the point where he would agree to anything.

In the eyes of the church, two types of informal marriage contracts were binding: *verba de presenti*, an exchange of promises between two people, in which they recognized that they were from that moment married; and *verba de futuro*, in which a mutual commitment to marry in the future was sealed by sexual intercourse. The events at Grafton covered both definitions. When, following Edward's announcement to his shocked council that September, a group of councillors explored whether the marriage could be annulled, they quickly found that it couldn't.[11]

It wasn't just Edward's flagrant disregard of one of the fundamental processes of kingship, his failure to seek advice, that caused such widespread consternation among his councillors; nor even that in marrying one of his own subjects, he had thrown away one of his greatest diplomatic cards. There was also the question of Elizabeth's family.

Elizabeth's mother Jacquetta was not the problem. With a lineage stretching back to Charlemagne and close family ties to the glamorous dukes of Burgundy, her nobility was undeniable. As a teenager she had made a sensational marriage to Henry V's powerful brother John duke of Bedford. But Bedford died soon after, leaving her, aged nineteen, a wealthy and highly desirable widow. Jacquetta's next marriage, to her dead husband's chamberlain, caused an uproar.

With a continent-wide reputation as a jouster, the Lancastrian knight Richard Woodville had all the seductive glamour of a great courtier-sportsman. But as the son of Northamptonshire gentry, even his subsequent ennoblement and membership of the Order of the Garter could not obscure the fact that he was, not to put too fine a point on it, common. Back in early 1460 Edward and Warwick, in their Calais bolt-hole, had taken turns to taunt the captured Woodville, now Lord Rivers, about his squalid lineage. He was, they had told him, a 'knave's son' who had 'himself made by marriage' and had been 'made lord': a social climber, entirely reliant for his wealth and status on his wife and his ability to advance himself at court. After Towton, however, Edward had delightedly accepted Woodville's pledge of loyalty, the insults apparently forgotten.

Indeed, for all the keen-eyed awareness of rank and precedence, there was rather less of a gulf between such 'made' lords and the 'old' nobility than the latter liked to pretend. New lords like Hastings and William Herbert wielded huge influence as part of Edward's inner circle.[12] Likewise, while the old nobility, rigidly conscious of their place in the social order, might have made a fuss about upwardly mobile marriages like Richard Woodville's to Jacquetta – which had itself followed on from another secret marriage that caused even more of an uproar, between Henry V's widow Catherine of Valois and her chamber servant Owen Tudor, at a stroke making Tudor stepfather to Henry VI – ultimately, they accepted them.

Social mobility may have provoked headaches among England's upper ranks, but it was rather more normal than most contemporary books of manners and courtesy let on: after all, these were books attempting to order society into a comprehensible ranking system. Occasionally, though, the messy reality of life defeated the authors of such tracts. One writer, attempting to tackle the question of commoners who married into the royal family, threw up his hands at the impossibility of it all. How should you rank poor noblemen or rich *arrivistes*; knights who had married 'ladies of royal blood'; or ladies of 'low blood and degree' who had married 'blood royal'? Confusion arose, the author said, for 'many reasons' and out of 'ignorance': people just didn't know.

Moreover, in courtly circles the nature of nobility itself was a live issue. One book circulating around court was the Italian writer Buonaccorso da Montemagno's *Controversia de vera nobilitate*. In it, an indigent, blue-blooded aristocrat and a virtuous low-born knight sought to trump each other's nobility, the latter maintaining that to dedicate yourself to the service of the state showed an innate nobility that counted for rather more than inherited wealth. Nobility, in other words, wasn't just something passed on down the generations; it could be earned, acquired.[13]

That, at least, was the theory. But while the urbanity and chivalric steel displayed by Elizabeth's father, Lord Rivers, and her oldest brother Anthony Woodville, may have delighted Edward, in the eyes of many it hardly compensated for their lack of blood and land. As one foreign dispatch put it, the grumbling among the 'lords and people' that greeted Edward's announcement was down to Elizabeth's status. The daughter of a 'simple knight', her lack of landed wealth – not to mention her widowhood and her two sons from her previous marriage – made her an entirely unsuitable proposition as England's queen. The way Edward had dithered before admitting his marriage suggested that he was quite aware what the reaction would be.[14]

Edward's mother was said to have exploded in a 'frenzy' of maternal fury at the news. Cecily, who had spent the last years luxuriating in her title of king's mother, had undoubtedly been bracing herself for the loss of status that would accompany her son's marriage. Having to concede that status to a great foreign princess was one thing; having to defer to the widow of a Lancastrian knight was another. In the decision that mattered most of all, her oldest son had proved an exceptional disappointment to Cecily and – according to Thomas More, giving the encounter extra literary spice – she had let him know it: Edward had, she scolded, 'defouled' his kingship by marrying a woman who was neither noble nor a virgin.[15]

If Cecily, who had laboured under the misapprehension that she could somehow 'rule' her son, was alarmed by this demonstration of his independent-mindedness, so too was Warwick. Working openly for a high-profile French marriage for Edward, apparently with the king's consent, the earl had been publicly blindsided. Almost immediately, in damage-limitation mode, Warwick had written to Louis XI saying how he and Edward had fallen out over the marriage, but that one of his secretaries would soon be in touch with some 'pleasing news'. According to a Milanese diplomat who had spent 'almost an hour' listening to the French king go on about it, Louis extrapolated wildly from Warwick's letter that the earl was about to overthrow Edward and make himself king of England – and, he added, he would give Warwick 'as much help as he could', as he counted Warwick one of his 'best and truest friends in the world'.[16]

The 'pleasing news', however, was not forthcoming. Warwick soon calmed down, at least in public; so too did Cecily. Edward did some belated massaging of bruised egos. Rather than turf his mother out of the queen's lodgings in Westminster Palace, he let her remain in possession. Still simmering, Cecily also reasserted her own queenly credentials, styling herself 'late wife unto Richard in right king of England'.[17] And on Michaelmas Day, 29 September, in an ostentatious display of family unity, Warwick and Edward's brother Clarence, now fourteen years old, escorted Elizabeth Woodville into the church of Reading Abbey, where a congregation of Edward's councillors honoured her as queen.

After the initial shock, people adjusted quickly to the new facts on the ground; whatever opinions they had, they kept to themselves. Nevertheless the Woodvilles, alert to the reception of their new status as royal family, kept their eyes and ears open. In response to an enquiry from Elizabeth's brother Anthony Woodville, the Norfolk knight John Howard was reassuring: he had taken soundings across East Anglia and only one of those he talked to had made difficult noises about the marriage.

Nobody, though, was more sensitive to Elizabeth's astonishing transformation than the new queen herself. Where her husband brushed aside the rigid ceremonial of court, she stood on it, sharply conscious of her new status and of the interrogatory gaze of the Yorkist establishment. Sensitive to her anomalous background, she reached for symbolism that would enfold it in the language of religious allegory: her new device, a deep red gillyflower, betokened the Virgin Mary's purity and motherhood, and carried associations of true love and matrimony.[18]

For although there was plenty about Elizabeth to explain away, as her gillyflower emphasized, there was every likelihood that she would be able to fulfil the crucial role of queen – bearing royal children. After all, she already had two of her own, while Edward had amply demonstrated his own potency: even as the pair wed, one of the king's mistresses was bearing his second illegitimate child.[19] As he put it breezily to his irate mother, 'neither of us is like to be barren'. Moreover, unlike Margaret of Anjou, it could at least be said of Elizabeth that she wasn't French.

Given that no amount of genealogical barrel-scraping could add lustre to her father's line, Elizabeth was quick to play up her mother's illustrious forebears. Of the six 'quarterings' in her new royal coat of arms, five referred to Jacquetta's Burgundian ancestry.[20] Which proved timely as far as Edward was concerned.

Early in July 1464, as Lord Wenlock was wining and dining with Louis XI and Philip of Burgundy, Edward was beginning to involve himself in another, off-the-record conversation, with Philip's estranged son and heir Charles of Charolais. It was a discussion that ran directly counter to the peace talks at Hesdin. Charles and Louis loathed each other: one of Louis' party pieces was a 'maniacal' impression, complete with hand gestures, of Burgundy's 'short-tempered, somewhat bestial' heir. For his part, Charles meant business. He was plotting with a group of disaffected French magnates to bring down the French king, and he was prepared to swallow his visceral Lancastrianism in order to include Edward in his plans. Edward, for his part, jumped at the chance of tearing Charles's sympathies away from Margaret of Anjou and the house of Lancaster.

That summer, unaware of the secret marriage that had taken place, Louis had written Edward a letter emphasizing his 'great desire' for a peace with Yorkist England, which, among other things, would leave him free 'to exterminate the duke of Burgundy and the count of Charolais'. Edward promptly forwarded the correspondence to Philip of Burgundy, who suddenly woke up to what his son had been trying to tell him for years: that in playing honest broker to an Anglo-French peace, he had been unwittingly preparing the ground for the destruction of his own state.[21]

As Edward and Charles searched for common ground meantime, messengers moving clandestinely between London and Bruges, they seized on Edward's new in-laws – who were only too happy to oblige. On 8 October, barely a week after Elizabeth Woodville had been presented to the assembled nobles in Reading Abbey, Edward authorized safe conducts for a Burgundian visit to England. The leader of this full-blown embassy was Jacques of Luxembourg, a military veteran from an ancient Burgundian family. The embodiment of Anglo-Burgundian détente, Luxembourg had been carefully chosen. Not only was he exceptionally close to Charles, he was maternal uncle to Elizabeth Woodville, the new queen of England.[22]

In London, merchants followed developments with mixed emotions. Anything that brought closer links with England's biggest trading partner was, of course, good news. But seen another way, Edward's cosying up to the bellicose Burgundian heir – a move which, in the minds of some, had been triggered by the king's new Woodville in-laws – could only serve to destabilize the delicate international equilibrium, and drag England into another ruinous war with France. London's mayor, Ralph Josselyn, was reported to have opined gloomily that Elizabeth's coronation 'would cost the lives of ten thousand men'. That autumn, though, the country's merchants had a more immediate problem on their hands. Just as Edward's relations with Charles of Charolais were softening, Philip of Burgundy, previously supportive of the house of York, suddenly snapped.

The protectionist laws that Edward had waved through Parliament the previous year had not gone down well in the Low Countries. Over the years, Philip had become wearily familiar with aggressive English mercantilism and had responded in kind, slapping embargoes on English cloth imports into his dominions. This time, perhaps hopeful of negotiating the laws' repeal, he had not immediately responded. But Edward's recoinage that summer, which further drained away scarce bullion from the mints of the Low Countries, was the straw that broke the camel's back.[23]

The existing trade agreement between England and Burgundy was due to expire on 1 November and, as the date approached, the city corporation wrote urgently to Edward to stress how 'behoveful', 'expedient' and indeed 'necessary' it was for it to be renewed. Edward's response was sluggish. On 19 October, barely two weeks before the treaty was due to expire, he ordered a group of representatives from Calais and London's Merchant Adventurers to open negotiations. It was too little, too late.[24] A week later, Philip tore up the trade treaty, banning all English cloth imports to the Low Countries. In doing so, he ripped through one of England's main economic arteries.

In the scramble that followed, English merchants reacted with practised efficiency. In the Low Countries, the governor of the Merchant Adventurers there, a bookish, cosmopolitan mercer in his mid-forties named William Caxton, had been part of Edward's negotiating team and had sensed what was coming. By the time the ban came into force a month later, the Bruges and Antwerp offices of the Merchant Adventurers were locked and shuttered, their stocks of cloth safely shipped out of the impounding reach of the Burgundian authorities. The merchants relocated a hundred miles northeast to Utrecht, the city outside Burgundian territory where, some three and a half years previously, Edward's young brothers had found refuge and which, keen to attract lucrative English trade, had promised Caxton a 'free market' there. Notwithstanding Caxton's decisiveness, however, the ban hit English commerce immediately and hard.

Cloth, piled high in London's warehouses and wharves, gathered dust; empty ships remained at anchor. In the Low Countries, Philip's officers moved through ports and towns, confiscating all the English cloth they could find. As autumn deepened into winter, the cost to London's export trade became apparent. Cloth exports plummeted. Trade with the Low Countries, in the doldrums for much of the previous decade, all but ground to a halt.[25] Now, desperate to re-establish relations with Burgundy, the city's merchants were only too happy to throw their weight behind England's new queen, whose family connections seemed to offer just such an opportunity.

With the city dying of the plague at the rate of two hundred a day, Edward and his new bride continued to give Londoners a wide berth, staying in the relative isolation of Reading Abbey with occasional forays up the Thames valley. In late November, skirting the capital's southern edge, they arrived at the royal manor of Eltham in the Kent countryside.

Elizabeth was growing into her role. She carried out the visible acts of piety demanded of a queen, from almsgiving and pilgrimages to the endowment of chantries and religious institutions; and quickly proved an effective lobbyist with her husband, on behalf of both the many petitioners who beat a path to her chamber and her own relatives, who luxuriated in their new status as royal family.[26] Elizabeth's parents, and her polished brother Anthony Woodville, were ubiquitous at court. Her large wider family, however, was not. Her parents' marriage had proved staggeringly productive; even more remarkably for the age, of their fourteen children only one had died in childhood. There was, besides, the matter of Elizabeth's two young sons from her first marriage, the ten-year-old Thomas Grey and five-year-old Richard. With Edward's marriage to Elizabeth, the house of York had not only changed in nature, it had ballooned. And Edward's new in-laws had to be provided for in a manner befitting their new status.[27]

By this point, Edward didn't have an awful lot of land to grant. The dower estates he now handed Elizabeth were worth strikingly less than those given to her Lancastrian predecessor, Margaret of Anjou – though Edward made a virtue out of his relative parsimony. Elizabeth's budget, a dower yielding an annual income of £4,500, was the same sum that his glorious Plantagenet forebear Edward III had given his wife Philippa of Hainault, a well-loved queen of impeccable Burgundian lineage.[28]

Determined to be a model of queenly prudence – and, perhaps, to earn comparison with the illustrious Philippa in the process – Elizabeth embraced her role. She seemed to have an instinctive sense of what was needed. From the outset her household operated in an atmosphere of careful, almost self-conscious economy, the queen surrounding herself with a notably scaled-down staff and keeping a restraining hand on expenditure. Elizabeth was also attentive to ways of augmenting her income and, if there was a hint of acquisitiveness in her control, she nevertheless strove to maintain the magnificence that her royal rank demanded. Sharing her husband's eye for fine things, she spent freely on furs and goldsmiths' work, and allocated over a third of her budget to building a lavish wardrobe.[29]

Together with her parents – in particular Rivers, who seemed to keep a tight grip on his daughter's new royal seal – Elizabeth set about doling out favour to her kinfolk. Her younger brother John Woodville became master of the horse, and her Kentish cousin James Haute was made one of her stewards; among her ladies-in-waiting was her sister Anne. Other key offices were given to her Bourchier in-laws, knitting the Woodvilles even tighter to this influential Yorkist family. But there were only so many posts that Elizabeth could give to her relations. If she were to keep a tight grip on her finances, and to sniff out revenue-increasing opportunities where they presented themselves, she also needed expertise.

Given that much of her dower came from the great estates of the duchy of Lancaster, now in royal hands, it made sense that many of her administrators were seasoned duchy officials, men who knew how such estates were run and, just as importantly, how to extract value from them. In typical Yorkist fashion, they also included men with close connections in the city of London. One man who spanned both worlds was the man appointed keeper of Elizabeth's Great Wardrobe, William Kerver.[30]

As receiver-general of the duchy of Lancaster, Kerver was an experienced accountant. He also had other qualities. As a mercer, he was a member of one of London's richest livery companies, one that dominated England's cloth trade with the Low Countries. In Kerver, as in so many of his colleagues, the worlds of royal administration and mercantile trade and finance blurred.[31] Someone who paid him close attention, who indeed may well have helped find him this key post in Elizabeth's household, was her father.

Whatever his demerits in the eyes of the nobility, Rivers' chivalric charm seemed to go down well among city merchants. Over the years, he had built up a reliable circle of London creditors, including the prominent draper Henry Waver and, very probably, Kerver himself. Alert to the opportunities presented by his daughter's extraordinary marriage, Rivers seemed to sense that Kerver was a very useful man to have onside.

Unusually, Elizabeth's receiver-general, her chief financial officer, had no record of royal service. In his early thirties, John Forster was the oldest son of an influential London couple – Sir Stephen Forster had been mayor some ten years previously; his wife, Agnes, was well known for her charitable work – and had trained as a lawyer before making an exceptional marriage to Joan, daughter of the powerful London draper Thomas Cook. John's head for business, and his in-laws' connections, had taken him into some heady but dangerous company. When in February 1461 Margaret of Anjou's ravening army threatened the city, Forster was on her wanted list. He had fled with his notorious grandfather-in-law, Philip Malpas, on the same ship as Edward's future close servants William Hatteclyffe and Thomas Vaughan. After they were captured by French privateers, the men had plenty of time to get to know each other as they awaited ransom. Forster's father-in-law Thomas Cook had found favour with the Yorkist regime: facilitating corporate loans that helped keep Edward's regime afloat, making large private donations out of his own coffers, and becoming mayor of London in the process. Perhaps Cook had had a few discreet words with royal officials; perhaps Hatteclyffe and Vaughan also had views. Whatever the case, Forster's appointment was a nod to the cabal of London associates who had proved such valuable creditors to Edward, another link between them and the newly remodelled Yorkist family.[32]

At Eltham, Edward and Elizabeth celebrated their first married

Christmas. The continuing plague and Philip of Burgundy's trade embargo only exacerbated another harsh winter which, coming after a poor harvest, meant there was little food around: livestock which might otherwise have consumed precious grain were slaughtered for meat instead. Edward, though, let nothing get in the way of his festivities. With Elizabeth not yet crowned and still awaiting the formal assignment of her lands, Edward advanced her £466 13s 4d 'against this feast of Christmas' for her wardrobe, chamber and stable expenses. Amid the liturgies and processions, the feasting, revelling and games, there was talk of another marriage.[33]

That January, one of Queen Elizabeth's brothers, the twenty-year-old Sir John Woodville, was betrothed to Edward's aunt, the wealthy dowager duchess of Norfolk – a 'slip of a girl' at eighty years old, snorted one chronicler, it was a *maritagium diabolicum*. In fact, the duchess was in her mid-sixties and the disparity in age was hardly unusual. What the duchess's expectant heirs did find diabolical was the prospect of their inheritance evaporating before their eyes: should the duchess die before her young husband, which looked likely, the chances of prising their jointure out of his grasp looked slim.[34] The betrothal, too, sent out a signal. With a clutch of unmarried siblings – only her oldest brother, Anthony Woodville, was already married – as well as her own sons from her first marriage, Elizabeth and her parents were a new and aggressive presence in the marriage market.

If the Woodvilles were on the alert for rich and influential matches, the process worked both ways. After all, marrying the 'queen's blood' was to marry into the royal family itself, bringing with it the chance to jump the long queue for favour and advancement either to consolidate your position within the regime or, at a stroke, to place your family at its heart. However, apart from the systematic speed with which Edward's new in-laws worked – the first betrothal, of Elizabeth's closest sister Margaret to the earl of Arundel's son and heir, had taken place weeks after the revelation of Elizabeth's own marriage – what prompted muttering in some quarters was the inevitably destabilizing effect of a large family entering the top end of the market. What was more, that family was backed by royal muscle. If Elizabeth and her parents were the driving force, the betrothals were clearly done, as one contract put it, at Edward's 'instance' and 'pleasure'.

Not long after, the Woodvilles landed one of the biggest fish of all. The Lancastrian nobleman Henry Stafford, duke of Buckingham, was one of England's greatest subjects and, as far as the lucrative market in wards was concerned, a great investment. With his father already dead, Buckingham had inherited his title aged four when his grandfather was singled out and slaughtered at the battle of Northampton. Early in 1464, Edward had shelled out the substantial sum of £1,830 to acquire control of the boy, his property and marriage rights. Now, he married the nine-year-old Buckingham off to the queen's sister Katherine, two years the boy's junior, handing him to Elizabeth to bring up in her household. It was a match that added another layer to Edward's new dynastic foundation. Few others could have afforded it, though one of them was the earl of Warwick, who had two daughters of his own to marry off. He was, it was rumoured, secretly furious at the news. What the young duke himself felt about his marriage went unrecorded. In any case, it was neither here nor there.[35]

In late January 1465, Parliament reassembled at Westminster. The atmosphere was fretful. With the Burgundian trade embargo predicted to have a drastic and far-reaching impact on the English cloth trade, with layoffs across the industry and the newly unemployed driven into 'sin and evil living', the Commons demanded reprisals.[36] They petitioned Edward to impose a blanket ban on Burgundian imports and, into the bargain, massive fines for anybody caught trying to evade such a ban by importing under royal licence. Edward, unsurprisingly, was evasive. At that moment, a delegation headed by one of his chamber servants, Sir John Donne, had arrived in Brussels. Announcing Elizabeth's forthcoming coronation, to be held on Sunday 26 May, Donne asked Philip of Burgundy whether her uncle Jacques of Luxembourg might attend as the state's official representative.[37] Amid these flickerings of Anglo-Burgundian détente, the last thing Edward wanted to do was antagonize Philip further; besides which, he had no intention of getting rid of the lucrative loophole that allowed him to issue import licences to anybody he saw fit. When, some two months later, he finally passed the Commons' ban, the loophole remained; moreover, though the Commons insisted that the ban should last 'forever', Edward stipulated that it should endure 'at the king's will and pleasure'. Not only could Edward bypass the ban whenever he wanted, he could repeal it too.[38]

At the Burgundian court, Sir John Donne and his fellow ambassadors found a fluid, fast-changing situation. Newly reconciled with his father, Charles of Charolais was now driving forward his offensive against his bitter enemy Louis XI. If Edward could be persuaded to join Charles's coalition of renegade French lords – who, styling themselves the *Ligue du Bien Public*, or League of the Common Wealth, were harnessing popular resentment in a bid to remove Louis from power – things would look very bad indeed for the French king.

Louis was rattled. Early that February, chuntering on to a Milanese ambassador about Edward's 'inconstancy', he waved around a letter from Margaret of Anjou.

From their base in eastern France, Margaret and her small circle of advisers, headed by the shrewd pair of Sir John Fortescue and John Morton, maintained a flimsy network of potential European support. Despite their isolated destitution – 'We be all in great poverty', acknowledged Fortescue frankly[39] – they persisted in reminding Louis that they were players at the table of international politics. That February day, Louis summarized Margaret's letter for the hovering ambassador. There was a rift between Edward and Warwick – old, out-of-date news, as far as Louis was concerned – and now was an ideal time for the Lancastrians to try to regain the English throne. Would Louis help her? And if not, would he be happy for her to seek assistance from the other 'great lords' of France? The threat was implicit: by 'great lords' she meant Louis' enemies in the coalition of nobles now being ranged against him. 'Look how proudly she writes', Louis said thoughtfully. Trying to work out the French king's attitude to the Lancastrian exiles, the ambassador gave up. 'Your lordship', he advised his master, 'will learn of English affairs better by way of Bruges than by this way.'[40]

Those affairs were progressing fast. The following month, as preparations began for Elizabeth's coronation festivities, the new queen's Burgundian uncle was back in London, urging Edward to join Charles's anti-French league. Edward's participation in the league, though, was out of the question. The Burgundian trade embargo was still in place, and in any case, England's beleaguered taxpayers would hardly be prepared to underwrite the colossal expense of a war against France. There also remained question marks over Charles's allegiances: he was still quietly funding prominent Lancastrians, including the new duke of Somerset, Edmund Beaufort. Jacques of Luxembourg, however, had brought Edward another invitation, evidence of Charles's new warmth towards the house of York, at which Edward's eyes lit up.

The invitation came from a figure even closer to Charles – his half-brother Anthoine, the 'Bastard of Burgundy'. The product of one of Duke Philip's countless liaisons, Anthoine wore his illegitimacy with as much flamboyance as he fought.[41] Now, in the spirit of closer Anglo-Burgundian relations, he was throwing down the gauntlet to Edward – or, rather, to Edward's new in-laws. Here was a chance for the Woodvilles to confirm their newly acquired royal status and their distinguished Burgundian heritage on a glittering international stage, through the activity they did best: jousting.

On Wednesday 17 April, Edward and Elizabeth had just finished celebrating high mass at the Thames-side manor of Sheen, west of London. The elaborate ceremonies of Holy Week, with their processions and crown-wearings, were in full swing and petitioners were out in force, trying to press requests for favour into the hands of those close to the king. As the royal procession made its way out of the chapel royal, Elizabeth's brother Anthony shouldered through the crowds of courtiers to speak to his sister about a business matter that he needed progressing. As he greeted her, dropping to one knee and sweeping his hat from his head, 'as my duty was', an extraordinary transformation took place.[42]

Suddenly, as if in a dream, beautiful women clustered about him. A pair of hands reached for his left thigh, tying around it a gold collar studded with pearls and with an enamel flower attached. The ladies explained to the befuddled Woodville that this 'flower of souvenance' or forget-me-not, one of Queen Elizabeth's emblems, was a token: he was being set an 'emprise', a chivalric quest. Then the ladies – the queen's gentlewomen – disappeared. Woodville came to and picked up the hat that had slipped from his grasp. Out of it dropped a letter, written on fine parchment and tied with gold thread, containing details of his quest. Wandering off to find the king, Woodville was admitted to his presence and, dropping to his knees, handed him the still-sealed letter, begging Edward to license him to take up the challenge contained in it, 'for the adventure of the said flower of souvenance'. Edward snapped the gold thread, handed the letter to one of the hovering lords around him to be read out and, having listened to it, gave his assent.

This moment of carefully stylized spontaneity was Anthony Woodville's response to the Bastard of Burgundy's proposal for a great Anglo-Burgundian tournament. In taking up the Bastard's challenge, Woodville proposed a great wargame, a *pas d'armes*, to be held in London, which would pit teams of the finest warriors in England and Burgundy against one another. Such encounters took place within a world of Arthurian make-believe, whose storylines imbued their real-life protagonists with a mythological lustre. Casting Anthony Woodville in the central role, this scenario focused international attention on the chivalric glamour of the queen's family. Then and there John Tiptoft, in his capacity as constable of England, handed a copy of the tournament rules, already carefully drawn up, along with Elizabeth's 'flower of souvenance' to a waiting officer-of-arms, Chester Herald, who was wearing Anthony Woodville's coat of arms.[43]

When the herald arrived in Brussels on the last day of April, Burgundy was on a war footing. Days before, Philip and Charles had brought their long conflict to a close with a very public display of reconciliation, Philip proclaiming his commitment to his son's anti-French league and to war with his former protégé, Louis XI. In the midst of the general mobilization, the herald presented Anthony Woodville's counter-challenge to the Bastard of Burgundy. While the Bastard, needing Philip's sanction to proceed, promised him a reply 'in haste', the herald was left kicking his heels for days, something he tolerated with diplomatic 'great cheer, as a herald pertained to have'. But while Philip, still seething at Edward's high-handed economic policies, was determined to make a diplomatic point, ultimately he gave his consent to the tournament: as his son Charles doubtless reminded him, if Burgundy was going to make war on France, it needed England onside. While Anthony Woodville's challenge to the Bastard was a private agreement between two individuals rather than a treaty between two heads of state, there was no mistaking its significance for future collaboration between Burgundy and the house of York.[44]

Weeks later, on 23 May 1465, Chester Herald disembarked at Edward's Thames-side manor of Greenwich. There, he related the story of his trip to the king and a clutch of attendant lords, among them two boys looking on dutifully: Edward's youngest brother Richard, now twelve years old and, three years his junior, the latest and most glorious addition to the queen's family, the duke of Buckingham.

Chester Herald's return from Burgundy had been impeccably choreographed. The next day, Elizabeth Woodville was due to set out from Greenwich on the first stage of her journey to Westminster Abbey where, the following Sunday, she would be crowned queen of England. London was ready to give her a royal welcome.

In the weeks leading up to Elizabeth's coronation, a subcommittee of London's corporation had drawn up plans for the reception that it was expected to lay on for significant royal events. Central to this civic street party were the pageants: multi-storeyed *tableaux vivants* that, constructed at strategic points along the queen's route through the city, would come to life as her procession approached. In the background, the queen's representatives – principal among them her parents, with their close connections to London's Guildhall – vetted the preparations, advising, recommending and insisting.[45]

The first two pageants would be staged on London Bridge, the great shop-lined thoroughfare with its twenty stone piers supporting two hundred buildings that hung over the river. A fortnight or so before the reception, three loads of 'old material' – stuff left over from previous royal receptions – had been taken out of storage in the Guildhall and carted over the bridge to a rented warehouse at its southern end. There, a team of carpenters and craftsmen worked, constructing the great timber stages and making the linen hangings with which they were covered, 'stained' with brilliant and expensively acquired colours: green verdigris, red brazilwood, vermilion, indigo, white and red lead and – for the faces and flesh of images – a gallon of pink-yellow, all mixed with alum to ensure the paint stayed fixed on the fabric. Eight lifelike effigies, figures from the Bible and myth-history, were made: their faces painted masks of leather over carved wood, their hair dyed flaxen. Reams of paper, gold and red, white and black, were cut into decorations; verses, spoken by actors to greet the queen, were written out ornately on boards, for the benefit of the literate. The labour was intense and thirsty. Even on the short, late spring nights, the men worked until the light failed, getting through four pounds of candles in the process and running up a tab of 46s 10d at the adjacent alehouse, The Crown.

On the afternoon of Friday 24 May, the bridge stood ready: pageant stages constructed, swathed in colour, the way swept and lined with forty-five cartloads of sand. Earlier in the day Elizabeth, dressed in white, and her party – a pack of noblemen, Edward's household servants and the queen's gentlewomen – set out from Greenwich to London Bridge, some five miles to the west. At the high point of Shooters' Hill, its archery butts deserted for the occasion, they were met by a reception committee: London's mayor and aldermen, and representatives of the city's companies, handpicked for their charisma, good looks and horsemanship, all dressed in gowns of Yorkist blue and mulberry. Riding up the Old Kent Road, the procession turned into Borough High Street and, at the Church of St George the Martyr, halted to hear a speech of welcome by the church's clerk, dressed as St Paul (a nod to the city's saint and to Elizabeth's Burgundian family, St Pol). Halting at the 'stulps', the thick wooden posts marking the approach to London Bridge, Elizabeth's procession was greeted by a choir singing from the upper window of an adjoining house and, as the first pageant came to life, presented with an illuminated souvenir booklet of the verses she was about to hear.

In wrestling with the twin problems of Elizabeth's genealogy and her widowhood, her advisers had decided to own them, to put them front and centre. They had done their work well. Playing up Elizabeth's maternal heritage – it was, as one chronicler stressed, the 'duchess of Bedford's daughter' that Edward had married – the symbolism of the festivities also smoothed away the issue of her widowhood. At the bridge's entrance St Mary Cleophas – the Virgin Mary's twice-married half-sister – stepped forward to address the queen. Elizabeth's procession then moved forward, passing through the tunnel of houses whose upper storeys met overhead. In the shadow of the Drawbridge Gate, on its tower a thicket of traitors' heads, an enactment of the Feast of the Visitation saw the Virgin's cousin, St Elizabeth, pregnant with John the Baptist, deliver a monologue. In both pageants, two London actors, Edmund Herte and Salomon Batell, played the Virgin Mary's relatives. By implication the starring role, that of Mary herself, was filled by the watching queen, who (it was noted) wore 'the attire of virgins'. Boldly acknowledging the new queen's complex marital history, the two pageants spun it adroitly into a compliment: remarriage and fertility were next to holiness.

Then the procession headed into the riot of noise and colour that was feast-day London. In the stands that lined the route were the city's livery companies; the rest strained for a view, leaning from windows, perched on rooftops. Hours later, Elizabeth and her retinue emerged on the city's eastern side at the Tower where, as custom demanded, she would spend the night, riding through its sequence of massive, fortified gates, the tumult outside subsiding to a distant roar.

Edward was already there. That evening, he created a new group of forty knights, leading them through the complex ritual of purification. Accompanied by Lord Hastings and a group of veteran knights, he visited each man in turn as the knight-to-be lay naked in his ceremonial bath. Advising him of the duties of his Order, foremost of which was to 'love the king thy Sovereign lord . . . and his right defend unto thy power', Edward dipped his right hand in the bath and touched the man's shoulders with his wet fingers. After this royal baptism, clothed and hooded in black, the men gathered in the chapel of St John, where they spent the night in vigil, stained glass and gold glinting in the light of their tapers. The following morning Edward enveloped each new knight in an embrace, then brought his hand down on the man's neck and, breathing the words 'Be ye a good knight', kissed him.[46]

Leaving the Tower, the royal procession nudged through the London crowds, Elizabeth a vision of white cloth-of-gold in a horse-drawn litter, blonde hair tumbling around her shoulders, on her head a gold circlet encrusted with precious stones. In front rode the phalanx of new knights, blue gowns billowing out behind them, their loyalties conspicuously bound to their king and his family. Among them the recovering Lancastrian nobleman John de Vere, to whom Edward had recently returned his family title of earl of Oxford, rubbed shoulders with an assortment of freshly knighted Woodvilles: the queen's brothers;

Thomas Grey, her oldest son by her first marriage; her cousin, the musician and composer William Haute. Leading them, as the precedent of his great rank demanded, was the nine-year-old duke of Buckingham.

For one London chronicler, however, it was only worth mentioning five names: members of the corporation whose knighthoods were a 'great worship' to the city – this was no overstatement, given that only eleven Londoners in the city's history had previously received the honour.[47] All five had been generous creditors of Edward's regime. Both the mercer Hugh Wyche and his successor as mayor, Thomas Cook, had negotiated thousands of pounds in corporate loans to the regime, as well as dipping their hands in to their own coffers on repeated occasions. There were two more drapers, along with Cook: Henry Waver, who had lent substantial sums both to Edward and to Elizabeth Woodville's parents; and the current mayor Ralph Josselyn who, whatever his privately expressed misgivings, had clearly proven supportive – besides which, he was Cook's brother-in-law. Finally, the influential goldsmith Matthew Philip was a regular supplier of fine plate to the royal household.

If the knighthoods were a compliment to the city, they were also a royal endorsement of the tight-knit London syndicate whose lavish credit had brought it close to the regime, and which had now bought into Edward's marriage.[48]

On Sunday 26 May Elizabeth, clothed in purple, was escorted into Westminster Abbey by England's two archbishops: Edward's uncle Thomas Bourchier, archbishop of Canterbury and – newly created archbishop of York – George Neville, both barefoot. Preceding the queen and her train of noblewomen, all in red, were the great officers of state, the newly made knights and, at the head of this 'solemn procession', Edward's brother Clarence.

Now fifteen, Clarence remained the king's heir, and Edward gave him the ceremonial pre-eminence his status demanded. He stood by while Elizabeth was crowned (her mother Jacquetta standing by her 'reverently', supporting the weight of the crown on her daughter's head) and held a basin of water from which the new queen refreshed herself after the arduous ceremonial. Back in Westminster Hall, Clarence supervised the coronation feast in his capacity as steward of England, directing operations astride a 'richly trapped' warhorse, its tack glittering with 'spangles of gold'. If the ceremonies were a picture of the newly remodelled regime, then Clarence – along with his new brother-in-law Anthony Woodville and the newly restored earl of Oxford – remained at its heart.[49]

While there were some notable absences, all were easily explicable. Etiquette demanded that Elizabeth's mother-in-law Cecily be absent, although she perhaps needed no second invitation.[50] Warwick and Hastings, meanwhile, had been sent abroad on a high-level mission to try to break the trade deadlock with Burgundy and reopen talks with France. Their brief for the Burgundian negotiations was to say much and do nothing: to make appropriately bellicose noises against 'our enemy' Louis while resisting all attempts to drag Edward into war with France.

As tens of thousands of Burgundian troops poured across the border into north-eastern France, Warwick's agents monitored the brewing hostilities. On 16 July at Montlhéry, southwest of Paris, the armies of Louis XI and Charles of Charolais' league fought each other to a standstill. While Louis had avoided complete disaster – his isolation and defeat of Charles's Breton allies had been key – he was forced to agree to humiliating reforms and to sign away a series of grants to the rebel lords, including the cession of a string of towns along the River Somme to Burgundy. So, it perhaps came as something of a surprise to Edward when, on the 22nd, Warwick returned bearing a freshly concluded agreement, not with Charles of Charolais – who, irritated by English foot-dragging, had aborted the talks – but with Edward's 'enemy' Louis. For the beleaguered French king, extracting an English commitment not to back Burgundy was essential. For Edward, Louis' reciprocal promise not to back the exiled Lancastrians had never seemed less urgent. Besides, it wasn't what Warwick had been sent for. In tying up an agreement with Louis, Warwick hadn't so much failed to fulfil Edward's brief as contradict it entirely.[51]

Meanwhile, shortly before sunset on Thursday 18 July, a rider had arrived in Canterbury from the north with urgent news for Edward, there with Elizabeth on pilgrimage to the tomb of St Thomas Becket. After over a year on the run, Henry VI had finally been chased to ground. Having narrowly escaped capture as he sat down to dinner at his latest safe house of Waddington Hall in Lancashire – his host's brother was said to have tipped off local knights loyal to Edward IV – the Lancastrian king had been detained in the nearby woods as he made for Brungerley Hippingstones, a ford across the River Ribble. After offering up thanks to God, Edward ordered the newly returned Warwick to meet Henry as he was brought south in chains.

On 24 July Warwick headed north out of London, up through the inns of St John Street to the village of Islington, where he took custody of the Lancastrian king. Formally arresting Henry, Warwick had him lashed to a donkey, legs tied to the stirrups, arms roped to his sides, a straw hat perched on his head. Then, in a grotesque inversion of a triumphal entrance, he led the helplessly swaying Henry – held on either side by ropes in case he fell off – back into the city and along the main thoroughfares of Cheapside and Cornhill, through jeering, mocking crowds. Warwick invariably knew what played well with the people. As one onlooker, a Hanseatic merchant from Danzig, put it, anybody who thought of 'doing honour' to a crowned king of England as he passed, wisely kept quiet 'for fear of his life'.

Following this public humiliation Henry was taken to the Tower and locked up. There, he was kept modestly, in a manner befitting his status: late king of England *de facto*, in deed, but not *de jure*, of right. Edward treated him well enough, paying for his attendants' expenses – one, Henry's aged and leprous secretary, Thomas Manning, was released and pardoned – providing him with a new wardrobe and occasionally sending him wine. After all, as one chronicler pointed out, people could then come and see for themselves this hapless example of Edward's benevolence, and listen to him try and justify why he once claimed the crown of England.[52]

In the wake of Edward and Elizabeth's marriage, scribes and illuminators set about updating their royal family trees and lines of descent. One man, an Oxford graduate called Thomas Haselden, had taken a fairly common-or-garden Lancastrian genealogy and, over the years, had made his own pro-Yorkist adjustments: underlining how Henry of Bolingbroke had incarcerated Richard II, 'true king of England', in the Tower, before 'unjustly' seizing the crown as Henry IV; emphasizing Roger Mortimer's central place in the line of succession. On a new page, Haselden now added a drawing of Edward IV and Queen Elizabeth kneeling before God, flanked by St George and St Margaret. As St Margaret prayed for a fruitful marriage for Elizabeth, God reiterated his gift of the kingdom of England to Edward. Haselden's summary was clear enough. The new reality and future of the house of York lay in Edward, Elizabeth and their offspring, whether people liked it or not.[53]

6

They Are Not to be Trusted

On Sunday, 22 September 1465, Edward IV's chancellor, George Neville, was enthroned as archbishop of York in a glittering ceremony in the city's cathedral. Neville had shown scant enthusiasm for his previous bishopric of Exeter, though admittedly in recent years he had had his hands full trying to hold together Edward's precarious regime. But the archbishopric of York was different. With a rich portfolio of estates and offices, it presented abundant opportunity to entrench and extend Neville rule throughout England's northeast, giving that authority an added dimension: spiritual, as well as temporal. Still only thirty-three, the rise of this brilliant politician seemed irresistible. His enthronement was a statement of his own and his family's pre-eminence in the north; so too was the celebration that followed, a meal so excessive that it would come to be known as the feast of the century. Lasting about a week and involving around three thousand diners, it dwarfed the festivities that Thomas Bourchier had put on for his enthronement as archbishop of Canterbury some ten years before. It also outdid Elizabeth Woodville's coronation feast in Westminster the previous May. Which was, perhaps, the point.

During the previous weeks, carts and wagons had streamed into the archiepiscopal castle at Cawood, south of York, with a staggering supply of provisions. There was a frenzy of butchery. The carcasses disembowelled, plucked, prepared and dressed for the occasion included 1,000 sheep, 500 deer of various varieties, 400 swans, 2,000 each of pigs and chickens, 104 peacocks, 12 'porpoises and seals' and 6 wild bulls. An army of pastry-makers produced nearly ten thousand pastries, pies and tarts, as well as the 'sugared delicates and wafers' with which the more privileged of the sated guests would idly toy as they digested the twenty-one pounds of meat that, on average, each was served. All this was washed down with three hundred tuns of ale and a hundred tuns of wine.[1]

Many of England's great and good were there, noted one chronicler, 'except', he added, 'the king and the queen'. Edward's non-attendance was hardly a surprise. Rather than make the long trip north, he had preferred a convivial progress through Essex, doing favoured house-hold servants like Thomas Montgomery – with whom Edward stayed at his manor of Faulkbourne – the great, and punitively expensive, honour of hosting the royal entourage for days at a stretch.[2] In any case, the Neville guest list was an expression of the regime's unity and inclusivity. On the archbishop's left hand, in an optimistic piece of seating, were two Neville brothers-in-law: the young earl of Oxford, John de Vere, and the man who had condemned his father and older brother to death, John Tiptoft, earl of Worcester. Presiding over the ceremonies, together with Warwick and John Neville, was yet another Neville brother-in-law, William Hastings. The king had even graciously provided his own ewerer for the occasion, to wash noble hands, proffer crisp linen, pour water, and lend a discreet ear to the table talk.

Behind the hall, in the seclusion of the private apartments, the noblewomen and ladies dined apart, as was customary. At high table, the women of the Neville family, including Warwick's wife and his two eligible young daughters – Isabel, just fourteen, and the nine-year-old Anne – were clustered around the thirteen-year-old boy whose educational development Edward IV had recently entrusted to his cousin Warwick. Seated with the women was the king's youngest brother, Richard.

Up to now, the question of what to do with Richard had, much like the issue of his appanage, been fairly low down the list of Edward's priorities. But as he approached *adolescentia*, Richard was entering a new phase of his education. This was the age at which noble boys left their childhood things behind, exchanging play swords for real weapons; when they began to enact the 'gests of battles', the great chivalric deeds of which they had been fed a constant diet ever since they were old enough to understand. Everything about this training – from archery and hunting to fighting with swords and maces, on horseback and on foot – prepared nobles for governing and defending the society of which they were the rulers.

Richard was a slight boy, not obviously robust. As contemporary theorists stressed, however, a noble education was about more than brute force and athleticism. It was what was in the mind that counted. To hunt deer, wrote one, to kill them and 'see them bleed', prepared boys for the violence of war, toughening them up and giving them 'hardiment' and courage; the chase, meanwhile, developed their tactical abilities and decision-making skills. It was also about a mentality, which pervaded all aspects of a noble teenager's education, from military training to courtesy, languages and music. Through all this, through rigorous discipline, 'temperate behaving and patience' and books – 'the example of the noble ancients' – boys absorbed the lessons and rules of the chivalric tradition of which they were the inheritors. If they did so successfully, in time they too would become virtuous knights.[3]

Richard wanted to be a virtuous knight as much as the next boy. A diligent pupil, he absorbed a working knowledge of Latin and law and – an indication, perhaps, of his comfort in the schoolroom – developed handwriting that was more precise than his brothers' extravagant scrawls. Brought up on standard texts like the Roman strategist Vegetius' *De re militari*, the staple military treatise of the age, Richard's education was conventional enough; so too was his conspicuous piety. But there were hints of a passionate intensity. One book that he kept by him was a collection of chivalric romances, including the story of Ipomedon, 'the worthiest knight in all the world', who, undertaking a quest for fame, glory and love, is scorned by his fellow knights and rejected by his beloved before, finally, winning her. At the bottom of one page, in his careful hand, Richard signed his name and the ardent phrase *'tant le desierée'*: 'I have wanted it so much', a phrase that was to become his motto.[4]

Giving his youngest brother into Warwick's care was a conspicuous act of trust and favour on Edward's part, one designed to underscore Warwick's continued place at the heart of the regime – whatever impressions anybody might have gained to the contrary following the king's marriage to Elizabeth Woodville. Warwick's household was the perfect place for Richard to continue his education. His formal introduction to the world of the Nevilles was George Neville's enthronement feast at Cawood that September. It perhaps struck the young Richard that it was comparable to anything he had experienced at his brother's court.

As Richard settled into life in Warwick's household at Middleham Castle in the north Yorkshire dales, his perspective, his centre of gravity, began to shift. His first thirteen years had been spent largely in England's southeast: London, Kent, the Thames valley. Now he encountered a different land with different customs, accents and dialects. Here was a watchful, battle-ready people, one whose cohesiveness was shaped by the intermittent violence in the borderlands to the north, and by the ever-present threat of Scottish invaders. It was an area hard hit by the economic slump of the last decades. Abandoned villages scattered the countryside, and while the once-prosperous port of Hull and the region's capital of York had seen commerce decline, the trade that remained was increasingly monopolized by London and the southeast. Here, far from the hub of royal power, people looked, as they always had done, to the region's great noble clans for lordship and the redress of grievances. The greatest of them all, dominating with vice-regal authority, was now the Neville family.

Richard made friends among the other boys who, brought up under Warwick's supervision, were his 'henchmen', his companions and servants. One, Francis, Lord Lovell, had become Warwick's ward after the death of his father. Warwick had brought the seven-year-old north from his native Oxfordshire, married him off to one of his nieces and installed him in his household. Perhaps, given the five-year age gap, Richard's relationship to Lovell – both southern boys in an unfamiliar land – was that of a protective older brother. Here, far away from Edward and Clarence, no longer just 'the other brother', Richard set about forging his own ties of affinity among those who would become close, not just as servants but 'lovers': intimate friends. At Middleham, as Richard watched, learned, imitated and grew, he flourished.[5]

Among the faces that Richard now began to encounter more frequently were the two young noblewomen who had shared his dining table at Cawood: Warwick's daughters Isabel and Anne. Warwick was a predatory operator in the marriage market and, with no sons of his own, had exceptional ambitions for his daughters. But he had not yet found them marriages. After all, the top of the market was thinly populated with suitable candidates – hence the earl's reported rage at the marrying-off of the duke of Buckingham to the queen's sister Katherine Woodville. Warwick's fury may have been whetted by the fact that, according to a story that later did the rounds, he had already made an audacious move on his daughters' behalf – and Edward, unhesitatingly, had shut it down.

Late in 1464, reported one chronicler, Warwick had convened a discreet meeting with the king's brothers Clarence and Richard to broach the possibility of their marrying his two daughters. It was an ambitious gambit, one that would strengthen still further the bonds between the Neville family and the house of York. When news of the conversation reached Edward, he had exploded and, incandescent, summoned his brothers for a dressing-down.

If they wanted to get married, he told the pair in no uncertain terms, they had to get his royal consent first. Clarence, his tongue running ahead of any sense of discretion, immediately shot back. Clearly, he pointed out acidly to his brother, marrying without any-body's consent had worked for Edward, since he had managed 'to gain entry to a good place'. When it dawned on him what Clarence was insinuating, Edward hit the roof. There would, Edward stated flatly, be no marrying Warwick's daughters. And that, he assumed, was that. As king, he naturally expected even the greatest of his sub-jects to obey him – and that included, first and foremost, his brothers. Edward's expectations of Clarence were especially high: 'more than others', he should be 'loving, helping, assisting and obedient'. The matter, he assumed, was closed.

Apart from this isolated case of fraternal friction, Clarence was obedient enough, and had cut a sensational figure at Elizabeth's coro-nation as master of ceremonies. Whatever his sour thoughts about Edward's marriage, he was probably less concerned about the nature of the match than its almost inevitable outcome: the royal offspring that would see him deprived of his status as heir presumptive. Clar-ence, moreover, had good reason to behave himself. Early in 1465, Edward had embarked on the latest stage of his plan to transform his brother into a 'great prince'.[6]

That February, Edward pushed through a parliamentary act of resumption. The closest thing to a royal spending review, this whole-sale re-appropriation of royal lands and offices from those to whom they had been granted was, this time, designed to provide a living for the king's family: his new queen and his brothers, especially Clarence. Out of this sweeping annexation, Edward granted his fifteen-year-old brother a vast portfolio of estates throughout the west country and the north: 'so large portion of possessions', Edward later commented, as if astonished at his own generosity, that 'no memory is' of a king ever having given 'so largely to any of his brothers'. It was hardly hyperbole. Worth a combined annual income of £3,666, Clarence's settlement would, when he reached his majority, make him one of the country's wealthiest noblemen.[7]

At the same time, as if to remind him of the nature of his staggering new endowment, Edward involved Clarence in the process of resumption from which his newfound wealth derived. When the act was announced, there was the usual mad scramble by people holding royal grants to ringfence their property from appropriation. If they were lucky – or, more to the point, had friends close to the king in a position to put in a quiet word – their frantic lobbying would bear fruit in a royal proviso for exemption, recorded for posterity on the parliament roll, enabling them to keep hold of their grants. Among those employed to deliver petitioners' provisos to Parliament on Edward's behalf was Clarence. It was a practical education to his brother in the reality of royal favour. What the king gave, the king could always take away.[8]

The same, of course, did not apply to hereditary lands – estates inherited by birth. But then Clarence, in Edward's words, was 'not born to have any livelihood'. The way for Clarence to acquire vast independent landed wealth was through a great marriage, but Edward was in no rush to find his brother a rich bride. Clarence's hand was a significant card to play and the king would do so when the time was right. But if Warwick had indeed offered his older daughter's hand, it would hardly have been surprising if Clarence, some twenty years his celebrated cousin's junior, had found it flattering. Nor if, notwithstanding Edward's refusal, he had continued to think about it.

In September 1465, as the gourmandizing at Cawood continued, away in London one of Queen Elizabeth's chamber servants left for the Low Countries. Thomas Wilde's trip was, in diplomatic terms, unremarkable: he stayed a few weeks, met some Burgundian councillors, and returned home the following month. Wilde, however, carried with him the significant announcement that Elizabeth was pregnant with Edward's first child. He returned to England with equally interesting news: Isabella of Bourbon, wife of the Burgundian heir Charles of Charolais, had died. Their eleven-year-long union had been good, albeit – with only one daughter, Mary, now eight years old – not especially productive. However Charles, one of Europe's most powerful princes, was looking to marry again and, with the growing détente between England and Burgundy, the house of York was an obvious place to look for a bride. Sometime that winter, a Burgundian envoy turned up at Edward's court with a marriage proposal – or rather, more of an enquiry, about Edward's third sister.[9]

At eighteen, Margaret of York was the oldest of Edward's unmarried sisters and highly eligible. Brought up for a while alongside her two younger brothers on an adequate but modest allowance, she was bookish and, like her mother Cecily, ostentatiously pious in the manner of the age, her devotion accentuating a natural reserve: she rarely smiled. People found her tall, slim good looks attractive, her grey eyes alive with intelligence. After Edward's marriage to Elizabeth Woodville, Margaret was regularly in the queen's company, her courtly education given an extra polish by Elizabeth's strict observance of protocol. And, as Charles of Charolais had heard, she possessed the most prized quality of all, being 'well built for producing heirs'.[10]

Whether Charles was entirely sincere about marrying her was another question. With his allies in his anti-French coalition backsliding, his priority was to get Edward involved; showing interest in the English king's sister would, Charles probably reasoned, help things along. At the same time, he was said to be seriously entertaining another marriage proposal, from none other than Louis XI, who had offered Charles the hand of his four-year-old daughter. Keeping his options open, Charles told his envoy to raise with Edward the subject of Margaret of York, but on no account to progress things. Edward, he knew, would be keen. He wanted to keep it that way.[11]

A month or so before she was due to give birth, Elizabeth went into confinement, retreating into her richly furnished apartments, her gentlewomen shutting the door on the outside, male world. There, in the still candlelight of her inner chamber – natural light and fresh air were all but blotted out by the decorated arras that hung heavy over its windows – her mother Jacquetta watched as the queen's midwives safely delivered her baby: a girl, born on February 1466, who was baptized Elizabeth.[12]

It was late March when the queen, having recuperated after child-birth, emerged for her 'churching', the ritual of purification that marked her return to the public life of the court. Among the waiting crowds was a Bohemian nobleman, Leo von Rozmital, and his entourage. Rozmital was brother-in-law to the king of Bohemia, George of Poděbrad. His country torn apart for decades by wars of religion, the king dreamed of a vision of a unified Christendom, based not on the supremacy of the pope and Holy Roman Emperor – and the typical aggrandizing and divisive treaties between individual states – but on a multilateral accord between all the kingdoms and principalities of Europe. This 'bond of alliance', founded on a common security policy, a single assembly and court, would ensure a peace and friendship between states that would 'endure and last forever'. It was, as Poděbrad may have admitted to himself, a far-fetched idea – but he was determined to try to achieve it. The man he dispatched to Rome on this mission, attempting to gain the support of Christendom's major states as he went, was his brother-in-law Rozmital.[13]

Having left his native Prague three months earlier, Rozmital's eventful journey up the Rhine and through the Low Countries culminated in a petrifying crossing to England from Calais. The first abortive attempt was abandoned after the Bohemians' ship 'sprung a great leak', the horses on board in water 'up to their bellies'; the second saw them hit by raging storms. Finally, slumped on the ship 'as if they had been dead', the Bohemians reached the Kentish coast: 'high mountains full of chalk', they wondered, which 'seem from a distance to be covered with snow'.

Progressing through Kent, taking in the elegance of Canterbury Cathedral and the richness of Thomas Becket's gold, gem-encrusted shrine, the saint's hair shirt hanging above it, Rozmital and his party started to acquaint themselves with English customs, including a beverage drunk by the common people, which, one of the party noted, was called 'Al'selpir' (though he didn't apparently realize that he was being offered a choice: 'ale' or 'beer'). In London, the Bohemians were put up by Edward in opulent lodgings, and deftly escorted by a royal herald around the city's most spectacular sights, its wealthy guildhalls, churches, shrines and goldsmiths' shops, and entertained in the Cheapside headquarters of the Mercers' Company. Noting Edward's freshly minted currency, 'nobles and other good coins' changing hands, they quickly formed the conclusion that London – a 'powerful' city, they appraised, with its face turned outward towards the world and 'rich in gold and silver' – was England. Despite the continued recession and trade war with Burgundy, there were plenty in the city, it seemed, who were continuing to do very nicely indeed. The visitors' impression was emphatically reinforced when, after a fortnight or so, they were summoned to meet the king.

The Bohemians were awestruck by Edward's court. Its formal splendour all seemed directed towards one thing: elevating the king above the greatest of his subjects. Even the mightiest noblemen were, like Edward's crisply dressed household staff, required to wear the Yorkist livery collar of suns and roses and, Tetzel remarked, 'had to kneel to him'. But what astonished them, thrown into relief by the precise ritual that framed it, was Edward's close physical intimacy. Shaking the hands of Rozmital and his servants, he settled down to listen with 'great friendliness' to Rozmital's account of his journey and mission. Some days later, he threw a dinner in honour of his Bohemian guests, a banquet involving 'fifty dishes', after which Edward personally hung livery badges – gold for the noblemen and knights, silver for those of lesser rank – around the necks of Rozmital and his attendants. As they basked in Edward's hospitality, they couldn't help noticing the ladies of various ages, 'women and maidens', who hovered in attendance: all 'of outstanding beauty'.[14]

Not long after, the Bohemians were summoned back to court as honoured guests at Elizabeth's churching. They watched agog as the procession – the child's godparents Warwick, Jacquetta of St Pol and Edward's mother Cecily, a stream of relic-bearing priests, musicians, choristers, noblemen, knights and sixty 'ladies and maidens', the queen in their midst, illuminated by the candelabrum she held – emerged from Elizabeth's apartments and wound through a succession of palace galleries to the chapel royal. Edward, now a beaming father, showed Rozmital 'our Lady's girdle and ring': the girdle of the Virgin Mary, one of Westminster Abbey's collection of relics, which Elizabeth had worn during her pregnancy to help ensure a safe birth.[15]

Following the processions and celebratory mass – the singing of the chapel royal choir, remarked a cultivated German in Rozmital's entourage named Gabriel Tetzel, was sublime – everybody sat down to dinner, the diners filling 'four great rooms'. This time, Edward was not present. Deputizing for him, sitting alone 'at the king's table, on the king's chair', was the newborn royal princess's godfather, the earl of Warwick, served as though he were the king himself. After dinner, Warwick escorted the sated Bohemians to a private chamber – 'unbelievably costly', murmured Tetzel of the interior décor – where they were ushered into a hidden alcove to watch Edward's queen eating dinner: her first meal back in the public world of court.

Elizabeth sat alone at a dining table, on a golden chair. As her ladies served the first course, two noblewomen – the queen's mother Jacquetta and one of Edward's sisters – who had been kneeling at a respectful distance as Elizabeth exchanged the odd word with them, now joined her at table. The meal, a succession of elaborate courses served over three hours, was eaten in complete silence: as the queen dined, her serving ladies waited on their knees. After dinner, musicians started playing and men were allowed into the room; couples danced carefully. At the heart of it all was the queen, still seated. The reverence paid her, Tetzel said, was astonishing. He had never seen anything like it.[16]

This vision of England, with its commerce, fragrant gardens and exceptional singing – the Bohemians had been gently propelled from one entertainment to another in a soundscape of the most 'pleasant and sweet music' – had been carefully choreographed for the visitors. It was, though, the richness of Edward's court that left the deepest impression. This was 'the most splendid court that could be found in all Christendom', at its heart a 'handsome' king who moved easily amid the ceremonial and his beguiling, exact queen. The dining in isolation, the prolonged silences at table weren't strange in themselves – they were, as foreigners had noted over the years, peculiarly English customs – but there was something about the sharp edges of the ritual on which Elizabeth insisted that caught the Bohemians' attention: an insistence, almost, on the fact of her queenship itself. To one member of Rozmital's party, a bibulous squire named Schasek, this rigid acknowledgement of rank masked something more slippery. The English, he wrote, were great observers of protocol, always ready to genuflect to power and authority. But 'no matter how they bend the knee', he concluded, 'they are not to be trusted.'[17]

If the Bohemians were left with the sense that Edward and Elizabeth had money to burn, it was hardly surprising. One of the men now responsible for supplying credit to the king's coffers was Elizabeth's father, Lord Rivers, whom, shortly after the queen gave birth, Edward made treasurer of England. As head of the Exchequer, Rivers took control of a government department whose role in the kingdom's finances was changing. Since the start of the reign, Edward had diverted income of various kinds – rents from land, loans, the proceeds of his recoinage, even the pope's taxes – into his own coffers. While, in theory, all payments still had to be declared and enrolled in the Exchequer, the government's account of record, the Exchequer's active role in collecting revenues and paying them out was diminishing. Its other role, that of borrowing on the crown's behalf, was fast expanding.[18] For decades, Exchequer officials had been selected for their business acumen and their ability to provide the king with funds: both as creditors in their own right and, drawing on their contacts in the mercantile community, as co-ordinators of credit syndicates. In the first years of Edward's reign, this arrangement had intensified and, in December 1465, the then treasurer of England, William, Lord Mountjoy, had secured the regime's biggest single loan to date, of £6,200.[19] When, three months later, Edward replaced Mountjoy with Rivers, he did so on the understanding that his father-in-law could do even better.

The treasurership had proved a tough job in the unforgiving economic climate of recent decades. Pestered by the crown's creditors, treasurers also carried the can for its financial failings: back in 1450, Cade's rebels had decapitated Henry VI's hated treasurer Lord Say, stuck his severed head on a pike and paraded it down Cheapside. But there were upsides. The treasurer enjoyed exceptional access to the king, with whom he had a daily audience, had huge political influence and controlled swathes of royal patronage. For all this, as well as preferential treatment at the Exchequer, petitioners and creditors were prepared to grease the treasurer's palm with 'rewards'. Besides which, treasurers were well paid – though at times, it wasn't entirely clear where treasurers' salaries stopped and peculation began: some clearly found their proximity to sources of ready cash an irresistible temptation. When appointing Rivers, though, Edward had awarded him an unprecedented financial package, including an annual salary of a thousand marks.[20] While this had much to do with Rivers now being family, Edward clearly also thought he was worth it. Rivers had the invaluable gift of convincing people to invest in Edward's regime. Which was just as well.

Over a year into the Anglo-Burgundian trade war, the effects of Philip of Burgundy's embargo were biting hard: English cloth exports had fallen by three-quarters. This, combined with Edward's various rounds of taxation and the crippling seigniorage fees that merchants were forced to shell out under the king's recoinage programme, meant that willing and reliable creditors were at a premium. London's corporate loans, on which the regime had relied so heavily in its first uncertain years, had dried up.[21] As fundraiser for the crown, Rivers' approach was much the same as that of his predecessors: targeting rich individuals with the promise of royal favour in return. The difference was that Rivers, as the king's father-in-law, sat as close to the heart of power and influence as it was possible to get. His promises carried weight – and he was exceptionally persuasive. The results were instant. Four days into his treasurership, working with a small group of colleagues – career officials like the Exchequer under-treasurer John Rogger, the teller Thomas Pound and William Kerver, the keeper of the queen's wardrobe – Rivers secured for Edward a loan of £11,200, a sum that put even Mountjoy's hitherto spectacular effort firmly in the shade. The money was delivered, as usual, straight into the king's chamber.[22]

Since the start of the reign, the king's chamber treasurer – who also went by the title of keeper of the king's jewels, the custodian of the valuable stones and plate that, when not adorning heads and sideboards on great feast days, acted as security for credit – had been an ageing Lancastrian relic named William Port, who had held the same post under Henry VI. Port's unobtrusive competence and experience – and, perhaps, his culture: he was a music fellow at New College, Oxford – had seen him transfer smoothly to Edward's service.[23] In June 1465, just after Elizabeth's coronation, Edward decided Port's time was up. The man who replaced him as 'architectour' or supervisor of the king's personal finances, his role as chamber treasurer confirmed not simply by the royal word of mouth but – for the first time – by letters patent, was no jobbing administrator but one of Edward's most valued servants, a man he held close to him: the esquire for the body Thomas Vaughan.

Since entering Edward's service back in autumn 1461, Vaughan had become one of an exclusive group of chamber attendants who, when not looking after Edward's daily needs, were abroad on various high-level diplomatic missions. In his new capacity as chamber treasurer, Vaughan now oversaw a system that, in addition to the annual £14,000 that it now received from the Exchequer, was raking in money from many and various sources, from the king's trade deals to the sale of royal wards. Answerable solely to the king, Vaughan occupied a crucial node in the network of political influence around Edward, working alongside men like the chamberlain Lord Hastings, the household treasurer John Fogge, and the man with whom, back in 1461, he had fled London only to end up in a French prison, the king's doctor, William Hatteclyffe. Like Vaughan, Hatteclyffe had spent a fair amount of his time over the past years away on royal diplomatic business; now, in January 1466 he had been made the king's secretary.[24] The control of royal finances, vested in a coterie of servants within Edward's household, was becoming ever more tight-knit: at the heart of this operation, in his influential new role as fundraiser to the regime, sat Rivers. When he heard about Rivers' appointment, Warwick, sensing himself further elbowed from the king's side, was reported to be livid.

Charles of Charolais had been right. When his ambassador to England had raised the idea of an Anglo-Burgundian marriage, Edward had jumped at it. In the spring of 1466, the king sent a full diplomatic mission across the Channel, again headed by Warwick and Hastings, for talks on a possible marriage between Charles and Edward's sister

Margaret, and the lifting of the damaging trade embargo. In his enthusiasm for a closer union with Burgundy, Edward had sent his ambassadors armed with another proposal: that his brother Clarence should marry Charles's only child and heir, the eight-year-old Mary.[25] What Clarence thought of the idea went unrecorded. For Warwick, who had continued to work assiduously for an agreement with France, the forthcoming discussions were an unpalatable prospect. If he wasn't keen on a treaty with Burgundy, less still did he want to negotiate away the hand of Clarence, whom he wanted for his own daughter Isabel.

Late that March, the English negotiators met their Burgundian counterparts in St Omer. The Burgundian delegation included some of Charles's closest advisers: the Bastard of Burgundy; Louis of Gruuthuse, an affable, cultured courtier–diplomat from Bruges; and a high-cheekboned, thin-lipped Italian in his late thirties, short black hair brushed severely forward. Tommaso Portinari was one of the most influential financiers in northern Europe, the new manager of the Bruges branch of the continent's greatest bank, that of the Medici of Florence.[26] Through Portinari, the Medici were heavily invested in the Burgundian state. What was more, they had every interest in bringing about a closer union between Burgundy and Edward IV's England.

Over almost a quarter of a century in the Medici offices in Bruges, Portinari had woven himself into the fabric of his adoptive country. It was remarked upon by his Medici colleagues, and not in a good way. By 1464 the tension between Portinari and his then manager, a morose accountant called Agnolo Tani, had reached snapping point. Unimpressed by Portinari's flamboyant lifestyle and his growing intimacy with Charles of Charolais, sources close to Tani informed head office in Florence that Portinari was spending more time swanning about at court than he was on the bank's affairs. Portinari huffed indignantly that it was just as well that he did because, unlike Tani – who had neither the ability nor the inclination to cultivate the bank's prestigious customers – he was winning new and lucrative contracts from the Burgundian state.[27] Portinari and Tani, chalk and cheese, clearly detested each other. But their spat was fuelled by something that went far beyond petty personal politics.

For decades the Medici had followed a general rule of thumb: that offering financial services to princes was very risky indeed. Such loans were difficult to secure and to amortize; besides which, banks often found it impossible to extract themselves from such agreements, being forced to extend further loans to their princely debtors in order to stand a chance of recovering the initial credit they had lent. Princes had a habit of squeezing banks until the pips squeaked, before defaulting. The Medici constantly held in mind the most notorious case, late the previous century, of the great Florentine bank of Bardi and Peruzzi: having failed to recover the series of massive loans that it had extended to Edward III of England in order to fund his military adventures in France, the bank had collapsed.[28] But there was a flip side. Supplying credit to princes brought with it access and influence. Doors magically swung open to new markets and business opportunities, from the importing of luxury goods to the exporting of wool. At a time of continent-wide recession, such opportunities were more important than ever to the Medici, who, like all banks, dealt in commodities as well as cash. If the Medici wanted growth, Portinari argued to his bosses, it had to take this route.

On 6 April 1465, worn down by his incessant lobbying, the Medici bosses made Portinari head of the Bruges branch. The results were instant. The following month, Portinari won for the Medici company the lucrative toll at Gravelines on the Calais–Flanders border, through which flowed all wool exports from England to the Low Countries, from under the long nose of his Lucchese competitor Giovanni Arnolfini. In the resulting contract, Portinari had acquired a notable new status: that of councillor to Philip of Burgundy. If the Medici bank now had a handle on Burgundian policy-making, the converse was also true: the bank had become more invested, more entangled, in Burgundian affairs.[29] What was more, this new spirit of Medici enterprise was drifting across the English Channel. And Edward's eyes had lit up at the prospect.

Gherardo Canigiani had arrived in London on Medici business as a twenty-two-year-old and had never left. Now, almost two decades on, he was a naturalized Londoner, who knew both city and court like the back of his hand and was a member of the Calais Staple to boot. In the first precarious years of Edward's reign, as the king cast around for sources of credit, Canigiani had obliged. At first the sums he lent were relatively modest – £200 here, 100 marks there – but, combined with the fine fabrics with which he was supplying the Great Wardrobe, they were substantial enough to get him close to Edward. There were pressing reasons why he needed to do so, chief among them the fact that the Medici relied heavily on exports of English wool to fill the convoy of galleys that docked each year at Southampton. To facilitate this operation, Edward's favour was essential.[30] Luckily, Canigiani had Portinari's knack for getting close to princes. With a moth-like attraction to power, he seemed to find the glow of Edward's favour irresistible; besides which, his twenty years in England had perhaps left him instinctively inclined to answer the king's call.

Edward liked everything about Canigiani: his excellent English, his superb contacts and, most important of all, the way that he never said no. In return, Edward granted him export licences and cut through red tape on his behalf. When one of Canigiani's ships, stuffed full of illegal imports, was detained at Sandwich by customs officials, Edward ordered the cargo returned to him, throwing in a licence to 'sell and dispose of it freely to his own profit'. By mid-1464 Edward, appointing Canigiani his factor, had gone into business with him and was employing him on sensitive diplomatic affairs, sending him to Scotland with hundreds of pounds of bribes to the pro-Lancastrian bishop of St Andrews in exchange for 'diverse secret matters'. When Canigiani decided to upscale his living arrangements in line with his fortunes, Edward wrote to the powerful merchant-financier Sir Thomas Cook, ordering him to rent Canigiani his grand house next to the stocks market in the heart of the city. Cook obeyed with alacrity. All of which fed back to the Medici head office in Florence. In August 1465, aware of Canigiani's closeness with the regime, Piero de' Medici appointed him joint manager of the bank's London branch. By late March 1466, after a bust-up with his colleague, Canigiani was in sole charge.[31]

In both Bruges and London, the Medici branches were now run by men who believed that cosying up to their respective regimes was the best way for the bank to do business. With Medici fortunes in northern Europe reliant on smooth trade relations between England and

Burgundy, both Canigiani and Portinari were anxious that the ongoing friction between Edward and Philip of Burgundy be resolved and the trade embargo lifted. That March, as Warwick's diplomats arrived in St Omer, Portinari was among those desperate to achieve progress. He was to be sorely disappointed.

It didn't take long for the talks to get bogged down. On 15 April, Warwick and Charles came face to face at Boulogne, in a meeting designed to further the *entente cordiale*. The pair, it was said, detested each other at first sight, their mutual antagonism fuelled by Warwick's barely concealed partiality for France. So much so that before the English embassy left, one of Charles's closest advisers, Guillaume Bische, was deputed to give Warwick a reality check.

Warwick needed to be aware, Bische buttonholed him, that Louis XI was an exceptionally slippery customer. There was absolutely 'no surety or firmness' in anything he promised, and if Warwick thought he could deal with the French king, he would inevitably find himself entangled. Reeling off a string of examples of Louis' untrustworthiness, Bische was blunt: 'if you put your faith in him, Monsieur de Warwick, you will find yourself deceived.'[32] Warwick ignored him.

In the back-and-forth over trade concessions, both sides proved equally intransigent, refusing to concede ground until the other had made the first move. England's Merchant Adventurers pressed for Edward's embargo to remain in place until Duke Philip lifted his own export ban; Philip refused to budge until Edward relaxed his punitive bullion laws – a subject on which the English king had deliberately avoided giving his diplomats any power to negotiate. Neither was there any progress on the proposed marriage between Edward's sister Margaret to Charles. The subject of Clarence's putative betrothal to Charles's daughter Mary, as disagreeable to the Burgundians as it was to Warwick, was quietly shelved.[33]

Next, in Calais, Warwick and his team entertained a delegation from the French king. In contrast to the stilted conversations with the Burgundians, the talks went swimmingly – not least because Louis, panicked by the possibility of an Anglo-Burgundian alliance, remained exceptionally keen for his ambassadors to wrap up a new agreement with England.

Early that summer, Warwick returned to England having concluded an Anglo-French truce, to last until 1 March 1468. He found Edward in a state of expectancy. A few weeks before, the king had started to push forward plans to host the great tournament, starring his brother-in-law Anthony Woodville and Anthoine, the Bastard of Burgundy, whose articles had been drawn up the previous year, and which would form a cornerstone of the new Anglo-Burgundian *entente*. On Edward's orders, the tournament's organizer John Tiptoft devised a new system of scoring for a 'jousts of peace', drawing on the latest continental fashions. Warwick's return to England, however, punctured the king's anticipation. It was the Burgundian track that Edward was keen to progress, not the French. On this front, Warwick had failed to achieve anything at all. And if Warwick and his agents could not be relied upon as far as Burgundy was concerned, neither, Edward was discovering, could his own chancellor, Warwick's brother George Neville.[34]

On 6 June, a week after Tiptoft had presented his new jousting rules to the king, then busy hunting at Windsor, Edward signed a warrant authorizing safe passage to England for the Bastard of Burgundy and his entourage. Reading over the warrant, George Neville raised an eyebrow and, instead of processing it, returned it to the king, highlighting two omissions: the lack of a limit on numbers in Anthoine of Burgundy's company, and the failure to stipulate that the king's 'English rebels' – exiled Lancastrians like Edmund Beaufort, duke of Somerset, who were still hovering around the Burgundian court – should be excluded from it. On the face of it, both seemed reasonable points. Edward thought otherwise.

The following day, he sent Neville another warrant, one dripping with irritation. The safe-conduct's expansive terms, he stated, had been discussed at length with many of his councillors. Neville knew all this perfectly well because, as Edward now twice reminded his chancellor, he had been part of the discussions: 'you being present'. What was more, Edward's chamberlain Hastings had already received 'clear' and honourable verbal assurances that no Lancastrian sympathizers would be included in the Burgundian party.[35] But, Edward concluded heavily, he would concede both points to Neville: the

Bastard was to bring with him no more than a thousand men, and no English rebels should be numbered among them.

Neville's punctilious attitude seemed to spark in Edward something more than the usual spasm of annoyance at having to ask twice for the royal will to be done. In the king's tone there was, perhaps, a suspicion that Neville was being deliberately obstructive, almost as if he were trying to entangle the king's great Burgundian project in red tape. Maybe, too, he disliked being corrected by a chancellor who seemed to find it difficult to modulate his intellectual superiority, even when addressing his own monarch.[36]

Some weeks later, Edward wrote to the pope regarding the appointment of an English cardinal, an office which, as he well knew, George Neville had publicly hankered after for years. The cleric whose name Edward put forward for papal approval was not Neville, but the archbishop of Canterbury, Thomas Bourchier. As well as being Edward's uncle, Bourchier was an uncontroversial conciliator whose opinions drifted serenely along in the wake of Edward's desires and whose family, blood relatives of the king, were becoming closely entwined with that of the queen: several Bourchiers now served in Elizabeth's household. Thomas Bourchier, Edward felt, was far better suited to represent English interests at Rome. He didn't tell George Neville.[37]

Through the summer, Anglo-Burgundian negotiations, robbed of much of their momentum by Neville foot-dragging, slowly began to pick up. Warwick's new treaty with France that June had an unintended consequence. Alarmed by the prospect of an Anglo-French alliance, Charles of Charolais' changeable attitude towards the house of York grew markedly warmer and, on 9 October, the tournament on which Edward and his wife's family had set their hearts was finally scheduled for the following spring. Passports were dispatched to the Bastard, his knights and a thousand men to visit England.

There was another reason for this new spirit of co-operation. In the intervening months Edward had decided he could no longer trust Warwick and his agents with the Burgundian talks, so he had quietly sidelined them. Diplomatic activity with Burgundy was now run from within the king's chamber, by his closest, most trusted staff.[38]

On 23 October 1466 Edward put his signature to a new agreement with Charles: a mutual defence pact in which they promised one another their help against any and all threats. But where Edward's other diplomatic achievements had been trumpeted, this pact was secret. Louis XI was not to get wind of it. Neither, for that matter, should Charles's ill, ageing father Duke Philip, who remained obstinately opposed to any deal with England. The other player from whom it had to be concealed was Warwick. Barely anybody knew except the few close servants of Edward's chamber and household who had helped bring it about: Hastings; Sir Thomas Montgomery, who had been in Bruges that summer; the chamber treasurer Thomas Vaughan and William Hatteclyffe, who as secretary kept the signet with which the king sealed his letters.[39] Central to the pact, too, were the queen's family, from the outset a driving force in Edward's détente with Charles.

In an attempt to thrash out a resolution to the trade war, and for other 'secret matters', the Anglo-Burgundian talks continued. As usual, the English negotiating team was headed by two figures. One was the familiar figure of Lord Hastings. The other, in place of Warwick, was the queen's father, Rivers. Having led his family's charge into the marriage market and muscled into the royal finances, Rivers was now establishing himself in Warwick's former sphere of pre-eminence – diplomacy. Warwick's thoughts on his exclusion by the king's father-in-law were unlikely to have been positive.[40]

That September, marriages were brokered for two more of the queen's sisters, bringing to seven the number of Woodville marriages since Elizabeth's own marriage to the king two years previously. Negotiated by Elizabeth and her parents, always with their eye for the main chance, they were facilitated by an enthusiastic Edward with grants of land and office. Elizabeth's ten-year-old sister Mary was betrothed to the heir of Edward's point man in Wales, William, Lord Herbert, who in recent years had extended his fearsome influence over much of the principality, all the while moving ever closer to the king and to the queen's family. If the marriage itself, celebrated in style at Windsor Castle, was uncontentious, the royal grant that accompanied it was not – at least as far as the earl of Warwick was concerned. Warwick had long had his eye on the Somerset lordship of Dunster, an estate now conferred on Herbert's son. That Edward was now privileging the claims of Herbert – a man who had once, as sheriff of Glamorgan, been Warwick's own retainer – only added insult to injury.[41]

If the Herbert marriage irritated Warwick, news of another Woodville marriage left him incandescent with rage. Some eighteen months previously, Warwick had arranged for his young nephew George to marry Anne Holland, only child of the exiled Lancastrian nobleman Henry Holland, duke of Exeter. George was one of the greatest prizes currently on the marriage market: as the son of Warwick's brother John Neville, he stood to inherit the earldom of Northumberland. Then the queen intervened. Following talks with the young girl's mother, Edward's oldest sister Anne – a discussion sweetened by a payment from the queen of four thousand marks – Anne abruptly cancelled the contract with Warwick. Instead the girl was married off to one of Elizabeth's sons by her first marriage, Thomas Grey. Warwick had been gazumped. Behind closed doors, his fury at the Anne Holland stitch-up was reportedly intense.[42] Publicly, his expression barely flickered.

If Warwick was vexed at these dents in his pre-eminence, Clarence appeared a model of decorum, undertaking governmental tasks with maturity and, when required, turning on a sparkling charm. At Salisbury that Easter, entertaining Edward's Bohemian visitors on their journey west, he proved himself a sophisticated host, treating them to an 'unbelievably costly' banquet. He had an immediate incentive. On 30 January 1466 Edward had set in train the formal process for his brother's coming-of-age. Clarence could now discern that threshold across which, in the adult world beyond, exceptional wealth and power awaited. Desperate for both, he had set out to display all the qualities Edward looked for in him. Edward had been convinced.

On 10 July that year, paying homage to his king, Clarence took possession of his lands. The customary age of majority was twenty-one; Clarence was still three months short of his seventeenth birthday. That autumn he rode to Tutbury in Staffordshire, where he began to acquaint himself with his landed inheritance in the north midlands, centred on the great estates of the duchy of Lancaster, and to involve himself in the region's complex web of local politics. There was plenty to keep him busy.[43]

Like any great lord, Clarence was quick to assert his authority, at the hub of which was his household, several hundred strong. His ducal influence rippled outward across his vast estates. These were maintained by the local landowners who looked to him for protection and advancement, and from whom he demanded loyalty in return; in times of conflict, the thousands of tenant-farmers who worked his lands would turn out for him, their billhooks becoming weapons of war.

Such authority, though, didn't just come with the territory; it had to be earned. And most of the time, conflict was something that a powerful magnate like Clarence was supposed to avoid. His job was to impose order and good rule, to ensure that his servants behaved themselves and, where necessary, to intervene in local spats, to arbitrate between the disputants, both – as he put it – for their 'quiet and rest', and for the benefit of the 'country' or region as a whole: in other words, to prevent local trouble escalating into feuds that, in turn, sucked in wider networks of influence and became something more troubling, more uncontrollable. Equally, if his own interests, and those of his associates, were challenged – or, indeed, if opportunities for self-aggrandizement presented themselves – active intervention on behalf of those interests was sometimes a necessity: intervention that carried with it the latent threat of litigation and violence. Clarence, with his neuralgic sensitivity to any perceived slight to his exalted status and rank, was alert to such challenges.[44]

For all his diplomatic progress with Burgundy, Edward was having a tricky financial year. With his recoinage nearing completion, the profits had stopped flowing, while the continuing Burgundian embargo had dented the enthusiasm of many of his regular creditors in the mercantile community. In the Exchequer offices at Westminster, Rivers and his officials were staring at a drop of almost two-thirds in annual revenues, which, even though increasing quantities of income were now being diverted directly into the coffers of Edward's chamber without appearing in the Exchequer accounts, told a grim story.[45] But the news wasn't all bad. Edward's, and latterly Rivers', cultivation of the Italian merchant-banking community was paying off. On 27 October, Gherardo Canigiani paid an exceptionally welcome call on the king.

Canigiani had taken the Medici's new policy of lending to princes to heart. But apart from the usual quid pro quo – a royal licence to export wool and cloth toll-free until the debt was repaid – there was another pressing reason why Canigiani and his bosses in Florence were so keen to have Edward in their debt: a mineral called alum.

Astonishingly versatile, potassium alum was coveted for medicine and cosmetics as an astringent, antiseptic and anticoagulant. But it was in the textile industry of northern Europe where it was used on an industrial scale, to cleanse and purify wool and as a mordant, or dye-fixer: properties that made it indispensable to the functioning of the wool and cloth trades of England and the Low Countries. As a result, alum was very big business indeed. It was, in short, a mineral without which Europe's economy would grind to a halt.

The best alum, rock alum, was to be found in the mines of Phocaea, near the city of Smyrna on the Anatolian coast. For centuries under Genoese control, Phocaea had in recent years been absorbed into the advancing Ottoman Turkish empire that was now menacing Christendom's south-eastern borders. While merchants from Christendom could still access the mines, prices had risen. What was more, every purchase of this indispensable commodity was now effectively funding the Ottoman military advance into Europe. So when, in 1460, huge deposits of high-grade rock alum were discovered northeast of Rome at Tolfa, in papal territory, it seemed to the cash-strapped Pope Pius II – still trying vainly to convince Christendom's princes to fund a crusade – that God had answered his prayers.[46]

In order to maximize profits, to control the sale of alum and keep prices high, Pius created a single company, the Societas Aluminum, to which he handed exclusive rights to the mining, shipping and sale of papal alum all over western Christendom, and which would deliver a proportion of its profits into the *camera apostolica*, the papal treasury. The company's enterprises were backed up by the full range of spiritual punishments. Christendom's merchants were forbidden from buying any alum except the papal stuff, on pain of excommunication. The fact that monopolies were forbidden in canon law was, it seemed, neither here nor there. Naturally, it made sense for the Societas Aluminum to be run by an organization with a continent-wide reach and influence, especially in the lucrative, alum-hungry markets of England and the Low Countries. It was hardly a surprise when, after a couple of false starts, the papacy struck a deal on 1 April 1466 with the Medici bank.

For the Medici, the Societas Aluminum presented an extraordinary opportunity. Even with a glut on the market, importers into England were achieving net profits of some 25 per cent. If the Medici could persuade Edward and Philip of Burgundy to enforce the papal monopoly, ceding them exclusive rights to sell the commodity in their territories, they and their papal clients stood to make a killing. So, it was hardly a surprise that when Edward IV came calling for a loan that autumn, Gherardo Canigiani fell over himself to oblige. Shown into the king's privy chamber on that late October day, Canigiani personally delivered into Edward's 'own hands' the sum of £5,354 19s 10d, in cash.[47]

In February 1467, the French king Louis XI was on pilgrimage in the cathedral city of Bourges. Among his entourage there was the usual flock of foreign diplomats, including a representative from the Burgundian court and the Milanese ambassador to France, Giovanni Pietro Panigarola, a man who missed little.[48] Dining within earshot of the French king one day, Panigarola overheard some intriguing table talk. Sitting by the king's side was his cousin Duke John of Calabria, the bitter, penniless son of René of Anjou. As the conversation turned from falcons and hunting to international politics, Duke John was loudly undiplomatic, insulting the attendant Burgundian ambassador and, as the conversation turned to England, the earl of Warwick. Louis, by contrast, was mildness itself. He liked winding people up and seemed to keep his cousin by him for precisely that purpose. Now, he enjoyed watching Duke John work himself up into a fury about Warwick, the man who had brought down his sister Margaret of Anjou.[49]

Warwick, John spat, was completely unreliable. Rather than waste time and energy cultivating the earl's friendship, Louis should instead help Margaret of Anjou regain the throne of England. The French king disagreed. Warwick, he pointed out, had been a better friend to him than his own family – indeed, he had prevented Edward from making war on France.

If Louis liked Warwick so much, Duke John snapped back, why didn't he then try and persuade the earl to change sides, and recover the throne of England for Margaret and the house of Lancaster?

Without missing a beat, Louis asked, banteringly, what security the house of Anjou would give him for his backing of such a venture? Margaret's oafish son, perhaps? At which point, Louis added a few sharp words about the Lancastrian heir, now a bellicose thirteen-year-old who talked about little else but 'cutting off heads or making war' – almost as though, Louis sneered, the boy were the king of England himself.

There was something absurdist about Louis. When the Burgundian ambassador protested about his persistent efforts to entice England into a military alliance against Burgundy, the French king, all wide-eyed innocence, denied everything: 'It was all an invention.' Equally, while Louis ridiculed John of Calabria's wild proposal about bringing Warwick and the exiled house of Lancaster together to overthrow Edward he was, as the onlooking Panigarola astutely put it, only 'half-joking'.

Even though Warwick had been a 'good friend' to him over the years, Louis – suspicious of everyone and everything – didn't trust him an inch. But the one thing the French king did not doubt was Warwick's influence with Edward. Over the years the Lancastrians had tried to bring to Louis' attention the growing coolness between Edward and the man who had once been his mentor. At the French court, however, the idea persisted of Edward as an impressionable young ruler under the thumb of the man who remained the 'first nobleman of England' – no doubt with the encouragement of Warwick's agents who, despite being sidelined from the Burgundian talks, continued to run the French diplomatic track. That things might be otherwise did not seem to cross Louis' mind. Soon, he would find out.

7

Love Together as Brothers in Arms

In late March 1467, shortly before Easter, the Norfolk knight Sir John Paston wrote home from his Fleet Street lodgings. Now in his mid-twenties, Paston was a long way from the nervous boy who, some six years previously, had been packed off to the royal household by his father to progress the family's claim to a contested inheritance, and had been too shy to ask for a meal there. In the intervening years, with the claim mired in violent local politics and interminable legal wrangles, Paston's frustrated father had come to think his son a spendthrift layabout, squandering his income at court; the pair had barely been reconciled when his father died. Paston, though, had found his feet at court, making friends in high places. He had ingratiated himself with the queen's family, while no less a figure than Edward's chancellor George Neville had promised to look after the family's interests, to be their 'singular good lord'. Meanwhile Sir John's embrace of all things chivalric and his reputation as a courtly lover – 'the best chooser of a gentlewoman', according to a friend – made him a natural addition to the virile circle around Edward: indeed, he was an almost exact con-temporary of his twenty-four-year-old king. Now, as Paston wrote breathlessly to his brother, he had just taken part in an exclusive royal tournament, organized by Edward himself, at the secluded manor of Eltham, deep in the Kentish countryside. 'I wish you had been there to see it', he wrote, 'for it was the goodliest sight that was seen in Eng-land this forty years of so few men.'

Paston's excitement was understandable. One of only three men on the king's team, the team 'within', his team-mates were the king's brother-in-law Anthony Woodville and the chamber servant Thomas St Leger, who was having an affair with the king's married sister Anne. On the away side, the team 'without', were two more powerful figures, William, Lord Hastings and Thomas Montgomery, and John Parr, a king's esquire from Westmorland.[1] This was about as good an opportunity as it got to make an impression, both with people who mattered around the king, and with Edward himself.

The tournament was match practice for something much bigger, the long-awaited chivalric showpiece between Anthony Woodville and the Bastard of Burgundy, which was to take place in London that spring. For Edward it represented a chance to bring together England and Burgundy in an ever-closer union, at the heart of which would be a spectacular marriage alliance. Following Charles of Charolais's polite enquiry regarding Edward's sister Margaret the previous year, Edward had clung on to the idea and had not let go.

Earlier that March a team of English negotiators, headed by Richard Beauchamp, bishop of Salisbury, and including the ubiquitous figures of William Hatteclyffe and Thomas Vaughan, had arrived in Bruges to progress the matter.[2] One afternoon in mid-April, one of the envoys, a canon lawyer in his mid-thirties named John Russell, was pottering around the city's booksellers. He picked up a copy of Cicero's *De Officiis*, *On Duties*, one of the Roman philosopher's most popular works. With its exemplary Latin style and advice on political behaviour, it was the kind of book that a man of Russell's learning probably owned already. This volume, however, was different. With its illuminated initials and neat Roman script, it looked at first glance like the scribal manuscript that it was designed to resemble, but it wasn't. The book had been printed in the German city of Mainz by Johann Fust who, some twelve years previously, had successfully sued his brilliant but impecunious partner Johannes Gutenberg for an unrecovered debt and, just as Gutenberg was about to go public with his new invention, walked off with his printing press as part-payment. Struck by the uniformity of the printing process – however painstakingly they were copied, no two manuscripts were ever exactly alike – Russell bought two copies.[3]

Despite the increasing diplomatic traffic between Edward and Charles, people in England still viewed the rumoured Anglo-Burgundian marriage as the usual horse-trading between princes. There was a vast gulf between discussing such spectacular marriages and bringing them to fruition, particularly given the massive amounts of finance needed to cover the festivities and the bride's dowry. In this case, too, there were other obstacles: Charles's equivocal attitude to the house of York; the papal dispensation needed for him to marry Edward's sister – as second cousins, they were within the proscribed degrees of consanguinity – and the ongoing trade war with Burgundy. If the marriage were to proceed, somebody would have to make big concessions. As spring advanced, such concessions didn't look likely. Edward seemed to be keeping his options open. So much so that the French king had convinced himself that, with Warwick's help, he had finally managed to prise Edward away from an alliance with Burgundy.

As Louis outlined it excitedly to the hovering Milanese ambassador Panigarola, Warwick had brokered a 'secret understanding' between England and France. This understanding, moreover, was ambitious and wide-ranging: nothing less than a perpetual peace, in which – so Warwick's agents told Louis – Edward had agreed to renounce the English crown's historic claim to France. The two kings would henceforth be 'brothers in arms', united in a 'war of extermination' against Burgundy, which would see the Low Countries carved up between France and England. This treaty would also involve two Anglo-French marriages: Margaret of York would be paired off with Louis' nephew, while Edward's youngest brother Richard would be offered Louis' second daughter Jeanne, then almost three years old. Edward's other brother Clarence, though, was already spoken for. As Louis explained, he was 'married to the daughter of the earl of Warwick'. In all this, Louis stressed, Edward and Warwick were of one mind. Indeed, Edward had given his personal commitment to the treaty, writing to Louis 'in his own hand': something, the French king said, that he had never done before.[4]

All of this was a direct contradiction of the Burgundian alliance that Edward had so earnestly come to desire; besides which, he was adamantly opposed to his brother Clarence marrying Warwick's daughter. Yet he seemed perfectly happy to let Warwick continue this conflicting agenda with France: so much so that he had put his own signature to the plans. It was a tactical move by the English king and his close advisers, one designed to keep the Burgundians keen. In this delicate, constantly shifting three-cornered relationship, nothing kept Charles of Charolais sweeter on Edward than the knowledge that Edward was making eyes at Louis. Nevertheless, the little touch of Edward had convinced Louis, constantly suspicious about English double-dealing, that he was serious about peace with France. It also persuaded Warwick. If in recent years Queen Elizabeth Woodville's family had helped swing Edward's affections towards Burgundy, Warwick was, he believed, finally tilting those affections back to what the earl saw as a much more advantageous settlement with France.

As Warwick prepared for a high-level diplomatic visit to Louis XI's court for talks on the 'perpetual peace', Edward encouraged him. There was, it was true, a few weeks' delay in processing the safe-conducts that Louis had sent through for Warwick's mission, pushing back his departure date to the end of May – but it seemed innocent enough.

In London, amid the May Day merrymaking, Sir John Paston placed a bet with a friend of his, a mercer called Thomas Lomnour. The wager's conditions were drawn up in a bill signed and sealed by both men. Lomnour had sold Paston 'an ambling horse'. If the Anglo-Burgundian marriage took place within two years of the date of the bill, Paston would pay 6 marks for the horse; if not, the price would be the rather lower sum of 40 shillings 'and no more'. The odds on the marriage taking place at all, Paston clearly thought, were long.[5]

On 18 May, having waited the best part of three weeks for storms in the Channel to abate, the Bastard of Burgundy's heavily armed ships set sail for England. His party, carefully selected to play up the Woodvilles' chivalric heritage, included some of Burgundy's most illustrious knights: men like Duke Philip's chamberlain Simon de Lalaing; Pedro Vasco de Saavedra, a Burgundian of Portuguese extraction who had fought Lord Rivers in a Smithfield joust some quarter-century previously; and Charles's close servant Philippe de Bouton, who had originally answered Anthony Woodville's challenge and who now wore the 'flower of remembrance' around his right bicep. With them was Charles's own household chamberlain, Olivier de la Marche, a punctilious military man in his early forties, and an obsessively Anglophile councillor and bibliophile named Jean de Wavrin. Just over half a century before, the fifteen-year-old Wavrin had watched transfixed from the French camp at Agincourt as Henry V's archers had obliterated the cream of French chivalry, an experience that convinced him thereafter to fight for the English. In his spare time, over the following decades, Wavrin had compiled a *recueil*, or collection of 'chronicles and ancient histories of Britain, currently called England', from Albion's foundation in the mists of myth-history to the death of Henry IV. Now, in his sixties, Wavrin was visiting England for the very first time. It would give him the chance to bring his chronicle fully up to date.

After an eventful crossing in which they had fought off a pack of French pirates with guns and hand-to-hand fighting, the Burgundians sailed round the north Kent coast, passing a 'fine town named Margate', and up the Thames. At Greenwich, they were welcomed by John Tiptoft and representatives of London's corporation, who escorted them into the city in a flotilla of gaudy barges. Disembarking at Billingsgate, they processed through the streets, past St Paul's, to their lodgings.[6]

One of the first of the great houses west of the city, lying south of Fleet Street with gardens running down to the water's edge, the bishop of Salisbury's Inn was empty – Beauchamp was at that moment away in Bruges – and Edward had furnished it lavishly for his guests, as well as laying on 'all manner of stuff in and without the town for his disport'. This included a training base, where the Bastard and his knights could practise away from the public gaze, at the bishop's house at Chelsea, a short boat ride up the Thames. As it turned out, there was rather more to the choice of location.[7]

Shortly after the Burgundians' arrival, on 28 May, Warwick left on his mission to the French court.[8] The next day, the Bastard and his men were training at Chelsea when Edward arrived 'secretly', with a small group of companions headed by Hastings and the queen's father Rivers – chief negotiators in his Burgundian talks – and the ubiquitous Thomas Montgomery. As wine and spices were served, Edward, Rivers and the Bastard huddled together in conversation. As much as a sporting visit, this was an informal summit meeting, one deliberately scheduled for the day after Warwick's departure, away from prying eyes in the seclusion of Chelsea.

As he pursued the Anglo-Burgundian alliance on which he had set his heart, Edward was well aware of Warwick's loathing for the idea.

He needed the earl and his meddling agents out of the way, and Warwick's summit with Louis XI was the perfect diversion.[9] With both eyes on his Burgundian prize, Edward seemed characteristically unbothered about what would happen when Warwick found out that, rather than the main event, his French trip was a sideshow. More than that, with Warwick safely off the scene, the king now moved against the man who, sitting at the heart of his administration, was proving a constant obstruction to his Burgundian ambitions: Warwick's brother, Chancellor George Neville.

In the following days the tournament build-up began. With the flaring of trumpets, shawms and clarions sounding his approach, Edward and his entourage rode through a city packed for the jousts and a forthcoming parliament, towards Westminster. In front of him, bearing the sword of state, was Anthony Woodville. To the crowd's delight, as they passed the bishop of Salisbury's house, Woodville turned to the watching Burgundians, brandishing his sword furiously at the opponent whom he had been waiting two years to fight.[10]

At Westminster Palace the next day the Burgundians, honoured guests, accompanied Edward into the Painted Chamber for the opening of Parliament. The chancellor George Neville was absent: a stand-in delivered his sermon to the assembled Lords and Commons. He had still not appeared two days later, when Edward approved the Commons' choice of speaker (the experienced financial administrator John Say, who as speaker in the previous Parliament had played a key role in raising taxes for Edward, was a shoo-in). In Neville's place, the man who delivered the king's reply to the Commons was Edward's increasingly omnicompetent father-in-law, Rivers.[11] Officially, Neville was unwell; unofficially, it seemed, he had been ordered to stay away.

The reason soon became clear. A few days later, on the morning of Monday 8 June, Edward and a dozen lords, including Hastings and Tiptoft, rode the short distance from Westminster to York Place, to the sprawling riverside mansion of the archbishop's London home. Walking into Neville's private apartments, Edward demanded that he give up the great seal, summarily dismissing him from the chancellorship that he had held since Edward and Warwick's triumphant return to England from Calais in the summer of 1460.

George Neville had been one of the regime's key architects, his value to Edward immense. But his record had been blotted by his failure to embrace the Burgundian vision so ardently desired by the king and his Woodville in-laws. He was no longer the future – a point made by the lords whom Edward had brought with him that morning. No fewer than five of those present had married into the queen's family, including Warwick's *bête noire* William Herbert and Edward's household treasurer John Fogge. As a roster of the new Yorkist establishment, the presence of these men around Edward was as good a way as any to drive home to Neville that he was now firmly outside it.

Meanwhile, the atmosphere in Parliament was restive. In recent years, tensions had grown over what the Commons considered the king's bad financial management. Like kings before him, Edward had repeatedly broken the unwritten compact that taxes were only to be raised for war or defence of the realm. Discontent over royal exactions, a major factor in the Lancastrian insurgencies of previous years, was helping drive an upsurge in lawlessness: 'murders, riots, extortions, rapes of women, robbery and other crimes.' On both his finances and law enforcement, the Commons informed Edward, he had to get his act together. The implication was that he was letting things slide.

Edward needed to make a big gesture. Enthroned, regal in his purple robes of state, he turned on the charm. Thanking the Commons effusively for their financial support during the first precarious years of his reign, he promised them that things would now be different. He would no longer ask for taxes for his 'own pleasure' – an implicit admission that up to now he had been doing precisely that – but would instead 'live upon mine own', from the income raised from his own lands and resources, except 'in great and urgent causes', when he would expect the Commons' unequivocal financial backing.[12]

The speech had its desired effect, Speaker Say remarking greasily 'how very pleasing' the Commons had found it to be addressed by their king 'with his own lips'. Whether or not the Commons were actually convinced was moot, given that monarchs regularly made loud pledges to live off their own financial resources before reneging on their word. But Edward had at least to look as though he was making an effort. Perhaps he genuinely believed that he could balance his books without resorting to taxation. Recently he had handed Rivers a new deal to 'encourage him to continue' in his post of treasurer – though his father-in-law presumably didn't need much encouraging to accept a financial package worth an eye-watering £1,300 per annum – and Rivers continued to come up with the goods. Three days after his new deal was announced, he and his credit syndicate deposited another large loan of £6,833 6s 8d into Edward's coffers.[13] But more, much more, was needed. To show that he was serious about fiscal reform, Edward announced a parliamentary act of resumption.

He had already carried out two sweeping re-appropriations of royal grants, the most recent of which had come a couple of years previously, in order to reallocate resources to his family: especially to his Woodville in-laws and to his brother Clarence. Now, Edward protected the endowment he had bestowed on Clarence, exempting his brother's massive portfolio of lands from the act of resumption. Clarence wasn't the only one: also ringfenced were the grants of a raft of establishment figures, from Rivers and Anthony Woodville to William Herbert, Hastings and various other men close about the king and – naturally – Edward's and Clarence's youngest brother Richard. The Nevilles, however, were not exempted. Edward clawed back several estates from George Neville and the absent Warwick, a gesture whose meaning was unmistakeable. Edward, it said, was in charge. If Warwick and George Neville wanted to continue to benefit from his great favour, it was up to them to mould themselves to his desires, not the other way round. And what Edward desired most of all, at this moment in time, was his treaty with Burgundy.[14]

It was a hot summer. On the morning of 11 June crowds started arriving early at Smithfield for the long-awaited tournament.[15] A space of some seventy by eighty yards had been transformed into a gladiatorial arena: the ground had been cleared and levelled, beaten flat by teams of men with mattocks, then covered in layers of sand and gravel and enclosed with fences and multi-storey timber stands, into which the spectators now filed. At either end were the two teams' entrances and the pavilions to which the combatants would retire after each round, to be towelled down, get a few words of advice from their trainers, refresh and re-arm themselves. On Woodville's blue pavilion, picked out in white antique lettering, was the slogan 'La nonchalance' – or, as the Italian courtier Baldassare Castiglione put it some sixty years later, believing it was a 'new word', *sprezzatura*. This quality of effortlessness, in everything from love to battle, was the way for the ideal courtier to express his innate nobility. Nobody encapsulated it more than the poised Woodville – though, just to make sure everybody was aware that his nobility inhered in his blue blood as well as his personal virtue, his pavilion was also festooned with a string of forty-three banners tracing the 'lineal pedigree of his descent'.

Around 9 a.m., after the king had appeared, hustled into the royal box through a side door to avoid the crowds, the two fighters who topped the bill made their entrances on horseback, circling the field to wild appreciation. Woodville appeared as England's hero, his horse caparisoned in white cloth-of-gold embroidered with a St George cross of crimson velvet. Before him, his in-laws, foremost among them Clarence and the young duke of Buckingham, carried his helmets and weapons.[16] Saluting the king, the combatants then retreated to their corners, the Bastard of Burgundy whipping up the crowd's anticipation further by arming himself 'openly', in full view. As the atmosphere built to fever pitch, the two knights manoeuvred their horses into the lists.

There was silence then, on a herald's shout of *'laissez les aller'* – 'let them go' – a wall of noise as the two riders spurred their horses. Visors down, gathering speed, they hunched over their lances, closing on each other at thirty miles an hour. Both missed.[17]

The next round of fighting, with swords on horseback, was close and furious, a twisting mass of armour and horseflesh. As they hacked away at each other, the two horses collided violently. The Bastard's horse reared high in agony, fell backwards and crashed to the ground, trapping its rider below it. As Woodville circled him triumphantly, holding his sword in the air, attendants rushed to free the prone Burgundian. The Bastard's horse, bleeding profusely, staggered to its feet and lurched a few paces before collapsing, dead.

In the royal box, Edward's agitated reaction spoke volumes about quite how much he wanted the Burgundian alliance. He berated

Anthony Woodville who, all wide-eyed innocence, denied any foul play – though, whatever it was, it was hardly *sprezzatura*. Edward called off the rest of the day's fighting. The Bastard, livid at the death of his favourite horse, was heard muttering something about Woodville having 'fought a beast' rather than a man. Overnight, tensions cooled and the diplomatic incident was smoothed over. Burgundian heralds refused to comment on speculation that the sliver of metal found in the dead horse's throat was in fact a shard of the sword that Woodville had rammed down it: the whole thing, they soothed, was pure accident.[18]

During the remaining fighting, Edward was tense. Inspecting and rejecting some of the combatants' weapons for being 'right dangerous' he sat, jittery, watching Woodville and the Bastard swing away at each other with axes. When, after warding off a frenzy of blows from his opponent, Woodville hit the Burgundian flush on the helmet, the king threw his white staff down, a signal to halt the fighting, and screamed at the pair to stop. They had to be forcibly pulled apart. The showpiece fight finally safely and honourably over, a relieved king commanded them to shake hands and 'love together as brothers in arms'. That evening, the *entente* was restored at a banquet hosted by Edward and Elizabeth at the influential Mercers' Company headquarters on Cheapside.

Over the following days, the games continued under Edward's watchful gaze. The king went out of his way to favour his guests: at one point, he pulled up one English jouster on a technicality, only allowing him to continue on the Bastard's say-so.[19] Meanwhile, the talks continued – and, as Thomas Howard, son and heir of Edward's bruising courtier and friend Sir John Howard, later put it, they were all about the marriage between 'Charles and Lady Margaret'.[20] Yet no amount of wining, dining and spectacular feats of arms could shift one major obstacle. While happy enough to sanction the jousts, Charles's father, Philip of Burgundy, had grown irascible, stubborn and withdrawn. He remained adamantly opposed to the match.

Then, on Friday 19 June, everything changed. A messenger arrived from Bruges with the news that four days earlier, at nine in the evening, Philip had died: 1,600 torchbearers had escorted the seventy-year-old's body through the Bruges streets to the Church of St Donatian, where he was buried in regal style. Charles was the new duke of Burgundy. Now, unimpeded by his father's peevish caution, he could do what he liked – which included marrying Edward's sister. As he expressed his solemn regrets to the Burgundians, Edward worked hard to conceal his delight.[21]

Charles had an expansionist vision far outstripping that of his temporizing father: his vicious, mulish ambition would earn him the soubriquet 'the Bold', or, depending on your point of view, 'the Rash'. He saw himself as ruler of a sovereign Burgundy, free of French over-lordship, whose lands extended far beyond its present frontiers. The most immediate obstacle to this great project was the man who Charles detested most in all the world, Louis XI. And while Charles remained lukewarm about the Yorkist regime in England, he knew that unless he came to an agreement with Edward, Louis would get there first – with potentially catastrophic consequences for the Burgundian state. As Charles put it, he wouldn't have entered into an alliance with Edward 'if Louis hadn't already tried to do so' and made such 'great offers and promises' to try and destroy him.[22]

On 24 June, as the Bastard and his entourage made their farewells, Warwick docked at the Kentish port of Sandwich. His reception by Louis had been lavish – indeed, he had been greeted as though he was Edward IV himself – and he returned to England weighed down with costly gifts and accompanied by a high-ranking French delegation to continue the progress that had been made in France. Besides the Anglo-French marriage, Louis XI had proposed a wide-ranging trade deal, including franchises for English merchants in France; he had even dangled the tempting prospect of further talks over the cession to England of the dukedoms of Normandy and Aquitaine, lost so catastrophically by the Lancastrian regime back in the early 1450s. With an eye on Edward's perpetual need for ready cash, Louis also offered to pay him an annual pension of 4,000 marks. The day after the English had left, Louis, convinced that the treaty was as good as signed, had gone public with it, sending details in a letter to all the lords and cities of his kingdom.[23] Returning with the French delegation, Warwick also seemed to think Edward's approval a formality.

From the moment Warwick landed back in England, however,

things didn't feel quite right. As the French envoys kicked their heels in Sandwich, awaiting the royal safe-conducts that would allow them onward travel, Warwick learned what had gone on in his absence, from the Burgundian talks to his brother's sacking as chancellor and Edward's resumption of some of his lands. When the French finally rode into a baking London on 1 July, they found Parliament prorogued; with an outbreak of plague sweeping the city, everybody who could do so was scrambling to leave.[24] In the circumstances it was unsurprising, though tactless, that Edward put them up in the same London lodgings just vacated by his Burgundian guests. When the French ambassadors caught up with Edward at Westminster, the royal household frantically packing up around him, the king greeted them with distracted geniality. He was off to Windsor to hunt. The ambassadors could, he said, catch up with him there.

At Windsor, the Anglo-French negotiations were conducted with leisurely affability by Hastings and Anthony Woodville, neither of whom – closely briefed by Edward – had any interest in reaching an agreement. Some weeks later the disgruntled French ambassadors finally departed with nothing except vague promises. A few pointed details suggested that the English, in fact, were laughing up their sleeves: the 'fine Burgundy wine' they had been served throughout their stay, and, along with the presents of cash and plate given them at their parting, more unusual gifts – 'great mastiffs, collars, leashes and horns', suggesting that Edward was wishing them better hunting elsewhere.

It was an outcome that eluded even Warwick's powers of spin. During their six weeks in England, the French ambassadors had been comprehensively disabused of the notion – built up over the years by Warwick and his agents – that 'everybody trembled before him'. His carefully cultivated image of powerbroker had been shattered. Indeed, although Edward treated the earl with the scrupulous courtesy that befitted his high rank, he didn't seem to have much influence on the king at all.

Warwick followed developments without a twitch of public emotion. But, after seeing the French off at Sandwich, he didn't return to court. Instead, he went north to Middleham Castle, to sulk.[25] Edward didn't seem particularly bothered. In fact, he seemed to gain satisfaction from the Nevilles' sidelining.

Later that summer, a papal messenger arrived from Rome with letters appointing Thomas Bourchier, archbishop of Canterbury, to the rank of cardinal. It was a fitting reward for this most useful of Yorkist servants, a devout son of the church who was nevertheless happy to order rounds of papal taxes in the knowledge that they would disappear into Edward's coffers, and whose allegiance, when push came to shove, lay with his nephew the king of England over a distant pope in Rome. When Edward received the letters, he forwarded a copy to the unsuccessful candidate for a cardinal's hat, his former chancellor George Neville. This, his gesture seemed to say, was what the reward for unquestioning loyalty looked like. Or maybe it was just a cruel joke on Edward's part. If so, Neville could hardly have found it very funny.[26]

That autumn, as Warwick fumed on his Yorkshire estates, the Anglo-Burgundian negotiations were pushed forward with a new urgency. Away in Rome, Burgundian ambassadors informed the pope of the putative marriage between Charles the Bold and Edward's sister Margaret, anxious to obtain both his holiness's blessing and the required papal dispensation. On 1 October 1467, as a high-powered delegation travelled to Flanders for talks on a perpetual peace between England and Burgundy, Edward and a great council convened at Kingston-upon-Thames, to listen to Edward's sister Margaret give her token consent to marry Charles the Bold.

At the heavily renovated Coudenberg Palace in Brussels, the two negotiating teams settled down to discuss the terms of the marriage. Heading the Burgundian side was Charles the Bold's seventy-year-old mother, Isabella, who, after years of estrangement from the old duke, was overjoyed to be back at court helping realize her son's aims – which, in this case, were also hers. Despite her Lancastrian blood, Isabella felt warmly towards her Yorkist cousin, Edward's mother Cecily, and had been toying with the idea of Charles marrying a Yorkist princess for well over a decade.[27] Whatever her inclinations, Isabella was a tough, experienced negotiator of trade agreements; her team was equally hard-headed. The Burgundians refused to move on to discussions over the marriage until a comprehensive trade settlement had been worked out. When, on 24 November, a new thirty-year free trade agreement between the two countries was unveiled in a formal signing ceremony, it was clear which side had been more desperate to get past the first phase.[28]

Edward had been only too willing to make concessions. Even before the English team had arrived in Brussels, he had given Charles permission to recruit a force of two thousand English archers to help suppress an uprising in the city of Liège; more significantly, he had signed a warrant lifting the embargoes on Burgundian imports into England, repealing the protectionist legislation passed in the parliaments of 1463 and 1464. The Burgundians had appeared to reciprocate, but in fact they had proved stubborn, refusing to repeal the ban on the one commodity whose export to Flanders was so vital to the English economy: cloth. So anxious was Edward to bring about the Burgundian marriage that he had signed up to a vastly imbalanced treaty. England's mercantile community was desperate to resuscitate the cloth export trade, and the deal would take some explaining. More widely, it was hardly likely to go down well among a population historically antagonistic towards 'Flemings' and 'Dutchmen'. For the earl of Warwick, who had never liked the idea of an alliance with Burgundy in the first place, it was a red rag to a bull.[29]

Since his diplomatic humiliation that summer, Warwick had remained in the north. As he saw it, the king's Woodville in-laws, having taken his place at the king's side, had stitched him up. Now, they were steering Edward towards a highly damaging agreement with Burgundy. It was an agreement that, Warwick felt, had to be stopped at all costs – and he was prepared to work with the French king to stymie it. By ignoring the earl's advice, prey instead to the blandishments of Rivers and his associates, Edward had shown himself to be a gullible fool. Or, as Warwick put it shortly to the French agents with whom he was in close contact, he was 'un peu simple': a bit thick.[30]

That autumn, Warwick was said to be building up his armed forces. In itself, this was hardly news: after all, Warwick's retinues were crucial to the security of the north of England. But with no ostensible threat either from Lancastrian rebels or from Scotland, as had been the case earlier in the decade, this renewed drive to take 'in fee, as many knights, squires and gentlemen as he might' inevitably invited speculation.[31] So too did reports that the earl was trying to push forward another project: the marriage between his oldest daughter Isabel and the duke of Clarence.

When, years before, Warwick had first suggested the match, Edward had categorically forbidden it. Such a marriage would have united his brother, his heir presumptive, to the Nevilles – who, Edward probably reasoned at the time, hardly needed any further enhancement to their pre-eminence. Since then, the king's relationship with the Nevilles had sustained more than a few dents, which only reinforced Edward's opposition to the marriage. Warwick, though, was still keen. So too was Clarence.

Clarence's enthusiasm was understandable. Isabel Neville was one of the country's great heiresses, bringing with her a vast inheritance: hereditary lands that Clarence, as her husband, could enjoy and pass on to his descendants in perpetuity, safe in the knowledge that – unlike the substantial but more precarious portfolio with which Edward had endowed him – they could not be taken away.

If, in Warwick's eyes, Edward was now proving a bar to Neville ambitions, the king's seventeen-year-old brother looked an altogether more promising project. For Clarence wasn't entirely happy. Huge as it was, the annual income allocated him by Edward was soon spoken for. Apart from embarking on an expensive programme of building works across his estates, Clarence had local loyalties to attract – which didn't come cheap – and a magnificent household to maintain, and he soon found himself needing more. There was no guarantee that more would be forthcoming: indeed Edward, with his parliamentary commitment to 'live upon his own', had more or less indicated that that would be that as far as royal grants were concerned. And with other members of the king's inner circle eagerly sniffing out possible opportunities to extend their wealth and power, nor were Clarence's existing grants especially secure.[32]

Throwing a mentoring arm around his young cousin, Warwick played on Clarence's anxieties: after all, the earl's own experiences that summer – and those of his brother, the sacked chancellor George Neville – showed that nobody, however close to the king, was immune to the whims of Edward's favour. The best way for Clarence to increase his income and future-proof his status, Warwick advised, was to marry his daughter Isabel. Dazzled by the attentions of his powerful relative,

Clarence quickly convinced himself that it was Warwick, not Edward – who had failed to let him marry who he wanted – who had his best interests at heart. With Clarence and Isabel related within the prohibited degrees of consanguinity, Warwick and George Neville set about trying to procure a papal dispensation for the marriage, dispatching a 'Rome-runner', a Master Lacy, who boasted good connections at the Curia.[33] And as autumn wore on, the uncertainties that Warwick had planted in Clarence's mind seemed to assume concrete form.

In north Wales, William Herbert was tackling a renewed outbreak of insurgency, focused on the fortress of Harlech. Despite everything, this formidable castle had remained in Lancastrian hands, its isolated garrison holding out with grim determination. Herbert's men had formed a ring of steel around it, watching for anything or anybody that came or went. That October, they had detained two Lancastrian agents carrying letters from Margaret of Anjou's exiled court to the castle's defenders. Herbert interrogated the men with his usual robustness, then sent them under heavy guard to Edward in London, together with a charge-sheet. Among the 'many things' that the men had confessed, Herbert told Edward, one detail was especially significant: while in France, they had heard 'suspicious talk' about Warwick transferring his loyalties from Edward to Margaret of Anjou.

The allegations seemed fairly run-of-the-mill. Margaret of Anjou had been unsuccessfully trying to prise Edward and Warwick apart for years. Nonetheless Edward – perhaps seeing the chance for clear-the-air talks with his disgruntled subject – invited Warwick to come and see him, to clear his name, offering to guarantee his security. Warwick refused. In a demonstration of his continued trust in the earl, Edward sent the accused men north to Middleham under armed guard so that Warwick could interview them himself. Warwick angrily dismissed the whole episode as 'frivolous'.[34] It had, though, confirmed to Warwick what he already knew: that his former retainer Herbert, who in recent years had made inroads into Warwick's Welsh territories, played a key role in sacking George Neville from the chancellorship and was now married into the queen's family, was, in conjunction with his Woodville in-laws, looking for every opportunity to alienate Warwick in the king's eyes.

If Warwick was now deeply suspicious of Herbert, so too was Clarence. Back in 1462, Edward had granted Clarence the earldom of Richmond and its valuable north Yorkshire estates, which abutted Warwick's lordship of Middleham.[35] The Lancastrian boy from whom Edward had confiscated the title and lands – Henry Tudor – had spent the last six years in Herbert's possession, growing up quietly in his luxurious Monmouthshire castle of Raglan. Sometime in 1467 Tudor, then ten years old, was joined there by another ward Herbert had recently acquired and who, at nineteen, was on the brink of his majority: Henry Percy, Lancastrian heir to the earldom of Northumberland.[36] In 1460, after his father had been killed at Northampton, Edward had given the young Percy into the dubious care of John Tiptoft, and had set about breaking up the family's vast estates. Some lands had gone to Clarence; others, along with the title of earl of Northumberland, to the Percy family's great rival, Warwick's brother John Neville. But Herbert had bought Percy's wardship for a reason, just as he had bought Tudor's. He planned to marry the two great young noblemen off to his own daughters.

Ultimately, Herbert presumably hoped to convince Edward to return to Tudor and Percy their hereditary titles – which in turn would trigger an almighty struggle for the return of their confiscated, redistributed patrimony. Given Herbert's close proximity to Edward, this scenario was hardly out of the question. It was one that threatened not only Warwick and his brother John Neville, but Clarence, who – if Herbert's bid were successful – stood to relinquish around a quarter of his grants. If Clarence, in particular, needed any reminding of how unstable was the ground on which his wealth and power rested, here it was.[37]

Meanwhile, the alarming increase in violent crime, which had so preoccupied the Commons in Parliament earlier in the year, was getting worse. Nowhere was the deterioration more marked than across the north midlands, where, Edward had been informed, 'great riots and oppressions' were constant.

Early in December 1467, a long-standing feud between two prominent Derbyshire families, the Vernons and Greys, ignited when a gang of sixteen men, servants of Lord Grey, waylaid and killed Roger Vernon, younger brother of Henry Vernon, the family's chief: a 'horrible murder', as one chronicler put it. As both sides looked to their powerful backers for protection, the killing's resonances rippled through the dense webs of affinity to deep within the royal household. As one chronicler pithily put it: 'Those around the king favoured Grey', while Clarence and Warwick – by implication not around the king – 'favoured Vernon'. It was the kind of situation that set people's political antennae twitching: a little local trouble threatened to become a fracture at the heart of the regime.[38]

Alive to the danger Edward, with a handpicked bodyguard of two hundred men for extra security, was soon in the midlands. Basing himself in Coventry Abbey, he ordered judicial commissions to be held across the region, probing the disturbances and punishing offenders. The names of Warwick and Clarence were listed among the commissioners, followed by those of Rivers, Anthony Woodville, Hastings, Warwick's nephew John, Lord Audeley – who, newly married into the queen's family, had been among the nobles complicit in the stripping of George Neville's chancellorship earlier in the year – and another man whom Warwick had come to dislike intensely, the king's household treasurer John Fogge.[39] But if Edward believed that, somehow, his bickering nobles would unite to investigate troubles that they had effectively endorsed and which reflected their own growing antagonism, it was wishful thinking.

On Thursday 17 December a ship from northern France, making for the Yorkshire coast, ran into strong gales in the English Channel and made unscheduled landfall at Sandwich. Among the passengers was Guillaume Monypenny, an expatriate Scot working for the French crown, whose long involvement in Anglo-French negotiations included the previous summer's fiasco at Windsor, and who was carrying letters from Louis XI to Warwick. Travelling with him was an equally seasoned diplomat, Warwick's secretary Robert Neville. Forced to continue their journey overland, they stopped off in London, where they met up with a number of Warwick's councillors, including two of his closest agents: John, Lord Wenlock and Thomas Kent. Over the years, both men had absorbed Warwick's views on England's foreign affairs. Both, like the earl, were hostile to Edward's Burgundian plans.[40]

Wenlock and Kent were impatient for news from France. Was it true, they asked Monypenny, that Louis XI and Charles the Bold had started talking again? When the envoy affirmed that they had, Wenlock practically rubbed his hands with glee. It was, he said, 'the best news Warwick could possibly have'. Inflamed by Edward's recent trade treaty, Wenlock continued, anti-Burgundian sentiment was rife in the city's taverns: it would only be fuelled by this evidence of Charles the Bold's untrustworthiness. People were saying that the 'traitors' who had advised Edward to reject France in favour of Burgundy – in other words, the circle dominated by the queen's family – needed beheading. Meanwhile, rumours circulated that Louis XI, tired of Edward's refusal to enter meaningful talks, was instead throwing his weight behind the exiled Lancastrian regime. There was renewed talk of invasion, and people were 'more scared than they had ever been'.

In his dispatches back to Louis XI, however, Monypenny revealed a further change in French attitudes towards Warwick. No longer was he the man who, with a judicious whisper here and there, could drip-feed French policies into the English king's mind. Rather, the earl was a populist, a disruptor: he would stop the Anglo-Burgundian treaty from going ahead by fuelling the widespread English discontent against it.

Warwick, Monypenny wrote, was breathtakingly popular. People loved him. Wherever Warwick and his glittering entourage travelled through England's regions and towns, it was 'like God had come down from heaven', crowds shouting chants of 'Warwick! Warwick!' As another chronicler remarked, his legendary hospitality kept him in 'great favour' with the public. Nowhere was Warwick's open-handedness more extravagant than in his London household, where 'six oxen were eaten at a breakfast' and anybody who knew anybody among his servants could take away as much boiled and roast beef 'as he might carry on a long dagger'. Warwick's investment was shrewd. As people in London's inns ate his food, they also talked about the affairs of the day.[41]

The friction at court was spilling over into city politics. One Londoner reported how 'many murmurous tales ran in the City' between the earl of Warwick's men and the 'queen's blood'. People walked around openly wearing the badges and colours of rival lords, the kind of provocation that led to increased tensions and fighting, forcing a concerned corporation to proclaim that if any citizen or city officer took or used 'the livery of any lord or magnate', he would lose his freedom and office. That Christmas, however, Wenlock, Kent and their colleagues had been ordered by Warwick to stay behind in London. Their mission was to 'cultivate those in the city', as Monypenny put it, who were opposed to both Edward's policies and the close advisers who had counselled him. Not to take the heat out of the situation, in other words, but to stoke the fire.[42]

Wenlock's demeanour was that of a faithful but disappointed subject, concerned that Edward had been badly led astray by the group around him. He urged Monypenny to seek an audience with the king, to see if he might sway his mind away from Burgundy and back towards France. Four days later, riding north, Monypenny duly broke his journey at Coventry Abbey, where, in a typical French slip of the tongue, he wrote that 'Warwick' was spending Christmas. He meant the English king.[43]

No sooner had Monypenny dismounted than he was brought to the king. Surrounded by a knot of his habitual friends, including Anthony Woodville, Hastings and Herbert, Edward asked Monypenny whether he had brought him any letters from Louis XI. No, came the answer. Yet, countered Edward, he was carrying letters for Warwick: did he know what was in them? No, replied Monypenny again, adding that he assumed they expressed Louis' surprise at Edward's failure to respond to French proposals for peace in the previous summer's talks. Edward, all seriousness, replied that he fully intended to act on Warwick's advice and send an embassy to France 'very soon'. To demonstrate his goodwill, Edward presented Monypenny with a gift of 25 marks and invited him to stay for Christmas.[44]

By February, a reconciliation of sorts had been brokered between Edward and Warwick. The earl finally agreed to attend a council meeting at Coventry, provided that the people he most loathed were absent. Persuading Rivers and Anthony Woodville to make themselves scarce, Edward laid on a lavish reception, greeting Warwick with exaggerated affection; the earl then made an awkward peace with a number of the lords with whom he was at odds, including Herbert. The man who acted as the go-between in this rapprochement, eager to work his way back into favour, was Warwick's brother, Archbishop George Neville. Returned to the king's good books, he was rewarded with two manors and, so it was reported, would soon regain the chancellorship.[45]

Yet the troubles and disorder continued, with rioting erupting in other parts of the country. At Maidstone in Kent, a local mob stormed onto Rivers' manor, the Mote, destroying parkland and slaughtering stocks of deer. Another uprising, in south Yorkshire, seemed more organized and more nebulous. A company of three hundred archers had assembled under a 'captain' – a word that carried ominous overtones of insurgency – calling himself, simply, 'Robin'. He had sent word to Warwick saying that he, his men and much of the local population were ready to turn out on the earl's behalf when needed.

Still hanging around at Edward's court, Monypenny believed that these were popular uprisings: spontaneous grassroots outbursts of frustration against Edward's rule and, in particular, his new alliance with Burgundy. Warwick, naturally, was the perfect figurehead for such opposition. There were, Monypenny reflected in a dispatch to Louis XI, two problems with Warwick: he tended to overthink things and was, besides, 'un peu lache', a bit of a coward. Nevertheless, affairs were bubbling nicely. If, Monypenny felt, the marriage between Margaret of York and Charles the Bold could somehow be prevented from taking place, the subsequent crisis would destroy all those around Edward who had supported it.[46]

Since the signing of the Anglo-Burgundian trade agreement, talks had moved on to the marriage treaty. The Burgundian negotiators put their price on the table: Charles wanted Margaret to come with a dowry of two hundred thousand crowns, or £41,666 – a sum not far short of the king's regular annual expenditure. It was a huge demand from which they refused to budge. Edward caved in, but it was unclear where the money was going to come from.[47] Although in recent months Edward had been raising yet more finance from the ever-obliging Medici banker Gherardo Canigiani, he had been spending it as fast as it came in.

Canigiani had been busy. In September 1467, he had brokered a thousand-mark loan to Edward, from a long-term creditor of Edward's and friend of the queen's family, the London alderman and former mayor Sir Hugh Wyche. Two months later, the Florentine surpassed himself. On 28 November, at Edward's 'special desire and commandment', he lent the king the massive sum of £8,468 18s 8d, paying it directly into the king's chamber account. The problem was, as indicated by an itemized schedule of recent payments authorized by Edward, the cash was already spoken for. That year, he had paid the Calais garrison over £6,000 in backdated wages; sent Tiptoft into Ireland with a large force of men to suppress rebellion there, an expedition that cost £2,896 16s 8d; handed Warwick 2,000 marks for the expenses of his pointless French embassy; and made various smaller but still significant payments to ambassadors and spies.[48]

A couple of months later, a lugubrious figure materialized in the Medici bank's London offices. Since leaving his post as head of the Bruges branch almost three years previously, Agnolo Tani had watched from afar as his successor, Tommaso Portinari, had embarked on what he considered the bank's ruinous policy of lending money to princes, making himself indispensable to Charles the Bold through a succession of large loans. As he riffled through the accounts of the London branch, the troubleshooting Tani took grim satisfaction in finding his misgivings thoroughly substantiated. Canigiani's loans to Edward were secured against everything from wardships to customs income and licences for toll-free shipping, which was all very well, but repaid this way, the debt was going to take a very long time to recover – with potentially catastrophic consequences for the bank's liquidity. Writing back to head office about the London branch's affairs, Tani remarked with gloomy relish that 'my assignment is to resurrect a corpse'.[49]

Edward desperately needed to find other creditors to help him fund his Burgundian commitments. He had been hoping that bringing Warwick onside would do the trick. As Monypenny reported it, Edward had asked Warwick to provide security for a loan of a hundred thousand marks to Charles the Bold. Taking the opportunity to explain to Edward the idiocy of his foreign-policy plans, Warwick refused point-blank.

Denying Edward credit was one way to stop the Anglo-Burgundian marriage coming to fruition. There was another line of attack. As Monypenny stressed to Louis XI, it was crucial to make sure 'by any means possible' that the pope did not issue the dispensation needed for the wedding to go ahead.[50] It was a strategy that Monypenny had clearly discussed with the Nevilles because, even as he was working his way smoothly back into Edward's favour, Archbishop George Neville was busy trying to entangle the dispensation in red tape. And he had an ideal tool at hand.

In the autumn of 1467, a representative of Pope Paul II disembarked at Dover. Stefano Trenta, bishop of Lucca, had set out from Rome over a year and a half earlier. In Bruges, he had kicked his heels for months waiting for diplomatic accreditation to continue his onward journey to England. Edward was not at all keen to see him.

While Edward was anxious to show himself a loyal son of the pope when it suited him to do so, his reluctance to let Trenta into the country was hardly surprising. Trenta's English mission involved three tasks: to find out what had happened to the proceeds of the papal tax raised by Edward back in 1464, not a penny of which had been delivered to Rome; to drum up fresh financial support, long promised by the Yorkist regime, for the papal crusade against the Turks; and another, equally critical task. This was to persuade Edward to cede the papacy exclusive rights to sell alum, the dye-fixer crucial to the functioning of England's cloth trade, now in the hands of the Medici bank. Edward did not want Trenta meddling in his financial affairs, especially given that the tax in question had disappeared into his own coffers. Neither did he want a papal legate going round the country making tax demands of his already hard-pressed subjects. He was also reluctant to antagonize the merchant-financiers of London and Calais – the very communities from whom he was hoping to secure the credit for his sister's dowry – by enforcing a monopoly that would push up the price of alum.[51] But the papal granting of a cardinal's hat to Edward's favoured candidate Thomas Bourchier demanded a quid pro quo, and Edward could hardly refuse a man so close to the pope.

At first, Trenta met with a warm reception from the king and his advisers. However, once it dawned on them that – unlike previous, pliable, papal officials – a sprinkling of royal graciousness and the odd backhander would not persuade the unswerving envoy to go easy in his investigations, the bonhomie soon wore off.[52] Soon, the legate came up against a wall of obfuscation; turning up to one meeting, he was confronted by an intimidating phalanx of royal lawyers. Warned to back off, and unable to trust anybody, Trenta shut himself away in his sumptuous accommodation in St Bartholomew-the-Less, near Smithfield, and turned down all invitations to socialize: he would, it was said, 'never come at no feasts nor dinners with no man, with king nor lord'. Londoners felt it was a shame that his visit should have been 'kept so privily', not least because of Trenta's reputation as a cultural giant. For his part, the isolated Trenta wrote back to Italy pleading to be recalled from the wasteland that was London.[53] However, by early 1468, he had found a friend whose cultural and political sympathies were in tune with his own: George Neville.

From his opulent Hertfordshire home of The More, the archbishop started a correspondence with Trenta, in which the homesick envoy took great comfort. Solicitous about Trenta's health – plague was still rife – and sympathetic to his predicament, Neville invited him to dinner. As soon as the wary Trenta realized Neville was back in the king's grace, he accepted – much to the astonishment of one Londoner, who was surprised to see him going out at all. Feeling he had an ally, Trenta allowed his guard to drop. In doing so he committed a rare written indiscretion, one that revealed precisely why Neville had been so keen to cultivate him.

In a letter of 1 February, Trenta reassured Neville that he had mentioned the archbishop's piety in his dispatches to the Curia. Neville clearly wanted it known that, in the pecking order of allegiances, his loyalty to the Most Holy Father took priority – even, so the implication went, over that of the English crown. Trenta then added that he was continuing to lobby the pope on behalf of Neville's *'fratre magnifico'*. By 'big brother', Trenta meant Warwick. And although he was careful not to commit the details to paper, 'this business', as Trenta referred to it obliquely, concerned the two papal dispensations: one that Warwick wanted to obtain, for the marriage of his daughter Isabel to Clarence; the other, permitting the marriage of Margaret of York to Charles the Bold, that he was equally anxious to quash.[54]

Grooming impressionable papal representatives was a strategy that the Neville brothers had used to stunning effect years before when, seeking international legitimacy for the Yorkist cause, they had co-opted the legate Francesco Coppini. Now, Trenta found himself caught up in the high-stakes game the Nevilles were playing against Edward, in co-operation with Louis XI, who had sent his own personal secretary to Rome to try to prevent the coveted dispensation being issued.[55]

Still, Edward and Charles had both done their own intensive lobbying at the Curia, and the signs looked good.[56] On 16 February, informed that the dispensation for his marriage was on its way from Rome, Charles put his signature to the marriage contract with England. Nine days later, a Burgundian envoy arrived back in Brussels with the paperwork from Rome and was instantly sent on to London. The document in question, however, was not itself a dispensation but a mandate instructing an officially designated papal executor to issue one. In England that executor was Stefano Trenta, now actively working on behalf of George Neville to make sure the paperwork never got issued.[57]

At the end of March, Trenta dropped his bombshell. He informed Edward that he had found some irregularities in the dispensation and would not be approving it. It had taken him an entire month to let the king know: a month in which Edward, assuming Trenta's approval was a formality, had publicly ratified the marriage treaty in a ceremony at Westminster, committing himself to the vast expense of his sister's dowry, and – openly now – stating his commitment to the Anglo-Burgundian defence pact that he had signed in secret some eighteen months previously. Irate, Edward ordered the envoy in front of his council to explain himself. Trenta refused to turn up.

Instead, in a letter dripping with offended dignity, he told Edward that there were problems with the documents. There was probably some truth in this: the process was a complex one and Trenta was a finicky man. But other considerations had informed his refusal to sign, among them his disgust at his treatment in England, now compounded by public calls for him to be stripped of his papal office for obstructing the dispensation, calls which, he said, stemmed from a 'certain prince' – in other words, Edward himself. Trenta, who liked things done the Italian way, 'secretly and quickly', had a horror of the English habit of airing dirty linen in public. Now, he was washing his hands of the whole business. Edward could inform Charles that as far as he, Trenta, was concerned, the dispensation was dead in the water.[58] The marriage treaty, on the brink of consummation, had been plunged into crisis.

Edward and Charles still had an ace to play. There was another organization that was exceptionally keen that the marriage should go ahead, which had invested heavily in both the English and Burgundian regimes, and which had every interest in ensuring an ever-closer union in which it saw substantial financial possibilities, not least in its role as the pope's official seller of alum, the mineral on which Anglo-Burgundian trade depended: the Medici bank.

A week after Trenta's revelation, Tommaso Portinari, chief of the bank's Bruges branch, wrote to the Medici head office in Florence. News of the fiasco in England had just reached the Burgundian court and Charles, apoplectic, had no doubt where the blame lay: 'He could not be less contented with the Pope.'[59] Nonetheless, Portinari continued, a solution was at hand. All Charles had to do to obtain the dispensation was to concede on the issue dear to the pope's heart: to agree to impose the papal alum monopoly throughout the Burgundian dominions. It would be a wildly unpopular measure. But the man perfectly placed to ensure, gently, that Charles agreed to it was his right-hand man and banker, as well as the agent responsible for the sale of papal alum in Burgundian lands – Tommaso Portinari himself.[60]

On 5 May 1468, barely a month after Portinari's letter, the ink was drying on a twelve-year agreement between Charles the Bold and the papacy. The agreement, which made illegal the importing of alum from non-papal sources, appointed Tommaso Portinari the sole authorized importer and vendor of alum into the Low Countries on behalf of the Bruges branch of the Medici bank.[61] Edward, though, had stood firm against the imposition of a similar agreement in England. Given that the bulk of his sister's dowry due to Charles would probably have to come from English merchants, a community whose dwindling goodwill would be eroded by the imposition of an alum monopoly, this was hardly surprising. Moreover, whereas Portinari and the papal legate to Burgundy had proved a persuasive team, their counterparts in England were not so minded. Canigiani, as English as he was Italian, was inclined to see things Edward's way; Edward and Trenta, meanwhile, were barely on speaking terms. The pope shrugged his shoulders: Charles's agreement would do for now.

Edward had already been given fulsome guarantees by Burgundian diplomats that everything was going to work out. On 11 April, he actioned the first payment of his sister's dowry, a bond of £10,000, with a promise to pay the remainder in three annual instalments. The money, naturally, would be deposited with Portinari.[62]

Following closely after were invitations – or rather orders – to the retinue that would accompany Margaret of York to Flanders for her wedding festivities. In the third week of April, Sir John Paston received his, its wax seal impressed with the king's signet: Paston was told to attend on Margaret 'every excuse or delay laid apart', in order to do 'jousts and pleasure' at the glittering ducal court in Bruges.[63] It was almost exactly twelve months since Paston had bet his friend Thomas Lomnour that the wedding would not go ahead within two years. Now, though Paston had lost, he was undoubtedly delighted to have done so: after all, he had been handed a courtier's dream opportunity to put himself about in the most glamorous of settings.

For Edward there was one large stumbling block still to negotiate. Despite having committed to pay his sister's dowry, he hadn't yet got the money together. Which was where Parliament came in.

Due to convene on 5 May, Parliament was informed by its new chancellor, Robert Stillington, bishop of Bath and Wells – a man heavily involved in Edward's Burgundian negotiations – that the session would be postponed while the king awaited news from 'certain other people'. Two weeks later, on Friday 17 May, that news finally arrived. Fresh from negotiating the alum treaty, the Burgundian agent Ferry de Clugny had arrived in England with confirmation that paperwork for the dispensation was now all present and correct. That morning, the recalcitrant Stefano Trenta was summoned to Westminster Palace, where he set his seal on the dispensation for Margaret of York's marriage to Charles the Bold. No sooner had he done so than, away in another part of the palace, Edward's new chancellor rose to address the assembled Lords and Commons about why it was that the king so earnestly desired money from them.[64]

PART THREE

A Season of Punishment

Spring 1468 – Summer 1471

'I will advise you in especial
To have good guiding and inspection
To every trouble in this nation
    For though by a little it beginneth
    It may destroy us all before it endeth.'
                George Ashby, *Active Policy of a Prince*

'Edward, late earl of March, usurper, oppressor, destroyer.'
            Proclamation by Warwick and Clarence, 1470

'He that is not against me is with me.'
                The Arrivall of Edward IV, 1471

8

Robin Mend-All

A biddable diplomat and civil servant, Robert Stillington had risen high during his two decades in royal service. He had made himself a fortune into the bargain, accumulating a portfolio of wealthy ecclesiastical livings and acquiring a notorious reputation for neglecting his flock. During his quarter-century-long tenure of the bishopric of Bath and Wells, he would appear in his see precisely once – but then, pluralism and absenteeism were necessary evils when serving the crown. As the keeper of the privy seal his legal expertise, experience and unquestioning usefulness had caught Edward's eye. Now, in his new role as chancellor, Stillington opened Parliament with the customary sermon to the lords and commons: the perfect opportunity to impress his enthroned, onlooking king.[1]

In a sweeping survey of Edward's achievements, Stillington expatiated on his king's tireless work in imposing the rule of law, restoring peace and order to a ravaged England, and on his exhaustive efforts – paid for out of his own coffers – to secure a succession of treaties and trading agreements with former enemies, now friendly neighbours with whom England could do business. Foremost among them, of course, were Charles the Bold, now about to marry Edward's sister Margaret, and Duke Francis of Brittany, the 'mightiest princes who hold their land under the crown of France'. Which brought Stillington to his point.

These alliances were part of a grand plan: to recover the French crown that rightfully belonged to the kings of England. Now, with Edward's allies urging him to invade Louis XI's lands and promising military co-operation, England's 'old and ancient enemy' was ripe for the plucking. Such opportunities were rare and had to be seized when they arose – and besides, domestic peace could be best achieved through foreign war. All of which, as many present were aware, was an

189

argument straight from the playbook of Henry V.[2] But, concluded Stillington, Parliament need not just take his word for it. The king would tell them himself.

Stirring himself, Edward expanded on the recent events that had led to his diplomatic crowning glory, the forthcoming Anglo-Burgundian marriage, which was the final piece in the jigsaw of anti-French alliances that he had been constructing. Then, after setting out his plans for war, he let Stillington pose the inevitable request for Parliament's loyal backing, in the form of a tax.[3]

Almost exactly a year before, Edward had assured the Commons he would not ask them for money except for 'great and urgent causes'. War with France was one of those causes, and the king's belligerence was infectious: Parliament duly voted him the funds. The snag was that the tax was already spoken for.

Just over a week before Parliament opened, the Medici troubleshooter Agnolo Tani, who had been so appalled by the state of the London branch's balance sheet, had written to head office in Florence with an unaccustomed lightness. In a private audience with Edward, he had received the king's personal guarantee that between '£3,000 to £4,000' of the forthcoming tax would be allocated to servicing the Medici debt.[4]

Yet the Medici bank was only one creditor in a complex web of loans that Edward had put in place to fund his sister's dowry, the first £10,000 instalment of which had to be paid before the wedding could proceed. Although Edward had already instructed a bond for the amount to be issued to Tommaso Portinari – the Medici, inevitably, were handling the transaction – he had struggled to raise the required finance, even the most reliable of his creditors by now being reluctant to lend.

The security provided by a parliamentary tax, however, made an instant difference. On 28 May, the Calais Staplers agreed to pay the first instalment of the dowry. Their loan was secured by bonds from sixty-two London merchants, themselves secured against the tax that Parliament had voted for Edward's war against France.[5] It was precisely the situation that Edward, the previous year, had given Parliament his solemn promise to avoid.

Edward had another burning issue to tackle. As a worried Commons repeatedly stressed, the kingdom was hardly in the state of tranquillity that Stillington had depicted. They demanded that the king do something about it.[6]

Edward made a conspicuous attempt to do so. He passed a new act against retaining – the private recruitment of men that, in times of tension or emergency, could see a nobleman's retinue swell alarmingly into a private army. Given that retaining was also the glue that held society together, allowing noblemen to extend their influence over the country and to mobilize troops on the king's behalf, the legislation, packed with loopholes, proved just as slippery as previous attempts to control lords' distribution of their badges and liveries. Neither, it seemed, did anybody take much notice. One eyewitness later recalled how he had seen the lords, gathered in Westminster Palace's Star Chamber, swear to obey the act they had just drawn up on the king's command. Less than an hour later, 'while they were still in the Star Chamber', he saw the same lords 'making retainers by oath' and generally breaking all the promises that they had just sworn to keep.[7]

Edward, it seemed, remained unswerving in his personal conviction that he could deliver both internal peace and a major military campaign against France. Parliament, for now, believed him. But that spring, there were palpable indications that the king was not in control of either process.

Dominated by its castle and rising above the tidal marshes of the Thames estuary, the Kentish port of Queenborough doubled as a bulwark of southeast England's coastal defence and, as one of two 'staple' ports in Kent authorized to handle the country's wool exports, a busy mercantile centre. That June, as the town returned to normal after the processions and feasting of Whit week, royal officials monitoring the incoming marine traffic from northern France, the Netherlands and beyond, stopped and searched a man coming into the country.[8] Identified only as 'Cornelius', a shoemaker, his unremarkable appearance was designed to evade suspicion, but the letters he was found to be carrying incriminated him. Cornelius was no shoemaker but the servant of Sir Robert Whittingham, a London draper and one of Margaret of Anjou's advisers-in-exile. He had travelled to England from Margaret's small court at Koeur to assess loyalties and raise funds for the Lancastrian cause.[9]

That spring Margaret's chancellor Sir John Fortescue, who had persistently lobbied the French king over the past years with scant results, sensed a new opportunity. Louis XI had tried everything to wreck the impending alliance between England and Burgundy: lobbying the pope, spreading lurid and baseless rumours about Margaret of York's promiscuity, cultivating Warwick. Nothing had worked. Angry and alarmed at the bellicose noises coming from Edward IV's government, he had shut down the Medici branch at Lyons in retaliation for the bank's facilitating of the Anglo-Burgundian marriage. And, clutching at straws, he began to pay attention to the Lancastrian agents who for years had hovered, ignored, on the margins of his court. Foremost among them was Fortescue, who told Louis that he knew a way to restore Henry VI to the English throne easily, cheaply and without the need for expensive military intervention, thereby solving Louis' Anglo-Burgundian headache at a stroke. Fortescue's was the alluring promise of exiled regimes throughout history: a plan for regime change that, in exchange for a modest investment, would bring the potential backer exceptional returns, including, in this case, 'perpetual peace' and the promise of a lucrative commercial alliance between England and France.[10] There were other 'more secret matters' that Fortescue would be happy to discuss in person with Louis or his representatives. The approach coincided with a marked increase in clandestine Lancastrian activity.

Edward's counter-intelligence operation, led robustly by Rivers and the royal household's treasurer John Fogge, went swiftly into action. Brought into the Tower of London, Cornelius was joined there by an Oxfordshire lawyer named Thomas Danvers, an addressee of one of his letters and a man with strong Lancastrian connections. Edward was concerned enough to interrogate Cornelius personally as he was tortured, the soles of his feet burned with hot irons.[11] One of the names Cornelius revealed was that of John Hawkins, a servant of Warwick's associate John, Lord Wenlock, who proved a fruitful line of enquiry. Racked exhaustively by Rivers and Fogge, Hawkins 'showed unto them many things', the pain so intense that he accused himself of treason to make it stop. From this forced testimony, Edward's officials constructed a disquieting map of subversion. Among the people that Hawkins incriminated were his boss Wenlock and a handful of prominent Londoners. One of the names he mentioned came as a bombshell to the inquisitors.

One of London's richest, most powerful citizens, the draper Sir Thomas Cook had been instrumental in marshalling the corporate loans that kept Edward on the throne, as well as being a major creditor in his own right: back in 1465 a grateful king had knighted him just before Elizabeth Woodville's coronation. Since then, Cook's dormant Lancastrian affiliations had been revived. Back in October 1466, he had been discreetly approached for funds by a Lancastrian agent. As Cook later told it, the approach simply involved an exploratory conversation over the possibility of a reconciliation between York and Lancaster: indeed, he had sought guarantees from the agent that there were no plans to dethrone Edward. Cook, however, had failed to report the conversation to the proper authorities. And that, in the view of Edward and his advisers, was treason.[12]

Cook was arrested and bailed. His release was down to the personal intervention of Edward's sister Margaret, who valued Cook's role as one of the sureties guaranteeing payment of her dowry. With the finance in place, the long-coveted marriage finally in view and Margaret's departure for Bruges imminent, Edward didn't want any more hold-ups. On 18 June, the chastened Cook was among the gaggle of city dignitaries that saw Margaret off on the first stage of her journey to the Low Countries, presenting her with a marriage gift of two fine silver-gilt bowls. In a gesture of familial rapprochement, Warwick had even deigned to turn up, Margaret riding pillion behind him through London. Five days later, Margaret and her glittering entourage, waved off by Warwick and her brothers Clarence and Richard, set sail from Margate for Sluis. With his sister safely on her way, Edward promptly re-arrested Cook. This time he was imprisoned, pending trial.[13]

Escorted by fourteen heavily armed ships – rumour had it that a desperate Louis XI would make a last-ditch attempt to scupper the marriage – Margaret's crossing was uneventful. Disembarking at Sluis, she was immediately plunged into the first stage of a ceremony of staggering scale and opulence. Charles the Bold was determined that his wedding, for which he had made Edward pay through the nose, would reflect his own stratospheric ambitions.

One chronicler in Margaret's wedding party scribbled down everything he saw: the procession, late in the warm midsummer evening, through Sluis' torchlit streets, and the mimed pageants, enacted opposite Margaret's lodgings, depicting her auspicious destiny as duchess of Burgundy. At a reception the following day, Margaret was presented to her new family, Isabella of Portugal peering into her prospective daughter-in-law's face, scrutinizing – 'avising' – it, as if committing her features to memory. When Charles met his bride-to-be, the chronicler likened the moment to when the heroic warrior Troilus first spotted Criseyde, pole-axed by love. Amid the welter of gift-givings and speeches was a florid oration by Elizabeth Woodville's secretary, John Gunthorpe. A master of the new style of Latin sweeping the courts and chancelleries of northern Europe, Gunthorpe deployed his full range of rhetorical tricks and recondite classical allusions. Not everyone was impressed by this revolution in eloquence: it was, grumbled one Flemish listener, windy and incomprehensible.[14]

Amid the meticulously planned splendour were some hasty last-minute recalibrations. The day before the wedding, Charles got round to giving notice to the small group of Lancastrian exiles whom he had been supporting financially over the past years. Given a sweetener of eight hundred livres to make himself scarce, Edmund Beaufort, duke of Somerset, left Bruges to rejoin Margaret at Koeur. Other Lancastrian sympathizers stayed in the city, going to ground. Whatever his newfound commitment to the house of York, Charles hadn't so much abandoned his Lancastrian loyalties as brushed them under the carpet.[15]

Early on the morning of Sunday 3 July, following a private wedding ceremony, Charles and Margaret set out on the short journey from Damme to Bruges. Dressed in white cloth-of-gold and wearing a crown adorned with the initials C and M and Yorkist suns and roses worked in precious stones, the new duchess of Burgundy was carried along on a richly dressed litter, surrounded by a phalanx of forty archers, their specially commissioned coats glittering with precious stones supplied by Charles's own jeweller Gerard Loyet, and accompanied by a 'noise of trumpets', English and Dutch musicians shoulder to shoulder.[16]

Bruges itself had been transformed into a land of chivalric fantasy. As the wedding party moved slowly through streets lined in

Burgundian black-and-crimson, clouds of roses and sweet herbs drifted down among the procession. Children leaned from windows showering the duchess with marguerites as she passed; flocks of pigeons were released from turrets. On street corners and in marketplaces, actors brought to life biblical and historical scenes depicting themes of Anglo-Burgundian unity. Entering the Prinzenhof, the ducal palace, guests were greeted by ingenious fountains of wine – red Burgundy, white Rhenish and sweet spiced hippocras – fired in a constant flow from the arrowheads of sculpted archers, before proceeding into a great dining hall built for the occasion: a hundred and forty feet long by seventy wide, all turrets, glass windows and gilded surfaces, its interior lined by the greatest collection of tapestries in Europe, silver and gold thread shimmering in the candlelight. The wedding supper was brought in a succession of thirty ships. Between courses, as the guests digested, a series of *entremets* – pageants – told the story of Hercules' labours. At one point, blaring trumpets announced the arrival of a tower, forty-one feet high, topped with a leopard clutching the banner of England and a marguerite. From it emerged a stream of performers dressed as animals: seven gambolling monkeys kept in line by a tambourine- and flute-wielding master; four donkeys singing, the delicate strands of polyphony weaving together; a dwarf duetting with the lion on which he rode.[17]

In the days that followed, the tournament that unfolded in Bruges marketplace was an epic spectacle that came complete with its own chivalric storylines, the combatants enacting a variety of quests. This, the *pas d'armes*, was fighting as drama, myth and legend made reality – though it didn't stop people and horses getting hurt. The fighting culminated in a *tournoi*: a mounted battle between the two twenty-six-strong teams on horseback. Sir John Woodville, one of Elizabeth's brothers, was proclaimed the winner. After their near-disastrous encounter at Smithfield the previous year, Anthony Woodville and the Bastard of Burgundy were kept well apart.

Amid all the feasting and junketing, the younger John Paston had taken time to write to his mother in Caister. Never, he wrote, did Englishmen have such a good time 'out of England'. Anything you wished for simply appeared, while the pageants were 'the best that ever I saw'; the fun-loving, courteous Burgundians were 'the goodliest fellowship I ever came among'. As for Charles the Bold's court, the only thing he could possibly compare it with was the fabled court of King Arthur. Nonetheless, the English wedding party, Paston wrote, was due to leave sooner than expected. Threatened by the new Anglo-Burgundian treaty, Louis XI had decided that attack was the best form of defence. French armies were on the move, marching fast towards Flanders, and Charles was scrambling to mobilize against them.[18]

Back in England, trouble was also brewing. In early July, as Paston and his friends caroused in Bruges, news reached Edward that the perennial Lancastrian troublemaker Jasper Tudor, sailing from the French port of Harfleur – Louis XI had, after all, proved receptive to Sir John Fortescue's suggestions – had landed in mid-Wales with a small band of armed men and was heading northeast to relieve the Lancastrian defenders at Harlech. Immediately Edward sent William Herbert, his ever-reliable 'cleanser' of Welsh troubles, to eliminate the problem; he also dispatched a seaborne force of marines, gunners and sappers to tackle Harlech, once and for all.[19] The day after Herbert left, a commission convened at London's Guildhall to start legal proceedings against the fifteen men whom Rivers, Fogge and their colleagues had identified as a Lancastrian support network. At the top of the list was Sir Thomas Cook.

Edward wanted a swift and decisive prosecution. Sensing the possibility of resistance, the commission he appointed was a model of political balance. Alongside Rivers was Warwick, their mutual loathing reduced to a simmer for the occasion. Clarence headed the panel: when, at one point, London's mayor Thomas Oulgreve, 'a replete and lumpish man', nodded off, Clarence snidely warned the assembled court to 'speak softly, for the mayor is asleep'. But the hearings soon ground to a halt. Perhaps through sympathy, perhaps because it didn't feel there was a case to answer, the jury was reluctant to indict Cook and his fellow defendants. It was promptly discharged and another jury appointed. The difficulties continued, the commission chopping and changing juries as it sought to secure indictments and verdicts.

Eventually, the Lancastrian agents were convicted of treason and condemned to death. Others, including Cook, were found guilty of misprision, failing to reveal a plot against the king: a lesser, but still exceptionally serious offence. Cook was hit with a fine of 8,000 marks and briefly imprisoned before, on 26 July, receiving a royal pardon. By this time his case had become a cause célèbre.[20]

The way Cook's case had been handled didn't look good. Rivers and Fogge, who had extracted forced confessions under torture, had been ubiquitous throughout: one of the juries was later said to have been rigged explicitly 'by the means of Fogge'. Cook's fine, imposed by a cash-strapped king on one of his wealthier subjects, was enormous. While Cook himself was still in custody, Edward ordered Rivers and Fogge to break into his property and seize his moveable assets in order to pay off the debt: a common, if harsh, practice that their men interpreted liberally, turning Cook's London townhouse upside-down, drinking his cellar dry and carting off large quantities of cloth, £700 in plate and jewels, and a series of exquisite, jewel-encrusted tapestries depicting the Siege of Jerusalem. They left the house in an 'ill pickle'. Some thought Cook deserved it: he was a vain, bullying man who was endured rather than liked. But soon his treatment was being seen in a different way.

As well as the parts played by Rivers and Fogge, two other stories were circulating. The queen's mother Jacquetta had long had her eye on Cook's magnificent tapestries. Enraged when he refused to sell 'at her pleasure and price', she quickly annexed them after Cook's house was trashed by her husband's men.[21] Meanwhile, following Cook's sentencing, Elizabeth herself had taken him to court to obtain a surcharge of eight hundred marks due on his fine, a prerogative tax known as 'queen's gold'. While little more than an expression of her propensity for wringing cash from whatever sources she could find, it was, as Elizabeth herself quickly recognized, a tactless move: her receiver-general John Forster – who, happily for Cook, was his son-in-law – agreed to waive the fine. But the damage was already done. Cook was cast as an innocent Londoner who had suffered the roughest of justice at the hands of the 'queen's blood'.

This tale of the victimized Cook, repeated and embellished, was a narrative that encapsulated the shortcomings of a failing regime: of a king who, rather than knowing his own mind, was prey to the Woodville-dominated cabal around him (though Edward was sufficiently in control to blow almost a thousand pounds of Cook's fine on several sets of exquisite Burgundian tapestries).[22] Given the earl of

Warwick's notorious reputation for spreading damaging rumours – back in the 1450s, Margaret of Anjou's men had been unable to stem the tide of insinuation about her infidelity – and the recent efforts of his agents to spread 'murmurous tales' against the queen's family, it would have been a surprise if, in the city's taverns, his agents weren't loudly sympathetic on Cook's behalf. They were also continuing to stir up indignation about the Burgundian alliance and the part the queen's family had played in forging it.

Towards the end of July, barely a fortnight after Margaret and Charles's wedding, civic authorities intercepted plans for a night-time riot against the Flemish community in Southwark, involving hundreds of men from various guilds. Fuelling it was the usual stew of economic and xenophobic grievances, one ringleader confessing that the plan had been to target Flemings, 'to cut off their thumbs and hands', thereby depriving them of the means by which they took away 'the living of English people'. One trigger had been talk about the poor hospitality Englishmen had received at the recent wedding – 'the Burgundians', wrote one chronicler, 'showed no more favour to Englishmen than they would to a Jew' – which ran counter to all the available evidence. Spread by people who knew perfectly well that, once in circulation, such false news was almost impossible to counter, it was immediately effective.[23]

That summer, rather than dampen down the toxic atmosphere, Edward and his councillors added fuel to the flames. In recent years relations with the Hanse, the mercantile league which dominated trade with the Baltic cities and the Rhineland, had been volatile at best. As English fleets tried to muscle in on trade in the North Sea and the Baltic, there were tit-for-tat reprisals, the latest of which had come that June. Failing to obtain redress for earlier English aggression, the king of Denmark seized six English ships anchored in the Øresund strait and sold off their cargoes in Danzig. Edward sought retribution. With few rich Danish subjects in England, he instead went after the Hanse. In retaliation for their tangential part in the Danish episode, all Hanse merchants in the country were arrested and imprisoned, their goods confiscated. While they might have played to the populist gallery, the reprisals were condemned internationally and at home, appalling everybody from London's own Merchant Adventurers – reliant on good relations with the powerful Hanse – to hard-hit clothworkers in Gloucestershire, who blamed the accusations against the Hanse on 'malice and evil', as well as 'singular profit' on the part of certain people who wanted them kicked out of England altogether. It wasn't difficult to work out who those individuals were. Edward had been pushed into this dispropor-tionate lashing-out by the 'verdict of the council' – in particular, councillors with substantial shipping interests who had sustained losses in the Danish incident, and who would themselves benefit from a lack of Hanse competition in England. Foremost among these councillors were Warwick and Fogge (for once, their shared financial interests had pushed them together) and the perpetually enraged Sir John Howard.[24] In the following months Edward, advised to rectify his mistake, released the merchants, rowed back on the fines he had imposed and tried to re-establish diplomatic relations with the Hanse. It was too little, too late.

Any residual glow of satisfaction from the Anglo-Burgundian wed-ding was fading fast. That summer Edward, never the most consistent seeker of advice, appeared vulnerable and overly susceptible to the cabal around him. The magnificent regal style that he had cultivated, a sun around whom all revolved, was fine when all the satellites were in alignment. When things were out of order, however, his motto of 'comfort and joy' began to look like laziness or, just as bad, helpless-ness. The king seemed to be floundering, unable to impose himself on the small group that, in the warmth of his favour, wielded his power with impunity, let alone to get a grip on the country's many ills or his nebulous, agile political opponents. His responses, when they came, were flailing, inconsistent and vindictive. Sir Thomas Cook's case had turned into a public-relations disaster, while his response to the Hanse fiasco suggested a king who was neither in control nor aware of the consequences of his actions. Meanwhile, he seemed unable to pre-vent a few well-placed rumours from turning popular opinion against a marriage that should have been a diplomatic triumph. This was a king who, in the eyes of many, was failing to fulfil his recent parlia-mentary commitments on unity, security and prosperity. His failure to do so looked like weakness and indecision, his actions ill-judged and erratic.

As the summer wore on, there were signs that the widespread

gossip and innuendo that had attached itself to the queen's family was starting to stick to Edward himself. As people questioned the king's fitness for his role, so – inevitably – they started to examine his right to rule: where issues of credibility were raised, issues of legitimacy were rarely far behind. In one case, a labourer called John Lacy was hauled before London's mayor and aldermen, accused of seditious language, and specifically of two statements: first, that Edward IV was not king by right; and second, that he was 'not born a gentleman' – which, in not so many words, implied that he was not the son of the duke of York but a bastard.[25]

At last, one good news story for the regime came from north Wales. In the face of Lord Herbert's overwhelming military muscle, Jasper Tudor's insurgent army had melted away. Tudor himself had escaped – disguised as a peasant, a bale of straw on his back, he had fled on a boat to France – but on 14 August 1468, after holding out for some seven years, the Lancastrian defenders of Harlech finally surrendered. Herbert's supremacy in Wales was now more or less total: he was, as one Welsh poet admiringly put it, Edward's 'master-lock' in the principality. He returned to London in triumph; there, a delighted Edward conferred on him Jasper Tudor's title of earl of Pembroke. Given the threat that Herbert presented to their interests, it was not a move to delight Warwick or Clarence.[26]

Despite its ultimate failure, Jasper Tudor's brief, high-profile incursion had in a way done its job. It had shown that the Lancastrian cause was alive and kicking, and that it had in Louis XI a sponsor who was prepared to support it, at least in an exploratory way. Coming at this time of heightened tensions, its timing had been impeccable.

Towards the end of September, a pale blue comet appeared in the sky. Astronomers in China minutely described its position, its northeast direction and its white-blue tail extending southwest, details that recurred in the reports of Japanese and Korean observers. In the Hungarian city of Pressburg, the Polish astronomer Martin Ilkusz wrote a report on it for his employer King Matthias of Hungary, saying it spelled danger; an observer in Paris noted its tail passing over the asterism of the plough, or 'chariot', as the French termed it. And in England, a chronicler noted how, 'shortly before Michaelmas', the blazing star appeared, moving from 'west to north', and stayed in the sky for the following five or six weeks, finally disappearing in the first week of November. Though he didn't try and explain it, like Martin Ilkusz he thought it a portent.[27]

That autumn, the wheels came off Edward's expensively assembled anti-French coalition. With French armies massing on his borders, Duke Francis of Brittany made desperate appeals to Edward for military aid. Even though Edward responded with alacrity, the agitated duke was pressured into signing a new treaty with Louis XI; in so doing, he ditched his agreements with Edward and Charles the Bold.

Charles, Edward's new brother-in-law, was proving equally unreliable. The alliance with Burgundy hadn't brought the breakthrough in trade talks for which England's businessmen desperately hoped: despite all Edward's concessions, the bans against English cloth imports into Flanders remained firmly in place. And Charles's own commitments to the Yorkist regime were looking distinctly equivocal. His Lancastrian friends, sent hastily away from Bruges a day before his wedding, were back in town, while Edmund Beaufort was fighting for the Burgundians against the French. Worse followed. On 14 October, in the Somme town of Peronne, Charles, while insisting on his treaty with Edward, signed a comprehensive truce with his arch-enemy Louis XI. Noting the utter incompatibility of being friends with both England and France, one puzzled Italian envoy remarked that Charles was 'trying to put two feet into one shoe'.[28]

For critics of Edward's Burgundian alliance, this was all grist to the mill. Barely three months after the spectacularly expensive wedding for which he had fought so hard – as well as some £18,000 subsequently shelled out on military backing for his flaky coalition partners – Edward's plans were in tatters, the foreign policy statement that he had trumpeted to Parliament unrecognizable. He now tried to reopen negotiations with Louis XI, who revelled in the irony: this time, it was Edward's ambassadors who returned from France loaded with gifts but 'without effecting anything for which they came'. Louis was enjoying himself. According to the Milanese ambassador Panigarola, the French king was putting it about that he planned to extend backing to the 'old queen of England', Margaret of Anjou – although, Panigarola added, 'I hear of nothing actual being done'.

When the talk reached an increasingly jittery Edward, he took it seriously.[29] The seaborne army originally mobilized in support of his former ally the duke of Brittany was now redeployed defensively; late that autumn, it roamed the English Channel on the lookout for a Lancastrian invasion force. And, at last, Edward turned to the two great lords who had so vehemently backed peace with France, and whom he had hitherto ignored: Warwick and his brother George Neville.

Suddenly, Edward seemed to wake up to the potency of the Neville brothers on the international stage and to their popular appeal back home: the 'hearts my lords hath gotten', as one correspondent put it. Both noblemen were once again treated to the king's closest attentions. Seen regularly at court and in Edward's chamber, they were even spotted talking amicably with the lords they loathed most, Rivers and Herbert. It was suggested that George Neville would soon be restored to the chancellorship from which Edward had sacked him some eighteen months previously. Edward seemed satisfied that this dose of royal charm had done the trick, dissolving the rancour and rivalries that had built up in the last months and years: that bygones were now bygones. He imagined that the Nevilles, back in the sun of his grace, felt the same.[30]

But as Edward stretched out one hand in conciliation, he punished with the other. That November, riding into various counties, detachments of his household men made a slew of arrests. Among those detained was the donnish figure of Ralph Makerell, one of Margaret of Anjou's close advisers, who was intercepted making his way secretly back to his native Suffolk to establish contact with the circle of plotters in England. In Wiltshire, two young lords were detained: Sir Thomas Hungerford and Henry Courtenay, heir to the earldom of Devon. Both had strong Lancastrian connections. Hungerford's father had been executed back in 1464; Courtenay's younger brother was in Flanders where, along with his Beaufort cousins, he was being funded by Charles the Bold. Accused of plotting with the exiled Lancastrians, the pair were taken to Salisbury and imprisoned, pending trial. So too was the twenty-six-year-old John de Vere, earl of Oxford, whose father and older brother had been convicted and executed back in 1462. Like Hungerford and Courtenay, Oxford's assimilation into the Yorkist regime had been thought complete – but, in the febrile atmosphere, his Lancastrian associations came under fresh scrutiny. Brought into the Tower, Oxford quickly folded under interrogation and 'confessed much thing'. Armed with a fresh list of names, royal agents rounded up more Lancastrian sympathizers: regional big men like the East Anglian knight Sir John Marney, and smaller fry like the London skinner Richard Steres and two esquires, John Poynings and William Alford, who had accompanied Margaret of York to Flanders the previous July and, while there, had allegedly been in 'familiar communication' with Edmund Beaufort and his men.[31]

With a slew of treason trials pending, Edward appointed a new constable of England to judge them. John Tiptoft was unavailable, having been sent to Ireland to sniff out suspect officials and reimpose English control in the volatile province. There, he had produced immediate and characteristic results. After condemning his predecessor, the earl of Desmond, to death for 'horrible treasons', Tiptoft took custody of the dead earl's two young sons, whom he was said to have used with 'extreme cruelty' before eventually having them beheaded: in his bewilderment the older of the boys, who had just turned thirteen, told the executioner to avoid a sore on his neck.[32] Despite widespread disgust at the killings, and his own vexation at the death of Desmond, a man he liked, Edward nonetheless left Tiptoft in Ireland to get on with the job. In his absence, the king's choice of constable was predictable – a man who, at the forefront of royal counter-insurgency, was scaling evergreater heights in Edward's favour, his father-in-law Rivers.

Rivers was soon in business. As the round-ups continued, Steres and his accomplices were duly found guilty of treason, dragged through London's streets and beheaded on Tower Hill. Londoners recorded Steres' execution with particular regret: he had, after all, been 'one of the cunningest players at the tennis in England'.[33]

Some days later, on 9 December, fifteen miles or so northeast of London at the Essex town of Waltham Abbey, three lords and their retinues convened: Warwick, Clarence and John Talbot, earl of Shrewsbury, another nobleman harbouring resentments against the Yorkist establishment.[34] There, the three lords put their signatures to a new set of ordinances for the 'rule and guiding' of Clarence's household. On the face of it, there was nothing remarkable about Clarence drawing up a new set of domestic regulations. Such ordinances, however, tended to be produced in response to specific contexts; here, the context leaped out of the document's wording.[35]

After a typical preamble, with its exhortations to piety, came several clauses with more than usual emphasis on conduct. Clarence's household men were exhorted to avoid 'vicious rule and suspected places' and to restrain from 'seditious language, variances, dissensions, debates and affrays'. This tone of admonition ran throughout the ordinance. Servants should 'break no doors nor windows, nor pick locks, by night or by day' to try and gain access to the duke's goods. The household's porters, who guarded the house gates, should be particularly diligent in ensuring that no foodstuffs, silver plate, pewter vessels, 'nor none other stuff of the said household, be embezzled out'.

While it was customary for household directives to instruct servants to be alert to indiscipline and deviant behaviour, the extent to which this point was laboured suggested that such behaviour was in fact prevalent in Clarence's establishment. Clarence appeared either unable or disinclined to exert control over his men. What was more, this 'misgovernance', as the ordinance noted, was evident not just 'within the duke's court', but 'without'.

Given the current state of emergency, with Edward's agents alert to any hint of careless talk and indiscipline, and royal spies clearly moving within noblemen's houses, somebody had decided that Clarence's establishment urgently needed taking in hand. That somebody was Warwick.

The ordinance also revealed something else. As befitted the foremost nobleman in the land, it made exceptionally generous provision for Clarence's household: from spices and exotic fruits – 'Pepper, Saffron, Ginger, Cloves, Cinnamon, Nutmeg, Dates, Licorice, Sugar, Raisins and currants, figs' – to Clarence's barge with its master and seventeen rowers, and the ninety-three horses in his stables. It also itemized £2,820 17s 8d on yearly wages to his 299 staff and fees to others, a staggering figure which nevertheless excluded sweeteners paid to 'lords, ladies, knights, and learned counsel and others'. With Edward's anti-retaining legislation of the previous May explicitly banning the recruiting of anyone other than household 'servants, officers, or men learned in the law', Clarence had simply expanded his household to accommodate extra men – not to mention the catch-all 'others' to whom he was distributing rewards.[36] Besides the borderline illegality of his actions, his ordinance vastly overbudgeted.

Clarence's annual income was some £3,400 – a very hefty sum but, following Edward's clawing back of lands in his act of resumption the previous year, substantially below the amount that had originally been intended for him. Yet his yearly expenditure, as laid out in the ordinance, came to £4,505 15s 10¾d. As well as emphasizing security and strict discipline, then, the ordinances set out details of Clarence's expanded retinue and a household budget that, given the massive gap between income and expenditure, clearly anticipated some change in the duke's financial circumstances. That December, anybody look-ing through the ordinances might have gained the impression that Clarence and Warwick were making plans for such a change in those circumstances – and, in cracking down on loose talk and indiscipline among his household servants, were keen to avoid any unwanted attention.[37]

In January 1469 the compliant earl of Oxford was released from the Tower, with sureties imposed for his future good behaviour. The others were not so lucky. At Salisbury, a high-profile commission assembled in the king's presence to charge Hungerford and Courtenay, the two lords arrested the previous November. Among the commis-sioners were the king's brother-in-law Anthony Woodville and the Devon nobleman Humphrey, Lord Stafford, a loyal Yorkist; backing Stafford in his local turf war against his Courtenay rivals, Edward was building him up to become the king's point man in the west country, just as Herbert had become the king's proxy in Wales. Head-ing the commission was the king's youngest brother Richard.[38]

Richard had just turned sixteen. Though the age of majority was twenty-one, children born to rule were often handed active responsi-bility well before then, just as Clarence had been: Clarence, indeed, had come into his inheritance at the age Richard was now. Richard's progress had been altogether more low-key than that of his brother: after all, he wasn't Edward's heir presumptive. Through adoles-cence, he had gradually emerged from the cocoon of childhood under Warwick's guidance, watching and absorbing the way his great older cousin commanded, governed and projected his power, and putting his schoolroom education to use as he started to comport himself in the adult world. At fourteen, Richard was cutting his teeth on legal commissions in York, where his active engagement was remarked upon, and appreciated: indeed, when the city had sent presents of red wine to Warwick and Richard, Richard's was the larger. It was high time, Edward thought, for Richard to be allowed to wield royal power and authority on his behalf.

Nonetheless, Richard's role in the trial of Hungerford and Courtenay was more or less a formality. The pair were charged with treason, on scant evidence. A cowed, intimidated jury returned its guilty verdict under the gaze of the king himself, who had journeyed down to Salisbury to ensure justice was done. Dragged west through the city streets to the outlying village of Bemerton, the two noblemen were put through the full ritual horror of a traitor's execution: hanged, cut down and eviscerated while still conscious, then beheaded. Some laid the blame for Courtenay's judicial murder squarely at the feet of his rival Stafford, who had his eye on the Courtenay earldom of Devon – which, months later, Edward duly handed him.[39]

With this rash of arrests and exemplary punishments, Edward and his agents seemed to believe they had grubbed up the plot that had taken root the previous spring. The clouds of suspicion and terror started to dissipate; the sun came out. Edward, once more, allowed himself to relax.

At Westminster Palace, Elizabeth Woodville gave birth to her second daughter, named Cecily, after her mother-in-law. Edward and his friends rejoiced enthusiastically with the help of two barrels of hippocras and a butt of Gascon wine laid in for the occasion – 'though', reported one Milanese correspondent from London, 'they would have preferred a son'.[40]

As he celebrated, Edward entertained ambassadors from Charles the Bold – who, as his brand new treaty with Louis XI collapsed, quickly rediscovered his love for his English brother-in-law – and Francis of Brittany, whose ambassador arrived sheepishly in London with a gift of £1,000 in cash and a renewed appeal for English military backing against France. As far as a gratified Edward was concerned, his anti-French coalition was back on. Perhaps more surprising, his patched-up relationship with the earl of Warwick also seemed to be holding together.

Warwick, indeed, even proved emollient, to the extent that Edward went so far as to trust him to maintain diplomatic relations with Burgundy. In Calais from mid-March, Warwick provided letters of safe conduct for the Burgundian ambassadors' onward travel to England and even swallowed his distaste for Charles the Bold, meeting with him on three separate occasions. There was, it was true, the odd moment of friction – at one point Warwick and his retinue tried to march into Charles's court armed, and were refused entry until the earl agreed to give up his sword – but by and large, things went smoothly. That May, Warwick was among the applauding guests in St George's Chapel at Windsor, as Edward received the prestigious Burgundian Order of the Golden Fleece. It was an honour Edward promptly reciprocated, admitting Charles to the Order of the Garter.[41]

Warwick knew perfectly well what was meant by these courtesies of ritual brotherhood. The Garter had been founded by Edward III with the express intention of helping recover the French crown to which he laid claim. No sooner had Charles received his garter than, in a blatant act of provocation against France, he was publicly wearing it.[42] Charles's newfound goodwill towards Edward seemed more committed than before: he expressed an eagerness to restart talks on the cloth embargo, and offered to broker English discussions with the Hanse, relations with whom were almost non-existent after Edward's ham-fisted aggression the previous summer. All of which Warwick seemed to accept without murmur. He was even prepared to do a little anti-French sabre-rattling of his own, his fleet roaming the western reaches of the Channel and France's Atlantic seaboard, provoking panicked rumours in France of English piracy and raids.

To Edward, it looked as though he had finally convinced the Nevilles of the vision that he had unfolded to Parliament a year previously. Back at the heart of Edward's government, Warwick seemed demurely accepting of his new status: no longer a first among equals but taking his place alongside the 'queen's blood' and those, like Herbert, whose new closeness to the king had punctured Warwick's former pre-eminence. The vicious rumours of the past years, which had sustained the hostility between the tight group around Edward and circles close to Warwick, seemed to dry up.

One hot day late that spring, a man turned up at court wearing a pair of waders 'as long as they might be' and clutching a spiked wooden staff. Recognized as a jester favoured by the king, he was admitted and brought to Edward, who asked what was going on with the outfit. The jester replied that he had been travelling through many regions of England, and wherever he went 'the Rivers were so high that I could scarcely escape through them'. As gags went, it was laboured: it was, explained one chronicler unnecessarily, about 'the great rule that the lord Rivers and his blood' had in the kingdom. Edward's response was to laugh.[43] At that moment the king seemed supremely, sprawlingly at ease, apparently as unbothered by the subtext of the joke as he was by the reports of popular uprisings that had been coming out of the northeast over the past couple of months.

In Yorkshire that April insurgency had broken out, led by a shadowy captain calling himself 'Robin of Redesdale'. It was a resonant name. The Northumbrian valley of Redesdale had a centuries-old reputation as a refuge for outlaws, reinforced in recent years by its use as a base for Lancastrian insurgents. The name Robin needed no explanation: stories of the outlaw and his deeds, resisting the evil councillors who had led their king astray and repressed his impoverished people, circulated widely. He was a popular hero, a righter of wrongs: or, as the insurgent captain's other *nom de guerre* put it, 'Robin Mend-All'.

A constant presence in the northeast, Warwick's brother John Neville reacted with typical decisiveness, mustering a large force of men 'to suppress Robin of Redesdale and other enemies of the kingdom'. Neville's uncompromising reputation went before him. The rebels melted away.

Shortly after, violence erupted again, some seventy-five miles away in Yorkshire's East Riding, led by a man who took his name from the coastal flatlands, 'Robin of Holderness'. This time, the uprising's proximate cause was clearer: local discontent at a regional tax levied by St Leonard's Hospital in York which, despite vocal protests the previous year, Edward had backed. Economic and political grievances mingled. The area was a hotbed of support for the pro-Lancastrian Percy family, whose heir, the twenty-one-year-old Henry Percy, was securely in the wardship of William Herbert away in south Wales: the insurgents wanted him restored as earl of Northumberland in place of the man who had supplanted him, John Neville. Late in May, some fifteen thousand strong, they reached the gates of York before Neville and his men materialized. There, after a 'long fight', Robin of Holderness was captured and beheaded.[44]

Edward ordered a judicial commission – headed by his brothers and an assortment of nobles including Warwick, Rivers and Hastings – to investigate the disturbances. Given the scale of the insurrection he also decided, reluctantly, to head north himself. Early in June 1469, mustering troops and having ordered the Great Wardrobe to supply 'banners, standards and coat armours', fifteen hundred jackets in the Yorkist blue and mulberry 'and such other stuff for the field', Edward set off, together with Richard of Gloucester and his Woodville in-laws: Rivers, Anthony Woodville and his younger brother Sir John. He was comfortable enough to schedule in a diversionary loop, a pilgrimage through East Anglia to the great north Norfolk shrine of Walsingham, during which he would recruit additional armed forces for his northern operation.

The pilgrimage was convivial and boozy. After a stopover at George Neville's Hertfordshire manor of The More, the king – waved off by the archbishop with an assurance of military help for his northern campaign – weaved his way hazily through Suffolk and Norfolk. At Norwich, the hospitality was so good that Edward pronounced himself 'well content' and promised to be back again 'hastily'. At the Lincolnshire town of Crowland, he went on a walkabout, praising its buildings and the fine triangular stone bridge spanning the two rivers that met there, and soaking up the adulation from well-drilled locals. Finally, he turned south to Fotheringhay, where Elizabeth was waiting for him and where he mustered more troops. A week later, he led his army north. In the second week of July he reached Newark.[45] There, the news of what faced him was stark.

Robin of Redesdale's uprising had reignited. An insurgent army, reportedly three times the size of Edward's, was now heading rapidly south. Scribbling orders for more troops to be raised, his tone now suddenly urgent, the king retreated twenty miles southwest for the greater security and strategic position of Nottingham Castle. Soon, he hoped, he would be joined by William Herbert's formidable Welshmen and the west-country archers of Humphrey Stafford, the new earl of Devon. It wasn't just the size of this 'great insurrection' that had suddenly made Edward sober up, but its nature.

The uprising had exploded out of Richmondshire, a region dominated by Warwick's fortress of Middleham and Clarence's lordship of Richmond. Talk had it that 'Robin' himself was Sir John Conyers, Warwick's household steward at Middleham and the former sheriff of Yorkshire: a man with an intimate knowledge of the region, its security networks, its people and their grievances. Other 'captains' in Robin's ranks were members of the extended Neville family.[46] This grassroots insurgency had been co-opted by Warwick and Clarence. Together, they were now driving it directly against Edward and his regime.

For months, Warwick and George Neville had presented themselves as Edward's dutiful subjects, happy to accept their place in the new order of things. Clarence had been equally decorous; so too had his household, brought into line by the ordinances of the previous December. Under the crust of observed formalities and protocols, however, the Nevilles stewed with resentment against an accumulation of slights, real and imagined. As Warwick saw it, his diminished standing with the king had had serious consequences. Edward, ignoring his counsel, had staggered from one disastrous piece of policy-making to the next, with serious consequences for England's well-being and security – not to mention those of Warwick himself. Seen another way, Warwick and George Neville were simply out of season. Edward had moved beyond them. Many of those around the king had adjusted to the new dispensation, but Warwick and his brother had not. Neither had Clarence.

Edward had gone out of his way to build Clarence up, to transform him into one of the mightiest nobles in the land. Yet Clarence, encouraged by Warwick, had come to fixate on his putative marriage to the earl's daughter Isabel as a way of insuring himself against fluctuations in the king's favour. In Clarence's eyes, it was not Edward – still contemptuously dismissive of the match – but his Neville cousins who had demonstrated a commitment to their shared future: that March, George Neville's tireless lobbying in the Roman Curia had finally borne fruit, Pope Paul II authorizing the dispensation for Clarence and Isabel to marry. Not that Edward's malcontent brother had needed much grooming. Whether or not Clarence was convinced by the need to take action for the good of the kingdom – and Warwick was rarely less than persuasive – he itched to do something for himself. Or, as one anonymous contemporary put it, he had 'a mind too conscious of a daring deed'.[47]

That June, as Edward was making his bibulous way through East Anglia, Warwick was at the Kentish port of Sandwich to inspect his fleet. There, he was joined by George Neville and Clarence – and, briefly, Cecily duchess of York who, perhaps with a mother's intuition, went to check up on her wilful son.[48] Over the following weeks, Warwick and Clarence started mobilizing their forces across the country, ostensibly to 'join the king in the north'. Then, with the papal dispensation in hand, they went public with their marriage plans, in defiance of Edward. On 4 July, joined by the Nevilles' brother-in-law John de Vere, earl of Oxford, whose chastening experience at the hands of Edward's interrogators the previous winter had only hardened his resolve against the regime, they crossed to Calais.

A week later, in Calais Castle, Clarence and Isabel Neville were married by Archbishop George Neville in a wedding that effectively made Clarence Warwick's heir. Wandering around Calais at the time was the Burgundian chronicler Jean de Wavrin, who had turned up at Warwick's vague invitation, hoping the earl would put him in touch with someone who could supply him with reliable sources for the history of England he was writing. Warwick's mind, Wavrin discovered, was elsewhere and his questions 'barely answered': the earl packed him off with the gift of a 'fine horse' and told him to come back in a couple of months. As far as Wavrin could see, the wedding venue was deserted; the festivities themselves, clearly cobbled together, lasted barely two days. There were, he thought, other 'big things' going on.[49]

The day after the wedding, Clarence, Warwick and George Neville issued a proclamation. It consisted of an open letter, signed by all three, to which was affixed the wax seals of their signets; and a petition which, they claimed, had been sent them by representatives of the king's 'true and faithful commons'. Identifying a group of 'seditious persons' at the heart of Edward's regime whose 'covetous rule and guiding' had led the king astray and the country into chaos for their own 'singular lucre and enriching of themselves and their blood', the commons called 'piteously' on the three lords to intercede with the king on their behalf with a view to reforming government: something that would not only be to the king's 'honour and profit', but to the benefit of the 'common weal' of England.

The petition itself painted a picture of misrule that would have been instantly familiar to anybody acquainted with the events of the previous two decades. In fact, the petition declared with menace, the situation that now faced England was similar to crises that had 'fell in this land' during the reigns of Edward II, Richard II and Henry VI, 'to the destruction of them'. For all that, the petition was also specific, both in its identification of the 'seditious persons' in question, and the charges laid at their door.

The named culprits were the queen's father Lord Rivers, his wife Jacquetta and their first-born son Anthony Woodville; 'Sir William Herbert' – pointedly not referred to by his newly acquired title of earl of Pembroke – and the new earl of Devon, Humphrey Stafford; the queen's younger brother Sir John Woodville 'and all his brethren'; their brother-in-law Lord Audeley; and, inevitably, Sir John Fogge, who with Rivers had led Edward's counter-insurgency operation the previous year.

This cabal, the petition asserted, had inveigled Edward to grant away to them much of the vast wealth that he had inherited on his accession, grants that, as well as being out of all proportion to the recipients' 'deserts and degrees', had plunged the king into poverty. They had been behind the recoinage of five years previously, persuading Edward to 'change his most rich coin'; behind the endless financial impositions on his subjects, from taxes to borrowing without repayment; behind, too, the siphoning off of papal taxes for the crusade 'without repayment of our said holy father'; and behind, among other things, the spike in violent crime of recent years, and the accusations of treason against anybody to whom they bore any 'evil will' – with the result that people of all ranks went in dread, uncertain of the security of their 'life, livelihood or goods'.

The charges were a skilful blending of genuine and confected grievances. There could be no doubt about Edward's appropriation of papal taxes, nor about his misleading of Parliament: indeed, in calling on him to carry out an urgent programme of financial reform, the manifesto quoted back at Edward the failed promises that he had made 'with his own mouth to us'. While the recoinage had been a success, the massive profits made by Edward and those involved in the process added to the widespread suspicion that something fishy was going on. Throughout the manifesto, individual voices seemed to surface: Warwick's indignation over his exclusion from the king's 'secret council'; Clarence's resentment about his 'impoverishment', and Edward's failure to give him 'sufficient livelihood or goods'. The most prominent of all the charges – and the catalyst for all the other wrongs – was, the petition stated, Edward's 'estrangement of the true lords of his blood'. If the commons' manifesto seemed as though it might have been written by Warwick, Clarence and George Neville themselves, it probably was.[50]

The three lords' proposed solution was drawn straight from the Yorkist playbook of the 1450s. Their proclamation was sent to potential supporters throughout England, urging them to mobilize with as many armed men as possible, and to join the trio as they went to try and make Edward see sense: a threatening deputation that could only end in bloodshed. The parallels with Edward and Warwick's return from exile in 1460 were also evident in what followed. Crossing back from Calais, the lords advanced through Kent towards London. There, the city gates were opened and the civic authorities, wary of Warwick's popularity with the commons, had a reluctant whip-round, lending the rebels £1,000. They then headed north out of the city, to link up with Robin of Redesdale's insurgents and to intercept the isolated Edward before Herbert's Welshmen and Stafford's west-countrymen could join the king.[51]

Complacent and lethargic, Edward had been caught out. Reading the commons' manifesto, a copy of which had been obtained and handed to him, his first act was to send the Woodvilles, now clearly public enemies, away from the region for their own safety. Rivers and his second son Sir John Woodville were dispatched to the safety of William Herbert's castle of Chepstow in south Wales; Anthony Woodville to his lands in Norfolk, on the other side of the country. With the latter, perhaps trying to mobilize more troops, Edward sent his youngest brother Richard.[52] He then dispatched the ever-reliable Thomas Montgomery with three letters to Clarence, Warwick and George Neville, stating that he could not believe the rumours of their treachery, that they would be 'right welcome' to him, and urging them to listen to what Montgomery had to say. Edward's astonishment was genuine. He made his way slowly south, hoping to rendezvous with Herbert and Stafford as they rode out of the southwest with reinforcements.

In the second half of July, Sir John Paston – like many in England – received two letters within days of each other. The first was from 'his especial true-hearted friend' the earl of Oxford, who asked Paston to supply three sets of horse-armour 'in haste', adding – with a meaningful nod to Paston's allegiance – 'I trust to God we shall do right well, who preserve you'. The second letter, from Edward, contained a double validation of his royal authority: signed with his monogram and sealed with his signet. Urgently, Edward ordered Paston to gather as many armed men as he could, and to meet the king at Doncaster, in order to fight the king's 'enemies, traitors and rebels'. Faced with this agonizing demand on his loyalty, Paston's instinct was probably to lie low, just as his father had done almost ten years before during the chaotic sequence of battles that had brought Edward to power.[53] But by the time Edward's letter reached him, it didn't matter anyway.

9

The Matter Quickeneth

That July William Herbert led his forces purposefully out of south Wales to put down Robin of Redesdale's renewed insurgency. He and his men were bullish. Feared across England, their confidence was fuelled by a Welsh prophetic tradition that foretold their extermination of the English oppressors. Notwithstanding his own place at the heart of the English royal establishment, it was a narrative that Herbert had skilfully cultivated. So too had Edward, whose Mortimer blood made him, as one bard put it, a 'kingly Welshman': the deliverer who would set their nation free. Besides, in the words of one Welsh poet, the northerners were 'a bunch of churls', a common rabble whose annihilation Jesus Christ himself would be happy to excuse.[1]

Reaching the Cotswolds, Herbert rendezvoused with Humphrey Stafford, earl of Devon. Together, Herbert's Welsh cavalry and Stafford's west-country infantrymen and archers were a formidable proposition. Nevertheless, on 24 July, as they made their way towards Northampton, an advance force clashed with a contingent of Robin of Redesdale's men and came off worst. The two lords halted for the night at the Oxfordshire market town of Banbury.[2]

That evening the two nobles' harbingers, the officers responsible for billeting arrangements, both laid claim to the same inn. This trivial 'variance', compounded by a quarrel over which of the lords got to sleep with the innkeeper's daughter, became a full-blown row. Though he had arrived first, Stafford lost out; honour slighted, he left in a fury, withdrawing his forces some ten or twelve miles distant. The following day, Herbert and his Welshmen advanced out of Banbury, eager for the battle to come, and aware of the need to fight the northerners before reinforcements turned up in the shape of Warwick and Clarence. They bivouacked on high ground to the northeast of

Banbury, 'at a place called Edgecote'. In front of them, open fields sloped into the valley of the River Cherwell; beyond, to the east and south, were rolling hills, and Robin of Redesdale's army.

As dawn rose on the morning of the 26th, the northerners advanced into the river plain, their archers loosing volleys of arrows into Herbert's ranks. Lacking Stafford's firepower, the Welshmen were exposed and Herbert ordered his men quickly into close combat. Through the morning, the fighting raged around the river crossing; finally, Herbert's men forced the rebels back. There was a lull as the battered armies regrouped. Then, over the eastern hills, new troops appeared. As they approached, Herbert's Welshmen could pick out the white bear and ragged staff on their standards and catch their battle-cries carrying on the air: the rhythmic repetition of 'A Warwick. A Warwick.'

As Warwick, Clarence and their forces rode north out of London, an advance force had raced ahead under the command of the bruising Essex soldier Sir Geoffrey Gate, one of Warwick's lieutenants. Now, joining the northerners, they surged into Herbert's men. Isolated, confronted by what they thought was the earl of Warwick's main army, they broke ranks and fled. In the carnage that followed, as many as two thousand Welshmen were killed.[3]

In Wales the news of Edgecote was greeted as a national catastrophe, a battle to end all fighting. The sense of apocalypse was intensified by weeks of 'savage weather', torrential rain and wind that wrecked harvests. Among the survivors who remembered the battle's horrors was Herbert's ward, the twelve-year-old Lancastrian Henry Tudor, who had been led to safety by the Shropshire knight Sir Richard Corbet. Edgecote would endure long in the Welsh memory. In the years and decades to come, it would become a byword for resentment against the English – in particular, 'northernmen'.[4]

What happened next was a frightening settling of scores, one which, in its concentrated fury and lack of due process, recalled the bloodletting of the 1450s. The reforming petition that Warwick and Clarence had issued shortly before Edgecote, it transpired, was also a hitlist. Now, in the battle's aftermath, the two lords dispatched squads of men to hunt down their targets. The first to be captured was Herbert. He was taken the twenty or so miles to Northampton, where Warwick,

Clarence and George Neville had arrived, to be tried. Even by the standards of recent years, their judgment was savage – and, given their complaints about Edward's indiscriminate accusations of treason, darkly ironic. But then, Herbert's beheading had nothing to do with the law, and everything to do with revenge.[5]

For one Welsh poet the execution of Herbert, Edward's 'masterlock' in Wales, was the moment his nation died. Nevertheless, Herbert's reputation as a cruel and arrogant man, a 'heavy lord', also went before him – something he had seemed to acknowledge in the will he made before his execution, when he asked for his body to be sent home quickly and secretly, to avoid abuse. People joked that his soul was past praying for.[6] As far as Warwick and Clarence were concerned, though, Herbert's judicial murder was only the start.

Other targets on their list were soon run to ground. Lord Rivers and his second son Sir John Woodville, fleeing Herbert's castle at Chepstow, were tracked down hiding in the thick woodlands of the Forest of Dean. Brought to Coventry, they were summarily executed. Five days later Humphrey Stafford, earl of Devon, whose monumental sulk before the battle at Edgecote had had such catastrophic consequences, was arrested and beheaded at the Somerset town of Bridgwater. Across the country in Norwich, Rivers' oldest son Anthony Woodville was detained in a city inn by local authorities acting on the orders of the king – or rather, of Warwick and Clarence, who now held the great seal. Woodville knew what awaited him. On the morning of Thursday 25 August, he slipped past his captors and disappeared.[7]

Meanwhile, Edward was moving south from Nottingham. He seemed to have no sources of reliable intelligence: days after Edgecote, he was apparently oblivious to the disaster that had taken place. As news finally reached him, and his hastily raised troops started to flee, the reality of the situation set in. Trying to swerve the rebel forces to the east, the king was finally run to ground by George Neville and a detachment of cavalry at Warwick's Buckinghamshire manor of Olney. He was taken north to Warwick's base at Middleham and imprisoned there.[8]

As Warwick and Clarence continued their savage round of reprisals, tearing down the new edifice of Yorkist power that Edward had been building for the past five years since his marriage to Elizabeth, they also started to undermine the foundations on which it was built.

That August, a messenger dismounted at Warwick Castle, where the rebel lords had based themselves. He brought disturbing allegations against the Woodvilles, from the influential Northamptonshire gentleman and former sheriff of the county Thomas Wake. A long-standing agent of Warwick's, Wake had married the earl's troubled, magnetic young kinswoman Margaret Lucy, who, it was rumoured, had slept with Edward.[9] Based at Blisworth, a short ride from the Woodville home of Grafton Regis, Wake was well placed to keep an eye on the activities of the queen's family. That summer, he had been involved in the fast-moving events on Warwick's side, turning out to fight at Edgecote. There, his son was killed. If he hadn't liked his aggrandizing Woodville neighbours particularly much beforehand, now Wake hated them: still raw with grief, he had been in the pack that had hunted down Rivers. And in the days after the battle he had come across a curious artefact, which he now sent to Warwick. It was a little lead figure of an armed man 'the length of a man's finger', which had been deliberately snapped in two, then bound together with wire.

This figurine, Wake claimed, was modelled to resemble Warwick himself. It had been made by the queen's mother Jacquetta, 'to use with witchcraft and sorcery' in order to bring about Warwick's death. Wake also had in his possession two more lead dolls representing Edward and Elizabeth, with which, so he alleged, Jacquetta had bewitched the king into his marriage.[10]

Back in 1464, the complaints about Elizabeth's suitability as a royal bride had quickly faded as people adjusted to the new reality. But with the tensions of recent years, and especially in the aftermath of Sir Thomas Cook's trial, they had resurfaced with a fresh malevolence. Accusations of witchcraft, however, were of a different order of seriousness. They could, and did, destroy even the greatest families: some quarter-century earlier, Eleanor Cobham, the wife of Henry VI's uncle Humphrey duke of Gloucester, had been sentenced to life imprisonment for 'treasonable necromancy', a conviction which had set in motion Gloucester's own downfall. Now, Wake was effectively asserting that Edward and Elizabeth's marriage was founded on nothing more substantial than an act of sorcery.

Wake's evidence was itself flimsy. His story was embellished around a few lead dolls that, discovered a couple of miles from the Woodville home of Grafton Regis, had been put on display merely as interesting found objects in the village of Stoke Bruerne. Nevertheless, it dovetailed nicely with the rebel lords' narrative – Jacquetta, after all, had the dubious distinction of being the only woman on Warwick and Clarence's roster of seditious persons – and cohered perfectly with their aims: nothing less than the total destruction of the queen's family.[11]

It hardly mattered that the allegations themselves didn't stand up. As Warwick knew perfectly well, the truth of the matter was irrelevant: it was the story that counted. Once rumours of witchcraft began to stick to Jacquetta and Elizabeth, there would be no washing them away. In the febrile atmosphere that August the rumours spread like a contagion. Soon, the 'common noise and slander' of Jacquetta's witchcraft had seeded itself through a 'great part of the realm'.[12]

Writing from an edgy London late that summer a Milanese envoy, Luchino Dalleghiexia, reported that the queen was still in the city. Scared for her own safety and that of her children, she was keeping 'scant state', a low profile. People were talking openly about how the queen's family had monopolized Edward's government, about how it was all the fault of Elizabeth, 'a widow of quite low birth', who had seized with both hands the chance given her by a bewitched king and who since her coronation had been tireless in her efforts 'to aggrandize her relations'.

It was clear where Dalleghiexia – who by his own admission was fairly clueless on English affairs – was getting much of his information: the earl of Warwick, 'astute as Ulysses'. With many of their political opponents eliminated, he continued, Warwick and Clarence were on to the next stage of their plan, to establish themselves as effective rulers of England, and had summoned a parliament in order to 'arrange the government' accordingly.[13] If this seemed like 1460 all over again, there were whispers of an even more radical change.

Warwick wasted no time updating his ally Louis XI. On 8 August, at his Loire chateau of Amboise, Louis held one of his regular private audiences with the latest Milanese ambassador to France, Sforza de Bettini. He was practically capering with joy.

In a letter to Louis, Warwick had apparently declared that he no longer believed Edward IV to have any right to the throne of England – because, Warwick had discovered, Edward was born 'a bastard'. He wasn't Richard of York's son at all, but the product of an affair of Cecily duchess of York, conceived while her husband had been away fighting the French. As a result, the crown of England didn't belong to Edward. The rightful king was his younger, true-born brother, the duke of Clarence.[14]

Warwick, of course, had form in this regard. Ten years earlier, he had used the same tactics against Margaret of Anjou and her son, the rumours of whose illegitimacy had been virulently effective. Now Warwick was prepared to do the same to Edward, in order to put his new son-in-law Clarence on the throne – and to resume his own position at the king's shoulder, his pre-eminence restored. But whatever Warwick told Louis, back in England any talk of making Clarence king was kept firmly under wraps.

While Warwick and Clarence commanded strong support on the streets, there was a rather more sceptical mood in the council chamber. Alarmed by the extreme violence of recent weeks, councillors instinctively loyal to the status quo and the rule of law were also perplexed about the two lords' motives. Having claimed to want to reform government, Warwick and Clarence had then locked the king up. Not only was it unclear on whose authority they were now acting, but they were struggling to control the popular energies they had unleashed against the regime. Disorder spread with news of Edward's imprisonment as people took the law into their own hands. Across the country, local vendettas blazed into life: insurgency spread unchecked in the northeast; in London, an epidemic of rioting and looting spread through the city.

Warwick and Clarence struggled to restore order. When they tried to raise troops, people ignored them, knowing perfectly well the orders hadn't come from Edward. In London, the mayor read out a letter from Charles the Bold, urging citizens to remain loyal to Edward. It was a message that now carried some weight given that Charles, with happy timing, had finally lifted the detested trade embargo on English cloth just weeks before. For Charles, the prospect of Warwick gaining power was worrying. England's elites agreed. Whether or not there was a case for reform, Warwick and Clarence's bid to control the government was met with a general shaking of heads: 'everyone', wrote Dalleghiexia, 'is of the opinion that it would be better not'.[15] The two lords bowed to the inevitable.

At Middleham Castle, sometime in early September, a month or so after his capture, Edward 'found his freedom': as if, somehow, all the doors had been quietly opened. He rode unhurriedly to York, hunting as he went. His appearance there was galvanizing. The troops that Warwick had found it so hard to mobilize were now raised and the northern insurgency extinguished, its leaders captured and executed. Progressing south, the king was joined by his loyal noblemen: men like his uncle Henry Bourchier, earl of Essex; Hastings, unswerving as ever; and Warwick's brother John Neville, earl of Northumberland, who – whether or not he had been tempted to join the rebel lords – had remained faithful to Edward. Among them, too, was the king's youngest brother Richard.[16]

In mid October Edward rode into London to an extravagant corporate welcome. Holding court at the bishop of London's palace the king seemed his usual expansive self, back at the centre of his universe, order restored. According to Sir John Paston, he had nothing but 'good language' for Clarence, Warwick, George Neville and the earl of Oxford, 'saying that they be his best friends'. However, Paston added meaningfully, the king's household men 'have other language'; in the privacy of the royal apartments, among Edward's closest servants, the animosity ran deep.

Nobody mentioned the reaction of Queen Elizabeth. She had emerged from the terrifying ordeal of the previous months, along with her surviving relatives, to resume her place at Edward's side, doubtless as poised as ever. In any case, she kept her head down, and her thoughts on Warwick's and Clarence's attempt to exterminate her family to herself.

There was, too, an edge to Edward's own conciliation. When George Neville and Oxford set out eagerly for court, his response was sharp: 'they should come when he sent for them', and not before.[17]

Whatever the private hatreds, a process of reconciliation was urgently needed. With the government and country destabilized and continued 'murmuring and doubtfulness' over Edward's ability to rule, the king's council stressed to him the overriding importance of resolving this 'deadly division' and restoring some semblance of unity. As Edward mobilized forces to deal with the aftershocks of the insurgency, representatives shuttled between the king and the rebel lords. Whether either side had any real appetite for peace remained to be seen, but for the sake of his kingdom, Edward had to try.[18] As talks continued, he set about rearranging his battered and bloodied government. Casting around for loyal, reliable noblemen, he settled on his youngest brother Richard, now seventeen years old.

Since the beginning of the year, Edward and Richard had spent prolonged periods in each other's company: during the trials of Lancastrian rebels in January; on progress through East Anglia, before the disaster of Edgecote; and that autumn, following Edward's release from captivity, when Richard had been quickly at his brother's side. Where Clarence had been found horribly lacking, Edward now reached for his other brother, in whose loyalty, ability and shared blood he found he could trust. Thanks to Clarence's volatility, Richard was now transformed in the king's eyes: no longer an afterthought, but a cornerstone of the reconstituted Yorkist regime, a royal duke deserving of power. Accordingly, Edward handed him the crucial role of constable of England.

In giving Richard the constableship, a role that carried with it the quasi-regal power to try and convict people for treason, Edward passed over two other candidates for this most politically delicate of posts: John Tiptoft, still away in Ireland; and Anthony Woodville, in theory entitled to the office that had been previously held by his father Rivers – though his appointment would hardly have helped engender a new spirit of conciliation. Richard, untainted by the rivalries of recent years, was a fresh start. Besides which, he clearly wanted the job.[19]

Richard's education had prepared him well. He was a keen student, constantly returning to the books that he kept by him, poring over the precepts laid out in staple texts like Egidio Colonna's *De Regimine Principum, On the Government of Princes* – his copy of which was especially dear to him, having previously belonged to his father. There was, indeed, something unbending in Richard's attitude to princely virtues and the zeal with which he sought to give them expression. In a directive to the officers of arms over which, as constable, he had jurisdiction, his language had a moralistic clarity. Heralds were to avoid 'openly slandered and defamed places and persons'; they were also to report to their superiors any colleagues who, they heard, had indulged in 'ungodly demeanour or slandering ways': the culprits would have to answer for their behaviour before Richard himself, and to accept 'punishment according to their deserts'.[20]

A certain inflexibility in Richard was hardly surprising. After all, he had barely known a time when England hadn't been at war with itself. For him, the binding forces of loyalty and obedience to the law, and the enforcement of the king's justice, were of supreme importance. Earlier that year, as judge in the treason trials of Hungerford and Courtenay, he had unblinkingly handed down the harshest of sentences. Now, he embraced the constable's judicial role.[21]

Richard's palpable commitment to the king's laws made him an ideal candidate to plug one of the gaping holes left by that summer's violence. In Wales, Herbert's beheading had been followed by an immediate upsurge in disorder. Edward needed somebody to reimpose control in the region, and Herbert's son, at barely fifteen, was hardly in a position to do so. Instead, Edward gave Richard the task of imposing control on the principality: stamping out rebellion and sedition, enforcing the law and wielding his power on the king's behalf. Richard had little local knowledge and barely any connections of his own – but, Edward judged, he had enough about him. In November, Richard left for Wales in the company of Herbert's brother-in-law William Devereux, Lord Ferrers, a hard Marcher lord who had fought at Mortimer's Cross.

After Herbert's beheading, Devereux had placed his Herefordshire manor of Weobley at the disposal of Herbert's widow, Anne, along with her daughters and one of their Lancastrian wards, the twelve-year-old Henry Tudor. The other Herbert ward, Henry Percy, was in the Tower, where Warwick had put him that summer. Aged twenty, he was on the brink of his majority. The Nevilles needed no reminding of the threat posed to their northern hegemony by this great Lancastrian claimant to the earldom of Northumberland.[22] Neither did Edward.

That autumn, as his search for a compromise with Warwick and Clarence continued, the king made fresh moves against Neville interests. Years before, Edward himself had built up the edifice of Neville power in the northeast: power that Warwick had then used to bring his regime to the brink of destruction. So, Edward decided to knock it down. His wrecking ball was Henry Percy.

Late that October, in a small chamber in Westminster Palace, Henry Percy swore an oath of allegiance to Edward, witnessed by a small knot of royal councillors including William Hastings and the archbishop of Canterbury Thomas Bourchier. In return, Percy was given his liberty. His release was seismic. Percy, everybody now knew, was to be restored to his earldom of Northumberland – with inevitable consequences for those who had profited from it: Warwick, Clarence and the earldom's current incumbent, John Neville.

Yet in removing John Neville from Northumberland, the king was breaking up one of the few pieces of his government that worked. Over the years, John Neville had been an exceptionally effective leader of counter-insurgency operations; not only that, but through the previous summer's upheavals he had remained loyal to Edward. Edward wanted John Neville to know that his future with the house of York was assured. The compensation package he received for the loss of his Northumberland earldom was correspondingly munificent: a new powerbase in the southwest, including a portfolio of lands previously belonging to the earls of Devon, and the title of marquess of Montagu. There was another, spectacular, bonus. Granting John Neville's small son George the royal dukedom of Bedford – a signal honour: the last magnate to hold the title had been Henry V's brother – Edward betrothed the boy to his oldest daughter Elizabeth. Binding the only male Neville heir into the new Yorkist line was a match that might one day see him on the throne of England. For John Neville, his northern identity bound up with the earldom that he had long desired and cherished, it was a wrench. But he seemed to accept it.[23]

So too did Warwick and Clarence. That December, after weeks of negotiations, the pair finally accepted Edward's guarantees for their security, arriving in Westminster with a 'slender crew' of soldiers. In the days that followed, Edward and the two lords were locked in 'long talk', shepherded along by the council. Over Christmas, residual antagonism gave way to seasonal goodwill. At a ceremony in the parliament chamber, Edward received Warwick and Clarence back into his grace 'and it was agreed that all disagreement should be abandoned'. Shortly after Epiphany, the reconciled lords left London.[24]

Away in France, news of the reconciliation sent Louis XI into a paroxysm of nervous rage. That February, in an audience with the Milanese ambassador Bettini, he had stamped about yelling that the English and Burgundians were coming – although, Bettini added, there wasn't much evidence to suggest an invasion was imminent. In any case, Edward had his hands full elsewhere.[25]

Through the last months of 1469 a newly alert Edward had sought to clamp down on further outbursts of regional violence, the kind of turf wars and grudges that, as Edward knew to his cost, had a habit of spiralling out of control – especially when given a helping hand by powerful noblemen with their own political agendas. The unrest in Yorkshire had spread south to Lincolnshire, where local law enforcement was overwhelmed by 'insurrections of the people'. One such riot came at the river port of Gainsborough, where a group of raiders ransacked and trashed the house of one of the region's big men, Sir Thomas Burgh, making off with 'all the goods and chattels that they might find'. Burgh was one of Edward's household knights, his master of horse, and a member of the king's council: the crown's eyes and ears in the region. The destruction of Burgh's house, on which he had lavished money, was more than just an attack on his wealth and power; it was an attack on royal authority that resonated at the heart of government.[26]

The raiders were led by Richard, Lord Welles, a Lancastrian whose father had died at Towton, and whose former pre-eminence in the region had been eclipsed by the *arriviste* Burgh. The feud between the two men had been simmering for years: Welles's attack on Gainsborough took it up a level.[27] With him was his son Sir Robert, and his two brothers-in-law, Sir Thomas Dymmock and the Gascon knight Sir Thomas Delalaunde, themselves both holders of royal office: Delalaunde, a fine jouster, had distinguished himself fighting alongside Anthony Woodville in the Smithfield jousts two years previously.

The attack on Gainsborough, moreover, sparked wider popular unrest. Burgh, who had done little to endear himself to the locals, was forced to flee the region. When Edward summoned the ringleaders to explain themselves, they refused to appear with the usual confection of excuses – Lord Welles pleading both 'want of health' and 'other business'.[28]

Throughout the first weeks of 1470 the Lincolnshire disturbances escalated. Early in February, Edward convened a council meeting in Westminster to discuss the security situation; both Warwick and Clarence were ordered to attend. Clarence didn't turn up. Warwick arrived in London to an unsettling reception. Overnight, anonymous bills had been posted across the city with lurid allegations about the two lords' continued sedition: Clarence's absence, it was said, could only be explained by the fact that he was away plotting against his brother the king.[29] Warwick took the hint, and swung into line.

With the previous summer's riots in Yorkshire constantly in mind, Edward and his council decided that the situation in Lincolnshire was serious enough to warrant royal judicial intervention. As Edward drew up plans to lead a force of men into the county 'for the suppression of our rebels and enemies', Warwick offered military aid, which Edward accepted. In another moment of reconciliation, Warwick was present when a commission investigating the virulent allegations of witchcraft brought against Edward's mother-in-law Jacquetta by Warwick's retainer Thomas Wake, reported its findings to the king's council. Jacquetta was cleared of all charges. As the council put her innocence on record, Warwick's demeanour was doubtless as unreadable as ever.[30]

Towards the end of February Warwick left London to mobilize troops for Edward's army. Before he set out, Edward appointed his 'gests', or stages of march, and confirmed with him 'the number of people he would come with to the king'. For a king to plan a campaign closely with his leading nobles was normal practice. But context was everything. Edward wanted to know precisely where Warwick would be at any given time, and who he was bringing with him. While he might have welcomed Warwick back into favour, Edward was watching him.[31]

Around this time, Sir John Paston wrote from London to his younger brother with his usual mixture of gossip, business and high politics: pointing him towards a young lady who was 'full of love';

promising him a delivery of oranges; and wonderingly describing the arrival at court of a Turkish dwarf – considerably smaller than the king's other dwarves, but with sons as tall as Edward himself. 'And', Paston added in awed tones, 'it is reported that his penis is the size of his leg.' Then, amid the fraternal ribaldry, he was suddenly sober. The king's imminent expedition to Lincolnshire, he wrote, had people worried. Talk was that Edward had assembled a vast army – the duke of Norfolk alone was said to have raised ten thousand troops – and was going to make an example of the Lincolnshire commons. The announcement that Warwick was going with Edward prompted further concern. 'Some men say his going shall do good', Paston hedged, 'and some say it doth harm.'

In Lincolnshire, there was growing anxiety. Royal commissions of the kind Edward was planning had a bloody history, and people had long memories. Such campaigns often did more harm than good; sometimes, they fuelled further trouble. Back in 1450 Jack Cade's Kentish rebellion was driven by fears that Henry VI, seeking retribution for the murder of his leading adviser the duke of Suffolk, was coming to devastate the county and turn it into a 'wild forest'. To any interested party, in Lincolnshire that winter the conditions for continued insurgency seemed perfect.[32]

Around Candlemas, the light-filled festival of renewal that alleviated the darkness of early February, two men of sober, clerical demeanour turned up unannounced at the Welles family home. The senior of the two, a man called John Barnby, brought with him letters of credence that he handed to Lord Welles. Barnby was Clarence's chaplain. The letters, from Clarence himself, were to guarantee that Barnby was who he said he was, and that he could be trusted. The message Barnby carried from Clarence to Welles was verbal, memorized: too explosive to be committed to paper.

Clarence had property interests in Lincolnshire. They weren't extensive but, combined with his royal status, enough to appeal to disaffected families like that of Lord Welles. Barnby reassured Welles and his son that Clarence and Warwick were assembling military support 'for their surety'; in return, the two lords needed their support. They should be prepared to raise all the men they could and try to incite an uprising among the commons whenever Clarence sent word. But, Barnby stressed, Welles and his son should not do anything yet: Warwick was still in London with the king, and it was imperative that they 'tarry and not stir' until he left, in case Edward worked out what was going on.

If the account of Barnby's visit was to be believed, Clarence and Warwick's newfound reconciliation with the king was nothing of the sort. And Warwick's proposed contribution to the royal army going into Lincolnshire masked another aim altogether.[33]

Lord Welles and his brother-in-law Dymmock, though, were cautious. Whatever their sympathies, they decided to clear the air with Edward. Belatedly responding to the king's summons, they made their long-delayed journey to London. Sir Robert Welles stayed behind in Lincolnshire and, encouraged by Warwick and Clarence, decided to make himself a popular hero.

On Sunday 4 March, proclamations in Sir Robert Welles's name were read out in churches across the county, to packed, fearful congregations. With Edward widely believed to be coming to the region with the intention of 'destroying the commons', Sir Robert called upon the people, in the name of the king, 'the duke and the earl' – Clarence and Warwick – to arm themselves and muster two days later, in order 'to resist the king'. Quite which king the commons were supposed to be supporting was left unclear. There was however no doubting the identity of the king they were opposing: Edward.

In London that same Sunday, Clarence finally put in an appearance at court, joining the rest of the family at Baynard's Castle for three days of Shrovetide feasting, hosted by Cecily duchess of York, before the abstinence of Lent. Under their mother's eye, Edward and Clarence were on their best behaviour – but, one chronicler noted, you could have cut the atmosphere with a knife, everybody making 'fair dissimulated countenances' to each other.

The following Tuesday, Edward finally rode out of London for Lincolnshire with a group of lords including Hastings and Henry Percy, newly restored to his earldom of Northumberland. Clarence, apparently surplus to requirements, headed southwest to meet up with his wife. Before Edward left, he handed pardons to Lord Welles and Thomas Dymmock. Then, just to be on the safe side, he detained them: hostages guaranteeing the good behaviour of the Lincolnshire rebels.[34]

That evening Edward arrived at Waltham Abbey, some fifteen miles north of London, to news of Sir Robert Welles's uprising. Over the following days, as he rode onwards, updates flooded in: the uprising was spreading like wildfire; in Yorkshire, men were heading south to join the Lincolnshire insurgents. Edward also received a message from Clarence, who proposed linking up with Warwick: the pair would then come to help him out with reinforcements. Edward replied, thanking him. He also sent for his two hostages, Lord Welles and Dymmock. Brought to him at the Cambridgeshire town of Huntingdon, they were interrogated apart. Both confessed to involvement in the uprising. Edward then forced Lord Welles to write to his rebellious son with a royal ultimatum: either he give himself up, or the hostages would be executed.

As Edward advanced, royal scouts monitoring the rebel forces noticed that, instead of moving south to confront the royal army, they were avoiding it, heading into the east midlands. Sir Robert Welles, it later transpired, was following instructions from Warwick, who told him that he and Clarence were raising men 'in all haste' and would be at Leicester the following Monday with twenty thousand men. The communication was done at arm's length, orders delivered to the rebel camp by various messengers – later, a confused Sir Robert remembered some of the names; others 'I remember not' – Warwick careful to distance himself from potential acts of treason until the decisive moment.

It was typical Warwick. Characteristically, he hedged – or, as Sir Robert Welles put it, 'seemed to tarry long'. This was the habit that the French ambassador Monypenny had contemptuously described as *'lache'*: cowardly. In fact, Warwick was trying to draw Edward into a trap. He told Welles on no account to engage the king's army, but 'to pass north and give them the way'. Then, Welles's rebels could form a barrier between Edward and the road back to London. Warwick's and Clarence's forces, under pretext of linking up with the king, would destroy him. Anybody fleeing south would be mopped up by Welles's insurgents.

That, at least, seemed to be the plan. Yet there seemed a tension in the rebels' movements, one perhaps inherent in the changing relationship between Warwick and Clarence, who strained against his older cousin's caution. The pair, it was reported, weren't getting on: indeed, they had left London 'on bad terms'.[35] Now, if Warwick remained a nebulous presence, the involvement of Clarence's men was markedly more open, from John Barnby to the presence in the insurgent army of one of the duke's chamber servants, 'Walter', whipping up the rebels with fiery speeches and shaping their tactics. Nonetheless, Warwick's caution predominated, the rebels following his instructions to the letter: these were the curious troop movements spotted by royal scouts. Then, on Sunday 11 March, a royal messenger arrived with Lord Welles's ultimatum and wrecked everything.

Realizing his father was in 'jeopardy', Sir Robert changed direction, leading the rebels straight down the Great North Road towards the king's army to rescue him. In their midst, urging them on, was Clarence's servant Walter, who repeated, again and again, that the rebels should 'destroy the king' and set Clarence up as king in his brother's place.[36]

Until now Warwick had been the senior partner, the guiding spirit, in challenging Edward's regime: manoeuvring cautiously, striking when he felt the timing was right, giving ground where necessary. At this point the momentum shifted, and an impatient, impetuous energy took hold of the insurgency. Now the rebellion was out of Warwick's control. It was all about Clarence.

Edward, though, was several steps ahead. Learning that the rebels aimed to ambush him as he arrived at the town of Stamford, he moved fast, reaching Stamford on the morning of the 12th, ahead of the insurgents. There, he found fresh dispatches from Clarence and Warwick, who told Edward they were coming to help the king 'against his rebels' and would be with him the following night. All Edward had to do was sit tight. He did exactly the opposite.

Advancing out of the town, he soon found the rebel forces in open country near the village of Empingham, tens of thousands of men drawn up in battle formation against him. Faced with this exemplary act of treason, Edward kept his promise. Lord Welles and Sir Thomas Dymmock were led out in front of the royal army, shoved to their knees under the king's banners and, in clear sight of Sir Robert Welles's insurgent army, beheaded. Then the royal guns opened up.

Despite their considerable numbers, Welles's men were mostly untrained, ill-equipped foot soldiers. Blasted by Edward's artillery, ridden down by his cavalry, their cohesion didn't last long. Their exposed lines fragmenting, they fled across the fields – the rebels' frantic shedding of the padded jackets that mostly served as their armour earning the battle the derisive name of 'Losecote Field'. Though Edward, in a populist touch, was said to have intervened repeatedly to prevent the slaughter of his 'poor and wretched commons', many were killed. Locals renamed a nearby patch of woodland 'Bloody Oaks'.

Brief as the clash had been, there had been enough to indicate its driving force. The rebels had advanced with a repeated yell of 'A Clarence. A Clarence. A Warwick.' Several – including their leader Sir Robert Welles – had worn Clarence's colours. On the corpse of one of them, hacked down as he fled, was found a casket stuffed full of documents, shocking pieces of 'great sedition' and 'abominable treason'. A servant of Clarence's, he had been the duke's go-between with Sir Robert Welles: perhaps it was Walter, who had grabbed a spear and gone into battle shouting death to King Edward.[37]

In the battle's aftermath Edward dispatched riders throughout the midlands and western England, proclaiming the victory and ordering a general demobilization. Nobody, he made it emphatically clear, was to raise troops on the commandment of anybody at all – no matter how high-ranking – unless that order came directly from the king. At the same time, he sent one of his close household servants, the trusted Welsh esquire John Donne, to Clarence and Warwick with messages written 'of his own hand'. Eventually tracking the pair down at Coventry, Donne presented them with the king's letters, which ordered them blandly to stand down the forces they had raised, and to come to him with their usual retinues. Attempting to read between the lines of Edward's instructions, the pair lost their nerve.[38] Warwick and Clarence set out, with the messenger in tow; soon after, Donne pointed out that they were going in the wrong direction. Concocting a flimsy explanation about raising more men on the king's behalf – something Edward had expressly forbidden without his say-so – they headed north, away from the king and the royal army.

Meanwhile, Sir Robert Welles and other rebel leaders were hunted down and brought to Edward at Grantham. At the king's side, newly returned from Ireland, was John Tiptoft, earl of Worcester, his inquisitor-in-chief. Interrogated separately, the rebels made full and frank confessions – which were obtained freely, 'not for fear of death' and with no resort to 'duress', the official account stated, unconvincingly. Then they were executed.

Warwick and Clarence, the confessions stated, had been the prime movers in the uprising, 'the partners and chief provokers of all their treasons'. Clarence's late arrival in London had been deliberately planned, aiming to delay the king for as long as possible, to give him and Warwick time to raise troops and co-ordinate with the insurgents. All the disturbances of the past months had had one overriding end in view: to destroy Edward and to put Clarence on the throne.

According to the official account, an artless piece of propaganda, it was at this point that the scales fell from Edward's eyes: a trusting king aghast at the 'false dissimulation' of his blood relatives. Even given Edward's exceptional confidence in his own personal qualities, it would have been surprising had a flicker of suspicion not crossed his mind. The more cynical might have thought that a vengeful king was giving his brother and cousin just enough rope to hang themselves. Whatever the case, he was now in hot pursuit.[39]

As Edward chased Warwick and Clarence into Yorkshire, remnants of the insurgency evaporated before him and the forces of the solidly loyal John Neville. As messengers rode between the king and the rapidly retreating lords, Edward was in no mood for mucking about. In response to their demands for sureties and pardons, he gave them an ultimatum. If they came to see him unconditionally, he would be 'pleased'; if they refused, he would deal with them as their 'unnatural demeaning' required. But at Rotherham Edward was forced to stop. Warwick and Clarence had fled through the Peaks into Lancashire. The king, not provisioned for a long campaign, headed north to York, where he could resupply his army and monitor any rebel movements in the northeast. He knew where Warwick and Clarence were headed – towards Manchester and the territories of Warwick's slippery brother-in-law Thomas, Lord Stanley.[40]

Lord Stanley had spent much of the last decade sitting on the fence. After the battle of Towton, where he had conspicuously failed to put in an appearance, his assimilation into the regime was smoothed by his family's dominance of England's northwest, which Edward needed him to secure, and his Neville connections: his wife was Warwick's sister Eleanor. But as Edward moved against the Nevilles, those connections had started to become a headache. And in March 1470, as the rebel lords headed towards him seeking refuge, Stanley's new neighbour, the king's brother Richard, was breathing down his neck.

About a year previously Edward had bestowed on Richard a collection of royal offices and lands in Lancashire and Cheshire, squarely in the middle of Stanley territory. Stanley had responded with active hostility. Richard, bristling, had stood his ground. As Warwick and Clarence arrived in Lancashire, he was still in the area, having waded into a longstanding local feud between Stanley and the staunchly Yorkist Harrington family – on the Harringtons' side. If it crossed Stanley's mind to lend Warwick a hand, Richard's presence probably made him think again; besides which, Edward was monitoring the situation closely. On 25 March, in a shot across Stanley's bows, Edward issued a proclamation commanding that nobody should use the 'variance' between his brother Richard and the Stanley family as an excuse to commit crime, on pain of death. His meaning was clear. Stanley sat tight.[41]

With their northern options shut off, Warwick, Clarence and their dwindling forces turned south. They did so with a price on their heads. In a proclamation distributed throughout the country, Edward pronounced them his 'great rebels' and traitors; anybody bringing them to the king would be given land worth £100 annually to his family in perpetuity, or £1,000 cash down. Meanwhile, royal agents moved onto the rebels' estates, seizing lands, buildings and assets in the king's name.[42]

Reaching Devon, where they were harboured by the sympathetic Courtenay family, the rebel lords joined up with Warwick's wife Anne and their two daughters. Isabel, Clarence's wife, was now heavily pregnant with the couple's first child. On Monday 9 April they set sail from Dartmouth, a cobbled-together flotilla carrying their remaining men.[43] To Warwick, it was déjà vu. Ten years before, pursued by Lancastrian troops, he and Edward had left south Devon for

Calais, first their refuge, then their springboard for invasion. Now, with Calais under the control of Warwick's deputy, Lord Wenlock, they had a similar plan. Edward, though, was several steps ahead of them.

In the Channel, a squadron of royal ships captained by John, Lord Howard was on the prowl; another fleet, including Warwick's impounded flagship *Trinity*, was being fitted out at Southampton under the command of Anthony Woodville. Warwick wanted his flagship back. As the rebels passed Southampton Water, he dropped anchor and sent a raiding party to seize it. Woodville's troops were lying in wait. Overwhelming the raiders, they took several rebel vessels; Warwick, Clarence and the rest of their ships headed rapidly for the open sea.[44] Shortly after, Edward and his army arrived in Southampton. The captives were handed over to John Tiptoft for trial.

Tiptoft condemned a number of Warwick's men to death – his close associate Sir Geoffrey Gate, an influential and potentially useful man, was spared – and the executions began. Not content with the full ritual horror of hanging, drawing, and beheading, Tiptoft went a stage further in underscoring the full coercive power of the Yorkist state. Stringing up the beheaded, eviscerated bodies by the legs, Tiptoft had stakes sharpened at both ends: one end was driven into each corpse 'at buttocks' until thoroughly wedged; the corpse's detached head was jammed on the other. News of the killings, and the sadistic personal flourish of Tiptoft's impalings, spread quickly among a horrified public.[45]

Sailing up the Channel, Warwick and Clarence managed to dodge Howard's patrols. Calais, though, proved no refuge. Trying to enter the harbour, the rebel lords were met with a hail of gunfire from the fortress of Rysbank and forced back into the open sea. Edward's orders to hold Calais against Warwick had already reached the garrison, which obeyed them to the letter. Its captain Lord Wenlock had little option but to fall into step.

Wenlock did manage to smuggle a message to Warwick, along with two flagons of wine for Clarence's wife Isabel, who was enduring a traumatic labour on board ship. Calais, Wenlock warned, was loyal to Edward; moreover, its officials had appealed to Charles the Bold for military aid. Marine reinforcements would be arriving any day, and Warwick should make himself scarce while he still could. In the bedlam, Isabel gave birth to a girl; she didn't live long. After burying the little body on the coast near Calais, the rebels headed back out to sea.[46]

In the days that followed, something changed in Warwick's thinking. Over the previous weeks, hunted down by an aggressive Edward, the earl's decision-making had been tired, cautious and predictable. The sea, though, tended to bring out an instinctive, counter-intuitive aggression in him. Bolstered by a flotilla commanded by his illegitimate cousin Thomas Neville, who had deserted Howard's fleet, Warwick went on the attack, raiding and pillaging the Flanders coastline and terrorizing the local population. Intercepting a Flemish merchant convoy off Calais, he seized the ships and their cargo, and threw the crews overboard. If this brazen act of piracy helped raise much-needed funds, it also seemed crazily provocative: with Edward trying to hunt them down and Calais' gates shut, the rebels now had Charles the Bold on their tail too. But there was method in Warwick's madness. What he and Clarence now desperately sought was the backing of the French king Louis XI. And the quickest way to achieve that, Warwick reasoned, was to stretch tensions between Burgundy and France to breaking point.

The rebel lords headed west along the Channel, towards the French coast. On Tuesday 1 May, their forty-odd captured ships in tow, they dropped anchor at the mouth of the Seine, some 150 miles west of Calais, and came ashore at the port of Honfleur, where a reception committee headed by the admiral of France gave them a cordial welcome. When reports of their arrival reached Louis XI at his Loire castle of Amboise, however, he was rather less pleased.

The French king's anxiety was understandable. No sooner had Warwick and Clarence reached Honfleur than they were using it both as a base to terrorize Channel shipping and as a marketplace for their plunder. Their presence on French soil threatened to trigger what was for Louis the disaster scenario: conflict with both England and Burgundy. As a livid Charles the Bold informed Louis in no uncertain terms, he regarded the French king's sheltering of the rebel Englishmen as an act of war. Publicly distancing himself from Warwick and Clarence, Louis ordered his commanders to get rid of them as fast as possible.

Nothing, however, was straightforward with Louis. He had instantly grasped the possibilities offered by the rebel lords' arrival in France. It wasn't so much that he wanted them gone but that, in an area crawling with Burgundian spies, any help he gave them would be immediately reported back to Charles the Bold. Louis told Warwick to leave the Seine estuary and go further west down the Normandy coast, 'away from the danger area'.[47]

Warwick, though, wanted to draw Louis into the conflict – with both Burgundy and Edward. He refused to budge. And, as the days passed, the idea that had for some time hovered on the edge of Louis' imagination finally seeded itself.

Through the first half of May the Milanese ambassador to France, Sforza de Bettini, noticed an increase in unusual comings-and-goings at Amboise. Louis was, he reported, constantly closeted away in secret discussions, while various advisers – chief among them the ubiquitous Monypenny – had been sent to Honfleur to talk with Warwick and Clarence. Then, Bettini wrote, events started to assume a surreal, free-floating quality, 'such that I seem to be dreaming as I write of them'.

Louis, Bettini had heard, was brokering an alliance between two apparently irreconcilable enemies: Warwick and Clarence on the one hand, and Margaret of Anjou and the exiled Lancastrian regime on the other. With French backing, Warwick and Clarence would return to England, throw Edward IV off the throne on which Warwick had placed him almost a decade previously, and restore the king and dynasty that Warwick had once been instrumental in deposing: Henry VI and the house of Lancaster. Warwick, Bettini wrote with a diplomat's succinctness, hadn't got what he wanted from Edward, so had decided to back Henry instead.[48] Where this left Clarence, whose royal claims seemed to have been set aside as quickly as they had been taken up, was unclear.

In the second week of June, Warwick and Clarence arrived at Amboise for talks. With Louis promising them the financial backing they wanted, the discussions over a potential Lancastrian alliance went smoothly. But where a jumpy Louis wanted to hustle the rebels off French soil as soon as possible, Warwick, characteristically deliberate, was not to be rushed into anything. The proposed alliance involved steering a delicate path through deeply entrenched loyalties, interests and hatreds. Louis' role was crucial. He would have to gain the trust of both parties – there was no way, in the first instance, that Margaret of Anjou would talk with the loathed Warwick face to face – and he would have to keep his promises of financial help.[49] All parties would have to hold their nerve.

Warwick and Clarence returned to Honfleur to spend the first instalments of Louis' cash. Assembling munitions, horses and men, they moved their ships west down the coast to La Hougue, a more convenient launch-pad for their invasion of England. Meanwhile, Charles the Bold's massive navy – an assortment of Flemish, Portuguese and German ships, with a handful of Hanse pirates thrown in for good measure – appeared off the Normandy coast. For Charles, the prospect of a French-backed regime on the English throne was unthinkable. Blockading Normandy's harbours, his fleet would make sure the rebel lords couldn't go anywhere.

On 24 July, after weeks of patient talks between Louis and Margaret of Anjou, the once unimaginable encounter took place. In a public ceremony in Angers Cathedral, Warwick abased himself in front of Margaret and her sixteen-year-old son, Edward of Lancaster; the earl begged her forgiveness – she kept him waiting on his knees for fifteen minutes before granting it – and swore loyalty to Henry VI, Margaret and their son. An official account was written up for Lancastrian consumption. Lingering over the details of Warwick's submission to the house of Lancaster, it figured forth a glowing picture of reconciliation: of ingrained enmities and old rancours painfully overcome, and of a new bond forged in the service of England and its people. This new unity between former foes would be sealed with the marriage of Warwick's second daughter Anne and Henry VI's heir Edward of Lancaster. Clarence, Warwick's first son-in-law, was pushed further down the pecking order. In this new settlement, Clarence's claims now came as something of an afterthought. He would be granted 'all the lands that he had when he departed out of England, and the duchy of York and', vaguely, 'many other'.[50]

Designed to convince diehard supporters on both sides, barely able to stomach the idea of such an agreement, the account's glossy brushstrokes hardly painted over the truth. The evanescent possibility of an alliance between Warwick and Lancaster had been in the water for years, but always dismissed for the fantasy it was. Now, with War-wick and Clarence as desperate as the Lancastrians, their worlds were for an instant superimposed: in that moment, they saw common interest. The account smoothed over the insuperable difficulties the alliance threw up. Most glaring was the problem of resetting the political clock to a time before 1461, when the great Yorkist land grab had seen titles, offices and estates snatched from Lancastrian loyalists and redistributed to followers of Edward IV – two of the greatest beneficiaries being Warwick and Clarence. Then there was the fact, indigestible to supporters of Lancaster, that Clarence had been written into the Lancastrian succession. Should the Lancastrian heir die without offspring, the crown would pass to Clarence and his descendants 'for ever more': a botched compromise whose pressure points were evident even as it was agreed.

Ultimately, too, Margaret was not quite able to put 'deeds past' out of her mind. As the new allies finalized invasion plans, she refused point blank to entrust her son to Warwick's care. Warwick and Clar-ence, along with a group of Lancastrian nobles, would have to prove their new-found commitment to Lancaster by doing the dirty work of regime change: getting rid of Edward IV, putting Henry VI back on the throne and stabilizing the country in his name. Only then would Margaret, her son and his betrothed – Warwick's daughter – leave France for England.[51]

In England that summer, tension built. As Edward's agents sent back information from northern France, he strengthened the Channel forts and bolstered the Calais garrison; Anthony Woodville's fleet joined the Burgundian blockade. He also tried to make Clarence see sense. That July, an unnamed lady had passed through Calais to the French court, carrying with her a letter from the king to his errant brother. If Clarence really thought he would benefit from an alliance with Marga-ret of Anjou and Lancaster, Edward told him shortly, he was deceiving himself. Edward's agents also reached out to Margaret herself, put-ting on the table a remarkable compromise. During her negotiations with Louis, Margaret showed the French king a letter she had just received from Edward, 'by the which was offered to her son my lady the princess'. Edward had tried to disrupt the Warwick–Lancaster talks by proposing a reconciliation between the two houses, the centrepiece of which would be a marriage between the Lancastrian heir and Edward's oldest daughter Elizabeth. If true, this bid for a joint Yorkist–Lancastrian future for England was a bolt from the blue. Whether or not Edward was serious, Margaret used the proposal merely as a bargaining chip in her discussions with Warwick: it was, she clearly thought, an impossibility.[52]

By early August, reports reached London of further disturbances in Yorkshire. 'There be many folks up in the north', Sir John Paston wrote to his brother with a southerner's fearful vagueness. Henry Percy, the new earl of Northumberland, was struggling to contain the rioters – so much so, Paston continued, that Edward had gone north himself with his household men 'to put them down'.[53] Given the events of the previous summer, Edward's new-found obsession with suppressing popular insurgency was understandable – yet, apprehensive Londoners feared, he had made the wrong decision. With rumours proliferating of the rebel lords' imminent arrival, people felt that Edward would do better to return south, and fast. 'I pray you be ready', Paston urged his brother: 'the matter quickeneth'.

Towards the end of the month, copies of a proclamation appeared overnight in London, posted to prominent landmarks: the Standard in Cheapside; the boundary 'stulps' in front of London Bridge; and church doors throughout the capital. Addressed from Clarence and Warwick to 'the worshipful, discreet and true commons of England', it expounded on familiar themes: the corrupt venality of 'seditious persons' around the king who had reduced England to a wasteland of violent disorder and poverty. The rebel lords would right wrongs, restore the rule of law and the 'common wealth', and make England 'free' again. London's mayor, Richard Lee, ripped down the letters as fast as they were put up. He also forwarded a copy to Edward.

Edward's response, again, was to write to Clarence. This time, he put his brother on notice. He told Clarence that he had seen the proclamations and other dispatches that his brother had been sending into England, 'no mention made of us'. Appealing to his 'nearness of blood and our laws', Edward ordered his brother to come and submit to him 'in all haste'. If he failed to do so, and if he continued in the 'unlawful assembly of our people', Edward would punish him and his followers. Any effusion of Christian blood that followed would be on Clarence's head.[54]

News of the instability rippled outwards. A thousand miles away in Florence, the new head of the house of Medici, Lorenzo the Magnificent, was finding the bank's affairs a headache. If Edward's regime, which Gherardo Canigiani had bankrolled so lavishly, were to be overthrown, there would be little chance of the Medici getting any of their money back. It was highly unlikely that a returning Lancastrian regime would honour the debts that had financed their rival – and Lorenzo knew it. Nothing, he wrote to Tommaso Portinari on 31 July, 'gives me more concern or greater trouble than this question of London'. Do something, he said to Portinari – and when things had settled down, it would be worth 'tying Canigiani's hands, so that they cannot soil us any more'.[55]

By 14 August, Edward was at the north Yorkshire city of Ripon, near the insurgency's reported epicentre. There he found nothing. Where the new earl of Northumberland had been utterly unable to impose order, the merest rumour of an approaching royal army had apparently been enough to disperse the rebellion, insurgents melting back into their communities.

As Edward, basing himself in York, picked at the various strands of the uprising, what he found hardly came as a surprise: almost every thread of affinity and allegiance led to Warwick. One name that cropped up again and again was that of Sir John Conyers, the self-styled 'Robin of Redesdale', a constant presence behind the insurgencies of the previous eighteen months. Although over the past year Edward had taken significant steps to dig up Neville networks of influence, their roots were deep. Now, he reconfigured military security in the Anglo-Scottish borderlands, removing the Nevilles altogether. Replacing the blameless John Neville as warden of the East March with his newly dominant rival in the region, Henry Percy, Edward stripped the absent Warwick of his wardenship of the West March, giving it to his youngest brother Richard. The appointment was a double-edged sword. This big national security command had been in Neville hands for so long it had come to be seen as a birthright.

Richard was profiting from Edward's destruction of Neville power. Warwick had been Richard's mentor: now, if things changed, he would be in the vengeful earl's line of fire.[56]

In early September, hearing that the rebel lords planned to make for the Kent coast, Edward sent orders to loyalists in the region to hold the line and, if they were unable to do so, to fall back on London, 'by which time we trust to be there in our own person or nearby'. Days later, Edward was still in Yorkshire raising men – John Neville had apparently agreed, grudgingly, to march south with him – when news came of Clarence and Warwick's arrival: not in Kent but far to the west, in south Devon. With them were a group of Lancastrians, including the earl of Oxford and that persistent troublemaker Jasper Tudor. They had returned, they proclaimed, 'in the name of our most dread sovereign lord, Henry VI'.[57]

Four days previously, accompanied by a heavily armed French fleet, the rebel lords had set sail from the Normandy port of La Hougue. By luck or good judgement, their timing was excellent. The blockading Burgundian fleet was nowhere to be seen, either disoriented by thick fog, or scattered by storms, or back in port revictualling. The rebels had a clear run.[58]

Making landfall at Dartmouth, the scene of their escape five months previously, Warwick and Clarence's proclamations revealed a cause transformed. A year before, their strongly populist manifesto had concealed a muddiness in their objectives, and in whose name they were being carried out. This time their message was unequivocal. It was a re-run of 1461, but turned on its head. Now, it was Edward who was cast as the illegitimate 'usurper, oppressor and destroyer' of England's true king, Henry VI.[59]

As Jasper Tudor headed into Wales to raise his forces there, Clarence, Warwick and Oxford marched unopposed through the west country, raising a 'great people' in a region where Lancastrian affinities, kept smouldering through loyalty to families like the Courtenays, now blazed into life. They made for Warwick's recruiting grounds in the midlands, where they were joined by Lord Stanley, finally revealing his political hand.

All over the country, people were hastily weighing loyalty and self-interest in the balance. Disturbingly for Edward, for many the decision seemed all too easy. One chronicler, a Cambridge scholar, summed up the situation succinctly. The 'common people', he wrote, had looked to Edward to restore all that was 'amiss' in England, and to bring 'great prosperity and rest' to the troubled country, 'but it came not'. Civil conflict had dragged on, with recruits having to march far from their own homes at their own cost; a string of taxes had been imposed under false pretences; and Edward's decision-making had 'hurt merchandise' and damaged the economy. All this had brought England 'right low'. The balance was tipping firmly towards the invaders.[60]

By the time they reached Coventry, Warwick and Clarence's forces were said to number thirty thousand men. Few, by contrast, were turning out for Edward. Tired of the constant commands to mobilize, aware of the growing power of Clarence and Warwick's forces, and simply not wanting to make the wrong call and find themselves charged with treason, when presented with Edward's summons people sat on their hands. With Edward as he set off south to confront the invaders were a knot of loyal men: his brother Richard, Hastings, Anthony Woodville, Tiptoft and John Howard. Their combined forces were nowhere near the numbers that Warwick and Clarence now commanded. Edward badly needed John Neville and his men. At Nottingham he stopped, waiting for them to turn up.

One night in mid-September, at Nottingham Castle, Edward was woken by a servant with urgent news: Warwick and Clarence were 'within six or seven miles' and closing fast. That news was even worse than anticipated. John Neville had recruited forces in Edward's name but then, still fuming about having been deprived of the earldom of Northumberland in exchange for lands which were not worth a 'magpie's nest', had changed sides. Declaring for Warwick, Clarence and Lancaster – his men were in their saddles shouting 'Long Live Henry VI' – he was now coming for Edward. Luckily, one of Neville's men had slipped away, rode to Edward and told him to 'avoid': to get away, while he still could.[61]

Edward, though, was trapped between Warwick's army, blocking routes west and south to London, and John Neville closing from the north. There was only one way open to him: east, through Lincolnshire and, skirting the great estuary of the Wash, to the Norfolk port of Lynn, where Anthony Woodville commanded local loyalties. It was a perilous route, the Wash merging imperceptibly into the shifting tidal marshes that stretched for miles inland. In failing light, crossing a notorious causeway across the mouth of the River Nene – the same place, perhaps, where King John had lost his royal treasure some 250 years earlier – Edward and his men nearly drowned. Darkness had fallen when, on the evening of Sunday 30 September, they reached Lynn.

Isolated, penniless, with dwindling support and his execution almost certain if captured, Edward took the only available option. The following Tuesday, he and his few hundred men embarked on a small fleet of ships and flat-bottomed boats that had been hastily commandeered, along with their English and Dutch skippers.[62] Weaving out through the treacherous shallows of the Wash and into the North Sea, they set course for the coast of Holland and the territories of Edward's brother-in-law Charles the Bold of Burgundy.

10

They Think He Will Leave
His Skin There

North of Bruges, the flat, low-lying polders of Flanders disintegrate into one of Europe's great deltas, a half-submerged, half-reclaimed world that gives the region its name, Zeeland. Here, where the Rhine, the Maas and the Scheldt disgorge into the North Sea, was Burgundy's mercantile heart; the series of interlinked ports at Middelburg on the island of Walcheren a constant pulse of activity, shipping and receiving goods from the Baltic to Asia Minor, and beyond. Some hundred miles beyond Zeeland, the Dutch coastline dissolves again into the Frisian islands. Tapering east and north into Germany and Denmark, this beautiful, desolate archipelago – constantly shifting, forming and reforming – marked the limits of Burgundian territory. On 3 October 1470, Edward's ship headed frantically towards the Frisian port of Texel. It wasn't where he wanted to end up – the Walcheren, probably, was his original destination – but he had little choice. It wasn't autumnal storms that had caused his small fleet to scatter, but the North Sea's other perennial danger: pirates. And in this part of the world, the pirates tended to be Hanse, the trading league of northern European cities with whom Edward's relations were at rock bottom.

In Burgundy the Hanse were seen rather differently. Among the Flemish cloth industry's most important customers, they maintained a high-profile presence through their *kontor* or office in Bruges, while their ships overwintered in Middelburg. They also had other uses. Their privateers bolstered Flanders' seaborne defences against raiders – most recently the earl of Warwick. In return, Charles the Bold did more than turn a blind eye to Hanse pirates operating out of Burgundian ports; he positively indulged them. When, in the winter of 1469, the notorious Hanse pirate Paul Beneke had captured the English cargo ship *John of Newcastle*, he towed it back to his base at the Zeeland port of Veere where, under licence from Charles, he sold off his stolen goods and converted the captured vessel into a warship.[1] As far as the Hanse were concerned, anything English was fair game. So when a pack of Hanse privateers spotted Edward's ships heading towards the Dutch coast, it started to hunt them down.

Trying to shake off their pursuers, Edward's ragged flotilla split up. One group of ships, commanded by his brother Richard and brother-in-law Anthony Woodville, made for the Zeeland coast, where they reached the shelter of the Walcheren. Edward, with seven ships, peeled off and fled north. Reaching Texel, the largest of the Frisian islands, his captains used the shallow draft of their flat-bottomed boats to escape. Nosing into the shelter of the Marsdiep, the channel separating Texel from the Dutch mainland, they left the larger Hanse ships behind, unable to follow for fear of running aground.[2]

Some days later, Edward's dishevelled band marched into the Dutch city of Alkmaar. There, they were warmly received by one of Charles the Bold's pre-eminent courtiers, the governor of Holland and Zeeland, Louis of Gruuthuse. In his mid-forties, Gruuthuse, a veteran of the recent Anglo-Burgundian negotiations and a member of the Order of the Golden Fleece, knew the familial and chivalric ties that bound Edward to Charles, and took his duties as host very seriously indeed. The fugitives' journey south was transformed into something more convivial. At Leiden, Edward and his entourage refreshed themselves with four jugs of sweet, spiced hippocras and three pounds of sweetmeats, washed down by more rounds of Burgundy and Rhenish wine; reaching The Hague, they sank with relief into the luxury of Gruuthuse's official residence, which he had placed at their disposal. Meanwhile, some two hundred miles south, Gruuthuse's messengers arrived at Charles the Bold's castle of Hesdin with news of Edward's arrival.[3]

Charles had been at Hesdin since August, monitoring the build-up of French troops in the Franco-Burgundian borderlands along the Somme. The new regime in England, headed by his nemesis Warwick, raised the prospect of an Anglo-French coalition against Burgundy. Fighting the French was difficult enough; fighting both England and France at the same time was all but impossible. Making Charles's nightmare that little bit worse was the knowledge that his Yorkist brother-in-law was on the doorstep, seeking help to recover his kingdom.

As reports flooded in of Warwick and Clarence's rapid progress through southern England, London had prepared its defences with a smoothness born of long practice. The city's oligarchs hardly needed reminding of Warwick's preternatural ability to spark into life smouldering popular resentment against hated elites, nor the threat to London posed by such resentment. News flooded in of uprisings in Kent, from where Jack Cade's insurgency had exploded twenty years previously. The city's levies were mustered, fortifications were checked, guns mounted and ammunition stockpiled; round-the-clock patrols watched from battlements and 'by water', and marched through the city's streets. Mindful of rumours that Warwick's supporters within the city – foremost among them the combative Sir Geoffrey Gate, who earlier that year had gone to ground after narrowly escaping Tiptoft's executions – were trying to co-ordinate a prison break, the authorities also kept a sharp eye on gaols and sanctuaries, especially Westminster, whose cramped lanes housed fugitives of all kinds.[4]

The attacks came towards the end of September. Kentish insurgents looted, sacked and torched London's eastern and southern suburbs, their chief targets the city's Flemish neighbourhoods, which were 'spoiled without mercy'. London's security, though, held firm. Then, on Monday 1 October, as the corporation's official journal tersely minuted, 'it was published by civic authority that Edward IV, king of England, had fled.' Any further attempt to hold out on his behalf was pointless. As it tried to beat back the Kentish mob on the city's outskirts, the best the city corporation could hope for was an orderly handover of power to Warwick and Clarence.[5]

Holed up in the Tower, her husband gone, Elizabeth Woodville quickly sized up the situation. Eight months pregnant with her third child, she, her mother Jacquetta and two small daughters made the three-mile journey across the city to Westminster, where she took refuge. Scared that any show of resistance on the part of Yorkist defenders would result in her and her family being dragged out of sanctuary, Elizabeth ordered them to surrender the Tower in return for guarantees regarding her personal security. Londoners appreciated the queen's

decisiveness, which helped prevent the city being turned into a bat-
tleground; for some, it may have called to mind Jacquetta's decisive
intervention with Margaret of Anjou a decade previously. They also
noted the studied calm with which Elizabeth dealt with the shock of
her husband's deposition and the personal danger she faced. Her private reaction was rather different: accounts filtered out of her 'pain',
'anguish' and 'weeping'.[6]

The following Sunday, Warwick and Clarence rode into London
at the head of their troops. With an anxious city looking to them
to restore order, they issued proclamations forbidding any acts of
violence and stressing the inviolability of the 'holy places of sanctuary' – including, first and foremost, Westminster.

The same day, Henry VI was hastily removed from his cell in the
Tower – where, as one chronicler noted drily, Warwick had put him
'rather a long time before' – and installed in the lavish apartments
recently vacated by Elizabeth. Henry's former chancellor, the cultured bishop of Winchester, William Waynflete, was sent in to explain
developments to the fragile Lancastrian king, who he found bewildered, dirty and 'not worshipfully arrayed'.[7]

Washed, brushed and changed into something more regal, Henry
was escorted through London's streets by the new chief representatives
of his regime – Clarence, Warwick, his brother George Neville, and
John de Vere, earl of Oxford, together with 'other lords, knights,
esquires and gentlemen' – to his new lodgings at the bishop of London's palace. There, in a swiftly arranged ceremony, all his prerogative
rights as king were restored to him. Some days later, on 10 October,
Henry processed, crowned, to St Paul's. The date would have been lost
on no one. Ten years before, to the day, Richard duke of York had
stormed into Westminster and laid claim to the English crown. Now,
the sovereignty of the house of Lancaster was being re-established –
and with it, as was soon apparent, the insoluble problem that had led
to its overthrow in the first place.

As a shuffling Henry was led the short distance to the west door of
St Paul's – Westminster, apparently, was too much of a stretch – his
physical frailty and mental instability were palpable. In the intervening decade he had become, if anything, more detached, more unearthly.
One Londoner followed the standard Lancastrian line, explaining

away Henry's 'ghostliness' as 'saintliness'; another delicately summed up the problem, observing that he was 'no earthly Caesar'. The Burgundian chronicler Georges Chastellain put it more bluntly. The king was 'ordered like a crowned calf', his uncomprehending gaze taken by his handlers as assent. 'And', Chastellain added, the real 'governor and dictator of the realm' was Warwick, who 'did everything'.[8]

Lancastrian advisers had been trying to solve the problem that was Henry for the best part of two decades. Foremost among them was Sir John Fortescue, whose propagandist skills had made him a bee in the Yorkist bonnet during the past years and who had helped mastermind Margaret's spectacular return from the political wilderness. During the crisis-ridden 1450s, as he witnessed first-hand Henry's slide into mental incapacity, Fortescue had developed a blueprint for governmental reform that attempted to counteract the unpredictable hazards of personal monarchy. Now, with Henry once again perched on the throne, Fortescue saw the chance to implement his plan.

That autumn, the sixteen-year-old Lancastrian heir Edward sent a letter from France to Warwick, his new father-in-law. It contained a series of instructions for government which, the boy wrote, Warwick could 'show and communicate' to Henry VI – and which, if Warwick thought useful for the 'common good', he could put into action. While Edward of Lancaster might have signed the letter, it had been written by his teacher Fortescue, and it contained an assortment of his key prescriptions.

Fortescue's concerns about the existing system were those that had run like a seam through the various Yorkist manifestos of the 1450s and early 1460s and, later, through those of Warwick and Clarence: the profligacy and favouritism of kings, and their propensity for being led astray by the whisperings of malign courtiers. But Fortescue's proposed solution to the problems that had ultimately plunged the country into civil war was very much his own. It involved the appointment of a council of twenty-four 'wise and impartial' men, twelve 'spiritual' and twelve secular, whose responsibility would be the 'good politic rule of the land'. These councillors would deal with all issues regarding 'the rule of the realm', from legal and mercantile questions to the processing of petitions for royal favour and the granting of lands and offices. Their impartiality was crucial, for it had to be remembered how the 'old council' comprised mostly great lords who looked out for themselves and their 'own matters' rather than the common good. This new council would be to the king's great benefit – and, moreover, to the benefit of those around him, 'whom', Fortescue hardly needed to point out, 'the people have sometimes slain for the miscounselling of their sovereign lord'.

Although Fortescue's prescriptions went out of their way to stress that this council was simply an advisory body – it would 'in no thing' restrain the king's power – there was no mistaking his vision. The king, he stressed, should take no major policy decisions, do 'no great thing' without first consulting this council, whose recommendations he should then follow.

Given that Warwick was now leading a rickety coalition of deeply conflicted interests, Fortescue perhaps thought that this kind of council, specifically designed to avoid faction and political rivalry, was an idea whose time had come. After all, Warwick had to show sceptics of all kinds that his government was a broad and non-partisan church. There were signs that he was anxious to do so: key posts went to a mixture of his own supporters (George Neville, naturally, got the chancellorship), Lancastrian servants and officers from Clarence's own household.

Governing by consensus, though, went against Warwick's restless energy and ambition, his constant hankering for a role – denied him by Edward – as the king's chief executive officer. This, more or less, was the position he now took up. The deal struck at Angers made him both 'regent' and 'governor' on behalf of Henry VI and his heir. An unprecedented position of power, it combined the two roles that governing councils had historically been anxious to keep out of the hands of powerful nobles of the blood who claimed the title of protector: head of government and custodian, or *tutela*, of the king's person. All of which was hardly inclined to convince sceptics that the restored regime would be anything other than a government run by and for the Nevilles. Those doubters, perhaps, had already started to include Clarence. For, if the duke had anticipated a role in running the kingdom, forming a duumvirate with Warwick, he was soon disappointed. It was to be the first of many such disappointments.[9]

One of Warwick's first moves was to appoint John de Vere, earl of Oxford as constable of England. No sooner had Oxford been handed the post than, in an irony lost on no one, he convicted for treason his notorious predecessor as constable: John Tiptoft, earl of Worcester, the man who had condemned Oxford's own father and brother. Incongruously for this most remorseless of men, Tiptoft had been found hiding up a tree in Huntingdonshire disguised as a shepherd. Now, as one chronicler dispassionately put it, he 'was judged by such law as he did to other men'. The fact that the new constable should never have been in charge of the process – whatever enormities Tiptoft had committed, they didn't include treason – was neither here nor there. Everybody knew what was going on, and why, and what the outcome would be.

On 18 October Tiptoft was led to his death on Tower Hill through crowds gawping with appalled fascination at the man they knew as the 'butcher of England'. An Italian priest at Tiptoft's side, a black-habited Dominican, put it to him that his imminent execution was the result of his 'unheard-of cruelties', foremost among which was his execution of the earl of Desmond's two young sons. If the priest's suggestion was designed to offer Tiptoft an opportunity to confess his sins, the earl's answer gave nothing away. Everything he had done, he replied impassively, was 'for the State'.[10]

In sanctioning what was effectively a private act of revenge, perpetrated by one of his own brothers-in-law against another, Warwick underscored the seriousness of his commitment to the new order. He sent out writs for a new parliament, to be convened at Westminster on 26 November: an assembly whose purpose was formally to destroy the Yorkist claim to the throne, pronounce Edward a usurper and to restore prominent Lancastrians to political life and to their confiscated lands. Meanwhile, people were watching the actions of the new regime closely: from its backers, like Louis XI, to its enemies; from the exiled Lancastrians now preparing to return, to those who had benefited from the Yorkist regime and who feared they would be deprived of their gains; from smallholders to big financial players like London's oligarchs, the wool merchants of Calais and the Medici, who had extended vast quantities of credit to Edward and who now, with his dethronement, despaired of making good on their loans. Warwick had his work cut out.

*

As Charles the Bold prepared his defences against the French onslaught that he feared was coming, one of his many concerns was the possibility of Warwick joining forces with Louis against him. An immediate anxiety was Calais, whose garrison, under the captaincy of Warwick's associate Lord Wenlock – now showing his true political colours – was showing every sign of mobilizing. Eager to find common ground with the new regime in England, Charles felt he had a card to play.

Despite his familial ties with the house of York, Charles had never lost his instinctive Lancastrianism, and had continued to be in close and clandestine contact with several of Margaret of Anjou's advisers.[11] On 10 October, as Henry VI was being led round St Paul's, Charles wrote an expansive letter to Wenlock at Calais, in which he pronounced himself overjoyed at the Lancastrian restoration: any friend and loyal subject of Henry's, Charles stressed, was a friend of his. Two days later, amid reports that four thousand troops were being sent from England to bolster the Calais garrison, Charles dictated another, rather more insistent letter to Wenlock, adding a personally handwritten postscript for good measure. Invoking St George – who, he wrote, 'knows me to be more English than the English' – Charles insisted that all the treaties of friendship he had made with Edward had not in fact been made with one king or another in mind, but with the English crown, whichever head it happened to be resting on. As far as he was concerned, Charles added hopefully, those agreements were still in force. Then he came to the crunch: 'the blood of Lancaster runs in my veins'. As the man to whom the Burgundian duke now entrusted delivery of his letter, an astute, sharp-eyed servant in his early twenties, pithily assessed, Charles was quite simply 'scared' of Richard Neville, earl of Warwick.[12]

During the two years that he had served in the ducal household, Philippe de Commynes had grown close to Charles. Though self-confessedly 'new to the sudden changes of this world', Commynes was already experienced in high-level politics – though not in the kind of daunting mission on which Charles now sent him. What followed was a diplomatic baptism of fire for a man who would become one of the greatest political commentators of the age, and whose memoirs, infused with psychological insight and laced with slippery ambiguity, bear comparison with those of his younger Florentine contemporary, Niccolò Machiavelli.[13]

As he rode towards the now aggressively anti-Burgundian Calais with an armed escort, Commynes encountered the first visible sign of trouble: a stream of Flemish locals fleeing the bands of armed Englishmen who now roamed the countryside around the Pale. Entering the enclave, he was struck by a new coolness towards him and his men. When he reached his lodgings, Commynes found pinned to the doors verses stating that Warwick and the French king Louis XI were an inseparable force. In case Commynes missed the point, the doors themselves had been daubed with white crosses: the badge of France. Commynes counted over a hundred of them.

Over dinner with Wenlock, Commynes remarked on the little golden ragged staff that Warwick's deputy wore pinned to his hat. Wenlock, imperturbable, replied that when the news had arrived from England, everybody in Calais had immediately thrown away their Yorkist badges and replaced them with Warwick's emblem. Apart from one Italian diplomat frightened out of his wits by the people 'turning and shouting "Warwick"', whom Wenlock had packed off to Bruges, everything had gone smoothly. The transformation, he told Commynes, had taken about fifteen minutes.

If Commynes was in any doubt about how quickly things could change, or the power of Warwick's popularity in these parts, he had his answer. While Wenlock had over the years developed quite the reputation – he was, spat the Burgundian chronicler Chastellain, a 'double and variable man' who bent whichever way the wind blew – Commynes found him honest, realistic and plain-dealing. He was less sure about Wenlock's men. Last time Commynes was in town, they had spoken glowingly of their king, Edward IV; now, they were violent in their hatred of him.[14]

Sticking to his brief, Commynes extracted an agreement from Wenlock that all existing Anglo-Burgundian treaties and alliances should remain in place, 'except that we should insert Henry's name instead of Edward's'. And he remained bland in the face of relentless cross-questioning about the fate of the Yorkist king, and whether he was really alive. Edward, a poker-faced Commynes assured his hosts, 'was dead'.

Nevertheless, as Charles the Bold continued his conciliatory approach – upbraiding Bruges' officials for their over-hasty confiscation of English goods; issuing proclamations throughout Flanders stating that any move against English interests would be punished; and sending a Burgundian embassy to London – he was under no illusions about the corner in which he now found himself. Neither was Commynes. As he noted flatly, if Charles had to go to war with both England and France at the same time, 'he would be destroyed'. The only hope for Charles, he wrote, was to 'sweeten Monsieur de Warwick' as far as he could, and to try to preserve commercial relations between the two countries: after all, conflict was incredibly bad for business, and the merchants of London and Calais wanted it no more than Charles did. Realistically, though, there was a sense of the inevitable being delayed. Wenlock would soon find out that Commynes had been lying about Edward's death. Charles's protestations of his Lancastrianism had bought himself time, that was all.[15]

As Commynes rode towards Calais, Charles dispatched two trusted servants to Edward and his group of refugees at The Hague; liaison officers who would stay with the Yorkist exiles and, at the same time, keep a close eye on their activities. At the start of November, Charles authorized a monthly pension for Edward of 500 ecus, backdated to 11 October. Not only, however, was the cash paid in arrears – by the time Edward had acknowledged the first instalment, scrawling an 'Edward R' at the bottom of the receipt, it was early December – it wasn't an awful lot.[16]

Trying to keep all his options open, Charles was faced with a dizzying exercise in plate-spinning. In the account book that itemized his first payment to Edward was also listed the latest payment to the Lancastrian dukes of Somerset and Exeter, now serving in Charles's army against the French. At the same time, his envoys were desperately trying to establish diplomatic relations with Warwick's regime. Just as his father had done with the young Clarence and Richard ten years previously, Charles kept Edward at a distance from the Burgundian court, at Louis of Gruuthuse's house in The Hague. Nor was there any mention of helping Edward regain his kingdom. Unsurprisingly, the modest pension Charles gave his brother-in-law suggested he was playing Edward's royal status down. The money was, as the ducal treasurer stipulated in his accounts, solely for Edward to 'maintain his estate' – and nothing more.[17]

Having arrived in Holland with little more than the clothes on their backs, Edward and his men were, apart from Charles's parsimonious allowance, almost entirely dependent on Gruuthuse's generosity. Together with William Hastings and a small clutch of nobles and knights, there were about eighty exiles comprising an assortment of royal servants, like the signet clerk Nicholas Harpisfield and the duchy of Lancaster official Nicholas Leventhorpe, and hangers-on like the Bristol gentleman and alchemist Thomas Norton. In mid-October, they were bolstered by a group of Calais deserters – shooed on to The Hague as quickly as possible by Charles – and by Richard. Coming ashore some 150 miles to the south, Richard and Anthony Woodville had found a sympathetic welcome: in Middelburg, the city's burghers had hosted a wine reception for them, and they had been loaned cash in the nearby port of Veere. Now, as they joined forces with Edward, his already slender resources were further stretched. Their meals consisted mostly of variations on rabbit – which, on the plus side, meant there were no temptations for Edward to resist.[18]

Adversity seemed to bring out the best in Edward, and his natural instinct for breaking through barriers of social rank to form intense bonds with the men around him. The crisis he faced seemed to absorb those obsessive drives that in quieter, more aimless times found release in his bingeing and womanizing. As Edward well knew, he could not risk his Burgundian exile becoming an established fact. It had happened to Margaret of Anjou's court at Koeur: resourceless and isolated, it had become an irrelevance, until the impossible had happened. As the days and weeks went by, people would become resigned to the idea of Lancastrian rule in England; Edward's own men would start to drift away. A few, in fact, had already deserted him, getting into a fight with some locals in a Bruges pub on their way to join Wenlock in Calais.

Whatever Charles the Bold thought, Edward had to start planning his return immediately, testing the visible fault-lines in the Lancastrian regime. As autumn deepened into winter, Edward's agents were already at work, crossing into England, sounding out allegiances.

Late in November 1470, Parliament opened at Westminster with a sermon from George Neville, who had slipped smoothly back into the chancellorship. Without apparent irony, he took as his text a verse from Jeremiah, 'Return, you backsliding children', urging all those who had fallen into the error of backing Edward to make their peace with the house of Lancaster; the political door, apparently, remained open.[19]

For all that Warwick's regime attempted to tread delicately through the thickets of competing interests in drawing up a new national settlement, the resulting compromises satisfied few. The most prominent case was Clarence. The previous summer in Angers, he had been confirmed in the Lancastrian line of succession. It was an agreement that put various noses out of joint – especially those of the Beaufort family, whose claims to the throne he had leapfrogged. With the Beauforts (among others) breathing down his neck, Clarence started to feel that the insecurity of his brother's rule was small beer compared to the situation in which he now found himself.

Meanwhile, one subject that went conspicuously unmentioned in Parliament was the matter that was rapidly becoming Warwick's biggest problem: the war against Charles the Bold that the French king was now pressurizing him to join. Louis XI's agents – headed by the ubiquitous Monypenny – had arrived in London just as Parliament opened. They had been closely briefed, right down to the opening pleasantries. Warwick was to be referred to as Louis' 'best friend', underscoring a sense of shared commitment and, now, obligation. Warwick, 'for many reasons', owed him.

Monypenny quickly cut to the chase. Louis was keen to invoke the secret deal at the heart of the Angers treaty: a 'special relationship' between England and France, focusing on a war dedicated to the total annihilation of the house of Burgundy. Louis' agents laid out three options for a joint Anglo-French offensive: Warwick could choose whichever he liked. Louis was also happy to discuss how the conquered Burgundian lands would be partitioned between England and France. Above all, the French agents confirmed, Louis was now placing 'everything' in Warwick's hands. Warwick should supply and pay for an English army, and confirm a starting date for the campaign, as soon as possible. The one thing that Louis 'did not desire' was any dithering on Warwick's part.[20]

The previous summer, Warwick had been desperate enough to sign up to whatever Louis wanted. Now, it turned out, he had got a very bad deal. Aggression against Burgundy in the form of piracy – something Warwick had proved good at over the years – was one thing. A full-scale war, which needed unified political commitment from the nobility and Parliament, was of a different order of magnitude. The earl was facing an uphill struggle convincing even his allies of the viability of his regime. Those to whom he looked for credit – English merchants in London and Calais – categorically did not want a war with their biggest trading partner. Moreover, having taken Edward to task for his exorbitant tax demands, there was no way Warwick could approach Parliament for funds without risking significant public opprobrium. He didn't even ask.

In London, below the flimsy veneer of business-as-usual, the mood was wary. The streets crackled with disorder; a night watch of three hundred armed men patrolled the city's wards; the entrances to Westminster sanctuary, filled with Edward's supporters, were kept under heavy guard. There, on 2 November, Elizabeth Woodville gave birth to a baby boy, an heir to Edward's throne. Christened in Westminster Abbey, he was named after his absent father.

The city's oligarchs, meanwhile, kept their thoughts to themselves and their heads down. The vengeful draper Sir Thomas Cook, now restored to favour, was on the prowl, going after those who he knew 'bore favour unto King Edward'. In the Guildhall, the common council's regular meetings were perfunctory, at least as far as the official minute-book was concerned: tellingly, little formal discussion was noted at all. Although it acknowledged the new regime, the city corporation's true attitude lay in the extent of its loans – or lack of them. It had handed Warwick £1,000 towards the defence of Calais: safeguarding the country's economic interests was, of course, a priority. That was more or less that, apart from £100 granted to Warwick himself, which in the circumstances was little more than pocket money. Whatever ordinary Londoners thought of the earl, those who ran the city kept their mouths, and their purses, shut.

In France, Louis quickly grew impatient. Not bothering to wait for Warwick, he unilaterally declared war on Burgundy.[21] And that, as far as Charles the Bold and Edward were concerned, changed everything.

*

That December, French troops advanced rapidly into the Burgundian borderlands of Picardy, taking the Somme town of St Quentin and menacing Amiens. For Charles the Bold, the time for equivocation was over: mobilizing his forces, he embargoed all trade with Lancastrian England. On Christmas Day, Calais shut its gates and didn't reopen them. Unable to do business, the Staple merchants started to haemorrhage money; away in London, the situation was no better, with ships stranded in port and warehouses stuffed with unsellable goods.[22] For England's businessmen, the outbreak of hostilities was catastrophic. For Edward, it was a godsend.

Now that he was facing an existential threat to his dominions, Charles finally had to be decisive. The best way to alleviate pressure on Burgundy was for Edward to regain his crown; Louis XI hardly possessed the resources to fight both England and Burgundy at once. Doubtless encouraged by some persuasive words from his wife, Edward's sister Margaret, Charles decided the time had come to rediscover his Yorkist side and embrace his English brother-in-law.

On Christmas Day, Edward, Richard and Louis de Gruuthuse, accompanied by a small group of Edward's closest followers, started on the two-hundred-mile journey south from The Hague to the town of Aire, south of Calais, where Edward and Charles were due to meet face-to-face for the first time. Arriving first, on 1 January 1471, the Yorkists were met by a ducal envoy bearing the news for which they had been hoping for months: Charles had signed off a massive loan of £20,000 to Edward, now unequivocally styled 'King of England'. As the duke's treasurer noted in his account book, the sum was explicitly intended to help Edward and his brother Richard 'to return to the kingdom of England'.[23]

At a stroke, Edward's prospects had been transformed. No longer the unwanted poor relation whose presence had so alarmed and embarrassed Charles, his aims and those of his brother-in-law now cohered exactly: to remove the Lancastrian regime from power as fast as possible. Edward had come in from the cold.

When Charles arrived the following day, the two men embraced warmly. Among the cluster of ducal attendants was Philippe de Commynes, who – not a man to lavish unnecessary praise – was transfixed by Edward's sheer magnetism. Seeing the English king in person for the first time, he seemed unable to tear his gaze away: Edward was, he recalled, 'the most beautiful prince my eyes ever beheld'. In fact, he added, he had never seen a 'more handsome prince' than Edward was at that moment, 'when my lord of Warwick forced him to flee from England'.[24] Crises, Commynes suggested, became him.

Edward had barely started talking before Charles cut in, offering whatever finance and military backing he needed. Charles's whole-hearted identification with Edward's cause had the zeal of a convert; it even extended to tackling his own split loyalties once and for all. In the following days, the pair headed south towards the front line with France and the town of St Pol. Awaiting them there were the two exiled Lancastrian noblemen whom Charles had been sheltering: Edmund Beaufort, duke of Somerset and Henry Holland, duke of Exeter. Rather than dismissing his former allies out of hand, Charles – careful to keep his new Yorkist friends well apart from their bitter enemies – settled down to chat with them.

Just possibly, Charles surmised, there was the chance of outdoing Louis' efforts at Angers the previous year and brokering an agreement between Edward and the Beaufort family. After all, if Somerset detested Edward, he also hated Warwick – a hatred that the new settlement in England, the Beauforts cut out of the Lancastrian succession in favour of Clarence and his heirs, had done little to dispel. But at St Pol, the impossibility of any reconciliation quickly became apparent, the Lancastrians emphatically restating their opposition to Edward and their loyalty to Henry VI.

As negotiations with the two Lancastrian nobles disintegrated, Charles moved to plan B. He told the pair that if they wouldn't come to terms with Edward, they would have to leave Flanders, their intermittent place of refuge for the previous six years. That Charles and Edward were prepared to risk the two lords going back to England spoke volumes. Around that time, another returning Lancastrian exile, the earl of Ormond, received a letter from his son urging him to set aside the implacable 'loathing and hatred' he had for Warwick and Clarence. If Somerset and Exeter went back to England in anything like the same frame of mind, Edward and Charles probably reasoned, their disruptive presence at Henry VI's court might prove a distinct asset to Edward's cause.[25]

Following the Lancastrians' departure, Edward and Charles talked through the night, stressing their common bonds of brotherhood and chivalry. As far as his own plans were concerned, Edward said, things looked good: he was receiving excellent intelligence from reliable sources in England.[26] Speed, however, was vital. It was crucial to return before Margaret of Anjou and her son arrived in England – that December, storms in the Channel had already forced them to abandon one crossing – and the Lancastrian regime, now some three months old, started to become a fact on the ground.

While Edward was constitutionally inclined to play up his own chances, he had reasons to be bullish. From their places of hiding, Edward's supporters in London had managed to evade Warwick's surveillance and establish contact with the exiles 'by the most covert means that they could', with updates on the political situation. Discouraging news – the general hostility of the commons – was offset by the more positive demeanour of the city's elites, who, whatever they thought of Edward, thought worse of Warwick.[27]

Meanwhile, Edward's men were probing loyalties elsewhere in England, with reasonably encouraging results. Among them was the chamber servant Nicholas Leventhorpe, sent clandestinely into his native northeast to make contact with Henry Percy, earl of Northumberland. While Percy's instincts were Lancastrian, Edward had restored him to his earldom the previous year: a decision that at the time looked a disastrous misjudgement but which now, with Percy's great rivals the Nevilles in power, might pay dividends. Leventhorpe had made landfall easily enough, evading local security, but his return journey had been problematic. With his ship impounded by suspicious port authorities and the northeastern ports on high alert, he had journeyed 150 miles north, across the Scottish border to Dundee. There, after five days trying and failing to put to sea in an inadequately rigged Dutch fishing boat, he forked out £4 on a fast and much more dextrous caravel that could go 'high in the wind'. Finally making it back to Middelburg, Leventhorpe brought positive news and, with him, evidence of Yorkist support in the region: a servant of the formidable Yorkshire knight Sir Ralph Ashton.[28]

All such intelligence, however, remained speculative. Until Edward set foot in England, he had no way of knowing whether anybody planned to keep their promises. And to make that happen, he had his work cut out to raise loans, mercenaries, materiel and supplies, and the ships that would transport them across the North Sea. On 10 January, he and Charles parted. Charles returned to the front, to oversee his defensive campaign against the French. Edward headed northeast, for the Low Countries' political and financial heart: Bruges.[29]

After Paris and Ghent, Bruges was the third largest city in northern Europe and one of its great entrepôts, ringed and interwoven by canals, the arteries that connected it to its North Sea outport of Damme and from there to the world. At its core lay the vast market-place, dominated by its belfry and cloth hall and a giant crane in constant motion, loading and unloading goods from the boats on to the Spiegelrei, children slogging round its twin treadwheels. Running north from the square, the heaving thoroughfare of Vlamingstraat opened out into a smaller place that took its name from a large, four-square building that stood in one corner. One of many multi-purpose *hofs* that provided lodgings, kitchens, financial services, warehouses, places of business and entertainment – or 'cabaret', as one such hostel described itself – the Beurse was named after its owners, the family of van der Beurse, whose coat-of-arms, three purses, was carved in stone above the door. Over time, the building's name had become synonymous with the business carried on inside it: in the years and centuries to come, the Bourse would lend its name to financial exchanges the world over. On the same square were the Genoese and Florentine consulates and, in the surrounding streets, the other 'nations' or resident merchant communities: the Hanse *kontor*, the extravagant Medici residence of Hof Bladelin and, east of the Crane, the 'English Street', with its own dedicated weigh house. An impecunious English king, trying to raise money and resources to reinvade his own country, could hardly have found himself in a better place.[30]

Along with the other cities and towns strung along the Flanders coastline, though, Bruges had been on edge for months. Anxieties were heightened by intermittent reports of Warwick's menacing fleet, commanded by his illegitimate cousin Thomas 'the Bastard' of Fauconberg, which attacked and looted ships irrespective of nationality. On 13 January, Edward and his men rode into a city on constant, agitated alert. Processions of clergy, praying for the safety of Bruges and Flanders, paced through the streets, intersecting with round-the-clock patrols. There, Edward was welcomed by the man who had been a reassuring presence at his side since arriving in the Low Countries three months previously, Louis of Gruuthuse.[31]

In the shadow of the Church of Our Lady, its bell-tower spiking the sky, Gruuthuse's Bruges townhouse would be Edward's base in the weeks to come. Gathered intimately round a central courtyard, the elegant brickwork and mullioned windows of its buildings exuded an urbane sophistication; inside, its tapestry-lined galleries were saturated with the culture of the Burgundian dukes. A constant refrain – painted on walls and ceilings, worked into the great ornamented fireplaces – was Gruuthuse's motto, *'plus est en vous'*: nobility and virtue, he believed, were to be found within.

In the exquisite comfort of Gruuthuse's home, Edward found much that was familiar. In recent years, his embrace of all things Burgundian had extended to investing heavily in its culture. While Edward yielded nothing to Charles the Bold in the small fortune he had spent on Burgundian tapestries – some £2,500 in 1467 alone on several sets of arras, including a nine-piece *History of Alexander* – there was nothing to indicate he had ever before come into contact with a library quite like Gruuthuse's: a collection second only to that of the dukes of Burgundy and which would come to define him as one of the great bibliophiles of the age.[32]

Produced by the finest studios in Flanders, these massive, luxurious manuscripts were works of art in their own right. With vividly ornamented initials, liberally scattered with Gruuthuse's arms and motto, their borders were a profusion of illuminated foliage and wildlife. Exquisite page-length illustrations depicted scenes from religion, history and chivalric romance: of knights wandering the Middle East, of loyalty and love, of glorious deaths in great battles. One manuscript, a *History of Jason and the Golden Fleece* by the Burgundian cleric and writer Raoul Lefèvre, recounted the tale of the Greek hero who journeyed through foreign seas and hostile lands, seeking the fleece whose possession would allow him to claim the throne that was his birthright. For the Burgundian dukes, this myth was the greatest of quests, one embodied by their own chivalric order, the Golden

Fleece. As a member of the Order himself, it was no surprise that the manuscript was one of the finest in Gruuthuse's collection; neither would it have been a surprise if he had shown the book off to Edward, an inspiring example of what the chivalric brotherhood could achieve.[33]

As Gruuthuse himself drummed up support for Edward among his fellow Burgundians, the Yorkists wrote letters, petitioned, bargained, raised loans and organized. Anthony Woodville was soon deep in talks with the civic authorities about fitting out a fleet. Edward managed to convince the Hanse merchants to loan him a number of ships: a feat of persuasion that owed as much to the Hanse's loathing of Warwick as to Edward's capacious promises, which included the full reinstatement of their trading privileges in England. Funds began to roll in from towns and cities across the Low Countries, including the ports of Middelburg and Veere, in exchange for similar guarantees. Money also came in from those who, having already invested heavily in Edward, had every interest in seeing him back on the throne.[34]

Richard, meanwhile, rode some sixty miles south, to the city of Lille. There, on 12 February, he joined his sister Margaret, bringing her news of the developing plans. Although, as duchess of Burgundy, Margaret had officially kept her distance from the exiles in the months following their arrival, she had maintained constant secret contact. Now, as Edward prepared to invade England, his sister's dual Anglo-Burgundian identity made her an unparalleled asset: indeed, as he headed to Bruges that January following his rapprochement with Charles, his own first stop en route had been Margaret's household at Lille.

It wasn't simply Margaret's fundraising abilities that made her invaluable to Edward's cause – though her energetic lobbying soon bore fruit in a substantial loan from a syndicate of Dutch towns. For Margaret, Warwick's regime threatened the destruction of both her blood family and, in Burgundy, her adoptive one. Reuniting her three brothers was now her great priority, and she made 'great and diligent' efforts to prise the errant Clarence away from Warwick and the Lancastrians and back to the family, sending a stream of agents into England. Her efforts dovetailed with those of William Hastings, who was masterminding Edward's efforts to reach out to Clarence and other disaffected elements within Warwick's administration.

Through all the upheavals of recent years, Warwick and Clarence had never expressed any beef with Hastings, who, despite being Edward's closest friend, had achieved the remarkable feat of never appearing on the rebel lords' lists of corrupt advisers. It was true that Warwick and Hastings, brothers-in-law, were close, and the pair had overlapping interests; neither had Hastings benefited from a close relationship with Queen Elizabeth's family. Besides which, Hastings' reputation as a likeable, honest and plain-dealing man went before him; his voice seemed to carry with it a candour and trustworthiness lacking in others.

That February, then, Richard's journey to Lille was not – or not only – about a reunion with a sister whom he had not seen for almost three years; it was about making sure Margaret's activities were closely aligned with those of Edward and his people. As they all knew, Clarence was ready to be turned.[35]

In the first weeks of January 1471, Warwick had his hands full with the war he had promised Louis XI. Overseeing the fitting-out of a fleet in the Cinque ports, and co-ordinating the first strikes into Burgundian territory by the Calais garrison – 'I will come and serve you as soon as I possibly can against this blasted Burgundian', he assured Louis – he was out of London much of the time. The earl's multitasking was beginning to take on a frenetic air. Unable to ask Parliament for money, and with credit from a sceptical mercantile community scarce, he was unable to commit himself in the way that Louis wanted; moreover, with rumours of Edward's planned invasion gathering strength, he was also mustering troops for home service. In a telling sign of his inability to rely on wider noble loyalties, Warwick entrusted the task of mobilizing defence forces to a mere seven lords, including himself, across the entire country. In his absence, the regime's nominal figurehead in Westminster and London was Clarence. But by this time, Clarence was feeling distinctly like a fish out of water.[36]

As Lancastrian exiles trickled back into England in anticipation of the return of Margaret of Anjou and her son, a nagging sense of his own vulnerability had begun to settle in Clarence's mind. Men intimately associated with the house of Lancaster, like the recently returned duke of Somerset, barely bothered to conceal their loathing. People were, Clarence felt, disrespecting him, looking down on him, treating him with 'great suspicion and disdain', even 'hatred'.

This disrespect took on a distinctly practical form. The earl of Ormond's son, in begging his father not to hate Warwick too much, pointed out that Warwick had gone out of his way to restore property to those Lancastrians whose lands had been annexed by Edward back in 1461 and redistributed it to his own supporters. Foremost among those beneficiaries, of course, was Clarence, whose vast estates had been carved out of a variety of confiscated lands. For diehard Lancastrians, a political map of England had no Clarence in it at all. If that map were now to be restored, the physical foundation of Clarence's power would disintegrate completely.

There were some safeguards for Clarence against predatory Lancastrian rivals. The Angers agreement stipulated that, unless Clarence received compensation in full for any lands restored to Lancastrian claimants, he could keep them – which, given that the new government had nothing with which to compensate him, seemed reasonable security. But from the moment Henry VI had been restored to the throne, the pressure on Clarence's interests had started. It had come from a predictable source: the Beaufort family. Despite the act of Parliament confirming Clarence's possession of the earldom of Richmond, its previous incumbent Henry Tudor – or, more to the point, his mother, Lady Margaret Beaufort, a diminutive twenty-seven-year-old who doted on her only son – wanted Richmond back.

Tudor's Lancastrian credentials were impeccable – if, that was, you discounted the flaw of bastardy that by act of Parliament had barred his mother's Beaufort family from ever laying claim to the throne. Among his cousins was the duke of Somerset; his uncles included Jasper Tudor, with whom the thirteen-year-old boy had travelled up to London that October, and Henry VI himself. Later that month, at the bishop of London's palace, Henry Tudor was presented to the tremulous king. Decades later, it was said that Henry VI had detected kingliness in him, going so far as to say that both 'we and our adversaries' – the houses of Lancaster and York – 'must yield and give over the dominion' to his nephew: in other words, that Henry Tudor would be the boy to unite the warring factions of England. Though that account may have been sprinkled with more than a little mythologizing

Tudor stardust, the encounter was a statement of intent on the Beauforts' part.

That autumn, as the Beauforts lobbied intensively for the earldom's return – Lady Margaret, not for the last time, pulling the strings – Clarence received a barrage of approaches on the topic, among which were no fewer than six visits from Henry Tudor's stepfather. On 24 February, with Clarence worn down, the parties settled on a fudged compromise: Henry Tudor would inherit the earldom of Richmond on Clarence's death. Neither side was particularly happy. Tudor was unlikely to get his hands on his estates for some time – unless, of course, something happened to Clarence. This unpleasant episode drove home to the duke the precariousness of his position in the new dispensation: what could happen to his Richmond estates could happen elsewhere. His growing sense of isolation only increased with the behaviour of all the Lancastrian families close to Henry VI, his wife and son. They were, he felt, constantly 'labouring' – scheming – 'among themselves'. All of this, Clarence was sure, led only in one direction: a growing and 'fervent' conspiracy to destroy him 'and all his blood'. Clarence was right to be paranoid. He was convinced that Lancastrian families like the Beauforts did 'not in any way have any righteous title' to the English crown. But then, they thought much the same about him.[37]

As a source close to Edward in exile put it, Clarence had begun to wake up to the fact that he was worse off in the new regime than he had been under the old. With the prospect of a 'mortal war' looming between the two sides, the division between him and his exiled brothers now made the disintegration of the house of York a distinct possibility. Even should Clarence emerge from the fratricidal showdown alive, he would be of no use whatsoever to the new Lancastrian regime that he had helped to bring into being: indeed, he would be in 'as great, or greater danger' than he was already. As Yorkist agents picked up on Clarence's increasing openness to suggestions that his quarrel with his brothers was 'unnatural' and 'against God', the channels of dialogue began to open, 'by right covert ways and means'.[38]

Although Clarence's relationship with Edward had splintered almost beyond repair, he had never lost contact with the women of his family. His first contacts with the exiles had come through the likes of his mother Cecily – who, as she had done in the crisis months of 1461, had remained entrenched and defiant at the family home of Baynard's Castle – and his eldest sister Anne, for whom the new regime had meant the doubly grim prospect of having to give up her lover, Edward's chamber servant Thomas St Leger, for her volatile Lancastrian husband Henry Holland, duke of Exeter, newly returned from exile. Other tracks of communication came through the loyalist Bourchier brothers: the Cardinal Archbishop Thomas Bourchier, that most dextrous of Yorkist mediators, who a decade previously had persuaded Edward's father Richard of York to retract his claim to the throne; and his older brother Henry, Edward's household steward. The previous October both men had been arrested, then released; both were now in close communication with Clarence.[39]

On 27 February Warwick left London for Dover to await the arrival of Margaret of Anjou and her son, who were again trying to make the crossing to England. Warwick's feelings about their impending arrival were probably mixed. On the one hand, they could lend his regime the credibility it continued to lack in the eyes of the Lancastrian nobility; on the other, their presence alone might begin to erode his authority. For now the question remained moot: Warwick 'tarried at the sea side' until it became clear that bad weather had once again prevented Margaret and her son from leaving port. Whatever was going on in Warwick's mind, something decisive had shifted in Clarence's. Whereas he had acted as Warwick's proxy in the capital during the earl's earlier absences, in late February he left the poisonous atmosphere of London, heading west to his Somerset estates. He had had enough.[40]

On 18 February Edward and his group of exiles left Bruges on the first stage of their journey back to England. Away at the port of Vlissingen, on Walcheren island, four large ships rode at anchor, provided, fitted out and provisioned by the energetic Gruuthuse and his influential father-in-law Henrik van Borsselen, who had loaned Edward his own ship, the *Antony*, and whose web of contacts had helped broker Edward's agreement with the apparently irreconcilable Hanse. In the fleet now assembled at Vlissingen were fourteen heavily armed Hanse warships. Having pursued Edward into exile, the Hanse were now tasked with carrying him back safely across the North Sea and for 'fifteen days after' – in case the invasion went badly and a swift get-away was needed.[41]

Edward's departure from the city that for the previous five weeks had been his adoptive home saw the king at his crowd-pleasing best. He left Bruges on foot, through streets packed with well-wishers, acknowledging the applause and roars of encouragement. Passing through the great gate of Dampoort, he walked the next five miles, the crowds milling around him, urging him on. At Damme, he and his men continued their journey by boat, weaving through the complex of canals and out into the North Sea, round the coast to Vlissingen and their waiting fleet.

The mobilization of Edward's invasion force had been rapid: barely six weeks. It was an impressive achievement, though one made easier by the fact that Edward's force was small; it numbered barely two thousand men, who, though 'well chosen', were hardly enough on their own to regain a throne. Edward's success would be heavily reliant on attracting loyalties in England – which, despite the assurances his agents had obtained, were by no means a given.

Impatient to get going, Edward and his close companions boarded the *Antony* on 2 March. While 'the wind fell not good for him', he refused to disembark.[42] Nine days later, the exceptionally stormy season, which had stymied Margaret of Anjou's two attempts to return to England, abated. On the 11th, seizing this window of 'good wind and weather', Edward's fleet weighed anchor and, sails spread, headed out of Vlissingen and into the open sea, west, heading for the Norfolk coast.

A week later Ferry de Clugny, a Burgundian diplomat with vast experience of English affairs, wrote to a friend with news. After optimistic updates from the Burgundian frontline against the French, where the Burgundians had mounted a successful counter-offensive – everything was going well, Clugny opined, and the war would soon be over – he remarked that Edward had left Flanders. While Charles the Bold had thrown money at Edward's invasion, Clugny continued, he wasn't sanguine about Edward's chances: 'England is opposed to him', Clugny ended hesitantly; 'I hope this thing is over quickly.' As news of Edward's quest to regain his throne filtered out of Burgundy and through Europe, the Milanese ambassador Bettini summed up his prospects pithily. It was, he wrote, difficult to leave a house by the door and then try to go back in through the windows: 'They think he will leave his skin there.'[43]

11

The Knot is Knit Again

The storms had slackened enough to allow Edward to leave Vlissingen, but they soon returned. Driven towards the East Anglian coast by gale-force winds, his fleet was quickly in trouble. A ship full of warhorses foundered and all the animals were lost – though, on the plus side, the foul weather kept hostile ships in port. On 12 March 1471, barely a day after leaving Vlissingen, he dropped anchor off the north Norfolk port of Cromer and sent a reconnaissance party ashore to check out the lie of the land. It soon returned. The news was bad. Anticipating Edward's landing, Warwick had rounded up the leading men of the region whom he suspected of Yorkist sympathies, chief among them the duke of Norfolk, taken them to London and locked them up. In their place, watching and waiting, were the forces of the Lancastrian John de Vere, earl of Oxford. Changing his plans, Edward headed north, back into the storms: that night, his fleet was scattered. Two days later, Edward's ship the *Antony* limped alone into Ravenspur, on the Holderness coast of north Yorkshire, the same port where, back in 1399, Henry of Bolingbroke had returned from exile to claim the throne as the first Lancastrian king, Henry IV.[1]

Taking Hastings and a small bodyguard, Edward disembarked and found shelter in a 'poor village' a couple of miles inland. Overnight, the winds slackened. The following morning the rest of his men came ashore; not long after, contingents from the other ships, many driven onto the north bank of the Humber Estuary, began to appear. They had been astonishingly lucky: not a single vessel had been lost. Soon, the whole force was assembled, including Richard with his three hundred men and Anthony Woodville, who had landed some thirteen miles away at a small fishing village called Paull.

As Edward knew, the local population was 'evil disposed' towards him. Though the carnage of Towton was now a decade ago, it lingered in the memory and everybody knew somebody who had died there: mostly on the Lancastrian side, fighting for Henry Percy, earl of Northumberland. Since then, the Nevilles had imposed themselves on the region, and Warwick's agents had been through the area in recent weeks, whipping up anti-Yorkist hostility. Riding warily inland, Edward's scouts reported back that armed groups – totalling, they guessed, some six thousand men – lay in wait along the road to York, some forty miles away; the nearest town, Hull, had also been ordered to resist him. At which point, Edward swallowed his regal pride and changed his story. He had returned, he proclaimed, not to regain the throne but simply to claim his patrimony as duke of York.

It wasn't a new tactic. Henry of Bolingbroke had used it when launching his bid for the throne seventy-two years previously. Such a move allowed potential supporters to rally to Edward without committing treason; by the same token, it gave those who had been ordered to resist him every excuse to stand off. Although Edward's two thousand troops numbered substantially fewer than the local forces, they were heavily armed, well drilled and came with a formidable reputation, while the cash and promises of future reward that Edward threw around helped potential combatants to make up their minds.

Anybody seeking control of the northeast needed York, the powerful, prosperous city at its heart. Edward made his way directly there. As he approached, York's authorities repeatedly told him support was out of the question. Hiding his growing anxieties – if his plans were to succeed, the city's backing was crucial – Edward convinced a civic deputation to admit him and a small group of his advisers for talks. Once inside the walls, he put on a consummate show of deceit: sporting an ostrich feather, Edward of Lancaster's badge; repeatedly and publicly proclaiming the names of King Henry and his son; and – to show York's mayor and aldermen he meant what he said – swearing on the gospels to be faithful to Henry VI and the house of Lancaster. As one chronicler grumbled, Edward was prepared to swear to anything, 'forgetting all religion and honesty', to get what he wanted.[2]

The lies worked. York's gates were opened to Edward's army. The following day, refreshed and resupplied, they started on the long journey south, through his father's former recruiting grounds of Sandal and

Wakefield, from where Edward hoped to attract more recruits to his cause – which, ostensibly, remained his claim to the dukedom of York.

The roads along which they moved were quiet, the lack of opposition marked. One factor above all others stood out: Henry Percy, earl of Northumberland. Despite his residual Lancastrian allegiance, Percy had weighed his loyalties in the balance and found there was no contest. If he disliked the idea of York, he hated Warwick and the Nevilles. Edward's restoration of the young nobleman to his birthright, to John Neville's disadvantage, now seemed a masterstroke. From the moment he landed, Edward was flourishing Northumberland's letters, the wax seal of Percy enough to make even the most antagonistic local pause for thought. Percy didn't turn out for Edward – an impossibility, given the regional loathing for York – but then, he didn't need to. He just 'sat still'. By letting Edward pass onwards, he sent out a signal to 'every man in all those north parts' to do the same. Simply removing his men from the equation was, remarked one of Edward's men with respect, a 'notable service', 'politiquely done'. At Pontefract, where John Neville himself was lying in wait, Percy's inactivity had particular repercussions. Unable to raise sufficient troops to oppose Edward, Neville hunkered down inside the castle and waited as he went by.

While support was slow to rally to Edward – at Wakefield, there was a disappointing trickle of recruits – the lack of resistance had a further effect. The longer Edward continued without being challenged, the more people assumed that it was safe to join him. There were positive signs at Doncaster, where he was joined by a handful of royal officials. These were followed at Nottingham by significant backing in the form of the north-western knights Sir James Harrington – Edward and Richard's support for his family against their regional Stanley rivals had proved key – and Sir William Parr from Westmorland (his loyalty to Edward overriding his connection to the earl of Warwick), bringing with them six hundred troops. Newly confident, Edward ordered his scouts to push further and further afield and, at Nottingham, they returned with news. Reaching Newark, some twenty miles northeast, they had found the town jammed with four thousand men: a Lancastrian army commanded by the earl of Oxford, the duke of Exeter and various other nobles. Unhesitating, Edward advanced. Since his landing, the speed and audacity of his decision-making, coupled with his brazen duplicity over his real ambitions, had caught potential enemies in two minds. As they hesitated, Edward moved forward.

At Newark, news of his coming panicked the Lancastrians into fleeing under cover of darkness, at two in the morning. When Edward heard that they were gone, their forces 'disperpled', scattered, he didn't bother entering Newark, but returned to Nottingham. Greater challenges were close at hand.[3]

Edward was still making his way towards York when, on 16 March, rumours of his landing reached Clarence at the Somerset city of Wells. The same day, Clarence wrote to his Derbyshire follower Henry Vernon. Back in 1467, Clarence and Warwick had backed Vernon in his blood feud against the Grey family. Now, as Vernon's lord, Clarence was calling in a favour. He wanted Vernon 'secretly' to plant 'sure and trusty men' in the northeast, keeping tabs on the behaviour of the earl of Northumberland – Clarence knew the importance of his role – and on two other northern lords with elastic loyalties, the earl of Shrewsbury and Thomas, Lord Stanley. Agents should work in pairs, he directed, one in place at all times while the other was 'coming to us', relaying information. Vernon was also to send spies to report on Edward, and – if he had indeed landed – to monitor his progress closely. Finally, Clarence ordered Vernon to raise as many armed men as he could, ready to mobilize on an hour's notice.

In his dispatch Clarence gave away almost nothing about his own plans or his own allegiances. A reader might have assumed that he was simply watching, waiting to see which way the wind blew, but for one detail: when writing of his brother, he referred to him by the initials 'K. E.', King Edward.

There was something inevitable about Clarence re-entering the Yorkist fold. His place in the Lancastrian settlement, precarious from the outset, had looked ever more unsteady as time went on: at that moment, away in France, Margaret of Anjou was planning the latest legal assault on his estates in favour of herself and her son and heir. Whatever Clarence's grievance with Edward, the family would always welcome him back: of that, Yorkist agents had stressed, he could be sure. He was also reassured by news from the north of Northumberland's sitting still and, following his uncharacteristic spasm of commitment to Warwick the previous autumn, of Stanley's return to his default mode of inaction.[4] Clarence wrote to Warwick, now marshalling his own forces at Coventry, to tell the earl to hold off attacking Edward until he arrived. Then, raising his men, Clarence headed off into the midlands to find his brothers.

Clarence's message might have jogged a memory in Warwick of the previous March, when he and the duke had sent duplicitous messages to Edward not to advance against the Lincolnshire rebels until they got there. As Warwick now probably guessed, the boot was on the other foot.

At Leicester, Edward received his biggest military boost to date: three thousand men, recruited by Hastings from his east midlands estates. With his now habitual directness, and mindful of the other Lancastrian forces in the region, he headed straight for Coventry, aiming to isolate Warwick. Cagey as ever, the earl retreated inside the city walls and stayed there, deaf to Edward's offers of fighting or negotiating. Leaving him to it, Edward marched on. He hadn't gone ten miles when, at the city of Warwick, news came that Clarence was approaching from Banbury with four thousand men. The news was good. Clarence was coming 'to aid and assist' Edward 'against all his enemies'.

On the afternoon of 3 April, Edward rode south out of Warwick. Three miles outside the city he halted in open country, his men drawn up in battle order, royal banners displayed. In the distance, Clarence's army could be seen: a 'great fellowship' moving towards Edward. Within about half a mile, it stopped.

With a few men, among them Richard, Anthony Woodville and Hastings, Edward rode out towards Clarence's lines. At the same time, a knot of riders detached themselves from the distant army. Soon, they were close enough for Edward's men to see the liveries Clarence's men wore on their jackets: the duke's gorget badge and, over it – an indication of superior allegiance – the white rose of York.[5] As the two groups faced each other, Edward and Clarence slowly advanced their horses, then stopped and dismounted.

Clarence fell to his knees, grovelling. Edward lifted his brother up, hugging him, smothering him in kisses, forgiving him everything. Then Clarence turned to Richard, the pair greeting each other warmly. As trumpets sounded, Edward and Clarence saluted each other's men to roars of 'Long Live King Edward'. For the first time since making landfall three weeks previously, Edward revealed his true aim: to regain the throne. The two armies then came together, the afternoon dissolving in smiles and embraces.

The reconciliation could hardly have gone better. As one onlooker put it, Edward, Clarence and Richard had been reunited with 'perfect accord'. There had been such 'kind and loving language' between them, such 'heartily loving cheer and countenance' that the bond between the three brothers was now, clearly, indissoluble: they were 'knit together for ever hereafter'.[6]

As they discussed their next steps, Clarence turned conciliator, pleading with his brother to let him try and broker peace with Warwick. Edward agreed, and sent messengers to the earl. Suspicious of Edward's intentions, and under pressure from his own Lancastrian allies to reject any Yorkist approaches, Warwick sat tight and refused to negotiate. In any case, time was on the earl's side. Lancastrian reinforcements were flooding into Coventry daily, while Edward's troops were having trouble finding food in a region already stripped bare by Warwick's men. The longer Edward waited, the stronger Warwick would get. After talking things through with his brothers, Edward struck camp. Detailing a force of spearmen and archers, 'behind-riders', to watch his back should Warwick come after him, he set out for London.[7]

Reaching Daventry, the Yorkists observed Palm Sunday, ten years to the day since the bloody victory at Towton. At the local parish church, Edward walked 'with great devotion' behind the sacrament-bearing priests, followed by townspeople clutching their 'palms' of yew and willow. Then, as the choir sang the customary anthem 'Ave Rex Noster', 'Hail our King, Redeemer of the World', the painted veil that had covered the church's crucifix through Lent was lifted; Edward knelt, fervently venerating the revealed cross.[8] As he did so, on an adjacent pillar a wooden box enclosing one of the church's statues gave 'with a great crack'. Through the slight opening could be glimpsed a little alabaster image of St Anne, a saint whose intercession Edward had especially sought during his exile. Mother of the Virgin Mary and grandmother of Jesus, Anne was divine validation of descent through the female line, on which the Yorkist royal claim depended. The boards seemed to close up again, then – all 'without any man's hand, or touching' – burst open, the image fully revealed to the entire congregation.

Coming as it did on Palm Sunday, the day Christ came in triumph to Jerusalem to save his people, the implications of this 'fair miracle' seemed undeniable: a 'good prognostication', pronounced one of Edward's men. St Anne's backing was manifest in two ways: the non-appearance of Warwick, following Edward with his usual caution; and the news that, away in northern France, storms continued to delay Margaret of Anjou and her son's voyage to England.[9]

Early that Holy Week, there was panic in London. Two letters were read out to the city council. One was from Edward, ordering the authorities to take Henry VI into custody; the other from Warwick, telling them to hold the city against Edward at all costs. The council dithered. Hearing the news the city's mayor John Stockton, who some six weeks previously had decided that discretion was the better part of decision-making and had 'feigned himself sick for fear of ministering of his office', remained in bed.[10]

Now leading Warwick's administration, George Neville tried to muster the city defences against Edward. Londoners' response was lukewarm. In a mirror-image of 1461, a stream of Lancastrian supporters, laden with whatever goods they could carry, headed down to London's port and sailed for France; among them was Sir Thomas Cook, whose political rehabilitation had been brief. As Edward and his army approached, the two senior Lancastrian commanders in the city, Edmund Beaufort, duke of Somerset and John Courtenay, heir to the earldom of Devon – both in any case inclined to do the opposite of what Warwick commanded – gave London up as a bad job and left for the south coast, to await Margaret of Anjou. '*Omnes fugierunt*', noted one chronicler simply. 'They all fled.'[11]

In a last-ditch attempt to boost Londoners' morale, George Neville ordered Henry VI to be put on a horse and led through the city's streets. Where, ten years previously, Edward's hastily constructed inauguration ceremonies had convinced most Londoners, this limp procession backfired spectacularly. His hand held all the way by

Neville – perhaps in reassurance, perhaps to stop him falling out of his saddle – Henry was dressed in a shabby long blue gown, 'as if', remarked one observer, 'he had no more clothes to change with', adding that the whole thing was more 'like a play than the showing of a prince to win men's hearts'.[12] Nobody seemed less convinced than Neville himself. With the fore-riders of Edward's army reported to be in the village of Stoke Newington, barely five miles to the city's north, Neville deposited Henry back in his lodgings and promptly 'shifted for himself', writing to Edward to ask for his pardon. Yorkist prisoners in the Tower overpowered their Lancastrian guards.

Towards noon on 11 April, civic officials ordered the city militia to stand down 'and go home to dinner'. A couple of hours later, Londoners watched as Edward and his 'fair band' of men rode unopposed through Shoreditch into the city. Offering up thanks to God at St Paul's, Edward walked into the bishop of London's palace, where George Neville prostrated himself and then, pouring out a stream of excuses, produced Henry VI.

Ignoring Edward's extended hand, the frail king embraced him: 'My cousin of York', he said, 'you are very welcome. I know that my life, in your hands, will not be in danger.' Edward replied that Henry didn't have to worry about anything. He would be taken care of.

With Henry secure in his lodgings, and the self-exculpatory George Neville and a group of Lancastrian bishops led away to the Tower, Edward took the royal barge upriver to Westminster. There, following a re-coronation ceremony in the Abbey – Edward's immediate priority was to reaffirm his royal right – he was reunited with his family: Elizabeth, his daughters and, 'to his greatest joy', the infant prince that had been born during his exile.[13]

As one London versifier put it, Edward's troubles 'turned to bliss'. Here was the devoted family man, surrounded by his queen and children, cradling his 'young prince' in his arms. Emphasizing Elizabeth's exhausted relief, the poet recalled her 'anguish' during the extreme uncertainty of the past six months. She had shown great strength in adversity, trying to get on with life as far as possible in Edward's absence, but 'when she remembered the king', found it impossible to control her emotions. 'Glorious God', the poet declaimed feelingly, 'what pain had she?'[14]

Bringing Elizabeth and his daughters out of sanctuary, Edward had them rowed downriver to Baynard's Castle, where they were welcomed by his mother Cecily, Clarence and Richard. Their reunion, though, was brief. The family observed the deep solemnity of Good Friday, creeping barefoot in the chapel towards the bare altar and the cross, which they kissed fervently. Outside, mounted scouts clattered into the courtyard with reports that the earl of Warwick was now coming south fast. His advance suited Edward, who knew he needed to fight Warwick before the main Lancastrian force under Margaret of Anjou materialized.[15]

Edward chewed over the situation with 'the great lords of his blood', his brothers foremost among them. What confronted them was daunting. The combined forces of Warwick, his brother John Neville and the earl of Oxford were reportedly 'far above' Edward's army; in firepower, too, they far outgunned the Yorkists. On Easter Saturday, 13 April, Edward sent Elizabeth, his children and his mother to the safety of the Tower. Then, he rode out of the city to St John's Fields, where ten years previously his Welshmen had acclaimed him king, and where his troops were now mustering.

The scene perhaps stirred memories of the battles Edward had fought as an eighteen-year-old, of Mortimer's Cross and the carnage of Towton. Since then, he had done little fighting. Either it had been done by his commanders, or the enemy had disintegrated, or he had fled. Edward's Burgundian exile and his rapid march through England had sharpened him, the instinct and muscle memory still there. Once again, he would have to fight his own subjects to assert his right to the kingdom. Around four in the afternoon Edward led his nine-thousand-strong army up St John Street and, through Islington, north.[16] With him, this time, were his brothers. And if Edward hadn't fought in anger for ten years, Clarence and Richard had never fought at all.

Both had been too young to experience the bloodletting of the early 1460s; Edgecote, meanwhile, was all over before Clarence could get there. Their education, though, had prepared them for this moment: hours upon hours of physical and military training, of practising combat with swords and lances; of learning the right way to tumble from horses and regain their feet in full plate armour; of how to fight in teams and to keep discipline. All this, drilled into them repetitively, was reinforced in the schoolroom by the standard texts of military theory, leavened by the inspiring tales of chivalric heroes from myth-history. It was a culture that Richard had inhaled since his youth: devoted to his training, he pored over manuals and romances alike. Now, his servants armed him in earnest for the first time. They moved around him, building up layers of padding and armour; tying his flexible steel sabatons over his shoes and, moving upwards, fitting the polished plate sections like a glove round his body; then, finally, attaching his visored helmet and buckling his dagger and short sword at his waist.[17] All commitment, Richard was ready. He had long wanted this: *tant le desierée.*

Edward continued to be impressed by his youngest brother, whose hunger belied his stiff, slight frame, and who pushed uncomplainingly through the dull back pain that had started to bother him. While the king kept Clarence close to him, just in case, he handed Richard command of his vanguard.

Six miles out of London, at Hornsey Park, the clashes began, Edward's 'scourers' attacking a pack of Warwick's scouts. As they fought against the setting sun, Warwick's men were chased up the escarpment that rose from the Middlesex plain, into the town of Barnet. In the half-dark Edward's men returned, breathless. Galloping through Barnet, they had run straight into Warwick's main army north of the town, half-concealed behind a great hedge. As night fell Edward had to decide, quickly, whether to stick or twist. Typically, he gambled. Not wanting to get trapped in the town, and aware of Warwick's powerful ordnance, he ordered his men to advance.

By now it was 'right dark', a thick layer of cloud obscuring any moon- or starlight. Creeping forward, muffling the clink of armour and horse harness as best they could, Edward's men started to deploy. With a hazy sense of the enemy's position in front of them, they drew up in the customary three 'battles': the left, under Hastings' command; Richard's forces on the right; and Edward and Clarence in the centre. Then, with no fires lit that might give away their position, they 'kept them still'.

Soon Warwick's guns opened up, firing into the dark. Deafened, the Yorkists realized that they had pitched camp practically on top of the enemy lines and – unknown to them – 'somewhat asidehand', the armies overlapping at either end. These errors saved them. Assuming Edward's forces to be further away and squarely in front, Warwick's artillery miscalibrated, firing over the Yorkists' heads. As Henry V had once done on the night before Agincourt, when his half-starved, disease-ridden troops had faced a powerful French army several times their size, Edward now commanded his men not to return fire: they should hold their nerve and make 'no noise'. Throughout the night, as Warwick's guns blasted blindly away, Edward's troops sat grimly silent, huddled in their armour, and waited for daybreak.

As the darkness began to lift between four and five in the morning, it gave way to an intense whiteness. Thick fog smothered the battle-field, reducing visibility to a few feet. Edward had already decided on surprise. With banners raised and trumpets rasping, his men advanced.

The fog lent the fighting a more desperate edge than usual. Hand-gunners and archers fired at the invisible enemy at point-blank range. Barely able to see in front of them, the combatants' fear and disorien-tation were total: the fighting, as one participant put it, was 'the more cruel and mortal'. Intensifying the chaos was the armies' skewed alignment. On the Yorkist left, where Hastings' men faced the earl of Oxford's much bigger force, the imbalance was driven home. Oxford's advancing troops swung round and piled into Hastings' exposed lines, which, after a fierce fight, buckled and broke. Their blood up, Oxford's men chased Hastings' fleeing troops back down the road towards London.

If the fog had helped Oxford, it had also concealed the destruction from the rest of Edward's army. There was no wash of panic spread-ing through the Yorkist ranks. In the centre Edward's troops, oblivious to the fate of Hastings' men, fought viciously. At their heart, massive in his plate armour, was Edward himself. Surrounded by his disciplined household men, forming a tight plate-armoured phalanx round their war-leader, he fought in a crazed fury, beating a bloody path towards Warwick's standards. Anything that stood in his way was battered down: 'nothing might stand in the sight of him'.

Then, two things happened. On the Yorkist right flank, Richard faced the equal but opposite situation encountered by Oxford's men. As his forces moved forward, all aggression, they curled round the Lancastrian left flank, squeezing and compressing the enemy lines into the path of Edward's inexorable advance. On Edward's now-vulnerable left, meanwhile, Oxford had failed to keep any discipline: his troops, pursuing Hastings' men, 'rifling' the nearby town and the bodies of the dead, were effectively out of action. According to one account, they were worse than useless. When Oxford's men belatedly regrouped and made it back to the battlefield, Warwick's troops mistook their badges for Edward's and attacked them: they turned and fled. With Oxford's forces scattered, there was nothing to alleviate the crushing pressure of Edward's advance.

Warwick, unusually for him, was in the thick of the fighting. Generally, he liked to marshal his troops on horseback, piling into the fighting if the momentum was with him, or escaping if things looked bad. While this was fairly common practice among noblemen, it nevertheless carried with it the whiff of faint-heartedness that had followed Warwick around over the years. This was probably why, as one story had it, his brother John Neville had insisted that Warwick dismount, send his horses away, and lead from the front, on foot. To the Lancastrians, however, the most reassuring presence was the resolute figure of John Neville himself. When, standing in Edward's path, he was killed, his banner listing drunkenly then, suddenly, swept away, the Lancastrian ranks started to disintegrate.

Seeing his brother dead, Warwick grabbed a horse and, spurring away from trouble, rode straight into a nearby wood. There, he was run down by some of Edward's troops and brutally killed; his body, according to one account, was 'despoiled naked'. One story had it that Edward saw what was happening and ran towards his soldiers as they pulled Warwick off his horse, but arrived too late: to his 'great regret', he found Warwick dead. It seemed an unlikely tale. Edward was not in a sparing mood.

The death of Edward's one-time mentor, the powerful nobleman who had made one king and remade another, the instinctive populist who had driven violent insurgencies against both monarchs to achieve his ambitions, the pirate whose unpredictable savagery had made him a bogeyman in Flanders as a 'drinker of blood', was met in Burgundy with unrestrained joy. Warwick's ignominious end was given an epic force. At the moment of his killing, recounted a Dutch chronicler, farmers working fields outside The Hague looked up and saw armies 'fighting across the great arch of the sky' and 'heard a sound like the roar of battle'.[18]

In London early on Easter morning, as bands of Hastings' shattered troops arrived, rumour spread that Warwick had won; sporadic fighting broke out in the streets. At around ten o'clock, the tide of hearsay began to turn. A horseman galloped through Bishopsgate bearing one of Edward's gauntlets, a token of victory for Queen Elizabeth. Soon, the victorious Yorkist forces were streaming through the gates. That afternoon, Edward himself arrived to the clangorous ringing of London's church bells, his army marching through the city's streets 'in great triumph'. Another onlooker, a Hanse merchant named Gerhard von Wesel, saw things differently. Those who had left London the day before with 'good horses and sound bodies' had returned almost unrecognizable, bloody and disfigured. Von Wesel was particularly appalled by the preponderance of 'bandaged faces without noses', the result of close-quarter hacking and stabbing in the fog of Barnet.

At St Paul's, to the singing of the Easter hymn *Salve festa dies*, celebrating God's victory over hell, Edward offered up his battle standards, ripped and shredded by gun- and arrowfire. He then had Henry VI paraded through London, to the Tower. In a spitefully effective touch, the Lancastrian king was dressed in the same blue gown that he had been wearing since his ineffectual display of regality the previous Thursday.

On Easter Monday, around seven in the morning, the bodies of Warwick and John Neville were brought to St Paul's and 'openly showed' on the floor in two open coffins, naked except for cloth covering their genitals. There, for the following days, they lay: incontrovertibly dead. Such was the power of Warwick's name, and of his 'subtlety and malicious moving', that rumours of his survival might in themselves have been enough to have caused 'new murmurs, insurrections and rebellions'. So one of Edward's officials put it, in language that testified to Warwick's magnetic hold over the people; 'right many were towards him', he concluded. In the following days, thousands upon thousands filed past the coffins, gazing at the two corpses, making the sign of the cross.[19]

Over the past months it had slowly dawned on Edward that he had never really managed to gain the hearts of the people. The previous autumn, barely anybody had answered his call to fight against Warwick and Clarence's armies: 'so little people', remarked one commentator, 'that he was not able to make a field against them.' On his march south in recent weeks, meanwhile, 'some folks' joined him, but – as one of Edward's servants put it, the bewildered royal ego all too evident – 'not so many as he supposed would have come'. Not for the first time, Edward's view of his own irresistible appeal was dented by contact with reality.[20] If Warwick had always sought to exploit the explosive potential of populism, Edward had come to mistrust the people and their destabilizing power, their instinctive attraction to the 'idols of the multitude'. During his Burgundian exile, he had done some thinking. From now on, his kingship would not seek to bend itself to accommodate the popular will: rather, the people would obey him, dread him – by force, if necessary.

One poem that did the rounds in the days following the battle made exactly this point. Urging people to reconcile themselves to Edward's rule, the anonymous versifier pointed to his 'just title' and his undefeated record on the battlefield, remarking that he had never read of a more famous knight 'since the time of Arthur's days'. Anybody who didn't love Edward, he added, was 'mad'. In the poem, belief mingled with pragmatism. 'He that loved division' – the versifier couldn't bring himself to mention Warwick's name – 'is gone.' The not-so-subtle subtext was that Edward was now the only game in town. People had better put their 'opinion', their subversive political views, aside and 'say Credo' 'I believe': to sign up unequivocally to Edward's rule. It was a message hammered home by the menacing refrain: 'Convertimini, you commons, and dread your king.'[21]

In London, Sir John Paston wrote furtively to his mother back in Norfolk. Both he and his younger brother had fought at Barnet on the wrong side, as part of the earl of Oxford's ill-disciplined force. His brother had been shot in the arm, but had been treated and was 'in no peril of death'. The medical care, though, had been expensive and Sir John was now out of cash. He was also scared. Through his friendship with the slippery George Neville, who had managed to pull strings even from his place of incarceration in the Tower, Paston had managed to obtain letters of protection, and was reasonably sure that he would escape execution. Nevertheless, Paston told his mother, he had been threatened and 'troubled' by Edward's men. There was in the city an overwhelming sense of fear and uncertainty – 'the world, I assure you, is right queasy' – and nobody knew what would happen next. It was crucial, he told his mother, that she not show his letter to anyone: 'it must be secret'.[22]

The next day, news reached London that Margaret of Anjou and her son had finally landed at the Dorset port of Weymouth. They had arrived on the evening of Easter Sunday, just hours after Edward's victory at Barnet. Linking up with the duke of Somerset and John Courtenay, they were heading southwest, raising troops as they went.[23]

Edward wasted no time. Standing down his injured men, he mustered fresh troops throughout the south and the midlands, and circulated a wanted list of Lancastrians, including the Beaufort brothers and Margaret's chief political adviser Sir John Fortescue. Engineers overhauled his artillery, of which – bolstered by the guns he had captured at Barnet – he now had 'great plenty', loading them onto custommade carriages. Ammunition was stockpiled: gunpowder, sulphur and saltpetre stuffed into leather bags; barrels of crossbow bolts; and chests packed tightly with bows, bowstrings, sheaves of arrows. Then, on Friday 19 April, as his scouts searched for the newly landed Lancastrian forces, the king and his brothers moved west up the Thames to Windsor Castle, his army's assembly point. As troops mustered in the castle grounds, Edward, Clarence and Richard celebrated the feast of St George and planned their next move.[24]

Leaving London was a risk. Attacks were expected from Kent, a hotbed of popular support for Warwick's cause; the Calais garrison, also loyal to Warwick, could be expected to march alongside an insurgent army. But the Lancastrian forces, and the galvanizing presence of Margaret of Anjou and her heir, could – if left to their own devices – be expected to garner huge popular backing. They had to be stopped before they could do so. Before he left, Edward tasked a force of men under the command of Anthony Woodville and the king's reliable uncle Henry Bourchier, earl of Essex, with protecting his family and co-ordinating the city's defences. Meanwhile, Yorkist scouts had found the Lancastrian army. Or so they thought.

Margaret, Edward's agents told him, had gone west to recruit men in Devon and Somerset. From there, the king and his advisers reckoned, she had two options: to march east, towards London, by either the inland or coastal routes, or to head into the Lancastrian-supporting northwest. Either way, Edward had to get to Margaret as soon as possible, before she could link up with other pro-Lancastrian forces. If Margaret advanced east, this meant cutting her off before she reached Kent, where Warwick's supporters would follow her banners; if she went north, Edward had to stop her crossing the Severn into Wales, where Jasper Tudor was raising his Welshmen. Margaret was hardly going to make it easy for him to work it out.

In the following days, as Edward set out from Windsor up the Thames valley, conflicting reports came in. Spotting a pack of Lancastrian fore-riders at the Dorset town of Shaftesbury, Edward's agents tracked them some twenty miles east to Salisbury. It was a feint, to convince Edward that the Lancastrians were heading towards London; so too was another detachment of riders that appeared shortly after at Bruton, in Somerset. Margaret's main army, however, had been detected. It was heading northeast, towards Wells, where it had stopped.

Still protecting the approach roads to London, Edward advanced slowly, barely ten miles a day. Then, on Monday 29 April, he changed pace. Moving fast and decisively, his army marched thirty miles from Abingdon to Cirencester, on the southern edge of the Cotswolds. Margaret's forces had reportedly made a move further northeast, towards Bath, from where they would 'come on straight' towards the Yorkist army.[25]

Now, Edward was on the prowl. The following day, his forces in battle array, he skirted the Cotswold escarpment slowly, 'seeking upon them'. At Malmesbury, he heard that the Lancastrians had diverted to the sympathetic city of Bristol, where they had resupplied and been given cash, troops and artillery, and were now advancing towards the strategic high ground of Sodbury Hill, an Iron Age fort on Edward's line of march. At midday on 2 May Edward reached Sodbury Hill. Everything was quiet. Scouring the surrounding river valley, his scouts found nothing. Margaret had given him the slip.

Over the previous days, as Edward had tried to narrow the Lancastrians' angles of advance, it had become clear which way they were trying to go. Feinting towards Sodbury, they had sidestepped the Yorkist army, swerving north again towards the Severn crossings, where the river became fordable, and Wales. Margaret was aiming to join up with Jasper Tudor. As the Yorkist scouts rode further and further afield trying to pick up the Lancastrian trail, Edward pitched camp on Sodbury Hill and waited.

It was still dark when, at 3 a.m., a group of riders returned to the king with a definite sighting. The Lancastrians were marching through the night, following the course of the narrowing Severn estuary, to Gloucester, the first practicable crossing point. Edward had to overtake them before they crossed. The race was on.

There was no chance of his army catching the Lancastrians before they reached Gloucester, and so Edward, after a hurried consultation with his council, sent messengers racing ahead. They carried orders for the city's governor Sir Richard Beauchamp, an appointee of Edward's, to defend Gloucester against Margaret; Edward would, they assured Beauchamp, be there soon. Edward was in luck. When, at around 10 a.m., Margaret's forces, weary from their night-long march, reached Gloucester, the gates were barred against them. Beauchamp ignored both the angry citizens, 'greatly disposed' towards the Lancastrian cause, and the increasingly desperate Lancastrian threats of violence unless he opened the gates. As both Beauchamp and Margaret knew, every minute that the standoff lasted brought Edward's pursuing army closer. Facing the prospect of being trapped against the city walls, Margaret decided to march on to the next crossing point at the small abbey town of Tewkesbury.

It was a hot, cloudless day and Margaret's army took the most direct route, the Severn a glinting, enticing presence on their left. It was a route entirely unfit for an army: not a road, but a lane, through a 'foul country'. In suffocating heat, weighed down by armour and weapons, the Lancastrian footmen, horses and pack animals stumbled along over 'stony ways', through thickets and woods, 'without any good refreshing'.

Before dawn that morning, Edward had set off in pursuit. He took a different way, up into the open 'champaign country' of the Cotswolds. As the day wore on, with no shade, his men were exposed to the blistering sun. Short of supplies, they were unable to find food or drink, nothing even for their horses 'save one little brook', its waters churned into mud by the horses and carts of his baggage train ploughing through it. Nevertheless, the Yorkists had one big advantage: where Margaret's troops struggled to make progress, they marched through open country. As Edward drove on his flagging men, 'travailing' them, his scouts kept 'good espials' on the Lancastrians, barely five or six miles away but in dramatically different terrain. Gradually the Yorkists began to gain ground. In late afternoon, after a forced march of thirty miles, they reached Cheltenham to the news that their enemies were at Tewkesbury, a few miles distant. There, they had stopped.

If the Yorkist troops were tired, the Lancastrians, having marched continuously for over thirty-six hours, were shattered and dehydrated; neither did they know exactly where Edward's army was. The river crossing at Tewkesbury, about a mile south of the town at Lower Lode, was not straightforward. The Severn was tidal, its currents unpredictable, and impossible to ford at high water. Any attempt to do so would have left the Lancastrian foot-soldiers horribly exposed to Yorkist attack, as well as the risk of being drowned.

When Edward had received 'certain knowledge' that Margaret's commanders had decided to dig in at Tewkesbury, he allowed his troops a brief pause, distributing what little food and drink remained, before continuing onwards. That night, the Yorkists camped some three miles outside the town.

Daybreak on Saturday 4 May saw Edward up and arming in his tent. Then, he inspected his men as they were formed up into their three divisions of around fifteen hundred troops each, armoured footmen interspersed with archers. As he did so, he and his commanders considered the task before them.

Edward's troops were marginally outnumbered. He knew, too, that the Lancastrians, entrenched south of Tewkesbury Abbey in a 'marvellous strong' position, would be difficult to dislodge. Somerset and his fellow commanders had chosen their position well. In front of them, an entanglement of 'evil lanes, deep dykes' and 'many hedges, trees and bushes' made an advance 'right hard', while screening their own deployments from the Yorkists on their slightly higher ground. Edward and his commanders, though, had been well briefed by their scouts.

With Somerset's forces drawn up on the Lancastrian right, Edward switched his own formation. His vanguard, commanded by his brother Richard – so successful at Barnet – was deployed not on the customary right wing but, facing Somerset, on the left. Hastings, meanwhile, was told to range right, opposing John Courtenay, earl of Devon. Confronting Edward in the centre was the Lancastrian heir Prince Edward who, eager for his first taste of battle, was surrounded by experienced men, among them the Warwick loyalist Lord Wenlock. As his own men manoeuvred into position, Edward noticed how beyond the Yorkist left wing, the rough terrain gave way to clear parkland, rising in a gentle incline towards a wood: precisely the kind of place that might conceal an ambush. He ordered two hundred handpicked spearmen to head for the wood and deal with any enemy forces they found. If there was nobody there, this mobile unit could operate as it saw fit.[26] Then, instead of ordering his men to advance against the well-dug-in Lancastrians, Edward wheeled out his artillery, which, incorporating the guns captured at Barnet, was now massively superior to that of his opponents. He would blast them out.

Edward concentrated his fire on Somerset's vanguard. In between punishing rounds of cannonfire, Yorkist archers advanced and loosed volleys of arrows. Somerset had to move. Skilfully, he manoeuvred his men along the skein of paths and hedges, skirting Richard's forces, before erupting into the open parkland that sloped down towards the exposed flank of Edward's own division, positioned behind that of his brother. Charging down the hill, over a ditch and through a hedge, the Lancastrians piled into Edward's men. It was, nodded one Yorkist commentator respectfully, a 'knightly and manly' manoeuvre. For Somerset and Lancaster, though, it proved a disaster.

From the outset, Edward had been alive to the possibility of a surprise attack. His well-drilled troops absorbed the initial impact of Somerset's onslaught. Whether because of the speed at which Somerset moved, or a breakdown in communication, or for some other unaccountable reason – pinned down by Yorkist gunfire, perhaps – the rest of the Lancastrian army failed to advance in support. Isolated on the Yorkist left, Somerset's men now faced not just Edward's forces but those of his brother Richard, whose vanguard turned in support. As at Barnet, the two brothers together counter-attacked 'with great violence', pushing Somerset's men back up the hill and into a trap. Edward's flying column of spearmen were concealed in the nearby wood. Seeing their chance – so perfect a conjunction of 'time and space', noted one Yorkist, that it might have been planned – they pounced.

Suddenly, Somerset's men were running for their lives. Edward's troops, though, showed iron discipline. Ignoring the easy target, they turned and, linking up with Hastings' troops on the right wing, headed straight for the Lancastrian centre, which, overwhelmed and demoralized, collapsed.

Carnage followed. Many were killed as they fled across the exposed open country or were cornered in the lanes and hedges as they made for the town and the sanctuary of the nearby abbey. Great numbers of men, drawn towards the river that they had tried so desperately to cross, were caught in a mill-race in the nearby water meadows, which turned into a death-trap. Those who didn't drown were slaughtered.

The Lancastrian cause was all but destroyed at Tewkesbury. Among the dead were John Courtenay, John, Lord Wenlock and, most significant of all, the sixteen-year-old Lancastrian heir, Prince Edward, caught fleeing towards the town by Clarence's forces. At the moment of his killing, according to one account, his precocious belligerence deserted him as he begged Clarence for mercy. Clarence himself was at pains to stress that the young prince had died 'in plain battle'.[27] Whatever the case, to the Yorkists Edward of Lancaster was more use dead than alive.

As his troops looted and pillaged their way through Tewkesbury, Edward and his household men made their way to the abbey, where a 'great number' of Lancastrians had sought sanctuary. Moving through the abbey precincts in a haze of bloodlust, the heavily armed Yorkist troops murdered cowering Lancastrians where they found them; others, including the duke of Somerset and other 'notable persons', were dragged out of sanctuary. While the official Yorkist account took refuge in a technicality – the abbey had never been handed the status of sanctuary, went the argument, so the king could do what he liked – other commentators were less coy. So 'polluted' was the abbey, observed one, that the monks refused to hold services there until it was re-consecrated a month later by the bishop of Worcester. Neither was this a one-off. Edward's troops systematically went round nearby parish churches and killed whoever they could find. There was nothing to suggest that the king had made any effort to stop them.[28]

Two days later, Somerset and the other Lancastrian leaders were charged with treason by Richard, reappointed constable of England for the occasion. The trial didn't take long. Not only had the defendants borne arms against Edward, they were for the most part recidivists, having accepted pardons from him before rebelling again. They were 'judged to death', then led to a scaffold in the middle of Tewkesbury and beheaded – though, as the Yorkist account stressed, they were given honourable deaths, 'without any other dismembering', or 'setting up' of heads and body parts. Along with Edward of Lancaster, they were buried in the abbey, which inadvertently became a Lancastrian shrine.[29]

In the days after the battle, messengers rode furiously across the country to the Channel ports and into Flanders with news of Edward's crushing victories. They carried with them eyewitness accounts of the campaign, written in real time by members of Edward's own household and secretariat, already helpfully translated into French for immediate consumption and circulation at an ecstatic Burgundian court. One account told how, rifling through the luggage of the dead Lancastrian prince, Yorkist soldiers had come across a text of the secret treaty made between the Lancastrians and Louis XI the previous autumn, specifying how the Burgundian state was to be dismembered and divided between the victors. Copying out the treaty, one Burgundian scribe was struck by Lancastrian accusations that Edward IV planned to exterminate the house of Lancaster – something which, he scribbled delightedly on his copy, 'was accomplished only a little later'. So many celebratory bonfires had been lit in Flanders, noted a Milanese ambassador sardonically, that 'one would imagine the whole country to be on fire'. In France, Louis XI was rather less sanguine. He was, reported one ambassador, very upset.[30]

As Edward took stock, updates came in on the Kentish insurgency and, from the north, fresh reports of 'commotions', of 'assemblies of people' arming themselves in the name of Henry VI and Lancaster. While Edward felt that London, its defences marshalled by Anthony Woodville, could be relied upon to stand firm, the northern insurrection bothered him. Raising fresh troops as he went, Edward headed towards the midlands and the city of Coventry. On the way, news came that Margaret of Anjou, after almost exactly a decade manoeuvring and masterminding Lancastrian resistance to Yorkist rule, had been detained. With her were several of her close advisers, including Sir John Fortescue. Among her ladies was Warwick's younger daughter Anne, doubtless in shock. In the past month's bloodletting, she had lost her father, her uncle John Neville and her husband Edward of Lancaster. Approaching her fifteenth birthday, Anne was already a widow; her family, along with the house of Lancaster, broken.[31]

At Coventry Margaret, bereft of her only son, submitted to Edward: she was, so she assured him mechanically, 'at his commandment'. She could hardly say otherwise. As news of the catastrophe at Tewkesbury percolated through the country, the northern rebellion evaporated, its cause newly uncertain. The one man who might have become a Lancastrian figurehead, Henry Percy, earl of Northumberland, distanced himself from the insurgents, announcing that he now stood 'utterly' with Edward and would put down any uprising to his 'uttermost power'. He was as good as his word.[32]

It was just as well. The reports from London, where Queen Elizabeth and her children remained in the Tower, had turned increasingly urgent, 'daily messages' arriving from the Yorkist commanders there. Many thousands of insurgents were swarming out of Kent towards the city, both by land and in boats up the Thames. Unlike the northerners, they had found a new leader. Their self-styled captain and leader of 'Henry VI's people in Kent' was Warwick's cousin Thomas, 'the Bastard' of Fauconberg.

London's mayor John Stockton had finally recovered from his fictitious illness when, on 8 May, a messenger arrived from Fauconberg, demanding passage through the city on his way to fight Edward. Stockton, the messenger added, was to deliver his reply to the insurgents' new base at Blackheath, the expanse of common heathland seven miles southeast of London, which was indelibly associated with popular revolt. To Stockton, as to most of London, it looked like Jack Cade all over again. Fortified by a letter from Edward with news of Tewkesbury, the mayor's response was robust. Enclosing a copy of Edward's dispatch, he reminded Fauconberg of the king's two devastating victories and that Warwick – 'who you suppose to be alive' – was dead: the earl's corpse recently on display at St Paul's was proof positive. Fauconberg should immediately disband his illegal mob.[33] Fauconberg ignored him. By the 12th his insurgents had reached Southwark. Edward was still a hundred miles away.

The rebel army that confronted London's defenders looked ominously familiar: an assortment of Kentish smallholders, labourers and tradesmen nursing much the same mixture of socio-economic grievances and desire for good government that had fuelled insurgents' violence over the past two decades and more. North of the Thames, rebels in Essex were also on the move. Many were dairy farmers, not so bothered by who was on the throne but incensed by the low prices they received for their produce in London markets. They marched on the city wielding 'great clubs', pitchforks and staves. This worrying situation was compounded by the volatile atmosphere in the city, with many ordinary Londoners minded to join Fauconberg rather than resist him. Some harboured a residual loyalty to Warwick; others to Henry VI and Lancaster; still others – the urban poor, menial servants, apprentices, who would have been 'right glad of a common robbery' – relishing the opportunity for looting and the chance to 'put their hands in rich men's coffers' that such chaos inevitably brought.[34]

That Sunday, Fauconberg's forces surged through Southwark, torching the southern end of London Bridge. The city's resistance was fierce; the Bastard, forced to retreat, changed his plans. The next day, he set out for Kingston Bridge, ten miles upstream, aiming to cross the river and launch a fresh attack on the city through Westminster and its western suburbs. Halfway there, he realized it was a bad idea. With a detachment of Anthony Woodville's men rowing fast to Kingston in barges, and knowing that Edward was approaching, he marched his men back to the place where they had started. There, aware that his window of opportunity was closing, Fauconberg threw everything he had at London.

The attacks came, it seemed to one citizen, 'on all sides'. From the south bank, a 'great number' of guns, hauled off the Bastard's ships, bombarded the city's river front. While the city defenders returned fire with concentrated accuracy, forcing the insurgents to abandon their positions and scramble for cover, the artillery exchange, as Fauconberg had intended, absorbed most of their available firepower. Picking their way through the ruined southern defences of London Bridge, the rebels set light to the bridge's teetering houses, trying to burn it down.[35] Meanwhile, Fauconberg's boats ferried some three thousand Kentishmen across to Blackwall and Ratcliffe, east of the city on the river's north bank. Linking up with the Essex rebels, they made co-ordinated attacks on four of the city gates. At Bishopsgate and Aldgate, amid a relentless barrage of handgun- and arrowfire, they torched the adjoining houses, trying to set the gates themselves alight. As Aldgate ignited, the insurgents managed to force their way in; retreating, the city militia released the portcullis, which slammed down, crushing and killing some attackers. With defences at breaking point, the Yorkist defenders' cool thinking told.

In the Tower, Anthony Woodville picked a force of four hundred troops, chosen from the garrison guarding the queen and her children. Emerging through a postern gate – a weak, tumbledown passage where City Wall met the Tower, unknown to the attackers – they crept round the city's walls to Aldgate, where they piled into the insurgents. Sandwiched between Woodville's men and the counter-attacking militias, the rebels fled. They streamed down Mile End Road, through Stratford, into Essex, or south to the river, through Stepney and Poplar, desperately trying to reach their moored boats and the safety of the river's south bank. Many were killed in the shallows or drowned.

His troops routed, Fauconberg pulled the remnants of his army back to Blackheath. In the next days, as an advance contingent of fifteen hundred royal troops reached London, he slipped away. Abandoned, the rebels dispersed: relieved Londoners woke up the next morning to find them 'vanished away'.[36] A few days later, on 21 May, Edward, Clarence, Richard and the Yorkist army were welcomed into the city by a euphoric twenty-thousand-strong crowd.

At the heart of this new Yorkist unity, noted one poet, was the bond between the king and his brothers. This fraternal love, he continued, was the best possible evidence that the rightful order of things had been restored. Edward, Clarence and Richard had been split apart by a 'subtle mean', but nature had thankfully compelled them to reunite, forging a relationship that was stronger than ever: 'the knot', he concluded triumphantly, 'was knit again'.

Of the three brothers, he singled out one for particular praise. The eighteen-year-old Richard, he felt, had a special quality. Still 'young of age' – within the phrase was a sense of astonishment that such a boyish frame was capable of such extreme violence – he had fought with a reckless bravery worthy of the great Trojan warrior Hector. It was a commonplace comparison, but a telling one. As the poet put it, 'I suppose he's the same as clerks of read'. Richard had become the kind of knight whose deeds, like those of Hector, literate people now read about in books: fitting praise indeed for a boy who yearned to emulate his chivalric heroes. 'Fortune hath him chosen', the poet reflected with a hint of wistful envy, 'and forth with him will go.'[37]

Though the poet had reached instinctively for the example of Hector, it didn't do to look too closely at the story. Like most heroes in the Greek myths, Hector dies a tragic death. In his last speech he rages against the gods for luring him to his destruction at the hands of Achilles, begging them not to let him die dishonourably but to go down in a blaze of glory, such that people would talk about him in time to come. Perhaps the poet knew all this, perhaps not. In any case, everyone used the example of Hector: it served nicely for Richard, 'victorious in battle'.

It was Rogationtide and the city was, as customary, awash with junketing and processions, parishioners beating the bounds of their communities, driving away evil spirits and sickness with the parish cross, the ringing of handbells and Gospel readings, and beseeching God for his protection.[38] On Ascension Eve, the last of the Rogation days, a procession emerged from the Tower and wove its way slowly through the city: a 'great company' of men from the Tower's garrison who, remarked one observer, bore weapons in the way they might have done when leading a convicted man to a place of execution. The man they carried in their midst, in an open coffin, was however already dead.

There had been a brusquely businesslike quality to Henry VI's killing; he was murdered, as one chronicler reported, on the day of Edward's arrival in London, between 11 p.m. and midnight. Who had done it was an open question – there were a few coy insinuations about Richard's presence at the Tower that evening – but, as everybody acknowledged, Edward had given the order. After all, for the best part of two months Henry had been in the close custody of two of Edward's household esquires, Robert Ratcliffe and William Sayer, who oversaw a security team that at times expanded to as many as thirty-six men. While there might have been a hint of plausibility in the official Yorkist line that Henry had died out of 'pure displeasure and melancholy' at the news of his family's destruction – possible given that the loss of Gascony had once plunged him into a fifteen-month spell of catatonia – nobody really believed it.[39]

Henry's body was put on open display at St Paul's so 'that he might be known', his coffin positioned against an 'image', a painting or statue, of the Virgin Mary. But there wasn't the insistent urgency that had accompanied the showing of Warwick's and John Neville's corpses: few people filed past. Although the nature of Henry's killing went unreported, his body continued to bleed from its wounds, first in St Paul's and then again after it had been brought down through the steep lanes west of the cathedral to Blackfriars, where it spent the night.

The following morning, guarded by a detachment of Calais soldiers, Henry was loaded onto a barge and taken thirty miles upriver to the Benedictine abbey of Chertsey, where he was buried respectably, though not royally. Chertsey itself was chosen deliberately: the kind of place where the memory of a king could moulder gently away to nothingness in the depths of Surrey.[40] That, at least, was what Edward hoped.

If Henry's murder was cruel, it was also logical. Previously, with Henry's son, a focus for Lancastrian loyalties, still alive, it would have been pointless to kill him. But following Edward of Lancaster's death at Tewkesbury, there was no plausible heir to Lancaster left. As one Yorkist put it confidently, with the air of a job well done: 'no one from that stock remained among the living who could now claim the crown'. Away in France, the Milanese ambassador Sforza de Bettini, driven to distraction in recent years by the impossibility of reporting on English affairs, received the news with a sigh of relief. Things had suddenly clarified, as there was only one king: Edward, the 'dominator' of England, who henceforth could rule 'without the slightest obstacle'.[41]

As Henry's corpse was being rowed to its resting place, in London the executions of captured rebels were just starting. Sending a force into Essex to mop up the rebels there, Edward and Richard rode into Kent. Fauconberg himself had gone to sea with ships he had stolen from Edward. Wanting the ships back, Edward offered him a pardon, which he accepted. On 26 May, he came ashore at Sandwich, where Richard received his fresh oath of loyalty on the king's behalf. Fauconberg aside, Edward was in no mood to be gracious. At Canterbury, royal agents compiled a list of 186 wanted men, most of whom had had the good sense to make themselves scarce before the king arrived. When Edward reached the city the mayor, Nicholas Faunt, detained as an associate of Fauconberg, was summarily hanged, drawn and quartered.

There was something calculated about Edward's vengeance. That summer, following his brief foray into Kent, royal commissioners prowled through the county, sniffing out treachery in what one commentator called a 'season of punishment'. The process was novel enough to attract comment. Those who were wealthy enough were 'hanged by the purse': given the chance to buy pardons with exorbitant cash 'gifts', and to enter into bonds for their future good behaviour; the poor were simply 'hanged by the necks'. Another chronicler painted a desperate picture of an indigent rebel scrabbling around to pay the seven shillings necessary to escape capital punishment: selling his clothes, borrowing money on exorbitant terms, then labouring to pay off the debt. From Kent, he said, Edward got 'much good and little love'.[42] For the first time in ten years, England now had only one king, Edward IV. If his rebellious subjects wished to be received into his grace, they could pay for it.

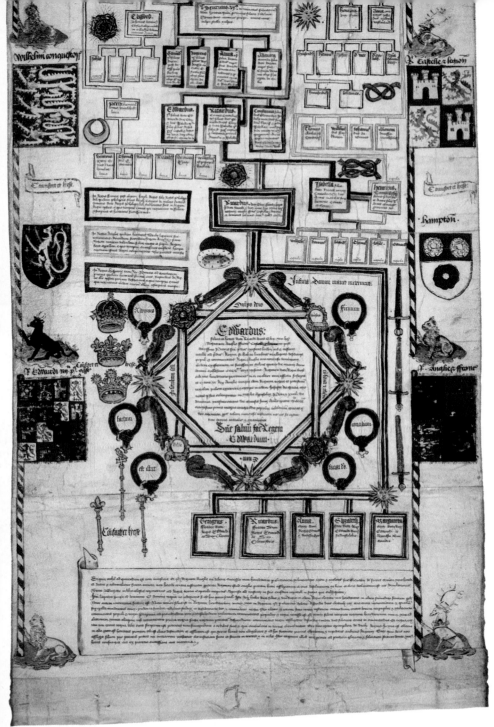

1. Detail from an illuminated genealogy, probably created to commemorate Edward IV's accession in 1461, showing the superior Yorkist line of descent. Here, Edward's claim to the crown is decorated with images of kingship and the Yorkist badges of the white rose and the sun in splendour; the fetterlock; the white lion of the Mortimer earls of March and the black bull of Clarence; the white hart of the Yorkists' ancestor Richard II; and Edward's own motto 'counforte et lyesse', 'comfort and joy'. Below Edward himself are listed his siblings, foremost among them his brothers George and Richard

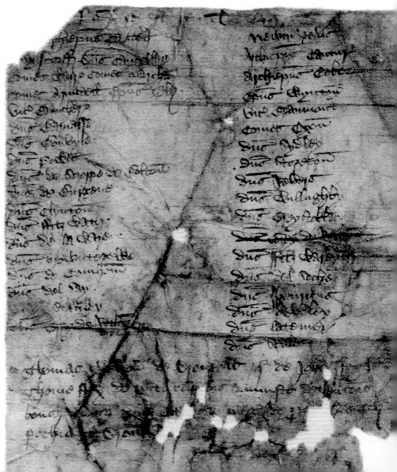

2. Letter from the young Edward and his brother Edmund to their father Richard duke of York, dated Ludlow, 'Saturday in Easter Week' (probably 1454), asking him for 'fine bonnets' to go with the 'green gowns' he had sent them (ll. 9–10); complaining of the 'odious rule and demeaning' of two boys in their household (l. 13); and hoping that York would prevail against the 'malice of your evilwillers' (l. 6)

3. Speculative list of Yorkist supporters (left hand column) and 'newtri', neutrals (right hand), drawn up in early 1461. Some names have been crossed out and moved from one column to another; the name of Thomas Lord Stanley appears in both columns

4. Baynard's Castle, London base of the house of York

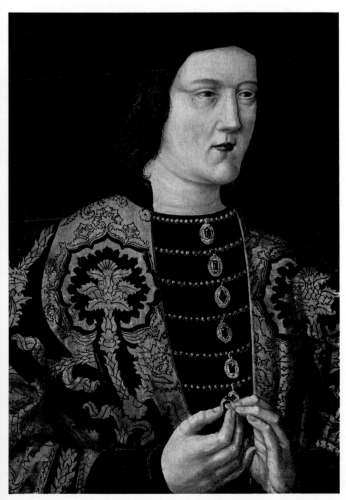

5. (*left*) Working his opulent wardrobe – beneath a cloth-of-gold cloak, he wears a fashionable black doublet and strings of pearls with pendant jewels – Edward is depicted here in his pomp: 'of visage lovely, of body mighty, strong and clean made', but showing traces of his later corpulence

6. (*above*) Energetic in the business of government, Edward habitually used his monogram 'R.E.' ('Rex Edwardus') to authorize documents

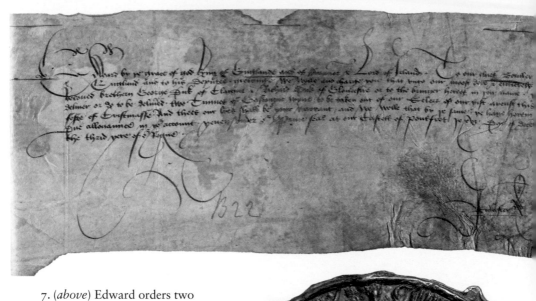

7. (*above*) Edward orders two 'tuns' (252-gallon barrels) of 'Gascon wine' to be sent to his 'most dear and entirely beloved brethren' George and Richard, for the upcoming Christmas festivities, December 1463

8. (*right*) Edward IV's great seal

9. (*left*) First minted in 1465, the gold 'angel' coin depicted St Michael the Archangel, who in Yorkist myth had prophesied Edward IV's coming. Together with another new coin, the rose noble, its introduction made Edward a tidy profit

10. The new reality and future of the house of York, c. 1465: Edward IV and Queen Elizabeth Woodville kneel before God, St George and St Margaret, patron saint of pregnancy and childbirth

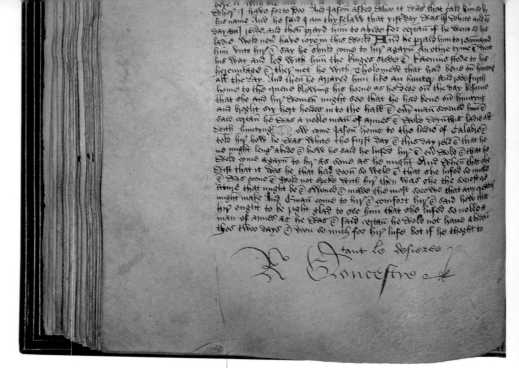

11. A hint of Richard's passionate intensity: his motto 'tant le desiérée' ('I have wanted it so much'), inscribed here in his copy of *Ipomedon*, 'the worthiest knight in all the world'

12 & 13. (*below*) Bitter enemies: Charles the Bold of Burgundy, and Louis XI of France. Edward's embrace of Charles and Burgundy, and his rejection of Louis, had an explosive impact on the house of York in the late 1460s

14 & 15. Margaret of York. Her sensational wedding to Charles the Bold was bankrolled by, among others, Tommaso Portinari (*below*, with his wife Maria), head of the Bruges branch of the Medici bank

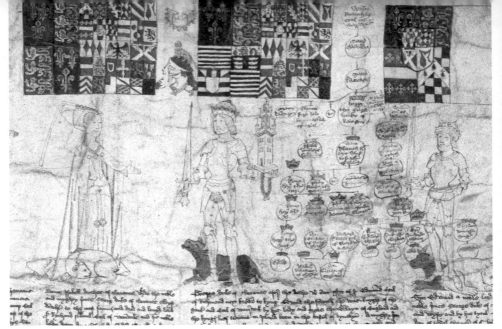

16. George duke of Clarence (*centre*) with his wife, Warwick's daughter Isabel Neville. Clarence's desperation to marry Isabel was the catalyst for his rebellion, together with Warwick, against Edward IV, who had forbidden the marriage

17. In spring 1471 Edward returned from exile and, with Richard and the reconciled Clarence, all but exterminated the house of Lancaster. Edmund Beaufort, duke of Somerset (shown here with his head on the block) was among the Lancastrians executed after the battle of Tewkesbury

PART FOUR

Brother Against Brother

Summer 1471 – Spring 1483

'The duke of Clarence makes himself as big as he can, showing as he would but deal with the duke of Gloucester. And
some men think that under this there should be some other
thing intended and some treason conspired . . .'

Sir John Paston to his brother, 6 November 1473

'You might have seen flatterers carrying the words of both
brothers backwards and forwards, even if they had been
spoken in the most secret chamber.'

Crowland Chronicle

'He said that the king intends to consume him in like wise as
a candle consumes in burning.'

Indictment against Clarence, 1478

12

A New Foundation

On 3 July 1471, some two months after the massacre at Tewkesbury, Edward processed into the parliament chamber at Westminster Palace. With him were his brothers and a clutch of loyalist noblemen and household officers. Restoring Yorkist rule across England would not be straightforward. Although the house of Lancaster and the Nevilles had all but been destroyed, the violent energies that they had unleashed continued to bubble; the Scots and Welsh, meanwhile, were reportedly 'busy'. The Lancastrian nobleman Jasper Tudor, who had watched helplessly across the River Severn as Margaret of Anjou's troops had been obliterated at Tewkesbury, was now fighting a running rearguard action across Wales against the pursuing Yorkist forces, counter-attacking viciously where possible. Alongside him was his teenage nephew Henry, now one of the last remaining sprigs of the Lancastrian line. Where the regime's troops tried to stamp out resistance, royal commissioners were quick to follow, rolling out across the country the procedure they were perfecting in Kent. Backsliders were offered the chance to buy their way back into the king's grace. From Cornwall to Yorkshire, bonds for future good behaviour were issued and fines extracted, funnelled directly into the coffers of Edward's chamber – a welcome injection of cash for a king desperately low on funds. As England's sole king, Edward now had the chance to create a new, solid foundation on which his royal authority would be built across the land, a political settlement that could bring peace and order to his troubled kingdom. The ceremony that unfolded in Westminster that July day, a ritual oath-taking, would be the start. Its focus was the king's firstborn son, Prince Edward, the boy to whom Queen Elizabeth had given birth in Westminster sanctuary eight months before.

One by one, the assembled councillors came forward to pledge allegiance to Edward's 'true and undoubted heir', the infant who now represented the dynasty's future. The first lords to do so were Clarence and Richard. They swore on the Gospels that, should the prince outlive his father, they would 'take and accept' him 'for true, very and righteous King of England', adding their names to a signed declaration for good measure.[1]

The oath-taking was a display of the new-found family unity that had powered Edward's astonishing victory, at its core the reforged bond between the king and his two brothers. It was also a vision of how, henceforth, he planned to rule. In keeping with this fraternal harmony, Edward had gone out of his way to secure Clarence's and Richard's approval for his plans for his little heir. The boy was handed the titles of prince of Wales, duke of Cornwall and earl of Chester; and, as was customary, had been set up with his own household and council, which would run his estates and affairs on his behalf until he was fourteen years old. The king's brothers had, naturally, given their consent. A formality it may have been, but it was a significant one: Prince Edward was now the king's heir presumptive. Which meant that Clarence, and by extension Richard, were not. Nonetheless, both brothers could console themselves with the fact that, as Edward carved up the political map of England, they were at the head of the queue.

As he distributed rewards and power, Edward placed a premium on loyalty. Those who had proved themselves during the king's 'late troubles', in particular those who had shared all his 'conflicts and journeys', now stood to benefit from his favour. As he had done back in 1469, trying to reimpose control after the orgy of bloodletting at Edgecote, Edward privileged his household men. Many of them had followed him into exile, and had fought with particular ferocity around their king in the recent battles. They were well represented at the Westminster ceremony: John Howard was there, so too Thomas St Leger and the northerners William Parr and Ralph Ashton. Chief among them, naturally, was Edward's close friend and chamberlain, William Hastings.

Among the prizes the king handed Hastings was control of Warwick's former stronghold of Calais. Edward had originally planned to grant the post to another of his companions-in-exile, the queen's brother Anthony Woodville, who had then expressed an ill-timed desire to go on pilgrimage. His wish elicited from Edward a snort of derision and accusations of cowardice – which, while unfair, was probably the king's frustration at the prospect of being deprived of one of his most useful servants. Woodville took the hint and stayed in England, but it didn't make any difference: Edward took Calais away from him and gave it to Hastings instead. The move made sense. It bound the workings of this critical but highly problematic enclave, a source of so much trouble over the years, closely to those of the king's household and chamber. Moreover, Hastings was appointed not captain of Calais, with all the independence of action that title implied, but its lieutenant, *locum tenens*, the king's representative there.

Woodville, who had coveted the role, was furious. Wisely, he expressed his frustrations in private. Besides, as he probably reasoned to himself, further opportunities would come his way: as uncle to the king's infant heir, he was now a blood relative of the dynasty.[2] And as Edward extended his rule across the country, it was his own blood to which he now turned, first and foremost his brothers.

Contrary to the rosy commentaries, Clarence's return to the fold that spring hadn't been down to a sudden outbreak of fraternal love and loyalty on his part. Or if it had, those impulses had been catalysed by an exceptionally attractive counter-offer from Edward. When, back in 1469, Clarence had married Warwick's older daughter Isabel, he had become heir to the vast portfolio of Neville lands that his wife stood to inherit – though at that point, getting his hands on them was a distant prospect. In the spring of 1471 Edward, happy to promise his brother almost anything to get him back onside, had honoured the arrangement; and Warwick's killing at Barnet had then clarified the situation marvellously as far as Clarence was concerned. Granted the Neville earldoms of Warwick and Salisbury in the battle's aftermath, along with a slew of other honours, he set about taking possession of the lands that came with them and, mediating with the king on behalf of Warwick's former supporters, taking them into his service. For Clarence, the seismic upheavals of the previous two years and more must have seemed entirely worth it.[3] Others, who had been at the sharp end of the bloodletting he had engendered, looked askance at the arrangement.

But it was Richard whose situation was now transformed. His loyalty to Edward had been tested in the king's 'time of great necessity', and it had endured. Not yet nineteen, his blood, his ability and his proven commitment to Edward's cause made him an automatic pick for a key role in government. Accordingly, Edward had already given him a string of great offices of state: the admiralty and great chamberlainship – both previously in Warwick's hands – to go with the constableship he hankered after.[4] But Richard also needed a landed portfolio commensurate with his status as a royal duke. For the first time in his life, he was in a position to ask for what he wanted.

Growing up, Richard had had to be content with what he got. When lands and offices were handed out he had been, if not at the back of the queue, then hardly a priority as Edward sought to satisfy the competing demands of key noblemen against a constantly shifting political landscape. Often, Edward had granted him lands only to take them away again, returning them to their previous owners as they were restored to favour, or giving them instead to Clarence. The episode of the lordship of Richmond – wrestled away from Richard by his older brother in a spasm of jealous rage – seemed to sum up the childhood relationship between the two brothers. It was one that Clarence had dominated, both in terms of his then status as heir presumptive and, given the three-year age gap between them, in physical development. At the time, Richard had little option but to take the path of least resistance. The grants he had received were a wide, diffuse scattering of estates and offices that, while they yielded the requisite income to maintain his ducal status, didn't give him the commodity that all great noblemen regarded as their birthright: a landed powerbase. In 1469, Edward had made a stab at setting up Richard, then sixteen, with an independent sphere of action in Wales, but with Edward and Richard soon fleeing into exile, it hadn't lasted long. Now Edward was in a position to bestow on Richard the kind of endowment he craved: the great northern patrimony of the earl of Warwick.[5]

The estates that Clarence stood to inherit through his wife were only one part of the Neville inheritance. The other half constituted the lands and offices of Warwick's northern power base, centred on his north Yorkshire castle of Middleham, which Edward now handed to his youngest brother. Edward's previous attempt to solve the intractable problem of the north, entrusting control of it to the Neville family, had blown up in his face. By transferring Warwick's patrimony and its networks of influence to Richard, Edward now aimed to impose a permanent solution.

Though Richard had spent time at Middleham as a teenager in Warwick's household, his associations with the Neville family weren't close: indeed, in the recent fighting, he had played a key role in destroying it. Neither was he especially familiar with the bonds of blood and intermarriage that knitted the region together, and the quarrels that simmered between leading local families. He was, in short, hardly a figure to prompt a visceral transference of allegiance among those who had looked to the Nevilles for protection and favour, and who had given their service in return. But then, Richard would not simply be the latest in a line of great regional lords. As the king's brother, he was the representative and mouthpiece of the crown. Local big men, aware of the influence that Richard could wield with the king, would find his lordship doubly enticing; Richard, meanwhile, would be backed by the full force of royal authority. Away in the south, Edward could rest easy in his Thames-side palaces, safe in the knowledge that the north was in his brother's reliable, trustworthy hands.[6]

This partition of the Warwick estates was, clearly, a division of spoils made after discussions between the king and both brothers. It was also far from straightforward – for the simple reason that the lands were not Edward's to give.

There were already legal heirs. The bulk of the lands Clarence now claimed through his wife were due by law to go to Warwick's widow, Anne. The northern lands now in Richard's possession, handed down through the male line of the Neville family, were to descend to Warwick's nephew, John Neville's young son, George duke of Bedford.

There was a neat legal solution to the problem of these Neville inheritors. Given that Warwick and John Neville had committed treason, all Edward had to do was to declare them and their heirs legally dead by a parliamentary act of attainder, and all their titles and property would be permanently forfeit to the crown; whereupon Edward could dole them out to his brothers. This, however, was a move that both Clarence and Richard were desperate to avoid. As the brothers knew all too well, what the king gave, the king could also take away. If they gained possession of the Neville estates by royal grant, their lands would for ever be in danger of being 'resumed' or reappropriated by the king.

Both brothers had first-hand experience of the insecurity provoked by these royal property reshuffles. Clarence had registered his frustrations in the most extreme way imaginable, by openly rebelling; Richard had just shrugged his shoulders and bided his time. Both perhaps felt that there was something in Edward – a tendency to indecision and whim – that now made it imperative to avoid such an arrangement. The far more secure way to hold their lands was somehow to inherit them from the legal heirs of the Neville family – which in turn meant that attainting Warwick, John Neville and their heirs was out of the question. On that, Clarence and Richard were agreed, and so they told their brother the king. It was probably the last time the pair were to agree on anything.[7]

As autumn came, many who had fought for Lancaster in the recent conflicts remained on edge. Sir John Paston wrote to his younger brother, still lying low at the family home of Caister Castle. Hearing that locals were denouncing him as a traitor, trying to provoke him into 'quarrels', Paston urged his brother to watch his step and to be 'chief of your language', to avoid loose talk. The royal pardon he had been promised was taking a long time to materialize. It would be good, Paston wrote worriedly, for his brother to be 'a little surer of your pardon than you are'.[8]

Woven into Paston's correspondence was a reminder of the dangers of straying loyalties. That summer the newly pardoned leader of the Kentish rebellion, Thomas Neville, the Bastard of Fauconberg, had gone north with Richard. His Neville connections and knowledge of the region would have been valuable to the young duke as he sought to assert his new authority; besides which, Richard could keep an eye on Fauconberg in case he was tempted to renege on his new oaths of Yorkist loyalty. Which, apparently, was what had now happened. As Paston reported, Fauconberg was 'either beheaded, or like to be'.

The trouble had come when Fauconberg returned south and, that September, had taken command of a ship and put to sea. Some days later, he sailed into the port of Southampton, where he was arrested 'for a new offence' and charged with treason: while at sea, his pardon had been revoked and royal agents were busy seizing his goods. What crime he had committed, nobody seemed to know. Given the naval expertise that he had already brought to bear against Edward's regime, Fauconberg's apparently unauthorized activities had perhaps been provocation enough to a twitchy government, especially at a time when prominent Lancastrian fugitives had broken out of sanctuary and disappeared.[9] Dealing with Fauconberg, however, wasn't straightforward. The government was anxious to avoid attracting public opprobrium for its procedurally suspect judicial killings (the most egregious example of which had come in Southampton the year before, with John Tiptoft's impalings). Besides which, Fauconberg's 'new offence' wasn't obvious, and it was highly irregular for kings to cancel pardons they had already granted.

Where the intelligence on Fauconberg had come from was unclear. It was probable that Richard had received it in his capacity as admiral, and taken it to the king; equally probably, he had reassured Edward that he would make the problem go away and Edward, relieved, had given him the go-ahead.

Richard took Fauconberg north to Middleham Castle where, away from the public gaze, he was summarily beheaded. If there had been a trial, nobody remarked on it. As Fauconberg's head was brought back to London – one Harry Capp was paid the substantial sum of thirty shillings for carrying it – and joined the thicket of heads on London Bridge, its sightless eyes gazing into Kent, people debated the killing: 'some men say he would have deserved it and some say nay'.[10] Whatever the case, Richard had laid down a marker. Anybody attempting to play fast and loose with the king's laws would receive the most rigorous justice at his hands.

For all the frightening uncertainty of Fauconberg's murder and the anxieties of former Lancastrians, Edward's punishments had, by and large, been calculated to offer the possibility of a way back into his grace – at a price. Those who had made the mistake of transferring their loyalties to Lancaster – from the Pastons to Warwick's one surviving brother, Archbishop George Neville – were pardoned. So, too, were diehard opponents of Edward's regime, like the group of Lancastrian advisers found sheltering with Margaret of Anjou after Tewkesbury. Foremost among them were the west-countrymen Sir John Fortescue, now in his seventies, and the fifty-year-old John Morton. For these men, the equation was simple. They had been unswerving in their allegiance to the house of Lancaster, through thin and thinner. Now, they were forced to acknowledge that their cause was irretrievably lost. John Morton put their line of thinking best. In an ideal world, he later observed, Henry VI's son would have been king, not Edward IV – but 'after God ordered him to lose it and King Edward to reign, I was never so mad that I would with a dead man strive against the quick.'[11]

Edward had always appreciated talent, wherever it came from; moreover, it was pleasing to be able to pardon those who threw themselves on his mercy. If this small group of highly able administrators and politicians – men who had been instrumental to Margaret of Anjou's decade-long survival in exile and her unlikely bid to regain power – were now prepared to commit themselves to the house of York, they promised to be considerable assets to Edward's regime. That autumn, Morton started a new job in the chancery offices in Westminster. Fortescue, meanwhile, wrote for his life, systematically dismembering the case he had made for the house of Lancaster's supremacy, and in its place offering a full justification for the house of York's rightful claim to the throne. Edward was gratified.

Besides pragmatism and self-regard, other impulses underlay Edward's conciliation. He had to move beyond the internecine bloodletting of the past years, to be seen as a unifier, a merciful healer as well as a deliverer of justice – which meant pardoning people for their misjudgements rather than executing them. There was another reason too.

Edward had been minded to throw the book at the families of Warwick and John Neville. They had tried to destroy him; in return, Edward would destroy the Neville line and confiscate its lands in perpetuity, through an act of attainder. But the king's brothers had twisted his arm, and he had changed his mind. The Nevilles would not be attainted in order that Clarence and Richard could benefit from the greater legal security of possessing their lands by inheritance, rather than by royal grant. But if Edward was not prepared to use this devastating political weapon against Warwick, the rebel-in-chief, he could hardly deploy it against the earl's supporters.[12]

With attainder no longer in the equation, Edward and his brothers had to find another legal justification for what amounted to a land grab of staggering proportions. In wrenching the lands away from their rightful Neville heirs, the claims of those heirs would somehow have to be dismissed – or the laws of inheritance would have to be overridden. Then came another twist. At nineteen years old, Richard was on the lookout for a suitable bride. One had recently become available: Warwick's younger daughter Anne, whose husband, Edward of Lancaster, had died at Tewkesbury. Richard wanted to marry her. If, up to this point, the interests of Clarence and Richard regarding the Warwick inheritance had been reasonably aligned, it was now that they violently parted company.

There had long been talk of such a marriage. If the rumours back in 1464 were to be believed, it was a match that Warwick himself had wanted. Richard and Anne had known each other for years, growing up together at Middleham. After Tewkesbury, however, she had come under the protection of her husband's killer, Clarence. Still only fifteen, 'amiable, beauteous and gracious', she was perhaps the most eligible young widow in the country – and Clarence knew it. She was now under house arrest, her every movement watched.[13]

Clarence had a particular reason for wanting to keep control of his sister-in-law. He held his own share of the Warwick inheritance through his wife Isabel. As joint heiress, Anne had an equally good claim on those lands. It was, therefore, entirely in Clarence's interest to prevent Anne from making such a claim – which would, of course, threaten his own.[14]

For Richard, Anne was more or less the ideal bride. While he already had his portion of Warwick's lands in the north, Anne embodied the familial link that his lordship in the region lacked. Marrying Anne, Warwick's daughter, would make Richard a true heir to the Nevilles, giving him more heft among the dead earl's followers in the region and allowing their allegiances to transfer more instinctively to him. It would also present a chance to muscle in on his brother's part of the

Neville inheritance: potentially, to claim a half-share on behalf of his wife.

When news of Richard's bid for Anne reached Clarence, he was livid. On her own account, Anne stood little chance of making good her claims. Backed by a powerful husband, however, it was a different story. Few could match Clarence for wealth and influence, but Richard was one of them. Clarence's agitation was driven not just by rage, but by anxiety. No sooner had he made good his right to the lands which he had coveted for years than that right started to look newly precarious – undermined, he feared, by his younger brother.

Clarence went to some lengths to prevent Richard getting his hands on his prospective bride. Disguising Anne as a cookmaid, he placed her in the precincts of St Martin's-le-Grand, a sanctuary north of St Paul's Cathedral, where the king's writ did not run. If Clarence took the view that possession was nine-tenths of the law, so too did Richard, who had no intention of negotiating with his brother for her release. Instead, he found out where Anne was and simply extracted her.[15]

Just as Richard had proved brutally uncomplicated in dealing with Fauconberg's shaky loyalties, so he now pursued his rights with direct aggression. Neither he nor Clarence was prepared to take a backward step over the young noblewoman whom both saw as their property. That winter, as talk of the two brothers' disagreement spread through the country and into northern Europe, their quarrel deepened.

The Christmas festivities of 1471 seemed more magnificent than usual. Through the feasting, plays and mummings, and the ribald antics of the abbot of misrule and his accomplices, Edward moved, sovereign in his own land. On Christmas Day, Westminster Abbey bore witness to a joint re-coronation ceremony: a magnificent reassertion of the dynastic order in which Edward and Elizabeth were crowned king and queen, followed by a banquet at nearby Whitehall. The ceremonial continued throughout the festive season. On Epiphany, one of the great 'days of estate', the king processed, crowned and in his velvet royal robes, Elizabeth alongside him; visibly pregnant with the couple's fifth child, she was excused from wearing the heavy gold crown. At the chapel royal, Edward offered up gold, frankincense and myrrh. Later, there was the usual Twelfth Night entertainment: following the Epiphany feast, a great bowl of wassail, spiced ale, was borne into the hall by John Howard and Edward's new household steward, Thomas, Lord Stanley. Awash with festive cheer, the king, queen and assembled court – including London's mayor and aldermen, and a group of specially selected citizens – listened appreciatively to 'fresh songs' sung by the gentlemen of the chapel royal, who then doubled up as a company of actors in the plays that followed.[16]

Meanwhile, Edward had plenty of time to reflect on his tumultuous year, in particular his exile in the Low Countries. Fondly recalling the help he had received from various Burgundian lords, his recollections of Charles the Bold himself were rather different. Edward remembered how, after his arrival in Holland, his Burgundian brother-in-law – scared of the very real probability of a joint invasion by Louis XI and the earl of Warwick – had at first dragged his feet, providing Edward and his men with a shoestring budget and not even acknowledging Edward's status as king, all the while protesting his Lancastrian affiliations. When some three months later the pair finally met, Edward, all warm hugs and fraternal bonhomie, had suppressed his irritation at these insults. Back in England, he gave it vent.

Beneath the continued Anglo-Burgundian *entente* and the frequent ambassadorial exchanges – Edward sending reports of his victories to Charles; Charles offering his sincere congratulations – the English king, reported one ambassador, was stewing over his 'savage treatment' by the Burgundian duke. For his part, Charles apparently 'did not know whether to be happy or not' about the news of Edward's victories: the 'bad grace' and 'much regretfulness' with which he had backed Edward weren't exactly conducive to their continued friendship.[17]

Away in France, these hints of mutual mistrust were seized on by Louis XI, his perpetual anxiety about a joint Anglo-Burgundian alliance newly inflamed by Edward's conquering return. He dispatched envoys to the English court who worked away on Edward's grievances against Charles the Bold, further stoked – in the endlessly tangled dance of northern European politics – by Charles's sealing of a truce with the French king, amid rumours of a marriage treaty between France and Burgundy. This, of course, was England's horror scenario:

an alliance that left it isolated and, as the Burgundian commentator Philippe de Commynes put it, 'in danger of destruction' – although, he added laconically, Edward and his council got 'unnecessarily worked up' about something that was never going to happen.[18]

Unnecessarily or not, Edward did get worked up. He refused to pay the remaining instalments of his sister Margaret's dowry due to his Burgundian brother-in-law. Payment of the outstanding balance – £30,000, or 75 per cent of the total sum – had fallen due on the second anniversary of their wedding, in July 1470. It was already late, for understandable reasons. Edward, who didn't have the money anyway, now refused to stump up. His well-ventilated grudges against Charles perhaps gave him an excuse to withhold payment, but his refusal to pay was almost inevitable, given that he was also defaulting on the sweeping financial commitments he had made to the Hanse when in exile, in return for their ships and men. The Hanse were unimpressed.

Charles was vexed in turn. Never the most temperate of men, he was exercised enough to abandon his recently rediscovered Yorkist loyalties – in private, anyway. In November 1471, he had held a secret ceremony in the city of Arras, in which he signed a statement to the effect that, through his maternal descent from John of Gaunt, founder of the house of Lancaster, he was the rightful heir to the Lancastrian king of England Henry VI, and would claim his throne as soon as chance arose to do so.[19]

Whether or not news of the ceremony reached Edward, that winter he was on the alert. As well as the substantial annual intelligence budget of £104 given to the monitoring station that was Calais, Edward handed its treasurer an additional £33 6s 8d 'for the exploration of rumours'. The money, another document stated, was to be used specifically on the surveillance of the plans 'of our adversaries'.[20]

As a chilly peace settled over northern Europe, Edward's brothers consolidated their hold on their new lands. In the north, Richard was recruiting. Former servants of Warwick flocked to him: pinning Richard's boar badge on their caps and their jackets, they pledged their allegiance to him and to the crown. Among them was Sir John Conyers, the man who as 'Robin of Redesdale' had sparked popular uprisings on Warwick's behalf. Further support came from committed Yorkists in the region, from the combative Sir Ralph Ashton – now sheriff of Yorkshire – and his son-in-law John Nesfield, to the Pilk-ington brothers John and Charles.[21] It wasn't just in the north that Richard had been busy. As Christmas drew to a close, and the royal household began to recover from the abbot of misrule's twelve days of benign disorder, he was seeking royal backing for his marriage to Anne Neville – and the king was inclined to listen.

As Edward well knew, Richard's proposal would be certain to cause trouble. The king had explicitly granted Clarence his portion of the Warwick estates, lock, stock and barrel. In allowing Richard to marry Anne, he was providing his youngest brother with a key to start unpicking Clarence's settlement. Then again, Richard had proved his loyalty and needed a bride of exceptional status. Edward was in the mood to give Richard what he wanted. Besides, the king was confident in his own ability to straighten out the argument between his two brothers, which, given their status as the regime's most powerful noblemen, threatened to destabilize whole swathes of the kingdom if it got out of hand.

On 17 February 1472, the first Tuesday in Lent, Sir John Paston wrote from London to his younger brother with distinctly unLenten thoughts. He was relaxed, skittish even. The Pastons' political reha-bilitation was almost complete. He and his on–off betrothed, Queen Elizabeth's cousin Anne Haute, had recently spoken at a 'pretty leis-ure'. Their marriage was on again – and, with it, Paston's relationship with the royal family. Paston asked his brother to dig out his copy of John Lydgate's poem of romantic courtly love, *The Temple of Glass*, and send it by return, to help him with his courtship.[22] Then he turned to political gossip.

The previous day Edward and Elizabeth, together with Clarence and Richard, had been rowed up the Thames to the royal manor of Sheen to attend a 'pardon', a ceremony at which papal indulgences were granted. In fact, Edward planned to use the occasion to thrash out the increasingly toxic spat between his brothers: away from the public gaze of London and Westminster, the relative seclusion of Sheen was as good a place as any to do so. 'Men say', Paston added delicately, that the brothers had gone 'not in all charity'. The atmos-phere could have been cut with a knife.[23]

Edward had already made one attempt to reconcile his brothers: it hadn't worked. Shortly before the Sheen trip he summoned Clarence and Richard to a council meeting at Westminster to rule on their claims to the Warwick inheritance. There, in front of the king and a panel of his close advisers, the brothers were ordered to put their cases in turn.

Both Clarence and Richard were used to heading commissions and presiding over courts; both knew how to debate, to turn a phrase. Even so, as one chronicler – a man either present in the council chamber, or close to someone who was – later recollected, the pair had astonished everybody present, 'the lawyers even', with their rhetorical pyrotechnics and their ability 'to find arguments in abundance' to support their cases. Edward, meanwhile, had kept order with a kingly affability. Then the writer paused, the scene recollected in his mind's eye. 'These three brothers', he continued, a hint of regret in his appraising tone, 'possessed such surpassing talent that their triple bond could only have been broken with the utmost difficulty' – 'if', that was, 'they had been able to avoid conflict.' It was a big 'if'. The meeting, increasingly heated, had reached an impasse and the panel had been unable to deliver a judgment. Calling proceedings to a close, Edward announced that he would deal with his brothers himself and be 'a mediator between them'. Which was where Sheen came in.

As the talks between the three brothers unfolded – Queen Elizabeth a silent, heavily pregnant presence at the king's side – it became increasingly clear that what Edward meant by 'mediation' was not independent arbitration: at least, not as far as Clarence was concerned. Rather, Edward was quite clearly 'entreating' Clarence on Richard's behalf, trying to persuade Clarence to let their youngest brother have what he wanted.

In the face of the king's pressure, Clarence's eloquence gave way to a sullen defensiveness. Richard could, he conceded, have Anne Neville – but, he added emphatically, 'there shall part no livelihood', no lands. It wasn't the marriage per se that worried Clarence, but the prospect of Richard launching counter-claims to his property on his new wife's behalf. But as all three knew, Clarence could argue as much as he liked. Edward had already made up his mind what was going to happen.

The king's ruling was unequivocally in favour of Richard: he was given the hand of Anne Neville, and with her a chunk of the 'livelihood' to which Clarence had clung so desperately. There was some horse-trading. Clarence was given a scattering of lands in compensation. He also extracted an assurance from Edward, on record, that henceforth none of the lands or possessions granted him by the king would be taken away from him or his heirs, 'neither by authority of Parliament' – Clarence had always been nervous about parliamentary acts of resumption – 'nor in any other way'. Inadvertently, this assurance revealed what had already happened at Sheen. Clarence had been presented with a choice: agree with the king, or lose everything.[24] Richard, on the other hand, had emerged triumphant as lord of one of the greatest blocs of territory in England. He was hungry for more.

There was something unwavering about Richard: the way he fought; the way he applied the king's laws; how he pursued what he believed to be rightfully his. Even more than most, his response to the uncertain, mistrustful world that had formed him – the years of blood-soaked instability, bookended by outbreaks of civil conflict and two flights into exile – was an unyielding insistence on rule and custom. The books he owned and acquired were a case in point. It wasn't so much that Richard was an exceptional reader. The volumes he read – chivalric romances, histories, 'mirrors' or guides for princes, prophecies and pious works – were fairly run-of-the-mill, the kind of books you might find in the chests and coffers of most noblemen of the time.[25] It was more his engagement with them, his identification with them – signing not the flyleaves, most at risk from being torn out, but the inside pages – and the way he strived to live by the ideals and virtues they depicted: of chivalry, piety and obedience. All of which provided reassurance and predictability in an unstable world – predictability that Richard seemed to crave. His mottoes seemed to sum this up: the heroic struggle of *tant le desierée*, 'I have desired it so much'; and the unconditional loyalty encapsulated in *'a vous me lie'*, 'I bind myself to you'.

Edward appreciated such sentiments, hitherto found so lacking in the emotionally incontinent Clarence. Richard's constancy found its expression in enduring friendships, from the 'servants and lovers' of his youth, like Francis, Lord Lovell and the lonely, resentful young Lancastrian duke of Buckingham, Henry Stafford; to Hastings, in whose company Richard had spent plenty of time during the recent upheavals, and the bruising John Howard. Now, the nature of those friendships was evolving, along with Richard's rapidly changing status. Back in 1468, when accompanying the fifteen-year-old Richard through East Anglia, Howard assured his regional boss, the duke of Norfolk, that when Norfolk said the word, he would instantly drop Richard and attend on him instead. There was little chance of Howard doing the same thing now. Indeed, all the signs were that those around the king were anxious to bind themselves close to Richard, with gifts and favours: a few days after the Sheen meeting, Queen Elizabeth had been quick to renew a grant to Richard that had been about to expire.[26]

Elizabeth's favouring of Richard was hardly surprising. The previous summer, when Edward's crushing of Warwick and the Lancastrians had finally brought to an end the period of agonizing uncertainty she had endured, a London poet had urged her both to 'remember old troubles and things past', and that Christ had 'delivered you out of woe'. Elizabeth undoubtedly kept in mind her profound debt to her Maker: always demonstrably pious, as her royal role demanded, she seemed to grow more devout as the years passed.[27] Equally, though, it would have been hard for Elizabeth not to recall 'old troubles and things past': the figure of Clarence, so instrumental in those troubles, was a constant reminder of them. Whatever she thought of Clarence, Elizabeth kept quiet. But her attitude manifested itself in one way – her backing of Richard in the brothers' quarrel.

Following his victory over Clarence at Sheen, Richard moved quickly to secure his prize. Away in Rome, on 22 April 1472, a papal clerk drew up the dispensation that allowed him to marry Anne Neville, his cousin; weeks later, a messenger arrived in England with the requisite paperwork. There had been a clerical error – the dispensation covered the third and fourth degrees of affinity, but not the first and second (Anne was both Richard's first cousin and sister-in-law). Still, nobody seemed particularly concerned about the mistake. Richard, presumably, put in a fresh application; soon after, the pair were married.[28]

Sometime that year, Richard ordered his secretary to begin a new work of reference: an exhaustive list of his titles and rights to land and offices, including grants made by Edward to his 'dearest brother', and those he had acquired through his wife's inheritance. Everything was itemized, even grants that Edward had made him in his youth and then, thinking better of it, cancelled and distributed elsewhere: the honour of Richmond, for instance, given instead to Clarence; and the lands of the earls of Oxford, subsequently handed back to the most recent incumbent, John de Vere.

Richard wanted a record of everything that he had ever been given, and to which he might therefore lay claim in the future. After all, the backsliding earl of Oxford, on the run since Barnet, had again forfeited his title and lands to the crown, following which Edward had regranted them to Richard. Like Clarence, Richard understood that there was no knowing when he might have to defend his rights – or when the opportunity might arise to reassert a once-dormant claim. When that time came, he would be ready. Over the coming years, this cartulary would grow, items written in by different hands in different inks at different times. It would become a map of Richard's consolidation and expansion of his ducal empire, and the expression of a great lord ambitious for the power to which his blood and his loyalty entitled him.[29]

Although the three brothers had thrashed out an agreement over the Warwick inheritance, the process at Sheen, rather than dispelling the mistrust between Clarence and Richard, only intensified it. With their slicing up of the dead earl's lands still to be ringfenced and protected in law, neither brother was happy. Clarence felt that he had been ganged up on. Richard suspected his brother was being deliberately uncooperative. When, according to the terms of the Sheen settlement, Richard relinquished some lands to his brother, Clarence refused to reciprocate. Clarence also seemed newly aware of his own political vulnerability. Realizing quite how few friends he had at court, he tried to buy some, handing plum offices on his estates to Edward's friend Lord Hastings – who, as a contemporary bluntly assessed, had more influence with the king and the lords than any man alive.[30] Meanwhile, that spring, conspiracy resurfaced.

On Saturday 25 April, at his spectacular Hertfordshire house of The More, Archbishop George Neville awaited a royal visit. Following the disasters that had overtaken his family in the past year, Neville, back in royal favour, had finally begun to relax. Earlier that spring, he and Edward had spent several days together at Windsor Castle, and had had 'right good cheer' hunting in the surrounding parkland; so much so that Edward had proposed to come and stay with him at The More, to 'hunt and disport with him' further. Delighted at this mark of grace, Neville's preparations were lavish. Some seven years previously, to celebrate his creation as archbishop of York, he had laid on a feast that people were still talking about; now, he was determined to prove an equally sensational host to his king. Fetching the vast quantities of jewels, plate, glass, tapestries and soft furnishings that he had hidden securely in London 'and diverse other places' after the battles of Barnet and Tewkesbury, and borrowing 'more stuff off other men', he had also laid in copious quantities of food and drink, ensuring that his newly constructed cellar was prodigiously stocked. He had prepared everything 'as richly and pleasantly as he could'. But that Saturday, Neville instead received a visit for which he was not prepared at all.

Late in the evening, a detachment of the king's household men clattered over the drawbridge, through the crenellated gatehouse and, brushing Neville's shocked servants aside, headed for the archbishop's apartments. Arresting him, they disappeared into the night. Where they had taken him, or whether he was still alive, nobody knew.

Some days later, people started to get wind of what had happened. Neville had been taken the twenty-five miles or so to the Tower, where he was imprisoned. Two nights later, he was marched down to London's docks and hustled on board a ship, which weighed anchor and headed down the Thames for the open sea and Calais, where he was locked up in the border fortress of Hammes.

It was unclear what Neville had done wrong. 'Men say that he hath offended, but some men say nay', observed John Paston noncommittally. For all his new-found geniality towards the archbishop, Edward had continued to keep an eye on him. Word had reached the king that Neville was receiving shady visitors – one had even brought letters to him at Windsor, right under the king's nose – and had idly discussed a plot to depose Edward. One of the servants hovering in Neville's attendance as he did so was his own treasurer, Edmund Chaderton, who had gone straight to the king with an account of the conversation. Neville's visitors were apparently agents of the exiled Lancastrian earl of Oxford, who that spring had launched several guerrilla attacks on the Calais enclave. After his arrest, Neville was charged with high treason for providing aid, probably financial, to this nebulous conspiracy. The indictment itself was thin: it didn't even mention Oxford, citing a number of unknown Yorkshiremen, of whom only one was named. But Edward wasn't about to take any chances with a man whose loyalties had over the years had proved exceptionally flaky. There was, too, another reason why he was inclined to accept Chaderton's evidence at face value.

As George Neville was shipped off to Calais, two of Edward's senior financial officers, his chamber treasurer Thomas Vaughan and William Parr, now controller of the royal household, turned up at The More. They summarily dismissed the archbishop's stunned entourage – 'every man his way', remarked John Paston – including the various hangers-on, 'great clerks' and 'famous doctors' from the University of Cambridge who comprised Neville's intellectual salon. Securing the house, Vaughan, Parr and their men then itemized and inventoried their way through its opulent interior with a practised efficiency, stripping it bare of 'all the goods that were therein'. The whole collection, they estimated, was worth a jaw-dropping '£20,000 or more'. Everything – the exquisite jewels, plate, furnishings, books and fine wine amassed by Neville over the years – was loaded onto carts and driven off.[31]

The haul was then given to the household of the king's son and heir – whose chamberlain, conveniently enough, Vaughan also was.[32] Edward kept one item for himself: the archbishop's jewel-encrusted mitre, which he ordered broken up and remade into a new crown. He also annexed Neville's ecclesiastical lands, the profits from which were, as usual, siphoned off into his chamber.[33] It was hard not to interpret Edward's proposed visit to The More as a way of getting Neville to bring out all his concealed riches into plain sight, before the king's men pounced.

To some, George Neville's treatment perhaps brought to mind the notorious case of Sir Thomas Cook, the London merchant whose victimization back in 1468 had done much to focus resentment against the Woodville family. It rather suggested that Edward either hadn't learned much from the episode – or that, as undisputed sovereign in his own land, he didn't care; now, people would think twice before sticking up for Neville. Besides which, in going out of his way to acquire the fine things after which he hankered, Edward was only doing what was expected, even demanded, of kings – even if the methods he used were a bit much.

Around this time the Lancastrian propagandist and political theorist Sir John Fortescue, determined to emphasize his new-found Yorkist allegiance, presented Edward with a treatise: 'On the Difference between an Absolute and Limited Monarchy'. Mining historical, legal, religious and political works, *The Governance of England*, as it would later become known, was a blueprint for the reform of England's monarchy.[34] In it, Fortescue – who in recent years had experienced up close the crisis that gripped England's monarchy – tackled the intractable problems that had come to obsess him and many of the country's ruling elites, and that had driven people to rise up in their multitudes in discontent. Central to Fortescue's vision of a renewed monarchy was a long-established idea, one that Edward had wholeheartedly embraced since first ascending the throne. The 'magnificence and grandeur' of the king's household was, Fortescue asserted, crucial in the projection of his, and the country's, power, wealth and honour: 'no realm may prosper, or be worshipful, under a poor king'. It was crucial that a king had enough money for great architectural projects, to enable him to buy 'rich clothes and rich furs'; to swathe his houses in the finest of tapestries and soft furnishings; to collect exquisite plate, jewels and knick-knacks 'convenient to his estate royal'. If a king was unable to live 'as befits his royal majesty', Fortescue warned, he would hardly be maintaining his unique, sovereign status. Magnificence, in short, was one way for a king to distinguish himself from even the greatest of his subjects – and it was crucial to do so, added Fortescue, for 'there may no greater peril grow to a prince, than to have a subject of equal power to himself'.[35]

But, as Fortescue was at pains to emphasize, a king could only be as magnificent as his finances allowed. Over the decades kings and their advisers had tried vainly to tackle the excessive spending, disorganization and peculation at the heart of the king's household. What the king now needed, Fortescue wrote, was 'a new foundation of his crown': a new financial settlement enabling him to govern the realm in the manner which his royal dignity demanded. Such an endowment, Fortescue recommended, should be another 'resumption' – a royal clawing-back of the crown lands that, over time, the king had granted to his leading subjects – but this time with a system of checks and balances that ensured the king would never again 'alienate' them, or give them away. But if this was ambitious, and almost impossible in practice, there were other ways in which kings could implement economic reform.

Soon after Fortescue had presented his treatise – almost as if in response to its advice – came the latest, comprehensive attempt at such reform. The *Liber Niger Domus Regis Anglie Edwardi Quarti*, or *Black Book of the Household of King Edward IV of England* was nothing less than a refounding of the royal household: a sweeping vision of an establishment that stood testament to Edward's idea of himself and his dynasty.[36]

There had never before been anything quite like the *Black Book*. An extravagant document, its preface, bursting into verse and citing biblical tags, explained in detail how and why it had been produced. The product of Edward IV's great council, it was the expression of a unified group of 'wise, prudent and well learned men', who brought to bear on the subject knowledge of the king's household, both from personal experience and through 'long study and deliberation'. Foremost among them were Edward's cousin, the cardinal archbishop of Canterbury, Thomas Bourchier, and his brothers Clarence and Richard. Citing some of the most celebrated royal households in history – from that of Solomon, famous for his 'great renowned richesse, welfare and high largesse', to Edward's illustrious forebear Edward III, whose household had been, quite simply, 'the house of very policy and flower of England' – it aimed to surpass them all. It would be the new, unified kingdom in microcosm, the 'new house of houses principal of England'.[37]

The *Black Book* presented the household in its customary bipartite structure: the 'house of magnificence', the glittering 'above stairs' through which the king moved, held audience, ate and slept; and the unseen 'below stairs', whose mechanisms ran with purring efficiency. That this would be a household of strictly ordered magnificence – 'the king will have his goods dispended, but not wasted', the ordinance warned – was clear from the prominence given to the workings of the counting-house. So detailed and intimate a picture did the *Black Book* provide that, despite its many idiosyncrasies, it was handed down through generations. In the early seventeenth century, it was still kept among the records of the counting-house, riffled through by the increasingly exasperated officials of James I as they sought solutions to his extravagance.[38]

The *Black Book* also detailed the institution at the household's core: the closely guarded sequence of apartments that formed the privileged world of the king's chamber. The chamber functioned separately, its staff a discrete unit who took 'no gift' given to the rest of the household, but were rewarded separately. These were the men under Lord Hastings' command: the specially selected servants who, on a constant rota, attended on Edward day and night. They formed his personal security, 'watching the king', and performed the most intimate service: they dressed the king from his personal wardrobe and made up his bed; kept his 'stool' or commode, his bows and personal armoury, his books, his dogs and his 'beast' – a pet monkey, perhaps – and his library. When not attending on the king, they often 'went messages', riding out on the king's confidential business.[39]

In stark contrast to its minute description of the household's financial workings, the *Black Book* was vague about the chamber's arrangements. The king's personal treasury now handled vast amounts of cash: income from the king's lands and his business deals, customs duties and the enforcement of his prerogative rights. The way it functioned – a breezy informality coupled with opaque close control – was characteristic of Edward himself. Describing the role of the chamber treasurer Thomas Vaughan, the *Black Book* stated simply that everything he actioned was to be done 'by the knowledge of the king and his chamberlain's record'. Vaughan, in other words, answered solely to William Hastings and to Edward himself.

Among its descriptions of the king's personal servants, the *Black Book* detailed his phalanx of medical officers, from the master surgeon and his groom, who looked after the household's medicine chest, to the apothecary who stocked it and who, when he made up the king's prescriptions, was paid out of the chamber's finances for his 'medicines and ingredients'. Ever present at Edward's side – when not in his own office 'devising the king's medicines' – was the king's physician.[40]

Like all monarchs, Edward numbered physicians among his closest servants. Unsurprisingly, given their crucial role in keeping the king in full working order – and their intimate, round-the-clock contact with the royal person – royal doctors could accumulate significant power and wealth. William Hatteclyffe, also Edward's secretary, was one of his confidential advisers and diplomats. During Hatteclyffe's frequent absences from court, other equally long-serving consultant physicians were on hand: William Hobbes, an unswerving Yorkist who had served Edward's father; and James Frise, a medic from Frisia. Back in 1461, Edward had welcomed Frise into his service with a golden handshake, a grant of several lucrative rents in the city of London that the determined physician terrified their former Lancastrian owner into handing over 'by inordinate, undue and damnable means', including death threats.[41]

On the face of it, the vigorous Edward was a rather more straightforward medical proposition than his unstable Lancastrian predecessor. His medics, though, earned their keep. While Henry VI's desperate consultants threw everything they could at the catatonic king – including 'laxatives, medicines . . . clysters, suppositories, medicines for clearing the head, gargles, baths, poultices, fomentations, embrocations, shaving of the head, ointments, plasters, waxes, cupping (with or without cutting the skin) and inducements to bleeding' – the challenge of Edward was a more subtle one.[42]

With so much of medicine being about prevention rather than cure, about keeping the king in full vital working order, Edward's medical advisers had long made concerned noises about his prodigious feats of consumption and sexual activity – rather suggesting that their efforts to regulate both had fallen on deaf ears. Nevertheless, from the outset of his reign, Edward also displayed an obsession about his health that was entirely in keeping with his compulsive tendencies, consuming sweetened powders and potions with the same gigantic appetite that fuelled his bingeing and womanizing. It was understandable enough. In what were years of almost constant plague and 'great pestilence', Edward and his doctors were preoccupied with warding off infection: anybody who could afford to do so – and most couldn't – did much the same. After all, people had little choice, even though they knew much medicine wasn't just overpriced and largely useless, but actively dangerous.

Sporadic government attempts at regulation of the medical profession had little impact. One wonder drug was theriac, popularly known as 'treacle', a remedy with a history stretching back to antiquity whose active ingredient was roasted viper flesh. It was prescribed to the well and the sick for everything from skin conditions to heart trouble, the inducement of menstruation and, inevitably, plague – when, advised one practitioner, it was to be taken twice a day, dissolved in a little 'clear wine or rosewater or ale'. Treacle was tricky to manufacture and almost always imported. With the medical industry eager to exploit the ill, scared and desperate, there was plenty of false product on the market, something eloquently summed up in a Scottish poet's collective noun for the manufacturers: a 'poison of treaclers'. In April 1472 a group of medical experts, led by Edward's physician Roger Marshall, examined a number of 'barrels and pots of treacle' seized in the port of London and declared it 'unwholesome', following which the consignment was publicly burned in Cheapside.[43]

Edward, inevitably, had his own recipe for treacle, which, despite the poet's scepticism, was used as an antidote to poison. He also had other expensive, bespoke remedies made for his 'preservation'; one, made up by Marshall, used the resinous leaves or root of the dragon tree, native to the Canary Islands.[44]

But while Edward's resort to medicine was hardly unusual, the quantities in which he consumed drugs, and the way he did so, raised eyebrows. In 1464 – admittedly, a plague-ridden year – his pharmaceutical bill came to a whopping £87, though given that this was a year in which his councillors became increasingly concerned about his sexual activity, these might have been prescriptions for a quite different sort of prophylactic.[45] His use of emetics – an otherwise standard remedy in the physician's cabinet – was eye-catchingly alarming. When full to bursting after one of his marathon sessions at the dinner table, he would 'take an emetic for the delight of gorging his stomach once more'. Instead of balancing the bodily humours, maintaining a state of physical equilibrium, Edward swung violently between extremes.

It wasn't so much that Edward ignored medical advice, more that he followed it selectively, inconsistently and – when he did so – to excess. Edward's reflexive gulping down of medicines seemed to betray an insecurity below the bombast, a sense that sickness and death awaited at every turn, whether from plague, or poison, or the invocations and experiments of astrologers and sorcerers. Such fears pervaded society. But in Edward, as with everything else, such anxieties were magnified and exaggerated: both because, as king, he mattered most; and perhaps because, despite everything, there remained something brittle at the heart of Edward's sense of himself and his kingship.[46]

Edward had another reason for getting his house in order. For years, he had toyed with the idea of invading France. A successful French campaign was in many ways the ultimate benchmark of English kingship. But in the decades after Henry V's triumphs, as his son's failing regime presided over the catastrophic loss of its French territories and England erupted in civil conflict, so this vision of a muscular, expansionist kingdom had faded from view. So too had a generation of men who, having fought and lived in Normandy and Aquitaine, had returned home only to die fighting each other instead. France, though, had stayed in Edward's mind: in 1468, he had even raised taxes for an invasion, only to squander them elsewhere. So when, in March 1472, Charles the Bold and his longstanding ally Duke Francis of Brittany, constantly searching for ways to distract the French king from menacing their respective borders, raised the idea of a joint invasion, Edward responded. He might not have liked Charles, but he did like the idea of becoming king of France.[47]

Beneath the vague, glorious notions of a quest for the French crown, other more practical considerations bubbled. Charles the Bold's rumoured alliance with Louis XI had been weighing on Edward's mind: would it be better to suppress his grudges against his Burgundian brother-in-law and ally with him, before the French king got there first? Besides which, local turf wars continued to flare in England and Wales. Political advisers commonly prescribed overseas invasion as a cure for internal ills: a war against France, Edward felt, could unify the country – and especially his bickering brothers – in a common cause. That spring, as Edward sent a force of archers to bolster Brittany's defences against a menacing France, Charles as usual couldn't wait. Itching to attack Louis, he led an army across the border, without his allies. While the Burgundian forces drew a breathless description from one English envoy, the invasion was badly planned. Within weeks, his men had run out of food; they retreated in a miasma of indiscipline. Although Charles detailed his soldiers' war crimes with pride, bragging in one letter about the effectiveness of his 'throat cutters', there was no getting away from the fact that his invasion had been a failure – nor that in order to do it properly, he needed the English.[48]

Edward needed no second opportunity. Stepping up the English naval presence in the Channel, he sent another force of two thousand archers to Brittany. In the meantime, his truce with Louis XI had lapsed: he didn't renew it. Early that September Edward signed a new treaty with Burgundy and Brittany. At its heart was a plan for a new joint invasion of France, England at its head, whose ultimate ambition was to see Edward regain the French crown. He would show Charles how it was done.[49]

Around the same time Charles the Bold's close adviser Louis of Gruuthuse arrived in England to patch up the tattered Anglo-Burgundian *entente*. Whatever Edward's suspicions of Charles, his gratitude to Gruuthuse – who had done so much to help Edward in his exile – was unbounded. He rolled out the red carpet.[50]

Met by English representatives at Calais, Gruuthuse progressed through southern England in a haze of hospitality. Stuffed with game and 'dainties', awash with fine wine and loaded with gifts, he rode through the gates of Windsor Castle to be greeted by smiling, familiar faces: William Hastings and a group of lords and knights whom he had last seen eighteen months before in rather different circumstances, waving them off from Bruges on the first leg of their uncertain return to England.

Embracing Gruuthuse, Edward took him into the heart of the royal family. With Hastings and other close servants a constant, solicitous presence in Gruuthuse's guest apartments – two exquisitely furnished, arras-lined rooms with expansive views over the surrounding parkland – he was led through a profusion of entertainments and ceremonies that revealed the house of York in all its splendour. Wandering over to the queen's apartments with Edward, the pair watched Elizabeth and her ladies playing indoor bowls and ninepins; later, as the games gave way to dancing, Edward danced with his oldest daughter Elizabeth, now aged five. The following morning, after a mass 'melodiously sung' by the chapel royal, Edward presented Gruuthuse with a gold cup, inset with a piece of unicorn horn – an antidote to poison – and on its lid a great sapphire. Then, after introducing the Burgundian to his two-year-old heir, dandled in the arms of his chamberlain Thomas Vaughan, the king took Gruuthuse and his men off for a day of sporting action in the 'little park', the carefully curated 650-acre expanse of hunting grounds that sprawled east and south of the castle, Gruuthuse riding the king's own horse and carrying another, extravagantly useless, gift: a silk-stringed crossbow with gilt-tipped quarrels, in a velvet case embroidered with Yorkist badges. The hunting was poor – late in the afternoon, they finally managed to run to death half a dozen deer with hounds – but it hardly mattered.

That evening, Gruuthuse was guest of honour at a banquet hosted by Elizabeth in her apartments. Sharing Gruuthuse's 'mess', a profusion of fine dishes, were the king and queen and various family and in-laws. Among them was the seventeen-year-old duke of Buckingham who, married to the queen's sister Katherine, had been festooning the Yorkist court for much of his short life and who now spent most of the evening dancing with the noblewomen in attendance. At an adjoining table, a 'great view' of ladies sat displayed for the appreciation of the other guests.

After the evening's dancing, Gruuthuse was ushered into another set of apartments in which he would pass the night: three 'chambers of pleasance', a vision in white silk and shimmering cloth-of-gold, the bed's silk curtains tied back to reveal bedlinen and pillows especially chosen by Queen Elizabeth herself. In an adjoining chamber were two baths: that evening, Gruuthuse and Hastings bathed together, an intimate expression of the close bond between England and Burgundy.

During Gruuthuse's visit, Parliament opened at Westminster. On St Edward's day, 13 October, in front of the king and the assembled Lords, the speaker William Allington gave a commendation, a speech of praise on behalf of the Commons. The first subject of Allington's oration was the queen, who had borne the trials of Edward's exile with 'great constancy': her 'womanly behaviour' all the more remarkable because, during this fraught time, Elizabeth had given the country the great 'joy and surety' of an heir to the throne. Both Anthony Woodville and Hastings were praised for their 'constant faith' during the king's Burgundian exile, while attention was drawn to the bravery and chivalry of the king's brothers, Clarence and Richard, in the recent fighting. Then came Gruuthuse's turn. In acknowledgement of the humanity and kindness he had shown Edward and his men, Gruuthuse was made earl of Winchester, the occasion celebrated with processions, feasting and – it being St Edward's day – the inevitable assertions of sovereignty, a crowned Edward processing around Westminster Abbey together with his little son.[51]

There was another point to Gruuthuse's appearance in Parliament. Living proof of the special Anglo-Burgundian relationship, he had also brought with him copies of the new tripartite treaty between Burgundy, Brittany and England, mandating them to make war on France. By parading Gruuthuse in front of the assembled Lords and Commons, Edward was able to show quite how committed Burgundy was to a joint invasion. After all, if he was to go to war, he needed to raise funds on the kind of scale that only Parliament could mandate. And Parliament was going to take some convincing.

13

Master of the Game

At the top end of the great London thoroughfare of Cheapside, in the shadow of St Paul's, stood the church of St Michael-le-Querne. Taking its name from a corn market once held nearby, the church marked the entrance to another district, one concentrated on the street that ran arrow-straight along the northern boundary of St Paul's Churchyard: Paternoster Row. Here, and in the adjoining lanes stretching north to the blood and noise of the shambles at Newgate, was the epicentre of England's book trade: the stationers, as they were known. On the Row itself, thirty-odd shops were crammed: small, two-storey units, little more than ten feet wide by ten deep. In them worked parchmeners, textwriters, illuminators and bookbinders, laboriously copying out everything from legal documents to romances in the uniform scribal hands of the day. Brightly coloured initials and coats-of-arms were worked, together with animals and foliage whose tendrils strayed and wandered through books' margins. The different texts – religious, historical, chivalric; from recipes and medical cures to navigational instructions and political tracts – were gathered together and stitched into the composite volumes that people kept by them. One such shop, next to St Michael-le-Querne itself, was owned by John Multon, a bookseller, translator and textwriter whose occasionally slapdash work was more than compensated for by his entrepreneurial spirit. Over the decades Multon had developed a keen eye for what sold and, with a thick book of city and courtly contacts, where to get hold of it. As well as an ever-popular backlist – Chaucer's *Canterbury Tales*, Hoccleve's *Regiment of Princes*, mountains of John Lydgate's interminable *rhyme royal* – he sold the texts everybody was talking about. Back in 1459, copies of the *Somnium Vigilantis*, the literary text condemning the Yorkist cause, could be found on his shelves; so too, in 1471, ballads celebrating Edward IV's all-conquering return. It was hardly a surprise that in the autumn of 1472, timed to coincide with the opening of the new Parliament at Westminster, Multon put out the latest work by a man with whom he had a long association: Sir John Fortescue, the Lancastrian propagandist now eagerly embracing the house of York.[1]

As Edward set out to persuade a sceptical public to fall into line with his renewed plans for an invasion of France, he needed all the help he could get. In the previous decade, he had twice gone to the parliamentary well to draw taxes for military campaigns against Scotland and France. On both occasions the money's disappearance into the bottomless pit of his dynastic plans had been a key driver of public anger against his regime. As Parliament convened that October, the king embarked on a sustained public relations exercise, one to which Fortescue's *A Declaration upon Certain Writings Sent Out of Scotland* was mood music.

A self-exculpatory disavowal of his former Lancastrianism, the *Declaration* was a masterpiece of rhetorical contortion. Fortescue had, he confessed, been a biased 'partial man', fighting his former master Henry VI's corner with any arguments that came to hand – arguments that had now, he was delighted to acknowledge, been comprehensively disproved in favour of the house of York. And what a blessing it was, Fortescue continued smoothly, that God had bestowed upon Edward IV the kingdoms of England and of France, because now his loyal subjects could, 'without any doubt or scruple of conscience', sign up to fight for him in France against the man who was currently occupying his throne there: Louis XI.[2] All these themes were taken up in the regime's opening salvo to Parliament: a lengthy peroration by John Alcock, bishop of Rochester, standing in for the absent chancellor Robert Stillington, being the first of 'many speeches of remarkable eloquence' intended to whip up war fever among the assembled Commons.[3]

Since the last time he had put the case for war to Parliament, back in 1468, Edward's grip on power had clarified spectacularly. There could, Alcock asserted, be 'no colour or shadow' in anybody's mind that Edward was now 'sole and undoubted king': king 'in deed' as he had always been 'in right'. Yet although the root cause of

England's troubles, the house of Lancaster, was 'extinct', the symptoms of civil conflict persisted, with 'many a great sore, many a perilous wound left unhealed'. The problem was, Alcock continued, that the armed retainers responsible for much of the recent and ongoing violence were those same people who, in times of conflict with external powers, the king would call on to defend England. If Edward were to mete out justice commensurate with their misdeeds, the country would be significantly weakened. There was, however, another solution: war against France. Such a campaign would redirect the violent impulses of 'idle and riotous people', restoring 'peace inward'. It would also pit the country against its number one enemy, Louis XI, who, in stirring up the 'most unnatural inward trouble' and backing the aggression of other international powers – notably Scotland – was the chief source of all England's problems, internal and external. Besides which, invading France would bring many material benefits: making the Channel safe for English trade; solving those niggling inheritance problems by providing land to redistribute to 'younger sons and others'; and permanently ridding the country of the said 'riotous persons', by resettling them in France where they would garrison the lands that Edward would conquer. In any case, as Alcock pointed out, since the Norman Conquest no king had managed to impose justice, peace and prosperity in England except through 'war outward'.[4] And never had there been a more perfect time to invade.

The king had, Alcock said, already done all the heavy lifting, assembling a grand anti-French coalition at vast personal expense – judiciously, Alcock glossed over the fact that much of that expense had involved credit raised against the security of parliamentary taxation – and obtaining promises of military support from Burgundy and Brittany, guarantees of which were 'ready to be shown and read' to Parliament.

Together, the drip-feed of parliamentary speeches and cheerleading pieces had the desired effect. Edward's invasion plans were, so it was reported, met by Parliament with ringing acclaim. Among those applauding loudest – their presence perhaps encouraging those inclined to give a more muted response – were the thirty-nine members of Parliament who were men of the king's household.[5] The tax was voted: a staggering £118,625 to keep an army of thirteen thousand archers in the field for twelve months; the invasion would take place on or before 1 April the following year. No sooner had Parliament signed off the tax than, with predictable inevitability, Edward's carefully assembled coalition began to unravel.

If the flaky loyalties of Francis of Brittany came as little surprise to Edward, given his vacillations of a few years before, the speed of his backsliding was remarkable. On 15 October 1472, barely a month after finalizing his treaty with Edward, and with French forces mobilizing threateningly on his borders, the Breton duke signed a panicky truce with Louis XI and sent envoys advising Edward and Charles the Bold to do the same. Charles promptly did so; three weeks later, the ink was drying on a new Franco-Burgundian truce. By early November, reports had reached London that the English taskforce sent to Brittany to bolster Francis's meagre army had been decimated by the flux – dysentery – 'and other epidemics': those not already dead were coming 'hastily home'.[6]

To add to the general sense of frustration that autumn, regional disorder and violence was increasing. Parliament fielded vocal complaints from representatives in the Welsh Marches about the 'outrageous demeaning of Welshmen'.[7] From the southwest to the midlands, the northwest and Richard's new stamping ground of the northeast, old hatreds were stirred into life by Edward's new political reordering of the previous year; by the deepening animus between his two brothers; and by talk of new conspiracy, involving Clarence.

On 25 November in the Flemish town of Gravelines, a few miles along the coast from Calais, the papal envoy Pietro Aliprando was fuming. Waiting to cross the Channel to England, he had had a run-in with customs officials at Calais. Rummaging through his baggage, they had found papal documents in support of the imprisoned George Neville – on whose behalf Aliprando was trying to intercede with Edward – and promptly frogmarched the diplomat off English territory. Aliprando poured out his frustrations in the first of a stream of dispatches to the duke of Milan, Galeazzo Sforza, for whom he was also working, on the political situation in England.[8]

Still steaming about his treatment in Calais, Aliprando's dispatches were long on speculation and snippiness. Edward might, he conceded, be a 'handsome and worthy prince', but his people were 'bad and perverse' and his council full of fat, ageing and anti-papal bishops. Relations between England and the Hanse merchants were once again at a low ebb, and Hanse pirates more or less controlled the Channel, plundering English vessels with impunity. Turning to the English plans for war against France, Aliprando thought there was little chance of Edward invading soon, given the mistrust between him and Charles the Bold – brothers-in-law they may have been, Aliprando added, but they were 'not good friends' – and the English propensity to be long on talk and short on action. Moreover, things in England were 'doubtful and changeable'. If Edward were really to lead an army into France, he would have to be very confident indeed in the people who would rule England in his absence.

For, Aliprando concluded, the people didn't love Edward. They saw him as weak and wobbly: 'a tavern bush', an inn sign swinging helplessly in the political breeze. They longed for a strong leader, someone who could get a grip on the country, and impose law and order with an iron rule: 'another Warwick'.

Reading between the lines, it was clear where Aliprando had got his information: George Neville, whose cultural sophistication and instinctive papal sympathies played well with Aliprando, as with papal envoys before him. Somehow, he had managed to make contact with the archbishop in his Hammes prison. Certain details, such as the fact that Edward still owed Neville 20,000 ducats, could only have come from the archbishop himself; so too, very probably, the contemptuous dismissal of Edward's wavering kingship.

On the face of it, the 'tavern bush' was an image that sat oddly with the implacable victor of Barnet and Tewkesbury. George Neville, though, knew Edward as well as anybody. During the late 1460s he had witnessed at first hand Edward's tentative, lackadaisical leadership, his tendency to let things drift and his inability to command the hearts of the people – weaknesses that, along with Warwick and Clarence, Neville had exploited and punished. While Aliprando and Neville both had their agendas, even those well-disposed to Edward remarked on similar flaws. At their annual conclave, the members of the Burgundian Order of the Golden Fleece underwent a process of self-examination, each knight's character and actions reviewed by his peers. This included absent members, of which Edward was one – and, with Edward having recently been among his brother knights during his Flanders exile, they had plenty of first-hand evidence to go on. Their analysis of Edward was full of praise: he was a courageous and skilled fighter, virtuous and a good friend. Then, however, came the criticism. Edward, his fellow knights agreed, was not blessed with foresight: with greater awareness, he might have spotted the dangers which had resulted in the reigniting of England's civil wars and his own exile. Moreover, the English king had 'so little self-confidence' that unless those trusted advisers close to him praised his plans and schemes, he would 'not dare to carry them out'; nor would he do anything unless backed by his men. Whether this trait was the fault of nature or nurture, the knights couldn't say.

Implicit in the knights' critique was not only the suggestion that Edward was fundamentally lazy, but that he was in the habit of leaning on a circle of friends whose approbation he craved, and without which he felt – as the knights' appraisal put it – 'diffident': doubtful, uncertain, fearful. If, in other words, you scratched the surface of Edward's awesome royal charisma, you found a thin-skinned insecurity, an inability to accept criticism and a constant desire for affirmation. All of which chimed with Aliprando's 'tavern bush' insult.

Aliprando found George Neville's character assassination of Edward seductive. If, he opined, Neville could escape from custody, 'he will yet accomplish something', not least because a new figurehead, 'another Warwick', was manoeuvring to overthrow the king: 'his brother the duke of Clarence'.[9]

Despite his professed aim to give Sforza 'truthful and agreeable advices', Aliprando was drawn to rumour like a moth to a flame: unfounded gossip about Clarence's intrigues was catnip to him. But while Clarence, still incensed at being deprived of a chunk of the Warwick inheritance that he believed to be rightfully his, continued to square up to his brother Richard, such talk of rebellion against Edward seemed wide of the mark. There was no specific information that Clarence was up to anything. As Edward knew from bitter experience, though, local trouble could, if effectively harnessed, quickly blow up into regime-challenging violence. It would pay the king to keep a particularly close eye on the way Clarence ran his estates, the activities of his followers, and the duke's own movements – and in all this Edward was reminded constantly by the people who clustered around him. Foremost among these were the queen's family, ever-mindful of the savagery with which Clarence had moved against them after Edgecote; the king's own household men, their memories of Clarence's serial disloyalties still raw; and Richard himself.

Throughout the early months of 1473, Edward tried tirelessly to resurrect his plans for war against France. Royal diplomats shuttled between London and Edinburgh, trying to prise Scotland away from its traditional alliance with France. In the Low Countries, Edward's secretary William Hatteclyffe sat down for talks with the Hanse merchants: still stewing over Edward's failure to fulfil his promises to them, Hanse privateers had launched a fresh onslaught against English shipping. Meanwhile, an embassy led by Lord Hastings arrived at Charles the Bold's court bearing terms and conditions for the joint Anglo-Burgundian invasion, on which Edward's 'affection was now greatly set'. Edward's demands included ten thousand Burgundian troops, under English command – and he wanted them by April that year, when he planned to cross to France.[10] The English ambassadors found Charles with his gaze turned eastward. Desperate to fulfil his long-harboured dreams of expansion into the Rhineland, and the transformation of Burgundy from a duchy into a sovereign state, Charles's military ambitions clearly lay, as far as Edward was concerned, in precisely the wrong direction. Charles, who didn't want Louis' armies bothering him while his back was turned, had already come to terms with the delighted French king. That March, his invasion plans clearly going nowhere for the time being, Edward followed suit, buying time by concluding a year-long truce with France. He didn't bother telling Parliament, which had just voted him another tax.[11]

It did so grudgingly. If Edward's slick public-relations campaign of the previous autumn had quelled the Commons' unease over his habitual misspending of taxes, those concerns quickly resurfaced. Even as the invasion was postponed, Edward – with the backing of the lords – was twisting Parliament's arm to hand over the money to him as soon as it had been collected. Throughout the country, as the impact of the taxes bit, Sir John Paston – one of the MPs who had voted for Edward's demands – received a letter from the family home in Norfolk: 'rather the devil, we say', grumbled his younger brother, 'than you should grant any more taxes', an observation which Sir John met with a discreet silence.[12]

Edward, as usual, was exploring other sources of credit. February found Louis XI chuntering about a familiar financial bugbear of his: the bank of Medici, which, not content with having underwritten Margaret of York's wedding and Edward's conquering return from his Burgundian exile, was continuing to extend finance to the English government. When a representative of the bank's newly reopened branch in Lyons arrived at the French court, one of Louis' advisers pulled him aside to tell him in no uncertain terms that Lorenzo de' Medici's money made the French king 'more wars than the enemy'.[13]

The Medici, though, had long since lost control over their own lending policies – at least as far as their London branch was concerned. Despite constant and increasingly emphatic reprimands from head office, Gherardo Canigiani had gone on lending to Edward. His total loans to the regime now stood at a vertiginous £26,000, making the Medici by some distance the largest single creditor of Edward's reign. For Canigiani, it made sense. His loans were always secured, mostly with the coveted export licences, and with Edward genuinely appreciative of Canigiani's support 'in our great necessity', the Medici were in prime position to take advantage of business opportunities as they arose.[14] The problem was, there weren't enough of them. From Florence, all Canigiani's panicked superiors saw was a massive balance of payments deficit, the value of English wool and cloth exports nowhere near offsetting the Medici's loans and imports – chiefly alum and fine textiles – into England. Writing to Tommaso Portinari in Bruges, Lorenzo de' Medici urgently told him to take control of the London office. Canigiani, he implied, had gone native – 'he has served the king with our money' – while his loans threatened to provoke a crisis with France that the Medici could ill afford.

All of which was compounded by disaster. Late that April, off the Flanders coast east of Calais, two Medici galleys loaded with alum and luxury goods for the English market were intercepted by Hanse privateers. One of the galleys managed to outrace its pursuers and reach the safety of Southampton. The pirates ran down and boarded the other, the *San Matteo*, towing it off to Danzig. Its cargo of alum, valued at 40,000 florins, was a huge loss to the Medici. Other injured parties included Agnolo Tani, the troubleshooter who had declared his experience of dealing with the London branch akin to that of trying to revive a corpse. On the *San Matteo* was an artwork he had commissioned from a Bruges-based artist called Hans Memling, a spectacular Last Judgment flanked by portraits of Tani and his wife, which was being shipped back to Florence; now, it was taken to Danzig, where it was given pride of place in St Mary's Church.[15] Then there was a group of London mercers, who had shipped goods in the *San Matteo* on the understanding that it had been fully insured. It hadn't been, and they now found themselves 'utterly deceived'. The man who now vigorously took up their case with Edward and the Medici was Canigiani. Both the loss of the *San Matteo* – itself hardly Canigiani's fault – and the arrival in London of a henchman of Portinari's, Cristofano Spini, who promptly swindled Canigiani in a business deal, tipped Lorenzo de' Medici over the edge. Later that year, Canigiani was sacked. He didn't seem to mind much. Promptly marrying the widow of a rich London merchant, he took English citizenship, whereupon a grateful Edward gave him a key post in Calais, as keeper of the exchange there. He was well aware of how well Canigiani had served him.[16]

In mid-April Edward left London on progress, in an effort to restore royal control in regions of chronic disorder. His itinerary would take him on an arc through the midlands to the Welsh borders. Apart from mollifying the disgruntled commons, the king had particular aims in view. For a start, it was all too clear that – in a reversal of the line that outward war would bring inward peace – a long military campaign against France could hardly be undertaken without first solving domestic political problems. For the problem of Wales and the Marches, Edward had alighted on an idea that dovetailed neatly with his ambitions for his own son and heir. He would hand the little boy – and the newly reconfigured council who represented his interests – sweeping powers to crack down on disturbances and to enforce royal authority. Before he left London, Edward sent the little prince on ahead, together with Queen Elizabeth and members of his council; he would link up with them at Ludlow later in the summer.

As Edward rode into the east midlands, it was turning into a fine spring. With him were some of his heavy hitters: his chamberlain William Hastings and Thomas, Lord Stanley, his steward and linchpin in England's northwest; Anthony Woodville; the duke of Buckingham; and, above all, his brother Richard – who, doubtless, took the opportunity presented by the long journey to discuss with Edward his aims and desires. Clarence wasn't with them. There was a sense of purpose in Edward's progress and, also, of vigilance. There would be trouble, people said, before May was out.[17]

On 16 April, Good Friday, Sir John Paston was riding eastwards. He was heading for the Kent coast to take ship for Calais, where he was serving under Hastings' command. Staying the night at Canterbury, he wrote to his brother. Edward's truce with France was now general knowledge, while the detachment of archers he had promised Charles the Bold the previous autumn – which, in fact, had never made it across the Channel – had been demobilized and were 'coming home by the highwayful'. Sir John feared for his belongings, brought on by carriage behind him, but in the end they turned up: 'all was safe'. In London, meanwhile, there were widespread rumours about a 'work' – a plot – of some sort. A soothsayer Paston knew, a man called Hogan from a well-to-do Norfolk family, had been arrested by royal agents and brought to the Tower: his 'old tales', apparently, prophesied unrest that spring. Hogan was interrogated and threatened with execution for provoking unrest. But, as it turned out, he was right.[18] A few days previously, Paston told his brother, the fugitive Lancastrian earl of Oxford had been spotted at the French Channel port of Dieppe, preparing to sail with a flotilla of twelve ships.

Since his raids on Calais the previous year, Oxford had sought backing from Louis XI. Casting around for ways to distract Edward from his invasion plans, the French king had thrown a modest amount of money the earl's way, fitting out a small fleet to carry him and his men to England 'to do what he can against king Edward'. A Milanese ambassador at Louis' court reported that Oxford was going to try to revive Warwick's networks and 'to become leader of the earl's party' – though in the same breath he acknowledged ruefully that he had little idea of what was going on in England, and had heard 'a great variety of things'. There was another interpretation: that Oxford was going to link up with the nobleman who had inherited Warwick's earldom and his networks in the midlands – Clarence.[19]

As the rumours escalated, so too did the arrests. A contact of Paston's told him that Oxford was due to attempt a landing on the East Anglian coast, where around 'a hundred gentlemen in Norfolk and Suffolk' had agreed to turn out for him. Shortly after their conversation, the same man was detained, accused of raising funds for Oxford's cause, and interrogated. For his part, Paston was anxious to put distance between himself and the earl. Back in 1471, the Pastons' decision to follow Oxford, and with him Lancaster, had seen Sir John narrowly escape execution and had left the family's fortunes on the brink of disaster. Now, writing to his brother in Norfolk, he dismissed the rumours of conspiracy as 'flying tales'. For all that, he seemed to know an awful lot, right down to the date of Oxford's proposed landing, which, 'if wind and weather serve him', would be on 27 May, eight days after the feast day of St Dunstan. All of which seemed to send a veiled warning to his brother: if approached by the plotters, don't get involved. 'God have you in keeping', he concluded, meaningfully.[20]

Paston's timings were only a day out. On 28 May, returning from a fruitless trip to Scotland in search of support – James III, now twenty and eager for a rapprochement with Yorkist England, batted the rebel earl away – Oxford made landfall at St Osyth on the Essex coast, a stone's throw from one of his manors at Wivenhoe.[21] Edward's intelligence, though, had been good. The area bristled with royal forces: the retinues of Henry Bourchier, earl of Essex, and lords Dinham and Duras. Oxford's supporters in the region wisely stayed at home. Equally wisely, Oxford made himself scarce. His small fleet retreated to the Isle of Thanet off the easternmost tip of Kent, where it remained, 'hovering', preying on passing ships.

News of the earl's attempted landing had, Paston wrote wryly, 'saved Hogan his head': now, the king was taking the soothsayer's prognostications seriously. Although Oxford's landing had been repulsed, the very fact of its attempt seemed to heighten the febrile mood. In London, people started to arm themselves; they didn't know quite why, but it felt good to be prepared. Armed men of the king's household appeared on the city streets; so too did Clarence's retainers, identifiable by the black bull badge conspicuously pinned to their jackets.[22]

Mention of Clarence led Paston on to news of the earl of Warwick's widowed countess, Anne, who remained under armed guard in the Hampshire abbey of Beaulieu. Anne was a much-sought-after lady, her dower estates – part of the Warwick inheritance – a particular bone of contention between Clarence and Richard. After the battle of Tewkesbury, Edward had initially granted the bulk of the countess's estates to Clarence; then, following the brothers' tetchy meeting at Sheen the previous year, he had reallocated them to Richard. Clarence refused to hand them over. Anne herself, appalled at the prospect of losing her hereditary lands to either brother, had energetically lobbied Edward and those close to him, pleading to be allowed to keep what was legally hers; questions had even been raised in Parliament. Finally, Paston heard, the countess was 'out of sanctuary' – but not on her own terms.

In a move sanctioned by the king himself, the countess of Warwick had been given into the custody of a group of Richard's servants. Now, she was being brought north to Richard's base of Middleham Castle, which had once been her home. Aiming to slice through the thicket of legal complexity preventing the transfer of the countess's estates to Richard, Edward and his brother had – perhaps in discussion on the king's leisurely progress into the midlands that spring – cooked up a plan. It allowed Richard, 'with the king's assent', to make a barefaced land grab, one that spoke volumes for the regime's priorities. And, Paston added with understatement, 'some men say that the duke of Clarence is not agreed'.[23]

Richard was proving remorseless in pursuit of his rights. Among the lands which he believed were rightfully his – given to him as a child by Edward, only to be taken back and regranted elsewhere – were the estates of the Lancastrian earl of Oxford. When, after Tewkesbury, Oxford had forfeited his title and estates, Richard (who had instructed his secretary to include the original, superseded grant in his cartulary of lands and offices) badgered Edward for the lands. Edward duly let his brother help himself. It wasn't only the exiled earl who suffered, but his family. His wife, Margaret, given not a penny of income by Edward or Richard, was said to be existing solely on charitable hand-outs. Then, at Christmas 1472, Richard had gone after Oxford's mother.

Elizabeth, dowager countess of Oxford, may have been sixty-three and infirm, but she wasn't stupid. Realizing what a precarious position she was in, with her sons declared legally dead and unable to inherit, she had attempted to protect her own considerable estates by 'enfeoffing' them, making them over to a number of trustees, with the aim of eventually handing them on to her heirs. Or so she hoped. Richard had other ideas. That Christmas, he rode over to the Essex nunnery of Stratford-le-Bow, where Elizabeth was living, and told her bluntly that 'the king his brother' had given him custody of the countess and her lands. Unmoved by the countess's evident distress – she wept, one of Richard's men later recollected, and made 'great lamentation' – he demanded that she hand over all her ready cash before abducting her. Imprisoned in nearby Stepney, the countess was kept under house arrest until, 'for fear of her life', she was forced to sign away everything.

That the king had, at the very least, turned a blind eye to his brother's rapacity was clear. Edward's indulgent attitude was hardly surprising. After all, it was in tune with his own actions: back in the freezing winter of 1464 he had subjected the duke of Somerset's mother to systematic, vindictive abuse as a way of getting back at the favourite who had abandoned him. For his part, Richard was simply taking a leaf out of his brother's book. Others helped him: Edward's chamber treasurer Thomas Vaughan, who lent Richard the Stepney house where he threatened the countess; and John Howard – the countess's own nephew – who 'gave great words of menace' to members of her entourage.[24]

If such behaviour on the part of the Yorkist establishment was shocking, it wasn't unexpected. It was a twisted manifestation of Edward's philosophy of 'family first', which maintained that power should be concentrated in the hands of the 'king's blood'. As close family, Richard deserved to be 'honoured and enhanced of right and power'; therefore, he was entitled to do as he pleased. Nonetheless, Edward knew perfectly well that what his brother was doing was wrong. When, a few years later, he was approached by a petitioner for advice on whether to buy from Richard a London townhouse previously owned by the earl of Oxford, Edward warned him against it. The title deeds, the king added, were secure in 'my brother's hands' but would be 'dangerous' for anyone else, given that – as Edward put it – Richard had 'compelled and constrained' the countess of Oxford to give him the property in question. Edward, in other words, knew exactly what his brother was doing, and didn't care.

When, five months after Richard's abduction of the countess of Oxford, the scenario repeated itself in the case of Warwick's widow Anne, it transpired that Edward was prepared not only to sit back and let Richard get on with it, but actively to facilitate the move. What was more, in doing so he was deliberately backing Richard against their brother Clarence.

Describing what happened to Anne countess of Warwick in the spring of 1473, Sir John Paston was studiedly neutral. But, reading between the lines, it was clear what was going on. While she may have been 'out of sanctuary', Anne had not been set at liberty. Richard had abducted her, keeping her securely at Middleham with the aim of forcing her to hand over her estates to him.

The man whom Richard entrusted with the mission was a young Suffolk knight named James Tyrell.[25] Tyrell's rise had been rapid. Abandoning his family's Lancastrian associations with the earl of Oxford – his father had been beheaded alongside the old earl back in 1462 – he had thrown in his lot with the Yorkists. At Tewkesbury, his fierce fighting had seen him knighted on the battlefield, following which he had quickly become one of Richard's closest servants and councillors. Three years younger than Richard, Tyrell was still only seventeen.

Writing from his chambers at Staple Inn, in the west London suburb of Holborn, the lawyer William Dengayn provided details of what was essentially a stitch-up between Edward and Richard. Apparently responding to the countess's lobbying, Edward had restored 'all her inheritance' to her and mandated her release from sanctuary, whereupon she had then – apparently of her own free will – 'granted it unto my lord of Gloucester with whom she now is'. The idea that the countess had spent so much time petitioning for the return of her lands, only to make them over to her son-in-law Richard, stretched credulity. Rather, this was a fait accompli, one that forced the countess to give away the lands to whose possession she was entitled in law. As Dengayn put it, with the hint of a lawyerly raised eyebrow, 'divers folks marvel greatly'.[26]

To Edward, it was a neat solution, a way of forcing Clarence to stick to the terms of the Sheen agreement; perhaps, too, it was a warning shot across the bows of a brother around whom talk of conspiracy continued to congeal. Whatever the case, it was evident that, as far as the Warwick inheritance was concerned, Edward was lending a sympathetic ear to his youngest brother. To Clarence, deprived of a large chunk of estates that the king had originally granted him, it looked suspiciously as though Edward was favouring Richard – and persecuting him, Clarence, in the process.

Late that spring, the fine weather turned remorseless. It was a 'great hot summer', reported one chronicler, 'for both man and beast'. With the heat came disease, and death was everywhere. Epidemics of dysentery took hold. Men out harvesting in the fields 'fell down suddenly' – though at least they had had a harvest to gather. In southern Europe, it was said, the heat had 'burnt away wheat and all other grains and grass', so much so that a bushel of wheat now cost twenty shillings. That a time of trouble was coming was confirmed in people's minds by fearful portents. A voice was heard 'crying in the air' at various places between Leicester and Banbury, shouting 'Bows! Bows!'; some said that the voice came from a headless man. Near St Albans, the River Ver burst its banks: heavy rainfall earlier in the year had slowly filtered through chalk to raise the groundwater, to spectacular effect. Such flooding at a time of drought was the phenomenon people knew as the 'woe water': a token of 'dearth, or of pestilence, or of great battle'. Similar floodwaters had been reported in Kent, Sussex and the west midlands. Those that saw them knew that 'woe was coming to England'.[27]

During these enervating months, the king circled the midlands warily, alert to signs of trouble. As Richard, hungry to impose himself, got to grips with the government of his adoptive northeast, Edward put a restraining hand on his brother's collar, showing him the necessity of pragmatism and flexible thinking in the pursuit of peace and order. Richard, all aggrandisement, had been offering cash payments and distributing his boar badge to servants of the powerful young earl of Northumberland, Henry Percy, trying to recruit the earl's men in his own backyard. Percy had bristled. The king, acutely aware of Percy's importance to royal control of the region, extracted a promise from Richard to back off, insisting that the pair thrash out their differences and find a way of working together.[28] The following month, he appointed Richard head of a commission to look into the entrenched feud between the two north-western families of Stanley and Harrington. Knowing full well Richard's commitment to the solidly Yorkist Harringtons, Edward ordered him to resolve the dispute in favour of the Stanleys – which made sense, given their practically hegemonic power in the northwest, and the fact that Lord Stanley was Edward's own household steward. Richard agreed to do so. Yet, faced with obeying his brother the king or abandoning the Harringtons – a family who, with close connections among Richard's own servants, looked to him for protection and lordship – Richard displayed another kind of flexibility. Over the following months the work of his royal commission gently ground to a halt, the Harringtons left unbothered. The case was quietly dropped.[29]

As summer wore on, Edward lingered in the Welsh borders, partly in an attempt to bring the independent-minded Marcher lords to heel, partly to be near the queen, now heavily pregnant. At Shrewsbury on 17 August, Elizabeth gave birth to a second boy, whom she named Richard. Then, towards the end of September, Edward set up his firstborn son and heir with a separate household at Ludlow, complete with a set of ordinances directing all aspects of his upbringing. The man to whom, that November, Edward entrusted the 'guiding of our said son's person' was the prince's maternal uncle, the queen's brother Anthony Woodville. Woodville was in many respects an ideal choice: polished, highly literate, with impeccable chivalric credentials and a record of unswerving loyalty to the dynasty of which he was now a blood relation. He was given oversight of the prince's upbringing and the smooth functioning of his household and council, whose servants were all answerable to Woodville himself. The prince's finances were secured in a coffer with three locks, the keys to which were held by Queen Elizabeth, Anthony Woodville, and the man appointed both the president of the prince's council and his tutor, John Alcock, bishop of Rochester.[30]

For all Edward's commitment to enforcing his laws, and his energetic judicial progress through the country that summer, disturbances continued to flare. According to a Milanese ambassador at the French court, the earl of Oxford had sent Louis XI the wax seals of twenty-four knights 'and one duke' who had committed to making war on Edward; along with this evidence of support for his project of regime change, Oxford was demanding for a 'good sum' of money from the French king. The identity of the duke was left unspoken: many believed it to be Clarence. Louis, though, demurred, apparently suspecting Oxford of exaggerating his support, and faking the seals. With no money forthcoming from the French king, that summer Oxford abandoned his hideout on the Isle of Thanet and with his small fleet drifted westwards along England's south coast, plundering hapless merchant ships – and, perhaps, hoping to find backing in the southwest, where Clarence was especially strong. Edward, though, was again one step ahead; early that summer he had put the sheriff of Devon and his networks on high alert, ordering him to prevent Oxford landing and to keep an eye out for any unlawful gatherings. At the end of September, running out of options, Oxford reached the western edge of England. He seized St Michael's Mount off the tip of Cornwall – the kind of place, remarked one chronicler, in which twenty men could hold out 'against all the world' – and hunkered down.[31]

On 6 November, Sir John Paston wrote uneasily to his brother from London: 'The world seemeth queasy here.' That autumn, fed up with what he saw as manoeuvres by his brother Richard, Clarence had had enough. Threatening to 'deal with' him, Clarence was openly recruiting as much hired muscle as he could. Richard, not one to take a backward step, was doing the same.

With the quarrel between the two threatening to explode into armed conflict, Edward again waded in. Preparing his own display of royal might – his household retinues made a conspicuous show of arming themselves – he announced that he would be 'a stifler' between his brothers, smothering their mutual antagonism. But if the king emphasized his own role as neutral arbiter, he was also prepared to follow through on his earlier warning to Clarence. If Clarence continued to be obstructive as far as the Warwick settlement was concerned, Edward was prepared to take away everything he had ever granted him.[32]

At Westminster, Parliament was again in session. Two of the items on its agenda were particularly significant. With Edward desperate to draw a line under his long-standing commercial war with the Hanse merchants, Parliament duly passed an act that conceded practically all the Hanse demands: the promises that Edward had made them during his exile in Flanders and which, back in England, he had then failed to fulfil. The act restored to the Hanse their lucrative trading privileges in England, with no reciprocal arrangements given to English merchants – but at least Edward could be sure that his seaborne invasion of France, when it eventually came, would not be harassed by Hanse pirates. Then came the second big piece of parliamentary business: an act of resumption.

Edward had carried out these sweeping re-appropriations of crown lands earlier in his reign; like others before it, this one was intended to convey the king's commitment to sound financial practice, to show that he was in control of his landed assets and his income. This act, as one commentator remarked, was especially severe, as it took back into royal control all grants made by Edward since his accession in 1461. There followed the inevitable frantic scramble by those possessing such grants to exempt their property from annexation. As usual, a substantial list of 'provisos', exemptions, was drawn up. Richard's name was on the list. Clarence's wasn't.[33]

Edward's reasoning appeared straightforward. Some eighteen months before, he had warned Clarence that any failure to co-operate would be met with royal confiscation of his lands. With Clarence intransigent, the king had duly activated his threat. But, in Sir John Paston's view, another motive animated Edward's move against his brother. Clarence's raising of troops wasn't simply a frustrated, flailing lunge against Richard: there was, Paston wrote, 'some other thing intended . . . some treason conspired'. Paston didn't elaborate, nor did

he comment on the source of the rumours – but given his own connections at court, it was a fair bet that they emanated from circles
close to the king himself. In this context, Edward's resumption of
Clarence's lands carried with it an implicit warning: that if his brother
was intent on trying anything silly, the king was watching.

Towards the end of November, Paston wrote home again. After
various requests – he was off again to Calais and, 'to avoid idleness',
was desperate for his musical instruments, stored in 'a chest in my
chamber at Norwich' – he updated his brother on the political situation. 'I trust to God', he commented, hoping that fraternal peace was
about to break out, 'that the two dukes of Clarence and Gloucester
shall be set at one by the award of the king.'[34] It was wishful thinking.
Passed that December, the act of resumption came as a devastating
blow to Clarence's status, the position of pre-eminence that he believed
was his by right.

Unlike the earl of Warwick, who back in the 1460s had typically
kept his emotions to himself until he could vent them in the privacy
of his own chamber, Clarence had always worn his heart on his
sleeve. (Although, it had to be said, Warwick had never experienced
the kind of humiliation that Edward was now visiting on his brother.)
Clarence made little effort to conceal his frustrated rage. He was,
people noted, 'extremely sore at heart'.[35]

No sooner was the Christmas feasting over than Edward moved
against his brother. On 9 January 1474, the king started to take
possession of Clarence's confiscated estates. In showing he meant
business, Edward targeted a portfolio of land stretching across the
north and east midlands, centred on the duchy of Lancaster honour
of Tutbury, possession of which had helped make Clarence a big
player in the region.

Back in 1472, as Clarence tried to make influential friends close to
the king, he had appointed William Hastings steward of Tutbury. His
gesture had had unintended consequences. Recent disorder in the
region had seen local families, sensitive to shifts in power, turn towards
Hastings for leadership and justice: Hastings had obliged, stepping in
to deal with regional disputes on Edward's behalf. Now, in repossessing
the Tutbury estates, Edward conferred them on Hastings outright. In

the spring of 1474, perhaps anticipating resistance from an intransigent Clarence, Edward rode into the midlands himself, Hastings by his side, to oversee the transfer of control to Hastings' men.[36]

Edward was doing more than simply redistributing lands from one nobleman to another. Hastings had few connections with the lands now coming under his control. What he did have – and what attracted locals to him – was exceptional influence with the king, to whom he owed all his power. Unlike Clarence, Hastings knew his position as the king's devoted servant and was perfectly happy with it. Accordingly, Hastings' possession of the Tutbury estates was to be qualitatively different. Granted control of the estates for life, he was a crown officer, a glorified estate manager who commanded allegiances as the king's representative in the region. That spring, Edward personally supervised the appointment of Hastings' regional staff. Some of Clarence's men were dismissed. Most, however, transferred easily to Lord Hastings, signing new indentures in which they were promised, as customary, 'good lordship' in exchange for their service – and, in becoming part of Hastings' network, they effectively became part of the king's own.[37]

As Edward toured the north midlands, the young Prince Edward's new council was flexing its muscles in Coventry, a city with close connections to Clarence. That April, Coventry welcomed the three-year-old boy with a sequence of pageants enacting scenarios from the house of York's history, accompanied by the city band and – in order to keep people really interested – conduits running with wine. At Bablake Gate, an actor dressed as Richard II revelled in the prince's ancient lineage, rejoicing that 'the right line of the royal blood is now as it should be'; further on, the sainted king Edward the Confessor reassured the little prince that he was watching over the house of York, reminding him how his father Edward IV had been driven from his throne 'by full furious intent', and giving thanks that England was now back 'in your father's hand'.[38] In playing up Coventry's special relationship with the prince, the city authorities also sought to gloss over its recent unfortunate associations with Henry VI's brief restoration: the prince's triumphant entrance confirmed that the city was back in the royal good books.

There was, however, more to the prince's visit. As Warwick's heir, he saw himself as the city's overlord; the city, it seemed, saw likewise. Back in June 1472, after the contrite citizens had spent hundreds of pounds trying to work their way back into royal favour, it was Clarence whose mediation with his brother the king had finally obtained Coventry's pardon. Yet in recent months Coventry had seen its fair share of disturbances, which Clarence had apparently failed to control. The prince's council, tacitly backed by Edward himself, had stepped in: the boy's arrival was a timely nod to the civic authorities as to whom they should be answering. Shortly before he left, the prince – or rather, his representatives, Anthony Woodville at their head – extracted from the mayor and corporation a new oath of allegiance.[39]

Seen one way, these were the actions of a concerned king, whose intervention through his son's administration was simply intended to help Clarence out in an unstable region. From where Clarence was standing, things looked rather different. Hastings was already muscling in on his lands in the north and east midlands. Now the prince and his council, dominated by the 'queen's blood', was encroaching on his authority in the west midlands, a region that Clarence ruled in his long-coveted capacity as inheritor to the earl of Warwick. Nor was that all. As he made this emphatic statement of royal control through his young son and heir, Edward was ramping up his involvement in Warwickshire, dispensing grants of land and office to local big men who already had links to Clarence. This was the kind of intervention that would inevitably result in the erosion of Clarence's networks of influence, as men instead looked directly to the king and his heir for favour and justice – just as, on the Tutbury estates, they now looked to Edward's representative, Hastings.[40] Clarence, perhaps, didn't have to be paranoid to feel that Edward was attempting to cut him down to size.

That year, a new book was in circulation at court. Back in 1471, shortly after Edward regained the throne, William Caxton had resigned his long-held governorship of the Merchant Adventurers. He was feeling tired – 'age creepeth on me daily and feebleth all the body', he wrote – and in need of a change of scene. He had journeyed the two hundred miles east from Bruges to Cologne, where, with the encouragement of Edward's sister Margaret, duchess of Burgundy, he settled down to finish a translation of the history of Troy on which he had been working fitfully for years. Cologne was a hub of the new technology of print. Ever the entrepreneur, Caxton was intrigued, then fascinated. He caught the bug. When, towards the end of 1472, he returned to Bruges, he took with him some cases of type and an assistant named Wynkyn de Worde; and he considered the business opportunities for the new technology back in his native England. In London and Westminster there existed a ready-made audience hungry for Burgundian culture. With his sharp eye for literary trends, Caxton would provide that culture, translated into English and in the most fashionable, up-to-date medium. One of his first books was an edition of a volume popular in Flanders but little known in England: the *Jeu d'Echecs*.

A book of advice, it was stuffed full of aphorisms and stories by 'ancient doctors, philosophers, poets and of other wise men'. Knowing the constant demand for fashionable books on public morality, Caxton – as was becoming his hallmark – added a prologue and an epilogue to provide some context for his English readers, did a print run of his translation and shipped it across the Channel. In the prologue of what he called *The Game and Playe of the Chesse*, he dedicated the book to the patron under whose 'noble protection' he had made it: George, duke of Clarence.[41]

For all that Caxton made of Clarence's support, there was little to suggest that the duke had had anything to do with the book at all. What encouragement there was stemmed, very probably, from the 'mighty and virtuous' princess who had already 'commanded' translations from Caxton: Clarence's sister Margaret of Burgundy. In suggesting Caxton dedicate the book to Clarence, Margaret – who shared her husband Charles the Bold's fear and loathing of the French king Louis XI – had a specific end in view. She wanted her brothers to stop quarrelling, make up and focus on the job in hand – the invasion of France.

In his epilogue, Caxton was a cheerleader for Edward's French war. The way for Edward to 'reign gloriously' in unity with 'the nobles of the kingdom', he advised, was through conquest of his 'rightful inheritance': the French throne. Echoing the prevailing wisdom, Caxton argued that war was a route to national virtue, peace and prosperity, a way for putting 'idle people' to work and for trade to prosper. If all this seemed like an echo of Edward's parliamentary propaganda, it was.[42] The message of the *Game and Playe of the Chesse* was evident. In dedicating the book to Clarence, Caxton was gently proposing that he sublimate his fraternal rage and focus on Edward's great project, helping to bring the king's long-cherished plan to fruition. Whether or not Clarence read the book, whether it even reached him, was unclear. But over the following months, he seemed to absorb the message contained in Caxton's epilogue.

During the first months of 1474, Edward's French war still seemed a long way off. Parliament had reassembled briefly, expecting an update on his plans, before again being prorogued. No business had been done, and the frustrated lords and commons left with a series of royal excuses ringing in their ears: Edward's chief partner in the invasion coalition, Charles the Bold, was distracted with his own expansionist military campaign; and besides, Edward had had his hands full with domestic problems. Foremost among which, of course, was the friction between his brothers.[43]

By the time Parliament was again recalled a few months later, a key cause of that unrest had been resolved. In mid-February the earl of Oxford, holding out on St Michael's Mount, finally capitulated. The siege had been more long-drawn-out than it should have been, and Edward had had to sack the besieging commander, Henry Bodrugan, for fraternizing with Oxford instead of fighting him. Finally, when his men had all been bought off by bribes and royal pardons, Oxford surrendered, on condition that Edward spare his life. Following an uncomfortable audience with the king at Windsor Castle, the earl was taken across the Channel to Calais, where he was immured in the border fortress of Hammes along with his fellow prisoner George Neville. Though Oxford's resistance had in the end proved little more than a costly nuisance to Edward, it had threatened much more.

Having tied up one loose end, Edward moved to knot another. The lesson he had tried to drive home to Clarence late the previous year had, it seemed, finally sunk in. That summer, Clarence finally agreed to the terms proposed by Edward for the splitting of the Warwick estates between himself and Richard. Then again, he had little choice: it was either that, or losing everything. In July, a mollified Edward returned most of Clarence's confiscated lands to his brother; all except the wealthy lands around Tutbury, which remained in Hastings' possession – as a reminder, perhaps, of what happened when you crossed the king.[44]

Having finally, as he thought, partitioned the Warwick estates to his brothers' satisfaction, Edward forced through a parliamentary act enshrining it in law. It was a squalid piece of legislation. Warwick's widow Anne was formally disinherited, her vast estates split between her two daughters – which in effect meant their husbands, Clarence and Gloucester. The Countess Anne herself was made 'naturally dead', the redistribution of her property 'as good and effectual in law' as if it had been passed on by inheritance. Edward had ridden roughshod over the accepted customs and laws of inheritance in order to promote his family's interests, and had used Parliament, the highest court in the land, to legitimize his actions. It would not be the last time.

As the self-exculpatory wording of the act put it, the settlement was done for 'various great and important reasons and considerations' – the quarrel between his brothers, which Edward had otherwise struggled to control, and which had become so disruptive that it had become a major obstacle in Edward's plans for his invasion of France. Now, Edward hoped, that particular boil had been lanced.[45] He could turn his attention to his long-delayed war.

The official date of his departure for France, agreed with Parliament, was Michaelmas, the end of September. That summer, however, he had neither an army nor the means to pay for it. In the last years, Parliament had voted taxes to the tune of £118,000, the sum Edward needed to keep an army in the field for twelve months. Now, commissioners announced that barely a quarter of that total had been collected.

Yet there was, finally, a sense of momentum. The resolution of his brothers' quarrel could now be added to breakthroughs on the diplomatic front. Following his settlement with the Hanse merchants, that July Edward trumpeted a new, wide-ranging treaty with Scotland, at its heart a marriage between his little daughter Cecily and the infant Scottish heir: one of France's hitherto most reliable allies was isolated. Then, to his surprise and delight, Charles the Bold – who had paused in his eastern campaign long enough to remember quite how much he hated Louis XI – agreed to sign a new treaty of perpetual friendship, the cornerstone of which was a military alliance against France. With the twin problems of Scotland and the Hanse neutralized, and the might of Burgundy onside, Edward could start planning in earnest – provided, of course, that the Commons were prepared to help him make up the massive financial shortfall he faced.[46]

Parliament caught the mood. Extending the deadline for the departure of Edward's army for France by two years, they reconfirmed the so-far-uncollected taxes. This still left Edward some £51,000 short, a sum that the Commons obligingly agreed to find. Given that they could hardly go back to taxpayers a third time, they cast around for fresh sources. Much of the shortfall was to be made up by targeting a demographic which, having 'not any or but little land, or other freehold', was usually exempt from taxation: the poor.[47]

Yet Edward's mistrust of Charles the Bold hadn't dissipated entirely – and with reason. As well as his new military alliance with Edward, Charles had, more or less simultaneously, renewed his truce with their mutual enemy, Louis XI. Edward also kept his options open. That August, an English herald arrived at the French court with a proposal from Edward. It was an offer of marriage, between his oldest daughter Elizabeth, now aged eight, and the dauphin, the French king's heir. At the French court, genuine anxiety about the possibility of an English invasion mingled with the belief that, when it came to the crunch, Edward wouldn't really go to war. As one Milanese ambassador reported, while people believed that Edward's offer was 'a sham', intended to lull Louis into a false sense of security, they also felt that it was the product of genuine ill-feeling on Edward's part towards his Burgundian brother-in-law. When pushed, the ambassador concluded, most believed that Edward wasn't serious about invading. Everybody knew his fondness for the easy life, inclined as he was 'towards quiet and peace rather than to war'.

Louis, though, was taking no chances. By September, with increasingly reliable reports confirming English military mobilization, he was reviewing his coastal defences and renewing his attempts to puncture Edward's diplomatic alliances with Scotland and Burgundy. Louis also sent an embassy to England, headed by the marshal of his household, a prying man called Christophe Lailler, with a present for Edward of two coursers from his stables.[48] When Lailler arrived a few weeks later, Edward was out of town, on progress. Lailler waited.

Along with the beautiful horses, Lailler brought another gift from Louis – or rather, three gifts: an ass, a wolf and a boar. The boar was the emblem of the duke of Brittany; the wolf, less heraldically evident, represented the slavering Charles the Bold. That left the ass, which, by extrapolation, could only be Edward. The ass didn't have any heraldic connotations with the house of York; it simply showed what Louis thought of the English king.

Over the years, Louis and Edward had got used to trading insulting diplomatic gifts. This one, though, had a particular resonance. A typically antic gesture on Louis' part, it brought to mind the tennis balls sent by the French dauphin to Henry V some sixty years before. Arguably, it was even more offensive. Edward's response, like Henry V's before him, was emphatic.

In October, in a letter widely circulated in England, he replied thanking Louis for his gifts, 'for they be very necessary for war'. Turning Louis' bestial analogy on its head, Edward confirmed that treaties had been made with both Charles the Bold and Duke Francis of Brittany, who had made a covenant with 'the beasts of my country, to teach them the way into France'. Invoking a variety of heraldic animals, all references to his leading noblemen, Edward conjured up a picture of himself as a huntsman at the head of a pack of slavering beasts, inciting them on a vicious hunt through France.

For those with long memories, the metaphor recalled Edward's relationship with Warwick back in 1460, the young bearward deploying his ravening bear against his Lancastrian enemies. Here again, in his letter to Louis, was the image of an English king in full control, forging his nobles' aggressively independent instincts into a powerful weapon of state. Foremost among these mighty lords were 'the black bull with the gilt horns' and another boar: his brothers, Clarence and Richard. 'Your mock', Edward concluded on a note of threatening triumph, 'shall turn you to shame,/ For I am master of the game.'[49]

14

War Outward

In November 1474, in a tent outside the Rhine city of Neuss, the Burgundian chamberlain Olivier de la Marche was putting the finishing touches to a document written at the special request of Edward IV. Winter was coming on and de la Marche, intimately involved with English affairs over the years, was probably grateful for something to do. That summer Charles the Bold, spotting an opportunity to further his glorious vision of a greater Burgundy, had marched his army east into the Rhineland. He headed towards Cologne, whose ruler had appealed to him for military aid against rebels who had taken control of the city. The nearby city of Neuss was also in rebel hands, and Charles decided to target it first; a less daunting proposition, it would provide an easy and morale-boosting win, a statement of intent – or so Charles thought. Having laid siege to Neuss at the end of July, he was still there four months later, having failed to make a dent in the city's defences. Louis XI, who was doing everything he could to distract Charles from joining forces with the English, was delighted. Edward, deep into the preparations for his French campaign, was not. Charles needed a nudge. That autumn, the victualler of Calais, William Ross – the man responsible for stockpiling and maintaining weaponry as well as supplies – had written to de la Marche on the orders of his superior Lord Hastings, with a special request from the English king.[1]

De la Marche was a master of organization. Having overseen the elaborate ceremonial of Charles's marriage to Edward's sister Margaret back in 1468, he had since supervised a complete overhaul of the Burgundian ducal household. Now, its shimmering glamour was underlaid by iron discipline: it was a well-oiled fighting machine. As Edward prepared his French campaign, he wanted a blueprint to follow. Edward had, of course, fought many battles in England, but these had been brief, often hasty mobilizations. Invading France was of a different order of magnitude: barely anybody now remembered the last time it had been done, by Henry V more than half a century ago. Edward's request had another purpose: a reminder to Charles that he, at least, was getting on with the invasion plans, it carried the implicit suggestion that the Burgundian duke might like to start doing the same.

That November, de la Marche sent Ross his *Estat de la maison du duc Charles de Bourgogne*, an ordinance detailing the Burgundian household in all its spectacular military precision, and the expense involved. It was, perhaps, a reassuring indication that Edward remained in Charles's mind. That winter, though, as the Burgundian army slowly froze at Neuss, Edward might have been forgiven for wondering how long Charles was going to stay there.[2]

Meanwhile, Edward was busy. Through the summer and autumn of 1474, he recruited the bulk of the thirteen thousand archers Parliament had promised to fund, their captains signing detailed indentures covering everything from muster details to the division of spoils. Across England, teams of craftsmen were contracted to produce all that was needed: from crossbows and longbows to gun carriages and ammunition: explosive, cannonballs, crossbow bolts and tens of thousands of sheaves of arrows.[3] At the same time, the king's envoys and ambassadors continued to lobby and negotiate in the courts and chancelleries of Europe, wrapping up treaties critical to France's diplomatic isolation.

Among them was an agreement with the powerful Italian *condottiere* Federico da Montefeltro, whose forces, English military planners dreamed, could be instrumental in launching a simultaneous attack on France from the south. Trying to win his backing, Edward handed Montefeltro membership of the Order of the Garter, an honour after which the old mercenary had long hankered. Foremost among the knights who lined up to sponsor his election – doubtless in admiration of his deeds as well as his legendary court at Urbino – were Richard and his friend Henry duke of Buckingham. A gratified Federico commissioned two paintings of himself to mark the occasion. One, a full-length portrait, showed him in his usual profile pose,

concealing his blind right eye and horrific scar – the result of a tournament injury years previously – and showing the absent bridge of his
nose, removed on his orders to give his good left eye a better field of
vision. Sitting in his study in full plate armour, reading a weighty
tome, Federico was portrayed as the epitome of the cultured, chivalric prince. Most prominent of all, buckled around the armoured left
leg that he turned out towards the viewer, was his new garter.[4]

Back at home, Edward's tax collectors raked in the exorbitant sum
Parliament had voted him for his war. Late in November, ten receivers rode across the country to gather the monies that had been
collected and deposited in designated secure locations, and which
they would take back to Westminster under heavy guard for accounting at the Exchequer. That was the theory. Weeks later, the frustrated
receivers reported a picture of widespread tax-dodging and peculation: collectors had failed to pay in the gathered taxes, instead keeping
the money for 'their own use'; or they had done so, only for the cash to
be appropriated by the officials appointed to keep it under lock and key;
or, the cash was simply not kept securely, people breaking and entering
with 'strong hand' and making off with it. So 'diffuse and laborious'
had the receivers found their job that some failed to pay in any money
at all to the Exchequer. The king and his councillors, though, had
anticipated such a shortfall.[5]

Edward was no stranger to creative fundraising. The previous June
he had granted two royal servants, David Beaupe and John Mar-
chaunt, a licence to 'practise the faculty and science of philosophy
and the turning of mercury into gold and silver', presumably on the
off-chance that these two would-be alchemists could somehow magic
up the necessary funds for his French campaign. The solution he now
devised, in conjunction with his chief financial advisers, was not so
much a forced loan as an extra-parliamentary tax on income and
property: 'an excellent device to raise money', as one half-horrified,
half-admiring Milanese merchant put it. There was, naturally, nothing optional about the 'benevolence', as it was called. All potential
donors received advance notification of what was expected of them,
royal letters explaining why extra funds were needed for Edward's
'mighty war' and instructing their recipients to give generously. Given
that the king himself interviewed potential donors one-on-one, from

lords to local gentry and civic authorities, there was little means of escape. It was a time-consuming and laborious process – but then, if there was one thing Edward backed himself to do, it was personal, intimate, seductive charm.[6]

As the same merchant remarked, Edward's approach was astonishingly successful. He himself had seen his London neighbours leaving in response to the king's summons, looking 'as if they were going to the gallows'; returning, they were positively 'joyful', apparently perfectly happy to have had large sums of cash extracted from them. The process went as follows. Edward greeted the reluctant interviewee familiarly, as though welcoming an old friend, softening him until he was putty ready to be moulded. Talk then turned to the king's invasion plans, following which Edward popped the question: what personal financial contribution might the interviewee like to make, out of his own goodwill or 'benevolence'? Most negotiated weakly, if at all. Edward's strategy was equally effective with women. After one Suffolk widow had put herself down for £10, Edward 'took her to him and kissed her', an embrace that she accepted 'so kindly' that she increased her gift to £20. But then, Edward had always had a way with widows.

If the bonhomie was vintage Edward, so was the narrow-eyed calculation that ran through it. As the Milanese merchant put it, this was a 'method', a strategy involving the deployment of as much royal spontaneity as the transaction demanded. By the king's side, a notary hovered. As Edward talked, he assessed, his mind recalling the 'names and estates' of potential donors 'as if he had been in the habit of seeing them daily'. If the sum offered was, he felt, commensurate with the contributor's wealth, his clerk would write it down; if not, Edward, adjusting the royal charm by a few degrees, would bring his interviewee 'up to the mark'. When the royal warmth failed to produce the desired outcome, it rapidly gave way to a menacing insistence: people were induced to give 'with shame, some with fear'.[7]

The fundraising campaign had been systematically planned, the king's itinerary targeting wealthy regions, towns and cities over a four-month period. That autumn of 1474 saw Edward heading west to Bristol, then doubling back through the cloth-producing Cotswolds before heading towards the rich cloth towns of Suffolk. Inevitably, he couldn't be everywhere. Some communities, expecting the king, had to make do with other 'solicitors'. Among them members of the royal household and key financial officers such as the queen's receiver-general, John Forster, and a man who – when not travelling abroad on the king's confidential diplomatic business – was increasingly to be found at his side: John Morton. Morton's invisible hand, indeed, may well have guided the benevolence; in any event, he was responsible for raising 'notable sums of money'. And, given that this was a gift rather than a tax, the proceeds – a staggering £21,656 8s 3d – were paid directly into the coffers of the king's household.[8]

In mid-November Edward returned to London to concentrate his charm on the mayor and corporation. The French ambassador Christophe Lailler was still hanging about, hoping to see him. Given that Lailler had already richly insulted Edward with his menagerie of gifts, it was hard to know what he expected: unsurprisingly, Edward refused. The king's *froideur* was as much as anything down to Lailler's reputation as a state-sponsored assassin: on Louis XI's orders he had recently poisoned two prominent French noblemen, one of whom, the duke of Berry, was Louis' own brother. Edward took no chances, detailing two of his chamber servants to wait on the ambassador at all times. When, finally, he granted Lailler an audience, he sat at one end of his presence chamber. Lailler was made to stand at the other end, forty feet away.[9]

But if Lailler had put the fear of God into Edward – an outcome that Louis, despite his grumblings about the English king's paranoia, had probably intended – it didn't appear to have softened his resolve. There was, remarked John Paston towards the close of 1474, 'never more likelihood' that Edward would go to war the following year 'than was now'.

As Christmas approached, a ship carrying Archbishop George Neville docked at Dover. Finally, after two and a half years in his Calais prison, he was free, his royal pardon the result of extensive lobbying. Richard, in whose youth the sophisticated Neville had loomed large, had put in a word with Edward, though the tireless representations of Pope Sixtus IV had probably had more to do with the archbishop's release. The latest papal envoy to England, the distinguished Greek intellectual George Hermonymos, had turned on been persuasive; for Edward – knowing that Neville, in ill health, was no longer much of threat – it was a cheap and easy way to curry favour with the pope. Riding slowly through Kent, Neville spent Christmas quietly at the archbishop of Canterbury's seat of Knole House, as a guest of Thomas Bourchier, the one-time rival who, years previously, had been awarded the cardinalate that Neville had believed was rightfully his.[10]

By the early months of 1475, the entire country was on a war footing. The king's warships were overhauled and fitted out, and from Cornwall to Sandwich ships were seized and requisitioned, towed 'to the Thames and elsewhere' in preparation for the embarkation of his army.[11] In Parliament, confronted with Edward's 'great displeasure' at the fact that almost half his tax had not yet been collected, the commons reluctantly agreed to another round of taxation. That spring, as collectors scoured the country alongside Edward and his representatives, still raising contributions through his 'benevolence', England's taxpayers were feeling the pinch. Margaret Paston, for one, was sick of the sight of royal officials: 'The king goes so near us in this country, both to poor and to rich', she complained to her son, 'that I know not how we shall live but if the world amend.'[12]

As Parliament authorized partition of the Warwick estates, formally burying the hatchet between Clarence and Richard, one issue remained to be addressed. The stitch-up had left a loose strand in the form of George Neville, duke of Bedford. Now nine years old, this son of Warwick's brother John Neville remained the legitimate heir to the earl's patrimony. His continued existence remained a headache – especially for Richard, now in possession of Warwick's great northern estates – but, given the Yorkist brothers' eagerness to hold the lands by inheritance rather than royal grant, a necessity. Oddly, then, the continued existence of the male Neville line validated the York brothers' inheritance of the Warwick lands. Unsurprisingly, the solution was a legal fudge.

Parliament ruled that Richard, Clarence and their heirs were to keep the lands for as long as the duke of Bedford or any of his male heirs – should he have any – remained alive. When his line died out, so the right of Richard and Clarence to pass the lands on to their own descendants would expire. It was a bodged compromise but the alternative, ripping up the laws of inheritance altogether, would have created a seismic political precedent that would have played exceptionally badly with England's landed classes, especially at a time when Edward most desired their unity and co-operation.[13]

Other problematic standoffs had been resolved. The long-running feud between the north-western families of Stanley and Harrington – which Richard, backing the latter, had been so evasive in tackling – was finally ended, the Harringtons buckling under furious royal pressure. The king had also brokered an agreement between Richard and the earl of Northumberland that formed the basis for a working relationship between the two in the northeast: Northumberland acknowledging Richard's pre-eminence, Richard promising to leave the earl's spheres of interest well alone.[14]

Reassuringly, too, the new treaty with Scotland showed every sign of holding and, that February, English messengers headed north to Edinburgh with the first instalment of Cecily's dowry. There were, inevitably, infractions. Much to Edward's annoyance, they came from the English side, from his brother Richard and his sidekick Northumberland. Both had been notably remiss in failing to attend cross-border meetings with their Scottish colleagues. Richard, too, had failed to keep in line the fiercely independent frontier communities of which he was now overlord, resulting in vocal Scottish complaints. There was also tension at sea, James III writing indignantly to Edward that one of his 'own proper' ships had been plundered by an English vessel under Richard's command. Perhaps it was slackness on Richard's part; that, or an unwillingness – or inability – to adjust to the new dispensation of peace with England's habitual enemy. A visibly irritated Edward gave his brother a ticking-off, telling him that he held Richard directly responsible for the act of piracy – 'considering that the said ship was his at the time' – and briskly reminding him to sort himself out and act 'according to the king's pleasure for his honour and surety' at all times. Richard duly fell into line. There would, Edward assured the Scottish king with a hint of gritted teeth, be no further 'cause of trouble nor breach' of the truce.[15]

By mid-March, Edward's invasion plans were well advanced. The king's massive figure could be seen most days at the Tower, obsessively inspecting the artillery that he was assembling there; new guns daily rolled off the production line. A muster date for the army was circulating: 26 May. People were going to extraordinary lengths to prepare for the campaign, commented one Italian observer. Yet he detected an undercurrent of scepticism, as though, at the last minute, the whole thing would be called off: a legacy, perhaps, of Edward's previous failures to follow through on his promises. 'Many', he added in a reference to the doubting apostle, 'are kinsmen to St Thomas.'[16]

The army that assembled in Kent late in the spring of 1475 was, people believed, the biggest English force ever to invade France – bigger even than Edward III's army at Crécy and Henry V's at Agincourt. At various muster stations across the country, men reported for duty under their captains and, in the last weeks of May and early June, their baggage trains stretching out for miles behind them, converged in long, snaking, ever-growing columns on the army's assembly point of Barham Downs, southeast of Canterbury, under the watchful eye of the army's provost, the queen's receiver-general John Forster. All Edward's personal commitment over the past years to the invasion – from the tortuous resolution of domestic problems (foremost among them his brothers' quarrel) to his energetic raising of cash and troops – had borne fruit. The most prominent banners were those of Clarence's black bull, under which marched some 1,200 troops, and Richard's boar: the retinues of Richard and his northern retainers numbered around three thousand men. The turnout also showed the significant pulling power of Edward's extended family and household, foremost among them lords Hastings and Stanley; the queen's brother Anthony Woodville; and Henry duke of Buckingham – who, finally, was allowed to do something other than hang around at court.[17] All told, the army stood at some fourteen thousand men, a formidable and well-drilled display of unity and firepower.

Yet the Italian commentator hadn't been mistaken in detecting a strong whiff of uncertainty running through proceedings. Even now, Edward was unsure about Charles the Bold's commitment. Despite all his attempts to prise his brother-in-law away from his eastern campaign, the Burgundian duke's armies were still entrenched in front of the city of Neuss, where late that April Edward had sent Anthony Woodville to 'stimulate and importune' him. Woodville delivered a warning. Edward, he told Charles, was ready – but if the duke did not leave Neuss for France immediately, Edward would not invade 'at all'. Charles, wearing his Garter robes, continued to make positive noises. But he showed no signs of moving.[18]

Around this time, Edward was presented with a manuscript by William Worcester, a swarthy, one-eyed Bristolian in his early sixties. A well-read man with an enquiring mind, Worcester loved to talk, and people happily paid his bar bill to hear him do so. Back in the 1450s he had written *The Boke of Noblesse*, a call to arms, urging Henry VI and his lords to embrace war against France. It had fallen on deaf ears, and Worcester had spent much of the intervening time plodding around the country in a vain attempt to sort out the entangled business affairs of his late master, the Norfolk knight Sir John Fastolf, whose secretary he had been. Now, on the eve of Edward's invasion, Worcester dusted off his treatise, added some new passages to freshen it up, and rededicated it to Edward for inspiration in his coming war. But in diagnosing the issues that had led to England's loss of its French territories in the first place – internal squabbling among its nobility; and the English army's dismal failures in courage, training, organization and discipline – Worcester's treatise inadvertently underscored the risks that they were now about to face.[19]

As Edward and his generals contemplated the war to come, they might have reflected that Worcester's criticisms remained valid. Edward, it was true, had won a string of battles. However, the brief, decisive encounters of civil war, despite their savagery, weren't much preparation for the rigours of a drawn-out campaign against a well-organized enemy in his own backyard. Besides which, almost a quarter of a century had elapsed since the English had been kicked out of France: there were now very few people with first-hand experience of what such conflict entailed. While Edward's preparations had been meticulous, he and his advisers hardly needed Worcester's treatise to remind him that Charles the Bold and his troops, schooled as they were in northern European conflict, were crucial to the invasion's success. It was looking increasingly likely, however, that Charles was not going to turn up.

As the English army mustered at Barham Downs, Garter King at Arms arrived at the French court. Edward's senior herald carried a final ultimatum for Louis XI: hand over the crown of France or face the consequences. The herald's visit, however, was less concerned with slamming the door shut on the French king, and more about keeping it ajar. Louis knew it, and beckoned him into a private room for a chat.

The French king was disarmingly frank. He knew perfectly well, he told the herald, that Edward was in a bind. With Charles the Bold's army in disarray, and the campaigning season now well advanced, it would be madness to proceed with the invasion – yet, Louis continued, he understood that Edward needed to keep up appearances, that he could hardly call the whole thing off now that he had raised so much money, mustered so many troops and generated such great expectation among the English public. But they both knew, Louis confided, that Edward would do better to make peace than war.

The herald had come prepared for such a conversation. In a reply scripted by Edward and his advisers, he stated that the English king was open to offers, but that negotiations could only start once Edward 'had crossed the sea', once the invasion was seen to be under way. When the English had landed, Louis should send a messenger to the English camp. There, he should ask for one of Edward's close advisers: John, Lord Howard, or his household steward Lord Stanley.[20]

That June, a vast fleet shipped Edward's army, together with artillery, supplies, carts and carriages, and twelve thousand horses, across the Channel to Calais. The transportation was well-planned – squadrons of escorting warships patrolled against possible attack – and the crossing was uneventful. Over the previous months, Edward's agents had effectively spread misinformation that the English beachhead would be the Normandy coast: Louis XI's armies, concentrated some two hundred miles west along the Channel, waited for an enemy that never materialized. The Hanse, mollified by the terms of their recent treaty with Edward, were quiet. On 4 July, with the bulk of his forces disembarked at Calais, the king crossed, together with his household. Before leaving, he had placed England in the care of his four-year-old heir – who, a nominal 'keeper of the realm', was looked after by his mother, Queen Elizabeth – and a governing council packed with the prince's own officers, at its head the president of his council John Alcock, bishop of Rochester. Edward also drew up a will: the queen, his 'dearest wife', in whom 'we most singularly put our trust', was one of the nine nominated executors.

Determined to campaign in a style befitting his status as king of France, Edward took with him a newly made coronation robe of satin-lined cloth-of-gold. As elsewhere, the organization of his entourage had left nothing to chance. Travelling with him was George Neville, taken along perhaps for his administrative knowhow, perhaps because he remained a security risk – though Neville, suffering from kidney stones, was in no condition to make mischief.[21] With the king too was a team of twelve surgeons and his usual coterie of physician-astrologers. Among them was an Oxford academic and astrologer named John Stacy, who received the substantial sum of £80 for his services on campaign. Edward, clearly, was impressed with his work – though he hardly needed his flock of prognosticators to tell him what he already knew. His brother-in-law, Charles the Bold, was going to let him down.

About ten days after Edward arrived in Calais, Charles turned up. A few weeks previously he had finally dragged himself and his ragged forces away from Neuss, after an unsuccessful year-long siege that had cost him some four thousand men. Belatedly trying to raise funds for a fresh army, he found the wealthy cities of Flanders disinclined to extend him further credit for a campaign that would only damage the international trade from which their prosperity derived. Arriving in Calais, Charles was accompanied by a modest detachment of sixty archers – which, it transpired, was the sum total of his military contribution to Edward's invasion of France.

Reaction in the English camp was predictably violent. Some felt the whole thing should be called off at once; others, vaingloriously, that they didn't need the Burgundians anyway. For now, at any rate, Edward and his advisers decided to continue the campaign. With the French army still in Normandy, he marched out of Calais and, unopposed, through Burgundian territory towards eastern France and his eventual target: Reims, the traditional coronation place of France's kings. On the way the English halted at Agincourt, pitching camp on the battlefield for inspiration. By early August they had reached the French borderlands. The weather was deteriorating but, so Charles had assured Edward, the renegade constable of France was prepared to hand over the strategic city of St Quentin that now stood before him.

Charles had added what Philippe de Commynes chucklingly described as 'a bit of fat' to his story. Approaching St Quentin to receive its surrender, an English deputation was met by a barrage of cannonfire and quickly retreated. With Charles refusing Edward and his troops shelter in the nearby Burgundian town of Péronne, the English were forced to camp in open country, in what was now torrential rain. For Edward, it was the last straw. He had always found the realities of a long campaign unappealing. Now, with summer nearly over, the weather foul and the English camp a breeding ground for disease; with cash running out and his hoped-for allies, including the flip-flopping duke of Brittany, sitting on their hands; with the regrouping French army now less than fifty miles away and closing fast, he made up his mind.[22]

On 12 August, the same day that Charles left in a cloud of promises to rejoin his own army some hundred and fifty miles away, Edward made contact with Louis XI, using as his go-between a French prisoner who had been briefed by lords Howard and Stanley. Recognizing the names that Garter herald had recommended to him weeks before, Louis moved fast. His own messenger, dispatched immediately, made emollient noises of friendship to Edward and his advisers: Louis had only ever wanted peace with England, his real enemy being the duke of Burgundy; he knew, besides, what vast expense Edward had gone to, and how much pressure he was under to make war on France, If he was now minded to discuss a treaty, Louis would most certainly make it worth his while.

Talks started almost instantly; indeed, the shopping-list of English demands, produced almost at once, seemed pre-prepared. Two days later, a delegation headed by Howard and the coolly appraising figure of John Morton met French representatives to discuss terms. Their demands were substantial: a one-off payment to Edward of 75,000 crowns for Edward, to be paid immediately; an annual payment or 'pension' of 50,000 crowns for life; a new Anglo-French treaty founded on a marriage between Louis XI's heir and one of Edward's daughters, the cost of which would be covered by the French king; and – a sop to English public opinion – a demand for independent arbitration over Edward's claim to the French crown. In return, Edward promised to lead his army back to England as soon as the paperwork had been signed and exchanged.[23]

Aware that negotiating would only slow things down, Louis agreed to everything. Delighted to usher Edward out of France as quickly and honourably as possible, he agreed to English proposals for a summit between the two kings, at Amiens. To keep the English troops sweet, Louis opened the gates of the city to them. Over the following four days, with its innkeepers ordered to serve Edward's men whatever they wanted, the city was effectively transformed into a free bar. Confronted by the prospect of unlimited booze, in time-honoured fashion the English entirely failed to control themselves. They staggered around, one bar reportedly running up a hundred and eleven separate tabs before nine in the morning, before Edward finally sent in guards to carry away his sozzled army.

On 29 August, some three miles downstream at the village of Picquigny, the atmosphere was rather more upright as Edward and Louis finally came face to face. With their respective armies lining opposing banks of the River Somme, the kings met in the middle of a specially constructed bridge over the river. Louis was mindful of a meeting between two French royal factions in similar circumstances back in 1419, when John of Burgundy was hacked to death on the orders of Louis' father. Accordingly, his encounter with Edward took place through a protective trellis. At his master's shoulder, one of the architects of the talks, Philippe de Commynes – who, having received an overwhelmingly attractive offer from Louis, had defected from Charles the Bold – watched attentively.

Despite their marathon drinking session the mounted English troops, drawn up in battle order, were an intimidating sight. Commynes looked on as the unmistakeable form of Edward approached the bridge, twelve close advisers at his back, foremost among them Clarence, Hastings and Northumberland. The last time Commynes had encountered Edward was in Flanders, five years before. Then, Edward had been a penniless, albeit magnificent fugitive. Now, dressed in cloth-of-gold and a black cap studded with a jewel-encrusted fleur-de-lys, Edward cut a regal figure 'but', said Commynes, was 'beginning to get fat': no longer the prince whose good looks had once taken his breath away.

Since their respective crownings within a month of each other back in the summer of 1461, the fortunes of Edward and Louis had been closely entwined. As they met, they perhaps felt a sense of mutual familiarity. Striving to outdo each other in elaborate courtesies, they embraced through the trelliswork, Edward towering over the diminutive, ageing form of the French king. Edward's French, noted Commynes, was 'pretty good'. After copies of the treaties were exchanged, Louis invited Edward banteringly to Paris to 'dine with the ladies', offering to provide a pliant confessor to 'absolve him from sin', before the talk again turned serious. The pair discussed France's neighbours and enemies, Burgundy and Brittany. At the mention of Charles the Bold, Edward shrugged – his brother-in-law was more or less dead to him – but he asked Louis not to make war on the duke of Brittany, whose friendship he valued. Shortly after, amid a profusion of mutual compliments, the two kings and their entourages parted.

Edward had done exceptionally well out of what became known as the Treaty of Picquigny: a seven-year truce that included a bilateral free-trade agreement, a mutual defence pact and a substantial financial settlement in Edward's favour. The one-off payment he had demanded, equating to £15,000, was delivered instantly; the annual pension of £10,000 would cover most of the running costs of his household or, depending on how Edward chose to spend it, the financing of the Calais garrison. Either way, a perennial headache had been solved. In addition, Louis had committed to providing a jointure of 60,000 crowns for the projected marriage at the treaty's heart, between Louis' heir and Edward's oldest daughter Elizabeth. To oil the wheels, Louis also distributed sizeable pensions and 'a lot of ready cash and plate' among Edward's most influential advisers, including Thomas Montgomery, John Morton, John Howard, the chancellor Thomas Rotherham and William Hastings, who received the biggest pension of the lot. All had been intimately involved in the negotiations. It was hardly surprising that – as one anonymous chronicler, a member of Edward's administration, put it – they considered Picquigny an 'honourable peace'. Others saw it differently.

When news of the treaty reached him, Charles the Bold reacted with predictable fury. He stormed into the English camp, where his vexation was met with collective indifference from Edward's advisers. One French envoy, reporting the meeting to the French king, did an impression of the frenzied duke of Burgundy, stamping his feet and swearing, calling Edward 'all the insults under the sun'.

Although he always enjoyed impressions of the volatile Charles, Louis remained wary. As his agents told him, the mood in the English camp was dark. One of Anthony Woodville's close friends, the hard-bitten Gascon Louis de Bretailles, told Commynes that Edward had won nine battles and had never lost – until now. The shame of returning home, moreover, 'was greater than the honour he had gained in winning the other nine'. What worried Bretailles most was the reception that they were going to face back in England, and precisely how they were going to explain themselves to an enraged public. Those of Edward's advisers who had accepted French pensions felt anxious about having done so. Louis' agents identified several leading Englishmen openly uneasy about the treaty – or, more to the point, uneasy about being seen to accept it. Foremost among them was Richard: he was, said Commynes, 'not happy'.

Richard's martial reputation preceded him, and he wanted war. His reluctance to accept the treaty terms alarmed Louis. At Amiens, the French king had thrown everything he had at Richard to bring him round, entertaining him lavishly, loading him with presents of fine plate, cash and horses, and assiduously flattering his martial pretensions. Louis' gifts included a 'great bombard', a gift that proved an ice breaker: 'I have always', Richard later wrote to Louis warmly, 'taken great pleasure in artillery.' Richard warmed up – or, as Commynes, a master of the apposite verb, put it, 'recollected' himself. Recognizing that Richard didn't want to be associated with the appeasement of Picquigny, Louis gave him a way out: as Edward signed the treaty, Clarence at his side, Richard was absent, inspecting the French troops at Louis' invitation. It was a neat way of distancing himself from the treaty in the eyes of his troops and those back home while at the same time accepting it.[24]

In France, widespread fear of the English had already given way to scorn. Songs circulated about how Edward's 'great army' had been washed away by a deluge of fine French wine and some pies – which, given quite how much it had cost Louis to buy Edward off, was a narrative he jumped on. In private, he mocked the English capitulation mercilessly. On one such occasion, the king realized to his horror that an expatriate French merchant, domiciled in England, was present, having been admitted to petition for an export licence. Ordering him not to return to England, Louis immediately had the merchant resettled in his native Bordeaux, where he was set up with a good job and reunited with his hastily repatriated wife. There was no way he was going to risk stories of his jokes getting back to Edward.[25]

Adding to the general air of malaise that hung over the English army was a fug of disease. As they marched dejectedly back through the malarial marshlands of the Somme valley, they finally managed to emulate Henry V's forces, in this respect if no other. 'I mislike the air here', Sir John Paston wrote to his mother from Calais. Having arrived in excellent health, he reported, he was now 'crazed' with sickness, his stomach in a terrible state.

Edward himself was noticeably subdued. He had, some conjectured, come down with ague, malarial fever – though it may have been the dawning realization that, despite having struck an excellent financial deal with Louis, there was little likelihood of him ever again having a crack at gaining the French crown.[26] That, and his preoccupation with how the deal was going to be received back in England.

The trans-shipment of Edward's army back across the Channel took most of September. Adding to the delay, so talk at the Burgundian court had it, was the king's refusal to let his brothers Clarence and Richard return to England before him. Apparently, Edward feared they might become a focus for popular discontent – especially Clarence, whose previous attempt to 'make himself king' was uppermost in the English king's mind. That, at least, was what Charles the Bold was saying. And Charles was in such a state about Edward that he was prepared to say any old thing.

For the Burgundian duke, Edward's peace settlement was a betrayal of chivalric values so profound that it could only be explained by his ignoble parentage. Edward, he fulminated, wasn't the son of Richard of York at all. Rather, he was the offspring of an affair between Cecily Neville and an English archer stationed at Rouen, whose name, as the infuriated Charles now called Edward, was 'Blaybourne'.[27] Such rumours had been floating around for years – at least since the bloodletting after Edgecote back in 1469, when Warwick and Clarence had spread talk of Cecily's liaison with the archer – though where the detail of the archer's name had come from was unclear. Whatever the case, Charles's rift with Edward now seemed irreconcilable. In his fury, the Burgundian duke even signed a new peace treaty with Louis XI, the man he hated most – though Edward now ran Louis a close second. In one paroxysm of rage, Charles tore his Garter into tiny pieces with his teeth.[28]

On 28 September Edward and his army entered London, battle standards aloft and trumpets blaring. Escorted by the mayor and five hundred citizens dressed in Yorkist colours, they followed the usual route of kings returning in triumph, over London Bridge and through the city, stopping to offer up thanks to God at St Paul's. Whatever his inward concerns, Edward brazened it out: this, the military parade seemed to say, was a victory as comprehensive as anything that might have been achieved on the battlefield.[29] In the days and weeks following the royal return, a slew of pronouncements continued to spin the official line. Edward's pension was in fact tribute money, acknowledgement by Louis of the English king's rightful claim to the French throne. Moreover, the new Anglo-French free-trade deal would be to the 'universal weal and profit of us and all our subjects'. All this seemed reasonable enough. There was no doubt that the lifting of restrictions on trade with France would benefit the country; the 'tribute', meanwhile, would go a fair way to easing the royal burden on the English taxpayer, something Edward emphasized in graciously waiving the last portion of his war tax, due for collection that autumn.[30]

But as Edward and those around him knew, it was the big picture that counted. Edward might have clinched the best deal in the world, but in the public imagination the more fine-grained fiscal, economic and commercial arguments were lost, swamped by the one truth that people understood. Having extracted a series of exorbitant taxes from them under what now looked like false pretences – a practice in which he had a long and undistinguished record – Edward had led a massive army to reconquer France and had returned empty-handed and humiliated. The English wanted their kings to deliver military glory, preferably over the French. Whatever the advantages of a king who preferred business 'aventures' to chivalric ones, the sense of national bathos was palpable.

Back home, Edward's discontented, newly demobilized troops prowled the country. Disorder spiked and, reported one chronicler, 'no road throughout England was left in a state of safety'. Edward had anticipated disturbances, and his response was quick and savage. Late that autumn, he rode through Hampshire and Wiltshire dispensing summary justice: anybody found guilty of theft or murder, even members of his own household, was 'instantly hanged'. Such brutal decisiveness, noted one government official approvingly, contained the disorder. People inclined to violent protest instead saw the wisdom in keeping their resentments to themselves.[31]

Edward, though, was disinclined to move far from England's southeast. The winter of 1475 saw him moving slowly between his Thames-side houses, from Westminster to Greenwich, then back upriver to Windsor. With regional troubles again bubbling up, exacerbated by Edward's absence in France and the ugly national mood on his return, he turned to the great family power bases that he had spent recent years establishing.

In the early months of 1476, attempting to get a grip on the endemic disorder in Wales and the Marches, Edward handed Prince Edward's council – at its head, the queen's brother Anthony Woodville – further judicial and military powers, which it was quick to deploy. Among the more visible councillors riding through the region and extending the young prince's authority ever further afield were the queen's sons by her first marriage: twenty-year-old Thomas Grey, recently created marquis of Dorset, and his teenage brother Sir Richard. The queen's family was establishing an ever-greater presence in the prince's council and household at the expense of other major players in the region. Notably absent from efforts to impose royal law and order were the earl of Pembroke William Herbert, son of Edward's Welsh 'master-lock', and Henry duke of Buckingham. Edward evidently didn't rate either of them.[32]

Despite absorbing him into the Yorkist family as an eight-year-old and marrying him off to the queen's sister Katherine, Edward had never seemed inclined to make Buckingham part of his plans. Perhaps Edward was wary of the great duke's Lancastrian blood; then again, perhaps he just didn't like him, refusing to give the duke any political responsibility whatsoever. Over the years, Buckingham's role had been restricted to that of a glittering court mannequin, wheeled out on great occasions of state – a role which, it had to be said, the elegant duke played to perfection. Obsessive about his appearance, he was a regular patron of the royal apothecary John Clark, who supplied him with various kinds of skin clarifier and whitener to obtain the aristocratic pallor prized especially by noblewomen; and a night-time face pack, to be washed off the following morning with an infusion of 'strawberry leaves, wild tansy, bean flowers and roses'.[33]

Buckingham, though, also wanted power – which, by early 1476, he looked ever further from acquiring. His poor relations with Edward had been aggravated by his insistence on parading his own Lancastrian credentials, incorporating the arms of his royal forebears into his own. If this hardly endeared him to the king, he and Edward then fell out during the invasion of France, when – perhaps vocally opposing the king's settlement with Louis XI – he had left for England with his four hundred troops even before the treaty was signed. Whether he had stomped off in a huff, or whether he had been ordered unceremoniously back by Edward, was unclear. Despite his family's traditional prominence in Wales, the twenty-year-old Buckingham was systematically excluded from the work of the prince's council.

Edward's aversion to Herbert, Buckingham's exact contemporary, was in marked contrast to the trust he had placed in Herbert's father. Youth was no disqualification: Herbert was the same age as the queen's son Dorset, who was now being heaped with regional responsibility, along with his younger brother. Perhaps, Edward felt, Herbert was simply less able than his brutal father; he had, it was true, failed to keep his own violent clan in check. As the prince's council spread its influence out from Ludlow through the region, methodically dismembering Herbert's networks of influence and ignoring Buckingham's claims, the two nobles sensed that the prince's men – the queen's family and their associates at their forefront – were hungrily acquiring power at their expense. If, previously, the Woodvilles had lacked a significant landed base of their own, now they had one – on behalf, naturally, of the prince and the king.[34] Buckingham and Herbert may not have liked it, but there wasn't an awful lot they could do.

Across the other side of the country, Richard and the earl of Northumberland toured an unsettled Yorkshire with a force of five thousand troops. At York, the duke told the feuding citizens to keep the peace: any and all violence would be punished, he warned, by imprisonment, fines and 'grievous pain', all at 'the king's will'. These were royal orders that Richard was delivering; likewise, as an arbiter and judge he would 'none otherwise do any time, but according to the king's laws'. The king's representative in the north, he worked tirelessly to prove himself the region's 'good lord', a great nobleman who would look after everybody who sought his favour – provided that, in the time-honoured equation, they gave him loyalty in return. This dual identity gave him an added attraction, as York's civic officers were well aware; that March, they lavished gifts on Richard, thanking him for his 'great labour' in lobbying the king for the city to retain its corporate privileges.[35]

This, of course, was how Edward had always ruled. With his family and close household servants entrusted with the rule of large swathes of the country, he was the splendid sun, even the greatest of his lords reflecting their master's regal light. Now, as Edward approached his mid-thirties, this quality seemed exaggerated. His furious bursts of activity – counter-insurgencies and judicial progresses – became fewer, his stretches in England's southeast longer. All of which made sense as far as the business of government was concerned, keeping him near England's financial and legal centres, and allowing him to react more immediately to developments across the Channel. More to the point, Edward liked his creature comforts – and, just because the French went out of their way to ridicule the English king's self-indulgence and sybaritism, that didn't make them wrong.

As Edward moved sedately, and not always soberly, from one pleasure-filled Thames-side manor to another, he had grand schemes in mind. With the clouds of recession and financial insecurity starting to lift, his coffers flush with Louis XI's cash, he started to invest in the grand architectural projects that would represent his dynasty's legacy.

In recent decades, funds for such schemes had been thin on the ground. Henry VI's great religious foundations of Eton and King's College, Cambridge – two of the few consistent preoccupations of his wandering mind – had proved a massive drain on the public purse. As the storm-clouds of civil conflict gathered in the 1450s, work on them had ground to a halt, the unfinished lines of the chapel at King's abandoned as finances were diverted to pay for troops and armaments.[36] Earlier in his reign, Edward improved the royal houses when he could, but the work had been piecemeal: funds were rarely available. Now, however, they were.

Windsor had always been one of Edward's favourite residences. Besides the hunting in its parks and the castle's sheer splendour, its chapel of St George was the spiritual home of the Order of the Garter, an institution that Edward had deployed to great effect to create a cult of personal chivalric loyalty to himself. For years, Edward had had the notion of transforming Windsor into the spiritual centre of the house of York. There was Fotheringhay, of course, but it was remote, a hundred miles away in Northamptonshire; besides which, as the creation of his ancestors it didn't reflect the new royal dynasty that he himself had brought into being.

Shortly before his invasion of France the previous year, Edward had plans drawn up for a new chapel at Windsor, a soaring, light-flooded vision in perpendicular Gothic. In a nod towards his ancestor Edmund of Langley's improvements at Fotheringhay, accommodation for the clerics in the castle complex was to be laid out in the shape of the family's fetterlock badge. As he embarked for Calais, Edward had told his master-of-works at Windsor, the bishop of Salisbury Richard Beauchamp, precisely where in the new chapel he wanted to be buried, in the event that he died in France.[37]

Groundwork for the new chapel had already started before Edward's return. In the months that followed, he threw quantities of Louis' cash at new architectural projects: a tower at Nottingham Castle, whose polygonal design and 'sumptuous' stonework would draw admiring appraisals in generations to come; and improvements to all his Thameside houses. One manor in particular, Eltham in Kent, now became the scene of Edward's most emphatic architectural statement.

Situated off the main London–Dover road, some eight miles south-east of the capital, Eltham, with its shady, vine-covered galleries and extensive gardens and parks, had for centuries been a house beloved of kings. Successive monarchs had left their mark on it, demolishing, adapting and rebuilding in a profusion of ever more luxurious apartments, though in recent decades it had, like much else, fallen into comparative neglect. Edward liked Eltham. He and Elizabeth had spent their first married Christmas there and, back in 1467, it had hosted the warm-up tournament in anticipation of the Bastard of Burgundy's visit. In winter 1475 work started on a building that was to become one of the glories of English domestic architecture. Eltham's new brick-built, stone-faced great hall would be over a hundred feet long and with a gilded hammer-beam roof. Light would flood in from the windows that ran along the hall's upper storey and from two deep bay windows, either side of the dais, that extended almost to the floor, and into which the royal coats of arms of York were glazed. Clean-lined, perfectly proportioned, it was an architectural statement of intent.[38]

As fast as he spent his money, Edward was as keen to keep it coming in. There were other windfalls. Part of the settlement with Louis XI had involved the ransoming of Margaret of Anjou – a figure who no longer posed a problem for Edward but, as a claimant to the powerful house of Anjou, and thus large swathes of provincial France, remained one for Louis. In early 1476 at Rouen, Thomas Montgomery handed Margaret over to the French king's representatives, in exchange for the first instalment of her £10,000 ransom. Aged forty-six, this resourceful, implacable queen had finally lost everything. Before leaving England, she was made to sign a document renouncing her claim to the throne; when she got to France, Louis forced her to relinquish her rights to the family patrimony of Anjou. Margaret retired to the small village of Reculée near Angers, where she lived off the modest pension that Louis had granted her and contemplated what had been.[39]

In constant pain from kidney stones, George Neville had spent the early months of 1476 in seclusion at the Neville family home of Bisham Abbey, immersed – when energy permitted – in diocesan administration and alchemy, trying to find cures for his ailments and misfortunes. The priest and alchemist George Ripley sent him prescriptions and a copy of his new book *The Marrow of Alchemy* – which, he told Neville, would restore to the ailing, friendless archbishop favour, wealth, and health and happiness, concluding that Neville had 'God before his eyes'.

Ripley was right, though not in the way he intended. In the spring, journeying slowly north to his see of York, Neville stopped at the Nottinghamshire village of Blyth, where he died.[40] Aged forty-four, the circumstances of his death seemed to mock the powerful flamboyance of his years as one of the regime's key architects. He left no will: after Edward's confiscation of his fortune four years previously, he had little to bequeath. No chantry chapel was built at York Minster; no money had been set aside to pay for the masses that would usher his soul through purgatory. Edward hardly seemed to notice Neville's passing at all.

That summer, the king was preoccupied with another interment. When, back in the winter of 1460, his father Richard and brother Edmund were killed in the massacre at Wakefield, they had been hastily buried in nearby Pontefract. There had always been other financial priorities, but now, over fifteen years later, Edward planned to bring the bodies back to their spiritual home of Fotheringhay. The reburial of Richard duke of York would be an epic statement of dynastic assertion and family unity.

Mid-afternoon on 29 July, at the entrance to Fotheringhay churchyard, a cluster of black-clad figures waited to greet Richard of York's funeral cortege. In their midst, bulky in a furred full-length habit of mourning blue, was Edward and, flanking him, Clarence and Richard, who as designated chief mourner had brought his long-dead father and brother south.[41]

At Pontefract, the two corpses had been exhumed from their resting place in the church of St John's Priory. There they lay in state as the office of the dead was sung, the coffins covered with rich palls of cloth-of-gold – and in Richard of York's case, topped with a life-sized effigy of the dead duke, dressed in royal blue, hands clasped in prayer, fixed eyes staring upward. Then, loaded onto funeral carriages pulled by teams of black-caparisoned horses, they set off on their final journey. With them, on foot, went four hundred 'poor men', black-habited, with black hoods pulled over their heads, carrying burning torches; a knot of royal officers-of-arms, heraldic coats of arms worn over their mourning black; and several noblemen and their followers, among them Northumberland, Lord Stanley and Richard, riding protectively behind his father's carriage.[42] Along the route, nightly vigils were held at pre-arranged locations, crowds gathering silently and solemnly to watch the processions and hear the masses.

Alongside the three brothers at Fotheringhay were other members of the family and their closest adherents: among them John de la Pole, earl of Lincoln, their fourteen-year-old nephew, and Henry Bourchier, earl of Essex; Anthony Woodville and his nephew Dorset; the omnipresent Hastings. After Edward tearfully kissed his father's effigy, the reception committee followed the coffins as they were borne into the church and laid under two extravagantly adorned, purpose-built canopies.

The following day, the royal family and a number of visiting dignitaries crammed into the church for the funeral service. After the obsequies were over, some two thousand guests sat down to a funeral feast in canvas pavilions erected in the adjacent fields, working their way through herds of beef and mutton and flocks of poultry, washed down with forty pipes of wine. Alms were distributed, a penny for each person, and twopence for pregnant women: in all, remarked one herald, 'up to five thousand people who came to receive alms were counted'.

Happily for Edward, the massive sums disbursed at Fotheringhay could be instantly recouped. Among the foreign representatives present was the Rouen merchant Guillaume Restout, who had come to hand over the first half-yearly instalment of Louis XI's pension. The day after the funeral, Edward handed Restout a receipt for 25,000 French crowns.[43]

By mid-September, London was finally shaking off the plague epidemic that had hung around all summer. People who had fled at the first signs of the outbreak cautiously began to return. Elizabeth Stonor, wife of the Oxfordshire knight Sir William, who had remained resolutely in her city home, wrote entreating her husband to join her – overburdened with business matters, she needed his help – and to send her children from her first marriage, whom she was missing.[44] Later that month William Caxton, former governor of the Merchant Adventurers, arrived back in the capital from his adoptive Flanders after a decade-long absence. Now in his fifties, Caxton had his head full of the new project that he had been developing in Cologne and Bruges for the past five years: printing.

As much as anything, Caxton's return was driven by a desire to be close to his target market: an aspirational readership eager for translations of the chivalric romances and histories fashionable in the courts of northern Europe. Nobody else was making them available in print: Caxton, with his bulky contacts book and knowledge of the Flemish literary scene, knew that he was the man to do so. He headed not to the heart of the city, where he would face competition from the publishers of Paternoster Row and other foreign printers who had settled there, but to Westminster. There, on 29 September, he took out a lease on commercial premises in the Abbey sanctuary. Soon, he was pasting up flyers with a notice advertising the sale of his new edition of the 'Sarum Pye' or *Ordinale Sarum*, the service book used around the country, including at its foot a note in Latin: *Supplico stet cedula* – 'Don't take this leaflet'. This, after all, was the first printed advert in England and, Caxton assumed, people would be drawn to its novelty value.[45] His timing was impeccable. Ten days after he opened for business, Edward and his court were back at Westminster. The king had summoned a great council – which meant that he had significant matters to discuss.

Having, as he hoped, fixed stellar marriages for two of his daughters – Elizabeth and Cecily to the French and Scottish heirs, respectively – Edward's thoughts were on his elder son and heir, now rising six. There was a marriage proposal on the table, to Juana, the second daughter of the Spanish monarchs Ferdinand and Isabella. As yet, though, this was a far-off prospect. There was a more pressing issue at hand: Edward's friendship with Charles the Bold, which had still not recovered from the battering it had taken at Picquigny.

Now wearing the golden handcuffs of Louis' pension, Edward's relationship with France had been reset in a way that had barely seemed possible two years before. For all that, the Anglo-French détente was still no more popular, as the king and his councillors remained uncomfortably aware. Late that year, the French envoy Restout arrived in London with the latest half-yearly payments for Edward and his inner circle. Calling in at Hastings' house south of St Paul's with his pension of a thousand crowns in cash, Restout's deputy, Pierre Clairet, was shown into a private chamber. When Hastings walked in, he indicated the money and asked pleasantly for a receipt. When Hastings demurred, Clairet persisted: could he please just have a few lines addressed to his master Louis by way of proof, so that the French king – 'somewhat suspicious by nature', he told Hastings, confidingly – would not think he had run off with his money? Hastings refused. Louis, he retorted, chose to give him the money: 'I didn't ask for it'. If Clairet wanted to leave the money, that was up to him. He would get no receipt. 'What I absolutely do not want', added Hastings emphatically, 'is people saying of me that the Lord Chamberlain of England is a pensioner of the king of France', nor did he want 'my receipts turning up in the French exchequer'. Whatever his feelings on the relationship with France, it was his public reputation that was most important to Hastings. While perfectly happy to accept French money, he saw no reason that people should know about it. Clairet got the point – and left the money. So did Louis. In future, when his envoys dropped off Hastings' cash, they never again asked him for a receipt.[46]

Louis was sensitive to his English unpopularity. That November, he was reported to be shipping Edward 700,000 butts – 126-gallon barrels – of French wine: 'a great and marvellous thing', wondered the Milanese ambassador to France, 'thought to be in order to ingratiate himself with the people of England'.[47] Whether or not Edward redistributed this vast quantity of wine was unclear. Perhaps, rarely able to resist temptation, he was more inclined to drink himself into a stupor instead. Louis probably considered it a win–win outcome.

Yet Edward's, and England's, relationship with Burgundy remained crucial: after all, many close personal connections bound the two states together. And while there was an economic upside to Edward's détente with Louis, the ill-feeling that festered with Charles continued to impact on English trade with Flanders, a problem that merchants persistently lobbied Edward to solve. Of equal concern to Edward and his council that autumn was Charles's behaviour.

Following the Picquigny meeting, Charles had returned to his ever-more compulsive obsession with expanding his eastern borders. His campaign against the independent cantons of Switzerland had limped from one fiasco to another, littered with atrocities – including his lynching of the entire 412-strong garrison of Grandson following the Swiss town's surrender – and beset by infighting among his mercenaries, the English being the worst troublemakers (they had no respect, reported one envoy, and were convinced of their 'superiority over all other nations'). Forced out of Switzerland, Charles reinvaded in the spring of 1476. He was camped outside his first objective, the fortress-city of Murten, when Anthony Woodville turned up. Delighted at this indication of renewed English support, Charles made much of him – and was correspondingly incandescent when, a few days later, Woodville suddenly recalled a prior engagement back in England, made his apologies and left. 'He is gone because he is afraid', was Charles's blunt verdict. Or maybe, something didn't smell right to Woodville. If so, his instincts were good. On 22 June, a relieving Swiss army routed Charles's forces, slaughtering thousands and capturing the bulk of his artillery. In the following months, Charles's denial of the disaster that had befallen him left observers unnerved: he just 'laughs, jokes and makes good cheer', reported one ambassador, appalled.[48]

Assembling yet another army, Charles seemed oblivious to his new vulnerability, and the dangers that accompanied it. Edward and his councillors, though, were deeply concerned. For around a century, the assertive Burgundian dukes had reshaped north-western Europe, their on–off alliance with England a crucial counterweight to the might of France. In his hubris, Charles seemed the last person to contemplate what the repercussions might be if Burgundy collapsed.

As the court celebrated Christmas that year, the festivities were dampened by news that Clarence's wife, Isabel Neville, was dead. Early in October she had given birth to the couple's second son; the delivery was difficult and Isabel had 'sickened' – a postpartum infection, probably, from which she had never recovered. Her baby boy, christened Richard, died soon after his mother, on 1 January. If the obsequies for his twenty-five-year-old wife were anything to go by, Clarence's grief was profound. At Tewkesbury Abbey, following a magnificent service and night-long vigil by members of his household, Isabel's body lay in state for a month before her burial. Clarence's mourning was sharpened by an awareness of his new dynastic precariousness, with a three-year-old daughter and a son rising two. As the death of their infant brother had shown all too clearly, there was no guarantee of them reaching the age of inheritance.[49]

Shortly after Epiphany, reports from eastern France of another death stunned everybody.

That winter, Charles the Bold's attempt to regain the strategically vital city of Nancy had hardened into another long siege. The weather was bitter, further weakening his already inadequate forces: some four hundred Burgundian troops froze to death. On 5 January 1477 the defenders marched out of the besieged city and, joining forces with a newly arrived contingent of Swiss troops, tore into Charles's army. In the chaos that followed, those who could, fled. The Burgundian duke's body was discovered two days later, frozen, naked and battered almost beyond recognition (following which, it was said, hungry wolves had been at it). It was finally identified by Charles's tell-tale scars and his customary long fingernails.[50] The future of the house of Valois-Burgundy now hung on the slender shoulders of Charles's only child and heir – his nineteen-year-old daughter Marie, now duchess of Burgundy – and the knowhow of her stepmother, Edward's sister Margaret. Within days, their enemies were on the move.

15

The Most Extreme
Purposed Malice

'It seemeth to me', Sir John Paston wrote home from London on 14 February 1477, 'that all the world is quavering.' With Charles the Bold's death, northern Europe trembled on the brink of a radical and bloody reshaping as Burgundy's great neighbours – the Habsburgs to the east and France to the west – clustered greedily around to claim the duchy for themselves. With the news came talk that England would get sucked into the devastating war that, as Paston put it, would soon 'reboil'; as a result of which, he added darkly, 'young men would be cherished'.[1]

In France, Louis XI had greeted the demise of the man he called 'the devil' – and who, the previous summer, he had variously cited a heart murmur, a headache and piles to avoid meeting – with ecstasy. Even before Charles's death was confirmed, he was mobilizing his armies. 'Now is the time', he told his commanders, 'to bring to bear all of your five senses on placing the duchy of Burgundy in my hands.' As they advanced into the disputed borderlands of Picardy and Artois, French forces met little resistance: one by one, fortresses and towns opened their gates and did homage to Louis. But in the great mercantile city of Arras people still hoped for a miracle, from England.

As the French approached, a poem circulated through the city, conjuring up a courtly world, a fragrant garden in which the heady perfume of the marguerite attracted the rose. On behalf of his beloved sister Margaret – the marguerite – Edward IV would send an army across the sea to rescue Arras, and Burgundy, from the ravening French. After all, the 'rose of England' was 'one of us', part of the Burgundian family. He would be here soon and then French war-makers would tremble.

The poem was partly right. The beleaguered new duchess of

Burgundy – her fearful leading advisers already trickling away to Louis XI, enticed by bribes and the promise of favour – confirmed that her stepmother Margaret was in intense negotiations with Edward, 'to persuade him to come to our aid'.[2] Whether Edward would heed his sister's call was another matter entirely.

If Louis needed no invitation to march into the lands he claimed as his own, in England the mood was more deliberate. At Westminster, wrote Paston, Edward had convened a great council to debate England's course of action in the face of this 'great change'. Clarence and Richard were riding to London to join the discussions 'in all haste'.[3]

The house of Burgundy was, as the Arras poet had pointed out, family. Blood and honour, as well as long-standing treaties of mutual defence, demanded that Yorkist England come to its aid. For those who, following the fiasco of Picquigny eighteen months before, had pocketed their substantial French pensions with a sense of shame, here was a golden chance to put England's chivalric reputation straight. As far as Paston had heard, though, there was no talk of war in the council chamber. The discussions, as far as he knew, revolved around more immediate concerns: the security of Calais and the preservation of peace, both with Flanders and especially with its aggressor, France.[4]

There were good reasons to keep out of any forthcoming conflict. The difficulties involved in assembling another invading army were self-evident. Given the outcome last time, Parliament was hardly likely to indulge requests for a fresh tax. War against France, too, would imperil all the concessions that Edward had wrung from Louis, foremost among them his lucrative pension and his daughter's planned marriage to Louis' son and heir: a match dear not only to Edward's heart, but to those of Queen Elizabeth and her family. Besides, the chaos of the new dispensation brought with it opportunity. Edward could hold over Louis the threat of English military intervention on Burgundy's behalf, making sure he fulfilled the terms of the existing treaty and, perhaps, squeezing him for more money into the bargain. As Paston hinted, Edward and his inner circle of advisers – as keen as the king not to relinquish their French pensions – now saw England's role not as aggressor but as power-broker, balancing its 'amities' with both France and Flanders to its best advantage. Sabre-rattling was part of this process. Going to war on behalf of the beleaguered duchy was not.

What was more, the great council turned out to be little more than a cosmetic exercise in consensus politics, presumably to satisfy those lords uneasy over Edward's distinctly unchivalrous abandonment of what they considered his obligations to Burgundy. Well before the council had even assembled, Edward and members of his inner circle had decided on their direction of travel, with John Morton and the trusted household knight Sir John Donne already on their way to the French court with a set of demands to extract from Louis XI. Hastings, so reluctant to leave a paper trail of evidence for his French pension, was part of the king's privy decision-making process. Edward's brothers, on the other hand, were absent. Riding furiously down from Yorkshire, Richard arrived late, to be presented with what was effectively a *fait accompli*. He accepted it blandly enough: after all, he was on good terms with the king's close advisers. But if Richard was sanguine, Clarence was not.[5]

As she urged Edward to intervene against Louis XI, his sister Margaret offered an inducement. Her stepdaughter Marie of Burgundy was now the most eligible heiress in Europe. She would, Margaret proposed, be the perfect match for the recently widowed Clarence. Not only might such a marriage stop Louis from reordering Burgundy to his own designs, it offered the house of York the chance to do some political redrawing of its own. Such a marriage would see Clarence, the brother of whom Margaret was reputedly 'more fond' than 'anyone else in the family', become duke of Burgundy.[6]

Clarence was still in mourning, his late wife's body still lying in state in Tewkesbury Abbey, when talk of his possible marriage to Marie started to circulate. It wasn't the first time the match had been suggested: Edward, indeed, had once proposed it over a decade previously, when feverishly pursuing his ever-closer union with Charles the Bold. Then, both the chief English negotiator Warwick – who had wanted Clarence to marry his own daughter – and the Burgundians, unwilling to entertain the prospect of Edward's brother as a potential heir to the duchy, had greeted the idea with alarm and it had been quietly dropped. Now, Clarence was said to be wildly enthusiastic about the proposal. He was in a minority of one.

Marie of Burgundy herself was said to be unimpressed by the idea.

Just a few weeks previously she had been betrothed to Maximilian archduke of Austria, son of the Holy Roman Emperor Frederick and heir to the great German house of Habsburg. As a counterweight to the existential threat presented by France, Maximilian was a more viable proposition than the brother of a king of England, something of which Louis XI was well aware. The French king had already made Marie a counter-offer: the hand of his seven-year-old son and heir, currently promised to Edward's oldest daughter. Finally, even though she was said to have 'devoted all her effort' to bringing Clarence and Marie together, Margaret knew that the proposal was speculative at best. Even as she aired it, she and Marie were getting on with the rather more realistic business of brokering a deal with the Habsburgs. Apart from anything else, Margaret knew that Edward was never going to agree to a marriage that would make Clarence one of the most powerful princes in Europe.[7]

For more than a decade now, Clarence's marital arrangements had provoked violent disagreement between the two brothers – for Clarence, indeed, they had been a catalyst for open rebellion against Edward – and his hankering after the Burgundian match only strengthened the king's continued suspicions about his wayward brother. Apart from anything else, the Burgundian dukes themselves had a decent claim to the English crown through their Lancastrian heritage, a claim that Charles the Bold had reasserted in recent years. Perhaps, Edward believed, Clarence planned to use the duchy as a springboard for another attempt to depose him.[8]

Edward's response to Margaret's proposal was deliberately obstructive. As one chronicler close to the heart of government put it, the king 'threw all the obstacles he could in the way of any such marriage taking place'. Edward told Marie that she couldn't have Clarence. Instead, he offered the young duchess another English nobleman with close Burgundian connections: the queen's brother Anthony Woodville. Although he might have brought with him 'a good number of soldiers', Woodville was hardly a prestigious option to give the Burgundians pause for thought. The marital options laid before Marie were the heir to the house of Habsburg, the heir to the French throne, or, as Philippe de Commynes sneered, 'a minor English earl'. Whether Edward genuinely thought Woodville a serious candidate for Marie of Burgundy's hand in marriage, or whether – as was only too likely – he was having a laugh at Clarence's expense, his brother was guaranteed to be deeply insulted. As usual, Clarence made no effort to conceal his fury. He was, as a contemporary put it, 'vexed'.[9]

Late that February, William Hastings sailed into Calais harbour. With him were sixteen men at arms, among them Sir John Paston, and 514 archers: a substantial company, but hardly the expeditionary force on which Burgundians had pinned their hopes. Sent to bolster the Calais garrison, its mission was clearly defined: to protect the English enclave and its borders, which 'stand in great jeopardy and peril' as a result of the 'comings of our enemies'.[10] Sending warm letters to senior French military officials, Hastings settled down to watch and wait.

Louis, twitchy as ever, was convinced that there was more to Hastings' arrival than a concern for Calais' security. Over the following weeks, the rumours grew. Hastings had not brought five hundred men, but twelve hundred; moreover, he was scheming with Margaret to spirit away the Burgundian duchess to England, where she would marry Clarence. It didn't help that the French advance had got bogged down, belatedly running into resistance in the Artois borderlands. Hesdin, the great castle of the Burgundian dukes, had been taken with difficulty – it had been 'packed with huge numbers of soldiers', grumbled Louis – while in Arras, uprisings flared against the occupying forces. Louis wanted to keep the English onside. Dispatching an envoy to Hastings, he stressed his commitment to the marriage between Edward's daughter and the dauphin – a matter on which he had been stalling, palming off Edward's ambassadors Morton and Donne with little more than the promise of future talks. He then asked Hastings to pass on to Edward a request for English military support against Burgundy. Hastings politely demurred. He didn't want to risk communicating such sensitive matters to Edward by letter; equally, his commitments in Calais prevented him from returning to England to talk with the king in person. He suggested that Louis would be better off sending a formal embassy to England – and, he added, the French king might also want to send the latest instalment of Edward's pension, which was now overdue.[11] As these exchanges took place, reports reached Louis that Hastings' men had been spotted twenty miles west of Calais in the port-fortress of Boulogne, offering military aid to its Burgundian defenders. Such manoeuvres flew in the face of Edward's official policy of appeasement with France – but then, there was nothing like a little military activity to remind Louis to stick to his English commitments.[12]

In the following weeks, correspondence between Hastings and the French king crackled with wary politesse. As Louis probed for inconsistencies in the official English line, Hastings stuck doggedly to it. Professing himself 'shocked' at French accusations of bad faith, he stressed that he was working hard for the 'continuance of the truces' between England and France. Then, in early May, Louis wrote to him with another query. He had been told 'by some Scots' that Edward IV had been laid low with some sort of infirmity or illness. Was this the case?

Suspended in the French king's artless enquiry was another question. If Edward was ill, perhaps his grip on affairs had slackened; perhaps others with instinctively Burgundian sympathies – such as Hastings – had taken it upon themselves to act on their own initiative. For instance, in quietly ramping up military action against France.

Hastings presented the straightest of bats. There was nothing remotely wrong with Edward, he replied on 10 May: indeed, 'God be thanked, he has been and remains in excellent health and prosperity and makes as merry as ever'. In fact, 'that very day', Edward was in Windsor Castle, presiding over the annual feast of the Order of the Garter, a picture of regal conviviality.[13]

Louis, though, was adept at spotting a hint of flame through the smoke. As he feasted and drank at Windsor, Edward's health was indeed a cause of concern, to both the king himself and those around him. The lateness of the Garter celebration that year, coming as it did weeks after the Order's feast day of St George on 23 April, was no accident. Royal agents had recently uncovered a plot against the king – specifically, to weaken and enfeeble him. Two days after the rescheduled Garter feast, Edward announced a high-profile commission to indict and try the conspirators. The two events were clearly connected because the seventeen lords named on the panel included eleven of the twelve adult noblemen present at the Garter celebrations. The glaring exception, the nobleman omitted from the commission, was Clarence – which was hardly surprising because, as Edward's men followed the trail of conspiracy, it led straight to him.

It was, one court insider speculated, the debacle of the possible Burgundian marriage that had proved the tipping point. To add insult to injury, that spring Edward had waved away another marriage proposal for Clarence, this time from the Scottish king James III on behalf of his sister. Edward replied that Clarence was still in his year-long period of mourning, and therefore off limits. There was nothing to suggest the king had talked with his brother before declining the proposal – but by that point, the pair were barely talking at all.[14]

Edward's apparent resolution of the quarrel between Clarence and Richard, in the months before his invasion of France, in fact hadn't settled anything – at least as far as Clarence was concerned. In the intervening months, he had continued to simmer at what he considered the unjust partition of the earl of Warwick's lands in favour of Richard, as well as at the encroachment on both his lands and his networks of influence by those close to the king, aided and abetted by Edward himself. These resentments were compounded by the deaths of his wife and infant son, which, Clarence was starting to believe, were no accident. And now there was Edward's refusal to let him marry again. If, in recent years, the chief object of Clarence's fury had been Richard, his anger was tilting back to its original target: Edward.

As far as Clarence was concerned, Edward had sought to frustrate his ambitions once before, in the late 1460s; now, he was convinced, the king was trying to destroy him completely. Edward, meanwhile, had come to think much the same of his mercurial younger brother: 'each', as one insider put it, 'began to look upon the other with no very fraternal eyes'.

Through the first months of 1477, Clarence was notable by his absence from court. Indeed, he made a point of 'withdrawing more and more from the king's presence'. When constrained to attend official business, he was a mute, glowering presence in the council chamber. On a rare appearance in the king's household, he abruptly turned down Edward's hospitality: a public insult that, as one commentator put it, 'severely disturbed' the king's glory. The implication was that Clarence feared being poisoned by his brother.

This atmosphere of distrust, reported the same chronicler, was fuelled by a constant flow of rumour-mongers, 'carrying the words of both brothers backwards and forwards, even if they had been spoken in the most secret chamber'.[15] Even allowing for embellishment – and there was little that made writers salivate more than descriptions of court intrigue – the observation had the ring of truth. Clarence had never been one to curb his tongue, and his example had rubbed off on his servants; back in the late 1460s Warwick had been concerned enough about his household's leakiness to take it in hand, without discernible results. As well as ostentatiously refusing the king's food and drink, Clarence was said to have been spreading stories that the king 'wrought by necromancy and used craft to poison his subjects'. For his part, Edward seemed increasingly fearful that Clarence was trying to do the same thing to him.[16] That spring, those anxieties came to a head.

In early May, Edward's agents arrested an eminent Oxford astrologer named John Stacy. The accusations against him were specific. Stacy had been approached by the adulterous wife of Richard, Lord Beauchamp to murder him by necromancy. Beauchamp, an officer of Clarence's, was from a circle of squabbling midlands noblemen and gentry who in recent years the duke had struggled to control. It was precisely the kind of situation that made Edward's ears prick up.

Stacy was tortured, during which ordeal he revealed a rather more significant plot: an attempt to murder the king himself, and his young son and heir, by witchcraft. He also named an accomplice, a gentleman named Thomas Burdet from the Warwickshire village of Arrow. Burdet was one of Clarence's men.[17]

The plot, so it was alleged, had been hatched some two and a half years previously, on 12 November 1474. At a secret meeting in Westminster, Burdet had asked Stacy and his Oxford associate Thomas Blake to 'calculate the nativities' of Edward and his eldest son, in order 'to know when the King and Prince should die'. Prognostication was common practice – after all, everybody at some point wanted to know what the future held, or what the outcomes of their actions might be, from harvests to business transactions – but the divination of future events often shaded imperceptibly into trying to control or shape them. This was why predicting the future lives of monarchs was strictly off limits: it was categorically forbidden without their explicit permission, and potentially treasonous. For all that, kings and princes were as anxious as anybody to predict events.[18] At times, Edward sanctioned his own coterie of physician-astrologers to dabble in prognostication. Back in 1474, that select group included the newly recruited, handsomely salaried figure of John Stacy himself.[19]

When Stacy accepted Burdet's request, performing two astrological consultations, he did so as a prominent member of Edward's own household. The divinations yielded some disturbing portents. On 26 May 1475, shortly after the second of these sessions and as Edward's army was embarking for France, Stacy and Burdet divulged to various of the 'king's people' what their calculations showed: Edward and his son and heir would 'in a short time die'.[20]

Whatever the impact of Stacy's findings, there was no immediate reaction from royal circles. Stacy travelled to France with the royal retinue and remained a valued member of Edward's household. But in spring 1477, almost two years after the event, the episode came back to haunt him.

Following Stacy's interrogation, Burdet was detained in the west London suburb of Holborn, where he had been caught circulating 'seditious and treasonable bills and writings, rhymes and ballads', urging people to turn against Edward and his son, 'and rise and make war' against them. On 17 May, the two men, together with their associate Thomas Blake, were brought in front of Edward's newly appointed commission at Westminster, a roll-call of the Yorkist establishment that included, among others, the queen's brother Anthony Woodville and his nephew Dorset.

Burdet, Stacy and Blake were charged with the treasonous offences of 'imagining and compassing' the deaths of Edward and his first-born son and trying to bring about their deaths by 'art, magic, necromancy and astronomy'. The indictment stated that in circulating the findings of his May 1475 consultation, Stacy had been trying to sap the people's confidence in Edward's regime by implying that the king would shortly die. Such a prophecy was designed to be self-fulfilling: this withdrawal of public love from the king would in turn sap his energies and his life would be correspondingly 'shortened'.[21]

From early in Edward's reign, those about him had been concerned about the deleterious effects of his promiscuous, self-indulgent life-style, not only on his physique but on his behaviour and, by implication, on his ability to rule. In recent months, those concerns had increased. By the spring of 1477, there was a heightened anxiety around the state of Edward's mood and health: an anxiety that Louis XI had picked up on, and that Hastings had brushed aside. Whether or not Edward was physically ill – the ague or malarial infection that he was said to have picked up in France had, perhaps, become chronic – or whether he was simply in a pensive frame of mind was unclear. Maybe it was both. Whatever the case, these concerns – as they tended to do – congealed around the idea that somebody was trying to harm the king through sorcery. In their frantic hunt for the source of this threat, royal authorities had alighted on Stacy.

Stacy, one insider said, was unmasked for what he was: 'a great sorcerer'. When, back in 1475, he had gone public with his worrying astrological findings about Edward and his son, Stacy had done so – as the indictment put it – in order that the king 'would be saddened thereby'. The word 'sad' carried with it a host of resonances: weariness, fatigue, lethargy and melancholy.[22] All of which rather suggested that the king was currently exhibiting these symptoms, and that Stacy's two-year-old prognostication was now deemed the root cause. At the time, Stacy's announcement, while known to 'the king's people', had passed entirely without comment. Now, somebody had recalled his prognostication and, realizing the astrologer's links with elements perceived to be hostile to the crown – Thomas Burdet and his boss, Clarence – had put two and two together. In arresting and torturing Stacy, royal agents were armed with prior knowledge about Stacy's consultation and his associations. They had been tipped off.

The indictment named only one of the people to whom, back in 1475, Stacy had revealed his findings: one Alexander Rushton, described as a 'servant of the king'. Yet until recently Rushton was both a servant of the duke of Clarence and an associate of Stacy's conspirator Burdet. It seems possible that Rushton kept Stacy's information to himself for two years – until such time as it became very useful indeed. Probably one of the rumour-mongers that moved between Clarence's household and the king's, Rushton mentioned Stacy and Burdet to one of the king's close advisers. If Clarence could believe that Edward was capable of poisoning him, it was hardly surprising if Edward – seeking explanations for his inexplicable 'sadness' – felt that his brother's guiding hand was behind this plot against the crown.[23]

The subsequent trial was short. Burdet and Stacy were convicted of treason. Dragged through the streets to the gallows at Tyburn, the pair were put through the full horror of a traitor's execution: hanged, then cut down and disembowelled, their entrails thrown onto a fire before, finally, being beheaded and quartered, their body parts 'to be disposed of at the king's pleasure'. Right to the end, at the foot of the gallows, the pair continued to insist on their innocence. Stacy's plea was 'faint', whether from the effects of his torture or the prospect of the ghastly execution he was about to endure.

For those with long memories, the episode recalled another case of necromancy. Back in 1441 two astrologers, Roger Bolingbroke and Thomas Southwell, had been arrested for trying to bring about the death of Henry VI. The pair had, it was alleged, been commissioned to read the king's horoscope by Eleanor Cobham, the wife of Henry VI's independent-minded uncle Humphrey duke of Gloucester, who was keen to see her husband on the throne in the event of the then-childless king's death. The astrologers were accused of revealing to many people that Henry VI would die of melancholia, an act that was intended to provoke the people into withdrawing their love from the king, whose consequent sorrow at this erosion of his subjects' loyalties would bring about his death. The charges were uncannily similar to those now levelled against Stacy and Burdet – so similar, in fact, that they might have been used as a template. Bolingbroke's declaration of his innocence – he had, he explained, simply 'presumed too far in his cunning' – could have been Stacy's also.[24]

For Edward, the executions eliminated a threat to himself and his family. They were also a warning shot to his brother with whom – however obliquely – Stacy and Burdet had been connected. Clarence saw the killings as something else: the latest in a series of royal assaults on his diminishing power, enabled by one of his former servants, Alexander Rushton, who – in what was becoming an all-too-familiar pattern – had become one of the 'king's people'. What was more, on the day Stacy and Burdet were executed, Edward announced the judicial review of a trial that Clarence had recently overseen. In doing so, he confirmed Clarence's deepest fears.[25]

Some six weeks earlier, in the early afternoon of 12 April, eighty armed men wearing Clarence's colours and led by his servant Richard Hyde rode into the manor of Keyford, near the Somerset market-town of Frome. Keyford was home to an elderly widow of some standing, Ankarette Twynyho. Sheep farmers and wool merchants, the Twynyhos were an influential local family; they were also part of Clarence's network. A number of Twynyhos had been in his service, including both Ankarette's sons and Ankarette herself, who had worked for his late wife Isabel. It was Ankarette who Clarence's men were now hunting.[26]

Breaking into her house with 'great fury and frenzy', the men seized Ankarette and rode off with her, heading into the midlands. Two days later, at sunset on Easter Monday, they arrived at Clarence's base of Warwick, some ninety miles northeast. Telling Ankarette's worried daughter and son-in-law, who together with a few servants had followed her abductors, to make themselves scarce 'on pain of death', they stripped the widow of all her jewels and money and locked her up.

At six the following morning the bewildered woman was brought in front of two Warwickshire justices and charged with having murdered Clarence's wife Isabel by giving the duchess 'a venomous drink of ale mixed with poison'. Two others were indicted alongside Ankarette: John Thuresby and Sir Roger Tocotes, both servants of Clarence's. Thuresby was accused of poisoning the duke's infant son; Tocotes with abetting both crimes. In the ensuing trial a hastily assembled local jury, intimidated by Clarence's baleful presence, found all three guilty. Convicted by this kangaroo court, Ankarette and John Thuresby – Tocotes, fortunately for him, had managed to evade arrest – were taken to a gallows on the city's eastern outskirts and hanged. It was still only nine in the morning. The whole process had taken three hours.[27]

People were wearily used to noblemen taking the law into their own hands. Even so, these judicial murders were shocking – particularly that of the defenceless Ankarette, who had been kidnapped and hauled across three counties to be subjected to a verdict that was, as several of the jury later confessed, blatantly 'untrue'. Running through the episode, though, was the hint of a ghastly, paranoid rationale on Clarence's part; one that had everything to do with an overwhelming sensation that his authority was fracturing and splintering, and that the walls were closing in on him.

The Twynyho family had been solidly loyal to Clarence: both Ankarette's sons had been involved in his rebellion against Edward back in 1470. But in recent times, as Clarence's sphere of influence was gradually encroached upon, the Twynyhos had like many others adapted to the resulting shifts in power. Where some had turned to Hastings and some to the king himself, Ankarette's kinsman John Twynyho, a noted Wiltshire lawyer, found advancement with the queen's family. Working for her son Thomas Grey, marquis of Dorset, he landed the plum post of attorney general to Edward's young heir, appointments to whose household were rubber-stamped by the prince's governor, Anthony Woodville. Perhaps Ankarette Twynyho, newly unemployed following the death of Clarence's wife, had drifted into Woodville circles, like her co-defendant Sir Roger Tocotes, another long-standing servant of Clarence's, who had taken up lucrative offices on the queen's Wiltshire estates. If the likes of John Twynyho clearly felt that it was acceptable to serve more than one master – a common-enough practice, especially for lawyers – Clarence didn't.

For the duke, who for years had watched his estates being eaten away at by his rivals around the king, his servants' loyalties trickling like sand through his fingers, there was an exemplary savagery in his pursuit of Twynyho, Thursby and Tocotes. In his deranged state, still mourning his lost wife and child, Clarence probably believed they had committed the crimes of which they were found guilty – though he had rigged the justices and jury just to make sure. But even if they hadn't, he perhaps felt, their disloyalty meant they had it coming.[28]

Edward thought otherwise. News of the Twynyho trial took a while to reach him, but on 20 May the case was transferred to Westminster for judicial review by the judges of King's Bench. Coming as it did on the day that John Stacy and Clarence's servant Thomas Burdet were hanged and eviscerated at Tyburn, the timing seemed more than coincidental.[29] The events of that May day seemed to unlock something in Clarence. His sense of discretion, perspective and self-control, always rickety, collapsed.

The following day, the king's council was in session at Westminster. Edward himself was absent, away at Windsor. Clarence barged into the council chamber, a grey-habited Franciscan friar trailing behind him. In front of the stunned councillors the friar, at Clarence's prompting, proceeded to read out the declarations of innocence that Burdet and Stacy had made before their executions, thereby effectively accusing Edward of a miscarriage of justice. To add fuel to the fire, the friar Clarence had chosen to challenge the king's supreme legal authority was William Goddard, a preacher notorious for his political sermons. Back in September 1470, when Clarence and Warwick had reclaimed the throne on behalf of Henry VI and Lancaster, Goddard had stood at Paul's Cross outside the cathedral, publicly elucidating Henry VI's rightful claim to the crown.

Seen one way, Clarence's act might have been a desperate, ham-fisted attempt to protest his own innocence, to ward off any accusations of guilt by association with Burdet and Stacy. But in light of the Twynyho trial, and his hyper-aggressive reaction to the leaching away of his power and authority, the duke's behaviour suggested the opposite: that he was actively identifying himself with the executed men. Moreover, in defending convicted traitors and identifying himself with their cause, Clarence had employed a man who had once denied Edward's very right to the crown.[30] His compulsive charge into confrontation with his brother's authority seemed driven by a desire to force matters to a head.

As news of Clarence's transgression reverberated around London, Edward met it with silence. For three weeks he stayed at Windsor, hunting, letting the implications of his brother's deranged behaviour roll slowly around in his mind. Then, he sent Clarence a summons to appear before him at Westminster.

Late in June, the two brothers came face to face, Clarence mute in the face of the king's precise, controlled fury. Edward told his brother that by intervening in the due process of law he had 'used a king's power', a crime known as 'accroachment'; what was more, he had committed embracery, trying to rig justice. His behaviour was 'a great threat to the judges and jurors of the kingdom'. Clarence was arrested and taken from Westminster across London to the Tower, where he was locked up.

After ten years of his brother's provocative insubordination, Edward's patience had finally snapped. The king's actions were saturated with anxiety about his own popularity. Clarence's undermining of the judicial system, bringing the king's justice into disrepute, was precisely the kind of behaviour guaranteed to impact on the people's love for their king. Around the time of Clarence's arrest, moreover, there were rumours that the Lancastrian earl of Oxford had escaped from his Calais prison and, resurfacing on the Cambridgeshire–Huntingdonshire border, was trying to raise an insurgency. The man – an impostor – was quickly detained, but for Edward it was a reminder of Oxford's plots of a few years before, through which Clarence's presence had seemed to flicker. That summer, as Clarence sat in the Tower, talk of another conspiracy coalesced around him.[31]

A week or so before the brothers' confrontation, Hastings arrived back in London for a whistle-stop visit after four months in Calais.[32] Hastings' return was intentionally timed: with a French embassy shortly due in London for wide-ranging talks, he could update Edward on the delicate international situation. The trip also gave Hastings, who firmly expected the visiting French to brief against him to his own king, the chance to get his own account of things in first. His instincts were good.

That July, the French ambassadors lodged an official complaint with Edward about his chamberlain's clandestine military operations against France; actions which Hastings had vociferously denied. Elegantly avoiding any direct accusation of Edward, the envoys claimed that Hastings was working secretly and independently, in league with Margaret of Burgundy and in opposition to the official English policy of neutrality. The French complaints had another purpose – obfuscation. In the ensuing talks, so much time and energy were spent dealing with their grievances that they returned to France having made no headway on the matters on which Edward wanted progress: the financial sureties for his pension and his daughter Elizabeth's marriage to the dauphin. Which was just how Louis wanted it.

The French king's frustrations were genuine enough. While his ambassadors were in England, the Habsburg heir Maximilian's wedding to Marie of Burgundy presaged a drastic shift in the geopolitical atmosphere. Although most in the Low Countries were sceptical of the whimsical young archduke's ability to resist the French – dawdling to Flanders, he had turned up with only four hundred horsemen and a modest war-chest – he was, at least in theory, backed by the might and resources of the Holy Roman Empire. Sensing his window of opportunity in Flanders closing, Louis ramped up military operations. French troops devastated the region south of Calais, burning towns and abbeys and destroying harvests. Rumour had it that Louis, thwarted by obdurate resistance from the strategically important town of St Omer, planned to bypass it to the north by marching his army through the wetlands of the Calais Pale. Just to be on the safe side, Hastings opened the enclave's complex system of sluice gates, flooding the marshy ground and rendering its causeways 'broken' and impassable. When one of Hastings' messengers turned up at the French camp, a frantic Louis raged at him, imprecating against his master. Amid widespread fears that the French were about to besiege the Pale – if he did, blanched one Calais inhabitant, 'Flanders will be lost' – Hastings tried to de-escalate the situation.[33]

Writing to Louis, the chamberlain again denied accusations that he had committed 'acts of war' against France. In fact, he had ignored all Margaret of Burgundy's pleas for help (this was a blatant untruth, given that he had sent her military aid on at least one occasion). Edward had, Hastings continued, invested 'special confidence' in him to maintain the relationship between England and France, and he would not displease Edward 'for all the goods in the world'. Hastings had been nurtured by Edward's father and by Edward himself. He had shared all the king's adversities, experiences which had led to the closest understanding between him and his master: there was no way he would do anything to cause Edward 'dishonour or displeasure', a point on which he was insistently sincere. If Louis was trying to drive a wedge between Hastings and Edward, went the subtext of Hastings' letter, he was wasting his time.

By this point, as Hastings knew, another high-ranking French embassy was on its way to England, armed with detailed instructions from Louis. Once again, the ambassador had a delicate balancing act to perform: to give every impression of progressing the negotiations without actually doing so and, in the process, to make Edward feel that Louis was his best friend in the world. As usual, Louis' technique was distraction. The ambassador was to brief against Hastings again, but this time with a subtle difference. Instead of telling Edward that Hastings was ignoring his orders, the ambassadors should inform the English king that Hastings was involved in a conspiracy against him – and that his co-conspirators were Edward's sister Margaret and his brother Clarence. As well as telling his representative what to say, Louis told him how to say it.

Arriving at Edward's court late in the summer of 1477, Louis' *chef de mission* apologized profusely for the delay in the talks. He said that his master would have given his previous embassy sweeping powers, had he not been deeply concerned about the warnings 'from all sides' that 'monsieur le chambellan' – Hastings – and Edward's sister Margaret had been in secret talks regarding a separate English deal with Burgundy. Here, the ambassador reminded Edward that the English had no business meddling in what was, essentially, an internal French affair involving 'rebellious subjects' of the French crown – the worst of whom was the 'widow of duke Charles', Margaret herself. And it wasn't just Louis against whom Margaret had been manoeuvring.

Many reports of private conversations at the Burgundian court, the ambassador continued, had reached Louis' ears. Edward clearly didn't know the truth of what was going on. If only he could have heard what his sister Margaret was secretly saying about her ambitions for a marriage between Clarence and the Burgundian heiress Marie, and about what Clarence planned to do in England should he become duke of Burgundy – try to seize Edward's crown, was the implication – Edward would realize that such a marriage would have done much more harm to him than to France. Louis wanted Edward to know all this purely out of the goodness of his heart. In any case, Edward should keep his eyes open.[34]

This was all typical Louis – a cluster of half-truths that, seeded in the recipient's mind, would blossom slowly into doubts and anxieties. But there was little in it to disconcert Edward and his advisers. They were experienced in the slippery game of international diplomacy, a game that they had played just as well as Louis in the past months. Edward, of course, had not gone anywhere near his sister's scheme to marry Clarence to the young duchess – a ship that had, in any case, sailed with Marie of Burgundy's marriage to Maximilian. Neither did he have any doubts about Hastings' loyalty. Meanwhile, Louis' latest efforts to draw Edward into a war against Burgundy were undermined by the breaking news that the French king, frustrated by Calais' flooded waterways, had disbanded his increasingly mutinous army, agreed a truce with Maximilian and gone home for the winter.[35]

Louis XI's innuendo about Clarence was similarly groundless. He had no evidence whatsoever for his claim that the duke, plotting with his sister, was planning to usurp the throne of England.

Yet here, the French king's insinuations fell on fertile ground. They fed the story that Edward had constructed for himself about Clarence's behaviour: a story of persistent disloyalty that had prompted Edward's close scrutiny of and active intervention in his brother's affairs, culminating in his imprisonment. It wasn't so much that Edward was taken in by Louis; rather, the French king simply confirmed what Edward already thought about his brother. There was no reason, in other words, for Edward not to believe him.

In mid-September, shortly after the French embassy had left, a Medici agent in the city of Arras wrote back to Florence with news from England. Edward, people were saying, had had his brother Clarence killed – 'but', the agent added, the news was 'not confirmed'.[36] He was wrong: Clarence was still in the Tower. That such rumours could even be given credence, however, was ominous.

At the start of November England's noblemen gathered in London, summoned by Edward to a great council. With it came the usual round of feasting, which involved a marked focus on the dynasty's future – Edward and Elizabeth's two boys. On the 9th Prince Edward, just turned seven years old, presided over a banquet given in his name. After dinner, the replete nobles lined up to pay allegiance to the younger prince, who stood by the ceremonial bed that festooned the king's presence chamber. First in line was his uncle Richard, who knelt and, after his nephew's little hands had clasped his own, did him homage and kissed him. The four-year-old boy thanked him – clearly enough for those in attendance to hear – for having performed the act 'so humbly'.[37] Over the next fortnight, the council pored over lavish plans for the upcoming wedding of this second son of Edward's to the three-year-old Anne Mowbray, only child of John, duke of Norfolk, who had died suddenly in his bed two years before.

The marriage was a typically predatory move on the regime's part. The wealthy Mowbray patrimony had been due to be divided between various co-heirs, including the late duke's widow and his cousin John Howard, one of Edward's staunchest supporters. In a stroke, Edward sliced through the complex inheritance. Making his second son duke of Norfolk, he bought off Mowbray's widow and settled the entire inheritance on the late duke's daughter Anne. In the event that Anne died without heirs, everything would go to her husband the prince. In his mid-fifties, John Howard was frozen out. It was the latest in a string of unethical legal sleights of hand that had seen great noble inheritances such as those of Warwick and Oxford carved up and settled on members of the royal family – and against which, in Howard's case, even years of long and loyal service to the family was no immunity. Given that Howard had helped Richard defraud the countess of Oxford some years before, he can hardly have been surprised. If he minded, he didn't say so – in public, anyway.[38]

For Edward, his family had always come first, with closeness of blood the index of entitlement: the 'higher' you were in the king's blood, the more you deserved to be 'honoured and enhanced of right and power'. His younger son was the latest beneficiary of this aggrandizing logic. The little prince's wedding to Anne Mowbray would be held the following January; the festivities would run alongside a parliament that would enshrine in law this latest act of Yorkist appropriation. The main business of the upcoming parliament, though, was to deal with the one member of the family whose face no longer fitted, whose very presence had become incompatible: Clarence.

That November, Edward and his councillors assessed the case to be brought against his brother. Towards the end of the month, there came hints that the king had already made up his mind: not just about the charges, but the trial's outcome.

As riders made their way through the kingdom with wedding invitations and writs for the forthcoming parliament, Sir Thomas Vaughan arrived up in Coventry. Representing both the king and his eldest son, within whose jurisdiction the city – formerly Clarence's stamping ground – now fell, Vaughan carried an uncompromising

message to the civic authorities. Anybody suspected of using seditious language was to be rounded up, 'openly punished' as an example
to others, and imprisoned. The authorities were to tell citizens that
anybody holding money, jewels or 'pledges' – sureties for debts
owed – from Clarence was to declare them immediately, 'without
concealment'.

The financial reckoning indicated that Clarence's property was
about to become forfeit to the crown; the tightened security suggested
a pre-emptive move by the king against any possible disturbances in
support of his brother. Which in turn suggested that, in Edward's
mind, Clarence was already guilty.[39]

On 15 January 1478, guests gathered at Westminster Palace for the
royal wedding. With Anthony Woodville holding her left hand, and
on her right Edward's teenage nephew John de la Pole, earl of Lincoln, the three-year-old bride was led gently into the richly decorated
interior of St Stephen's Chapel. Ensconced under a canopy were the
royal family: Edward, Elizabeth and their children, and the dynasty's
matriarch Cecily duchess of York. After the requisite papal dispensation was flourished for this wedding between two relatives of such
'nearness of blood', Anne was taken to the high altar where her little
prince awaited her. The marriage over, Richard stood at the chapel
doors, delving into gold basins filled with coins, flinging showers of
gold and silver over the waiting crowds outside. Then, he and the
duke of Buckingham accompanied the new bride out of the chapel to
the wedding feast. So many were the 'famous' names and so great the
crush of people, noted one herald, that he had been unable to write
them all down.[40]

The following day Parliament was opened and quickly adjourned
in order that the gathered Lords and Commons could enjoy the festivities: a jousts royal, which would take place in Westminster Yard,
transformed for the occasion into a temporary stadium. The revels
absorbed most people's attention – as, perhaps, Edward had intended.
From Norfolk, Sir John Paston's younger brother wrote eagerly for
news 'of the marriage of my lord of York and', he added vaguely,
'other parliament matter'.[41]

Over the following week, the tournament unfolded in front of

Edward, Elizabeth and their sons, the assembled nobility, French and Imperial ambassadors and 'other strangers', twenty-four new knights created by Edward for the occasion, and hordes of retainers, servants and hangers-on. There was a marked emphasis on youth in the two teams of jousters: among them was Richard's servant Sir James Tyrell and Edward's master of horse, a giant Kentishman called John Cheyne, who had been brought up in the queen's household and who, at six feet eight inches, looked down even on the king himself. Most evident of all was the participation of four members of the queen's family, all of whom were officers in Prince Edward's household: the Grey brothers Thomas and Richard, her cousin Sir Richard Haute and, most spectacular of all, Anthony Woodville.

As the joust opened, knights rode into Westminster Yard in a riot of colour, their flamboyant entrances heralded by a rasping of trumpets and an explosion of noise from the crowds crammed into the stands built for the occasion. Woodville stole the show. At thirty-seven, he had lost none of his glamour: his entrance, drawing on the latest continental fashions, was pure sporting drama. A team of horses drew a wheeled tableau or 'pageant' depicting the ascetic Franciscan preacher St Anthony, played by Woodville himself. In front of a stylized hermitage of black velvet and glass, he sat motionless on an armoured horse, swathed in a hermit's white robe and hood. When the tableau halted in the arena, Woodville's servants ripped off his white habit to reveal a dazzling coat of arms: tawny satin, woven with golden trees and flames.

For all Woodville's glory, another moment best summed up the pre-eminence of the queen's family. Dressed in his colours of white and mulberry, the marquis of Dorset rode into the arena in 'great triumph' surrounded by a pack of 'great estates, knights and esquires'. Foremost among them, carrying Dorset's helmet, was his brother-in-law the duke of Buckingham. At twenty-two, the pair were exact contemporaries. But where Dorset had been loaded with royal favour and office, Buckingham, who had spent a lifetime at court waiting for something to turn up, had not. Since falling out with Buckingham some years before, Edward's indifference towards him had become more pronounced: characteristically and scrupulously acknowledging his high rank, the king refused to give the duke any political responsibility whatsoever. The jousts royal was precisely the kind of occasion that rammed home to the aristocratic Buckingham the gulf in power that existed between himself and Dorset, a commoner who had been 'made lord'. Ten years previously, the twelve-year-old duke had borne Anthony Woodville's helmet and weapons into the lists at Smithfield for his fight against the Bastard of Burgundy. Now, as he rode into Westminster Yard bearing arms for another of his Woodville in-laws, Buckingham perhaps reflected quietly to himself that, in the intervening decade, nothing had changed.

After a day's fighting, documented by a gaggle of heralds and chroniclers – the 'furious' swordplay of 'this famous earl' Anthony Woodville was breathlessly noted – the wedding celebrations dissolved into an evening of music, dancing, drinking and prizegiving. The trophies, including a great 'E' of gold inset with a ruby, were awarded smilingly by Edward's oldest daughter, the blonde, blue-eyed Princess Elizabeth, who was just turning twelve.[42] As a glittering display of family unity, it was complete.

The festive mood evaporated as the Lords and Commons filed into the Parliament chamber, MPs like James Tyrell and John Cheyne exchanging their armour for more sober attire. The opening sermon was preached by Edward's chancellor Thomas Rotherham, who held forth on everything that Edward had done for his subjects. Invoking Psalm 23, 'The Lord rules me and I shall lack nothing', he stressed that those obedient to the king would be well looked after. Those, conversely, who did not submit to his authority should 'be afraid'. Here, Rotherham veered off into St Paul's letter to the Romans. The king did not carry a sword without cause. Indeed, as God's representative, he was a 'revenger', come to 'execute wrath upon him that doeth evil'. It didn't take an expert in exegesis to understand what Rotherham was talking about.[43] Parliament knew what was coming.

If the Lords had already been brought onside during the previous autumn's great council, the Commons had been equally well arranged. Edward and those close to him had gone to considerable lengths to pack the lower house with compliant MPs. Among those who interfered in borough elections – bringing in their own candidates, rigging ballots and tampering with returns, erasing names and writing others in their place – were Richard, who had at least five associates among the assembled MPs, and Hastings, with seven. Of the 296 members of the Commons who took their places in the chamber that January, some 20 per cent were royal servants, of whom 43 were members of the king's household. At their head, the new speaker William Allington – who had previously delivered on Edward's tax demands for his French invasion and who, that summer, had quashed the insurgency led by the impostor earl of Oxford – was an exceptionally safe pair of hands, close to both Edward and Queen Elizabeth.[44] The stage had been set.

Brought from the Tower, where he had spent the last six months, Clarence was led into the Parliament chamber and led in front of Edward who sat enthroned, massive in his parliament robes. As he stood there, alone, the king charged his brother with treason.

The role Edward now took was unprecedented in a parliamentary trial. Over the years, his regime had resorted to treason laws reflexively in the face of opposition, the king's ability to discern treason a quick, clean solution to chronic political problems. What followed was this instinct pushed to its logical conclusion: an act of calculated legal destruction that one appalled observer, an anonymous civil servant, found so traumatic that when he tried to describe it his mind refused, 'ran away'.[45]

Incorporating the full dossier of charges that he had compiled against Clarence over the years, Edward's indictment was saturated with the emotive language of fraternal betrayal. He had always wanted the best for a brother who, from his 'tender youth' until now, he had always 'loved and cherished'. In living memory, no king of England had ever heaped such great wealth and power on one of his brothers – so much so that in his 'livelihood and richesse', Clarence had been second only to the king himself. In return, Edward continued, he had asked only for his brother's love, help, and his obedience 'to all the king's good pleasures and commandments'. Time and again Clarence had failed him; time and again Edward had forgiven him, even wiping the slate clean following his rebellion in 1470.[46] His love hadn't worked.

In recent years, Clarence had perpetrated new treasons, 'more heinous and loathly than ever before', plotting the 'extreme destruction and disinheriting of the king and all his issue'. This accusation – that

Clarence was plotting to destroy Edward, Elizabeth and their heirs and to place himself on the throne of England – echoed through the indictment. In language redolent of Stacy's and Burdet's indictments the previous year, Clarence stood accused of persistent efforts to incite rebellion: from his spreading of vicious rumours about the king's malign treatment of his subjects in order to provoke the people 'to withdraw their hearts, loves and affections from the king'; to his accusations that the king planned to take away his livelihood and destroy him; to his illegal retaining of men, whose contracts purpose-fully omitted the customary overriding oaths to the king and his heirs. There was more. Clarence had in his possession a copy of the agreement between himself and Margaret of Anjou – made back in 1470, as the duke and Warwick thrashed out their accord with the house of Lancaster – which, stamped with Henry VI's great seal, guaranteed Clarence the crown should the main Lancastrian line fail. He had also breathed life into the allegation that he and Warwick had first spread in the late 1460s, following the bloodletting at Edgecote: that Edward himself was illegitimate, a 'bastard', and that he and his heirs were consequently 'not begotten to reign'.

The last straw, for Edward, was news that had just come to his know-ledge of a conspiracy against Edward, Elizabeth and their family that was 'more malicious, more unnatural and loathly' than any treason yet perpetrated. In preparation for a fresh insurgency, Clarence had mustered large numbers of troops, ready to 'raise war' against the king at an hour's notice, and planned to send his little son out of England and out of danger should his uprising fail. But the erosion of Clarence's networks was complete: the people he had enlisted to smuggle the boy abroad had betrayed him. Roger Harewell, a mem-ber of Clarence's household; John Tapton, formerly Clarence's own chancellor; and another man with close links to Clarence, the abbot of Tewkesbury John Strensham – all had been in Clarence's closest trust. They had gone straight to the king with news of the plot.[47] Clarence's manoeuvrings, Edward concluded, could only be con-strued as the 'most extreme purposed malice'.

Edward had tried the path of mercy, and it had proved fruitless. For the sake of the royal family, for the greater good of England, just-ice had to be served. In a phrase that resonated with Rotherham's sermon and with the political trials of recent decades, justice was not only concerned with rewarding the good, but was also about the 'punishment of evil doers'.

For all the sorrowful rage of Edward's indictment, there was something coldly detached about the progress of the trial, every aspect of which had been contrived to steer it towards its inevitable outcome. Various people – probably including those members of Clarence's household who had already denounced him – were produced to give evidence on the crown's behalf, though their role in proceedings was ill defined. The onlooking chronicler couldn't tell whether they were witnesses or accusers – or, as he put it acidly, both 'at the same time'. Clarence, allowed to defend himself, met each charge with the same automatic reply of 'not guilty'. With nobody prepared to speak out on his behalf, he called no witnesses. At one point, in desperation, he offered to settle the trial by single combat with his brother the king, an offer that was unsurprisingly rebuffed. It was hard to avoid the impression that, as Clarence put it, Edward was destroying him as inexorably 'as a candle consumeth in burning'.[48]

On 7 February, after going through the motions of considering its verdict, Parliament pronounced Clarence guilty of treason. Sentence was handed down by Buckingham, whom Edward had temporarily appointed to the role of high steward, the great officer of state who customarily delivered such convictions. Even Buckingham, it turned out, occasionally had his uses. The duke duly condemned Clarence to death. Now, all Edward had to do was give the nod.

Clarence was taken back to the Tower and time passed. Perhaps, his brother's life in his hands, Edward pondered the enormity of his next, irrevocable command. A week or so later, with Parliament still in session, Speaker Allington and a group of MPs walked over to the house of Lords and, with all decorum, requested that they ask the king to get on with it.

Insisting that the king order his own brother's liquidation was hardly something that Allington would have done on his own initiative. The source of the nudge could be guessed at. A key member of the Yorkist establishment, Allington's effusions about Queen Elizabeth and the little prince of Wales were a matter of parliamentary record; the queen had rewarded him handsomely, appointing him one of the prince's councillors and making him chancellor of the boy's administration.[49]

The Woodvilles' fear and loathing of Clarence had never gone away. No amount of reconciliation could make up for the killing of Earl Rivers and Elizabeth's brother John after Edgecote almost a decade previously, and Clarence's smearing of the queen's mother as a witch and Elizabeth's marriage to Edward as illegitimate, together with their offspring. In the years that followed, the innuendo around Clarence's ambitions had fed their hate and encouraged their backing of Richard against him. If Edward was anxious that Clarence was out to destroy him and his children, Elizabeth – who had already experienced the raw violence of which Clarence was capable – was infinitely more so. But if, as one later commentator put it, it was Elizabeth who persuaded Edward that unless Clarence were dead, their children would never come to the throne, the queen was hardly alone.

On 18 February, deep in the Tower and away from public view, Clarence was executed. The manner of his killing was obscure: even those close to events were unsure of its nature. Soon, word leaked out that rather than being beheaded, Clarence – in a nod, perhaps, to his excessive drinking habits – had been drowned in a butt of *malvasia*, sweet Greek white wine.[50] Even at the last, Edward had been unable to resist indulging one of his typical poor jokes. It was a gag of exquisite tastelessness.

Within hours of his brother's murder, Edward was trying to mitigate the enormity of what he had done. Pronouncing that he intended to do 'right worshipfully' for Clarence's soul, he gave orders for his brother's body to be escorted honourably to Tewkesbury Abbey, where he would be buried alongside his wife, Isabel. Edward further smoothed Clarence's passage into the afterlife by paying off his outstanding debts.[51]

If all this constituted simply a formal tying-up of loose ends, later chroniclers didn't think so. According to Thomas More, who got his account of proceedings from Edward's close adviser John Morton, Edward 'commanded' his brother's execution then, as soon as he was told it had been done, he 'piteously bewailed and sorrowfully repented'.

More's contemporary, the Italian historian Polydore Vergil – who based his narrative on first-hand interviews with those who had been around at the time – added a telling detail. From that time onwards, whenever Edward was confronted with somebody petitioning him on behalf of a condemned man, Clarence would come into his mind and he would 'cry out in a rage: "Oh unfortunate brother, for whose life no man in this world would once make request".' In order to avoid the shattering guilt of his brother's murder, Edward constructed for himself a new, more comforting, reality: that it had been everybody's fault but his own. Edward, Vergil said, had convinced himself that his brother had been 'cast away by envy of the nobility', who had failed to intercede with the king on Clarence's behalf. Vergil saw straight through this elaborate act of self-exculpation: 'it is very likely', he concluded simply, 'that king Edward right soon repented that deed'.[52]

Given the lengths to which Edward had gone to stitch up both council and Parliament, the lack of support for Clarence was hardly surprising. There was one hint of an objection, by the king's former chancellor Robert Stillington – locked in the Tower shortly after Clarence's killing, he was pardoned months later for having made unspecified 'utterances' prejudicial to the king – but that was it. Even before his death, those who might have had the power to influence the king's mind were hungrily eyeing Clarence's vast agglomeration of lands and offices that, now forfeit to the crown, were available for redistribution. First in the queue was Richard.[53]

Later, Richard was said to have been overcome with sorrow at his brother's death. It seemed unlikely. The pair had after all been at odds since childhood, their youthful squabbles eventually metastasizing into a malignant vendetta over the Warwick inheritance. In any case, outward displays of grief were hardly incompatible with business. On 15 February, as Clarence awaited execution, Edward conferred the condemned duke's title of earl of Salisbury on Richard's small son and heir, in what was clearly a prearranged deal. Days later Richard was handed the great chamberlainship of England, one of those grants that he had been forced to hand over to Clarence. With typical singlemindedness Richard had recorded the obsolete grant in his cartulary: its return to him was justice done.[54]

There were other favours, including the tidying-up of a persistent worry. As Parliament had ruled back in 1475, Richard's hereditary title to the Warwick patrimony – the estates that now formed the heart of his northern power base – was dependent on the continued survival of the legitimate male Neville heir, Warwick's nephew George, and his family line. With George now in his late teens, his presence both validated Richard's claim and threatened it. Richard had to ensure that, on reaching adulthood, the boy would be in no position to mount a challenge for his lands. Parliament now passed an act asserting that the boy had insufficient income to maintain his high rank of duke of Bedford – true enough, given that Richard had taken all his lands – and correspondingly demoting him from his dukedom to the rank of earl. Unable to do away with George Neville physically, Richard could at least make him disappear politically.[55]

By the time of Clarence's death, however, Richard had removed himself from the claustrophobic atmosphere of Westminster, riding north to make a quick tour of his Yorkshire estates. Much to his satisfaction he had acquired Richmond Castle, one of those grants over which he and Clarence had fought and which now, finally, he had prised from his brother's stiffening clutches. The whole of the north Yorkshire fiefdom of Richmond was now his. Whereas for Clarence, it had brought with it persistent problems – back in 1470, the Beaufort family had aggressively sought its return on behalf of the previous claimant Henry Tudor – there was hardly any likelihood of the attainted, exiled Tudor returning to claim his patrimony.[56]

Three days after Clarence's death, more royal paperwork came through for Richard: approval of Richard's petition to found two chantry colleges, at Barnard Castle in Durham, and at his north Yorkshire home of Middleham, to pray for the 'good estate' of the royal family, including Edward and Elizabeth and – delicately eliding Clarence – 'the king's brothers and sisters'. It was a judiciously timed request on Richard's part, given the king's ongoing preoccupation with his health and his morbid self-chastising over Clarence's execution.[57] Richard, as he always had done, knew how to bend with the king's increasingly extreme fluctuations of mood. Nonetheless, Richard seemed glad to be back in the north. As he described his arrival in York, with perhaps just a hint of relief, it was a 'homecoming'.[58]

16

Diamond Cuts Diamond

With the spring of 1478 came growth. As Edward's free-trade agreements with France and the Hanse continued to hold, England's ports flourished, exports surging to double the amount of the recession-hit 1460s. The wealth was unevenly distributed; London, as ever, did best, inexorably sucking the mercantile trade away from other great entrepôts like York and the slow-declining Southampton. In the capital, the mayor Ralph Josselyn embarked on an energetic fundraising campaign for long-needed repairs to the city walls, riding around the Sunday markets with a collecting box. Nobody embodied the sense of financial boom more than Edward. The memory of Clarence's killing was subsumed in a frenzy of royal spending, Edward reiterating to England and its neighbours – and, perhaps, to himself – the power and magnificence of the house of York.[1]

At Windsor, where the perpendicular lines of Edward's new chapel were now reaching skywards, an army of masons and carpenters was at work; so too at Eltham, where the king's new hall was taking shape. In the east midlands Nottingham Castle, which dominated the surrounding region from high on its sandstone cliff, was undergoing a major upgrade: new royal lodgings were bolted on to the ancient fortress, in the form of a 'right sumptuous' three-storey polygonal tower with 'marvellous fair' bay windows.[2] Besides these great projects – whose combined budgets alone came to an annual £3,250 – and a proliferation of other architectural works, Edward was busy acquiring. With the cash to feed his appetites, he bought everything from fine wine to clothes, textiles and soft furnishings, jewels and plate. He employed an agent, the Flemish merchant Philip Maisertuell, paying him £240 to source the finest Flemish illuminated manuscripts. He paid £160 for three 'images', including an exquisite golden Virgin and Child studded with 'great numbers' of precious stones, from the duke of Suffolk; and he bid the staggeringly large – and, incredibly, unsuccessful – sum of £3,000 for a 'mighty' diamond and ruby ornament being hawked around the courts of Europe by the Genoese dealer Luigi Grimaldi.[3]

As fast as the money flowed out of Edward's coffers, it was coming in. Along with the rest of his family and inner circle, the king remained alert to new business opportunities proposed to him, as they had been from early in the reign, by a coterie of advisers and leading merchants. With the new openness in trade, such 'aventures' were increasingly plentiful, from the king's Italian factors, who – on the king's account and their own – bought up all the wool they could lay their hands on (to the inevitable chorus of grumbles from English exporters) to the English merchants with whom Edward went into business, their fleets protected by the navy into which Edward had poured money over the past years. Long interested in his merchants' ambitions to break into the lucrative Portuguese-dominated north African trade in ivory, gold and slaves, Edward was also intrigued by sailors' accounts of other possibilities: the rumoured island of Brazil, a country of fabulous wealth that lay some hundreds of miles west of their usual trading routes.[4]

A new spirit of expansion was, almost imperceptibly, percolating through England's mercantile trade. English ships started appearing in Italian ports, exporting on their own account; among them, sometimes, appeared Edward's own great ships. That summer, the Florentine state galleys that had habitually brought luxury goods to England and exported massive cargoes of wool and cloth, weighed anchor and left Southampton Water for what would be the last time, never to return.[5]

At the same time, balancing magnificence and prudence in the prescribed way, Edward issued a new directive designed to tackle wastefulness: slashing the royal household's wage-roll; reducing allowances of food and fuel; tightening up procedures of service. On his council's advice, he made strenuous efforts to tidy up the long-standing mess between the Exchequer and his chamber treasury, where real financial power lay, and – flush with his annual French pension and the income from the dead Clarence's forfeited estates – to tackle the regime's debts. The man appointed by Edward to spearhead this programme of fiscal reform was the ex-Lancastrian who in recent years had become one of the house of York's most dedicated servants, John Morton, whose forensic clarity Edward appreciated.[6]

Top of the list of the regime's creditors was the city of London, which had bankrolled Edward since 1461 and had never been properly paid back: now, he granted the city a slew of profitable offices. The initiative, however, came too late for Edward's greatest creditor. In 1478 the London branch of the Medici bank closed its doors for the final time. Coming during the Medici's *annus horribilis* – a year of family assassinations and financial disaster – its failure was the result of embracing a lending policy so reckless that, rather than owning Edward through its loans, as the Medici had hoped, Edward ended up owning, and ultimately ruining, the bank.[7]

Running through these reforms was the sense of a tightening royal grip, of a king determined to exploit his resources and rights to the full. To do so, he could hardly have chosen better than Morton, a man whose reputation for 'hard dealing' already went before him. Through England's customs houses, from Dartmouth in the southwest to the Norfolk port of Great Yarmouth, royal agents moved, 'searching' the income streams due to the king from the increased movement of goods in and out of the country. In London, as other ports, a new post was created: a royal surveyor of customs, given sweeping powers to look for and investigate customs evasion, and 'entertainment' or bribery of royal officials. The city found Edward's renewed attentions uncomfortable. That summer saw a blizzard of prosecutions, followed up by royal accusations that members of the Merchant Adventurers were trying to 'embezzle greatly' the subsidies due him through the Port of London. When a deputation of merchants, anxious to resolve matters, turned up, Edward directed Morton to have a chat with them about the 'very truth' of the matter. Some time later they emerged, chastened, acknowledging their guilt and agreeing to pay the king £2,000 in settlement.[8]

If a fresh sense of hesitancy pervaded people's dealings with the king, it was hardly surprising. Even when young, Edward possessed the ability to flip suddenly from his default mode of expansive bonhomie to boiling rage if he felt he was being mucked around. Now, people tiptoed around him, and with reason: a king who was prepared to kill his own brother would clearly do anything to anybody. When news reached the king of a fight between some of his household men and a gang of Londoners, the city rushed to soothe his fury, then passed a ruling that never again were citizens to provoke members of the royal household. Calm was restored: the sun came out again. Courtiers seemed more than usually alert to the royal cues. When the royal esquire Thomas Norton, summoned to court to explain his malicious accusations of treason against the mayor of Bristol, was shown into the king's presence, Edward simply slid his eyes away from the kneeling figure, 'estranging his look'. The assembled courtiers instantly did the same. Norton made his way out, alone, friendless, out of favour.[9] As one close observer of Edward's behaviour put it, the king 'seemed to be feared by all his subjects, while he himself feared no man'.

Norton's opponents had known who to lobby. This was the nexus of family and close servants around the king, his handpicked group of chamber servants, the ever-constant Hastings at their head; and the queen, her 'blood', and their advisers who dominated the household and council of Edward's heir, the prince of Wales. It was this tight group through whom Edward could 'rule as he pleased', and who wielded his power with impunity.

Outside this charmed circle, however, it was noted that people began to 'desert' the king, to distance themselves from the regime, perhaps convinced that the game of courtiership just wasn't worth playing. Some years later, one of Edward's servants, John Blount, Lord Mountjoy, categorically advised his sons not to 'desire to be great about princes', adding with feeling 'for it is dangerous'. Clarence's death had shown precisely how dangerous it was.[10]

That winter, plague re-erupted. Sweeping across the country, this epidemic proved devastating. The usual precautions and remedies were taken. Those who could afford it clutched pomanders packed with aromatic herbs to ward off the poisonous air and took medical advice – not that they generally expected the prescriptions to work. In London, as usual, the wealthy fled. Chief among them was the king.[11]

Throughout the early months of 1479 the royal household kept a safe distance from the pestilential city, moving regularly and often between the king's Thames-side houses, their rooms cleaned and scrubbed with a fretful thoroughness, from the Berkshire manor of Easthampstead, skirting London to the south through Croydon, to Eltham and back again, settling by late February at Sheen. The expansiveness of the previous year seemed to have evaporated, replaced by a fear-filled caution.

As usual, both Edward and his doctors watched anxiously for any signs of diminished vitality in the king's body. In his privy chamber, the pungent aroma of burning aloeswood and ambergris mixed with camphor and rosewater hung in the air: one of the special fumigations, prepared by the royal apothecary John Clark to ward off the pestilence, which Edward inhaled before going to sleep. As well as ingesting various potions, syrups and waters – including the inevitable treacle and *aqua imperiale*, a concoction designed to ward off all manner of poison and pestilence – prescribed by his solicitous medical team, Edward obtained a papal dispensation to eat meat and eggs during Lent. If in all this there was something of the hypochondriac, it was hardly surprising. Despite all the precautions, plague penetrated the royal establishment. That March, Edward and Elizabeth's one-year-old son George fell sick and died, the little boy buried in the king's unfinished chapel at Windsor.[12]

The charged atmosphere seemed to suffuse Edward's ongoing negotiations with Louis XI over the issue closest to his heart: the marriage of his daughter Elizabeth to the French king's son and heir Charles. That February, the princess reached the legally marriageable age of thirteen, which – according to the treaty Edward and Louis had signed three years previously – triggered the marriage and Louis' provision of an annual jointure of 50,000 crowns. In the face of English insistence, the French king dispatched a team of negotiators to England. Their message was blunt. Though Edward's daughter might be ready, the eight-year-old dauphin Charles was not: there was no way that the betrothal could take place nor the jointure be paid.

In Edward's council chamber, there was uproar. An uncompromising John Morton told the French representatives that this was a deal-breaker. If Louis failed to move the marriage forward, the Anglo-French alliance was off. Instead, Edward would reach an agreement

413

with France's sworn enemy, the Burgundian duke Maximilian, who was offering rather more favourable terms: an annual pension of 60,000 crowns, trumping Louis' pension to Edward by 10,000. Worn down by the combination of Morton and the xenophobia he encountered in England – on one occasion, in Windsor, Edward's household men watched unconcernedly as a mob attacked his servants – the beleaguered French ambassador was browbeaten into signing all the documents the English put in front of him. In the meantime, Morton didn't add, Edward had gone ahead and signed a new, secret, treaty with Maximilian anyway.[13]

As the year progressed, an ambitious vision seemed to settle in Edward's mind, one fuelled by the belief – shared by the more bellicose of his advisers – that he held all the cards: that foreign powers were in equal measure eager for England's support and tremblingly fearful of its military might. Hitherto, Edward had pursued relationships with Burgundy or France: both, by nature of the mutual hostility between the two states, tended to be exclusive. Yet both Louis and Maximilian were desperate for English backing. Or, rather, Louis was desperate that Edward should stay out of any war between the two; Maximilian, on the other hand, was doing everything humanly possible to drag him into a new conflict against France.

In July 1479, Edward's envoys concluded a preliminary agreement to marry Edward's little daughter Anne to Maximilian's infant heir, Philip. Following the marriage treaties for his daughters Cecily and Elizabeth to the Scottish and French heirs respectively, this was another, potentially sensational, dynastic trophy: as well as the dukedom of Burgundy, Philip stood – if the stars aligned themselves fortuitously – to inherit the great Habsburg Empire itself. If, Edward seemed to reason, Burgundy and France needed England more than England needed them, then it might be possible for his daughters to marry the heirs of both. In so doing, he could entwine the dynastic future of the house of York not only with those of the French kings, but of the Burgundian dukes and the Habsburgs into the bargain.

That summer, events seemed to bear out Edward's thinking. A resurgent Maximilian crushed French forces at Guinegatte in the Franco-Burgundian borderlands. Edward was gratified: his renewed friendship with Burgundy had so far cost him nothing except the acquisition of large quantities of fine Burgundian plate, bought by his agents at knockdown prices from the impecunious Maximilian as he looked to raise funds for his armies. Louis XI, now ageing fast and still recovering from a cerebral haemorrhage that had poleaxed him some months before, was increasingly anxious about the renewed Anglo-Burgundian *entente*. Which was just how Edward and his councillors wanted it.

Louis, who had bought off Edward spectacularly at Picquigny some years before, knew that cash was the way to the English king's heart. Since that time Edward's reputation for avarice had spread; the Milanese ambassador warned his boss against becoming entangled in a marriage agreement with Edward's daughters, the English king's sole interest in the match being the duke of Milan's exceptional wealth. But when, that autumn, Louis' envoys offered Edward an annual payment of ten thousand crowns towards his daughter Elizabeth's expenses, in lieu of Edward's marriage demands, he swatted it away.

Edward was engaged in a bigger game now: playing France and Burgundy off against each other. It was a strategy of triangulation that, Edward apparently believed, would allow him to control and profit from the quarrel between the two states, to clean up on the European marriage market and, perhaps, to collect an annual pension from both. Indeed, he offered to mediate in talks between Louis and Maximilian, a self-styled honest broker. Louis, who knew perfectly well what Edward was about, turned him down flat. Nonetheless, Edward was convinced of his own desirability in the eyes of France and Burgundy – and, as long as they were at odds, he had a point.[14]

Autumn 1479 saw Edward ensconced in the Surrey countryside at Woking, a sprawling manor that he had once confiscated from the Beaufort family. Others returned cautiously to the still-diseased London, seeking to pick up the threads of their businesses and lives. Among them was the Norfolk knight Sir John Paston who, with his family still mired in their intractable property dispute, arrived in the capital to lobby those close to the king, hoping to obtain royal support for his case. Paston was, he wrote to his mother, in great 'fear of the sickness' – the grubbiness of his London lodgings especially worried him – but he tried to put it to the back of his mind. On 5 November he distracted himself drawing up an inventory of his 'English books': romances and histories, a copy of *Le Morte d'Arthur* borrowed from his hostess at the George Inn, and his prized 'book of knighthood'. By the end of the month, Paston was dead, killed by the epidemic he had feared. He was buried outside the city walls in the church of the Whitefriars south of Fleet Street.[15]

Submerging his sorrow in activity, Sir John's younger brother rode to London to pursue the family's litigation. Once there, he aimed to speak with William Hastings, the man perhaps closest of all to the king, and to another influential figure increasingly friendly with Edward's chamberlain, John Morton. But with both men besieged by petitioners and lobbyists there was another – and as far as Paston was concerned, more likely – route to Edward's ear. This lay through the servants of the king's chamber: men like Paston's uncle Sir George Brown, who, in their intimate physical proximity to Edward might have the chance to mention his case on his behalf. For all his brisk purpose, Paston found his grief for his lost brother overwhelming, almost incapacitating. 'I have so much more to write', he told his mother, 'but my empty head will not let me remember it.'[16]

Meanwhile, the diplomatic dance continued. That winter, French and Burgundian diplomats trailed after Edward, who spent Christmas at Windsor before heading downriver to Greenwich, the royal barge rowing hastily through the city. Away at the French court English envoys were turning up the heat on Louis. The Milanese ambassador there, a discerning man, worked out what was going on. The English, he noted, were obsessed with pushing through the Anglo-French marriage: a marriage that, while the threat of English involvement in a new anti-French coalition was still real, Louis could hardly disavow. But the moment the French king succeeded in bringing Maximilian under control, either by force or diplomacy, the marriage would be off. 'And so', the ambassador meditated on the sharpness of the relationship between the two kings, 'diamond cuts diamond.'[17]

Another of Edward's portfolio of marriages looked newly vulnerable, too. Recent months had seen a surge in Scottish raids across the border, threatening the precarious peace between the two countries.

The spike in violence had been catalysed by the presence in the border-lands of the Scottish king James III's disaffected younger brother, the duke of Albany. The previous spring, their relationship had collapsed in a way that had observers of Edward and Clarence nodding know-ingly. Opposed to everything the Scottish king stood for (which included peace with the English), Albany did what he could to restore Anglo-Scottish relations to their default setting of chronic hostility. In the spring of 1479, after murdering one of Edward's representatives and taking several more hostage, he dodged James III's attempts to arrest and indict him for treason, and fled to France, where Louis XI welcomed him with open arms. The violence continued to escalate. In England, people strongly suspected that Louis, with Albany in his pocket, was up to his old tricks: attempting to distract Edward from any European adventures by creating a distraction in his back-yard. It had to be said that Louis could hardly have done a better job than the incapable Scottish king; nevertheless, Edward was not happy.[18]

In January 1480, Edward's envoys presented James with an ulti-matum and a list of demands in recompense for various breaches of their truce, foremost among which were that he hand over Berwick and various border towns to which the Scottish king had 'no right', and that he send his son and heir south to England as security, to ensure the marriage with Edward's daughter Cecily went ahead. If he failed to do so, Edward would carry out reprisals.

These were excessive demands, but Edward seemed entirely ser-ious. As he emphasized, this ultimatum had been made with the advice and backing of his council. The one councillor who had done most to persuade Edward of this sea-change in policy, to convince him that war with Scotland was both desirable and achievable, was the man responsible for the security of England's northern border – his brother Richard.[19]

Since Clarence's murder, Richard's stature as the king's only surviving brother had grown still further. In the autumn of 1479, as he turned twenty-seven, his authority ran throughout England's northeast. There, the energy and drive of his rule belied his slight, stiff frame and the scoliosis that, unseen by most, was probably now manifesting in a constant background pain along his spine. Now, as his power spread inexorably into all corners of the region, it was to Richard and his council that people turned as the ultimate arbiter of disputes, from property cases to violent assaults. As the oligarchs of York, the region's elegant political and commercial capital, sought Richard's 'good and benevolent lordship', so his household men obtained plum posts in the city's corporation and citizens of York found their way into his service.[20] The same systole–diastole of Richard's rule was at work in the great palatinate of Durham, where he made inroads into the authority of the prince-bishops: his servants sitting on the episcopal council, palatinate families bypassing the bishop and looking to Richard for favour, the bishop himself increasingly seeking Richard's authorization on matters concerning the bishopric – developments that would have had his warlike, independent-minded predecessors spinning in their graves.[21]

Aggressive and aggrandizing, there was also a certain upright quality to Richard's government: the rigid commitment to rule and precept that made him such an effective right-hand man to his brother the king. Having inhaled the principles of good government through his education and the constantly expanding library that he kept by him, ready to consult over any knotty point of procedure or morality, Richard seemed determined to impose them to the letter. Volumes like Colonna's *De Regimine principum* stressed the importance of governing truthfully, magnanimously and honourably, with a commitment to the impartial rule of law, the protection of the poor and the common good. The key to such government – as one of the most popular books of advice, the *Secretum Secretorum*, 'Secret of Secrets', put it – was self-government. A prince had to be 'most of excellence', had to eradicate vice and 'shine in virtue' above all his subjects. This was common, conventional enough advice drummed into most noblemen from childhood. But, more than most, Richard seemed to take it to heart.

Besides his energetic commitment to the imposition of justice, this striving for princely perfection shone through in Richard's piety, a spirituality that was no less sincere for being entirely conventional in its expression. It manifested itself in the usual public ways: rigorous enforcement of his household servants' daily attendance at mass, with punishments for lateness or non-appearance; the disbursement of appropriate financial gifts to churches, chantry chapels and religious houses as he rode about the region; and his foundation of religious institutions. Richard did this charitable work on a scale befitting his role as lord of the north: plans for his new collegiate church at Middleham Castle, drawn up in the summer of 1478, made provision for one hundred priests. His own devotions displayed the self-conscious humility typical of the piety of the age, with its sharp focus on the precariousness of human fortune and the transitory nature of existence. As Richard put it in the preamble to the statutes for his college at Middleham, he was God's 'most simple creature, nakedly born into this wretched world', reliant on God's grace for his exalted rank and great riches.

This was a piety in which Richard and his wife Anne Neville consciously and publicly shared. Together, they inscribed their names on the flyleaf of a copy of *The Book of Ghostly Grace*, the thirteenth-century mystic Mechtild of Hackeborn's vivid recounting of her revelatory visions: a book of lingering descriptions of the angels, the Virgin and Christ himself, appearing to Mechtild clad in rich heavenly garments, and an aid to private meditation.[22]

Richard's piety reflected his Neville affiliations. Though hardly an intellectual of the calibre of George Neville, one of the figures who had loomed large in his youth, Richard was no slouch either. He followed in Neville's footsteps, patronizing religious institutions associated with the late archbishop and, especially, finding places in his own household for members of the Cambridge intelligentsia who had populated Neville's salons. All of which showed a personal commitment to religion that was markedly different in tone from that of his brother Edward, who had never gone out of his way to lead by pious example. It was rather more like that of their father, Richard of York.[23]

Richard didn't always practice what he preached. In York, there were sporadic mutterings about the factionalism and cronyism of the Richard-controlled corporation, one city saddler opining that 'he did nothing for the common people but grin at us'; while the finance for his college at Middleham dribbled in and eventually dried up altogether. By the late 1470s, though, Richard's dominance of the northeast was all but total. Feuding and unrest remained, of course, but he proved to be a unifying figure, bringing to a close that most nationally destructive of the region's turf wars, the feud between the Percy and Neville families. Even Richard's on–off quarrel with the Stanley family, whose lands bordered his to the west, had been reduced to a low simmer: where they had to, he and Lord Stanley swallowed their mutual distaste and got on with the business of government.[24] There could be little doubt that this enforced harmony was in large measure down to Richard's own personal 'excellence', as contemporary books of advice put it: a figure whose strong, upstanding leadership inspired loyalty, respect, even love.

If Richard's lordship was a contributing factor, there was also no denying that his dominance was a result of who he was – not simply a great magnate, but the king's brother and representative, a conduit to the heart of royal power. It was a fact of which Richard was always aware, insisting repeatedly that he would proceed only 'according to the king's laws'. If God, 'of his infinite goodness', had ultimately been responsible for handing Richard his titles and lands, so too had Edward. The king's continued backing, investing Richard with astonishing authority and lifting him above the region's other noblemen, had made him what he was. Richard's rigorous leadership and his insatiable hunger for power, bound up in his quest for self-perfection, did the rest.[25] In the early months of 1480, Richard turned his gaze on the kingdom that bordered his dominions to the north, with a sense of possibility.

Richard hardly needed the Scottish lords' needling to ramp up hostilities. He shared their frontier state of mind, pricklingly alert to the tensions between feuding families whose cross-border 'reiving' or raiding might, with a little government backing on either side, flare into something more significant. Back in 1475, Richard's lackadaisical attitude towards the Treaty of Edinburgh had earned him a reprimand from Edward. Although he was the king's chief representative in the region, an Anglo-Scottish peace didn't suit Richard. War, however, did.[26]

The abortive invasion of France three years previously had only increased Richard's itch to lead an army into battle. A Scottish campaign would be an opportunity to further his reputation as a war-leader;

more to the point, it would consolidate his hold in the north, where the idea of conflict against Scotland was more or less a reflex, and even extend his rule into Scotland itself.

On the face of it, war with Scotland made little sense for Edward. A diversion from his negotiations with France and Burgundy, it would be a drain on his finances into the bargain. But Edward, his thoughts gently led by his brother, was irate at the dishonour done him by the Scottish king – and, perhaps, he recalled the prophetic notion in which England and Scotland would be united in one Yorkist Britain. Besides which, he now seemed inclined to give Richard free rein. His brother had demonstrated his qualities of loving obedience time and again. If he now wanted to fight a war against Scotland using his own northern forces, that was fine by Edward. It would be a useful outlet for Richard's belligerence; the upsides were glory and territorial gain for the house of York. In May 1480, with James III having failed to meet any of his demands, Edward handed Richard the post of the king's lieutenant-general in the north, and with it the power to raise an army.[27]

Meanwhile, Louis XI's evasions were becoming ever more desperate. When, in the latest attempt to keep the French king to his commitments, an English delegation arrived in Paris, he retreated behind a shower of gifts and excuses and fled the city.[28] The episode made up Edward's mind for him. Where Louis equivocated, the ailing Burgundian state had proved eager for Edward's friendship, a stream of Burgundian diplomats – old, reassuringly familiar faces from Edward's exile a decade before – beating a path to his door. Driving this renewed charm offensive was the dowager duchess of Burgundy, Edward's sister Margaret.

In recent years, Margaret had done everything possible to draw Edward into the conflict with France, playing the family card time and time again. Edward had been stolid in the face of his sister's entreaties, unmoved even by a desperate, reproachful letter of March 1478, in which she described how she had been deserted by everyone, 'especially by you'. On 24 June, Margaret left Flanders for talks with her brother, talks that, she hoped, would lead to a new Anglo-Burgundian alliance. It would be her first return to England in a decade. Whether Edward actually wanted an alliance, or whether he just wanted to twist Louis' arm with the threat of military action, was unclear. But he was prepared to show his sister 'great pleasure', with no expense spared.[29]

In early July Margaret and her entourage were met at Calais by the queen's youngest brother Sir Edward Woodville and a hundred of Edward's household men, crisply uniformed in jackets of Yorkist mulberry and blue, embroidered with white roses. On the royal ship *Falcon*, the Burgundians were taken across the Channel and round the Kentish coast under heavy escort to Gravesend; from there, transferred to a royal barge, they were rowed up the Thames to London.[30]

All poised Burgundian glamour, Margaret was embraced warmly by the family whom she hadn't seen for so long, and in some cases – her nephews, Edward and Elizabeth's young sons – not at all. She was escorted to her lodging, the great house of Coldharbour on Thames Street, where Edward's gift of ten fine horses adorned with exquisitely worked trappings awaited her. A welcome banquet at Greenwich was attended by many of the family, among them her mother and fellow guest of honour Cecily, the dynasty's matriarch, and Richard, who had left the Scottish border to make the long journey south to see his sister. As she looked about her, Margaret could hardly have been more conscious of the one glaring, unspoken absence: that of her favourite brother, Clarence. But Margaret knew what she was in England for. She praised the king's wine – Edward, gratified, sent her a barrel a few days later – and concentrated on the job in hand.[31]

That summer, Edward and his court went out of their way to articulate the bond between Burgundy and the house of York. The king flaunted his Burgundian credentials. His expensively acquired Flemish tapestries adorned the walls of his palace; also on display were eight exquisitely illuminated manuscripts, newly sourced from the ateliers of Bruges and Ghent and transformed into objects of Yorkist luxury. Adorned with Edward's coat of arms, and those of his two sons, the books had been bound and 'dressed' under the supervision of his wardrobe keeper Piers Curteys: the edges of their pages gilded, covered in crimson velvet, blue and black silk, with gilt clasps engraved with white roses, and laces and tassels supplied by the London silkwoman Alice Claver. Meanwhile, Edward had chosen the courtiers deputed to attend on Margaret carefully, with an eye to their

Burgundian sympathies and literary credentials: Thomas Thwaites, the treasurer of Calais and a noted bibliophile; William Hastings and his brother-in-law Sir John Donne, who some years before Margaret had presented with a *Deeds of Alexander the Great* in the vain hope that he might intercede with Edward on her behalf; and Anthony Woodville, with whom Margaret found common ground in, among other things, their shared Burgundian heritage and their patronage of William Caxton.[32]

This shared cultural landscape appeared to translate into an abundance of political will. The talks went well and by 1 August a succession of secret documents, their terms concluded by an experienced negotiating team including John Russell, bishop of Rochester, Lord Stanley and the ubiquitous Thomas Montgomery, were drawn up. The chief signatory was Richard. But if Margaret had hoped that Edward would curb his deal-making instincts in favour of family sentiment, it was wishful thinking.

In order to get her brother's commitment to a fresh Burgundian alliance, including a force of six thousand English archers – recruited, naturally, at Burgundian expense – and the house of York's guaranteed backing in the event that Burgundian talks with France broke down, Margaret had little choice but to give Edward everything he asked for.[33] This included underwriting Edward's annual pension of 50,000 crowns in the event that Louis stopped paying it, and – the cornerstone of the new alliance – the marriage between the Burgundian heir Philip, who had just turned two, and Edward's four-year-old daughter Anne. Edward, still stung by the memory of the vast sums that Charles the Bold had wrung out of him for Margaret's own marriage back in 1468, insisted that he pay no dowry. Even so, Edward still believed he was doing his sister a favour. After dinner one late July evening, he handed Margaret a dispatch from John Howard, fresh from the French court: a panicky Louis XI was now prepared to give in to all Edward's demands if he promised not to sign a new treaty with Burgundy. But, Edward soothed his sister, there was no way he would make another agreement with the French king.[34]

If Edward was inured to Louis' diplomatic shenanigans – 'dodges and lies', as Howard put it dismissively – he was less alert to Maximilian's whimsy. In late August, Margaret was still in England when news came that the Burgundian ruler, a prince who Machiavelli later judged to be impossibly fickle, had wandered off and concluded an independent truce with Louis with a view to a lasting peace with France. The rest of Margaret's stay was an exercise in damage limitation: smoothing Edward's ruffled feathers, assuring him that there would be no further secret discussions with Louis, and keeping the Anglo-Burgundian treaty on track while supervising the hiring and shipment of a force of English archers to Flanders. Finally, after a weekend's entertainment on Anthony Woodville's Kentish estates en route to Dover, Margaret made her farewells and sailed for Calais.

Not long after, the veteran envoy Chester Herald returned from the French court. Chatting with one of the king's secretaries, he gave an unvarnished account of Louis XI's reaction to the news of Edward's alliance with Burgundy. The French king, 'fantastically angry', had raged against Margaret, ranting that she had hated him ever since he had refused to support Clarence's 'treasons' against Edward. In his fury, Louis had initially refused to see the herald and his fellow envoys. Then, calming down, he had summoned them in, and presented them with proof of his own secret understanding with Maximilian, along with copies of supposedly confidential correspondence between Edward and Burgundy that Maximilian had subsequently passed on to Louis. On being told this news, the envoy added with understatement, 'Edward had marvelled'.[35]

Rather than clarifying the diplomatic situation, the new treaties simply added to the haze of mutual suspicion between the three rulers. These were conditions in which Louis thrived. That autumn, despite his professed 'understanding' with Maximilian, he again mobilized an invading army against Burgundy – his troops 'on the front all ready', as one panicked Calais merchant reported. He also cancelled planned peace talks with Maximilian – talks that Edward, playing to his role of 'honest broker', had been keen to mediate – and refused to pay any more instalments of Edward's pension.

Louis had called Edward's bluff. In massing his forces against Burgundy, the French king dared Edward to get off the fence and side openly with Maximilian, as his recently signed treaty demanded. Aware that this irrevocable step would result in the loss of his French pension and the Anglo-French marriage for which he continued to hold

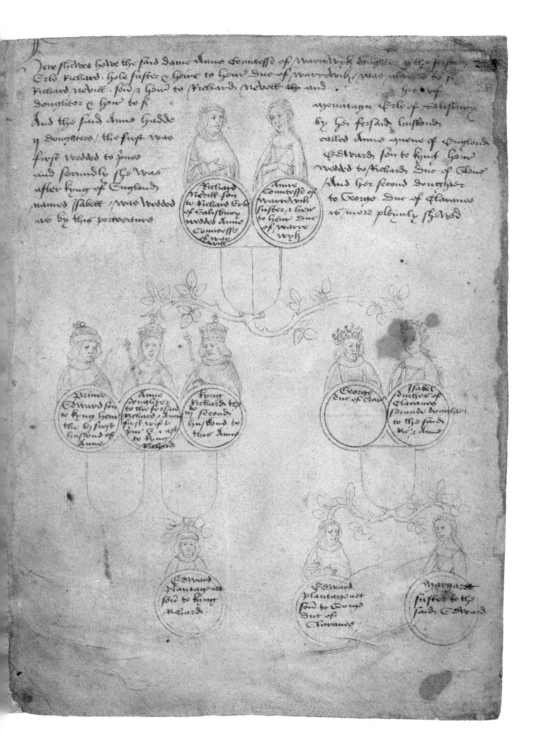

18. In the 1470s, the vast landed inheritance of Richard Neville, earl of Warwick (*top*, with his wife Anne) was the subject of an increasingly violent quarrel between Clarence and Richard (*centre right* and *left*, with their wives, Warwick's daughters Isabel and Anne), a fraternal conflict that Edward IV struggled to control

19. Edward spent substantial sums on exquisitely illustrated Flemish manuscripts, their margins decorated with his badges and mottos. Here, his rose-en-soleil appears in a lozenge of murrey (mulberry) and blue, the Yorkist colours

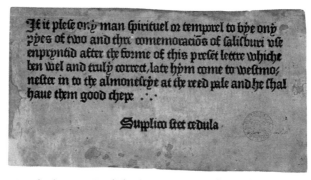

20. The first printed advert in English. Caxton's 1476 flyer advertising his new edition of the 'Sarum Pye', the widely used service book. At its foot is the Latin phrase 'Supplico stet cedula': 'Don't take this leaflet'

21. (*above*) The Garter 'stall plate' of Edward's close friend William Lord Hastings – indicating his seat in St George's Chapel Windsor, the Garter's spiritual home' – depicts his coat of arms, the 'maunch sable', or 'black sleeve'

22. This page from the prescription book of the royal apothecary John Clark details two recipes for 'ceruse', skin whitener and clarifier: one made of wheat flour, one of roots. The recipes were supplied by – and/or for – Henry Stafford, duke of Buckingham, who spent his formative years at Edward's court before helping Richard seize power in 1483

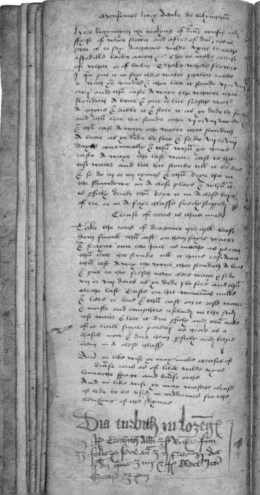

23. (*above*) Edward IV towards the end of his life. Decades of self-indulgence have clearly taken their toll

24. (*right*) One of Edward IV's daughters, probably Elizabeth of York, at prayer

25. (*below*) The signatures of the boy king Edward V and, below it, the two figures who usurped his throne: Richard and Buckingham. Above his signature, Richard has written his motto 'loyaute me lie', 'loyalty binds me'

26. Richard III and family: his wife Anne Neville (*left*) and son Edward of Middleham (*right*). At the feet of Richard and his son lies his boar, Richard's family badge; at Anne's feet is the bear of Warwick

27. Detail of a charter granted by Richard III to the Worshipful Company of Wax Chandlers, 1484. In the illuminated initial 'R', two of Richard's boars (his personal emblem) support the royal coat of arms

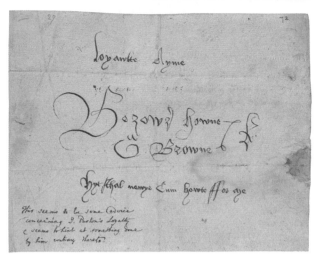

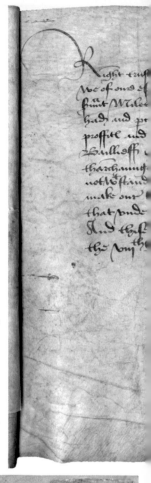

28 & 29. Rebellion, autumn 1483: (*above*) A message from George Brown, one the Yorkist rebels, indicating his opposition to Richard III: 'Loyalte a me' (a variation on Richard's motto), 'it will never come out for me'. (*below*) Richard orders the great seal to be sent him after receiving news of Buckingham's rebellion. His scribbled note details his fury at the treachery of his right-hand man: 'the most untrue creature living'

30. (*right*) Richard's grant of a pension to the wife and son of the recently deceased Miles Forest, formerly wardrobe keeper at Barnard Castle, 'for diverse causes and considerations us moving' (line 1). Later, Thomas More identified Miles Forest as one of the two murderers of Edward IV's sons

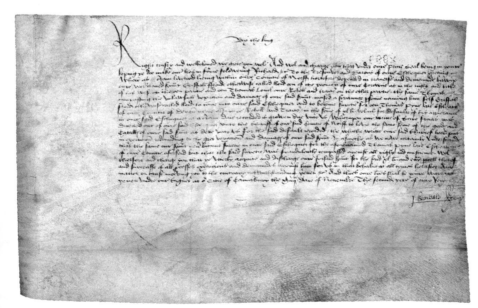

31. Tudor rebels aimed to disrupt the workings of Richard's government. In this case of fraud and identity theft, a 'strange person' sent by Tudor's right-hand man Thomas Lovell assumes the identity of Griffith Lloyd, a royal official, causing 'vexation and damages' (ll. 5–6)

RICARDVS · III · ANG · REX

32 & 33. Richard III (*above*) and, his battle standard (*top*)
depicting the English cross of St George, the Yorkist white rose
and sunburst, and his personal boar badge, against the Yorkist
livery colours of murrey and blue

out, not to mention committing himself and England to a potentially ruinous war in France, Edward couldn't bring himself to do it. Besides which, he had another conflict to deal with. After months of phony war with Scotland, it had sparked into life.[36]

In September Richard had returned north to news of a massive Scottish raid along the Northumbrian coast as far as the castle of Bamburgh, which was torched. There were rumours that the raid, led by an ally of the exiled duke of Albany, was guided by the unseen hand of Louis XI, a distraction to stop Edward meddling in the conflict between France and Burgundy. If so, it worked to perfection. Nobody was happier to escalate the situation than Richard, eager for war. His reprisal raids had the hapless James III urgently begging Louis for military aid and artillery, and sending envoys to Westminster in a fruitless last-ditch effort to avoid conflict. That November, at a belligerent meeting of his great council, Edward decided to invade Scotland. What was more, perhaps stirred by hazy memories of his northern campaign nearly twenty years before, the king declared that he would not leave matters to Richard but would lead the army himself.[37]

Edward's announcement was a game-changer. No longer was the campaign simply a question of Richard assembling his northern forces. Rather, it involved mobilizing a national army, a process that would require massive planning – and massive funds. Though Edward was now solvent, the finance at his disposal was hardly enough to bankroll a prolonged military campaign: troops' wages, munitions and supplies, and a supporting navy to ferry them up the coast. Given the residual public hostility over the fiasco of his French invasion, he could hardly approach Parliament for financial backing. Instead, he resorted to the creative fundraising that, from the moment he acceded to the throne, had been a hallmark of his kingship. This time, its centrepiece was a new 'benevolence': another round of forced loans and gifts extracted from England's taxpayers under the guise of voluntary, public-spirited contributions to the king's wars.

If the previous benevolence, collected in the run-up to Edward's French invasion of 1475, was dressed in at least a pretence of negotiation with donors, this new initiative cut straight to the chase. Anybody worth more than 20 marks was to contribute; anybody failing to do so would, it was strongly implied, be sent to fight in the north. This time round the process, under the direction of the king's council rather than the royal household, was more systematic, more rigorous, more intrusive. Commissioners fanned out across the country, examining potential donors and compiling extensive lists of names and contributions that were returned to the council, in order that – the phrase carrying with it a faint air of menace – 'we may know and understand the behaving and merits of every person in this behalf'. Supervising the benevolence were experienced financiers like the queen's receiver-general John Forster and, unnamed but hovering in the background, John Morton.[38]

In the spring of 1481, as Edward's commissioners assessed, documented and collected, invasion plans were drawn up, and supplies and weapons stockpiled. Meanwhile, Edward gently deflated the hopes of his new Burgundian allies, informing them that owing to his Scottish war he was unable to fulfil any further promises of military aid against France. What he didn't tell them was, in the latest convolution of his increasingly baroque diplomacy, he had quietly reopened back-channel negotiations with Louis XI. If such thinking was flexible, it was also increasingly tortuous: a product of the enduring mistrust that riddled relations between Europe's princes, and of Edward's persistent belief that he could both have his cake and eat it.

Initially, Edward's approach seemed to pay off. That winter, Louis had suffered his second stroke in as many years. Despite his scheming, the French king remained anxious about the prospect of Anglo-Burgundian co-operation, and he jumped at Edward's informal offer of reconciliation, which came as a discreet message from William Hastings.[39]

Hastings was back on the diplomatic scene after some months in his east midlands heartland, where he had been catching up with the regional big men and the coterie of legally minded business advisers and estate managers who, like all noblemen, he employed to look after his lands and interests. Satisfied that things were well in hand – men like the Northamptonshire lawyer William Catesby, effectively his second-in-command in the county, had everything covered – Hastings spent much of his tour poring over plans for the redevelopment of his ancestral home of Kirby Muxloe into a magnificent crenellated vision in brick and glass, surrounded by an ornamental moat and deer-filled grounds. By the winter, Hastings was back at Edward's side, actioning the latest of his foreign policy contortions and, in March 1481, sending his 'thoughts' on the importance of peace between England and France to Louis. As Louis knew perfectly well, Hastings' thoughts were Edward's own.[40]

Agreeing to everything Edward asked, including his marriage demands, Louis again turned on the taps of his French pension. Edward, accordingly, continued with his plans to invade Scotland. He appeared to think that Louis had genuinely changed tack; that the French king now wanted to embrace the marriage treaty that he had spent the last six years trying to avoid. Given the French king's approach of balancing 'sheer weight of cash' with 'dodges and lies' – a strategy with which Edward and his advisers were long familiar – this seemed optimistic at best.

With spring came the first act of Edward's Scottish war. In recent years, the king had invested heavily in England's once negligible navy; now, he reinforced what was already a formidable seaborne force with nine new vessels. Squadrons of warships patrolled the Dover Straits and the west coast of Scotland; meanwhile English privateers, with a nod and a wink from the government, opportunistically hunted down Scottish shipping. In mid-May, a fleet under the command of John Howard nosed out of Sandwich, waved off by an enthusiastic Edward and his ten-year-old heir, and sailed up England's eastern seaboard towards Scotland on a softening-up expedition, prior to the land invasion that was to take place later in the summer.[41]

Howard had ensured that his three-month tour of duty would be as comfortable as possible. His flagship, the *Mary Howard*, was crammed with necessaries: rugs, tapestries, featherbeds, pillows stuffed with down and fine linen, a silver 'pissing basin', silver dishes and cutlery, a case with four glass goblets, and – to liven up the monotonous on-board fare – 'a pannier of spices' and five sugar loaves. He also took clothes for all occasions, including a jacket of cloth-of-gold and one of 'popinjay colour'. To while away the long stretches of time on board ship, he had with him several barrels of white wine and malmsey; his chess boards and 'a bag with chess men'; and a portable library of twelve books, all in French, including strategic military reading like the ever-popular *Tree of Battles,* and two books on dice and chess.[42]

Just over three weeks later Howard's ships materialized in the Firth of Forth, spreading panic and mayhem. In a lightning sequence of raids, his troops burned towns and villages all the way up to the key port of Leith, destroying a number of ships and capturing eight others. Having obliterated Scotland's naval power, he returned to Newcastle to await news that Edward's army was on the move. And there he waited.[43]

Meanwhile, Edward's mobilization had gone smoothly. His inner circle was well represented: Anthony Woodville had recruited a thousand men and his nephew Dorset six hundred; Lord Stanley, in a demonstration of his regional muscle, contributed three thousand archers. With the Scots divided, disorganized and underfunded, now was the time for Edward to strike. Despite continued bellicosity, however, he stayed put.

In the north, Richard and the earl of Northumberland waited with their assembled forces for Edward's main army to join them: Howard remained in port with his fleet, ready to escort supply ships when the signal came. Weeks, then months ticked by.[44] Finally, in mid-July, Edward rode unhurriedly west out of London and up the Thames to Windsor, where he stayed for over a month assembling his armies and hunting. Then, amid incessant summer rain, he dawdled further up the Thames valley to his Oxfordshire manor of Woodstock.

The window of opportunity for an invasion was fast closing. Late in August, with Edward nowhere in sight and Howard's ships long since returned to their Kentish base, Richard and Northumberland laid siege to the key border fortress of Berwick. As the Scots – growing in confidence with each day that passed with the non-appearance of the English army – surged across the border 'in great number', Northumberland wrote urgently to his followers for reinforcements. Edward was still three hundred miles away at Woodstock, hunting and working his way through the eighty butts of malmsey ordered 'for the use of him and his army'. On 22 September he, his commanders and a 'multitude of men' rode over to nearby Oxford, their sunset entrance to the city illuminated by a forest of burning torches, where they spent the following days being wined and dined as guests of the university's chancellor, the queen's brother Lionel Woodville.[45] Eventually, in early October, Edward arrived in Nottingham, still two hundred miles away from the English front line. With winter approaching, he eventually decided against leading his army into Scotland and instead returned south. By the end of the month, he was back in the comforting surroundings of Greenwich.

Later, in a letter to Pope Sixtus IV – to whom, months before, he had trumpeted his invasion plans – Edward put the failure of his campaign down to *adversa tempestas*. The 'bad weather' into which Edward's army had run was real enough. The weather that summer had been appalling and, with the second terrible harvest in as many years, there was little to sustain an army on; corn was scarce and prices high, which, combined with the effects of Edward's 'benevolence', had led to unrest and rioting in the north.[46]

Yet there was no denying that it was the king himself, at his erratic worst – the wavering 'tavern bush' of scathing ambassadorial report – who had scuppered his own invasion. Not for the first time, Edward's vaunting military ambitions had been followed by a limp afterthought of a performance. His desire for comfort overriding his impulse for glory, he had found it all but impossible to tear himself away from the luxuries of his Thames valley houses, and his compulsive triangulations with Maximilian and Louis, until it was too late. In his own mind, Edward perhaps felt that the army had served its purpose: his new treaty with Louis was signed and the latest half-yearly instalment of his French pension duly paid.[47] The uncomfortable truth, though, was that he had blown at least twice that sum on an invasion which, as a result of his indolence, had run into the sand. Once again, he had raised massive sums from his subjects, and had failed even to try to deliver. Neither did he seem particularly bothered about it.

None of which, by now, came as a surprise. Edward, after all, was no longer capable of moving anywhere fast. In previous years, commentators had hesitatingly suggested that this once-beautiful king was carrying a little extra timber. Now, as he approached forty, the havoc he had wrought to his body through decades of self-indulgence was horribly evident, his massive frame and fine, delicate features blurred with fat. Englishmen and foreigners alike unhesitatingly reached for the same word: 'gross'. But while foreign commentators were quick with their digs about Edward's preference for the bed and the banqueting table over the battlefield and the tent, domestic opinion was growing altogether more scathing. One contemporary chronicler, a councillor of Edward's, later wrote how people in England of all walks of life marvelled at how a king 'so addicted to conviviality, vanity, drunkenness, extravagance and passion' could continue to function. When it came to money, if nothing else, Edward had total recall.[48] Even now, to the consternation of his subjects, Edward's razor of a memory managed to slash through the sybaritic haze that his life had become, instantly recalling the names, details and personal wealth of men scattered through his kingdom 'as if they were daily within his sight'.

There had always been an obsessive edge to Edward's bingeing. In earlier years, the furious energy that fuelled it had also found release elsewhere: during his lean, dry months in the Low Countries, in his drive to regain his kingdom, he had glowed with the superhuman vitality that had floored Philippe de Commynes. Now, that compulsiveness had turned in on itself, evident in Edward's insatiable hunger for deal-making, for cash and, above all, in what Commynes, tellingly precise with his adjectives, described as a 'violent' addiction to pleasure.

Edward's court had always had the atmosphere of a hunting ground. But where, over the years, some in the king's inner circle had tried to curb his appetites, such advisers were now dead – like William Hatteclyffe – or, afraid of the consequences of 'counselling or answering' him, had fallen quiet. Now, Edward had nobody to step in with quiet, authoritative advice on his lifestyle, and he gave his impulses free rein. His companions egged him on. The younger Woodvilles – men like the queen's brother Sir Edward and her two sons by her first marriage, Dorset and Sir Richard Grey – were among the 'principal promoters and companions of his vices'. Hastings, Edward's longstanding fixer-in-chief and pimp, was said to have been the chief culprit, 'secretly familiar with the king in wanton company', a phrase of Thomas More's that left everything to the imagination. Edward was in the habit of passing on to his companions the women discarded from his bedchamber once he had tired of them, a practice that caused widespread distress among its victims who, as one chronicler noted grimly, were used 'much against their will'. Queen Elizabeth, hardly able to visit her wrath on members of her own family, was said to have loathed Hastings, his relationship with her husband a constant, humiliating reminder of the way he had once facilitated her own entrance into Edward's bedchamber.

As his councillors had long feared, Edward's prodigious consumption was finally catching up with him. Doctors such as the Cambridge- and Ferrara-trained physician John Argentine, 'standing in the presence of the king's meals', stood by in silent horror while Edward, crammed with food and awash with drink, left the table to take an emetic then came back for more. His body exhibited the imbalance of humours that resulted from his lack of moderation and self-government; meanwhile, the prolonged spells of listlessness and sadness into which he was regularly plunged in recent years left his physicians shaking their heads in rueful acknowledgement of what they already knew – that excessive sexual activity stripped men of their virility and left them enervated, 'effeminate', suffering the effects of 'women's conditions'.[49] Whatever *adversa tempestas* had prevented Edward from leading his army into Scotland, it was nothing, it seemed, compared to the increasing personal tumult in the king's body and mind.

Edward's army had not been entirely disbanded. Before winter closed in, Anthony Woodville, Dorset and Lord Stanley rode north on the king's orders. Joining forces with Richard and Northumberland, they drove the raiding Scots back across the border in an orgy of 'incontinent great burnings, robbery and destruction'. Meanwhile, Edward's new treaty with France started to bite. That winter, Louis studiously ignored the Scottish king's increasingly desperate pleas for aid, James III writing to him 'diverse times' and getting 'no answer' in return.[50]

Woodville and his fellow commanders soon returned south, leaving Richard and Northumberland, watchful, to hold the line. As Edward worked out his next steps, what he needed above all was his brother's constancy, to keep the border against the Scots until something turned up. It was a hard winter. Amid plummeting temperatures and further Scottish incursions, Richard's men were unpaid, hungry and restive. Richard himself spent much of his time trying to keep a grip on discipline and, with troops on the West March suffering a 'daily increasing dearth and scarcity of victuals', requisitioning scarce food supplies.[51] As 1482 came round, he was forced to ship in quantities of wheat, barley, oats and rye from Wales and Ireland to feed his hungry men. The lengthening days finally brought relief in the form of a succession of cash payments from Westminster, including £10,000 in backdated wages for his army. Richard duly fulfilled his brother's expectations. As he slogged through the dark, dreary months on the border, he perhaps asked himself why Edward had so spectacularly failed to invade Scotland the previous autumn, and whether the king's increasingly haphazard manoeuvrings had any concrete end in view at all.

For by this point, the involutions of Edward's foreign policy seemed finally to have worked themselves to stasis. That January, when Burgundian ambassadors turned up at court demanding that he fulfil his promises to Maximilian and to know what was going on with Louis, Edward shrugged. There was nothing he could do until he had dealt with Scotland. Meanwhile, his advice to Maximilian was simply to sit tight and wait for the ailing Louis to die – 'which', he said, 'wouldn't be long in coming'.[52] Then, suddenly, the diplomatic pressure was unexpectedly released.

Late that March, Maximilian and his wife were out hunting when her horse tripped and fell, throwing her and breaking her back; days later, she died. Marie of Burgundy had been Maximilian's key to the great cities or 'members' of Flanders, who had put up with his mercurial autocracy largely because of their loyalty to her and her family. Having borne the brunt of his destructive and costly foreign policy, they now refused to acknowledge him as regent, claimed guardianship of Marie's two children, the three-year-old Burgundian heir Philip and his little sister Margaret, and forced a reluctant Maximilian to open talks with France. Which was fine as far as Edward, confident in his position as power-broker, was concerned: at least it stopped Maximilian pestering him for military backing. Besides, Edward had other fish to fry. His invasion of Scotland was on again.[53]

For well over two years, the Scottish king's disaffected brother Albany had been kicking his heels in France. In recent months Louis, having abandoned his friendship with James III in favour of his new treaty with Edward, began to look at the duke with renewed interest. If Edward still wanted to invade Scotland – and Louis, who wanted Edward off his back, was exceptionally keen that he should do so – he needed a figurehead for a regime change. With some gentle nudging from the French king, Albany formally petitioned Edward for help. Edward responded with alacrity. A short, victorious war followed by the installation of a compliant puppet king on the Scottish throne seemed the ideal solution to what was becoming an intractable problem.[54]

That spring Edward seemed possessed, the lassitude of the previous summer replaced by a manic energy. In April, a ship carrying Albany and twenty attendants nosed into Southampton harbour. Styling the duke 'king of Scotland', bringing him to London and installing him in the Erber, the great stone townhouse formerly belonging to the earl of Warwick, Edward again moved on to a war footing.[55] Ordering his forces to be ready to mobilize on two weeks' notice, he bolstered them with two thousand northern European mercenaries fresh from the battlefields of Flanders and Switzerland, including several hundred gunners, all kitted out in new red-and-white battledress. In mid-May, the king went down to Dover to review his fleet, before returning to London to inspect his troops before their march north. During those days the death of his second daughter, the fourteen-year-old Mary, a few miles downriver at Greenwich, seemed to pass almost unnoticed: her coffined body was rowed up the Thames, past the Tower where her father was absorbed in his preparations, to Windsor. On the 29th she was lowered into the ground in the half-finished St George's Chapel, the king's eleven-year-old heir Prince Edward a solemn figure by her grave. At that moment the king himself, Albany at his side, was riding north out of London to rendezvous with Richard at the family's home of Fotheringhay.[56]

They had been there a full week before Richard turned up. The day he arrived, as though waiting for his imprimatur, Edward and the duke of Albany signed their deal. In the treaty, which formally acknowledged Albany as the rightful king of Scotland, Edward promised him military aid to regain his crown; in return, Albany – regally signing himself 'Alexander R' – would pay Edward homage as his overlord, marry Edward's daughter Cecily as soon as he could wangle a papal dispensation to free himself from his French wife, and cede Berwick and a large swathe of southwest Scotland to the English crown.[57]

Richard, in fact, had just returned from raiding this area, his forces pillaging and burning their way twenty miles into Dumfriesshire. The raid, it turned out, was audition and dress rehearsal rolled into one. Finally accepting that he was not the man to lead an invasion of Scotland, Edward handed his brother leadership of the campaign and with it, Richard's chance to confirm his status not just as lord of the north, but as the kingdom's undisputed war-leader. As usual, events in mainland Europe were monopolizing the king's attention. With Maximilian newly vulnerable and Edward's eyes turned towards Scotland, Louis had seized his opportunity. French armies were once more on the march towards Flanders, provoking frantic demands from Calais for increased security and a hasty attempt by Maximilian to convene a peace conference.[58] The day after the Fotheringhay treaty was signed, Edward promptly headed back south.

By mid-July Richard's army was on the move. Most of his twenty thousand men were northerners: Richard's private forces and those of his right-hand man Northumberland, supplemented by contingents led by Lord Stanley, the queen's son Dorset and her youngest brother Edward Woodville. In Richard's lengthy baggage train was a closely guarded war-chest of some £15,000: wages to keep the army together for four weeks. Ample time, so it was felt, to destroy the meagre, divided forces of James III and to place his brother Albany on the throne. Nevertheless, the clock was ticking. Richard had to crack on.

In late July he was still on the English side of the border when news came that James's army, mustering at the Scottish border town of Lauder, had disintegrated. The Scottish king's resentful, fractious nobles, all too aware of the potentially catastrophic military mismatch that awaited them, had taken matters into their own hands. Arresting and summarily hanging a number of the king's household officials, they seized James and hustled him back to Edinburgh Castle, where he was locked up. Richard's way to Edinburgh lay open. With the citadel of Berwick holding out, Richard bypassed it and made his way unopposed up the coast at speed, plundering and burning everything in his path. On 2 August, he entered the Scottish capital.[59] There, his problems started.

First, it had become abundantly clear that, with not a single Scot rallying to him on their march north, Albany was not a viable figure as king. With commendable realism, Albany himself sized up the situation and, abandoning his claim to the throne in exchange for his restoration to his ducal titles and lands, instantly swapped sides. His puppet king gone, Richard had an urgent need to get hold of the man who, despite his manifest inadequacies, Scots still viewed as their rightful king. The problem was that James III, locked in Edinburgh Castle, remained the prisoner of his own noblemen – and though Richard had entered Edinburgh easily enough, the castle, crouched on the volcanic cliffs that rose sheer above the surrounding city, was all but impregnable. Neither could Richard get his hands on James's young sons, sent well away to Stirling with their mother for safekeeping. Regime change was now out of the question. Unequipped for a siege and with his army's wages running out, Richard led his army back south with secret – and not especially reassuring – promises from Albany that, despite having been received back into the Scottish political fold, he planned to reassert his claim to the crown when the chance arose. Re-crossing the border, Richard besieged Berwick Castle, which capitulated. For the first time since 1461, when Margaret of Anjou had handed it over to the Scots, this key border fortress was in English hands. In terms of what Richard had to show for his vaunted march to Edinburgh and back again, though, Berwick was more or less it.[60]

Given the campaign's time limit, however, Richard had made the best of a bad job. He had acquired the lustre of a national war-leader, at least in some quarters. Away in Calais, Hastings – who got on well with Richard – ordered celebratory processions and bonfires, and the town's artillery was 'shot for joy'. This outpouring of public sentiment was led by Edward. 'Thank God', he exclaimed in a letter to Pope Sixtus IV, to whom he had used the Scottish campaign as a constant excuse for avoiding contributions to the papal crusade against the Turks, 'for the support received from our most loving brother.' Such was Richard's stature, Edward added, that he could probably beat the entire kingdom of Scotland on his own. Nevertheless, there emanated from the letter a sense that Richard was managing the king's expectations: the conquest of Scotland, Edward puffed to the pope, would not be long in coming, 'especially as the duke of Albany so influences their policy'.[61]

Those actually involved on the campaign, by contrast, were under no illusions about what it had, or rather hadn't, achieved. On their way back to York, one contingent of troops grumbled incessantly about how boring it had been, having spent all their time guarding the artillery and baggage train. Neither had the campaign been exactly a picture of unity. On his way into Scotland, Richard had left Lord Stanley and his men behind, handing them the unglamorous and far from simple task of trying to capture Berwick. On his return from Edinburgh, the relationship between the two, saturated with mistrust from years of friction in the north of England, reached a new low, Stanley simmering with resentment at the way he had been left 'in great danger' at Berwick. At Salford Bridge, there was a stand-off between armed retainers of the two lords: in the fight that followed, Stanley's men made off with one of Richard's banners.[62]

For Richard, it was clear that his inability to get hold of the Scottish king had cost him his grip on the Scottish capital, indeed on Scotland itself. As the earl of Warwick had shown during the civil wars of the preceding decades, for anybody ambitious to bring about regime change and wield power, possession of the king was nine-tenths of the law. In Scotland, that rule had been driven emphatically home to Richard. It was a lesson that, over the coming months, he would absorb and reflect on.

17

They Have Taken Away
the Rose of the World

In the corridors of Westminster during that summer of 1482, the afterglow of Richard's Scottish campaign soon subsided. Among the more financially minded of Edward's councillors there were mutterings about an expensive fiasco. Berwick had been a 'trifling' gain; besides which, it could only be a drain on royal resources, its upkeep costing some ten thousand marks a year. Talk had it that £100,000 had been squandered on Richard's campaign: it was an exaggerated sum, put about by Westminster-centric civil servants with an equally caricatured view of the north – a region from where, as one of them put it dismissively, 'all evil spreads'. Nevertheless, the whispering got to Edward. Having basked in the news of Berwick's capture, he was soon obsessing about how much money had been spent on it – especially when it became clear that Richard's campaign hadn't actually solved his Scottish problem. He had renewed concerns about matters at the other end of the country too.[1]

In Calais, tensions were as high as they had been for years. Following Marie of Burgundy's death earlier in the year, Louis XI had sought to exploit the resulting chaos. With his armies marching towards Flanders, Calais was as usual in the firing line. In between news of shipments and fluctuating exchange rates, the wool merchant William Cely reported how French troops had taken the town of Aire, a day's ride south of the Pale, and a castle near St Omer 'by means of treason'; now, they were marching on Gravelines, the key trading post through which English wool exports flowed to Flanders. Soon, Cely feared, the French would control all the overland routes out of Calais, leaving the business community there at the mercy of Louis. Given the situation, it was hardly surprising that William Hastings, head of the Calais garrison, had been a constant presence there since May: the town and its outlying defences bristled with his troops and a newly recruited force of a thousand Kentish archers.[2] It wasn't just the Pale's external defences that preoccupied Hastings, but – with talk of treason in the air – security within Calais itself.

That August, Hastings' agents uncovered a potentially catastrophic security breach: somebody had tried, and perhaps succeeded, in counterfeiting the keys to the city gates. The Calais council ordered a 'great inquiry' into the incident, following which blame was placed squarely on the shoulders of the man responsible for the town's defences: its porter, Robert Ratcliffe. The council, headed by Hastings himself, took no chances. Ratcliffe and all the men in his pay were to be 'put out of wages', and were to leave Calais and the marches with 'wives, children and goods' by the following Friday 'on pain of death'.[3]

Notwithstanding the febrile atmosphere, the Calais council's response seemed an overreaction. A trusted Yorkist veteran, Ratcliffe had served in Calais since the early 1470s, and had proved his loyalty to the regime time and again, especially as a naval commander in the recent war against Scotland. He hardly seemed capable of a security lapse, let alone treason. Hastings, though, had eyes and ears throughout the Pale. It was one of these informers, one John Edwards, who had made detailed allegations against Ratcliffe. Edwards had thrown fuel on the fire by alleging that Ratcliffe hadn't been acting alone. There were other, more powerful figures behind him: the queen's brother Anthony Woodville, and her son Thomas, marquis of Dorset.[4]

There was a political edge to the allegations and the Calais council's uncompromising response. Ratcliffe, Hastings' man, also had close connections with Anthony Woodville.[5] In Hastings' eyes, it was these increasingly cosy links with the Woodvilles that made Ratcliffe a problem.

Back in 1471, Edward had handed Woodville the crucial command of Calais, before changing his mind and giving it to Hastings. For Woodville, the loss rankled. He asked for an 'exemplification' or official copy of his one-time appointment as Calais' governor – just in case, at some unspecified point in the future, a chance to reclaim the post might arise. He had apparently gone further, whispering in the king's ear about Hastings' unreliability in Calais. Woodville, indeed, may have been the source of talk, back in 1477, that Hastings' Burgundian sympathies had got the better of him – jeopardizing both Edward's cordial relations with Louis XI, and Calais itself.

Dorset was also apparently 'suborning informers' to brief against Hastings, going so far as to accuse him of treason, though the friction between the two had a different source. There was much to suggest that the convivial Dorset was muscling in on Hastings' role as the fixer of all Edward's desires – and that Hastings, sharply attuned to any challenge to his pre-eminence around the king, didn't like it. Their mutual antipathy, whetted by a simmering regional rivalry in the east midlands (barely six miles separated Dorset's manor of Bradgate from Hastings' Kirby Muxloe), had long been common knowledge at court.[6] Back in the spring of 1481, when Hastings left court for Calais, an agent of the Oxfordshire knight Sir William Stonor – then attempting to push forward some business matters with the help of influential contacts close to the king – wrote to his master urgently. Stonor should come to court as soon as he could, 'for my lord of Gloucester, my lord Chamberlain, be gone, and now here be your friends'. Stonor's friends were the Woodvilles, above all his brother-in-law, who was none other than Dorset himself. The implication was clear. Hastings and Richard disliked Dorset and his 'friends' enough to try and obstruct routes to the king's favour. With both men absent, Stonor's way to Edward, smoothed by his Woodville in-laws, was clear. Since that time, things had not improved.[7]

All this made Hastings and the Calais council ready to believe the explosive allegations against Ratcliffe, and that he was acting on the Woodvilles' behalf. It was almost as though Ratcliffe had engineered the security breach in order to discredit Hastings, blame for which would be laid unequivocally at his door. In the robustness of the Calais council's response, there was more than a hint of the bad blood between Hastings, Anthony Woodville and Dorset. And when the case was quickly referred to a high-profile panel at Westminster – Hastings' informer John Edwards was hustled in front of the king and a group of his close councillors including Morton, Montgomery and the ever-reliable earl of Essex – there was a sense that Edward was moving to smooth over this growing friction between three of his leading subjects before it got out of hand.[8]

In the hearing that followed, Edwards retracted his original allegations with emphatic speed. He claimed that he been coerced into
making the story up 'of his own false imagination', and threatened
with 'the brake', the rack, unless he complied. He had made the allegations 'for fear of his life': they were, he confessed, a pack of lies,
'utterly false and untrue'.⁹ If true, Edwards' tale painted a picture of
factionalism that had taken root at Calais: that Hastings or his supporters were trying to concoct smears against the Woodvilles and
those close to them, to paint them as unreliable, disloyal and a threat
to national security. In Westminster, through the king's swift and
independent arbitration, the matter was shut down, Anthony Woodville and Dorset officially exonerated.

Yet such accusations were not washed away quite so easily, as the
queen's family knew all too well. Back in 1469, allegations of witchcraft against Elizabeth and her mother had stuck, to near-catastrophic
effect. For the Woodvilles, the nerve endings were still raw. Later that
autumn Anthony Woodville, ever-sensitive to public opinion, wrote
to his attorney general, the Middle Temple lawyer Andrew Dymmock, enclosing the text of Edwards' confession to the king's council.
He instructed Dymmock to make more copies for circulation, together
with a protestation of innocence on behalf of himself and 'my lord marquis', which was to be 'made up in as sure form as can be'.¹⁰ If Woodville
and Dorset had been cleared, the allegations of treason had done their
work. Though Edward had interposed his intimidating form between
his noblemen, the Woodvilles' quarrel with Hastings bubbled on.

After a leisurely few weeks on pilgrimage to the north Norfolk shrine
of Our Lady at Walsingham, Edward returned to London. By mid-
October he was at the Tower, closeted away with his close councillors,
discussing international affairs. Since the summer, the sclerosis had
deepened. Edward's baleful attitude towards Scotland, carefully nurtured by Richard, now manifested itself in his demand for the
repayment of his daughter Cecily's dowry. With it, Edward stamped
out any lingering hopes of her marriage to the Scottish heir, once the
hoped-for foundation of a new peace between the two kingdoms.¹¹
Across the Channel, Edward also continued to do nothing, ignoring
Maximilian's frantic pleas for English military aid, pocketing his

French pension and waiting for Louis XI to die. Even a desperately ill Louis, however, was capable of mischief. That autumn, he published the secret treaty agreed with Edward the previous spring. In the great cities of Flanders there was horror. Constitutionally disinclined to war, they had always resisted Maximilian's military ambitions. Now, with Louis' treaty proof positive that their English ally was prepared to abandon them at the drop of a hat, they clamoured for Maximilian to come to terms with the French king.[12]

To add to the general muddiness, there emerged from Edward's council meetings yet another vague notion of military action against France, the king ordering Hastings, Anthony Woodville and Dorset to form a working party to explore various options.[13] Perhaps it was nothing more than an attempt by Edward – as always, invoking the idea of a French war in order to resolve domestic dissent – to corral his bickering nobles into some kind of unity. That, and the time-honoured excuse to raise cash.

Late that autumn, Edward invited the new mayor of London, William Heryot, the city's aldermen and a number of carefully vetted citizens to hunt with him in Waltham Forest. A prosperous merchant, Heryot had a track record of showing 'pleasures to the king'. A notable donor to the regime, he had partnered with Edward on various business initiatives: Edward was keen that his willing attitude should rub off on his fellow Londoners. After shooting the king's deer in the company of a number of household knights, the assembled Londoners were brought to a newly built hunting lodge, where they were wined and dined, working their way through 'all manner of dainties' washed down by a variety of Gascon wines from the king's cellar. During the feast Hastings made cheery table talk on Edward's orders; following the meal, the Londoners were privileged with a sodden afternoon's hunting in the company of the king himself. Typically, too, the king remembered the absent ladies: in the days following, gifts of venison and a tun of Gascon wine arrived for the wives of the city's notables.[14]

Here was the king in his element: a nod and smile here, a 'good word' there, his intimacy edged with calculation. This was the corporate environment in which Edward had always thrived, and which had come to encapsulate the character of his reign. Content to get, spend and consume, luxuriating in his own charismatic majesty,

Edward's rule combined bonhomie, greed, rapacity and – through the haze of his excesses – a narrow-eyed watchfulness, alert to financial irregularities and wandering loyalties alike. Not that anybody contemplated disloyalty – at least, not in public. Under the practised charm, the threat of a terrifying, indiscriminate violence lay ready to erupt against anybody who crossed the interests of the king or his family. This was what Edward's rule had come to – and, for some, especially its beneficiaries, these blurred, limited horizons were enough. England was at peace, with itself and with its neighbours, ruled by a solvent and more or less functioning king. If that meant a country held tight in the grip of the royal family and an autocratic monarch who, all ambition spent, seemed content to let his kingship spool out in an endless round of self-pleasure and the empty repetitions of a worn-out foreign policy, so be it.

Christmas that year, at Westminster, seemed to one onlooker even more extravagant than usual, a display of opulence befitting a 'mighty kingdom'. The preparations had involved an extensive renovation of various 'ruinous buildings', a new privy kitchen, and the installation of a new great chamber in Queen Elizabeth's apartment complex, no expense spared.[15] The palace was 'filled with riches': cupboards adorned with the contents of Edward's jewelhouse on public display, glinting richly in the candlelight; tapestry-lined walls, including the king's latest acquisition, a vast multi-piece arras depicting the history of Thebes, newly imported from Flanders for the princely sum of £300; cellars fully stocked with wine. Enjoying the festive hospitality was an international guest list including 'men from every nation', underscoring England's place at the centre of world events.

At the heart of the festivities was, of course, the family. On show was the dynasty's future, Edward and Elizabeth's 'handsome and delightful' children. Foremost among them were the two princes – Edward, recently turned twelve, a confident boy whose sophisticated education enhanced his natural authority; and his nine-year-old brother Richard – together with their older sister, the blonde, beautiful sixteen-year-old Elizabeth, and the king's bastard son Arthur Plantagenet, a boy of 'virtuous and lovely disposition'.[16] The king, though, was not to be upstaged.

Always sensitive to the latest fashions, that season Edward appeared in public in a succession of the 'costliest clothes', in head-turning style: the robes with full sleeves, styled after the 'monastic frock', their insides lined with the most luxurious of furs. This new wardrobe, declared one bystander, had a sensational impact, the king displayed 'like a new and incomparable spectacle' – though, he added, the king naturally 'always stood out because of his elegant figure'.[17]

It was this last observation that gave the game away. Edward's habit of showing himself off in lingering public displays and walkabouts had turned into a distorted self-parody. He seemed oblivious to the extent to which his 'fine stature' had become bloated with years of gorging; oblivious, too, to the fact that onlookers praising his regal appearance did so with tongue firmly in cheek.[18] In the last days of December, though, came a hammer-blow against which Edward's self-love was no protection at all.

On 23 December 1482 in the city of Arras, Louis XI and Maximilian finally came face to face: Louis ill and frail, the youthful Maximilian exuding barely disguised frustration. Sick of the Burgundian duke's inability to offer any kind of governance in war-torn Flanders, the Flemish cities of Bruges, Ghent and Ypres had taken matters into their own hands, negotiating a peace with the French king. That day, Louis and a reluctant Maximilian put their signatures to a peace treaty in which 'all rancors, hatreds and malevolences' between the two warring princes were to be forgiven. At the treaty's heart was a marriage between Maximilian's two-year-old daughter Margaret and Louis XI's son and heir Charles – the boy who had been previously, and in Louis' case unwillingly, promised to Edward's daughter Elizabeth. In wording that dripped with condescension, it was Louis' 'pleasure' that the king of England be included in the new agreement. This was window dressing. Edward had had no involvement in the treaty at all. He had been blindsided.[19]

Edward shouldn't have been surprised. For years, his envoys and advisers had been telling him that Louis was using every trick in the book to entice Burgundy away from an alliance with England. But in playing Louis and Maximilian off against one another, Edward had characteristically convinced himself of his own desirability, that both princes needed him more than he needed them. Increasingly, though,

Edward's foreign policy vacillations had become the projections of his own inner turmoil – and, perhaps, his inability both to relinquish the idea of an aggressive, conquering England and to put that idea into practice. Edward had effectively been negotiating not with his neighbours but with himself. Now, reality had intruded. As the light poured in, it dawned on Edward that, in the great game of international power politics, he had been spun along by Louis – the king on whose imminent demise he had been relying – and, finally, snared in his web.

Edward's once-special relationship with Burgundy was in tatters. To add insult to injury, two of the noblemen on the pro-French regency council of Burgundy, now mandated to govern the principality, were the sons of Edward's old ally Louis of Gruuthuse, and the Bastard of Burgundy, whose joust against Anthony Woodville some fifteen years previously had appeared to herald a new dawn in Anglo-Burgundian relations.[20] Ripped apart too was the French marriage alliance over which Edward had obsessed, that of his daughter Elizabeth to the dauphin. His brusque rejection of the Scottish marriage now looked horribly premature, especially as James III had refused to return his dowry. Worse still, the taps of Edward's French pension had now been firmly and conclusively turned off. Humiliated on the international stage, his dynastic plans in shreds, Edward was 'deeply troubled and grieved', a grief quickly transmuted into a vicious, vindictive rage.[21]

That January, as Parliament opened in a wintry Westminster, a small printed pamphlet was doing the rounds. Called 'The Promise of Matrimony', it had come from the press of a Flemish printer named William de Machlinia. From Mechelin – or, in its French iteration Malines, the adoptive home town of Edward IV's bibliophile sister Margaret – Machlinia had set up shop on Fleet Street near the inns of court, specializing in the printing of lawbooks. Although a legal document, 'The Promise of Matrimony' was far removed from his typical output. It stitched together two contracts. First was the nuptial agreement – the so-called 'Promise' of the title – signed by Edward and Louis at Picquigny back in 1475; the second was a recently obtained copy of the Treaty of Arras, in which Louis, so the English narrative went, had broken the marriage contract behind Edward's back. Combined, they amounted to a damning portrayal of French perfidy: a simple and powerful piece of rhetoric clearly intended to whip up anti-French antagonism and win support for a new round of parliamentary taxation for a war against France. Back in 1472 Edward's then chancellor, John Fortescue, had done something similar in conjunction with the manuscript copyshops of Paternoster Row. This time, Edward – or rather, his chancellor John Russell, a man with a deep appreciation of the printed word – had enlisted the power of new technology to create the first known piece of printed political propaganda in English.[22]

As usual, Edward had done everything to ensure a complaisant Parliament. The house of Commons was stuffed with MPs loyal to the regime's key figures. Anthony Woodville, writing to his attorney-general Andrew Dymmock, had urged him to fix parliamentary seats for five of his own retainers and advised him to 'get yourself one' into the bargain. In addition, the speaker, John Wood, a veteran Exchequer official, was a royal servant steeped in financial knowhow.[23]

In a regal harangue Edward revealed to the Commons 'the whole series' of Louis XI's 'great frauds', perhaps brandishing Machlinia's pamphlet as he did so, and asked them to help him 'take vengeance' on France. The tactic worked: a tax was duly voted – along with a tax on wealthy foreigners, which always played well.

War, though, was a chimera, and everybody knew it. For all his fury, there was no chance of Edward mounting another invasion of France. As had been abundantly clear in his failed campaign of eight years before, the resources needed were so substantial, the preparation so complex, that even the most generous parliamentary tax wouldn't cover it – and this time, Parliament hadn't been particularly generous. Given his track record, Edward didn't dare ask for more. As he put it lamely to Parliament, vengeance on France was to be exacted 'as often as opportunities of time and circumstance might permit': hardly a ringing declaration of war.

In an effort to underscore the regime's martial credentials, Edward put on parliamentary record his gratitude to his 'entirely beloved brother' Richard for having secured a foothold in the Scottish borderlands, which Richard now aimed 'to get and subdue' in future'.[24] In the wreckage of the king's foreign policy, Richard's modest achievements of the previous summer took on an added lustre.

Edward seized desperately at his brother's triumphs, and at the possibility of further conquest: days before Parliament's opening, envoys from the Scottish pretender Albany had arrived in London, announcing his fresh defection to England. In order to support Richard in his ambitions of Scottish conquest, Edward now handed him an astonishing grant – one that, he told Parliament, had recently been agreed in talks with his brother.

First, he conferred on Richard the hereditary wardenship of the West March – the western borderlands with Scotland – along with a large portfolio of estates in the region. This was a prelude to the main event: the creation for Richard of a new county palatine, over which Richard and his heirs would have exclusive and perpetual jurisdiction. While it wasn't everything it looked at first glance – the county, which consisted of all the land Richard could annex for himself and the English crown in the western Scottish borderlands, as yet only existed on the parchment roll of parliamentary record – it nevertheless confirmed Richard's unprecedented domination of England's north. No English nobleman since the Norman Conquest had possessed the power that Edward now placed in Richard's hands.[25]

All of which was consistent with Edward's 'family first' strategy of placing as much power as possible in the hands of those 'high in the king's blood' – for it was they who bore the primary responsibility for 'the great security, honour, defence and politic governance' of the kingdom. Where the policy had failed spectacularly with Clarence, Richard was proof positive of its success. Consistently alive to the king's 'good pleasures and commandments', Richard had reaped dazzling reward.[26]

That February, a new sumptuary law underscored Edward's familial vision. The wearing of cloth-of-gold and purple silk was restricted to the king and queen, the king's mother Cecily duchess of York, his children and his brothers and sisters. Nobody else, 'of what estate, degree or condition he be', however exalted in rank, could wear these luxurious fabrics. For Edward there was the family, then a vast gulf and then the rest of the nobility. All this was now evident in parliamentary legislation that represented the latest stage of Edward's familial carve-up of his kingdom. In Wales and the Marches, where his firstborn son's household and council – dominated by the queen's family – held sway,

William Herbert, son of Edward's Welsh 'master-lock', was formally removed from the principality that his father had once dominated on the king's behalf. Even those in the king's favour suffered, Parliament ratifying the most egregious land grab of recent years: the transferral of the vast estates of the duke of Norfolk to Edward's second son, whose little child-wife Anne Mowbray, heiress to the dukedom, had died two years earlier. Now, instead of reverting to their original heirs, the lands became the property of Edward's son – again falling under the control of his mother's Woodville family, in whose care he was – and, should he die childless, the crown. Prominent among those who lost out was the Norfolk knight John Howard. Over the years, Howard's loyalty to the regime had been constant. But in this case, at any rate, it went unrewarded. As far as the king was concerned, family came first. Like Herbert, Howard had no option but to put up with it. [27]

As the days lengthened, Edward's fury subsided into one of the bouts of listlessness, 'sadness', with which those close to him had become all too familiar. Physicians and leading councillors alike were concerned about the 'pensivous thoughts', the 'greatest melancholy' in which Edward was now submerged. If the king's bingeing and promiscuity formed the underlying cause, they opined, Louis XI's 'crafty and fraudulent dealing' had been the trigger. But it wasn't just Edward's mind that refused to function. His body had had enough.[28]

On Tuesday 25 March, in Holy Week, Edward made the journey from Windsor downstream to Westminster. There over Easter he fell ill and was closeted away in his privy chamber, unable to move, let alone get out of bed, despite the allure of the great feasting going on elsewhere in the palace.[29] Opinion varied as to the diagnosis. One commentator heard that he had gone fishing and had come back with a chill, which had become complicated; another suggested that the malaria Edward picked up on his French campaign had returned with a vengeance. Amid general medical ignorance – Edward, physicians pronounced with authority, 'was not affected by any known type of disease' – rumours of poison abounded. Perhaps the most convincing explanation came from Philippe de Commynes away in France. Having already seen his master Louis XI survive an apoplexy, Commynes suggested that the same thing had now happened to Edward, his massive consumption of alcohol and hypertension-inducing lifestyle now catching up with him in one massive cerebral haemorrhage.[30]

In the fevered, speculative atmosphere at court the king's death was reported prematurely by one twitchy agent in the pay of his brother Richard. Carried fast up the Great North Road, news reached York on 6 April. A hastily arranged funeral mass in the Minster the following day was invalidated with equal haste after it turned out the king was still alive.

Over the next days Edward carried on, prone and immobile but apparently lucid. Surrounded by his coterie of helpless doctors, servants padding silently around his chamber, the bedridden king started to prepare for the death whose approach he had already started to discern. In consultation with the executors – men like John Morton and Thomas Rotherham – who now hovered at his bedside, Edward reviewed the will and testament that he had drawn up back in 1475 before his abortive invasion of France, adding codicils here and there.[31] As he put the kingdom in readiness to hand on to his twelve-year-old son, one issue above all gnawed at Edward's mind: the messy squabbles between certain of his lords, whose control would be rather more tricky for a king on the verge of adolescence, however fine his political education.

The vendetta most urgently in need of resolution was that between his closest friend Hastings and the queen's family. Anthony Woodville was away in Ludlow with Prince Edward, so it was Dorset who, along with Hastings, was ushered into the presence of the dying king, his bulk propped up on a mound of pillows. As they stood at his bedside Edward weakly urged them to reconcile for the sake of his sons; then, finding the effort too much, lay down on his right side and gazed up expectantly at the two lords. Moved by the sight of their ailing king, Hastings and Dorset told Edward what he wanted to hear, tearfully clasping hands with each other in mutual forgiveness and reconciliation. Perhaps, at that moment, they convinced themselves they meant it.[32]

Two days later, in the early hours of Wednesday 9 April, Edward died. He was a few weeks short of his forty-first birthday. In the glimmering rushlight, air thick with incense, his close servants wept by his bedside. At its head was the confessor to whom the dying king had made his remorseful last confession, promising, desperately, to make amends for any financial wrongs done and debts owed before he was summoned to God to make his own final accounting. He had, remarked an anonymous member of his government, made 'the best of ends for a worldly prince' – although, as the same chronicler drily put it, it helped that Edward was 'carried off immediately' before he could change his mind. Then the deferential tone was resumed: the late king had, he concluded, put his affairs in order impeccably, and had made 'full and wise' arrangements for the succession.

Yet Edward's end had come suddenly. It had caught many by surprise and left England with a young monarch who, while widely acknowledged to be kingly material, was not yet of age. The question now, as the late king's confessor bent over his body, fingers sliding eyelids over his sightless gaze, was how to put those arrangements into practice.[33] And, as Edward's corpse began to stiffen, people's thoughts began to turn towards the new dispensation, and their place in it.

It was still dark when people started to slip out of Westminster with news of Edward's death. In the depths of the palace, Queen Elizabeth summoned her dead husband's councillors to discuss next steps. Two were sent to the mayor of London, with orders for him to review the city's security arrangements in light of the king's unexpected demise; and messengers were dispatched to Ludlow, to tell Prince Edward that his father was dead and that he was now Edward V, king of England. As bells tolled across Westminster and London, a stream of agents left court carrying the news to nobles and gentry across the country: to Richard, at his Middleham base; and to Hastings' garrison at Calais.[34]

Later that morning Edward's washed, anointed body, massively naked except for a cloth from his navel to his knees, was placed on a board in Westminster Hall. For some ten hours people filed past, witnessing the fact of his death: members of the late king's household, lords who happened to be 'in London or near about', the mayor of London Sir Edmund Shaw and other city dignitaries. That evening the body was taken away, eviscerated and embalmed with spices, wrapped in fine linen bound with silk cords, then in layers of silk, velvet and cloth-of-gold. Next morning, the coffined corpse was carried into St Stephen's Chapel, which was draped in black, and placed on a hearse illuminated by thousands of candles. Over the next eight days there unfolded an elaborate sequence of divine offices for the dead sung by the chapel royal, intercessions for the late king's soul; by night, selected lords and members of Edward's household, their names drawn up on a watch roll, kept vigil over his body. As they watched, in another part of the palace the royal council, in its customary role as caretaker government, deliberated the transference of power from the old regime to the new.[35]

There were some key absences. Most significant were those of the new king's two uncles: Anthony Woodville, at Ludlow with the king himself; and Richard, still in the north. Also missing were great magnates like the earl of Northumberland and the duke of Buckingham, away on his Gloucestershire estates. Yet around the council table sat a group of experienced royal councillors, loyal to the wishes of the late king whom they had served, and now to his son and heir. Alongside the likes of Edward's chancellor Thomas Rotherham and John Morton, both of whom had been involved in the recent additions to the royal will, sat William Hastings and John Howard, John de la Pole, earl of Lincoln and the young heir to the duke of Suffolk, and household men like Sir Thomas Montgomery and Edward's brother-in-law Thomas St Leger. Prominent too were members of the queen's family, chief among them the marquis of Dorset and, at the head of the table, Elizabeth Woodville herself. Behind her regal poise she was still absorbing the shock of her husband's death and her new role, at the age of forty-six, as mother to the king of England.[36]

Among the councillors there was, in the words of one anonymous commentator – a man then present in the palace, if not in the council chamber itself – complete consensus about what should happen next. 'All who were present keenly desired that this prince should succeed his father in all his glory.' In other words, Edward's young son and heir should be crowned and should rule in person. This keenness was manifest in the early date agreed for his coronation: 4 May, barely three and a half weeks away.

On the face of it, the crowning of a twelve-year-old might have seemed unusual. But to a council packed with men steeped in legal and historical precedent, and with sharp memories of the dynastic upheavals of recent decades, it was an obvious step. While Prince Edward was a minor, he was by all accounts an intelligent and active boy, who would provide the ideal focus for his subjects' loyalties. Besides which, there were precedents. The great Edward III had ascended the throne at fourteen, while – an admittedly less auspicious example – Richard II had been crowned at the age of ten. In his will, Edward IV had underscored his desire for continuity: what more continuous than for government to continue seamlessly under his son? Here was a rare chance to effect a smooth handover of power, one in which everything might, more or less, remain the same.[37]

The councillors, accordingly, threw their collective weight behind the new king. But, as everybody knew, just because the king was crowned did not mean that he would begin to rule. His majority, indeed, was four years away. In such situations, the precedent of previous royal minorities suggested that a governing council should rule in the boy's name, until he was able to do so himself. Here, too, the arrangement seemed to make sense. But, as the council got down to business, its fleeting unanimity began to buckle and splinter over the role of the queen's family in the new regime.

The problems started with the provision for the new king's continued upbringing, his 'government' or 'tuition'. His current governor, who had supervised his education for the last decade, was his maternal uncle Anthony Woodville – and indeed, Woodville's authority over the young boy had been reconfirmed only weeks before by Edward IV. This authority, however, applied to the boy as prince of Wales, not as king. When it was proposed that existing arrangements continue, and that the boy be placed in the custody of his mother's Woodville family, trenchant objections were raised by a knot of council members. There was no way, they stated emphatically, that the young king should be given into the care of the 'uncles and brothers on the mother's side'. Members of the queen's family, indeed, 'should be absolutely forbidden to have control of the person of the young man until he came of age'.[38]

There was a trace of moral concern in these objections. It was one thing for the Woodville 'uncles and brothers' – Dorset and Sir Edward Woodville to the fore – to have been the ringleaders in Edward IV's life of vice and dissipation; quite another for them to have the rule of his twelve-year-old son. But what concerned the council most of all was to balance conflicting political interests: interests that, in the absence of the late king's massive centripetal force, threatened to destabilize the government. While Edward was alive, the 'queen's blood' were part of the extended royal family. Now, with Edward's vast shadow removed, they were exposed in plain sight as a discrete political bloc. Suddenly, Anthony Woodville's reinforced 'authority' over the prince, and his power to raise men in the Welsh Marches, combined with Dorset's control over the Tower and the royal treasury, assumed – at least for some on the council – an actively menacing valence, as though Woodville custody of the prince threatened to transmute into Woodville control of the kingdom.[39] For those old enough to remember the council's unavailing attempts to control the virulent factionalism of the 1450s, it was essential to avoid a repeat. Unity was vital.

Quickly, these concerns focused on the upcoming coronation. It would, certain councillors stated, be difficult to preserve a status quo among the lords 'if those of the queen's relatives who were most influential with the prince' – Anthony Woodville and Sir Richard Grey – were allowed to escort the new king to London 'with an immoderate number of horse'.[40] Nobody wanted noblemen and their private armies facing off in London's streets for control of the boy. The most vocal advocate for restricting the size of the king's escort, and for the reining in of Woodville influence more generally, was William Hastings. And while Hastings' views may have been 'sound', as the anonymous commentator put it, he had more pressing reasons than most to hold them.

Days before, Hastings and Dorset had shaken hands over the body of their dying king. As far as Hastings was concerned, the reconciliation was purely cosmetic. The Woodvilles' position now had worrying implications for his own: should they get their hands on 'supreme power', they would 'sharply avenge' the injuries he had done them. While the extent of this bad blood was unclear, it was unsurprising that Hastings should feel exposed. All his wealth and power derived from the late king, with whom he could 'do anything', in whose all-enveloping shelter he had spent the last quarter-century and alongside whom, in his will, he had stipulated that he should be buried. But Edward was now gone – and, as Hastings knew perfectly well, changes of regime tended to be accompanied by wide-ranging reshuffles, in which the new king's household men took the places and offices of the old. In this case, Edward V's establishment was currently ruled by the queen's family, which had a deep-rooted animus against Hastings.[41]

Hastings' anxiety gave force to his protestations. If the new king did not come with a 'modest force', he stated flatly, he would 'flee' to Calais and await developments there. Nobody present needed reminding of the significance of Hastings' threat to retreat to a base that had been the springboard for Edward's own march on London in 1460, and Warwick and Clarence's rebellion nine years later; a base which, given the continued insecurity on the Franco-Burgundian border, was currently bristling with some fifteen hundred troops, more than double its usual strength.[42]

Queen Elizabeth was quick to conciliate. Keen to 'extinguish every spark' of antagonism, she assured Hastings that she would write to her son the king, recommending he bring with him no more than two thousand men. With this gesture, Elizabeth acknowledged the council's concerns about balance and showed that her family, too, wanted unity. After all, it was to the Woodvilles' advantage for arrangements regarding control of the young king to stay precisely as they were. Given this, reducing the size of the king's retinue was an easy concession to make. Hastings pronounced himself happy. He was sure that Richard and the duke of Buckingham, men in whom he had 'the greatest trust', would bring with them similar numbers.[43] Balance would be preserved.

On 14 April, five days after leaving Westminster, a royal messenger dismounted at Ludlow Castle, and news of the 'lamentable and most sorrowful tidings' of his father's death was broken to Prince Edward. Updates on the council's deliberations followed soon after. Within two days the prince, comforted in his 'sorrow and pensiveness' by his uncle and governor Anthony Woodville, was echoing the council's resolution. In a letter to the town of Lynn on the north Norfolk coast – a letter almost certainly penned for him by Woodville, whose

town it was – the boy proclaimed his intention to 'govern, rule and protect this our realm of England', and to be 'crowned at Westminster'.[44]

Word of Edward IV's death had already reached Richard at Middleham, on the other side of the country. Since the first rumours of his
brother's demise, Richard had probably been anticipating news – but,
in any case, he had his ear to the ground. His lines of communication
with London and the southeast were exceptional: the previous summer, the system of posts put in place to ensure rapid communication
between him and Edward during his invasion of Scotland had brought
news to the king of Berwick's surrender – a distance of some 340
miles – in an astonishing thirty-six hours.[45] Now, in the days following his brother's death, a constant stream of messengers shuttled
between Westminster and north Yorkshire with news of discussions
in the council chamber. Many of these agents, according to 'common
report', were from Hastings. As Richard assembled the retinues that
would accompany him south to his nephew's coronation, he digested
the council's discussions, filtered for him through Hastings' uneasy
perspective on events.

Edward IV's final journey started on the evening of Wednesday 16
April. Following mass in Westminster Abbey, his coffin was heaved
onto a carriage draped in black velvet and, over the coffin, a black
pall with a cross picked out in white cloth-of-gold. Atop it was a life-
size effigy, 'like to the similitude of the king', dressed in his royal
robes and crown, orb and sceptre clutched in its stiff hands. Drawn
by six black-caparisoned coursers, and protected by a canopy of
imperial purple borne by four of the late king's household knights,
the solemn cavalcade set off up King Street towards Charing Cross, a
company of banner-bearing knights and squires headed by John
Howard, themselves led by a gaggle of heralds and bishops. After
overnighting at Syon monastery, the procession halted the following
day at Eton; there, bishops John Russell and John Morton censed the
coffined body, bathing it in drifts of incense as the college's assembled students knelt murmuring prayers, white-surpliced, bare-headed,
tapers in one hand and psalters in the other. Then the procession
moved on, crossing the Thames at Windsor Bridge and towards the
castle with its great drum keep.[46]

In the castle's lower ward stood Edward's new chapel of St George, a half-realized vision in perpendicular Gothic. His coffin was borne up the nave, whose lower walls had begun to rise from their foundations, and into the choir, in a more advanced stage of completion: its pendant vaulting soaring overhead, windows glazed and carved stalls in place, walls and floor lined with black cloth. At the north-eastern end, ready to receive the body, was the newly finished 'sepulture' and, above it, the chantry chapel where masses would be sung in perpetuity for the dead king's soul. Dominating the choir was a massive wooden hearse, a multi-storey wooden stage, 'marvellous well wrought', festooned with banners, flags and escutcheons, in which the coffin was placed. That night, after the Office of the Dead had been sung, a 'great watch' was kept over the body by lords, knights, squires and yeomen of the late king's chamber and household.[47]

Inside the candlelit hearse stood a group of lords, among them Hastings and Dorset, uncomfortably close, Edward's household steward Lord Stanley, and John Howard. The rest, hooded and in mourning black, stood in concentric circles radiating outward from the hearse: from the late king's brother-in-law Thomas St Leger and his giant master of horse John Cheyne; to the Oxfordshire knight Sir William Stonor and the gentleman usher William Collingbourne. Throughout the night they remained shoulder to shoulder, constant and motionless, their shrouded faces illuminated by the burning brands they held, the last collective expression of a household's unswerving loyalty to the king they had served.[48]

The next morning the final rites began, commendations of the departed soul followed by masses and offerings. Edward's richly embroidered coat of arms, shield and crowned helmet were all offered up to his former chancellor Thomas Rotherham in his capacity as archbishop of York. Then, through the doors in the temporary west wall, came John Cheyne leading a warhorse in black trappings; riding it was Sir William Parr, bareheaded and in white armour, gripping a battleaxe point downwards. Riding the length of the choir, Parr dismounted and, led by the heralds of the absent Richard and the duke of Buckingham, made his way to the high altar, offering himself to God.

The solemn ritual was punctuated by an unseemly scuffle between the two offerors, lords Berkeley and Maltravers, as to who should stand on the favoured right side. Berkeley lost out, his claims of senior rank trumped by Maltravers' lineage. Along with John Howard, Berkeley was one of those who, due to benefit from the death of the old duke of Norfolk, had been passed over when Edward IV settled the duke's entire inheritance on his second son, Richard. Having kept his head down while Edward was alive, Berkeley was now flexing his muscles. While his spat with Maltravers was brief and quickly resolved, it was a sign that, with Edward not yet in the grave, the political order was already loosening.[49]

The mass ended, offerings of cloth-of-gold were laid on Edward's coffin. One herald, vainly trying to scribble the offerors' order of precedence as he peered over the packed crowds, managed to note that the last to offer – first in 'nearness of blood' to the late king, was Edward's teenage nephew John de la Pole, earl of Lincoln, who, in the absence of the dead king's brother Richard, was designated chief mourner.[50]

Finally, with the great officers of Edward's household gathered round the open grave, the coffin was lowered into the ground. Together, Hastings, Stanley, the treasurer Sir John Elrington and Sir William Parr, all weeping openly, snapped their staves of office and threw them into the grave, after their king. One herald, a Portuguese named Roger Machado, glossed the self-evident symbolism. They were now, he said, 'men without a master and without office'.

It was a sentiment echoed in one of the many verse epitaphs and laments for the king's soul that, painted on placards and boards, hung around his tomb: a poem that came from the heart of Edward's household, told in the voice of one of the servants left bereft by his passing. This was a narrator struggling to deal with the shock of the king's death: he 'was here yesterday', went the uncomprehending refrain. For him, Edward was the peerless war-leader, the wellspring of knighthood, the 'freshest' in battle, the 'most dread' prince whose deeds were immortalized 'in gests, in romances, in chronicles near and far'. In his eyes, even Edward's debacle in France eight years before had acquired the lustre of an epic enterprise, the French miraculously subdued both by 'force and might' yet 'without stroke'. Edward, too, had made Scotland 'yield' – almost, it seemed, in person. This, though, was no sycophant. Rather, it was the hard, unyielding loyalty of the household retainer: a man who had followed his king willingly into battle and who had seen him 'in every field, full ready for our right', whose identity and cause were inseparable from those of his king. For him Edward, magnificent in his robes of estate, was an affirmation of his own place in the world: indeed, 'it was a world to see him ride about'. He was the 'sun, the rose, the sunbeam' – never had Edward's badges seemed more apt – and his 'royal company', his household men, bathed in his lustre. The king's household was this author's universe: his mind's eye recollected Edward's retinues, 'his lords, his knights all', his 'palaces made of lime and stone' and his household servants dining together, breaking bread in the hall. Then, suddenly, that constant, glorious light had been snuffed out.

Now, a desolate present stretched before the narrator. In the Westminster streets, Edward's weeping, black-clad retinue shuffled towards him – mere 'wretches' now, deprived of 'the lantern and the light'. Coming to terms with this barren, insecure new reality, he choked, 'makes my heart quake'.[51]

What now could loyal followers of Edward IV do? For the poet, the answer was simple: there was 'no choice, no other grace' than to be faithful to the memory of their dead master, to death. But for the late king's servants, as they accompanied Edward's coffin to its last resting place at Windsor and stood vigilant together through the night, the pressing question was what form that fidelity might take. After all, masterless in this insecure new world, they needed to find a new light to follow. This was no literary conceit. Back in 1461, after the death of Charles VII of France, his former chamberlain summed up perfectly this reactive compound of loyalty and self-interest. Addressing the late king's household, he told them that he 'and all other servants had lost a master'. And, he continued, with brutal clarity, 'every man must think for himself, and each one should provide for himself.'[52]

Now, in that spring of 1483, Edward's servants were thinking along much the same lines. Nobody more so than the man whose perspective adhered most closely to that of the devastated, lamenting poet, and who perhaps gave a similar speech to the late king's household: his own chamberlain, William, Lord Hastings.

*

On Saturday 19 April, the day after Edward's last rites, as London's mayor and aldermen met to discuss their reception of the new king, the council convened again. In the meantime, two letters had arrived from Richard. The first – warm, comforting, 'loving' – was written to Queen Elizabeth Woodville herself. Consoling her in her loss, Richard assured her that he would offer 'submission, fealty, and all that was due from him to his lord and king, Edward V, the first-born son of his brother the dead king, and queen'. The second letter, a precise edge to its courtesy, was addressed to the council.

Apprised of the council's deliberations, Richard set out his own position clearly. Drawing attention to his record of unimpeachable loyalty to his brother the late king, 'at home and abroad, in peace and war', he pledged an equal loyalty to the new king, and indeed all his brother's offspring if – 'God forbid' – the youth should die. He would lay his life on the line to protect the children from danger. Then, he came to the crunch.

Richard asked the councillors, as they made their plans for the new government, to bear in mind his own 'deserts'. He was, he stated, entitled to the government of the kingdom: both by law and as set out in his brother's will. Asking that the councillors consider his record of service and what was best for the country, he ended with an emphatic reiteration: 'nothing contrary to law and his brother's desire', he told the council, 'could be decreed without harm'.[53] While Richard's request was open-ended, everybody knew what he meant. He wanted to be protector.

Richard's demand had the council scrambling for historical precedent. The previous century was littered with useful examples of 'protectors', from Humphrey duke of Gloucester's rule during the long minority of his nephew Henry VI to Richard duke of York's two protectorates during the adult Henry's incapacitating bouts of mental illness in the 1450s. None, however, adumbrated what Richard now had in mind.

Over the previous hundred years or so, when councils tried to establish a working government in the absence of a sane or adult monarch, they had always come back to the same problem. If you appointed a protector of the realm, usually the foremost nobleman of royal blood, you risked handing that nobleman quasi-regal authority.

Such powers were temptingly open to abuse: indeed, back in 1377, Richard II's uncle John of Gaunt was forced to issue a public denial to Parliament that he wanted the throne for himself.[54] Consequently, councils had always resisted demands for a full regency, in which royal powers were conferred on a proxy king. More than that, they had always split the role of protector in two. Nobody, however close to the king by blood, was allowed to hold the post of 'tutela' – tutor or governor of the king – and 'defensor', defender of the realm. Back in 1428, when Henry VI's uncle Humphrey of Gloucester had lobbied incessantly to be given the care of the young king, the council was unmoving: in handing him the title of 'protector', they clarified that it was explicitly not 'the name of tutor, lieutenant, governor, nor of regent, nor no name that should import authority of governance of the land'. Protector, here, was simply another term for 'chief councillor', with special responsibility for the kingdom's security – a sop to Humphrey's sense of his own dignity rather than anything else. During Henry VI's periods of insanity, Richard of York was handed precisely the same powers as Humphrey: powers which York swore not to use without the council's backing.[55]

Yet this combined governance – protectorship of the realm and custody of the king – was apparently what Richard had now requested, citing both 'law' and his 'brother's desire'. In his last will and testament Edward had, so it was said, entrusted his sons 'to the tuition' – the upbringing – 'of Richard his brother'. Yet even if Edward had granted these powers on his deathbed – which, given the lack of precedent, was highly unlikely – it was academic, given that a dead king's will had no permanent force in law. Neither did Richard's close blood relationship with the new king carry any legal weight.[56]

To a council determined to preserve a delicate balance between interest groups, such precedent was a helpful prop. Nevertheless, one caucus of conciliar opinion – the same group that had protested so vigorously against the dominance of the Woodville 'uncles and brothers' – insisted on tabling Richard's request. Accordingly, the council was presented with a choice. The first was that Richard head up a regency government. The second was that he be offered precisely the same role that Duke Humphrey had been given some half-century before: the role of chief councillor in a governing council that would help the new king to reign in his own right, with the honorific title of 'protector'. The council voted 'in a majority' for the second option. Edward V would rule with the guidance of a council, his uncle Richard at its head.

Even now, there were voices of caution. Such decisions about the government's composition and the coronation needed to involve Richard, the realm's greatest magnate of royal blood: they were too important to be finalized in his absence. If Richard arrived with everything settled, especially his own role in his nephew's government, he might receive the council's decision 'reluctantly'. He might, indeed, 'upset everything'.

At which point Thomas, marquis of Dorset cut in: 'we are so important', he breezed, 'that we can make and enforce these decisions, even without the king's uncle'. On a point of procedure Dorset was right: the council did have executive power. But to some on the council, the comment dripped with contempt and impunity – and, moreover, it indicated the Woodvilles' real agenda to arrange the government to suit themselves.

Dorset then proceeded to back up his words with deeds. The new government's structure was ratified, and the council took immediate steps to combat French aggression, mandating Dorset to 'keep the sea'. The queen's youngest brother, Sir Edward Woodville, was instructed to assemble a navy and an expeditionary force of two thousand marines, for which he was given £3,670 in cash out of the royal treasury now under Dorset's control in the Tower. A detachment of three hundred men was dispatched to reinforce the garrison at Calais: an urgent and necessary intervention for the defence of the realm, or – seen another way – an attempt to prevent the enclave's lieutenant, Hastings, from asserting his military independence. The Woodvilles had played everything by the book. Through the council, it seemed that they were set to dominate the minority rule of Edward V.[57]

By this time, Richard was on his way south. At York, he stopped to hold obsequies for his brother in the Minster – a funeral service 'full of tears' – and to make a public commitment to the new regime. Summoning all the region's nobility, he made them swear binding oaths of loyalty to the new king, Edward V. Richard, it was noted, led by

example: he 'swore first of all'.[58] The summons also had another purpose: some of these nobles and their men would accompany Richard
to London, swelling his company to the permitted two thousand
men. And, as well as receiving updates from Hastings, while in York
Richard received another messenger, this time from the duke of
Buckingham.

Buckingham's adult life had been an exercise in frustration. One of
the greatest noblemen in the land, married to one of the queen's sisters, he was exceptionally close to the centre of power but, under
Edward, excluded from it. He had been shouldered out of his family's
traditional spheres of influence in the Welsh Marches, where the
prince's council now dominated, and the north midlands, where the
lands he coveted were bestowed instead on Hastings. Buckingham's
role in the Yorkist establishment had been restricted to walk-on parts,
as a glittering courtly bauble and occasional useful idiot: in his honorific role of high steward, he had rubber-stamped Clarence's guilty
verdict and death sentence. Whether or not Buckingham resented his
childhood marriage to Katherine Woodville – though vocal in his
'loathing' for women in general, there was no sign that he detested
his wife with any particular vehemence – he resented her family, who
had come to represent everything that he felt had held him back.

During Buckingham's childhood years in Edward's household,
Richard had been a regular presence at his side, the two boys appearing together in the regime's rituals and ceremonies. The relationship
appeared to have endured. Shortly after Buckingham received news
of Edward's death, he sent a trusted messenger to Richard, promising
his support in this 'new world', and offering to attend on him with a
thousand men should need arise. Richard, it was said, sent the messenger back with thanks and 'diverse privy instructions by mouth'.

Meanwhile, both Richard and Buckingham were in touch with the
new king at Ludlow. Edward V and his advisers were happy to accept
Richard's proposal of a rendezvous on the way to London, so that
they, together with Buckingham, could escort the king into the city
together, a picture of the new regime's unity. While Northampton, on
Watling Street, was on Richard's route south, for the king's retinues
it represented a substantial detour through the midlands. For them,
the more direct way to London was down the Thames valley, the

road Edward and his Marcher men had taken after Mortimer's Cross over twenty years before. Reflecting the prevailing spirit of compromise, however, they agreed to the meeting point.[59]

As a fretful Hastings waited in London, raising his own men – 'I will and desire you', he wrote urgently to John Paston the younger in the Pale fortress of Guisnes, 'to come over in all goodly haste' – Richard rode south out of York, still in mourning black, at the head of six hundred horsemen, recruiting more as he went. On the other side of the country, the young king's household left Ludlow on 24 April; shortly after, Buckingham rode out of the west country. The three retinues would converge at Northampton on the 29th, to enable them to stick to the council's planned date for the king's arrival in London: May Day.[60]

PART FIVE

The Gaze of Our Inward Eye

Spring 1483 – Summer 1485

'How much pureness in heart is needed by one who is both king and general, how much self-control in all situations, how much good faith, how much liberality, how much intelligence, how much humanity ... nor can he be strict in passing judgement, if he fails to allow that others should be strict judges in his own case.'

Archibald Whitelaw, 'Address to King
Richard III', 12 September 1484

'O most sweet lord Jesus Christ, deign to release me from the affliction, temptation, grief, sickness, need and danger in which I stand ... deign to free me, your servant king Richard, from every tribulation, sorrow, and from the plots of my enemies; and to bring to nothing their evil plans that they are making or wish to make against me.'

The prayer of Richard III

'Wales shall be armed, and to Albion go.'

Streets of London prophecy

18

Old Royal Blood

On the evening of 30 April 1483, London was in holiday mood. The next day, it would erupt in the city-wide street party that was the 'maying', which, with its associations of anarchy and sex, was one of the more eagerly anticipated feast days. In the early morning, Londoners would walk through the city gates out into the surrounding countryside, bathe their faces in dew, and return with garlands to adorn houses, doorways and churches in preparation for the day's junketing. In the heart of the city, outside St Andrew Undershaft, stood the great corporate-sponsored maypole from which the church took its name. Each parish, too, had prepared its maypole, its feasts, bonfires, stages and 'warlike shows' of archery and gunfire, its batteries of drummers and its pageants that would sway through the streets. At the heart of each pageant were the 'lord and lady of May', the young May king and queen. Their procession, a triumph of 'honour and glory', marked spring's conquest over winter, whose discord and duplicity, 'heaviness and trouble', was replaced by universal peace, the spring flowers of 'perfect charity' and the buds of 'truth and unity'. That year, London's preparations acquired a particular intensity. Amid the festivities, the city was due to welcome a real May king, the twelve-year-old boy whose choreographed arrival would promise a new start for both the city and the country – Edward V.[1]

Late that evening a rider dismounted at the Tower, where Elizabeth Woodville, her second son and her four daughters were in residence. He brought shattering news. Earlier that day the young king, who had set out from Ludlow six days before, had been detained barely fifty miles outside London, along with his uncle Anthony Woodville, Sir Richard Grey – the queen's son by her first marriage – and other close servants. Now Edward V was in the town of Northampton, in the custody of his other uncle, Richard duke of Gloucester.

Clustered around its hulking Norman fortress, Northampton, with its crumbling walls, tumbledown houses and abandoned plots, had seen better days. But its strategic position at the heart of England, at the intersection of main routes west and north from London, had kept it at the centre of national events. People still remembered how, back in the summer of 1460, the eighteen-year-old Edward and the earl of Warwick had fought through the mud to take control of the hapless Henry VI, and with him the kingdom; how, three years later, the commons of Northampton had rioted in protest at the exceptional favour shown by Edward to the renegade Lancastrian duke of Somerset; and how in 1469 Warwick and Clarence, based in the town following the battle of Edgecote, had had Edward's right-hand man William Herbert unceremoniously executed there. Northampton, indeed, had close links to the Yorkist regime: the town's dominant figure was Edward IV's great friend William Lord Hastings. Hastings' reach stretched through the northern half of the county into the east midlands, his influence sustained by the assortment of local big men, business managers and lawyers who managed his affairs during his prolonged absences at court or in Calais.[2]

Earlier that April, he agreed to Richard's proposed rendezvous in Northampton, Anthony Woodville was doubtless mindful of Hastings' influence in the area – an awareness sharpened by the bad blood between Hastings and the queen's family, and the recent testy exchanges in the council chamber. When, some four days after its departure from Ludlow, the young king's household approached Northampton, it neatly swerved the town and continued south for fifteen miles, finally halting at the base Woodville had chosen for it: Stony Stratford.

It was a practical choice. There was hardly room in Northampton to billet the royal retinue as well as Richard's and Buckingham's men; besides which, it was always as well to keep rival retinues apart. The small town of Stony Stratford, clustered either side of Watling Street, the main road out of London to the midlands, was used to hosting royalty. But Woodville's decision was also strategic. To him, this was reassuringly familiar territory. A few miles to the north lay Grafton, the queen's childhood home: at Stony Stratford, almost two decades before, Edward IV had gone out hunting one May morning and had come back married. And in the event of any trouble, the king and his Woodville uncle would be fifteen miles closer to London, on a fast road.

Trouble, however, seemed highly unlikely. Conciliation was in the air: Edward V in particular was anxious to 'deserve well' of his paternal uncle, to acknowledge his central place in the new regime. He now wanted to run all the council's plans past Richard, 'to submit everything that had to be done' to his judgement – though as the council had already taken the key decisions in Richard's absence, it had to be said that this was little more than a nice gesture.

With the coronation scheduled for 4 May and the king due to arrive in London on May Day, the clock was ticking.[3] The king's party were already settled into their Stony Stratford lodgings, their men billeted in the scattering of surrounding villages, when on 29 April news came of Richard's arrival in Northampton. Buckingham still hadn't turned up. With barely two days to conclude discussions with Richard and ride the seventy-odd miles to London, the young king sent Anthony Woodville, Sir Richard Grey and a group of attendants over to Northampton for talks over dinner. A deferential gesture, it was also an impatient one.[4]

The royal delegation rode into Northampton that evening to find Richard awaiting them, so one account put it, 'with a particularly cheerful and merry face'. Over a convivial meal, they talked through plans for the new regime – plans which Richard, to their relief, seemed to accept without demur. Late into the evening the duke of Buckingham finally arrived. It was night before the party broke up, the guests escorted back to their respective lodgings. Richard and Buckingham stayed up.[5]

If William Hastings owed everything he had to Edward IV, so too, in his own way, did Richard. It was Edward who had built him up in the north; who had backed him in his dispute with Clarence over the Warwick inheritance and facilitated his marriage to Warwick's daughter Anne; who, after Clarence's killing, had made Richard into

England's greatest nobleman; and whose indulgence of his youngest brother had helped reinforce in Richard the sense of entitlement and impunity that came with royal blood. If, as part of the royal establishment, the queen's family had been instrumental in Clarence's death, so too had Richard, who had been a direct beneficiary of it. And if there had previously been hints of a coolness between Richard and those around the queen, it had seemed no more than the usual court manoeuvrings. Now, however, Richard felt his pre-eminence challenged. The council's decision to hold an early coronation, taken in his absence, suited the queen's family rather better than it did Richard, whose newly bestowed protectorate would end the instant the crown was placed on the boy-king's head.[6] If Richard feared that the Woodvilles were ordering the new regime to suit themselves, both Hastings and Buckingham – each nursing their own resentments – now fed those anxieties and the ambitions that shadowed them. Later, some commentators were convinced that Richard was already preparing to make the ultimate move, to 'usurp the kingdom'; perhaps this was the direction in which Richard's steps were taking him, even if he hadn't consciously admitted it to himself. Whatever the case, Richard knew perfectly well the impossibility of controlling power without controlling the person of the king – a lesson that had been driven home to him during his ineffectual attempt at regime change in Scotland the previous summer. That night, as the two dukes talked, Buckingham held up a mirror to Richard's desires, urging him on. The groundwork, though, had already been prepared – by Hastings.[7]

For while Hastings may have been absent, away in London, his men weren't. One of his councillors in particular had been central to the communications with Richard and Buckingham. This was the Northamptonshire lawyer William Catesby, Hastings' deputy in the county, whose expertise and discretion he prized. According to Thomas More – who knew a thing or two about lawyers – Catesby dealt with Hastings' most 'weighty matters' and was in his most 'special trust'. It helped, too, that Catesby had the confidence of Buckingham, another of his clients. Apart from the power he wielded as Hastings' representative, Catesby had exceptional local influence on his own account. His father had been three times sheriff of Northamptonshire, head of the county's law enforcement and security; so too, only the year previously, had his brother-in-law. Catesby also had cosy ties with the current sheriff, his son-in-law Roger Wake. Close to Hastings, the Wakes were no strangers to national politics; what was more, they harboured an abiding grudge against their Woodville neighbours.

Back in 1463 it had been Roger Wake's father, Thomas – a client of both Warwick and Hastings – who, as sheriff, had turned a blind eye as Northampton's citizens rioted in protest against Edward IV's closeness to the duke of Somerset. It was Thomas Wake, too, who in 1469 had helped hunt down the queen's father Lord Rivers after Edgecote, a battle in which his own son had been killed fighting for Warwick and Clarence. Thomas Wake had also produced the lead figurines that – discovered at Stoke Bruerne, equidistant between the Woodville seat of Grafton and the Wakes' adjacent manor of Blisworth – had provided the fuel for Warwick's incendiary allegations of sorcery against Elizabeth's mother Jacquetta, leaving a stain that the Woodville family had never quite eradicated. After 1471, the Wakes' close links to Hastings had aided their political rehabilitation. When Thomas died, his son and heir Roger had stepped into his shoes. An effective networker, he served on royal commissions alongside Hastings and his brother Ralph, and another up-and-coming lawyer named Richard Empson. On one of these panels, after Clarence's murder, Roger Wake and his half-brother John worked alongside Catesby to appropriate the duke's vast estates on the king's behalf. After making an advantageous marriage to William Catesby's daughter Elizabeth, it was hardly a surprise when, in March 1483, Roger Wake was appointed sheriff of the county. By this time, the mutual loathing between the Wakes and the Woodvilles had subsided to a smouldering suspicion. It merely needed some fresh fuel to reignite.[8]

Quietly, efficiently, in the weeks since Edward IV's death, Catesby had been busy stitching together an understanding between Hastings, Richard and Buckingham and secretly mobilizing local networks, at their heart the Wake family. If, that April, Anthony Woodville felt that he had taken adequate precautions, he had been hopelessly outmanoeuvred. In riding over to Northampton that evening, he had been lured into a carefully prepared trap.

In the early hours of 30 April, as he chewed over the situation with Buckingham, Richard knew that everything was prepared. Hastings and Catesby had provided the ammunition. In firing it, Richard triggered the sequence of events that, as one appalled supporter of Edward IV later put it, would lead to the 'extreme detriment' of the kingdom and 'utter subversion of his own house': the destruction of the house of York.[9]

At daybreak, Richard made his move. In the spring half-light his men, billeted in lodgings around Northampton, armed themselves quietly and harnessed their horses. Woodville, Grey and their companions woke to find their inns surrounded. Trying to leave, they were arrested and imprisoned. Northampton itself was sealed off, all the roads out of town watched – with the connivance of sheriff Roger Wake and his men, whose local knowledge would have been invaluable in preventing the king from being tipped off. Anybody attempting to head south out of Northampton was stopped and turned back.

Richard and Buckingham rode fast to Stony Stratford. There, they entered the royal lodgings and detained the king's close servants, foremost among them his veteran chamberlain Sir Thomas Vaughan. Finding the king in his apartments, both noblemen removed their hats and knelt. One eyewitness, possibly the royal physician John Argentine, recalled how a sombre Richard addressed the boy. Expressing 'profound grief' at the death of Edward IV, he placed responsibility for the late king's untimely demise firmly at the door of the 'companions and servants of his vices' – the queen's son the marquis of Dorset, her youngest brother Sir Edward Woodville, and their hangers-on. These same men, Richard continued emphatically, could not be allowed near the young king. An echo of the objections raised in the council meeting, it also modulated them. In Richard's argument, the question of the protectorship hinged not so much on issues of protocol, precedent and political balance, but of morality.

By encouraging the late king's 'vices', so Richard's argument went, the Woodvilles had destroyed his health and, by extension, that of the country. Their own excessive sexual appetites, moreover, had rendered them 'puny': men utterly unfit to participate in government. There was more. It was 'common knowledge' that they planned to deprive Richard of the protectorship that his late brother had promised him. Worse still, Richard had intelligence that they were plotting to kill him: to ambush him before they reached London or, failing that, in the capital itself. For all these reasons the Woodvilles had to be removed. Richard would take on the role of protector in their place. Besides the late king's approval, he had the experience and, he added, the popularity: the people loved him.[10]

If Richard expected the young king to accept his reasoning without demur, he was disappointed. With the poise for which he was acquiring a reputation, Edward V replied that he had 'complete confidence' in the servants his father had chosen for him; they had served him faithfully, and he saw no reason to dismiss them. As far as the government was concerned, he was equally confident in the council and his mother Queen Elizabeth, whose decisions he thoroughly endorsed. Effectively, the twelve-year-old told Richard he was getting ahead of himself.

The king's self-possession infuriated Buckingham, who spat that women had no business governing kingdoms and that the boy's confidence in his mother was mistaken. Richard was self-contained, cooler, more dangerous. His deference acquired an edge. He repeated the explanations 'insistently'. This was not a matter for debate. It was how things were going to be.

Outside the king's lodgings, a proclamation was read out. Edward V's Marcher men were ordered to disperse, and not to come near him on pain of death. Anthony Woodville, Richard Grey and Thomas Vaughan were sent north under armed guard. The rest of the royal household was dismissed, with the exception of a few close servants, among them the physician John Argentine, whom the boy was allowed to retain.[11] Escorted back to Northampton, Edward V put his signature to a letter placed in front of him by Richard, ordering the aged archbishop of Canterbury, Thomas Bourchier, to take possession of the great seal, the Tower of London and its treasury. In Richard's eyes, the current chancellor and keeper of the great seal, the archbishop of York Thomas Rotherham – possibly one of the councillors vocal in opposing his claims – was not to be trusted. The aged Bourchier, a man of unimpeachable integrity, was a safe pair of hands.

*

Early on May morning, news rippled through London's streets that Elizabeth, her younger son and her daughters had, along with Dorset, left the Tower and had made their way upriver to Westminster, where they were now in sanctuary. Elizabeth, of course, had been here before, in 1470, as Warwick and Clarence had advanced on London in the name of Henry VI. For one commentator, the panic on the streets felt horribly familiar, 'like Barnet' all over again. As the day wore on, there were reports of armed men assembling in Westminster in the queen's name: an attempt, perhaps, to hold the city against Richard. If so, this resistance quickly evaporated in the face of a formidable display of armed force by William Hastings, who had for weeks been preparing for this moment, urgently summoning men to the capital from Calais. Meanwhile London's corporation, in receipt of a letter from Richard justifying his actions, reacted to the changed circumstances with a practised efficiency. After all, compared with the agonizing over whether or not to open the city's gates to Edward in 1460 and 1471, this was straightforward. The steadfast presence of Hastings, a long-time friend to the city's business communities, assuaged their concerns – and besides, even if he was now in the care of his uncle Richard, the king was still the king.[12]

On 4 May, the day of Edward V's now-postponed coronation, the royal party rode into London, accompanied by the corporation's reception committee, clad in Yorkist mulberry. Proclamations were shouted to the onlooking crowds. The young king and the nation had been rescued from a terrible fate and, to prove it, four cartloads of weapons were produced, confiscated from Anthony Woodville and his men, seeming proof positive of the intended ambush. As the procession wound through the streets to the bishop of London's palace opposite St Paul's, where Edward V would take up temporary residence, people saw that the royal retinues now also wore Richard's boar badge.

With the young king securely lodged, Richard – who based himself at Crosby Place, a sumptuously modernized merchant's house on Bishopsgate – convened a meeting of the council who, along with London's mayor and aldermen, swore oaths of loyalty to Edward V. In the following days, people's worries subsided. The way forward seemed clear: the young king, with uncle Richard at his side, was an arrangement that 'promised best for future prosperity'. As Hastings, 'bursting with joy', put it to anybody who would listen, the transfer of power had been achieved with no killings and about as much blood spilt 'as might have come from a cut finger'. This, he said, was how to bring about a 'new world'. Two blood relatives of the queen – Anthony Woodville and Dorset – had simply been replaced in the king's administration by 'two nobles of the blood royal', Richard and Buckingham.[13]

The council's first piece of business was to confirm Richard as protector. As Richard started to govern, he did so with a reassuringly studied observance of protocol, seeking the council's consent and goodwill in his decision-making. A revised date for Edward V's coronation was quickly confirmed: it would take place on 22 June, with Parliament convening three days later to ratify the new order. Meanwhile the new order itself, as Hastings was stressing, looked very much like the old.[14]

There were a few notable exceptions. Head and shoulders above everybody else was Buckingham who, having been denied almost any power by Edward IV, was now deluged with favour by a grateful Richard. He was handed a staggering portfolio of land grants that together amounted to what was, more or less, an independent fiefdom in Wales and the Marches, regions recently controlled by the Woodville-dominated council of the prince of Wales. Indeed, the role of Buckingham – a constant, insistent presence at Richard's shoulder 'with his advice and resources', as one commentator put it – seemed almost a power-sharing one.[15] Catesby, meanwhile, was handed the chancellorship of the earldom of March, a powerful post that brought him further within Buckingham's orbit. Others, from Yorkist veterans like John Howard to Richard's childhood friend Francis Lovell, received a smattering of patronage; there were, too, a few minor reshuffles. By and large, though, the status quo was preserved. It had been the Woodvilles whose grasping ambitions had endangered the future of the Yorkist dynasty – or so the story now went. They had been neatly removed, no harm done.

To many besides the overjoyed Hastings, the message was clear. Richard was the continuity candidate, the keeper of his late brother's flame, and clearly the most appropriate protector of his heir Edward V.

When the question of the young king's accommodation was raised, Buckingham's proposal of the Tower met with a general nodding of heads. After all, it was the traditional pre-coronation venue, and it was secure. On Cheapside, people turned out to watch the boy being escorted to his new residence, enjoying the spectacle with a few drinks.

Nevertheless, there were plenty of loose ends. It quickly became clear that the late king's finances were in something of a mess. If the general impression was that Edward IV had left a kingdom awash with cash, the reality was rather different: his treasury and coffers were found to contain some £1,200, plus a quantity of silver plate minted into coin and some dodgy currency. Factoring in anticipated incomings from his wool exports, the sale of one of the king's jewels and some loans, the available liquidity came to around £6,040 2s 8d. None of which should have come as a surprise, given Edward's two costly campaigns against Scotland and the extra annual expense now involved in the upkeep and garrisoning of Berwick, but for an administration facing immediate security challenges it was not an encouraging picture. Hastings had written immediately to his brother in Guisnes advising him that there was no extra money for reinforcements or wages: he should make do with what he had.[16]

Blame for the kingdom's precarious finances was now placed squarely on the Woodvilles. The recent cash payments to Dorset and Sir Edward Woodville for naval protection of England's southern coastline, authorized by the royal council, were construed as theft, the pair having absconded with Edward's 'immense treasure'. Judiciously, Dorset hadn't hung around to argue his case. Sir Edward was already at sea. Richard monitored the fleet's progress off the south coast, all the while removing Woodville-appointed officials from key coastal fortresses and replacing them with other men who, having served Edward IV, were happy enough to transfer their loyalties to the new regime. When Sir Edward's ships materialized in Southampton Water, Richard's men were waiting. His fleet captured, Woodville himself got away, fleeing with a pair of royal ships.[17]

After the first cautious days of his protectorship, Richard grew more aggressive, confident of the council's backing. He ripped up Woodville networks by the roots. Moving onto their lands, Richard's men turfed out their occupants with the flourish of official letters, confiscating all the moveable goods they could find and riffling through accounts and paperwork: among those annexing Anthony Woodville's estates was a gratified Roger Wake.[18] Nor did the extended Woodville family escape. In Kent, the manor of Ightham Mote was confiscated; its owner Sir Richard Haute, the queen's cousin and a household official of the young king, had been among those arrested at Stony Stratford and sent north. With Richard's escalating belligerence, however, came renewed tension. The council may have conceded the fact of his protectorship, but it wasn't prepared to let him off the leash.

In the following weeks, concerns were raised in the council chamber about the impunity with which Richard was acting. Councillors expressed vocal anxiety about the well-being of his prisoners, currently detained without charge. They pointed out, too, that Richard didn't seem particularly bothered about the queen's 'dignity and peace of mind': in sanctuary, Elizabeth Woodville was already living hand to mouth.[19]

In response, an indignant Richard went on the offensive. He told the council that Anthony Woodville and his associates had plotted to murder him. The evidence was damning, and they were clearly guilty. He directed the council to convict them of treason.

The council debated Richard's appeal at length before rejecting it. There was, it declared, no convincing case to be made – a polite way of saying that Richard had in fact provided no good evidence to support his accusations. Even if there had been evidence of a Woodville plot, the council added, it could not be construed as treason, for at that point the council had not yet invested Richard with the protectorship. It was a clever ruling. While not disputing Richard's claim that the laws of treason should apply to him as protector, it was an implicit reminder to Richard of the temporary and conditional nature of his role. He was protector by authority of the council, and ultimate power rested with the council, not with him.[20]

Richard's insistence on the death penalty for his opponents was the kind of move made all too often in the last few decades: seeking legal endorsement for what was essentially a political settling of scores.

Richard was convinced of the Woodvilles' guilt. But his demand also carried with it a hint of vulnerability and an awareness of the growing unease within the council. For the sake of unity it had been happy to sanction Richard's initial seizure of power, but with young Edward's coronation barely weeks away, there was an upswell of sympathy for the new king's maternal family: it would not do for them to be in prison while he was crowned.

As Richard knew, such sympathy brought with it resentment against his rule. While they were still alive, the Woodvilles remained a threat. They needed to be permanently removed. But the council, packed full of experienced legal minds, had emphatically dismissed Richard's case. Its judgment was perhaps influenced by the disconcertingly regal way Richard was now going about government. The consensus-driven approach of his first weeks in office had evaporated. Now, he was 'commanding and forbidding in everything like another king'.[21]

Around this time the new chancellor John Russell, bishop of Lincoln, promoted by Richard from his post of privy seal, sat down to draft his opening sermon for the Parliament that would follow Edward V's coronation.[22] Typically, such orations set forth a monarch's vision for government and it was striking quite how much the new king's aims, as articulated in Russell's sermon, now suited Richard. A masterpiece of radicalism dressed as conformity, it outlined a continuation and dramatic extension of Richard's powers as protector – powers that Parliament was expected to endorse.

Russell opened by making all the right noises on political and financial reform. Reaching for an assortment of tried and tested ideas, his speech called for renewal and unity. He praised the nobility as the key to good government – islands of stability in the choppy seas that were the perpetually revolting commons – while at the same time reproving them for the self-interest that had been the source of so much trouble and ordering them to pull together 'amiably' for the sake of their new young king and the well-being of the country. There were a few sneery references to recent events. The 'tempestuous Rivers', which threatened to overwhelm the islands of the nobility, was a mouldy pun on the monopoly of favour enjoyed by the queen's father at Edward IV's court back in the late 1460s. Russell now dusted it off to deploy against the imprisoned Anthony Woodville – the current Earl Rivers – and the queen's family more widely. It was a cheap gag but, Russell probably reasoned, it would raise a laugh. More crowd-pleasing metaphors followed. Acknowledging the heavy tax burden of recent years with a wry nod to Edward IV's ballooning weight and greed, Russell noted that the belly of the body politic had 'waxed great'. The new government would be lean, its fat trimmed. Taxes would be consumed in responsible moderation, and king and council would work hard to digest the 'great and weighty matters' with which the kingdom was confronted. All this was predictable and, to a nation concerned about both security and taxes, welcome.

At this point, Russell shifted focus. What great good fortune it was, he stated, that 'during his years of tenderness' the young king's uncle Richard should be at hand to take on the role of his 'tutor and protector'.

Clearly, Russell continued, Edward V wasn't yet old enough to rule in person. Until he was, the best arrangement was for Richard to continue to wield power and authority on his behalf. Richard was an exemplary public servant, comparable to the Roman consul Lepidus in his disinterested loyalty to the common good. He possessed that rare combination of virtue and birth inherent in true nobility, as well as wisdom, experience and 'martial cunning': attributes from which the young king would benefit immensely as he learned how to rule. Of all the new Parliament's business, Russell concluded, this confirmation of Richard in his role of protector was the most urgent and should be done immediately. It would bring enormous relief to the king who, in conclusion, Russell now ventriloquized: 'Uncle', the boy's voice said, 'I am glad to have you confirmed in this place to be my protector.'

The erudite cadences of Russell's sermon could not conceal a dramatic departure from the plans agreed by the council following the late king's death. Following Edward V's coronation, Richard would not only continue in his role as protector; he would do so in an enhanced role. Russell was asking Parliament to vest unprecedented powers in Richard: both the 'tutele' or personal control of the king, and the protectorship of the realm. Precisely that combination of

roles, in other words, which had been denied to Humphrey of Gloucester some sixty years previously, and which the council had explicitly
withheld from Richard in the days after Edward IV's death.[23]

There was more. If Richard's credentials were impeccable, Russell
stated, so was his lineage; indeed, he was 'next in perfect age of the
blood royal'. Some weeks before, in his letter to the council laying out
his claim to the protectorship, Richard had sworn fealty to Edward V
and, in the event of his death, to all his late brother's offspring. Implicit
in Russell's comment, though, was a rather different definition of Richard's position: should anything happen to the young king, Richard
would be next in line to the throne.[24]

This was a sermon written under Richard's close direction. It contained the distinct sense that Richard, increasingly uncomfortable
about what would happen after Edward V's coronation, was redefin-
ing his role, not simply as the young king's protector, but – and here
were shades of the Parliament of 1460, which had made his father
Richard of York and his heirs next in line to Henry VI – as his
successor.

The sermon carried a hint of Russell's own discomfort. As he put
it uneasily, he hoped that his proposals would have 'such good and
brief expedition in this high court of parliament as the ease of the
people and the condition and the time requireth'. Very probably, he
was expecting the opposite: that, at best, the plans would have a
rocky ride through Parliament. In the end, he was spared the trouble.
His speech would never be made.

On Monday 9 June, Simon Stallworth, an agent to the Oxfordshire
knight Sir William Stonor, wrote from London to his master with an
update on the political situation. Stonor, Dorset's brother-in-law, was
anxious for news. Stallworth, however, didn't have much to tell him.
The queen, her second son and their supporters – Dorset among them –
continued to sit tight behind the heavily guarded walls of Westminster
sanctuary, immune to Richard's efforts to persuade them out; Dorset's
goods were still being seized wherever they were found. That day, a
four-hour-long council meeting, headed by Richard and Buckingham
and involving 'all other lords', had been held at Westminster – Edward
V, still in the Tower, hadn't been present – but, as usual, nobody had
bothered to update Elizabeth Woodville on its business.[25]

For all that, Stallworth reported, London and Westminster buzzed with the 'great business' of preparing for the upcoming festivities: the sense of expectation was palpable. And at that point, he continued, Stonor would be in London himself for Edward V's coronation, 'and then shall you know all the world'.

If Russell's draft sermon stressed that it would be business as usual for Richard's protectorate following Edward V's coronation, in public the atmosphere seemed different. Running through Stallworth's comments was a sense of anticipated catharsis. The boy king would be brought out of the Tower, into the open – and then, things would change. This was what Elizabeth Woodville hoped. And what Richard feared.

The following day a messenger left Richard's household at Crosby Place, rode out of London through Bishopsgate and headed north fast. A bruising military man from Cumberland in the far northwest, Richard Ratcliffe was one of Richard's close councillors, his loyalty proven through years of service in the northern borderlands and on campaign in Scotland. Ratcliffe's uncompromising reputation preceded him: in Thomas More's pithy character assassination, he was 'as far from pity as from all fear of God'. The messages Ratcliffe now carried with him, from Richard himself, were urgent, shocking and highly confidential. In them Richard called on his northern supporters, chief among them the earl of Northumberland, to raise an army and head south to London as rapidly as possible. One letter to the mayor and corporation of York, requesting as many armed men as they could provide, explained why.

The queen, her family and followers, Richard stated, were plotting to 'murder and utterly destroy' him and Buckingham, and 'the old royal blood of this realm'. The threat, indeed, was more widespread even than this. The Woodvilles plotted the 'final destruction and disinheritance' of all other 'inheritors and men of honour that belong to us' – anybody of note, that was, who had any connection with Richard.[26] Ratcliffe, the letter concluded, would communicate everything more fully by word of mouth.

These were sweeping allegations. Yet the letter to York's corporation, at any rate, contained little that was new – or, indeed, concrete.

From the outset, Richard's seizure of power had been based on the threat of Woodville aggression, charges repeated constantly in the six weeks of his protectorate. Something had triggered his sudden, apparently panicked demand for military aid: the question was, what?

The letter mentioned the Woodvilles' use of the 'subtle and damnable' practice of 'forecasting' – the use of astrology or witchcraft – to try to bring about the deaths of Richard and Buckingham. A serious charge, though as Richard admitted, it was already 'openly known', old news. Indeed, he may have been referring to the allegations of sorcery against Jacquetta and Elizabeth Woodville back in 1469: allegations which, despite having been dismissed by Parliament itself, had lingered in the popular memory.

But with most of the Woodville ringleaders in prison or on the run, the nature of the plot and the question of who was masterminding it remained unclear – at least, in Richard's letters. Perhaps Ratcliffe, committing the names and details to memory, told the recipients in person.

On the morning of Friday 13 June, three days after Ratcliffe left for the north, several leading councillors made their way to the Tower for a council meeting summoned by Richard the day before. On his orders, the council had been split into two: one group, consisting of the majority of the lords – effectively a working party to discuss the coronation plans – was convening upriver in Westminster under Chancellor Russell; the other, at the Tower, would be chaired by Richard himself. As well as Hastings and Catesby, this second group included councillors who had been associated with the conciliar pushback of the previous weeks: men like Edward IV's former chancellor Thomas Rotherham, John Morton and, a man who had never been entirely well disposed towards Richard, the late king's household steward Thomas, Lord Stanley.[27]

As the councillors arrived at the Tower, Richard greeted them with pleasant small talk, asking Morton for some strawberries from the garden at his Holborn residence, which, Richard had heard, were particularly good. The doors of the council chamber were closed. The attendees took their seats around the council table and waited for Richard to speak.[28]

At first Richard said nothing but sat in his place looking increasingly agitated and chewing on his bottom lip, his characteristic nervous tic. An uncomfortable silence settled on the chamber. Then he started talking. He had, he told the assembled councillors, called the meeting for one specific reason: he wanted to show them in what 'great danger of death' he stood. In the last few days, he had been ill, unable to eat or drink, and had grown weak and short of breath: what was more, some of his body parts had begun to 'fall away'. By way of proof he held out his arms, straight, in front of him: one was shorter than the other. This was the result of his scoliosis, which made his right shoulder slightly higher than his left – and it was a moment later seized on with relish by Tudor chroniclers. Richard then repeated the accusations he had made a few days before in the letters carried by Ratcliffe: Elizabeth Woodville was plotting, by witchcraft, 'to destroy me, that am so near of blood unto the king'.[29]

For some moments, nobody said anything. Hastings broke the silence. If the queen was found guilty, he offered, she should certainly be punished. Richard replied sharply that he knew the queen had done it – evidence enough. Hastings unhesitatingly offered the same reply.

Suddenly Richard rounded on Hastings, shouting at him, banging on the table, accusing him of being a ringleader in the queen's plot. It was the signal for a group of Richard's men, stationed secretly in a room next door. They barged in, weapons drawn, and arrested Morton, Rotherham, the late king's secretary Oliver King, Lord Stanley, who had narrowly avoided a flailing sword – wielded, probably, by his hostile north-western neighbour Robert Harrington in an opportunistic attempt to settle their long-standing feud – and Hastings. The men were marched out of the council chamber and detained separately in the Tower's many cells. All except Hastings, who was forced outside to Tower Green, hastily shriven by a priest from the Tower chapel of St Peter ad Vincula, pushed to his knees and beheaded.[30]

In Richard's eyes, Hastings had transformed from close supporter to existential threat. Over the past weeks, Richard had taken the temperature among certain influential councillors – men like Morton, Rotherham and Hastings – regarding the proposed extension of his protectorate, as laid out in Russell's parliamentary sermon. These were men loyal to Edward V, the living continuation of Edward IV's regime; men who, while acquiescing in Richard's protectorate, had in recent weeks raised concerns about the way he was exercising power. Richard had been alarmed to find that these councillors habitually 'foregathered together in each other's houses'. He tried to find out what was being discussed. What apparently did for Hastings were private conversations with the man he regarded as being in his 'special trust' – William Catesby. In these conversations, Hastings reiterated his unyielding allegiance to Edward V and revealed his misgivings about Richard's plans for power; he also gave the names of other councillors with similar concerns. Catesby dutifully reported everything back to Richard and Buckingham.

To Richard, Hastings' intransigence was a source of extreme frustration. Hastings' initial endorsement of Richard's protectorate had been crucial in securing the backing of the old Yorkist establishment. But Hastings now unequivocally wanted Edward V to be crowned – which inevitably meant the ending of Richard's protectorate and, in practice, some sort of accommodation with the Woodvilles. To Richard, such a scenario was unthinkable. Not only would it leave him open to counter-accusations from the Woodvilles, but the upcoming Parliament – whose business he was trying so hard to dictate – represented the perfect chance for his opponents to move against him. His sense of vulnerability was increased by the recent death of George Neville, the boy whose portion of the Warwick patrimony had been handed to Richard and had become the foundation of his northern power. With his passing, the male Neville line was extinguished – and so too were Richard's hopes of passing the inheritance on to his own son. As decreed by Parliament back in 1475, when Richard died so too would his family's ownership of the lands.[31]

The political situation was now very muddy. Richard, who more than most craved the certainty of a clearly ordered world, found what he perceived to be Hastings' lack of loyalty confusing and overwhelming: so excruciatingly unbearable that he had to rid himself of Hastings as soon as possible. At Richard's side, Buckingham was equally concerned. With hungry eyes on a portfolio of north midlands estates currently in Hastings' possession, lands which he believed were his by right, he was emphatic in his belief that Hastings had to go.[32]

In attending the council meeting at the Tower that morning Hastings, like Anthony Woodville before him, had walked into a trap. He had, according to Thomas More, ignored the curious nature of the meeting itself, Lord Stanley's repeated warnings not to attend and, on the way to the Tower, a handful of bad premonitions. But then, Hastings perhaps reasoned he had nothing to fear. After all, as he saw it he was not being disloyal to the protector, but faithful to the family that he had served for almost a quarter of a century.

Richard's agents quickly arrested a go-between. John Forster, Elizabeth Woodville's long-standing receiver-general, had been in regular contact with Elizabeth in sanctuary; he was also a close friend and colleague of both Hastings and Morton. Imprisoned in the Tower, Forster was kept without food and water for forty-eight hours until he signed over his profitable stewardship of the abbey of St Albans, held jointly with Hastings, to William Catesby.[33]

As news of the arrests spread, Richard sent a herald into the city to announce to anxious Londoners that a plot against the regime had been foiled: the conspirators had been arrested and their ringleader Hastings executed. The situation was under control. If there was shock at the murder and what it portended – especially among those who like the goldsmith Hugh Brice and London's current mayor Edmund Shaw had been closest to Hastings and the old Yorkist establishment – people kept their thoughts to themselves. A city chronicler offered an explanation for Londoners' subdued response. Despite their misgivings people simply refused to believe what was happening; there was, he wrote, 'some hope' that Richard had simply acted as 'an avenger of treason and old wrongs', not as a man with ambitions to seize the throne.[34] For the next two days, it seemed as though this hope might be borne out. The preparations continued for Edward V's coronation, now only a week away. Then, on 16 June, everything changed.

At Westminster that Monday morning boats disgorged a mass of Richard's men, heavily armed, who deployed round the sanctuary, sealing it off. Through the sanctuary gates, heading for Elizabeth Woodville's lodgings, came a knot of councillors, foremost among them Chancellor John Russell and the elderly figure of Cardinal

Bourchier, archbishop of Canterbury. Over the weekend, Richard had convinced the council that Edward V's nine-year-old brother should be present at the coronation. A man practised at smoothing out the knottiest of situations – over two decades before, he had confronted a glowering Richard of York, talking him down from claiming the throne – Bourchier had been deputed to persuade Elizabeth Woodville to hand over her second son. Wisely, Richard and Buckingham had stayed behind in Westminster Palace.

Talking through things with the queen, Bourchier was all persuasive reassurance. It wasn't right, he told Elizabeth, that the young prince should be absent from Edward V's coronation. It looked improper and besides, the young king wanted his brother at his side, for comfort. Elizabeth should release the boy: he would play a full and honourable part in the ceremonies and would then be returned to her afterwards. Besides, if Elizabeth refused, Richard's troops would come and take the prince by force. Elizabeth agreed.[35]

Bourchier led the boy out of sanctuary and across Westminster Palace Yard to Richard and Buckingham, waiting in the doorway of the council chamber. Greeting his nephew with 'many loving words', Richard helped him onto a waiting boat that ferried him downstream to the Tower, now under the command of one of Richard's household servants, the Durham man Robert Brackenbury.[36] With both Edward IV's sons in his custody, Richard made his move.

Later that day, he ordered Edward V's coronation to be postponed until 9 November, almost five months distant. Parliament was cancelled. The next day, London's mayor and aldermen announced the return of monies collected for the king's coronation gift to their donors; in Westminster, a chancery clerk processed the appointment of three men to provide meat for the king's household in the Tower. These were to be the last official mentions of Edward V's reign.

Soon, the workings of government started to betray tell-tale signs of regime change. Officials, uncertain of Edward V's authority, dated documents by the year of grace rather than the regnal year – or, increasingly, did nothing. Business ground to a halt.[37]

Across the city at Crosby Place, Richard kept ostentatious open house. In the following days, he issued a proclamation calling men to join him – 'his highness', now – in London, and publicly broadcast his accusations against the Woodvilles, who had tried to destroy his 'royal person'. Replacing his mourning black with purple robes, he went on procession through the London streets with a thousand horsemen. Londoners were unimpressed: he was 'scarcely watched by anybody'. Anticipating unrest, the city corporation ordered companies of militia onto the streets, detachments stationed on Cheapside and Cornhill.[38]

The following Saturday, the 21st, Simon Stallworth wrote again to Sir William Stonor, a letter markedly different in tone to the one he had written less than two weeks previously. Running through the sequence of events triggered by Hastings' beheading, he reported 'much trouble' and a general sense of unease: 'every man doubts other'. Londoners were anxious about the imminent arrival of Richard's northern armies. There was general uncertainty, too, over the fate of John Morton and the other detained councillors, still in the Tower: 'I suppose they shall come out nonetheless', Stallworth wrote, then paused and drew a line through the sentence. He mentioned, too, the arrests of 'Foster' – John Forster – and 'Mistress Shore', Edward IV's former mistress Jane Shore, who was also rumoured to have been in relationships with Hastings and his enemy Dorset. Then, Stallworth signed off, shakily: 'I am so sick I may well not hold my pen.'[39]

On the morning of Sunday 22 June, Edward V's cancelled coronation day, a huge crowd comprising Richard, Buckingham, several more lords and their retainers and hangers-on gathered at Paul's Cross to hear a sermon by the Cambridge theologian Ralph Shaw. Brother to London's mayor, Ralph was an eloquent and popular speaker; people hung on his words, which was why he had now been chosen to deliver the bombshell that everyone had, consciously or otherwise, been anticipating. Taking as his theme a verse from the Book of Wisdom, *Spuria vitulamina non agent radices altas* – in Thomas More's forceful translation, 'bastard slips shall never take deep root' – Shaw proclaimed that Edward V was not the real king of England after all.

Edward IV's marriage to Elizabeth Woodville, Shaw elaborated, had been found to be bigamous. When the pair were wed, back in the spring of 1464, Edward had failed to disclose that he had already signed a precontract of marriage with another woman – which meant that Elizabeth was no lawful queen and, consequently, that her children were bastards. There was more. Edward IV himself was illegitimate. Back in 1441, while Richard of York was away at the front, valiantly trying to hold back the French advance through Normandy, his wife Cecily was sleeping around. Edward had been the result. You could tell Edward was a bastard, Shaw explained, because – a strapping, strawberry-blonde six-footer – he looked nothing like his father. Neither, for that matter, did Clarence. Richard, on the other hand, 'little' and dark, did.

There was little that was new about Shaw's sermon. The rumours around Edward IV and Elizabeth Woodville's marriage, and indeed Edward's own illegitimacy, stemmed from the bloody summer of 1469: then, on top of his allegations of sorcery against Elizabeth's mother Jacquetta, the earl of Warwick had written to the French king Louis XI declaring Edward a bastard. The letter's contents had circulated widely, on the international stage at least, and had taken root. Six years later, following Edward's aborted invasion of France, an irate Charles the Bold had started calling him 'Blaybourne', after the name of Cecily's alleged lover. Clarence had apparently tried to fan the flames in the last fevered year of his quarrel with Edward. Then, with his death, the rumours had gone cold. Now, Richard blew life back into them: blazing up, they acquired a new ferocity, fuelled by Richard's resolute belief in the illegitimacy of Edward's offspring.

In churches throughout the city congregations listened agog to their parish priests, relaying Shaw's allegations in their Sunday sermons. People were equally titillated and appalled. One bystander echoed a prevailing view when he fumed that such preachers were both irresponsible and immoral in equal measure: 'they should have blushed'. What was more, in alleging Edward IV's bastardy, the preachers – their words tacitly endorsed by the new regime – were accusing Cecily duchess of York, the family's matriarch, of adultery. In indulging these stories, Richard seemed perfectly happy to dishonour his own mother.[40]

Another uncomfortable parallel perhaps occurred to those long enough in the tooth to remember. Back in 1461 Edward IV's inauguration ceremonies, masterminded by George Neville, had contrasted the 'unnatural', illegitimate Lancastrian line with the purity of York.

Richard was now doing much the same to define himself against his late brother and his brother's children.

It was now the height of summer. On St John's Eve, crowds turned out for the Midsummer Watch, the annual civic display of military might that saw two thousand heavily armed militiamen parading through London's streets, accompanied by a battery of drummers and fifemen, armour gleaming in the torches and bonfires that illuminated the city – a procession put on for the 'honour of the king'. Amid the 'neighbourly drinking' and the children running loose with wooden spears and blunted swords, people now knew who England's new king was going to be.[41]

The following day, the duke of Buckingham arrived at the Guildhall to set out Richard's right to the throne and reassure the concerned corporation. All sweet reasonableness, his face an 'angelic mask', Buckingham again laid out the evidence for the illegitimacy of Edward IV and his children before turning to the truly noble qualities that, besides his untainted royal blood, made Richard undeniably England's king. First and foremost were his 'blameless morals' – here, Buckingham glossed over the fact of Richard's own bastard children, John, now in his teens, and Katherine – which were a 'sure guarantee' of the order and good government he would bring to the realm.[42] Then there was Richard's liberality, which Buckingham was in no doubt would come as a relief to London's business leaders after years of Edward's 'insatiable covetise'. The new regime, Buckingham implied, would be strongly inclined to treat the city's mercantile and financial affairs with a much lighter touch.

Buckingham's thirty-minute peroration was a masterpiece in public relations and rhetorical skill: even its pauses, noted one chronicler, were perfectly judged. But when he had finished, there was silence among the assembled Londoners. Then, suddenly uproar. Among the crowd, a group of men led by Richard's household servant John Nesfield shouted: 'King Richard, King Richard', flinging their caps in the air in stage-managed spontaneity in an effort to coax acclamation out of the uncertain corporation.[43]

Richard now moved against his political opponents. Thomas marquis of Dorset, in Westminster sanctuary with his mother Elizabeth Woodville, knew what was coming. He fled and, eluding a manhunt with 'troops and dogs', went to ground. Meanwhile, two hundred miles north at Pontefract Castle, Richard's urgently summoned forces were ready to march south under the command of Northumberland and Richard Ratcliffe. Before they did so, a brief, vicious ritual took place. Freed from the constraints of Edward V's council, Richard had sent orders for the immediate execution of Anthony Woodville, Sir Richard Grey and Thomas Vaughan.[44]

Even in the most excessive of Edward IV's treason trials, there had always been a veneer of due process, a sense that the judgment handed down 'belongeth after the law', as John Tiptoft had once put it: a sentiment that found its most extreme expression in the horrifying parody of a trial that was Clarence's judicial murder. Richard was a man intimately acquainted with the law of treason. Yet as Thomas More put it – and whatever More's politics, he knew his law – Woodville and his fellow prisoners were condemned 'hastily, without judgement, process or manner of order'. When it came to ridding himself of knotty problems, Richard was making a habit of putting necessity first and law a distant second. It was a way of operating that resembled not so much Edward IV, but both brothers' one-time mentor, Richard earl of Warwick.

As they stood in the open air, awaiting their turn to kneel and put their heads on the block, Woodville and his friends were reportedly denied the chance even to say a few last words in their defence. A man whose pious obsession with mortality was more pronounced than most, Woodville had, along with his last will and testament, left behind a poem in which he reconciled himself to what he knew was coming. 'Such is my dance', he shrugged, 'Willing to die.'[45]

With Richard's coronation scheduled for 6 July, the search for legitimation and unity found expression in the inauguration rites that, for all his disavowal of his brother's reign, Richard had repurposed from Edward IV's equally confected accession ceremonies of April 1461. On 26 June, at the family's Thames-side home of Baynard's Castle, a group of lords, gentlemen and leading London citizens – representatives, so Richard asserted, of the 'lords spiritual and temporal and the commons of this land' – looked on as Buckingham presented Richard with a petition setting out his claim to the throne and, on the assembled group's behalf, formally requested him to take the crown.[46] After a dramatic, overlong pause, Richard assented. Next, accompanied by Buckingham and the other petitioners Richard rode in state, sword borne before him, to Westminster Hall. Swathed in royal robes, sceptre in hand, he walked through the crowds, up the half-dozen steps to the marble chair of King's Bench, where, just as his brother had done, he sat and announced that he would begin to reign, as Richard III.

Following the usual formulas, Richard promised to rule on behalf of all his subjects, and to be a just and impartial lawgiver. To maintain the rule of law, he told the assembled crowd in a 'pleasant oration', was the king's foremost duty. He wanted to heal divisions and unify the country, to which end he would 'pardon all offences against him'. Following his peroration the long-standing Yorkist servant Sir John Fogge – one of the Woodvilles' close associates, who had been extracted from his bolthole in Westminster sanctuary – was led in front of the new king. Richard clasped his hand, a public welcome back into the political fold.[47]

In all this, Richard was at pains to paint himself as Edward IV's natural successor. The allegations of his brother's bastardy – so loudly trumpeted in recent days – were now quietly dropped from the official narrative. As quickly as he had been erased from the Yorkist line, Edward IV was painted back in, Richard embracing the memory of 'our dearest brother, late king of England'. Now that the lineal aberration of Edward's sons had been excised, his family's line could continue on its serene, ordained path.[48] In turn, all those former servants of Edward IV could be assured of Richard's favour. If any of these men, who had naturally – but, as it turned out, mistakenly – transferred their loyalties to Edward V, were worried about what Hastings' execution meant for their own relationship with the new regime, Richard wanted to set those worries at ease. His conciliatory handshake with Fogge spoke volumes. Bygones could now be bygones.

A more than usual sense of his royal mission suffused the new king's pronouncements and paperwork. Beside him in Westminster Hall sat John Howard, rewarded for his loyalty to Richard with the dukedom of Norfolk that he had quietly craved and which Edward IV had denied him. The royal charter enshrining Howard's title was exaggeratedly loquacious. God's eternal radiance shone upon 'those who share in his goodness', it pronounced, and Richard III was one of those fortunate creatures. Irradiated by God's 'grace and liberality', he was determined to reward Howard, the most noble and deserving of his subjects.[49] Indeed, Richard had been sent by God for the benefit of all England. He would be a perfect king: obedient to the law, he would rule in accordance with all the virtues – or, as the catch-all term had it, to 'loyaute'. It was a commitment that Richard wore publicly in a new royal motto, *'loyaute me lie'*: 'loyalty binds me'. His God-given virtues would transmute into a tireless commitment to the common good, and to bringing peace, order, unity and prosperity to England.[50]

The bewildering reality was rather different. In Calais, Hastings' erstwhile deputy John, Lord Dinham – a man who, back in 1459, had helped Edward and Warwick, on the run from Lancastrian forces, escape England to Calais and who had remained staunchly loyal ever since – wrote to Richard for clarification of the new order of things. Could he explain, Dinham asked bluntly, how the new oaths he was now being asked to swear to Richard squared with the oaths he had already made to Edward V? Even though they might not have risked Dinham's tactlessness, across the country people were asking themselves the same question.[51]

In the following days, the new regime started to take shape. As royal favour was redistributed, Buckingham was naturally first in the queue. To go with the grants Richard had already made him, the duke was handed a slew of high offices, including the constableship of England, an assortment of posts previously held by Hastings, as well as a substantial portfolio of duchy of Lancaster lands, which he had long claimed but had been denied him by Edward IV. Together with his coveted dukedom of Norfolk, John Howard was given a swathe of estates through East Anglia, turning him into Richard's point man in the region, and made admiral of England; his eldest son Thomas Howard, a pugnacious forty-year-old, was made earl of Surrey.[52]

That, though, was more or less it. With the emphasis firmly on continuity, there wasn't a great deal of new patronage to go around. Richard's childhood friend Francis Lovell was given Hastings' old post of chamberlain; Richard's trusted servant Robert Brackenbury was confirmed in the key role of constable of the Tower. Besides that, the changes were minimal – with one further exception.

William Catesby was made chancellor of the Exchequer, an esquire of the body in Richard's household and a member of the king's council; along with these posts, he was given offices and lands in his native Northamptonshire, all of which had been held by his former boss, the man he had betrayed, Lord Hastings.[53] Catesby's meteoric rise from mere lawyer to one of the key architects of the new regime spoke volumes for the critical role he had played in the seismic events of previous weeks, one that had earned him both Buckingham's and Richard's intimate confidence and trust.

Some way down the food chain of favour, Catesby's Northamptonshire connections received substantial rewards for their part in the rise of the new regime. Prominent among them were the Wake family. Both Roger and his brother William were given lands from Anthony Woodville's confiscated estates. It was, though, their half-brother John who did best. He was made a gentleman usher of the king's chamber, an influential and confidential post that involved him being constantly in Richard's presence and supervising the smooth functioning of the chamber, from the drawing up of servants' rotas to the greeting of noblemen and diplomats. What made Richard single out John Wake in this way was unclear, though he was, it seemed, especially close to Catesby. Perhaps it had something to do with John's parentage.

John Wake had been the product of his father's second marriage to the earl of Warwick's troubled young kinswoman Margaret Lucy; his birth, indeed, may well have resulted in her death, aged twenty-eight, in August 1466. During her short chaotic life Margaret, who clearly had something about her, had been constantly harassed by men. After her first husband was killed by her lover at the battle of Northampton, she was stalked for years by an Oxfordshire lawyer, Thomas Danvers. Convinced that he had made a marriage contract with Margaret, which she strongly denied, Danvers had launched legal proceedings against her and, during the notorious court case that followed, spread noxious, defamatory and highly upsetting rumours about her. Around this time, with the intervention of the earl of Warwick, she married his follower Thomas Wake instead.[54]

Years later, Thomas More wrote that Margaret Lucy had been one of Edward IV's mistresses and had borne him a child. The story was hazy: More couldn't even get her name right, calling her 'Dame Elizabeth Lucy'. But in other circumstantial respects it made sense. A young, attractive, vulnerable widow throwing herself on the king's mercy, Margaret Lucy was Edward's type; moreover, she could conceivably have been the young woman in Warwick's household that Edward, while staying there, had impregnated some two decades previously, to the earl's fury.

Now, in June 1483, Richard's claim to the throne had focused on proving the invalidity of Edward IV's marriage to Elizabeth Woodville, and the corresponding bastardy of their children. Various stories of marriage precontracts were floating around and, as Richard sought to build a case against his late brother, it was possible that the identity of John Wake's mother acquired a fresh significance. Richard's exceptionally generous treatment of Wake was undoubtedly down to the service he had already done Richard, and his own excellent connections. But it might also have helped that, when need arose, Wake could tell anybody who cared to listen the story of how his mother was once exploited mercilessly by the late king of England.

Under the direction of Buckingham and Howard, the plans for Richard's coronation were drawn up. On 27 June, the keeper of the Great Wardrobe, Piers Curteys, reconfirmed in his post by the new regime, signed indentures for work to be completed by 3 July – which, even though he was largely repurposing the work done for the cancelled ceremonies of Edward V, still gave him barely six days to deliver his contract. Artists painted flags, trumpet banners and heralds' coats-of-arms with brightly coloured oils, fabric setting stiff as the paint dried thick; embroiderers fringed, corded and 'powdered' jackets, robes, banners and hangings with finely worked motifs and badges. Some of the work was outsourced to suppliers, from the London haberdasher Thomas Sunnyff, who produced thirteen black bonnets, and the merchant William Melbourne, supplying 13,000 cloth boars, Richard's badge, to be stitched onto uniforms and handed out; to the Lucchese Ludovico Bonvisi, who supplied fine gold-woven damasks and 'baudekin', the silk brocade named after Baghdad, its place of origin.[55]

Also specified in Curteys' indentures was the customary list of 'liveries': the distribution of fine textiles and clothes to all those attending the coronation, guests and servants alike. Compiled by Richard in consultation with 'the lords of his most honourable council' and drawn up with acute attention to fine gradations of rank, it also evinced solicitude for Edward IV and Elizabeth's recently bastardized children. The three-year-old Bridget, sick and unable to attend the ceremony, was supplied with down-stuffed pillows and pillowcases of fine Holland cloth. Another of their offspring, though, was named among the honoured guests: the recently deposed Edward V, now styled 'lord Edward, son of late King Edward the Fourth'.

The clothes to be supplied to 'lord Edward' were opulent and extensive, virtually a new wardrobe in itself: eight gowns, each made of various colours of damask, velvet and satin; and a variety of eye-catching accessories, including thirteen bonnets, five hats, six pairs of gloves and seven pairs of shoes made of the softest Spanish leather. His place in the royal procession was indicated by the two pairs of gold spurs provided, and the nine horse harnesses of velvet and silk, garnished with buttons of Venetian gold. He was to be accompanied by seven henchmen, close servants, dressed in black doublets and gowns of quartered green and white.[56]

Less than a week before the pre-coronation ceremonies were due to start, Richard and his advisers were working on the assumption that the attendance of 'lord Edward' would symbolize the new spirit of unity which the new regime aimed to engender. His presence at the rites would be the most powerful, most persuasive symbol of all. If he was prepared to acknowledge Richard III as king, so too, it was clearly hoped, would all those whose loyalties still lay with Edward IV's children.

Nevertheless, Richard was taking no chances. Security around the forthcoming ceremonies would be exceptionally tight. In the first days of July, his northern forces, some four thousand men under the command of the earl of Northumberland and Richard Ratcliffe, arrived in the capital: Richard greeted them bareheaded as a sign of respect. The troops' presence had the desired effect. Helmeted, heavily armed men, they seemed to some to possess superhuman strength, 'with hands and arms of iron' – although, muttered one Londoner disparagingly, they were 'very evil apparelled', fitted out in rusty and ill-maintained armour. As Richard imposed a 10 p.m. curfew and banned the carrying of unlicensed weapons, his men took up positions throughout the city and its suburbs, detachments stationed at crossroads, gates and other strategic points 'for safeguard of the king's person'. If anybody tried anything, Richard was prepared.[57]

Early on the morning of 6 July Richard and his wife, Anne Neville, emerged from Westminster Hall. Visions in crimson cloth-of-gold, their trains borne respectively by Buckingham and Margaret Beaufort, countess of Richmond, they walked barefoot along a path of red cloth to the adjacent abbey, their approach heralded by blaring trumpets and a train of clerics, noblemen, knights and civic representatives, the crowds held back by heavy security. Entering the packed abbey, its interior swathed in rich cloth, they climbed the steps to the specially constructed stage where their thrones awaited them. There, they were anointed and crowned, Archbishop Bourchier setting St Edward's crown on Richard's head with a murmured *'coronet te deus'*, just as he had done with Edward IV, in the same spot, almost exactly twenty-two years before.[58] Richard recited the ancient coronation oaths with fervour. Wanting all his subjects to know what they could expect from him, he had the oaths translated into English, for the first time.[59] Characteristically, Richard was obsessed with these ideals of good government: during his reign, he would return to the oaths again and again.

That afternoon, the guests filed through Westminster Yard, its conduits running with red wine, and into the hall for the wedding feast. Running the length of the cavernous space were four tables, the seating plan done, as customary, according to strict precedence. At 4 p.m., England's new king and queen were announced. Richard and Anne took their places at King's Bench, now transformed into a banqueting table, on their left a sideboard glinting with gold plate; with servants hovering attentively, the ceremonies were directed from his horse by John Howard, revelling in his new place in the regime. The feast unfolded in a succession of extravagant dishes paraded triumphantly through the hall, the arrival of each course announced by a phalanx of thirty trumpeters. Richard accepted the obeisance of the king's champion Robert Dymmock and, in response to the heralds' customary shouts of *largesse*, tipped them extravagantly. In between courses, as minstrels played, he chatted attentively with guests, a picture of gracious, regal informality. The royal socializing went on late into the evening; a 'void' of 'wafers and hippocras' – sweet cakes and spiced wine – signalled the end of the feast.

In the gathering darkness, a stream of servants bearing flaming torches processed into the hall. The assembled lords rose and, one by one, filed past Richard making obeisance. Then the party broke up into the July night, guests making their torchlit ways 'where it liked them best': Richard and Anne, surrounded by a cluster of lords, into the palace and their apartments; London's dignitaries through Westminster's silent streets, following the curve of the river east, back to the silent, curfewed city.[60]

That evening, in the privacy of his chamber, Richard perhaps reflected that things had gone as well as they possibly could have done. The guest list had been a reflection of the Yorkist unity towards which he aspired. There had been a few obvious absences. Elizabeth Woodville had refused to emerge from sanctuary; her sister Katherine, Buckingham's long-suffering wife, wasn't invited – though this was probably more a reflection of their sullen marriage than anything political. Others, like John Morton, sent far from London to Buckingham's secure Welsh castle of Brecon, were behind bars.[61] But more or less all England's nobles had been present, along with seventy knights. The vast majority of his brother's men had become Richard's own: from the late king's *éminence grise* Sir Thomas Montgomery, to Sir George Brown and Sir William Parr, Edward's former master of horse Sir John Cheyne, his chancellor of the Exchequer Sir Thomas Thwaites, and Thomas St Leger, the chamber servant who had married Anne of York and in the process had become Edward's – and Richard's – brother-in-law.[62] Even Lord Stanley was there, having recovered from the fracas in the council chamber a few weeks before – all smiles, his cut head healed, no harm done. Stanley's dominance in the northwest made him a crucial node in any English king's government – and, if not onside, a potential threat. Accordingly, both he and his wife Lady Margaret Beaufort had occupied prominent places in the coronation ceremonial: Stanley walking in front of the king carrying the great mace of state; Margaret bearing Queen Anne's train.[63]

Quite how much this reflected loyalty to the new regime was unclear. Most people were in London anyway, having arrived for another coronation entirely. Invited to Richard's crowning, people were expected to stay. Leaving would have been unwise.

One sign of the new regime's insecurity was a glaring absence from the coronation guest list. Barely a week before, a delivery of fine clothes had been sent to the Tower for Edward V, 'lord Edward', in anticipation of his attendance. But in the meantime, Richard had changed his mind. When it came to the coronation itself, the boy wasn't there. There were rumours of a plot to break both princes out of the Tower, which in turn prompted a change in their security arrangements: they were, it was said, 'holden more strength'. It clearly wasn't a good time for Edward V – a living, breathing rebuke to Richard's claim to the throne – to be paraded at his uncle's coronation.

People started to grow anxious about the boys. Where before they could be seen playing in the Tower gardens and doing archery practice, now they no longer appeared outside. Their faces were seen at the barred windows of their apartments with less frequency as the days went on. Finally, they were no longer seen at all.

Around this time, most of the household servants that Edward V had been allowed to keep with him were dismissed. According to one of his remaining attendants, his doctor John Argentine, the boy, increasingly agitated, had developed the habit of confessing his sins daily, 'like a victim preparing for sacrifice'.

The man to whom Argentine talked was a black-habited Augustinian friar named Domenico Mancini. A cultured man, steeped in fashionable humanist learning, Mancini had moved north from his native Rome to Paris, looking for work. Arriving in England sometime towards the end of 1482 – sent, possibly, by a French government increasingly worried about a vengeful Edward IV's plans to invade France – he had stayed and, fascinated and appalled by the political upheavals that had followed Edward's death, tried to make sense of what he was witnessing.

Mancini didn't know England and couldn't speak much of the language. His sources were mostly people like him: members of London's

Italian mercantile community, and cosmopolitan, internationally educated Latinists like Argentine and the itinerant scholar Pietro Carmeliano, who, unknown to his new employers the English government, was also a Venetian spy. But though reliant on hearsay and at times ill-informed speculation – in which he was hardly alone – Mancini was an inquisitive, investigative sort. As he moved around London prompting, questioning and listening, he was concerned to get his facts straight as far as he could and to report the truth of what he experienced. Returning to Paris shortly after Richard's coronation, Mancini would write a vivid account of the revolution he witnessed – the first and only immediate, first-hand account of Richard's seizure of power.

Shortly before he left England in July 1483, Mancini picked up on the widespread concern over Edward V's disappearance. Mention of the young king's name, he found, elicited a common – and to him, frustratingly incoherent – response: people 'burst forth into tears and lamentations'.[64] In place of words, they simply grew distressed.

19

No Long Time in Rest

A fortnight after his coronation, Richard's travelling household left Windsor Castle and rode west up the Thames valley on the first stage of his summer progress, a journey which would take in a swathe of the west country before curving back on itself, heading through the midlands and northeast towards its final destination – York. It was an ambitious itinerary, particularly in the context of Edward IV's torpid parades of recent years, and one with a set of traditional aims in mind: for Richard to see as much of his new kingdom as possible, and for him to display those kingly qualities to which he had publicly committed himself in his coronation oaths. The royal cavalcade was boosted by the presence of Buckingham, Richard's partner in power, and Lord Stanley, whom Richard had reconfirmed in his role as steward of the king's household and, for good measure, made a knight of the Garter. But as Richard knew, he had to watch his back. Talk of Woodville plots continued to bubble. The royal absence from London would provide perfect conditions for conspiracy to breed.[1]

Earlier that July Richard had dispatched his trusted chaplain and envoy Thomas Hutton to Brittany, to reassure Duke Francis of his commitment to tackling the English pirates that had plagued the western reaches of the Channel since Edward IV's death. Hutton was also given another set of instructions. Having sailed over the horizon two months previously, Elizabeth Woodville's brother Sir Edward and his men had resurfaced at the Breton court, which was also home to another political refugee. This was the twenty-six-year-old Lancastrian Henry Tudor, only son of Lady Margaret Beaufort, who – despite various attempts at reconciliation and extradition – had been in Brittany for the past twelve years. But that July it was Sir Edward

Woodville, not Tudor, who occupied Richard's mind. As Hutton moved about the Breton court, Richard told him, he was to 'feel and understand' Duke Francis's attitude to the Yorkist fugitive. In particular, Hutton should find out 'by all means to him possible' whether there were any Breton plans to send Woodville into England to stir up insurgency, to carry out some manner of 'enterprise'. He was to update Richard 'with all diligence'.[2]

Richard wasn't inclined to let grass grow under his feet. As one chronicler, a man in government circles, put it, he 'never acted sleepily' but 'incisively and with the utmost vigilance'. In any case, Richard himself hardly needed reminding of the real danger of plots by foreign-backed English exiles. Back in 1470, he had fled England with Edward as a result of Warwick and Clarence's French-backed plot and, six months later, had taken part in Edward's vengeful return. Now, as Richard set out from Windsor, his right-hand man John Howard turned back towards London: the newly created duke of Norfolk had been handed exclusive power to muster troops throughout southeast England in the king's name. With plenty of business to attend to in his native East Anglia, Howard was well positioned to keep an eye out for disturbances.[3]

The first days of the royal progress passed sedately enough. At Reading on 23 July, Richard granted Hastings' family lands to his widow, Katherine, along with custody of their son and heir – the kind of conciliatory gesture for which the new king was gaining a reputation and which, he perhaps hoped, would help dispel any lingering tensions provoked by his summary beheading of Edward IV's close friend.[4] A short stay at Oxford followed, offering Richard the chance to display his credentials as a patron of learning. At Magdalen College, he sat through a day of scholarly disputations in the great hall, presenting the celebrated humanist scholar William Grocyn with a deer and 5 marks for his performance. Then after a tour of the university, dispensing largesse as he went, Richard left for the crumbling royal manor of Woodstock, where he spent a couple of days hunting. On the 29th, he made the ten-mile journey west to Minster Lovell where, in a mark of special favour, he planned to lodge with his friend and chamberlain, Francis Lovell. That day, as the royal household's carts and carriages rumbled through the Oxfordshire lanes, a messenger from London, riding frantically up the Thames valley, caught up with Richard's slow-moving cavalcade.

Amid widespread anxiety over the 'human fate' of Edward V and his brother, a group of conspirators had been arrested in London for plotting an 'enterprise', an attempt to break the two princes out of the Tower, which was to involve starting decoy fires in various locations in the city to distract officials. With around fifty conspirators involved, the plot had sprung leaks: the ringleaders had been detained before they could act. Reaching Minster Lovell, Richard wrote to his chancellor John Russell with orders to put them on trial.[5]

Soon after, four men were convicted and executed. Two of them had been royal servants: Stephen Ireland, a wardrober in the Tower and John Smith, a groom in Edward IV's stable. Their involvement was especially worrying. It suggested both that bigger, more powerful forces lurked behind the conspirators – John Smith's former boss was John Cheyne, Edward IV's master of the horse – and that, for all the apparent willingness of the late king's servants to turn out for Richard's coronation, loyalties had not transferred so smoothly to him after all. Moreover, the condemned men had been found guilty of planning to send letters to the English fugitives in Brittany. These messages were addressed not to Sir Edward Woodville, but to the long-exiled Henry Tudor and his uncle Jasper earl of Pembroke, the diehard Lancastrian who was a constant presence at his nephew's side.[6]

A few weeks before, Richard had sent Hutton to Brittany to unearth details of a possible Woodville-led plot. But the situation was changing fast. The charges against the London conspirators now made clear that they were seeking to bring on board the exiled Tudors in a move to restore Edward V to the throne of England. And the initiative for this new Woodville–Tudor partnership had come from Henry Tudor's mother, wife to Richard's steward Lord Stanley: Margaret Beaufort.

Over the years, Margaret had worked hard to bring her exiled son in from the cold. Her most recent attempt, in June 1482, had seen Edward IV approve terms for Henry Tudor's restoration to the king's 'grace and favour'. But, advised by his uncle Jasper – a man deeply sceptical of Yorkist gestures of conciliation – Tudor had stayed put in Brittany and the plans were shelved. After Richard seized the throne, Margaret revived them.

Approaching the new king, Margaret proposed an idea that had been mooted some years previously: that her son should marry one of Edward IV's daughters. Richard, it seemed, made equivocal noises.[7] In any case, Margaret and Stanley, though willingly aligning themselves with Richard's regime, were experienced political operators and used to hedging against all possible outcomes. Accordingly, Margaret also engaged with the other, disaffected, side of the newly fractured house of York, opening secret talks regarding the same marriage proposal with the girls' mother, Elizabeth Woodville.

Quite when the two noblewomen started talking was unclear, though Margaret may well have waited until Richard was safely on progress before making contact with Elizabeth, who was still hunkered down in Westminster sanctuary. Their go-between was an eminent Welsh astrologer–mathematician named Lewis Caerleon, who, physician to both Margaret and Elizabeth, had the perfect cover, walking gravely past the unsuspecting guards Richard had posted around the sanctuary perimeter.

That summer, communication between the two women blossomed into something more ambitious: regime change and the possibility of restoring Edward V to the throne and his mother's family to power. Margaret had much to offer – if, that was, she could persuade her notoriously inscrutable husband to swing the might of his north-western forces behind a Woodville-led uprising, and if the exiled Tudors could exploit their contacts at the Breton court to raise funds and men for an invasion. For Margaret, too, the stakes were high. Henry Tudor's marriage to one of Elizabeth Woodville's daughters would tie him to the house of York. If that marriage produced children, they would then take their place in the Yorkist line of succession. It was an agreement rich in historical irony. In previous decades Lady Margaret's cousins, the dukes of Somerset, finding themselves unable to live with Edward IV, had done their utmost to destroy him before being destroyed in turn. Now, the Beauforts promised to secure the future of Edward's family line.

In late July and early August, Margaret was a flickering presence in Woodville insurgency, in the plotters' attempts to contact Henry

Tudor and in the flight of her half-brother John Welles, who was apparently among the conspirators. Evading arrest, Welles eventually resurfaced among the exiles in Brittany.[8] At this point, Margaret's aim still seemed to be the restoration of her son to his earldom of Richmond – whose title and lands now belonged to Richard, a crucial node in his northern hegemony – and as a key figure in the restored regime of Edward V. But, in the following weeks, things changed.

As Richard continued westward, he displayed the open-handed liberality and ostentatious piety demanded of a good prince. Determined to define himself against his late brother's reign, with its increasingly creative and grasping efforts at fundraising, he graciously declined the customary corporate gifts of cash from the communities, towns and cities that he passed through. He left a trail of regal largesse in his wake: from Woodstock, where he regranted to the local community lands previously annexed by Edward; to the city of Gloucester, which he granted various liberties, with all the political and financial benefits they entailed; to Tewkesbury, where he repaid a long-standing debt of £310 owed by his brother Clarence to the abbey there.[9] Meanwhile, he continued watchful. And the situation continued to escalate.

By mid-August, events were tumbling over themselves. Amid reports of a desperate bid to smuggle Edward IV and Elizabeth Woodville's daughters out of Westminster sanctuary and out of the country – so that, as one chronicler put it, if anything happened to the princes in the Tower, the kingdom might 'some day return to its rightful heirs' – Richard reinforced security around the sanctuary's perimeter, saturating the abbey and its precincts with troops under the command of one of his trusted northern servants, the Yorkshireman John Nesfield. The whole neighbourhood, said the same chronicler, 'took on the appearance of a castle'.[10]

In addition, Richard sent an urgent request for reinforcements. His demand for two thousand Welsh troops, to be dispatched to him 'in all haste', echoed his frantic summons to his northern supporters back in June. Shortly after, Richard sent orders to Buckingham – who had peeled off from the royal progress, to return to his own lands in Wales – to head a commission into treasons throughout southeast

England. The threat of insurgency in support of Edward V seemed to be spreading outwards from London, leaching into the surrounding home counties as far afield as Kent and Oxfordshire: regions dominated by the late king's household servants.[11]

As the threat intensified, so too did the pressure on Richard. Since his brother's death four months previously, he had responded to the newly uncertain world with a savage decision, fuelled by his craving for order and predictability, and his instinctive tendency to reach for extreme methods to impose it. That summer, as a nebulous opposition coalesced around the blameless figure of Edward V, Richard was perhaps reminded of his own formative years: of a time when there had been two kings of England, and of the chaos and bloodletting begotten by this divided royal authority. Now, with history set to repeat itself, it was hardly surprising if Richard just wanted the problem to go away.[12]

During these last weeks of summer, as Richard's household progressed regally through the east midlands, stopping off at Nottingham Castle, and on into south Yorkshire, talk spread that the young princes had been murdered. If, during the last couple of months, there had been whispers about the boys' killing, now the rumours came in a torrent. In the absence of concrete information, stories proliferated. Buckingham, so one report had it, had egged Richard on, just as he had done from the moment Richard seized power at Stony Stratford. Later, Thomas More's elaborate retelling had the constable of the Tower, Robert Brackenbury, refusing to carry out the orders, and Richard's sidekick Sir James Tyrell – a man to whom he had for years delegated the most sensitive tasks – ordering two of the princes' guards to kill them. These men were Miles Forest, a wardrobe keeper from Richard's Durham fortress of Barnard Castle, who had probably made his way south with the king's entourage and taken up a post in the Tower, and Tyrell's own household servant John Dighton. Likewise, opinions varied as to how the princes had been murdered: smothered between feather mattresses, or drowned in malmsey (an echo, this, of Clarence's killing), or injected with a 'venomous poison'. Whatever the details, one dominant narrative soon established itself. The boys had been killed, and on Richard's watch: 'the people', wrote one chronicler, 'laid the blame only on him'.[13]

As commentators acknowledged, whatever Richard had – or had not – actually done soon came to be irrelevant. It was the story, 'common report', which mattered; 'hard it is to alter the natural disposition of one's mind', the same chronicler reflected, 'and suddenly to extirp the thing therein settled by daily conversation'. Once people had made up their mind to believe something, in other words, it was all but impossible to make them change it. Unable to offer any positive proof of the princes' continued survival, Richard lost control of the narrative.

In Westminster sanctuary, an uncomprehending grief descended on the small Woodville establishment. Elizabeth Woodville's misery was absolute. She passed out, then, when revived, was frenzied in her distress: crying, tearing her hair, her shouts of pain echoing throughout her lodgings, calling out the names of her disappeared sons. Finally, 'after long lamentation', her pain began to congeal into anger. She besought God for revenge.[14]

Having lived through the violent upheavals of recent years, people weren't easily shocked. But if, following Richard's brutal assumption of power that spring, many in the Yorkist establishment had shuffled hesitatingly into line, widespread reports that the two blameless royal children had been killed while in his care convinced them that their initial misgivings had been right. Among the former household servants of Edward IV there remained a fierce allegiance to the memory of the late king and his two sons. That allegiance now acquired a new sharpness.

Late that summer, Sir George Brown wrote a brief message to his nephew John Paston the younger. Brown was a Yorkist loyalist; his stepfather was the late king's recently executed chamber treasurer Sir Thomas Vaughan. One of Edward IV's close chamber servants, Brown had been knighted on the battlefield at Tewkesbury back in 1471; following the king's death that April, he had carried the banner of St George at his funeral and was among the household men keeping watch over his body the night before its burial. Now, Brown's message to Paston read, simply, 'Loyalté Aymé. It shall never come out for me.' Scrawling a variation on Richard III's new royal motto, Brown dismissed it out of hand. There was no way that Richard's idea of loyalty would work for Brown: he didn't trust the new king an inch.[15]

When rumours of the princes' deaths reached Margaret Beaufort, still at her husband's London house, she saw a new possibility. She made a fresh proposal to Elizabeth Woodville through the indefatigable Lewis Caerleon, who continued to carry messages between the two women 'without any suspicion'. Now that Edward IV's sons were assumed to be dead, a marriage between Henry Tudor and the widowed queen's oldest daughter, Elizabeth of York, offered both a new focus for the loyalties of disaffected Yorkists, and a different way for the heirs of Edward IV and Elizabeth Woodville to regain power.

In his secret talks with Elizabeth Woodville, Caerleon spoke fluently and persuasively and, presumably, with exceptional sensitivity; going off script, he talked 'off his own head'. Soon after, he walked unassumingly out of Westminster sanctuary having extracted a promise from the widowed queen that she would do everything she could 'to procure all her husband King Edward's friends' to join forces in a conspiracy with Henry Tudor to 'obtain the kingdom' and, having done so, to make her daughter Elizabeth of York his queen.[16] In the privacy of Westminster sanctuary, these two noblewomen and their Welsh middleman concocted an astonishing plan. In place of the missing princes, Henry Tudor, the fugitive Lancastrian son of Lady Margaret Beaufort, would become the heir to Edward IV and his dynastic line. The question now was whether those loyal to Edward IV and his heirs would accept it.

The plotters moved fast, Margaret sending a messenger to Brittany to update Tudor. Meanwhile an intermediary, a 'chief dealer' between Margaret and the pro-Woodville Yorkists, was agreed on: Margaret's receiver-general Reynold Bray, a nerveless, blunt-speaking midlander. Within a few days, Bray had made contact with sympathetic plotters across southern England: former servants of Edward IV including John Cheyne, George Brown and the Somerset knight Giles Daubeney, and friends of the Woodvilles like the Kentish Guildford family. Not long after, Bray received a message from the duke of Buckingham, now at his castle of Brecon in south Wales. Buckingham knew Bray, who had worked for the duke's late uncle, Sir Henry Stafford – who had himself been Lady Margaret Beaufort's third husband (before his death in 1471 and her marriage to Lord Stanley). It wasn't, however, Buckingham who had instigated contact with Bray, but the man who was now the duke's prisoner: John Morton.[17]

Now well into his sixties, Morton's experience of the crises of past decades was practically unrivalled: indeed, he had been at the heart of many of them. From St Albans to Towton, to a decade-long stretch in exile plotting the restoration of the house of Lancaster, to the political conversion after Tewkesbury that saw him become one of Edward IV's closest advisers, Morton's extraordinary journey had now brought him, via the devastation of Richard's fateful council meeting in the Tower that June, to Brecon, where he sat chatting comfortably and confidentially with the proud, greedy young nobleman who was his gaoler.

Earlier that summer, Richard and Buckingham had had a spat. When the duke demanded the grant of some of his ancestral lands now held by the crown, Richard, in a rare display of anger against the ally whom he had already so richly rewarded, slapped him down. Perhaps, the king felt, Buckingham's persistent grabbiness would carry on unless checked. Whatever the case, the argument summed up a change in their relationship. During Richard's protectorship, commentators had seen Richard and Buckingham, 'these dukes', as two sides of the same coin. Since Richard's coronation, this balance had, inevitably, tilted. Richard, now, was king; Buckingham, however exalted, was his subject. And the duke didn't like it.[18]

In Thomas More's account, Morton played Buckingham with consummate skill. Teasing out the duke's envy of Richard, playing on his frustrated royal ambitions as a Lancastrian descendant of Edward III, Morton then introduced an ominous note. Ruminating on the widespread resentment against Richard, he suggested that Buckingham would be far better off, not to mention safer, by distancing himself from the king and aligning himself instead with the Woodville–Beaufort conspiracy. All the while, like the experienced councillor he was, Morton 'rather seemed to follow' the duke's train of thought 'than to lead him'.

When Morton was done with him, Buckingham had come to believe that rebellion against Richard III was the obvious best step, of 'infinite benefit' to the kingdom – and that it was all his own idea. According to Thomas More, Morton even insinuated that Buckingham himself should be king. Gratified, the duke told Morton that he was keen to use his 'faithful secret advice and counsel'. Reynold Bray shuttled unobtrusively between Brecon and Lady Margaret Beaufort, who adjusted her plans accordingly. By the end of the summer Buckingham had been sucked into a conspiracy against Richard III, the king that he had put on the throne, on behalf of 'the blood of king Edward' – the Yorkist line that, only months before, he had helped overthrow and tried to destroy.[19]

On 29 August 1483, his progress swelled by seventy northern knights and gentlemen that had joined him at Pontefract, Richard entered York in triumph, together with his wife and their ten-year-old son Edward. The boy was in delicate health, brought by chariot the fifty miles south from Middleham Castle, though he had managed to get on a horse for the procession into York. For Richard's latest, triumphant homecoming, the city corporation had laid on a spectacular welcome. Its plans, as was customary, had been drawn up in close consultation with Richard's household, the fretful demands of his secretary John Kendall betraying a king who, beneath the expansive exterior, was anxious to make the right impression on his new royal entourage. Richard, wrote Kendall, wanted plenty of pageants, speechifying and spectacular décor, 'for many southern lords and men of worship are with them'. These southerners, Kendall added, would 'mark well' the kind of welcome they got in York: its extravagance would reflect the love northerners had for their lord, now England's king.[20]

Richard needn't have worried. The following days unfolded in a haze of wining, dining and corporate hospitality – York's mayor spent a ruinous amount hosting two banquets for the king and select members of his retinue – as well as the required pageants and plays. At his lodgings in the archbishop's palace, Richard graciously received civic notables and their gifts, laying on feasts and entertainments 'to gain the affections of the people'.[21]

During those days, one of the king's advisers, Bishop Thomas Langton, wrote to his friend William Sellyng, one of England's finest scholars and the prior of Christ Church, Canterbury. Both in their early fifties, the two men were old friends; Langton kept an eye out at court for Sellyng's interests. Desperate to find a secure way to ship a much-needed consignment of Bordeaux wine back to England – in the Channel, English and French ships continued to attack each other at will – Sellyng wrote anxiously to Langton, who provided reassuring advice and promised to put in a word with the king. He then turned to the subject of Richard himself.

The king's progress north, Langton wrote, had been an astounding success. Richard had the popular touch: 'he contents the people wherever he goes, best that ever did prince.' Open-handed and magnanimous, he went out of his way to redress injustices, especially among the poor and needy who had previously 'suffered wrong' and who were 'relieved and helped by him and his commands'. Truly, Langton pondered, 'I never liked the conditions of any prince so well as his' – which, given that he himself was currently luxuriating in the king's favour, was unsurprising. Only weeks before, Richard had bestowed upon Langton the Welsh bishopric of St Davids; Langton, though, already had his eye on the much richer see of Salisbury, recently vacated by Lionel Woodville – and was expecting to get it. As he put it to Sellyng with a nod and a wink, he hoped soon to be 'an English man and no more Welsh', adding, in Latin, *'sit hoc clam omnes'* – 'mum's the word'.

Yet Langton's assessment of Richard was sincere enough. The king was showing a keen desire to deliver on the sacred oaths he had made at his coronation two months previously. As he watched Richard go about his work, Langton was judging him against those ideals and, implicitly, against the government of his late brother Edward. In short, Richard was a bright new dawn for England: not simply a monarch for a privileged few, as Edward's reign had increasingly come to be seen, but for the many. 'God hath sent him to us for the weal of us all.'

If such an encomium might have been made to order by Richard himself, the king would have been less delighted with Langton's comment on his household, in which 'sensual pleasure holds sway to an increasing extent'. Richard, apparently, was enjoying the well-stocked royal cellars – though such an observation was not, Langton added hastily, to detract from his words of praise.[22]

The high point of the royal visit came on 8 September, the feast of the Nativity of the Blessed Virgin. That day, Richard and Queen Anne processed, crowned, through York's streets to the Minster, where they celebrated mass in a ceremony that to one observer seemed like a 'second coronation': a way, perhaps, of acknowledging the special relationship between Richard and this great northern city. Then, they returned to the archbishop's palace, where Richard created his son prince of Wales, investing him with the role that Edward IV had once given his own heir, the boy who had become Edward V.[23]

In a proclamation announcing his plans for his son, Richard set forth his own vision of kingship: the well-worn simile of the king as the sun, bathing the orbiting planets – his noblemen – in his 'outstanding light'. Despite its ubiquity, there was something distinctive about Richard's use of the image. For him, kingship combined both power and heavy responsibility. If Richard was all-seeing, training the 'gaze of our inward eye' on his kingdom and its subjects, he could also discern the 'immensity', the magnitude, of the task that confronted him – the 'great responsibilities that press upon us'. There was little here of Edward IV's 'comfort and joy'. Richard's was a burdensome power.[24]

Soon after Richard's arrival in York, an envoy came from Brittany with a letter from Duke Francis. Expressing profuse gratitude for Richard's friendship, Francis asked for English military support against Louis XI. Having menaced the duchy's borders for years, Louis was now putting immense pressure on Francis to hand over Henry Tudor, threatening war unless he did so. With conflict looming, the Breton duke urgently needed Richard to supply and pay for a defence force of four thousand archers. Otherwise, Francis regretted, he might be forced to give Tudor to the French king – something he was 'very loath' to do, given the harm Louis was capable of inflicting on Richard and England.[25]

Richard hardly needed reminding about Louis' propensity for meddling in English affairs. But over the decades, he had also become familiar with Francis's wheedling demands for military aid. It was true that the duke was only following up on promises made him by Edward IV – shortly before his death, in his violent fury against Louis XI's double-crossing, Edward had assured Francis of his support – but to Richard, it looked suspiciously like blackmail.[26] Barely had he received Francis's request, however, before the situation in France changed suddenly and dramatically.

On 30 August Louis XI died, the cumulative impact of multiple strokes finally catching up with him. While sometimes too artful for his own good, this absurdist French king had often run rings round his enemies, and had been a constant, antic presence in the upheavals of Edward IV's reign. His death brought to the throne his thirteen-year-old heir, Charles VIII. A tantalizing ten months short of his majority, the boy was surrounded by a cluster of predatory French nobles seeking to control him and wield power – a mirror-image of the circumstances that had confronted England on Edward IV's death five months previously.

With the French crown now gripped by its own internal troubles, the situation seemed turned on its head. For Richard, the international outlook was now rich with promise. During the last years of his brother's reign he had watched Edward's increasingly tortuous diplomatic manoeuvrings, his own frustrations barely relieved by the occasional charge across the border into Scotland. Richard yearned to show himself to his subjects as a royal war-leader: now, here was the opportunity. At the very least, he could turn up the pressure on a newly vulnerable France; there was even perhaps the chance of getting Edward's French pension restarted that, earlier in the year, Louis XI had cut off. By the same token, there seemed no need to respond to Brittany's nagging pleas for military support: Richard duly ignored them. And, in the meantime, Richard's expansionist ambitions in Scotland had been given a welcome boost by the return of the Scottish pretender Albany, who had – predictably – fallen out with his brother James III's regime once more and had again fled south of the border. Determined to dominate his European neighbours, to show that neither he nor England would become entangled in the way his brother had been, Richard started to flex his muscles.

After three weeks in York, Richard started out on the journey back south to Westminster, where Parliament, after two abortive summonses during the recent upheavals, was due to convene on 6 November. He left in a cloud of goodwill, having bestowed on the city a raft of generous tax breaks. Never before, wrote his secretary, had a king done 'so much' for the city. For all that, the extent of Richard's grants was vague: so much so that three representatives of York's corporation hurried after the royal party to 'speak with his good grace' and find out what he had actually given them.[27]

In the second week of October, the royal household was making its leisurely way from Gainsborough to Lincoln when royal agents, riding across country from Wales, caught up with it. The messengers brought news that Henry duke of Buckingham, Richard's right-hand man, had raised an army and was marching out of Wales against him.

It was perhaps their altercation that summer that had made Richard suspect something was up. Whatever the case, his agents had been watching Buckingham for weeks. Reluctant to believe ill of the duke, Richard did what kings tended to do in such situations, summoning him with 'exceeding courtesy' to court to explain himself. When Buckingham refused, citing a stomach bug, Richard sent another, sharper message, telling him to stop temporizing and come immediately. Buckingham's response was a declaration of war. By the time his defiant message reached the king, Buckingham had mustered his troops at Brecon and was on the move.[28]

Whatever the extent of Richard's suspicions, he was unprepared for this devastating betrayal. Reaching Lincoln, he scrambled to raise troops and wrote to his chancellor John Russell in London, urgently demanding the great seal, the supreme symbol of royal authority that would give added weight to his commands. Alongside the precise formal text of his secretary's letter, Richard scrawled his own personal postscript. Picking up mid-line where the clerk had finished, he wrote in a neat, crabbed hand whose speed left a trail of smudges and inkblots; when space ran out, he turned the letter ninety degrees, his message crammed perpendicular in the left-hand margin.

Ordering Russell to bring the seal in person immediately, and to send it securely if not – the chancellor was, apparently, ill – Richard then slid into incredulous rage at Buckingham's treachery. The duke had 'best cause to be true', he wrote, yet had proved to be 'the most untrue creature living'. Why, Richard seemed to be asking himself, should somebody he had loaded with rewards now betray him so completely? Struggling to rationalize Buckingham's behaviour, Richard was itching to deal with him: 'never', he ended his postscript grimly, was 'false traitor better purveyed for'.[29]

As Richard mobilized his forces, the full extent of what now faced him became clear. News came in of another rebel front on the other side of the country, in Kent. Following the disturbances that summer, Richard was alert to goings-on in the southeast. The snag was that the nobleman he had appointed to lead the commission into treasonable activity in London and the surrounding counties was Buckingham himself – who, it now transpired, was part of the problem. Luckily for Richard, John Howard also happened to be in the area. In mid-September, touring his new ducal properties in Surrey, Howard had sniffed conspiracy. As he returned to London in early October, reports of uprisings flooded in.

At first, it looked to Howard like the kind of local trouble that had erupted out of Kent for generations – 'the Kentishmen are up in the Weald', he remarked, and aimed 'to come and rob the City' – though he was also long enough in the tooth to know that apparently spontaneous popular protest was often shaped by bigger political forces. Howard set about raising more troops, secured the Thames crossings and the city, and waited.

Soon, two things were disturbingly apparent. The revolts were more extensive than Howard had at first thought, spreading not just across the Thames into Essex and East Anglia, but throughout southern England. As one insurgency ignited, so another caught, carried like brushfire through the forest and heath of the Weald from Kent, through Sussex, westwards.[30] What was more, the uprisings were co-ordinated.

In barely two months, the circle of conspirators around Lady Margaret Beaufort and Elizabeth Woodville had given fresh impetus and focus to the disaffection against Richard and, in co-ordination with Buckingham's rebellion in Wales, had stitched together local cells of resistance in a series of armed uprisings. Their ringleaders were men at the heart of the political establishment, former household men of Edward IV, loyal to his two disappeared sons. In Kent the trouble was spearheaded by the local Woodville-supporting Guildford family and their associates, bolstered by men from East Anglia like Sir William Brandon; further west, in Wiltshire, it was driven by men like John Cheyne, Giles Daubeney and Walter Hungerford, all of whom had been coffin-bearers at Edward IV's funeral. In the southwest, another rebel cell was headed by Thomas St Leger, members of the disgruntled Courtenay family (including the bishop of Exeter, Peter Courtenay) and Elizabeth Woodville's son Dorset, who had resurfaced after months on the run, at his side a square-jawed lawyer named Thomas Lovell who had, it was said, saved Dorset's life. As the uprisings spread, others joined them: men like the Oxfordshire knight, and Dorset's brother-in-law, William Stonor who, receiving an order to mobilize on Richard's behalf, ignored it and linked up with the rebels instead.[31]

Rising up, the rebels attacked royal authority wherever they found it, ripping up the infrastructure and networks of which they had been an integral part, and disrupting Richard's lines of communication. As the king's officers moved across the country on routine business, reporting to central government in Westminster, they were stopped, their documents and funds seized. One customs official, John Kymer, travelling from the Dorset port of Poole, realized that men like him were being targeted: there was no way, he wrote, that he could travel to Westminster, as rebels were out 'in great number' along his route. He stayed put.[32]

As further updates came in, Richard seemed torn between marching south to safeguard London, and combating Buckingham's forces as they marched out of Wales. The rain that autumn was incessant, turning roads to mud, hampering the king's progress and the mobilization of troops – which, even without the foul weather, was proving problematic. With funds low, Richard was forced to scrape together money from his own advisers and to ask his supporters to fund themselves, with a promise to repay them when he could.[33] Besides which, there was widespread hesitancy. Writing from Lancashire, the gentleman Edward Plumpton reported how people were faced with conflicting orders from both Richard and Buckingham, 'in the king's name and otherwise', and froze: 'they knew not what to do'.

Plumpton's candid assessment of the situation was coloured by his own context, as secretary to the twenty-three-year-old Lord Strange, son and heir of Lord Stanley. Stanley was now a key figure in Richard's regime, but the pair had history and Stanley's reputation for slipperiness preceded him; besides which, his wife Margaret Beaufort was one of the main drivers of the rebellion. From the noises that Plumpton made about the duke of Buckingham's 'malice' – an echo of Richard's own language – it looked like the Stanleys had decided to throw their weight behind the king: Lord Strange, indeed, was due to march south with ten thousand men. But the note of doubt remained. Where Strange was headed, Plumpton added coyly, 'we cannot say'.[34]

At Grantham on 19 October, Richard came to a decision. Howard was pushing back successfully against the southern insurgency, imposing control in Kent. Forced to retreat, the rebels were being forced west through southern England. Richard himself headed southwest. He was aiming for Salisbury, one of the centres of insurgency, where he could trap the rebels, sandwiching them between his army and Howard's forces to the east. There, too, he could block any attempt by the southern rebels to link up with Buckingham's forces as they moved out of Wales and into England.[35]

On the 23rd, as he led his assembled army out of Leicester, Richard issued a proclamation against the rebels. The initial bewilderment of a few days earlier was replaced by an implacable conviction. Richard, the proclamation stated, had gone out of his way to demonstrate his commitment to the regal virtues of mercy and justice, hoping through his personal example to persuade evildoers back to the 'way of truth and virtue'. But this had not happened. Instead, a group of traitors had plotted his destruction – and Richard had identified precisely what was fuelling their treason.

On seizing power back in April, Richard had loaded his actions with moral justification, portraying his late brother's court as a pit of iniquity. At his coronation, with most of Edward IV's men apparently reconciled to his kingship, this narrative had faded from the official discourse, Richard instead presenting himself as his brother's natural successor. Now, in his October proclamation – or, as it was officially titled, 'Proclamation for the reform of morals' – these original accusations acquired a fresh intensity, a sharper internecine edge. Not only Edward and his wife's Woodville family, but all those loyal to the late king, were tarred with the same brush.

The rebels, the proclamation stated, were 'oppressors and extortioners' of the king's subjects and 'horrible adulterers and bawds'. It was unsurprising that Elizabeth Woodville's son Dorset should have rebelled. Such behaviour was entirely consistent with his rotten morals: his 'devouring, deflowering and defouling' of countless 'maids, widows and wives', behaviour summed up by his adultery with that 'unshameful' and 'mischievous' woman, Edward IV's former mistress Jane Shore. The late king's former household servants-turned-rebels – all listed by name, from Sir George Brown and John Cheyne to bishops John Morton and Lionel Woodville – were similarly tainted. Their treasonous uprising, evidence of their moral depravity, was nothing less than a war on truth and virtue by the forces of damnable 'vice and sin'. In this view, the house of York had fractured into black and white. Edward IV's line was rotten to the core; Richard III's was the only true way.[36]

As Richard headed towards Coventry, Buckingham's rebellion was already beginning to disintegrate. The duke was a notoriously bad landlord, 'a sore and hard dealing man'; as he belatedly realized, such poor lordship failed to translate into solid support. No sooner had he ridden out of Brecon then the castle was sacked by members of the local Vaughan family – nominally the duke's own supporters – who abducted his two daughters. The news reached Buckingham at the Herefordshire castle of Weobley, where he was trying unsuccessfully to mobilize the locals. Morale was already plummeting among his forces: Welsh tenant-farmers of Buckingham's, who hated him at the best of times, had been coerced into mobilizing 'without any lust to fight for him'. This general reluctance to take up arms was exacerbated by the continued terrible weather, widespread flooding and news of a well-organized royal army that faced them across the Severn – that was, if they could cross at all. Having destroyed all the bridges, Richard's troops were blocking all the routes into England.[37]

As Buckingham's army fragmented, he and John Morton split up. Morton made his undercover way out of the country to Flanders. The duke wasn't so decisive, or so lucky. He hid in the Shropshire house of one of his childhood servants, Ralph Bannaster, who, enticed by the large royal reward on offer for Buckingham's capture, promptly handed him over to the authorities in the shape of the ubiquitous Sir James Tyrell. Tyrell then brought him south to Salisbury, where Richard arrived on 1 November. Now, it was Buckingham who begged for a meeting with Richard. Richard refused to see him; he also refused the duke a trial. The following day, All Souls, Buckingham was beheaded.[38]

The southern uprisings, meanwhile, were already running out of steam; now, following Buckingham's execution, and confronted by a large royal army, they crumbled. The ringleaders scattered. Many fled headlong into the southwest, in front of the pursuing royal army, trying to link up with the rebels led by Dorset, St Leger and the Courtenay family. They aimed, too, to link up with the leader on whom their hopes were now pinned. In co-ordination with Buckingham's rebellion and the southern insurgents, Henry Tudor was sailing from Brittany with a large force of men. Tudor, though, was nowhere in sight.[39]

Communication between the rebels had been poor and Tudor was late. By the end of October, when Tudor set sail from the Breton port of Paimpol with a fleet of fifteen ships and some five thousand troops, Richard's men had secured all the major ports along the Hampshire and Dorset coast. At dawn the following day, shoreline patrols at Poole Bay spotted two ships limping into harbour. Tudor's fleet had run into storms and had scattered. Most of his ships had turned back; Tudor had ploughed on. From the strand, royal troops tried to entice him ashore, shouting that they were Buckingham's men come to rendezvous with him. Wisely, Tudor ignored them.[40]

As he sailed further west, hoping to link up with the southern insurgents, Tudor was harassed by detachments of seaborne marines off the east Devon port of Exmouth and, further south, at Dartmouth, Saltash and Plymouth. Finally, a boatload of his men managed to get ashore, where they heard the news of Buckingham's death and the failure of the southern insurgency. An attempt to proclaim Henry Tudor king of England at the Cornish town of Bodmin – involving the bishop of Exeter Peter Courtenay, a handful of Edward IV's household men, some of Buckingham's rebels and a few local loyalists – was fruitlessly symbolic.[41] By now Richard, based in Exeter, was hunting down the remaining insurgents: in Rougemont Castle he beheaded several, chief among them Thomas St Leger.

Tudor turned back. As he made for Brittany, storms swept him up the Channel as far as the Cotentin Peninsula, adding an extra two hundred weary miles overland back to the Breton court at Vannes. His prospects bleak, he worried that his long-time backer Duke Francis might come to see him as a liability rather than an asset.[42] However, as autumn deepened into winter, there was one consolation: the situation had clarified. As a stream of rebels fleeing Richard's wrath arrived in Brittany to bolster his ranks, it had become evident to anybody opposing Richard that Henry Tudor was now the only game in town.

In just a few weeks Richard had put down a potentially catastrophic challenge with what was, on the face of it, a display of crushing royal authority. Those not executed or in custody were on the run. As the king mopped up resistance in the southwest, his men were already busy at work, moving onto the rebels' lands and seizing property, assets and goods in the king's name.[43] Where, following his coronation, Richard had a smattering of patronage with which to reward his followers, he now had a flood – not only the lands, but the royal offices held by many of the leading rebels, between a third and a half of whom had been servants of the late king, Edward IV. And that, for Richard, was the problem.

Across the shires of southern England these men, influential figures in their local communities, had been crucial nodes in the network of royal authority: men 'through whom may be known the disposition of the counties', imposing justice and security in the king's name, enforcing the crown's rights and collecting its income, and when necessary raising cash and troops on the king's behalf. Just under fifty such men were convicted in their absence as rebels – which, of course, left many more people who weren't, ostensibly at any rate. Yet for each man that rebelled, there were plenty more who had the same instincts but just chose to keep their heads down. That, at any rate, was how Richard saw it. Dealing with two counties at the heart of the insurgency – Wiltshire and Hampshire – he issued an order to confiscate the lands not just of the rebels involved, but of all significant property-owning gentry. The rebellion had shaken Richard's trust not simply in certain named insurgents, but in the entire network that he had inherited from his brother and which, he hoped, had transferred its loyalties to him. Now, he realized, he couldn't rely on it at all.

In the rebellion's aftermath, Richard's solution was instinctive. Needing trusted, reliable servants to patch the gaping holes in these torn networks, he reached not for local replacements, but men with whom he was long familiar, who had worked for him as duke of Gloucester and who were – barring one or two exceptions – northerners. No sooner had he annexed rebels' lands and offices than he regranted them away to his supporters, even transferring the ownership of land before its forfeiture by the rebels concerned had been recognized in law.

In the weeks and months that followed, 'strangers' with unfamiliar accents took possession of estates across southern England, stepping into the shoes of local officers and elbowing their way into tight-knit communities. From Devon to Kent, these northerners were transplanted into local society as substantial new landowners. They were men who – as Richard wrote to the town of Tonbridge in Kent regarding the arrival of his household knight Marmaduke Constable – had come 'to make his abode among you and to have the rule within the honour and town'. These were visible and uncomfortably dominant bearers of royal authority, their presence intended to detect, disrupt and block any further attempts at insurgency and to ensure that Richard's will and laws were obeyed. It was hardly a move to broaden the base and appeal of Richard's regime – but in the current climate he prioritized absolute loyalty, even if it meant relying on a smaller pool of tried and trusted servants. These 'plantations' were the gaze of Richard's 'inward eye' in action. Property-owning southerners didn't like it; they found it, as one chronicler put it, a 'tyranny'.[44]

The atmosphere was still heavy with coercion when, on 25 November, Richard rode across London Bridge into the capital, accompanied by the usual cluster of corporate representatives. With the south of the country in a state of emergency, and rebels still on the run, the Channel ports were in lockdown; travellers were stopped and searched, and documents of all kinds confiscated. For the last month, wrote the wool merchant William Cely from Calais, nobody travelling to London was prepared to act as a courier. The aggravation wasn't worth it: 'no man went that would bear any letters for searching.'[45]

On Tower Hill there was a further round of beheadings, among them Sir George Brown, the chamber servant of Edward IV who had rejected Richard's motto and his authority. Driving home his moralistic mission, Richard ordered the public shaming of his late brother's mistress Jane Shore, whose liaisons with Hastings, Dorset and 'other great estates' made her, in Richard's eyes, the living embodiment of everything that had been wrong with Edward IV's regime. She was made to walk through London's streets in her kirtle – which, for the higher ranks at least, was considered underwear – holding a lighted taper. The move backfired, at least according to Thomas More. Londoners, he said, had only sympathy for the exceptional dignity with which she bore her 'great shame'.

A sense of expansive relief and gratitude pervaded Richard's rewards to his followers, while the Christmas celebrations that year provided a welcome release of tension. At court, the wine flowed. The invitees to a Twelfth Night banquet included the mayor of London and a select group of citizens. Richard was eager to cultivate the city, whose donations had shored up the early years of his brother's reign, and whose leading businessmen he now approached in person for fresh loans to cover the 'great charges' he had sustained in putting down the rebellion, pledging fine plate from the king's jewelhouse as collateral. At the festivities, the king presented the mayor with a fine gold cup encrusted with pearls and lapis. Then, in a moment of sozzled largesse, he promised to London the independent borough of Southwark south of the River Thames, together with a £10,000 grant to extend the city walls round it. The corporation didn't bother following up the offer, made in a moment of festive overindulgence. It was hardly feasible and besides, Richard hardly had £10,000 to give.[46]

Meanwhile, away in Brittany, another ceremonial was being enacted. On Christmas Day in Rennes Cathedral, Henry Tudor made his group of exiles a solemn promise. His first act, on gaining the crown of England, would be to marry Edward IV's oldest daughter Elizabeth, currently still in Westminster sanctuary with her sisters and mother. In return, the fugitives swore oaths of loyalty to Tudor 'as though he had already been created king'.

With this exchange of pledges, Tudor officially became the leader of the Yorkist rebels loyal to Edward IV and his sons. In the absence of Edward's two heirs – missing, presumed dead – the late king's servants now preferred to take their chances with a long-exiled Lancastrian of sketchy blood rather than accept the rule of Richard III.[47]

*

Following the bloody upheavals of the previous months, an unspoken, unanswered question lingered. It was the question associated with the foundation of Richard's rule, and with the new stature of Henry Tudor among the Yorkist exiles in Brittany. What had happened to Edward IV's sons? In France, they thought they knew the answer. In January 1484, the French chancellor went on the record: Richard, he stated, had had the princes killed.[48] In England, by contrast, there was a collective *omertà* at the heart of power. Either people didn't know what had happened to the boys – or, if they did, they weren't saying.

The uncertainty affected government departments. Exchequer officials in Westminster, trying to process ongoing business, kept bumping up against the problem of how to refer to Edward V. There were signs of formulas having been written out, then rejected and redrafted. One official wrote up a memorandum in which 9 April was mentioned: the day of Edward IV's death and, consequently, the first day of his son's reign. Somebody else had come along and erased the original wording, in its place writing simply 'the xxiijrd year of King Edward the Fourth' in a capacious hand, adding a couple of horizontal lines to fill up the space of what had clearly been a longer formula – one perhaps too tellingly revealing of Edward V's fate. In official documents, the wording eventually settled on was 'Edward bastard, late called Edward king of England'. 'Late', or its Latin equivalent 'nuper', was used to refer to people in the past tense. Depending on the context, it meant either 'former' or 'dead'. In the cases of Edward IV and Buckingham, the latter killed and stripped of his title and lands by Parliament, it meant both. In the case of the disappeared Edward V, 'late called king' was an ideal hedge.[49]

Whether or not Richard was anxious about the uncertainty, he redoubled his efforts to establish his rule in the minds of his subjects. Towards the end of January Parliament finally convened at Westminster. Chancellor John Russell got to his feet and delivered the sermon that he had waiting to give since the previous June – though, in the meantime, he had revised his text, now obligingly lingering on the threat presented by the enemy within, from such 'as ought to have remained the king's true and faithful subjects'.[50] The following day the Commons elected their speaker, a man whose exceptional closeness to the king compensated for his complete lack of previous parliamentary experience: William Catesby. Catesby had some delicate business to see through. First on the agenda was the ratification of Richard's right to the throne of England, and the invalidation of his late brother's line.

The parliamentary declaration setting out Richard's royal title, or *titulus regius*, laid out in lurid detail the now well-rehearsed reasons for Richard's claim. First among them was the 'ungracious feigned marriage' between Edward IV and Elizabeth Woodville. A specific reason for the marriage's invalidity had now been pinpointed. Edward, while sleeping around in the early 1460s, had apparently made a secret marriage, a 'pre-contract', to Eleanor Butler, a noblewoman who – perhaps conveniently – was how long dead and unable to tell her side of the story. It was a promise perhaps made, as was Edward's habit, in a haze of lust, as he tried to get her into bed. The revelations had come, so it was said, from Robert Stillington, bishop of Bath and Wells and Edward's former chancellor. From Edward's bigamy had resulted the perversion of all 'politic rule' in England, and the bastardy of his children. Given that Parliament had already declared the duke of Clarence's children 'barred from all right and claim to the crown' on account of his treason, there was as a result 'no other person living' except Richard, undoubted son and heir of Richard duke of York, who was rightfully entitled to claim the crown 'by way of inheritance'.[51]

The *titulus regius* was not, or so it was claimed, Richard's declaration of his own title. Rather, it was the ratification of the people's will, the rubber-stamping of a ceremony which, so the declaration now asserted, had been carried out back in June 1483 at Baynard's Castle: then, an assembly of the lords and commons had 'elected' Richard king, presenting him in person with this very document. Yet as the *titulus regius* now stated, this informal deputation hadn't carried with it the weight of parliamentary authority – which, in turn, had made many people doubt Richard's claim to the throne. Therefore Parliament, whose authority 'commands before all things most faith and certainty', would enlighten the people, by putting on record its statement of the king's title. If anybody was still unsure whether Richard was the lawful king of England, Parliament had pronounced.[52]

There followed an act of attainder, confirming in law the permanent disinheritance of the rebels. Going out of his way to prove his commitment to the coronation oaths he had sworn, to justice and the common good, Richard also passed a slew of more progressive measures. These included a series of legal reforms in a genuine attempt to address the muddle of legislation on property ownership; the outlawing of his late brother's deeply unpopular practice of forced loans or 'benevolences'; and – this time taking a leaf out of Edward's book – protectionist legislation aimed at guarding domestic workers against the 'devious and crafty means' of foreign craftsmen and merchants, with Italians, as usual, the prime target for English xenophobia. An exemption was made for any foreigners involved in the book trade, who were free to import and sell 'any kind of books, written or printed': always a keen reader, Richard was perhaps unwilling to deny himself the pleasures of European literature.[53] All of which, if the parliamentary record was anything to go by, showed a government in control, listening to the will of the Commons and addressing its concerns; an authoritative display of kingship.

Others saw it differently. One anonymous chronicler was furious that Parliament saw fit to endorse Richard's title to the throne. The validity of Edward IV's marriage, he fulminated, was no business of Parliament's; rather, it was a matter for the church courts, which alone had the authority to adjudicate matrimonial cases. As far as this, admittedly hostile, chronicler was concerned, Richard had intimidated parliamentarians into endorsing his title: mute with fear, they waved the legislation through. The act of attainder, meanwhile, was a travesty: a land grab unprecedented in history, allowing the king to seize 'great numbers of estates and inheritances', which he then parcelled out to his northern followers.[54]

As well as driving home the validity of his rule, Richard intensified his efforts to eliminate resistance to it. Furious at Brittany's backing of Tudor, he tried to batter the duchy into submission. Ratcheting up the English piracy of recent months, making it official government policy, the king intensified it into an indiscriminate naval war against Breton shipping. Nor was it just Brittany. Determined to pursue the Scottish war he had been forced to abort back in September 1482, Richard ignored the Scottish king's overtures of friendship and

initiated preparations for a fresh invasion. And, following the prescribed policy advice for unifying a divided country, he gave his sea
captains licence to attack French vessels wherever they found them (in
the process letting England's current truce with France lapse). One
command, on 12 February, summed up the military fronts to which
Richard had, almost involuntarily, committed himself. It gave the order
to fit out and supply a number of royal ships 'to resist our enemies the
Frenchmen, Bretons and Scots'.[55] Richard's way of proving himself a
war-leader, it seemed, was to declare war on everybody at once.

There were some belated signs of conciliation on Richard's part.
One was enforced. If Lady Margaret Beaufort had played a crucial
role in the uprisings, her husband Lord Stanley had, after some customary vacillation, turned out for Richard. Taking into account
Stanley's 'good and faithful service', Richard spared Lady Margaret
'for his sake'. However, he tied her hands, transferring all her property and wealth to her husband and others, and extracting a promise
from Stanley to keep her in isolated house arrest. At the same time,
Richard tried to drive wedges between various elements of the resistance: among those to whom he offered a pardon was Lady Margaret's
fixer Reynold Bray. Bray ignored it.[56]

Then, Richard scored a coup. After weeks of negotiation with Elizabeth Woodville and her representatives, attempting to detach
Edward IV's queen from association with the rebels, a deal was brokered. With the lords and London's mayor and aldermen as witnesses,
Richard swore on the gospels to protect Elizabeth and her five daughters; to provide for and treat them as his 'kinswomen'; to find the girls
good marriages, and make sure their husbands treated them right.
Elizabeth, 'late calling herself queen of England', would be given a
quarterly stipend of £466 13s 4d to maintain her household, head of
which would be Richard's servant John Nesfield. Elizabeth Woodville's decision to leave the safety of Westminster sanctuary was
driven, very probably, by a mixture of impulses: resignation; a sense
of futility; a desire for some sort of security for her and her daughters
in the likelihood of Tudor's rebellion being destroyed – or more likely,
as time went on, simply petering out into nothingness. On 1 March,
she and her daughters, foremost among them the girl whom Henry
Tudor had sworn to marry, emerged cautiously from the cramped

sanctuary lodgings where they had passed the previous ten months and gave themselves into Richard's care.[57]

Reports of another recent ceremony might also have swayed Elizabeth's mind. One day in late February, the lords spiritual and temporal, together with a number of the king's more senior household knights and squires, gathered in 'a certain downstairs room' in Westminster Palace. Each in turn added his signature to a written declaration pledging allegiance to Richard's son, 'should anything happen to his father'. The oath-taking, however, was not so much about Richard's fears as his dynastic hopes.

Back in 1471, following Edward IV's destruction of the Lancastrian cause at Tewkesbury, noblemen and knights loyal to the regime – Richard and Clarence foremost among them – had gathered at Westminster to pledge loyalty to his son and heir, the boy who became Edward V. Now, Richard re-enacted this dynastic statement of intent. News that the lords and commons, or a representative sample of them, had recognized Richard's ten-year-old son as England's future king perhaps signalled to Elizabeth Woodville that the door was closing on any prospect of an alternative. Early that spring, after months of conspiracy and rebellion, it seemed as though Richard III had started to lay the foundations of his rule.[58]

20

The Castle of Care

In early March 1484 Richard travelled north with Anne, his queen, to Nottingham. With Edward IV's costly new state apartments almost complete, Nottingham Castle was a fitting home for a king: 'a place full royal', as one of the elegies on Edward's death had put it, approvingly. Both Richard's planned five-month-long absence from the southeast, and his choice of Nottingham – positioned on the River Trent, the traditional dividing line between north and south – as a base, confirmed the royal shift in gravity. A self-assertive move, it suggested that Richard felt he had repaired the damaged political landscape of southern England following the previous autumn's rebellion, and had secured his own rule there. Whatever the case, his focus was north.[1]

Progressing up the Great North Road, Richard and Anne had stopped for a few days at Cambridge, where they were given an effusive welcome by university officials; although Richard had displayed his credentials as a patron of learning at Oxford the previous summer, it was Cambridge whose northern graduates predominated in his close circle of advisers. There, Richard basked in an encomium from the university's chancellor, Thomas Rotherham, praising his 'royal munificence'. (Rotherham, Edward's former chancellor, so hostile to Richard's seizure of power the previous summer, was now apparently reconciled to the fact.) Among the gifts Richard distributed was a grant of £300 towards the construction of King's College Chapel, whose stop–start works were testament to the upheavals of the last decades. Now, though, it was taking shape, recognizably the building that would become, as Rotherham put it with spectacular but justifiable hyperbole, 'the unparalleled ornament of all England'.[2]

The king and queen reached Nottingham in mid-March. They had been there a fortnight when news reached them from Middleham Castle that their son and heir, always in fragile health, had fallen ill and died.

Richard and Anne were devastated. For a long time after, remarked a contemporary, they were 'almost out of their minds'. The ten-year-old-boy had carried all Richard's hopes of dynastic succession: he and Anne had no children left. The tentative foundations he had started to put down were wrecked. For some, it was divine judgment. This was what happened, remarked the same chronicler unfeelingly, when a king 'tried to regulate his affairs without God'.[3]

It was late April by the time Richard, recovering himself, moved slowly north to Pontefract, York and Middleham. On the way, an envoy from the Holy Roman Emperor Frederick III caught up with him: a nobleman named Nicolas von Poppelau, from Silesia on the Empire's eastern borders.

Von Poppelau was the ideal ambassador. Equally at home in the tiltyard, court and library, he possessed sensational strength – he carried with him a lance so heavy that only he could lift it – and could turn a well-worked oration. As he travelled up from London, however, he concluded he didn't like the English very much. In his league of national stereotypes, they more or less came bottom, outdoing the Poles in pretension, the Hungarians in violence and the Lombards in duplicity. Their women, though stunning, were rather too independent-minded for his liking. And their cooking was atrocious. Von Poppelau arrived at Pontefract on the first day of May with something like a sense of relief. There, he was given a magnificent welcome from Richard III – and, if he wasn't so keen on the English, he liked their king.[4]

In the following days, Richard sublimated his grief, entertaining his visitor with an expansive display of regality – an awkward simulacrum of his late brother's easy intimacy, albeit with less of the physical contact (where Edward hugged, Richard stuck out an awkward hand). He showed off the magnificent chapel royal in which, following Edward, he was investing heavily, and invited von Poppelau to dine with him each day. On one such occasion the king beckoned over one of his attendant noblemen, relieved him of his gold livery collar, and hung it round his guest's neck.

Von Poppelau, who saw Richard at close quarters for some eight or nine days, had plenty of opportunity to assess him. Though England's king was somewhat taller than himself – by 'three fingers', von Poppelau estimated, almost as though he had measured the difference between them in person – his slightness was thrown into further relief alongside his visitor's muscular frame. In fact, von Poppelau struggled to find the right words for Richard's stature: the king was, he put it tactfully, 'a little thinner', 'much more lean' than him, with 'delicate arms and legs'. Whether or not it escaped him – Richard had always effortfully concealed his physical condition, except when it suited him to do otherwise – von Poppelau said nothing about his scoliosis. His abiding impression was the striking contrast between the king's thin body and the 'great heart' that burned within it.

On 2 May, the day after his arrival, von Poppelau was given the honour of a private audience with the king: the pair were left together, 'quite alone'. Richard quizzed his guest about the political situation in the Empire, and the Turkish armies encroaching on its southeastern borders; and listened hungrily to the Silesian's embellished account of a recent victory over the Ottoman forces in Hungary. At one point, unable to contain himself, Richard burst out: 'I wish my kingdom shared a border with Turkey', adding that he would love – 'with my own people, without the help of other princes' – the chance to drive away 'not just the Turks but all my enemies.'[5]

For decades, a succession of popes had urged England's support in the fight against the Ottoman advance. Edward IV had constantly disappointed them. While making all the right noises, he had seen papal demands as an irritant to his sovereignty and kept Rome at arm's length, only approving papal fundraising in order to help himself to the proceeds. Richard was different. He venerated England's crusading kings, monarchs like the lionhearted Richard I, and longed to emulate them.[6] For all this a different, more complex desire seemed to animate his words to von Poppelau. To Richard, the idea of crusade had become rolled up into one definitive confrontation against, as he put it, 'all my enemies'. Hovering in his mind's eye was the vision of one great existential battle, a final victory which would solve the various troubles that now pressed upon him.

Most of those troubles, it had to be said, were fights that Richard had started himself, provoking hostilities with Brittany, Scotland and France. That spring, rumours persisted that there would be war with France by the summer; speculative talk, given there was neither the finance nor the political will for such a huge campaign, but there was something in the air.[7] When Richard talked to von Poppelau about 'all my enemies', he meant it. He was running three separate conflicts against three separate international powers at the same time, apparently in the God-given conviction that he could win the lot.

As in his observations on Richard's physicality, so there was in von Poppelau's comment on the king's 'great heart' a hint of diplomatic circumlocution. While, as a crusading knight himself, the envoy admired Richard's passionate belligerence, he may also have been taken aback by the number of simultaneous battles the king was picking.

In recent weeks, though, Richard had seemed to sense that he was overreaching himself. The loss of his son was a shattering reminder of the precariousness of his kingship. Just as significantly, his thin financial resources could hardly stretch to such ambitious operations, while his aggressive foreign policy was not popular with his main source of credit, the merchants of London and Calais. As much as anything else, his change of mind was bound up with the manoeuvrings of the man he was trying to force the duke of Brittany to hand over. Around the time Richard's son died, rumour spread that Tudor and his exiles 'would shortly land in England'.[8]

One unanticipated side-effect of Richard's destructive naval war was to force France and Brittany, suspicious neighbours at best, into a defensive alliance against England. Persuaded by the French and by Tudor, the Breton ruler agreed to fit out another small fleet to carry the exiles to England.[9] As it turned out, the fleet – its details entered neatly in the Breton receiver-general's account book – consisted of no more than six ships, with a capacity of 890 men. Richard, though, wasn't taking any chances. On 1 May, he issued orders to put the entire country on high alert, instructing his chief officers in each county to be ready to raise troops at a moment's notice. This was not an offensive move, but a defensive one: against Tudor.[10]

In the intervening weeks, however, the political situation in Brittany had shifted abruptly. That April, Duke Francis's powerful treasurer, Pierre Landais, shoved aside his rivals and, with the duke increasingly ill and absent-minded, took control of government. A resolute believer in the duchy's independence, Landais was hostile to its French overlords. Reaching out to opposition forces at the French court, he tried to stir up the antagonistic factions around Charles VIII, while attempting to revive the network of international alliances against France. Key among them was England. That spring, Breton ambassadors arrived on Richard's doorstep with the now-customary demands for military aid – in return for which, support for Tudor would be suspended. This time, Richard was eagerly receptive. Early that June, a truce was agreed which was to last until April the following year.

Détente with Brittany was soon followed by a thawing of relations with Scotland. While Richard, overseeing operations from the Yorkshire port of Scarborough, was winning his seaborne war against the Scots, this success was offset by the English-backed duke of Albany's latest failure. When, that July, his forces were destroyed at the town of Lochmaben, Albany slunk off to France. Ineffectual, unlikeable and highly unreliable, Richard's Scottish puppet had nevertheless been key to his Scottish invasion plans. Without him, Richard grudgingly accepted the Scottish government's offer of talks, to take place at Nottingham the following September. All of which eased the pressure on Richard's finances and his military and intelligence resources – which was just as well, given that insurgent activity was once again bubbling in the south of the country.[11]

By July 1484, royal agents were focusing on pro-Tudor plotting in the far southwest, where, the previous autumn, rebels had been the first openly to proclaim him king. But it was in London that rebel activity, emboldened by Richard's prolonged absence – he had been away from the south now for over four months – was most boldly evident. On 18 July, Londoners awoke to find 'seditious rhymes' put up in prominent locations around the city. One, pinned to the doors of St Paul's, was memorable and damning. It ran, simply,

> The Cat, the Rat, and Lovell our Dog
> Rule all England under a hog.

The verse didn't need much deciphering. The Cat and the Rat were, respectively, Richard's counsellor William Catesby and the Cumberland man Sir Richard Ratcliffe, who had grown ever more influential, leading negotiations with Scotland and wielding exceptional power in the northeast. Francis Lovell, Richard's childhood friend and chamberlain, clearly wielded as much influence with Richard as his predecessor William Hastings had done with Edward IV: besides, the inclusion of his name made the rhyme scan nicely. The hog, a scathing reference to his white boar badge, was – of course – Richard.[12]

Pinned up in one of the most prominent locations in the entire kingdom, the rhyme was immediately and memorably insulting, a blow against the public royal image that the king was so carefully and self-consciously tending. But it also made a serious political point. In the months after his coronation, Richard had emphasized that he would rule on behalf of the entire country, for rich and poor: 'for the weal of us all', as Thomas Langton had put it. Yet following the previous autumn's rebellion, Richard had turned to men of proven loyalty who had worked for him as duke of Gloucester, rewarding them with illegally seized property and offices confiscated from the southerners whose communities they now dominated. Anxious about the uncertain commitment of those in the south, Richard had either punished them or simply ignored them – or that was how many now felt, a sense reinforced by Richard's marked absence from the south of the country. There was an increasingly prevailing view that, far from governing for the common weal, Richard was ruling by and for a privileged clique.[13] That July, all this was summed up in the damning couplet pinned to the doors of St Paul's Cathedral.

The city authorities, it was said, carried out 'much search' for the culprits, but despite many arrests nobody was charged. By the time royal agents had worked out who they were meant to be hunting, the perpetrators had gone to ground. William Collingbourne and John Turberville were west-countrymen. A loyal member of Edward IV's household, Collingbourne had been among the Wiltshire insurgents the previous autumn, but where other Yorkist rebels had fled to Brittany he had stayed on, smuggling messages, funds and men out of the country to the exiles. Turberville was a relative of John Morton. Both, in other words, fitted the profile of the committed Yorkist dissident who now saw Henry Tudor's claim to the throne as the best chance of overthrowing Richard, the king they hated.

Their scurrilous rhyme was only the tip of the pair's activities that summer. In regular contact with the rebels, and – in Collingbourne's case – cultivating unrest among disaffected Londoners, they were among the dissidents trying to help Tudor co-ordinate another landing for the following autumn, again on the Dorset coast. However, with Richard's new truce with Brittany showing every sign of holding, and so frustrating rebel attempts to provoke insurgency, they urged Tudor to change tack and seek backing elsewhere. Collingbourne suggested sending the reliable John Cheyne – a man he knew well from Edward IV's household – to the court of the French king on a fundraising mission.[14]

Meanwhile, Richard prepared to return to his restive capital after his long tour of the north. He was aware that he could hardly be at both ends of the country at once, and characteristically, even as he castigated his late brother's methods of government, he looked to them for a solution. In the 1470s, Edward IV had handed the rule of Wales and the Marches to his young son's council, an arrangement that allowed him to delegate the everyday running of the region, while keeping it in the family and under his personal control. Richard had planned to do much the same thing for the north, placing his own son at the head of a dedicated council. Now, though, his son was dead.

Late that July, shortly before he returned south, Richard signed a set of articles for a new council in the north, now clearly defined as a sub-department of the king's own council. Casting around for an appropriate figurehead, the king passed over the claims of leading regional lords, chief among them his ally Henry Percy, earl of Northumberland. While Northumberland had supported Richard's seizure of power in the hope that the king would restore to him his family's traditional authority in the northeast, Richard had no intention of letting that happen. The idea of putting the earl at the head of royal networks in the north seemed exceptionally unwise. Like their detested rivals the Nevilles, the Percies had historically proved themselves dangerously independent-minded: a challenge, rather than a support to royal authority. There seemed no point in risking this again. Instead, Richard appointed as president of the council in the north his nephew, and now his closest adult male relative, John de la Pole, the earl of Lincoln.

Son of the duke of Suffolk and Richard's older sister Elizabeth, John de la Pole was close Yorkist family. Visible at court during Edward IV's last years, he had easily transferred his loyalties to Richard and played a leading role at his uncle's coronation. For all that, de la Pole had spent the twenty years of his existence shuttling between his family estates in East Anglia and the Thames valley. He knew next to nothing about the vast region over which, as president of the Council of the North, he now had nominal control. For Richard, though, that was the point. De la Pole was a figurehead, a conduit for Richard's authority, heading a council of royal servants who between them possessed a wealth of local knowledge and administrative expertise. As a continuation and expansion of Edward's methods of extending royal control through the regions, it made sense. The earl of Northumberland didn't like it very much, however. Nor was he impressed by the terms of his renewal of his wardenship of the East March, overseeing the security of England's northeast. This was an office customarily renewed in five- or even ten-year periods – though Northumberland regarded it as his by right. That August, Richard reappointed him for a year. There had always been some needle between the two as far as the northeast was concerned, Northumberland perpetually in Richard's shadow. Now that prickly relationship continued, Richard making it emphatically clear who was in charge. Northumberland brooded.[15]

Back in London that August, Richard made renewed efforts to woo the mercantile community, lending a sympathetic ear to their concerns and, where he could, paying off his debts. In addition to the rumours of war with France, civil conflict had again erupted in Flanders, making it too hazardous to trade safely; the Merchant Adventurers imposed a blanket ban on commerce with the region. Assuring them of his support, Richard issued a proclamation cracking down on English pirates, now forbidden to attack ships of any nation. It was a welcome, if belated, volte-face and a sign that he was attempting to engage with business, though in fact he made one exception: French ships were still, apparently, fair game. In return, London's mollified corporation responded to his appeal for funds, extending him a substantial and much-needed loan of £2,400.[16]

Meanwhile, in an act of political penance and reconciliation, Richard ordered the remains of the Lancastrian king Henry VI to be disinterred from their sequestered location at Chertsey Abbey, and royally reburied in the choir of the near-completed chapel of St George at Windsor, close to the body of the man who had destroyed him and his family, Edward IV. Edward, of course, had designed the chapel specifically as the last resting place of the Yorkist kings. The symbolism of Richard's gesture was lost on no one: in death, at least, the houses of Lancaster and York were to be unified. Perhaps, Richard hoped, some of the Lancastrian king's saintliness would rub off on him by association. And, as a flood of pilgrims descended on Windsor to venerate the bones of the saintly Lancastrian king, Richard redoubled his efforts to get hold of his rather more troublesome living descendant, Henry Tudor.[17]

In Brittany, Richard's agents reassured the duchy's de facto leader Pierre Landais that its long-desired military support would soon be coming, in the form of six thousand English archers. The arrival of Richard's right-hand man James Tyrell at the Breton court, then resident in the city of Vannes, was enough to trigger rumours that the soldiers were already on their way: the French government was concerned enough to investigate the reports. To Tudor and his supporters, scattered in lodgings across the city, Tyrell's presence was alarming. It suggested that the Breton government was preparing to hand Tudor over to Richard.[18]

For Landais and his regime, Tudor and his growing band had become not only a financial burden but a political liability. That summer, as Landais scaled back support for the exiles, Tudor had followed Collingbourne's advice and reached out to the French king. It was a move that threatened to upset Landais' own manoeuvrings. With Tyrell communicating Richard's fulsome assurances of military aid, and promising that Tudor would be well treated back in England – restored, indeed, to his earldom of Richmond – Landais knew that the time had come to cash him in.[19] But Tyrell was too late.

Shortly after his arrival in Brittany, Tudor vanished. He had been tipped off.

Since escaping to Flanders after the previous autumn's rebellion, John Morton had sat tight, monitoring events in England and Brittany, watching and waiting. His contacts were good. Hearing about the plan to extradite Tudor, Morton sent one of his own entourage, a priest named Christopher Urswick, the four hundred and fifty-odd miles across northern France to Vannes, with a message for Tudor to get out of Brittany as soon as he could.

Tudor left Vannes on horseback with five friends, pretending to pay a call on a local acquaintance. Once out of the city, he disguised himself as a servant; the small group then fled towards the French border. Their absence was soon noted. As detachments of Breton troops rode furiously in pursuit, the fugitives crossed into France by the skin of their teeth.

Finally, news of Landais' machinations reached Duke Francis. Angry and ashamed at his treasurer's betrayal of Tudor, whom he had protected for over thirteen years, the duke summoned representatives of the three hundred English exiles remaining in Vannes – Sir Edward Woodville, and the Kentish esquire Edward Poynings, a capable military man who had risen rapidly to become 'chief captain' of the rebel army. Giving them travel funds, Francis told them they were free to rejoin Tudor in France. Within weeks, Tudor and his group were at the Loire city of Angers and the court of Charles VIII. Greeting them warmly, the boy-king 'promised him aid, and bade him be of good cheer'.[20] For the English king, the threat from Tudor had suddenly got a whole lot worse.

That summer, Richard had successfully ended his conflicts against Brittany and Scotland in order to concentrate his resources on eliminating renewed domestic insurgency and extinguishing the rebellion at source by extraditing Tudor to England, while maintaining a belligerent stance towards France. These latter warlike ambitions dovetailed perfectly with his aim of shutting down the rebel threat – so long as Tudor remained in Brittany. Now, having eluded Richard's grasp, Tudor had found shelter with a French government with whom Richard was aggressively at odds. Charles VIII and his advisers were deeply concerned about Richard's manoeuvrings – his intensifying of the naval war against France, and his dabbling in a resurrected anti-French coalition. For the French, Tudor was not simply a political card to be played; he was a weapon to be deployed against Richard.

For many involved, the echoes of recent history were all too clear. Back in 1470, the French king Louis XI had backed an insurgency against Edward IV: an insurgency which, led by two renegade Yorkist figureheads in Warwick and Clarence, aimed to restore the Lancastrian Henry VI and his heirs to the throne. The scenario that now faced Richard III was its obverse: the French government was backing a group of mainly Yorkist exiles, using a Lancastrian figurehead to topple a Yorkist king and restore the line of Edward IV. In an added historical irony, Charles VIII's promises to Tudor had come at Angers, scene of the Louis XI-brokered agreement between Margaret of Anjou and the earl of Warwick some fourteen years previously. The repercussions of this new conjuncture were soon being felt in England.

As Tudor rode headlong into France, Richard was returning north. At Nottingham that September, he received a Scottish diplomatic mission, listening to an elegant oration from James III's secretary, Archbishop Whitelaw. Through Whitelaw's unctuous flattery – 'Never before', he oozed to Richard, 'has nature dared to encase in a smaller body such spirit and strength' – ran a clear message: war was expensive and pointless. For once, Richard concurred. Signing a new Anglo-Scottish truce, he brought a halt to his own decade-long obsession with Scottish conflict.[21] There were more pressing matters on his mind.

That autumn at Nottingham, Richard settled down to tackle the problem of his rickety finances. Emulating his brother, he aimed to delve into the furthest recesses of his kingdom, to know everything 'that might be most for the king's profit'. As Edward had done, he targeted the great royal estates, which provided a huge proportion of the crown's regular revenues. In a new 'remembrance', or set of guidelines, he set down procedures for the 'hasty levy' of income from these lands, aiming to maximize that income, ensure its efficient collection and audit, and swift payment into the depleted coffers of his chamber. All of which depended on the reliability and trustworthiness of the king's network of local officials, and their effective communication with central government – the Exchequer was directed to use 'hasty process' against any dilatory financial officers and aggressively pursue debtors to the crown – and the king himself.[22]

Among the business that Richard processed that autumn was a set of instructions to one of his key officers in Ireland, the earl of Desmond. Writing to Desmond, Richard – as he increasingly seemed to be – was in reflective mood. As his recent reburial of Henry VI indicated, political killings of the past were much on his mind. In his letter to Desmond, he recalled John Tiptoft's 'extortious slaying' of the earl's father back in 1468 'against all manhood, reason and good conscience', and urged him to seek legal redress. For Richard, the episode brought to mind a 'semblable chance' – similar thing – that had since happened in England: the judicial murder of his brother Clarence. Clarence's killing, Richard told Desmond, had been wrong, and he felt distinctly uncomfortable about it. Not, it had to be said, that Richard's unease had stopped him from lobbying for the duke's forfeited property at the time; nor that it now extended to seeking justice for his murdered brother's family.[23]

This sense of seeking exculpation, of making good, perhaps informed another of Richard's actions that October. Among the warrants that he authorized – payments for building works; £270 to two Calais merchants for a consignment of wine – was a grant to a widow, Johanne, or Janet, Forest, and her son Edward.[24]

Johanne's husband Miles Forest, the wardrobe keeper at Richard's fortress of Barnard Castle, had recently died. On hearing the news, Richard converted his salary, an annuity of 5 marks, into a pension to Johanne and her son, payable as long as either of them lived. According to Thomas More, Forest had been one of the murderers of Edward IV's sons. He had died not long after, 'rotting away' in the London sanctuary of St Martin's-le-Grand – which, in the 'very bowels' of the city, housed the usual assortment of social outcasts, 'a rabble of thieves, murderers, and malicious heinous traitors'.[25] More's emotive language aside, the question of whether Forest had sought shelter in St Martin's – or, indeed, whether he had been involved in the boys' killing – was moot. What was certain was that Forest was now dead, and that Richard had made his widow and son not only a generous settlement, but an unusual one. This pension was paid, not in recognition of a lifetime of service on Forest's part – rewards for 'good service' tended to be recognized explicitly as such – but 'for diverse causes and considerations us moving', a formula kings habitually used when referring to confidential business carried out on their behalf.[26] It was impossible to say for sure what 'diverse causes and considerations' might have moved Richard. But whatever Forest had done for him, it merited an exceptional royal response.

The impact of Tudor's flight to France was soon being felt in the autumn of 1484. In England, there was a marked upsurge in clandestine activity. Richard responded fast, ordering his agents to make more arrests in the 'west parts of the realm'. At Berkeley Castle in Gloucestershire, royal officers presided over the confessions of three west-country merchants who had sent funds to Tudor's men in Brittany, their punishment to be 'in fearful example of other'.[27] But if Richard thought he was getting a handle on the conspirators, he was mistaken. What was more, the rebels' activity seemed organized, purposeful and with a definite aim in view.

That November, Exchequer officials in Westminster, following Richard's orders to move aggressively against slack financial practice, took action against a Devon official called Thomas Pyne. Pyne was the county's escheator, the officer responsible for enforcing the king's rights, a potentially lucrative area of royal income that Richard had been trying to tighten up. Typically, royal officers were required to provide financial sureties to ensure they fulfilled their roles properly: failure to do so would trigger the penalty. Such sureties were underwritten by others, family and friends. When Pyne failed to file his accounts at the Exchequer, his surety of £40 was triggered. Following Richard's recent instructions, Exchequer officials duly carried out 'hasty process' against the man who had given the surety, a king's yeoman named Griffith Lloyd, turning up at his home to seize goods and assets to the required value. They were confronted by an outraged Lloyd, who swore blind that he had never stood surety for Pyne at all.

Investigating further, royal officials pieced together an altogether more disturbing picture. Lloyd had been the victim of both fraud and identity theft. Earlier that autumn, a 'strange person' had walked into the Exchequer claiming to be Lloyd, put his name down for Pyne's surety, and then vanished into thin air. The scheme had involved Pyne himself: probably disgruntled at having to work for the man Richard had planted in Devon as the county's sheriff, the Yorkshireman Halneth Mauleverer, he had defected to Tudor and fled to Brittany. As royal agents discovered, however, the man behind the operation was a figure who would become one of Henry Tudor's closest, most uncompromising advisers: Thomas Lovell.

This wasn't a headline-grabbing case, but it was an audacious one. It was designed specifically to cause disruption – or as Richard put it, 'vexation and damages' – in the workings of government, to prevent the smooth and efficient flow of funds to his impoverished regime and, in doing so, to erode trust between the king and the network of royal officials on whom he relied.[28]

There was nothing isolated about the Pyne case. That autumn, the regime's nervous system seemed under attack. County sheriffs and other local officials, aware of their king's jumpiness, took care to acquire royal pardons: insurance against any failure to fulfil their duty that might be construed as disloyalty. Another official who failed to account to the Exchequer was the escheator of Worcestershire, Robert Hunde; elsewhere, the sheriff of Lincolnshire John Meres, demonstrably reluctant to take up his post in the first place, was proving to be a serial foot-dragger. Both men, unbeknownst to Richard, were now working for Tudor. By simply failing to do their jobs – and, probably, re-routing their unpaid revenues to the rebels in France – they were slowly bringing the everyday mechanisms of local government and revenue collection to a grinding halt.[29]

Richard was a diligent man. He was, very probably, sharply aware of what the rebels were trying to do, and how they were doing it; accordingly, he tried to keep the system functioning smoothly, to tighten up procedures against financial malpractice, to make sure funds were paid in and the wages of government officials were paid. Yet it was all but impossible to work out who was being slack, and who was actively committing treason. As one chronicler put it, where 'some man of name passed over daily to Henry', others 'favoured secretly some partners of the conspiracy'. If the former included men such as Pyne, the latter were exemplified by the likes of Hunde and Meres.[30]

Among Richard's vulnerable pressure points was Calais, whose garrison had been at the heart of attempts at regime change over the last decades. Around the same time as Lovell's 'stranger' was spreading confusion in the Exchequer, Richard was tipped off about a plan by Tudor and his rebels to free a long-term Lancastrian prisoner, John de Vere, earl of Oxford, from the Calais fortress of Hammes where he had been incarcerated for a decade. In the intervening years, Oxford – who, over the previous two decades, had careered from reconciliation with the house of York to outright opposition, from conspiracy with Warwick and Clarence to disaster in the fog at Barnet and increasingly aimless manoeuvrings in the 1470s before his final arrest at St Michael's Mount – had been all but forgotten. Following one leap into the moat at Hammes that might have been either an attempted escape or a suicide bid, he seemed resigned to dying in prison. Tudor's arrival in France, though, had given this Lancastrian loyalist a new political significance and a new lease of life. When Richard sent one of his chamber servants to Calais to transfer the earl to the greater security of the Tower, the servant arrived to find him gone. Together with his gaoler James Blount – another disaffected friend of the late William Hastings – and a handful of sympathizers, Oxford was making for Paris, the French court and Henry Tudor.[31] Once again, Richard's grasp closed on thin air.

Around the same time, insurgency flared in the Essex town of Colchester and moved west, into Hertfordshire. It quickly became clear that these new troubles were connected to those in Calais, the skeins of conspiracy looping and threading across the Channel. A central node was the earl of Oxford, who had been tapping up residual loyalties in his family's Essex heartland. Another shadowy figure in the uprising was John Morton, busy pulling strings from his Flanders hiding place, exploiting his regional connections built up as bishop of Ely. Again, however, the troubles spread fast through the system of local government. The Colchester uprising was led by a handful of Edward IV's former servants, at their head Sir William Brandon, who had been involved in the previous year's rebellion. Richard reacted fast to put down the uprising, and the rebels scattered. Brandon's two sons William – leaving behind him a baby boy named Charles – and Thomas fled to the windswept tidal island of Mersea, where they commandeered a boat and disappeared in the direction of France.[32]

The effects of the abortive Essex uprising rippled through south-eastern England. Richard put the armed forces of neighbouring counties on half a day's notice to resist 'any sudden arrival', any surprise attack by the rebels; he also commanded the Calais garrison to besiege Hammes Castle, where the remaining rebels were holed up.

That November, as sheriffs across the country finished their annual term of office, Richard took the opportunity to weed out officials suspected of colluding with the rebels, who had displayed an apparent lack of commitment, or who had failed to respond with sufficient alacrity to royal commands – which now, in Richard's eyes, were more or less one and the same. From the west country to Wiltshire, East Anglia and the southeast, more of Richard's tried-and-trusted household men replaced recalcitrant locals. Robert Percy, controller of the king's household, was made sheriff of the problematic county of Essex; John Wake, one of Richard's gentleman ushers, was given the equally febrile counties of Cambridgeshire and Huntingdonshire. Decades before, when forced to send his close adviser Thomas Montgomery to investigate disturbances in East Anglia, a young Edward IV had grumbled that Montgomery was a servant he could not do without. For Richard, this lack of reliable human resources was becoming the norm.[33]

In early December, as royal agents tried to stamp out the fires of insurgency, they seized copies of a letter from Henry Tudor to potential supporters in England. Confident and intimate in tone, it asked for help in pursuing 'my rightful claim' to the crown, and in overthrowing 'that homicide and unnatural tyrant' on whose head it currently rested. Describing himself as 'your poor exiled friend', Tudor urged people to raise what forces they could, to cross the sea and join him in France, thanking them in advance for their 'loving kindness'. The letter concluded with a regal flourish, sealed with 'our signet' and signed with the monogram 'H' – Henry.[34]

Tudor's open declaration of his royal ambitions was an audacious move. When, back in 1471, Edward IV returned from his Burgundian exile, he concealed his attempt to regain the throne under protestations that he simply wanted to reclaim his dukedom of York: this from a man who was a crowned king of England. Tudor, who barely had a claim to the throne at all, nevertheless owned that claim, putting it front and centre of his appeals for support. To Richard, Tudor's letter, allied to the surge in insurgent activity across southern England, signalled one thing: his invasion was imminent.

Back in Westminster, Richard issued a proclamation condemning Tudor and the leading rebels, from the marquis of Dorset and Sir Edward Woodville to the earl of Oxford, newly arrived in the rebel camp. He denounced Tudor for his claim to the throne, 'wherein he hath no manner interest, right, or colour'; for allying with France, England's 'ancient enemy', and for signing away England's claims to the French throne in the process. He added, for good measure, a lurid portrayal of the horrors that a Tudor regime would visit on England's people, and an appeal to all Englishmen to resist the invaders. Alongside the proclamation, Richard ordered another general mobilization; and with it, instructions to commissioners in each county to carry out a detailed review of their defence plans, to ensure all was in readiness.[35]

Meanwhile, after months of conspirators slipping through his fingers, Richard finally ran one insurgent cell to ground. The west-country rebels Collingbourne and Turberville were found guilty of treason in a perfunctory trial. Turberville was imprisoned. Collingbourne – whose derisive couplet had caused fury at the heart of Richard's regime – was subjected to the full ritual horror of a traitor's execution. On Tower Hill, in front of a fascinated crowd, he was hanged until semi-conscious, then 'cut down and ripped': his stomach slashed open. The butchery was swift and expert. Collingbourne was still alive to witness his intestines pulled out and thrown on a fire, one bystander hearing him gasp: 'Oh lord Jesus, yet more trouble.'[36] This, Collingbourne's execution was presumably intended to convey, was what happened if you messed with Richard – though as a deterrent, it was hardly likely to work. By now, the rebels had worked out the risks.

There seemed something impulsive, impatient about Richard's response that winter. That Tudor's threat was real was beyond doubt. Yet it didn't appear to occur to Richard that his overblown proclamation against Henry served only to magnify his opponent's credentials and attractiveness to those disillusioned with Richard's rule. Indeed, Richard could scarcely have advertised better how seriously he was taking this obscure nobleman who most in England otherwise barely knew at all; who even those in relatively information-rich London were describing simply as 'a gentleman named Henry'. Likewise, Tudor was hardly on the brink of invading England. His own letter, copies of which Richard had seen, was little more than a speculative and hopeful plea for sympathizers to join his small band in France. Moreover, while Charles VIII had welcomed Tudor with open arms, and had given him 3,000 livres towards his military costs, it wasn't a sum that would go very far: more a symbolic gesture than anything else. The French government, too, continued to keep the diplomatic door open to Richard, sending envoys to the English court. After all, situations could quickly change.

Richard found both his elusive enemy and the contradictions of foreign policy unsettling; his response, as usual, came in clear, straight, unambiguous lines. Seen one way, his military preparedness made sense. But his orders to his commissioners betrayed an anxiety about his own troops' state of readiness, about their allegiance – men were to report to only those commanders whom Richard had appointed, 'and none other' – and about the availability of defence funds: money raised by local officials was either not being paid in at all, or was being embezzled from, 'taken out of the keeping of', those officers appointed to look after it.[37] More than anything else, however, Richard's anxieties were all too evident in the way he put the entire country on a military footing, waiting for an invasion that might never come, and through his increased hostility towards Tudor's new backer, France – at a time when an outstretched hand might have worked wonders. As Christmas approached, Richard re-imposed his control, stamping out the latest wave of insurgency and securing Calais. Yet his dependence on his small pool of trusted servants was self-perpetuating, and increasingly problematic. His coterie of close advisers was being spread exceptionally thin. Despite having become the king's linchpin in south Wales, James Tyrell was redeployed to Calais and made lieutenant of Guisnes Castle, in order to shore up the creaking security apparatus there; Robert Brackenbury, delegated to tackle 'arduous business concerning the king's right', was also over-stretched.[38]

The architects of Tudor's strategy of disruption – Morton, Lovell, a sharp Lincolnshire canon lawyer in his late thirties named Richard Fox and the group of experienced, knowledgeable Yorkist officials with them in France – were making a devastating impact, as much as anything else on Richard's mind. For one Tudor commentator, the Italian Polydore Vergil – a man who constructed his history of England from first-person interviews with precisely these men – the impression was of a king 'as yet more doubting than trusting in his own cause', and who by this time was 'vexed, wrestled and tormented in mind with fear almost perpetually of the earl Henry and his confederates' return'.[39] Vergil's sources, and the context in which he wrote, naturally gave his history an ingrained bias. Yet his description of Richard's fears suggested that this was precisely the effect that Tudor's rebels, with their constant worrying away at the government's connective tissue, hoped to produce. They knew Richard, and they knew the effect political uncertainty had on him. As much as anything, theirs was a strategy of mental disintegration. And there were signs that it was working.

Around this time, Richard acquired a book of hours. Designed for personal, everyday use, this prayer book was small, its illuminations – initials, sprays of foliage, the occasional illustration picked out in pink, blue and warm orange, with gold leaf – simple and practical, designed to guide the reader around the text in the course of their devotions. It was a book to be carried, to be kept close and consulted frequently.[40] Into this book, a scribe had copied a prayer tailored to Richard himself. Its wording drew on a long tradition of appeals for heavenly protection from danger: invocations which, when muttered repeatedly, mantra-like – one rubric advised saying the prayer on thirty consecutive days for its full power to take effect – were intended to soothe the mind of the anxious supplicant.

Yet there was nothing generic about the mood of claustrophobia that clouded Richard's prayer, with its appeal to Christ to ward off the king's adversaries, to 'turn aside, destroy and bring to nothing the hatred they bear towards me'; to deliver Richard from 'the plots of my enemies'; and to send to his aid St Michael. This was the angel who in Yorkist prophecy had foretold the reunifying of England under the kings of the house of York, and who, back in 1465, Edward IV had credited with his destruction of Lancastrian insurgency, the saint from whom his newly minted 'angel' coins had taken their name. Along with the repeated exhortations to Christ to free him from the 'tribulations, sorrows and troubles' that seemed to press in on him from all sides, Richard begged for a release from *dolor, infirmitas* and *paupertas*: abstract nouns that all, nevertheless, spoke to his own afflictions – the grief of his son's sudden death; the discomfort and sudden spasms of pain from his twisted back; his ever-present financial problems.[41] Months before, Richard had told Nicolas von Poppelau of his desperation to confront 'all my enemies'. The wording of Richard's prayer suggested that desperation was becoming ever more acute.

For all Richard's money problems, Christmas at Westminster that year was magnificent, the habitual crown-wearing at Epiphany more than usually majestic: like being 'at his original coronation', as one onlooker put it. Richard seemed to submerge himself in the light relief of the festivities: in the prurient words of one commentator, 'far too much attention' was paid to 'singing and dancing'. Even Richard's own supporters had expressed reservations about the 'sensual pleasure' in which the king indulged, and the implied contradiction with his own moralistic trumpetings on his late brother's faults. In particular, Richard seemed to be drinking more and excessively. Just maybe, he sought solace from his 'tribulations, sorrows and troubles' at the bottom of a wine glass.[42]

One piece of royal frivolity struck observers as genuinely shocking. Following Richard's guarantees of protection the previous March, the Woodville ladies had made a quiet re-entry into political life. In the intervening months they had kept a low profile, their public appearances few and far between. That Christmas, however, Richard lavished attention on the former queen – Dame Elizabeth Grey, as she was now styled – and her family, as honoured guests at court. Richard's way of emphasizing the Woodvilles' political rehabilitation was to order his wife, Queen Anne, and Elizabeth, the blonde, blue-eyed eighteen-year-old daughter of Edward IV and Elizabeth Woodville, to swap costumes and, with them, identities.[43]

In a way these 'vain exchanges of clothing' were of a piece with the seasonal atmosphere of license and misrule, the order of things subverted. But this upending of sumptuary laws placed the eighteen-year-old Elizabeth on a par with Richard's own queen. It was the king's way of publicly resuming control of the young woman who, betrothed by Yorkist exiles to Henry Tudor in Rennes the previous Christmas, had been transformed into a political figurehead for the rebels: their queen-in-waiting, in whose person the regime of Edward IV would be restored. The clothes-swap was bound to set tongues wagging – and that was the point. It would reach the clandestine cells across England and the exiles in France; and, by signalling the Wood-villes' total reintegration into Richard's regime, indicate the favourable treatment their supporters should expect, should they desert Tudor and seek a return to the king's grace.

For all their success in infiltrating Richard's networks, and in stretching his already scant resources to the limit, the rebels were themselves hardly well placed. Although the arrival of the earl of Oxford had given Tudor's cause some added aristocratic lustre and military experience – Oxford immediately proved his credentials by returning to Calais to break the remaining rebels out of Hammes Castle – French interest in the exiles' project was proving predictably uneven. With civil war threatening to erupt in France, Charles VIII's belea-guered government had its hands full: the cause of Tudor and his allies had fallen rapidly down its list of priorities. By the early months of 1485 morale was beginning to sink among the rebels who, 'weary with continual demanding of aid', began to believe they were getting nowhere. Some among them felt that Henry was hopeless, that nothing 'went forward with him'. There were signs that Richard's attempt to divide the exiles, to entice Yorkist rebels back to grace, was working. A trickle of Woodville adherents accepted pardons from the king and agreed to financial bonds for their future good behaviour. Among them were the queen's younger brother Richard Woodville, and Sir John Fogge, whose handshake with Richard back in June 1483 sig-nalled an apparent rapprochement with supporters of the young Edward V before things had gone horribly wrong. Richard almost landed one of the biggest fish of all. His arch-enemy Thomas Grey, the marquis of Dorset, was in constant correspondence with his mother Elizabeth Woodville, who assured him of the lavish settlement that awaited him should he return to Richard III's court – the king had, apparently, 'promised mountains'. Fed up with kicking his heels in France with Tudor waiting for something to happen, Dorset left Paris secretly one night and headed for Flanders. He was run to ground by John Cheyne's brother Humphrey some fifty miles northeast of Paris at the town of Compiègne and hauled reluctantly back to the capital.[44]

Though Dorset's break for the border had failed, it signalled two related points. The exhausted, shattered Elizabeth Woodville, desperate for a quiet life and a stable future for her daughters, now saw her best chance of achieving these goals with Richard. If Elizabeth and Dorset felt that way, as time passed there was every chance that other Yorkist rebels, fed up with the boredom and penury of exile, would arrive at a similar conclusion.

Richard's own problems, however, were continuing. His attempts to improve his finances the previous autumn hadn't worked: constant mobilization against his elusive enemy – from soldiers' wages to much-needed upkeep of defences and the supply of weapons and ordnance – and the disruptive manoeuvrings of Tudor's agents were proving a drain on his already depleted coffers.[45] In early 1485 he turned to his late brother's favoured mechanism for raising funds: a forced loan. That February, royal officials sent out targeted letters to potential creditors across the country, stipulating the required sum each lender was expected to stump up: 'every true Englishman', the letters said, should be willing to contribute to the defence of the realm.[46] This appeal to patriotism could hardly mask the fact that having made financial reform a central plank of his government, Richard was now engaging in precisely those practices that, the previous year in Parliament, he had unequivocally condemned and sworn never to use.

Richard's opponents seized eagerly on this about-turn, painting him as a hypocrite and tyrant who 'extorted great sums of money' from his subjects. At the very least, this desperate attempt at fund-raising suggested a king who had come to power in a welter of high ideals that he was now manifestly failing to live up to. Richard's constantly reiterated professions of liberality, generosity and open-handedness had disintegrated on contact with the realities of kingship. What was more, this new round of loans was designed to tackle a conspiracy that the king – who had from the outset presented himself as the figure most likely to bring 'surety and firmness here in this world' – had clearly failed to get a handle on.[47] Far from bringing peace to England, his reign had descended into a near-constant state of emergency. Even to his supporters, it didn't look good.

For Richard, as ever, the root of the problem was morality – not his own, but other people's. Since seizing power two years previously, his obsession with the spiritual health of the nation had run like a seam through his public pronouncements, the forces of 'sin and vice' explicitly equated with his enemies. On 10 March, at Westminster Palace, Richard wrote a letter to Archbishop Bourchier and his other bishops about a matter that, amid all the other 'businesses and cares' that preoccupied him, was constantly on his mind. His 'principal intent and fervent desire', he wrote, was to promote 'virtue and cleanness of living' throughout the country, and correspondingly to punish vice. It was imperative that those of high rank set an example to the lower orders in this regard. Richard was keen that the archbishop identify those in his jurisdiction who were involved in the promotion of 'sin and vices' and see to their 'sharp punishment' – an action which, Richard assured him, would be gratifying both to God and to himself.[48]

Less than a week after this letter was sent came an event that, for his enemies, highlighted Richard's own moral shortcomings; and which caused even his closest supporters to question his kingship.

In London on the afternoon of Wednesday 16 March, at around twenty minutes to three, people noticed the quality of daylight begin to alter as the moon moved between the earth and the sun. Within an hour, the sun was almost completely obscured, its corona glowing faintly. Around that time, in her apartments in Westminster Palace, Anne Neville, queen of England, died. Nobody was particularly surprised. Though her end might have been betokened by the solar eclipse, people had been expecting it for weeks.[49]

Ill since the turn of the year, Anne had declined rapidly. Her physicians tried everything, yet nothing had worked and the cause of her death quickly became the subject of wild speculation. Talk had it that her sickness had been triggered by the attention Richard had been paying his teenage niece Elizabeth of York and exacerbated by his avoidance of his wife's bed. It was true that Richard's marriage to Anne hadn't proved especially fecund and, with almost a year having passed since the death of their son, there was no sign of Anne becoming pregnant again. Richard, it was said, had complained 'unto many noble men' about the lack of an heir. So desperate had Richard been to rid himself of his wife, it was alleged, that he had spread rumours of her impending death, in order to 'bring her in great dolour' and thereby exacerbate her illness; alternatively, he was killing her with a slow-acting poison. Hearing the talk, Anne had tearfully confronted her husband, demanding to know why he had 'determined' her death. Richard had comforted her with kisses and loving words: 'signs of love', it was said, made expressly for public consumption, 'lest that he might seem hard-hearted'. In the battle for moral supremacy, his pro-Tudor opponents seized gleefully on the rumours: his 'wicked intent' towards his late wife, they proclaimed, was proof positive that Richard was 'wayward from all righteousness'.

None of these stories had much to substantiate them. Anne probably died of tuberculosis, exacerbated by the doubtful medical concoctions of her doctors; equally, Richard may have been advised to stay away from his wife given the risk of contagion.[50] The problem for Richard was that people seemed all too ready to believe the whispers. Indeed, the mechanisms by which Anne's death were said to have been procured were all too believable. After all, back in 1477, Edward IV had believed himself threatened by prognostications of his imminent death that were intended to make him fall sick through 'sadness'; Clarence, meanwhile, had ascribed his own wife's death after childbirth to poisoning by one of her close servants. Then, shortly after Anne's death, it was reported that Richard was planning to marry his niece, Elizabeth of York.

Though indecorous, it was hardly unusual for nobles to wed again quickly after a spouse's death. Clarence himself had been proof that grieving and playing the marriage market were hardly mutually exclusive. For Richard, marrying his niece made political sense. Not only would it deprive Henry Tudor of his putative matrimonial link with the Yorkist rebels, it could also give Richard an escape route from the increasingly narrow power base on which he had come to rely. Such a marriage could conceivably reunite the house of York, re-establishing Edward IV and Elizabeth Woodville's royal line by a lineal sleight of hand: not in their own right – Richard's proclamation of their illegitimacy had, after all, enabled him to seize the crown in the first place – but through marriage to Richard. Through this marriage, Richard might refound his reign on a much broader political base. Any heirs that he and Elizabeth produced would embody this newfound unity. The Woodville family, the original source of all Richard's anxieties, was no longer the problem but the solution. All of which was, of course, the mirror of the Yorkist exiles' vision for Elizabeth's marriage to Henry Tudor.

Whatever the substance of the story, it was taken very seriously indeed. The rumours were said to have convulsed Henry Tudor, 'pinched him to the very stomach', and prompted a frantic search for a new bride for him in case the unthinkable happened. It also sent a shockwave through Richard's regime. Members of his own government were alarmed enough to convene a council meeting, at which the king was called upon to explain himself. At the meeting, Richard appeared to cut a cowed, defensive figure, protesting that 'such a thing had never entered his mind'. His denials, at least to some of his councillors, weren't convincing.[51]

Talk of Richard's remarriage to his niece was especially alarming to the tight-knit group of Richard's supporters who, if such a marriage were to take place, had most to lose under a refounded, reunited Yorkist regime. In the council chamber, Richard was now taken to task by two of these advisers: Catesby and Ratcliffe, the Rat and the Cat.

It wasn't enough, the two now told the king 'to his face', for him to refute the rumours in front of his own councillors. Unless he went public with his denials, they warned, the northerners 'in whom he placed the greatest trust' would rise up against him, believing him to be responsible for the death of Queen Anne. The two councillors could hardly have put it more bluntly. Richard, they stressed, owed the loyalties of his northern following to his late wife – who was, after all, the daughter of Richard Neville, earl of Warwick. Now, unless Richard could regain control of the situation, there was every chance that those loyalties would evaporate. In any case, the councillors told Richard, citing the opinion of a dozen or so theological experts who had been wheeled into the council chamber for the occasion, such a marriage was within the prohibited degrees of consanguinity. It was, they declared – in language presumably intended to press Richard's moral buttons – positively incestuous, an offence in the eyes of God.

Naturally, it was their own fortunes that Catesby, Ratcliffe and the rest of Richard's inner circle were especially worried about, should the rumoured marriage come to pass. A resurgent Woodville family would be hungry to avenge the deaths of the queen's brother Anthony Woodville and her son Richard Grey, while those Yorkists loyal to the memory of Edward IV and the princes wanted the return of their confiscated lands and offices, which Richard had since redistributed to his own inner circle. If, back in spring 1483, William Hastings had been worried enough about the impact on his own fortunes of a Woodville-dominated Edward V to urge Richard into regime change, the urgency with which this Cumbrian esquire and Northampton-shire lawyer now told a crowned king of England what he had to do spoke volumes.[52] So too did the way in which Richard followed their advice to the letter.

On 30 March, London's mayor and aldermen, and other influential citizens, trooped north out of the city to the priory of St John's in Clerkenwell, where the king had summoned them at short notice. They assembled in the great hall, along with many of the lords and – equally anxious about the implications of a Woodville remarriage – most of Richard's household men, foremost among them his chamberlain Francis Lovell. As the king spoke, they listened.

Talking loudly and distinctly, Richard rebutted the rumours that, he noted, had been spread among the people by 'evil disposed persons': that Queen Anne had been poisoned by his 'consent and will', so that he could marry his niece. The idea of such a marriage, Richard continued, had 'never come in his thought or mind'; moreover, he was as sorry and heavy-hearted at the death of his queen as it was possible to be. As the clerk of the Mercers' Company put it – with a hint of the restive businessman sharply aware that every second spent listening to the king's laboured harangue was costing him money – Richard's speech was long. Finally, Richard wrapped up with a detailed admonition to the mayor, his own household officers and servants and all 'faithful subjects' to report any loose talk and remove any 'seditious bills'. In early April, Richard sent similar instructions to the city of York, and doubtless to other towns and cities throughout the country. All of which suggested that there was in fact plenty of seditious language and flyposting going on – and not only in London.[53]

Although Richard 'doubted not' that his denials and instructions had been taken on board, it was proving impossible to shift the toxic haze of uncertainty that now blanketed his regime. One material consequence of this, as a London chronicler noted, was evident among the city's businessmen. Some had already loaned 'great sums of money' to Margaret Beaufort back in the autumn of 1483: now, her agents were again busy. At their head was Reynold Bray, persuading 'tender and loving friends' among the city's mercantile community – men like the goldsmith and former mayor Edmund Shaw and the mercer Henry Colet – that their allegiances and best interests lay with Tudor. Typical of many who, as one chronicler put it, 'were in such a doubt that they knew not which party to lend unto', Colet covered both bases, extending credit to Richard and smuggling funds out of the country to Tudor. Others were more resolute. The goldsmith Hugh Brice, who had been a regular lender to Edward IV and close to William Hastings, didn't give Richard anything. Funds were moved out of England and across the Channel to the exiles, along with a now-constant stream of support. Others, like the former keeper of the Great Wardrobe Piers Curteys, deserted the regime by taking sanctuary.[54]

In attempting to extricate himself from the political corner into which he had boxed himself, Richard had only succeeded in provoking doubt among the very supporters on whom he had come to rely, and who, as rumours of his planned marriage to Elizabeth of York continued to circulate, eyed the intentions and actions of their king with fresh uncertainty. Imperceptibly, mistrust spread, and loyalties were loosened.

In mid-May the long, meandering train of Richard's travelling household left Westminster for Nottingham, whose castle had become his principal base. It was here that news of his son's death had reached him, and he had come to associate its familiar apartments with the interminable stretches of watching and waiting. It was, he wrote in a nod to the great allegorical poem *Piers Plowman*, his 'Castle of Care'. The reference was telling. From the start of his reign, Richard had conceived of kingship as a burden; in the intervening months, it had only become more oppressive. His citation also contained within it the shade of another meaning.

In *Piers Plowman* the narrator dreams of a landscape with a tower on a hill and a great valley in which was a dungeon, separated by a beautiful field in which all kinds of people lived and worked 'as this world demands'. The sight of the dungeon 'struck terror' into the narrator. It was, he was told, 'the Castle of Care'. Whoever entered it would curse the day he was born. Inside, there lived a being called Wrong: the father of lies, the creator of original sin. Wrong had built the castle. Those who placed their trust in his 'treasure' – the word carried with it associations of custodianship, of safekeeping – 'are betrayed soonest'.[55]

Ever since his seizure of power two years before, Richard had castigated his political opponents for their immorality, vice and sinfulness. Unable to acknowledge his own mistakes, Richard had blamed everybody but himself. Here could be glimpsed something else, a flickering moment of profound, agonizing self-awareness: the buck stopped with him.

What was also glaringly evident was that Richard could find no relief – or, rather, such relief could only come with the elimination of his nemesis, Henry Tudor. In mid-June, a fortnight after his arrival at Nottingham, reports reached him that the rebels were accelerating their invasion plans. Richard's reaction was instantaneous.[56]

On 21 June he issued another nationwide proclamation, spicing it with further graphic details about Tudor and his band of 'rebels and traitors'. Tudor was a foreigner, a betrayer of England, a rebel without a claim: 'son of Edmund Tudor son of Owen Tudor' – the baldness of these plain names emphasizing his lack of lineage – he was 'descended from bastard blood' on both sides of his family. If true Englishmen valued their own welfare, and that of their family and country, they were duty bound to turn out on Richard's behalf, against him.

Alongside the proclamation, Richard gave orders for yet another general mobilization. Commissioners were to ensure their troops were well armed and ready to assemble on an hour's notice. They should do so 'in all haste possible': a phrase that ran like a mantra through the royal orders. Indeed, it seemed to sum up Richard's rule over the last year and more, during which time, in response to Tudor's phantom threat, men had been repeatedly and urgently mustered and, as the menace evaporated, stood down again.[57]

This time, Richard's information was good. Leaving Paris that spring, Tudor and his men had travelled some eighty miles northwest to the Norman capital of Rouen, the port-city on the Seine that would be the base for their return to England. There, Tudor set about raising an army, and a fleet to carry it. As well as loans scraped together from various sources, including the drip-feed of cash smuggled out of England, the regime of the young Charles VIII had finally put its money where its mouth was, injecting a timely 40,000 livres – £10,000 – into Tudor's bid for the English throne.[58]

This funding had less to do with Tudor's persuasiveness, and more to do with France's vulnerability. That spring had seen an increase in aggressive manoeuvring from the kingdom's habitual enemies: Burgundy, Brittany and England. In both Flanders and Brittany, pro-French forces were on the retreat. Richard, meanwhile, had signed a seven-year truce with Brittany (this time committing to supply the long-promised detachment of archers). If this was intended to distract the twitchy French government from any move against England, or even to intimidate it into coming to terms with Richard, the move had the opposite effect, catalysing French support for Tudor from warm words into hard cash.[59]

In the weeks that followed, Richard scrambled to mobilize his forces. He could count on the retinues of his committed household men on whom he had lavished rewards and also, it seemed, great noblemen like Howard, Stanley and Northumberland, who together would supply several thousand troops. But a sense of uncertainty continued to pervade Richard's orders to 'all sheriffs', men whose co-operation in 'mustering and ordering' troops was crucial. Sheriffs, or their deputies, were ordered to base themselves in the 'shire towns' of their various counties, so that Richard and his commissioners would know where to find them. If they failed to do so, Richard added emphatically, they would answer to him at their 'uttermost peril'. It was almost as though he half-expected most of them to desert him.[60]

Meanwhile, the king tried to work out where Tudor might land. In recent decades, challengers to the English throne had made landfall everywhere: from the northeast, where Richard had returned together with Edward back in 1471; to Calais and Kent, the sites of Edward's invasion in 1460 and Warwick and Clarence's challenge in 1469; to the Devon coast, where Warwick and Clarence had arrived from France a year later and where Tudor had made his abortive attempt in 1483. Then there were the various Lancastrian efforts at stirring up insurgency over the years, up and down the Welsh and north-eastern coasts. Richard had to make an educated guess.

The southwest coast, directly across the Channel from the mouth of the Seine, was an obvious potential landing zone that Richard quickly moved to seal off. Operating out of Southampton, an armed fleet under the command of his chamberlain Francis Lovell patrolled the coastline, paying particular attention to Poole Bay – the site of Tudor's failed landing back in 1483 – and the village of Milford, which, so one prophesier had forecast, was where Tudor would make for this time.[61] The long, exposed Welsh coast was another possibility, especially in the southwest of the principality and the Tudors' own sphere of influence around Pembroke Castle. Although Richard had been bolstering his defences throughout Wales, his resources could only be spread so far. His authority was strongest along the principality's south-western coast, where his household man Richard Williams controlled much of the security infrastructure; to the east, the deputies of James Tyrell held sway. (Tyrell himself was still in the Calais fortress of Guisnes, where he had been redeployed the previous January and where he was still needed in the event of a Tudor assault on the Pale.[62]) Further north, Richard relied on the loyalties and influence of the Stanley family.

Since demonstrating their loyalty to Richard in the rebellion of autumn 1483, Lord Stanley and his brother Sir William had reaped rich reward from a grateful king. But though Richard had given them much, there were signs that both Stanleys wanted more. Despite his influence in north Wales, Sir William hadn't perhaps attained the pre-eminence after which he hankered. Meanwhile Lord Stanley, lavished with high office, expected a further boost to his north-western pre-eminence: in February 1485, Richard had instead picked open the scab of Stanley's decades-old feud with his regional Harrington rivals by bestowing a royal grant on them. For all that, Stanley was Richard's constable of England, a military linchpin. So when, that July, Stanley asked for permission to leave the royal household, where he was still steward, and return to his Lancashire base of Lathom, Richard let him; after all, Stanley would need to muster his troops in readiness to combat Tudor. But though Stanley had been as good as his word in keeping his wife Margaret Beaufort under house arrest, Richard didn't entirely trust him. His one condition was that Stanley send his son and heir, Lord Strange, to him at Nottingham, as surety for his continued loyalty. Stanley duly did so. On 1 August, with Stanley still absent, Strange turned up at court.[63]

Throughout the country that summer, with forces mobilizing and the threat of renewed civil war in the air, the prevalent response to Richard's call to arms seemed to be fatigue. For most, the demand to prove themselves 'good and true Englishmen' by marching halfway across the country to endanger their lives in a conflict of remote significance was, as it always had been, something best avoided. Meanwhile, in villages and towns, marketplaces, churches and inns, life continued. People discussed the usual subjects and anxieties, the usual hopes and fears: the harvest – better, this year, than the appalling yields of recent times, despite the damp weather; property disputes; exchange rates, business deals and the price of cloth; and a virulent new sickness, its hallmark a violent fever, which killed in hours.[64] Yet somehow the constant enervating state of emergency had to be resolved; sides had to be chosen. The instinctive impulse of many, when presented with Richard's letters and a flourish of the great seal, was to turn out for their sovereign lord against rebels who, as Richard's proclamation put it, had confounded 'all truth, honour and nature' by 'forsaking their natural country'. In the minds of others, the blame for England's instability was to be laid firmly at Richard's door.

On 31 July, as troops assembled, William Caxton brought out an edition of the late Sir Thomas Malory's *Morte d'Arthur*. The story of King Arthur and his knights of the round table was a perennial favourite – Caxton had, he said, been prompted to publish by 'many noble and diverse gentlemen' – and Malory's version was an obvious choice. Malory had fought in Edward IV's wars against the

Lancastrians and had completed his book in prison during the tumultuous late 1460s. All human life was here, Caxton explained in his prologue: 'herein may be seen noble chivalry, courtesy, humanity, friendliness, hardiness, love, friendship, cowardice, murder, hate, virtue, and sin.'

The printed book included a number of alterations to Malory's manuscript. In one episode, a sleeping King Arthur dreams of a mortal fight between a ravening bear, 'a tyrant that torments your people', and a dragon, which kills it. In Caxton's edition, someone changed the bear to a boar. The allusion was unmistakeable: the boar was Richard. And the dragon? Back in 1461 Edward IV had claimed that beast, portraying himself as heir to the mythical British king Cadwaladr – 'rubius draco' – who would unite England, Wales and Scotland and whose heirs would reign to the end of the world. But now, in the summer of 1485, 'rougedragon' denoted somebody different: the man who, in the absence of Edward's children, loyalists to the late king now saw as the heir to his cause – Henry Tudor.[65]

On 11 August, days after Caxton's publication of the *Morte d'Arthur*, messengers arrived at Beskwood Lodge outside Nottingham, where Richard was hunting. Tudor had landed. The prophecy was right, in a way. Tudor had landed at Milford, but not the Dorset village: he had come ashore at Milford Haven, on the westernmost tip of Wales. Richard, it was said, was jubilant: 'the day he had longed for, had now arrived'. The same day, he fired off urgent orders. The final confrontation with his elusive enemy was at hand. Nobody, he told his followers, was to miss it.[66]

21

A Beginning or End

That unsettled August, messengers rode through England with Richard's letters. As always, his language, underscored by his neat signature, was categoric. His supporters should come in person with the forces they had promised: as fast as possible, no excuses. Those who failed to do so would be punished with the loss of 'all that you may forfeit and lose', including, so the implication went, life itself. Richard himself stayed in Nottingham, not moving until he had celebrated one of the most significant feasts of the religious year, that of the Assumption of the Virgin Mary on 15 August. It was an act of piety that masked something else. Richard was finding it hard to raise men.

Partly it was down to the season – harvest time, when extra labour was needed in the fields. Yet the signs of foot-dragging were all too evident, even among his supporters. On receiving Richard's summons, the city of York sent not a detachment of troops but a messenger to the king, 'to understand his pleasure': to find out, in other words, whether this mobilization would be any different from any of the other false alarms the king had raised since his first such alert back in April 1484. Other royal officials enacted a deliberate go-slow. Some failed to raise troops at all; some did so and took them instead to Tudor.[1]

On the 19th, over a week after Tudor's landing, Richard rode the twenty-five miles south to his army's muster station of Leicester.[2] There, he took stock. Prominent among the assembled forces were the banners, badges and colours of the earl of Northumberland; and those of John Howard, who had come from East Anglia together with his son Thomas. Robert Brackenbury had made the journey from London, bringing guns from the Tower armoury. If some contingents still hadn't yet turned up – most notably the forces of Lord Stanley and his brother Sir William – the turnout, at around ten thousand men, was still substantial. It was big enough, Richard presumably felt, to deal with Tudor's ragtag assortment of exiles and foreign mercenaries, who were now moving through the east midlands, aiming hopefully for London. Time was an important factor: the longer Tudor went without being intercepted, the more convincing his claim would become. In any case, Richard was eager to get on with it.

On the morning of 21 August, Richard's army rode west out of Leicester in battle formation in 'great pomp', banners flying. Flanked by John Howard and the earl of Northumberland, Richard wore his crown; the cross was borne before him. A dozen miles or so out of town, scouts rode in with reports that Tudor had halted south of Watling Street, the straight Roman road to London, in the grounds of Merevale Abbey, near the village of Atherstone. Richard headed for nearby high ground and pitched camp.

If Tudor's campaign of misinformation, his gnawing away at the structures of Richard's government, had worked well from a distance, it was now proving harder to attract drifting loyalties to his cause. As he and his four thousand men slogged through the rugged Welsh terrain, through the Marches and into the English midlands, many of those who had promised their support now stood off. Richard had left the uncommitted in no doubt of the consequences of opposing an anointed, crowned king.[3]

To Tudor's horror, those sitting on the fence included the Stanley family: his mother's in-laws, of whose support – despite their public pledges of allegiance to Richard – he had been quietly confident. Lord Stanley's equivocations weren't so surprising: his motto *'sans changer'* stood in ironic counterpoint to his slipperiness of the last decades; besides, his son and heir was now in the custody of a suspicious Richard. But Tudor had hoped for more from Sir William Stanley. A former household knight of Edward IV and household steward to his son and heir, Sir William was precisely the kind of unswerving Yorkist loyalist whom Tudor now claimed to represent – and his three thousand men could make all the difference. But when Tudor and Sir William met at Stafford on the evening of Friday the 19th, the pair had a short, positive but inconclusive talk. Sir William then went away again.[4]

By this point, Tudor was 'full of fear'. Over the next two days, as his forces marched southeast through the midlands, he spent much of his time in increasingly frantic attempts to reach out to the Stanleys. On the evening of the 20th, Tudor disappeared altogether. He returned to his camp at dawn the following morning, assuring his anxious troops that he had good news from certain 'secret friends'. But later that day, after reaching Merevale Abbey, a clandestine meeting with Lord Stanley in person didn't change matters. Remarking, surprised, on how few men Tudor had, Stanley refused to give him any guarantees. Tudor, who had hoped for so much, was on his own.[5]

Richard awoke early on 22 August 1485. He had slept badly, it was later reported – restlessness as likely to have been down to adrenalin and nerves as much as a troubled conscience. The king's jitteriness rubbed off on those around him. When he wanted to hear mass, his half-awake chaplains scrambled to find what they needed for the divine service, even managing to mislay the sacrament: when they had 'one thing ready, evermore they wanted another, when they had wine, they lacked bread, and ever one thing was missing.' Neither, added another chronicler, was Richard's breakfast ready. Then, a rogue Scotsman apparently walked off with the king's battle coronet before he was apprehended and the crown returned.[6]

A general sense of suspicion and unease pervaded Richard's camp. As dawn rose, Richard's right-hand man John Howard emerged from his tent to find a note pinned to it: 'Jockey of Norfolk', it ran, alluding to Howard's ducal title, 'be not so bold/ For Dickon thy master is bought and sold.' The story was a Tudor one, but the atmosphere of mutual distrust it conveyed was real. If Richard had spent much of the previous two years trying to ensure that people turned out for him, he was equally concerned that when push came to shove, those who did turn out would actually fight – and on his side. He was, it seemed, almost anticipating betrayal, or at least indifference.[7]

Once he was armed, Richard summoned his commanders to his tent. In front of them, he held a ceremonial crown-wearing and took an oath to go on crusade against the Turks in the event of his victory: acts designed to emphasize that his was the righteous cause. In his pre-battle speech, Richard was said to have told his men that the battle to come would, either way, 'totally destroy' the kingdom of

England. If he won, he would 'ruin' those who had lined up with his enemy; if victorious, Tudor would, he knew, do 'exactly the same' to Richard and his supporters.[8] This vision of total destruction was not one to which many were prepared to subscribe. In the minds of many of his supporters, Richard's apocalyptic world of black and white dissolved into shades of uncertain grey.

Around seven in the morning, Richard drew up his men and gave the order to advance. First to move off, leaving the high ground of their encampment, was John Howard's vanguard, archers protected by spearmen, and in their midst Brackenbury's gunners. Behind them, watching the deployment – and keeping an eye on Lord Stanley, whose red-jacketed troops could be seen taking up position on the slopes of an adjoining hill to his left – was Richard with his elite household knights; in the rear, with several thousand men, was Northumberland. Reaching the plain below, Howard took up position and waited.

Meanwhile Tudor's mixture of Yorkists and Frenchmen, Lancastrians, Scots and Bretons marched in battle formation, east, through the ripe cornfields. His last-ditch plea to Lord Stanley had been batted away. Sitting tight, Stanley offered him the token support of four of his knights and their followers – that was it. Already 'vexed', Tudor now 'began to be somewhat appalled'. But, as his troops drew within bowshot of Richard's army, he had to get on with it.

Tudor himself was in the rear, protected by his own household men and a phalanx of French pikemen. His 'slender vanguard' was commanded by the earl of Oxford. The last battle Oxford had fought in England was fourteen years before, in the fog at Barnet, when the indiscipline of his troops had proved fatal. Now, he had a highly unlikely shot at redemption – against John Howard, the man who, following Edward IV's near-extermination of the Lancastrian cause in 1471, had been handed many of his family lands. With around three hundred yards separating them, the two vanguards eyeballed each other, fastened their helmets and prepared to fight.

Then Oxford advanced. Trying to avoid a patch of boggy ground, and the destructive combination of Howard's arrowfire and Brackenbury's artillery, he targeted the right-hand extremity of the enemy lines. As the two lines came together in a frenzy of hacking, stabbing and slashing, the earl, fearful of a repeat of Barnet, ordered his units of infantrymen to stay tight to their divisional standards and 'throng thick together' to avoid being split up in the fighting. Briefly, the lines disengaged: Howard's men paused, bewildered and suspicious, 'supposing some fraud'. The lull gave Oxford time to reshape his entire vanguard into an 'array triangle', a wedge formation protected on both sides by French pikemen, before punching again with concentrated force into the enemy lines, aiming for Howard himself. Soon, Howard's ranks, comprising lightly armed archers and foot soldiers, began to disintegrate under the disciplined ferocity of Oxford's onslaught. When Howard was killed, his banners swept away, panic rippled through the rest of Richard's vanguard.

Richard had been following the fighting with increasing impatience. As updates of Howard's collapse came in – the vanguard, as one of Richard's panicked household knights put it, 'breaketh on every side' – it was clear that Lord Stanley's forces were not about to intervene on Richard's behalf. Equally alarming was the realization that the earl of Northumberland, with his three thousand-odd troops at the rear of Richard's army – 'stationed in a part of the field where no encounter was discernible and no battle-blows given or received', as one chronicler put it understatedly – was showing no inclination to get involved.

Back in 1483, Northumberland's military might had been instrumental in Richard's rise to power. But, with Richard refusing to hand Northumberland control of the northeast, all the earl's resentments about Richard – of how, in the 1470s, Richard had muscled into the region he regarded as his birthright – had come flooding back. Now, Northumberland stayed where he was. Later, some tried to explain away his inaction, stating that the earl had been physically unable to advance through the boggy ground in front of him. But Northumberland had a history of 'sitting still'. Back in 1471, as Edward IV advanced south to reclaim his throne, Northumberland had done nothing: a non-intervention that, as one of Edward's men had remarked, was in fact a 'notable service'. Whatever the case, with both Stanley and Northumberland refusing to budge, Richard had to act. There was an opportunity, his scouts told him: Tudor's own forces, detached from Oxford's marauding vanguard, were alone, isolated and vulnerable.

As Richard contemplated a cavalry charge against Tudor, one of his advisers, a Spanish mercenary named Jean de Salazar, worriedly counselled him against the move. Richard himself was exposed, Salazar said: there were blatantly treasonous manoeuvrings among his own men. The king should retreat, seek safety while he still could. Richard's reply was entirely in character. Having waited so long for the chance to resolve the uncertainties of the past two years, he wasn't about to wait any longer. He wouldn't retreat one step, he told Salazar unequivocally. 'This day, I will die as a king or win.' Later, the Tudor historian Polydore Vergil reflected on Richard's words: 'such huge great fierceness and such huge force of mind he had', Vergil wrote, 'he came to the field that thereby he might either make a beginning or end of his reign.'[9]

Over his armour, Richard put on his royal coat of arms, and fixed his gold coronet to his helmet.[10] Leading his mounted household knights, gripping his battleaxe in one hand, reins in the other, Richard skirted his collapsing vanguard and rode down the hill towards Tudor, circumspectly at first, then, when he could see Tudor's banners clearly, faster, stabbing his spurs furiously into his horse's flanks, charging at the enemy he had wanted to meet for so long.

Tudor's men bunched together, preparing to absorb the shattering impact of Richard's horsemen. Tudor himself dismounted – 'he wanted to be on foot in the midst of us' – recalled one of the French mercenaries at his side. Packed tightly around him were the Yorkist loyalists faithful to Edward IV and his sons, their commitment transferred to Tudor: Sir William Brandon, clutching Tudor's red dragon standard; the giant figure of John Cheyne; Sir Edward Woodville, the dowager queen's brother; Giles Daubeney, Edward Poynings, Richard Guildford.

Richard's cavalry crashed into Tudor's lines, the shock partly absorbed by the marshy ground through which they had charged and by a hastily redeployed wall of French pikemen. Richard hacked his way towards Tudor with the white heat for which he was renowned, his rage fuelled by the sight of his nemesis, by the foreign mercenaries who had blunted his charge and who he cursed as he fought, by the treason in his own ranks. He got close, killing William Brandon – Tudor's standard briefly listed – and felling John Cheyne. The two men, king and pretender, were face to face. Then, with Tudor almost overwhelmed, relief arrived. Sir William Stanley's forces had been concealed behind the brow of a hill, out of Richard's eyeline. Now, they piled in. As Salazar had feared, Richard and his household knights were now beyond help.

Richard fought fiercely: even his enemies agreed. As he did so, according to many commentators, he shouted repeatedly and wildly that he had been betrayed. The indifference and disaffection that had set in over recent months, much of it shaped by Tudor's own long-distance phony war, had been carried onto the battlefield, fulfilling all Richard's anxieties.

Finally, he stumbled, or his horse lost its footing and threw him. His helmeted head was battered; blades sliced through his head, shearing off bone; a dagger was forced through the top of his skull. It was said that Welshmen killed Richard, their bloodlust fuelled by memories of Edgecote over fifteen years before, when 'northernmen' had massacred a generation of Welsh gentry. Now, they had their revenge against Richard and his northern knights – Brackenbury, Ratcliffe, Sir Robert Percy – whose bloodied bodies lay around their dead king: they 'killed the boar', puffed the Welsh bard Guto'r Glyn, 'shaved his head'.

With Richard's killing, it was all over. His men streamed across the surrounding fields in flight, shedding armour as they ran. They were pursued and slaughtered by Lord Stanley's troops: belatedly, and ingloriously, Tudor's father-in-law had got involved. Those who could, surrendered. William Catesby was captured, along with the quiescent earl of Northumberland and Thomas Howard, son of the dead duke of Norfolk. And, as his soldiers picked at the corpses of their enemies, stripping them bare of valuables, a disbelieving, traumatized, elated Henry Tudor made his way up a nearby hill, along with a clutch of his commanders, nobles and knights.

There, to shouts of 'God save King Henry!', Lord Stanley placed Richard's coronet – apparently found in a hawthorn bush – on the head of his son-in-law. Tudor, it was said, gave orders for the wounded to be tended, and for the dead to be buried honourably. If the orders applied to Richard, they weren't carried out.

As the battlefield was cleared, bodies piled onto carts, Richard's body was stripped of its fine armour and clothes, trussed up 'like a hog' – a sneering reference to his badge of the white boar – and heaved, naked, over the back of a horse, a noose round its neck. On the way back to Leicester, it became a plaything for Tudor's victorious, blood-drunk troops: somebody stabbed it in the right buttock with a dagger, so hard that the dagger blade penetrated through to Richard's pelvis.[11]

The indignities weren't over. Back in Leicester, Richard's body was put on display in the Franciscan Priory there 'for all men to wonder upon' – and to make sure, just as Edward IV had done with Henry VI back in 1471, that everyone knew he was dead. But if the custom was common enough, the manner of it was not: Richard's body was lain out still covered in 'mire and filth'. Neither was his interment. He was buried 'irreverently', without the appropriate funeral rites: 'in a ditch like a dog', some said.[12]

Commentators made no attempt to airbrush this treatment. Even pro-Tudor writers were appalled by the lack of humanity afforded Richard's corpse. But this savage treatment of him, they pointed out, was in a way the point. This was a 'miserable spectacle', remarked Vergil, but 'not unworthy for the man's life'. In other words, Richard got what was coming to him. He was no true king but a usurper, who had abused his vows of 'allegiance and fidelity' to his own nephews: the abuse of his body drove home the fact. But, added another chronicler, the natural order of things had been righted. Richard had tried to destroy his late brother's family line, and now, those faithful to the memory of Edward IV and the disappeared princes had triumphed. It was 'King Edward's sons whose cause, above all, was avenged in this battle' – a battle which would come to be named after a nearby town: Bosworth.[13]

On 7 November 1485, Henry Tudor's first Parliament opened at Westminster. His title to the throne was declared. Unlike the circumlocutions of Richard III's *titulus regius*, it stated briefly and simply that, for the avoidance of doubt, the crown of England and all its possessions belonged to Tudor, his lawful heirs, 'and no-one else'. There was no further validation needed. Richard III's reign, meanwhile, was swiftly delegitimized. Backdating his reign to the day before Bosworth – when the battle was fought, therefore, Tudor was the king and Richard the usurper, his supporters by definition traitors – Tudor annulled Richard's *titulus regius*, eradicated it from parliamentary record, and ordered that all surviving copies should be seized and burned, in order that Richard's claim may be 'forever out of memory and forgotten'. Tudor understood perfectly well the power of such documents. And in convicting Richard's key followers – among them Ratcliffe, Catesby, Lovell, Brackenbury and the Northampton-shire sheriff Roger Wake – he made a wry nod to the rhetoric by which Richard had tried to sustain his own kingship. All kings, Tudor observed, had a duty to promote and reward virtue, and to oppress and punish vice.[14]

Dealing with the Yorkist line of Edward IV, which had brought Tudor to power and whose cause he had embraced to add legitimacy to his own, was not so straightforward. Tudor duly rewarded those who had fled into exile with him, but as Yorkist loyalists quickly found, he had no intention of turning the political clock back to a time before Richard III's reign. That November, there was no men-tion whatsoever in Tudor's own claim to the throne of his bride-to-be, Edward IV's daughter Elizabeth of York. As one dismayed former councillor of Edward put it, Tudor could supply all that 'appeared to be missing' in his own title to the throne by marrying Elizabeth: why, the implicit question ran, didn't he do so?[15]

Although Tudor had been happy for people to paint him as the 'avenger of the white rose', he was not about to allow his own claim to the crown to depend on that of his wife. Tudor wanted to draw a line under the fratricidal Yorkist conflict that had brought him to power; besides which, the fate of Richard had shown what happened when kings came to lean on an overly narrow base of support. Tudor had avenged the white rose – but he had no intention of making good its claims. He would be king in his own right, and if people refused to acknowledge him as such, he would make them.

When Parliament was prorogued for Christmas, the Commons made a humble request to the new king. Given that Parliament had now unequivocally decreed that the right to the crown of England should 'rest, remain and stay in the person of the lord king and the heirs lawfully begotten of his body', they suggested, he was now safe to marry 'that illustrious lady Elizabeth, daughter of Edward IV'. From such a marriage, people hoped for offspring 'from the stock of kings, to comfort the whole realm'. After the Commons' petition had been made, the Lords spiritual and temporal rose collectively from their seats, bowed to the still figure who, swathed in his purple robes of state, sat on the throne of England, and asked, again, whether the king would marry Elizabeth of York. Acknowledging their request, Henry VII replied that he was content to do so.[16]

Epilogue

Sometime in 1486, the year after Bosworth, an ageing Warwickshire antiquary called John Rous finished his *Historia regum Angliae*, a history of the kings of England that he had been working on for the previous six years. Originally commissioned by one of the surveyors working on St George's Chapel, Windsor, as a way of giving Edward IV some ideas about which past monarchs he might like to commemorate in the new building, Rous's book had been overtaken by Edward's death and the cataclysmic upheavals of Richard's reign. At first, Rous had been highly complimentary about Richard, writing verses in his praise. But then Bosworth had happened. Dedicating his history to Henry VII, Rous painted a grotesque pen-portrait of the king's predecessor. The infant Richard, Rous claimed, had emerged from his mother's womb after a gestation period of two years, sporting a full set of teeth and shoulder-length hair. As an adult he had developed markedly uneven shoulders – right higher than left – and was a 'despicable' person: smooth-mannered, duplicitous and exceptionally cruel. The princes, Edward IV's sons, had been slaughtered in his care, and he ruled 'in the way that Antichrist is to reign'. Richard had, Rous grudgingly admitted, met an honourable death, fighting nobly 'despite his little body and feeble strength' – though even here he couldn't resist a dig. Richard, he wrote, shouted 'Treason' over and over again, 'tasting what he had often administered to others'.[1]

Rous's damning portrayal of Richard was an exercise in self-preservation. He was hardly alone. In the aftermath of Bosworth, many who had profited from Richard's rule conveniently found that they had been averse to it all along. Petitioning against his attainder in Henry VII's first parliament, Catesby's brother-in-law Roger Wake, who had played an instrumental role in Richard's seizing of power at Stony Stratford, claimed that it had been against his 'will and mind' to fight for him – an impulse that, by the last desperate days of Richard's reign, was shared by all too many. But in his presentation of Richard, Rous was making Henry Tudor's own point for him. Just as Richard was a physical anomaly, so was his reign, an unnatural deformation in the true lineal descent of kings that had now been corrected and straightened out.[2]

In the first years of Henry VII's rule there were many who didn't see it that way. Yorkists of 'old royal blood' abounded: men such as Richard's informal heir John de la Pole who, grooming a boy to impersonate Clarence's young son – another who, on paper, had a far more convincing claim to the throne than Tudor – raised conspiracy, international backing and an army. On a hot June day in the English midlands, De la Pole and his forces were massacred at the Nottinghamshire village of East Stoke. One man who got away was Richard's former chamberlain, Francis, Lord Lovell, who spent the rest of his days in the obscurity of a Scottish exile. The young pretender, the son of an Oxford joiner named Lambert Simnel, was put to work in the royal kitchens as a spit turner. The threat from Richard's supporters seemed contained. Contained enough, at any rate, for Henry VII in 1495 to commission a new alabaster tombstone for Richard's grave, together with an epitaph commending the dead king's bravery and complimenting Henry himself on honouring Richard 'piously' and – a nod to Henry's priorities – 'at your expense'.[3]

It was, however, the other side of the Yorkist family that proved most problematic for Henry Tudor. As everybody knew, his opportunity had only come because of the supposed deaths of Edward IV's heirs, a fact that he both simultaneously acknowledged and disavowed, continuing to downplay the claims of his wife's family: it wasn't until 1487, after Elizabeth of York had given birth to their first son, the new dynasty incarnate, that Henry finally had her crowned his queen. By then, her mother had also left court. Restored to her royal dignity, Elizabeth Woodville had since proved an uncomfortable reminder of the true origins of Henry's claim, while her equivocations during Richard's reign suggested that she was a less than fully paid-up member of the Tudor project. Perhaps subject to some gentle arm-twisting, she took up residence at Bermondsey Abbey; Henry, meanwhile, transferred her dower lands to her daughter the queen. On her death in 1492 Elizabeth Woodville was buried at Windsor Castle alongside her dead husband, as both she and he had wished. Her funeral, mirroring her own directions, was a paltry affair: economies had even been taken with the ceremonial lighting, which used 'never a new torch but old torches ... and torches ends'. All her daughters were there, except the heavily pregnant queen, and alongside them a young woman called Grace, 'a bastard daughter of King Edward' who had, perhaps, grown to love her adoptive mother. Elizabeth Woodville had nothing to bequeath, no worldly goods to leave the queen, 'my dearest daughter', nor to 'reward any of my children, according to my heart and mind'. Instead, she left them all she could: her blessing.[4]

Yet dissident Yorkists were already targeting the fundamental flaw in Henry Tudor's claim to the throne. Backed by Margaret, the dowager duchess of Burgundy – who had always been closer to her brothers Clarence and Richard than Edward, whom she had never really forgiven for his failure to come to Burgundy's aid – conspirators claimed to have found another Yorkist heir: the younger of Edward IV's sons, who had not been murdered by his uncle Richard after all, and had come to claim his throne. Although the Tudors dismissed him as the son of a Flemish boatman named Perkin Warbeck, the boy was convincing – and he stirred visceral loyalties in the Yorkists who had since transferred their allegiances to Henry VII. Turning the political clock back to April 1483, Warbeck's appearance threatened to wreck the settlement represented by Henry VII and Elizabeth of York's marriage and offspring.

Alarmingly for Henry, Warbeck managed to reunite plotters on both sides of the Yorkist divide. Ex-servants of Clarence joined forces with those who had fought for Richard III and those loyal to Edward IV's sons; even the Yorkist matriarch Cecily, now approaching eighty years old, was linked with the conspiracy.[5] Yorkist loyalists had become the enemy within: having absorbed them, Henry now purged them. Identified as a ringleader, Sir William Stanley – who had been Henry's chamberlain, responsible for his personal security – was beheaded, but the conspiracy endured. Henry did what he had to do. Warbeck was captured, tortured and executed; so too, to prevent him becoming a focus for rebellion, was Clarence's real son, a harmless, backward child. In 1502 Richard's close adviser Sir James Tyrell – who had, astonishingly, managed to transition to the new regime – was found guilty of plotting with another of the De la Pole family and executed for treason. In the days and weeks after his beheading, word spread that Tyrell had confessed to arranging the murders of Edward IV's sons, a confession which, the Tudor regime hoped, would put the matter to bed once and for all.

Through all this, Henry VII's relationship with Elizabeth of York endured. This was a true union. When, in 1503, she died in childbirth, Henry was devastated, as much for his personal loss as for the political catastrophe it represented. With his first son already dead, the future of the dynasty now lay in their second, the boy who would become Henry VIII. The last illness-ravaged years of Henry VII's reign were a desperate exercise in hanging on until the boy could reach his majority: anything to prevent a re-run of spring 1483.

Over time, though, Yorkists of both camps came to identify with the Tudor regime. John Howard's son Thomas – wounded at Barnet fighting for Edward, and at Bosworth in Richard's cause – was persuaded to follow the long road back to Henry VII's favour, eventually inheriting the dukedom of Norfolk that Richard had conferred on his father. When Henry VII died in April 1509, having dragged his family to the brink of a first untroubled dynastic succession in over a century, among the select few gathered at the king's bedside in his privy chamber was George, Lord Hastings: grandson of Edward's chamberlain William, he had also inherited his political instincts. Others, like the inscrutable figure of Thomas Montgomery, had woven an even more dextrous path. One of Edward IV's most valuable advisers, Montgomery had transferred to Richard's service – adding to his already substantial personal wealth in the process – and, having put in a discreet appearance at Bosworth on Richard's behalf, had adroitly fallen into step with the Tudor regime with no discernible change of pace.[6]

His maternal grandfather incarnate, the young Henry VIII embraced

Edward IV's lifestyle, surrounding himself with the descendants of Edward's household men: Parrs, Greys, Brandons, Guildfords and Bourchiers. Deeply aware of his own Yorkist inheritance, he had also inherited Edward's suspicion of the other side of the family. Still on the run, Richard III's youngest De la Pole nephew, Richard, became known as 'White Rose': a badge the Tudors now associated with their enemies. When in 1514 De la Pole threatened to invade England to claim his inheritance – backed, in time-honoured fashion, by French funds and using Brittany as a launchpad – Henry scrambled to make peace with France. He wasn't about to make Richard III's mistake again.

As the sixteenth century unfolded, the faultlines in the house of York, overlaid now with the religious conflict sweeping Europe, continued to shape Tudor fortunes. This time it was Clarence's descendants who were at the heart of the problem. His grandchildren, foremost among them Cardinal Reginald Pole, deplored Henry VIII's treatment of his first wife Katherine of Aragon, his religious choices, and his inferior claim to the throne. For Henry, the Poles – together with other Plantagenet families the Courtenays and the Nevilles – became an existential threat. He tried to eliminate them in a frenzy of torture and execution, and in 1541 had his seventy-year-old aunt, Clarence's daughter Margaret, executed for treason: a killing that echoed Edward IV's judicial murder of his brother over sixty years before. But Reginald Pole endured, spearheading England's return to the Roman religion under Henry's daughter Mary. On 17 November 1558, now back in London, Pole died of flu; that same day, across the city, Mary also died and Henry VIII's younger daughter was proclaimed Elizabeth I of England.

In Elizabeth's reign, a time when the civil wars had finally passed from living memory, the story of York finally ceased to be a live issue for the Tudors. Moralizing histories of the conflict became simply a way of throwing the Tudor achievement into starker relief while entertaining the public with the ghastliness of the Yorkists' fratricidal relationships. In decades to come, accounts of Edward's self-indulgence, Clarence's vaunting ambition and Richard's tyranny were offered to monarchs as examples of how not to do it, their authors often more concerned with flattering or pointing out the foibles of their dedica-tees than with the accuracy of their history.

When the clouds of civil disorder once more started to gather in the mid-seventeenth century, the story of the house of York again assumed a terrible immediacy. It was crucial, William Habington urged Charles I in his *Historie of Edward the Fourth*, that these 'rugged times' be explored, 'in order to avoid the byways of error and misfor-tune'. Back then, he wrote, the conflict had finally been resolved and 'sovereignty found a happy calm'. It was a comparison made more in hope than expectation. A year after Habington's book was published, England was once again at war with itself.[7]

Acknowledgements

In the course of writing this book I have met with immense generosity from the community of fifteenth-century scholars: my debt to their work, and to the work of historians past, will be evident. I've benefited greatly from conversations and correspondence with Jim Bolton, Alex Brondarbit, Helen Castor, Linda Clark, Ralph Griffiths, Sam Harper and David Rundle. Rosemary Horrox, Joanna Laynesmith, Tony Pollard, Carole Rawcliffe and John Watts, equally generous with their time, have all read parts of the manuscript and offered invaluable and thought-provoking advice. So too have Sean Cunningham and James Ross, to whom I owe a particular debt: their insight and friendship have been a constant source of illumination.

I'm grateful to Hugh Doherty for his enthusiasm and erudition; to Barrie Cook, in the British Museum's Department of Coins and Medals, for talking me through Edward IV's recoinages; and to Turi King for discussing with me her ground-breaking work on the genetic analysis of Richard III.

Thanks are also due to the staff of the British Library, The National Archives, the Corporation of London Records Office, Cambridge University Library, the Bodleian Library, and the Archives du Nord in Lille. I want also to acknowledge three scholars, Cora Scofield, Charles Ross and, again, Rosemary Horrox, whose landmark studies of Edward IV and Richard III are crucial to an understanding of the two reigns spanned by this book.

At Penguin Press, I'm especially grateful to Stefan McGrath, Stuart Proffitt, Pen Vogler, Rosie Glaisher, Ingrid Matts, Dahmicca Wright, Jim Stoddart, Jon Parker, Ellen Davies, Chloe Currens, Richard Duguid and Lou Willder. Rebecca Lee has been a model of calm. I'd also like to thank Charlotte Ridings for her eagle-eyed copyediting and Cecilia Mackay for her deft picture research. At Simon & Schuster US, Bob Bender has been encouraging, enthusiastic and exceptionally forbearing. My agents Catherine Clarke and Anna Stein have been a constant source of clear-eyed advice and reassurance.

I am deeply indebted to my editor and publisher Simon Winder, for his perspicacity and boundless patience, and for his uncanny ability to say the right thing at the right time.

My sons Guy and Louis fill me with joy. They surprise and delight me every single day, and keep me going. And this book could not have been written without Kate, who inspires and guides me: I owe her everything.

Finally, I want to thank my parents, who have given me so much. This book is for them.

Notes

Abbreviations

ADN	Archives du Nord, Lille
BL	British Library, London
BN	Bibliothèque Nationale, Paris
CC	*Crowland Chronicle*
CCR	*Calendar of Close Rolls*
CChR	*Calendar of Charter Rolls*
CLRO	City of London Records Office
CPL	*Calendar of Papal Letters*
CPR	*Calendar of Patent Rolls*
CSPM	*Calendar of State Papers, Milan*
CSPV	*Calendar of State Papers, Venice*
EETS	Early English Text Society
EHD	*English Historical Documents*
EHL	*English Historical Literature*
GC	*Great Chronicle of London*
HMC	Historical Manuscripts Commission
Household EIV	*The Household of Edward IV*, ed. Myers
JCC	Journal of Common Council
LMA	London Metropolitan Archives
LP RIII/HVII	*Letters and Papers Illustrative of the Reigns of Richard III and Henry VII*
LP WF	*Letters and Papers Illustrative of the Wars of the English in France*
LREF	*Life and Reign of Edward the Fourth*, Scofield
ODNB	*Oxford Dictionary of National Biography*
PL	*Paston Letters*
POPC	*Proceedings and Ordinances of the Privy Council of England*
PROME	*Parliament Rolls of Medieval England*
RP	*Rotuli Parliamentorum*
STC	Short Title Catalogue
TNA	The National Archives

1. Three Suns

1 Griffiths, 'Sense of dynasty', pp. 19-26; Allan, 'Political Propaganda', pp. 266 n. 2; Given-Wilson, 'The chronicles of the Mortimer family', pp. 67-86, 200-201. 2 Bennett, 'Memoir of a yeoman in the service of the house of York', pp. 259-64. 3 Ward, *Livery Collar*, pp. 60-71; *Historical Poems*, nos. 90, 92; Ormrod, *Edward III*, pp. 588-9; Wise, *Medieval Heraldry*, pp. 21-2 and fig. 56. 4 Watts, 'Pressure of the public', passim; Starkey, 'Which age of reform?', pp. 14-16. 5 'Bale's Chronicle', p. 135; BL Cotton MS Julius II 23, cit. Harvey, *Jack Cade's Rebellion*, p. 191. 6 John Watts, 'Richard of York, third duke of York (1411-1460)', *ODNB*; Johnson, *Duke Richard of York*, p. 226; Harriss, *Shaping the Nation*, p. 569. 7 Laynesmith, *Cecily Duchess of York*, p. 44. 8 John Watts, 'Richard of York, third duke of York (1411-1460)', *ODNB*; Laynesmith, *Cecily Duchess of York*, p. 56. For Henry IV's clause excluding the Beauforts from the succession, and doubts over its validity, see Jones and Underwood, *The King's Mother*, pp. 21-6. 9 Jones, 'Somerset, York and the Wars of the Roses', pp. 286-7; Watts, *Henry VI*, p. 269. 10 PROME, XII, 1450 November, Introduction, p. 160; *John Vale's Book*, p. 186; Griffiths, 'Duke Richard of York's intentions', p. 189; Watts, *Henry VI*, pp. 271-3. 11 PL Gairdner, nos. 142, 143; Watts, ' "Common weal" and "Commonwealth" ', p. 148. 12 PROME, XII, 1450 November, Introduction, p. 171; *Annales*, p. 770. 13 'William Gregory's Chronicle', p. 196; 'Short English Chronicle', p. 69; *Chronicles of London*, p. 163; *EHL*, p. 373; Watts, *Henry VI*, pp. 276-9; Hicks, *Warwick*, p. 81; Virgoe, 'Some Ancient Indictments', pp. 258-9; Ross, *Edward IV*, pp. 7, 13-14. 14 Laynesmith, *Cecily Duchess of York*, pp. 60-1. 15 J. A. Giles, *Incerti Auctoris Chronicon Angliae* (London, 1848), pp. 43-4, cit. Ross, *Henry VI*, p. 65. 16 PROME, XII, 1453 March, Introduction, p. 219; Griffiths, 'Local rivalries and national politics', p. 337. 17 PL Gairdner, II, no. 235; Griffiths, 'The King's council', pp. 309-17; Johnson, *Duke Richard of York*, p. 127. 18 PROME, XII, 1453 March, Introduction, pp. 221-5, items 32, 33 (pp. 258-60), Appendix, item 20 (p. 323); Roskell, 'Protector', pp. 226-7; Hicks, *Warwick*, p. 95; Griffiths, 'The King's council', p. 314. 19 *Original Letters*, ed. Ellis, vol. 1, pp. 9-10; Kleineke, *Edward IV*, p. 30. 20 'Bale's Chronicle', p. 141; PL Davis, II, no. 512; CSPM, no. 23. 21 Watts, *Henry VI*, pp. 313-15; Goodman, *Wars of the Roses*, pp. 22-3. 22 PL Gairdner, III, no. 283; Watts, *Henry VI*, pp. 316-17; Armstrong, 'Politics and the Battle of St Albans, 1455', passim. 23 'William Gregory's Chronicle', p. 212. 24 'William Gregory's Chronicle', p. 198; *English Chronicle*, ed. Davies, p. 72; *John Vale's Book*, pp. 190-3. 25 PROME, XII, 1455 July, items 23, 24 (p. 343); PL Gairdner, III, no. 299. 26 PL Gairdner, III, no. 303; PROME, XII, 1455 July, items 31-9 (pp. 348-57). 27 PROME, XII, 1455 July, Introduction, p. 329, item 47 (pp. 381-5); TNA KB 9/287, no. 53, cit. Ross, *Henry VI*, p. 73; Griffiths, *Henry VI*, pp. 751-3. 28 PL Gairdner, III, no. 322; Watts, *Henry VI*, pp. 321-2. 29 PL Gairdner, III, no. 334; Jones and Underwood, *The King's Mother*, pp. 39-40. 30 Griffiths, *Henry VI*, pp. 777-85; Harriss, 'Struggle for Calais', pp. 45-6. 31 GC, p. 189; MS Gough London 10, in *Six Town Chronicles*, p. 160; *Registrum . . . Whethamstede*, I, p. 296; Bennett, 'The Medieval Loveday', p. 369; Watts, *Henry VI*, pp. 343-7; Griffiths, *Henry VI*, pp. 804-7; Hutton, *Stations of the Sun*, p. 173. 32 Hicks, *Warwick*, pp. 138-47. 33 'Bale's Chronicle', p. 147; Hicks, *Warwick*, pp. 146-51; Allmand and Keen, 'William Worcester', pp. 98-9. 34 *Chronicles of London*, p. 169; Hicks, *Warwick*, pp. 152-6; Bolton, 'City and the crown', pp. 17-20. 35 *English Chronicle*, ed. Davies, pp. 81-3; 'John Benet's Chronicle', p. 223; PROME, XII, 1459 November, items 14, 15 (pp. 458-9); Watts, *Henry VI*, p. 350; Johnson, *Duke Richard of York*, pp. 185-6; Goodman, *Wars*

of the Roses, pp. 26–8. **36** Griffiths, *Henry VI*, pp. 821–2; Bellamy, *Law of Treason*, p. 200. **37** 'William Gregory's Chronicle', p. 205; *PROME*, XII, 1459 November, items 16–19 (pp. 459–60); Goodman, *Wars of the Roses*, pp. 30–1. **38** Hicks, *Warwick*, p. 169; Scofield, *LREF*, I, p. 41. **39** *English Chronicle*, ed. Davies, p. 83; 'William Gregory's Chronicle', p. 207; Laynesmith, *Cecily Duchess of York*, p. 70. **40** Gilson, 'Defence of the proscription of the Yorkists', passim; *PROME*, XII, 1459 November, items 7–22 (pp. 453–61). **41** Wavrin, *Anciennes Chroniques*, V, p. 282; Hicks, *Warwick*, p. 174; Scofield, 'The capture of Lord Rivers and Sir Antony Woodville', pp. 253–5; Richmond, 'English naval power', pp. 4, 8–9; Jones, 'Edward IV and the earl of Warwick', p. 345. **42** TNA DL 37/32/79, repr. in Jones, 'Edward IV and the earl of Warwick', p. 351; Barron, 'London and the crown', p. 95; Watts, *Henry VI*, pp. 349–54; Johnson, *Duke Richard of York*, pp. 199–200. **43** Harvey, *England, Rome and the Papacy*, pp. 195–6; Lunt, *Financial Relations*, pp. 142–3; Head, 'Pius II and the Wars of the Roses', pp. 146–51. **44** Hicks, *Warwick*, pp. 192–4; *Original Letters*, ed. Ellis, 3:1, pp. 83–8; *English Chronicle*, p. 94; Pius II, *Commentaries*, III, pp. 269–70, quoted in Head, 'Pius II', p. 152; *CSPM*, nos. 31, 32, 37; Watts, 'Polemic and politics in the 1450s', p. 30; Jones, 'Edward IV and the earl of Warwick', pp. 349–51; Thielemans, *Bourgogne et Angleterre*, p. 375. **45** 'A warning to King Henry', 'The Ballad set on the Gates of Canterbury', in *Historical Poems*, pp. 208–11, 218–21; *English Chronicle*, pp. 91–2; 'Articles of the commons of Kent at the coming of the Yorkist lords from Calais, 1460', *John Vale's Book*, pp. 210–11; *Three Fifteenth-Century Chronicles*, p. 73; Watts, 'Polemic and politics in the 1450s', p. 30; Harvey, *Jack Cade's Rebellion*, pp. 183–4. **46** *Annales*, p. 772; *English Chronicle*, pp. 91–4; Harvey, *Jack Cade's Rebellion*, pp. 184–5; Grummitt, 'Kent and national politics, 1399–1461', p. 249; Scofield, *LREF*, I, pp. 65–9. **47** *English Chronicle*, p. 94; *Annales*, p. 772; LMA Journal 6, ff. 237–9v; TNA E404/72/1/23; Bolton, 'City and the crown', p. 11; Barron, 'London and the crown', p. 97; Ross, *Edward IV*, pp. 16–7. **48** *English Chronicle*, p. 96. **49** 'Battle of Northampton', in *Historical Poems*, p. 212. **50** LMA Journal 6, f. 257; 'Battle of Northampton', p. 212; Barron, 'London and the crown', pp. 97–8; 'John Benet's Chronicle', p. 227; Scofield, *LREF*, I, pp. 92–3. **51** *CSPM*, no. 38; Hicks, *Warwick*, pp. 184–5. **52** Pius II, *Commentaries*, III, pp. 269–70, quoted in Head, 'Pius II', p. 152. **53** More, *History of King Richard III*, p. 4; Mancini, *Usurpation*, pp. 79–80. **54** 'Battle of Northampton', p. 215; Watts, 'Polemic and politics', pp. 31–2. **55** *PL* Davis, II, no. 613; TNA E404/72/1/108. **56** *POPC*, VI, p. 303; TNA C266/82/31, CHES 2/135 m. 3, cit. in Jones, 'Edward IV and the earl of Warwick', p. 347; 'Private indentures for life service', pp. 56, 164–5; McFarlane, 'Wars of the Roses', p. 237 n. 14; Johnson, *Duke Richard of York*, pp. 210–11. **57** *Registrum . . . Whethamstede*, I, pp. 376–7, trans. *PROME*, XII, 1460 October, Introduction, pp. 508–9; *Chronicles of London*, p. 171; Jones, 'Edward IV and the earl of Warwick', pp. 342–52. **58** Johnson, *Duke Richard of York*, pp. 213–19. **59** *PROME*, XII, 1460 October, pp. 517–18, items 11–19 (pp. 517–23). **60** *PROME*, XII, 1460 October, items 20–27 (pp. 523–5); 'William Gregory's Chronicle', p. 208; Armstrong, 'Inauguration ceremonies', pp. 52–3; Morgan, 'Political afterlife', pp. 869, 874. **61** 'Letter from Prince Edward to the City of London, 1460', in *John Vale's Book*, pp. 142–3; 'William Gregory's Chronicle', p. 210; *CC*, p. 113; *Annales*, pp. 774–5; LMA Journal 6, ff. 279, 284; Pollard, *North-Eastern England*, pp. 279–80; Jones, 'Edward IV and the Beaufort Family', p. 259. **62** *Annales*, pp. 774–5; *Three Fifteenth-Century Chronicles*, p. 154; *Registrum . . . Whethamstede*, pp. 381, 384–5; Scofield, *LREF*, I, p. 120 n. 3. **63** Dockray, *The Battle of Wakefield*, pp. 10–11, 23–7; Hall, *Chronicle*, pp. 250–1. **64** 'William Gregory's Chronicle', p. 210; 'John Benet's Chronicle', p. 228; *Annales*, p. 775; *English Chronicle*, p. 107; *Registrum . . . Whethamstede*, I, p. 382.

2. The Rose Stands Alone

1 *English Chronicle*, pp. 108–9; Griffiths, *Henry VI*, p. 872; Gillingham, *Wars of the Roses*, pp. 122–3. 2 'The Battle of Towton', ll. 12–13, *Historical Poems*, no. 90, p. 216; *PL* Davis, I, no. 114; Pollard, *North-Eastern England*, p. 282. 3 *CSPM*, nos. 56, 58; *CSPV*, no. 364; *POPC*, VI, pp. 307–10. 4 *Six Town Chronicles*, p. 153; 'John Benet's Chronicle', p. 229; *PROME*, XII, 1460 October, Introduction, p. 511; TNA E163/28/5; Richmond, 'The nobility and the Wars of the Roses', pp. 261–9; McFarlane, 'Wars of the Roses', pp. 244–5. 5 *CSPM*, no. 76. 6 *CSPM*, nos. 54, 59. 7 'William Gregory's Chronicle', pp. 211–14; *CSPM*, no. 63. This account of the battle follows Gillingham, *Wars of the Roses*, pp. 124–9 and refs. 8 'William Gregory's Chronicle', pp. 211–14; *English Chronicle*, p. 108; *Registrum . . . Whethamstede*, I, pp. 389–90; *CSPM*, no. 64; Smith and DeVries, *The Artillery of the Dukes of Burgundy*, pp. 48, 237–8. 9 'William Gregory's Chronicle', p. 214; *CSPM*, no. 71; *Registrum . . . Whethamstede*, I, pp. 394–6. 10 'The Battle of Towton', no. 90, in Robins, *Historical Poems*, p. 216. 11 *CSPM*, no. 64; LMA Journal 6, original ff. 10, 35; *English Chronicle*, pp. 108–9; *John Vale's Book*, p. 142; Barron, 'London and the crown', p. 98, Table 2, pp. 103–4 and refs; Bolton, 'The city and the crown', pp. 11–12, 21, 98. 12 Lucia Diaz Pascual, 'Luxembourg, Jacquetta de, duchess of Bedford and Countess Rivers (c.1416–1472)', *ODNB*; *John Vale's Book*, p. 83; Scofield, *LREF*, I, pp. 145, 147; Laynesmith, *Cecily Duchess of York*, p. 83. 13 *CSPM*, nos. 64, 65; Scofield, *LREF*, I, pp. 144–8; Barron, 'London and the crown', p. 97; *John Vale's Book*, p. 83. 14 *John Vale's Book*, pp. 77–8, 83, 160; *Chronicles of London*, p. 174; R. A. Griffiths, 'Vaughan, Sir Thomas (d. 1483)', *ODNB*; Rosemary Horrox, 'Hatteclyffe, William (d. 1480)', *ODNB*; Laynesmith, *Cecily Duchess of York*, pp. 82–3. 15 Laynesmith, 'The piety of Cecily', p. 29; Laynesmith, *Cecily Duchess of York*, p. 61. 16 *English Chronicle*, pp. 109–10; *GC*, p. 195; 'Hearne's Fragment', *Chronicles of the White Rose*, p. 6; Laynesmith, *Cecily Duchess of York*, pp. 82–3. 17 'William Gregory's Chronicle', pp. 214–15; *English Chronicle*, p. 109; Fleming, 'The battles of Mortimer's Cross', pp. 100–102; Bolton, 'The city and the crown', pp. 11–12. 18 'William Gregory's Chronicle', p. 215. For the changing Yorkist line on Henry VI, see *Three Fifteenth-Century Chronicles*, p. 76; *PROME*, XIII, 1461 November, item 14 (pp. 20–1); *Foedera*, XI, p. 471; Fleming, 'The battles of Mortimer's Cross', pp. 99–100; Evans, *Wales and the Wars of the Roses*, pp. 130–1. 19 'William Gregory's Chronicle', p. 215; *English Chronicle*, p. 110; *Chronicles of London*, p. 173. 20 Michael Hicks, 'George Neville (1432–1476)', *ODNB*. In what follows I draw on Armstrong, 'Inauguration ceremonies', passim. 21 *Chronicles of London*, pp. 173–4; MS Gough London 10, in *Six Town Chronicles*, pp. 161–2; *GC*, p. 195; Armstrong, 'Inauguration ceremonies', pp. 54–6; *LP WF*, II, p. 777; for the debate over 'many others unnamed', see Ross, *Edward IV*, p. 34 n. 3 and Lander, 'Marriage and politics', pp. 103–4. 22 Sermon in Halliwell, 'Observations upon . . . Edward the Fourth', pp. 128–30. 23 *CSPM*, no. 78. 24 TNA E404/72/1/19, 22, 23, 24; Scofield, *LREF*, I, pp. 158–9. 25 TNA E404/72/1/36, 68; Barron, 'London and the crown', Table 2. 26 TNA C54/313, no. 38d; *CCR 1461–1468*, pp. 54–6; Scofield, *LREF*, I, pp. 154–6. 27 *Chronicles of London*, p. 175; *CSPM*, no. 78; *CPR 1461–1467*, p. 31; TNA E404/72/1/29, 80; Tucker, 'Government and Politics', p. 338. 28 Gillingham, *Wars of the Roses*, pp. 60–1. 29 'William Gregory's Chronicle', p. 216; Wavrin, *Anciennes Chroniques*, II; 'John Benet's Chronicle'; Goodwin, *Fatal Colours*, pp. 153–4; Goodman, *Wars of the Roses*, pp. 50–1; Scofield, *LREF*, I, pp. 157–72; Colin Richmond, 'Mowbray, John (VI), third duke of Norfolk (1415–1461)', *ODNB*. 30 *GC*, p. 198, cit. in Payling, 'Edward IV and the politics of conciliation', p. 94. 31 In this account of the battle I draw on Goodwin, *Fatal*

Colours, ch. 10 passim; Goodman, *Wars of the Roses*, pp. 50–2; Maurer, *Margaret of Anjou*, p. 202. **32** Strickland and Hardy, *The Great Warbow*, esp. ch. 19. See also Richmond, 'The nobility and the Wars of the Roses', pp. 76–7; Hall, *Chronicle*, p. 255. **33** GC, pp. 196–7. **34** *Three Books . . . Vergil*, p. 111; Commynes, *Memoirs* ed. Jones, p. 187. **35** Hounslow, 'Scattered skeletons', passim; Novak, 'Battle-Related Trauma', pp. 90–102. **36** Sutherland, 'Recording the Grave', pp. 40–1; Knusel and Boylston, 'How has the Towton Project . . .', pp. 185–6; Hall, *Chronicle*, pp. 255–6. **37** TNA C81/382; *PL* Davis, I, no. 90; *CSPM*, nos. 78, 79, 83; *Chronicles of London*, p. 175; Ross, *Edward IV*, pp. 37–8. **38** Hicks, *Warwick*, p. 237. **39** *PL* Davis, II, no. 628; *CPR 1461–1467*, pp. 29, 45, 95; Pollard, *North-Eastern England*, p. 285. **40** *Registrum . . . Whethamstede.*; 'The Battle of Towton', *Historical Poems*, p. 216. **41** Payling, 'Edward IV and the politics of conciliation', pp. 81–94; Ross, *Edward IV*, p. 45; Kleineke, *Edward IV*, p. 210; Scofield, *LREF*, I, pp. 173–4; CC 110–11. **42** *CSPM*, nos. 85, 86. **43** Wavrin, *Anciennes Chroniques*, pp. 357–8; *Chronicle of John Stone*, p. 83; Scofield, *LREF*, I, p. 178; Hicks, *False, Fleeting Clarence*, pp. 6–7; Colvin, *History of the King's Works*, II, pp. 998–1001. **44** *Chronicles of the White Rose*, p. 10; 'The maner of makynge knyghtes', in *Three Fifteenth-Century Chronicles*, pp. 106–13. **45** TNA E404/72/1/114. **46** 'The Battle of Towton', ll. 66–71, *Historical Poems*, no. 90, p. 218; TNA KB/145/7/1, Kleineke, *Edward IV*, p. 49; Scofield, *LREF*, I, pp. 182–4. **47** Free Library of Philadelphia, Lewis E 201, sec. 7, https://libwww.freelibrary.org/digital/item/3335. **48** BL Harleian MS 7353; BL Additional MS 18268A. **49** Hicks, *False, Fleeting Clarence* (1992 edn), pp. 7–8. **50** 'Brief Latin Chronicle', p. 174; Armstrong, 'Inauguration ceremonies', p. 71 and n. 4. **51** E.g. *CPR 1461–1467*, p. 19; *Foedera*, V (II), pp. 66, 106; TNA E72/1/71, 75, 109. Further examples are cited by Allan, 'Political Propaganda', pp. 345–6. **52** Gillingham, *Wars of the Roses*, p. 154. **53** TNA E404/72/1/10.

3. The World is Right Wild

1 *CSPM*, no. 117; Vale, *Charles VII*, p. 177; Peyronnet, 'The distant origins of the Italian wars', p. 41. **2** *CSPM*, nos. 117, 120. **3** Fortescue, *Laws and Governance*, p. 10; *Household EIV*, pp. 45–6; Scofield, *LREF*, I, p. 283; Ross, *Edward IV*, pp. 261–2 and refs. **4** TNA E101/82/10; *CSPM*, no. 117; *Henry the Sixth . . . Blacman*, p. 8, cit. in Ross, *Henry VI*, p. 24. **5** *CSPM*, no. 120; *CPR 1461–1467*, p. 97. **6** Vaughan, *Philip the Good*, pp. 353–4; Scofield, *LREF*, I, pp. 157–62; Vale, *Charles VII*, pp. 189, 192–3. **7** See e.g. TNA C81/1377 and TNA C81/1486-8, passim. **8** *CSPM*, nos. 81, 117. **9** *PL* Davis, I, no. 117. **10** *Foedera*, XI, p. 473; Linda Clark, 'Bourchier, Henry, first earl of Essex (c.1408–1483)', *ODNB*; Anne Crawford, 'Howard, John, first duke of Norfolk (d. 1485)', *ODNB*. **11** More, *History of King Richard III*, p. 52; Mancini, *Usurpation*, pp. 69, 89; Rosemary Horrox, 'Hastings, William, first Baron Hastings (c.1430–1483)', *ODNB*. **12** TNA E28/89/29. **13** TNA E28/89/28; TNA SC 8/29/1435A; *Original Letters*, ed. Ellis, 1st ser. 1, p. 116; Ross, *Edward IV*, p. 49; Bellamy, 'Justice', p. 136; Scofield, *LREF*, I, pp. 197–200. **14** Jones and Underwood, *The King's Mother*, pp. 40–3; Scofield, *LREF*, I, pp. 203–4. **15** TNA E404/72/1/55B, 96; *Household EIV*, pp. 111–12. **16** *Household EIV*, pp. 123–4; Rawcliffe, 'More than a bedside manner', pp. 72, 84. **17** Kisby, 'The Royal Household Chapel', pp. 195, 221; Ross, *Richard III*, pp. 9–10. **18** PROME, 1461 November, item 7, pp. 11–13; Lander, 'Attainder and forfeiture', pp. 119–20. **19** Wolffe, 'Management of royal estates', passim; Wolffe, *Royal Demesne*, pp. 162–3, 168 n. 73, 169–71. **20** *Household EIV*, pp. 45–6. **21** *Household EIV*, p. 127; *CPR 1461–1467*,

p. 101. **22** *PROME*, XIII, 1461 November, items 38–9 (pp. 63–6). **23** *PL* Davis, I, no. 63; II, no. 662; *PL* Gairdner, IV, pp. 32, 235; *CPR 1461–1467*, pp. 100–1; Ross, *Edward IV*, p. 44; Richmond, 'English naval power', p. 8–9. **24** *PL* Davis, II, no. 6361; I, no. 167. **25** *Chronicles of London*, p. 177; *CPR 1452–1461*, p. 465; 'John Benet's Chronicle', p. 232; *CSPM*, no. 125; Ross, *Foremost Man*, pp. 36, 41–7; Scofield, 'Early life of John de Vere', pp. 228–9. **26** Benjamin G. Kohl, 'Tiptoft [Tibetot], John, first earl of Worcester (1427–1470)', *ODNB*. I am grateful for David Rundle's perceptive thoughts on Tiptoft's character and outlook. *CPR 1461–1467*, p. 74; MacCulloch, *Reformation*, pp. 76–7; 'A Letter Preface from John Free to John Tiptoft', pp. 101–3, tr. Wakelin, *Humanism, Reading and English Literature*, p. 71. **27** Keen, 'Jurisdiction and origins', passim; Keen, 'Treason trials', p. 88; Bellamy, 'Justice', pp. 140–1. **28** *GC*, pp. 198–9; Warkworth, *Chronicle*, p. 5; 'Hearne's Fragment', p. 289 (I am grateful to James Ross for this reference). **29** Ross, *Foremost Man*, pp. 49–51; ibid, 'Treatment of traitors' children', p. 135. **30** Renewing companies' privileges e.g. *CPR 1461–1467*, pp. 242–3 (Goldsmiths); Tucker, 'Government and Politics', pp. 251, 253, 338, 342–3; Scofield, *LREF*, I, pp. 205–6. **31** Calmette and Périnelle, *Louis XI*, pp. 19–21; Scofield, *LREF*, I, pp. 251–4; Harriss, 'Struggle for Calais', p. 51. **32** Scofield, *LREF*, I, p. 258. **33** *Three Fifteenth-Century Chronicles*, pp. 158–9; Jones, 'Edward IV and the Beaufort family', p. 259. **34** LMA Journal, pp. 170–1, 7, ff. 6–9; *John Vale's Book*; *CPR 1461–1467*, p. 231; *Annales*, pp. 779–80; Tucker, 'Government and Politics', p. 253. **35** *Three Fifteenth-Century Chronicles*, pp. 158–9; Allan, 'Political Propaganda', pp. 306–7; Morgan, 'House of policy', p. 55. **36** P. J. C. Field, 'Malory, Sir Thomas (1415x18–1471)', *ODNB*; TNA C67/45, m. 14 (24th October 1462); Field, 'Last years', pp. 436–7; Barber, 'Malory's "Le morte Darthur"', p. 138; Carpenter, 'Sir Thomas Malory', pp. 31–43. **37** Malory, *Works*, book XXI, p. 724. **38** Piccolomini, *Commentaries*, pp. 22–5; Goodman, 'The Anglo-Scottish Marches', pp. 18–33; Pollard, *North-Eastern England*, pp. 15, 21, 41–2, 171–2. **39** *GC*, pp. 199–200; 'William Gregory's Chronicle', pp. 218–19. **40** *John Vale's Book*, pp. 171–2; Hicks, *Warwick*, pp. 241–3. **41** *John Vale's Book*, pp. 170–1; LMA Journal 7, ff. 8, 9; Warkworth, *Chronicle*, p. 2; Hicks, *Warwick*, pp. 241–3. **42** *PL* Davis, I, no. 320. **43** Warkworth, *Chronicle*, p. 3; *Annales*, pp. 780–1; Ross, *Edward IV*, p. 52. **44** *PL* Davis, II, no. 675; *Extracts from the Municipal Records of York*, p. 33; *John Vale's Book*, pp. 149–50; *Annales*, p. 781; *GC*, p. 200; Hicks, *Warwick*, pp. 242–3. **45** *Three Fifteenth-Century Chronicles*, p. 176 (tr. Ross, *Edward IV*, p. 52); Jones, 'Edward IV and the Beaufort family', pp. 259–60; Payling, 'Edward IV and the politics of conciliation', pp. 89–90. **46** Warkworth, *Chronicle*, pp. 2–3; 'William Gregory's Chronicle', p. 219; *CPR 1461–1467*, p. 262. **47** Jones, 'Edward IV and the earl of Warwick', pp. 351–2, cit. TNA DL 37/32/79. **48** Jones, 'Edward IV and the Beaufort family', pp. 259–60. **49** *PROME*, XIII, 1463 April, Introduction, p. 84, item 1 (p. 92); Jurkowski, 'Parliamentary and prerogative taxation', pp. 273–4. **50** *PROME*, XIII, 1483 April, item 18 (p. 105). **51** Postan, *Hanse*, pp. 97–9. **52** 'Libel of English Policy', in *Political Poems and Songs*, 2, pp. 172, 176; Holmes, 'The "Libel of English Policy"', pp. 200–1; Harriss, *Shaping the Nation*, pp. 269–70; Tucker, 'Government and Politics', pp. 127, 344–5; Bolton, *Medieval English Economy*, pp. 311–15. **53** 'On England's Commercial Policy', *Political Poems and Songs*, 2, pp. 282–7. **54** *PROME*, XIII, 1463 April, items 18–22 (pp. 105–15); 'On England's Commercial Policy', *Political Poems and Songs*, 2, p. 284; Munro, *Wool, Cloth and Gold*, pp. 160–1. **55** Hicks, *Warwick*, p. 244. **56** 'William Gregory's Chronicle', pp. 219–21. **57** 'William Gregory's Chronicle', pp. 219–22; *GC*, p. 200; Jones, 'Edward IV and the Beaufort family', p. 260 n. 17; Scofield, *LREF*, I, p. 273. **58** *CPR 1461–1467*, pp. 13, 134, 266; TNA E101/82/6/4; Ross, *Edward IV*, p. 75; Payling, 'Widows', p. 112. **59** 'William, Gregory's Chronicle', pp. 221–2. **60** Waurin, *Anciennes Chroniques*, III, pp. 159–60; *Priory of Hexham*, I, no. 85; *Annales*, p. 781; Bittmann, 'La campagne Lancastrienne', pp. 1061–2, 1082–3; Pollard, *North-Eastern England*, p. 227; Macdougall, *James III*, p. 54.

4. Two Kings of England

1 Emery, *Greater Medieval Houses*, II, pp. 238–42; Colvin, *History of the King's Works*, II, pp. 649–50; Scofield, *LREF*, I, p. 268. 2 Scofield, *LREF*, I, p. 297. 3 Scofield, *LREF*, II, App. I, p. 300; TNA E101/411/15, f. 14v; Chastellain, *Oeuvres*, IV, pp. 279–80; *Annales*, p. 781; Kleineke, *Edward IV*, p. 79; Sutton, 'Chevalerie . . .', pp. 117–18. 4 *Chronicle of John Stone*, p. 88; CPR 1467–1477, pp. 295–6; Hicks, *False, Fleeting Clarence* (1992 edn), p. 14; Keir, 'George Neville', pp. 193–4. 5 RP, VI, p. 168; Hicks, *False, Fleeting Clarence*, pp. 156–7. 6 RP, VI, p. 193. 7 TNA E361/6 mm. 53d, 54; E403/825, m. 2; E404/72/3/47; E404/72/4/2; CPR 1461-1467, pp. 52, 197, 212–13; Hicks, *False, Fleeting Clarence* (1992 edn), pp. 8–11; Ross, *Richard III*, pp. 9–11. 8 Scofield, *LREF*, I, p. 216. 9 *Chronicle of John Stone*, p. 88; TNA DL 37/31/36. 10 Chastellain, *Oeuvres*, IV, pp. 282–5; Thielemans, *Bourgogne et Angleterre*, pp. 367–410; Vaughan, *Philip the Good*, p. 357; Scofield, *LREF*, I, pp. 301–23. 11 *Mémoires d'Olivier de la Marche*, II, pp. 214–17; Vaughan, *Charles the Bold*, pp. 156–7; Ballard, 'Du sang de Lancastre', pp. 83–6. 12 Commynes, *Memoires*, ed. Dupont, III, pp. 201–2; Meek, 'Conduct and Practice', p. 67 and n. 16. 13 Vaughan, *Philip the Good*, pp. 336–54; Ballard, 'Du sang de Lancastre', pp. 83–6. 14 *Foedera*, V (2), p. 117; Meek, 'Conduct and Practice', p. 70. 15 Kekewich, 'Lancastrian court in exile', p. 96. 16 TNA E404/72/3/57, 68; CPR 1461-1467, pp. 280, 292–3; Hoare et al., *Old and New Sarum*, p. 158. 17 Scofield, *LREF*, I, p. 309. 18 Wavrin, *Anciennes Chroniques*, III, pp. 173–4; Jones, 'Edward IV and the Beaufort family', p. 260, citing Scofield, *LREF*, I, p. 296 n. 2. 19 *Three Fifteenth-Century Chronicles*, p. 177; LMA Journal 7, f. 65v; Tucker, 'Government and Politics', pp. 339–40. 20 'William Gregory's Chronicle', p. 221; PROME, XIII, 1463 April, items 8, 11 (pp. 97–8); Jurkowski, 'Parliamentary and prerogative taxation', pp. 273–4. 21 Dunlop, *James Kennedy*, p. 242. 22 Warkworth, *Chronicle*, p. 3; 'William Gregory's Chronicle', p. 223; TNA C81/796/1301; Jones, 'Edward IV and the Beaufort family', p. 261 and n. 31. 23 Wavrin, *Anciennes Chroniques*, III, pp. 178–81; Jones, 'Edward IV and the Beaufort family', pp. 260–62. 24 PROME, XIII, 1463 April, item 28 (p. 122); point made by Pollard, *Wars of the Roses*, p. 39. 25 CPR 1461-1467, p. 292; TNA C81/1494/3953; E159/240, brevia Hill.3 Edw.IV m.1; Ross, *Richard III*, p. 10. 26 Jones, 'Edward IV and the Beaufort family', pp. 261–2. 27 PL Gairdner, IV, pp. 88, 91; EHL, p. 356; Bellamy, 'Justice', pp. 136–7; Scofield, *LREF*, I, pp. 318–20; Ross, *Edward IV*, p. 398. 28 PL Davis, I, no. 321. 29 'Short English Chronicle', p. 80. 30 Bolton, *Medieval English Economy*, pp. 75–80; Spufford, *Money and its Use*, pp. 331–2, 360–1; Roover, *Rise and Decline*, pp. 358–60, 480–1; Wavrin, *Anciennes Chroniques*, III, pp. 182–6. 31 CCR 1461–1468, pp. 230, 259; Jurkowski, 'Parliamentary and prerogative taxation', p. 274. 32 TNA E404/72/2/44, 45; Scofield, *LREF*, II, pp. 331, 406; Lander, 'Council, administration and councillors', p. 195; Ross, *Edward IV*, pp. 351–3. 33 CC, pp. 138–9; Power, 'English wool trade', pp. 20–2; Gray, 'English foreign trade', pp. 45–8; Ross, *Edward IV*, p. 352. 34 Scofield, *LREF*, II, pp. 331, 404–7; Lander, 'The Yorkist council', p. 39. 35 Meek, 'Conduct and Practice', pp. 119–27. 36 Meek, 'Conduct and Practice', p. 70, cit. BN MS Français 2811, f. 53; Hicks, *Warwick*, pp. 253–6. 37 Wavrin, *Anciennes Chroniques*, III, p. 184. 38 *Dépêches . . . milanais*, II, pp. 75–81. 39 Scofield, *LREF*, I, p. 320. 40 Getz, *Medicine in the English Middle Ages*, p. 63. 41 *Three Books . . . Vergil*, pp. 117–18; Kleineke, *Edward IV*, pp. 79–80; Payling, 'Widows', p. 112. 42 *Foedera*, V (2), p. 123; CSPM, no. 132. 43 Wavrin, *Anciennes Chroniques*,

III, pp. 164–75, at pp. 173–4; 'William Gregory's Chronicle', pp. 223–4; Macdougall, *James III*, p. 56; Dunlop, *James Kennedy*, pp. 242–3; Pollard, *North-Eastern England*, p. 152. **44** Gillingham, *Wars of the Roses*, p. 152. **45** 'William Gregory's Chronicle', p. 224; Warkworth, *Chronicle*, p. 4; Ross, *Edward IV*, pp. 59–60. **46** 'William, Gregory's Chronicle', pp. 224–6; *Three Fifteenth-Century Chronicles*, pp. 178–9; *Annales*, p. 782; Warkworth, *Chronicle*, p. 4; *Priory of Hexham*, I, pp. cviii–lxi; Keen, 'Treason trials', pp. 99–101. **47** Warkworth, *Chronicle*, pp. 39–40; 'William Gregory's Chronicle', p. 226; TNA E404/72/4/54; *Chronicles of London*, p. 178; *Annales*, p. 782; *CPR 1461–1467*, pp. 295–6; Hicks, *Warwick*, p. 246. **48** Warkworth, *Chronicle*, pp. 37–9; Keen, 'Treason trials', pp. 90–92, 95, 97. **49** TNA C81/1377/27. **50** *CPL*, XI, p. 654; Harvey, *England, Rome and the Papacy*, pp. 85–6; Scofield, *LREF*, I, p. 336. **51** Lunt, *Financial Relations*, pp. 146–50. **52** In what follows I draw on Allen, *Mints and Money*, p. 209; Challis, *A New History of the Royal Mint*; Reddaway, 'The king's mint', pp. 16–17. I am grateful for Barrie Cook's perceptive thoughts on the impact of Edward IV's recoinage. **53** Tucker, 'Government and Politics', pp. 427–8; Cowley, 'Urban Capital', p. 34. **54** Griffiths, *Henry VI*, pp. 339, 363, 369; Tucker, 'Government and Politics', pp. 359, 427; see also Challis, *New History of the Royal Mint*, pp. 210–12. **55** TNA E 101/294/18; Scofield, *LREF*, I, p. 362; Tucker, 'Government and Politics', p. 346. **56** *CCR*, p. 216; Morgan, 'Political afterlife', pp. 861, 864–5; Hughes, *Arthurian Myths*, pp. 83, 108–9, 143–4; Kleineke, *Edward IV*, p. 193. **57** *History of the Kings of Britain*, ed. Monmouth, Book IX, Ch. IX; Laynesmith, 'Telling tales', p. 204.

5. Now Take Heed . . .

1 Wavrin, *Anciennes Chroniques*, II, pp. 326–7; Chastellain, *Oeuvres*, V, pp. 23–4; *Dépêches . . . milanais*, II, pp. 213–14; Meek, 'The practice of English diplomacy', pp. 72–3. **2** *CSPM*, nos. 137, 138, 139; *Dépêches . . . milanais*, pp. 276, 292. **3** Hicks, *Edward V*, pp. 43–4. **4** Hepburn, *Portraits of the Later Plantagenets*, pp. 54–60. **5** Hicks, *Edward V*, p. 45; Payling, 'Widows', pp. 113–15. **6** HMC, Hastings MSS (1928–47), 1301–2; Lander, 'Marriage and politics', pp. 106–7. **7** Fabyan, *New Chronicles*, p. 655; Payling, 'Widows', p. 106 n. 16, cit. TNA E163/29/11, m. 5; Hicks, *Edward V*, p. 41; Scofield, *LREF*, I, pp. 332–3. **8** Malory, *Morte d'Arthur*, cit. Laynesmith, *Last Medieval Queens*, p. 63; 'William Gregory's Chronicle', p. 226. **9** Mancini, *Usurpation*, pp. 60–1, 66–7; *Three Books . . . Vergil*, p. 117; Fahy, 'Italian Source', p. 665. **10** *Peter Idley's Instructions to his son*, bk 2, ll. 1661, 1674–5, p. 135. **11** Helmholz, *Marriage Litigation*, pp. 34–40; Visser-Fuchs, 'English events in Caspar Weinreich', p. 31. **12** Horrox, 'Introduction', in *Fifteenth Century Attitudes*, p. 6. **13** John Russell's 'Boke of Nurture', in *The Babees Book*, pp. 189–90; *Declamacion of Noblesse*; Wakelin, *Humanism*, pp. 162, 168–71; Allmand and Keen, 'History and literature of war', pp. 103–11. **14** Wavrin, *Anciennes Chroniques*, II, pp. 327–8. **15** More, *History of King Richard III*, p. 62. **16** *Dépêches . . . milanais*, II, pp. 304–5. **17** Colvin, *History of the King's Works*, I, p. 537 (I am grateful for Joanna Laynesmith's clarification on this point); Laynesmith, *Cecily Duchess of York*, pp. 116–17. **18** Crawford, *Yorkist Lord*, pp. 43–4; Sutton and Visser-Fuchs, 'The device of Queen Elizabeth Woodville', passim. **19** Hammond, 'Illegitimate children of Edward IV', p. 230. **20** Laynesmith, *Last Medieval Queens*, p. 183. **21** TNA C81/1377/45; *Dépêches . . . milanais*, II, pp. 181, 295–310; Meek, 'Conduct and Practice', p. 10; Ballard, 'Anglo-Burgundian Relations', pp. 26– ; Watts, *The Making of Polities*, pp. 349–51; Vaughan, *Philip the Good*, pp. 336–46, 374–5; Scofield, *LREF*, II, App. V, pp. 469–70; Scofield, *LREF*, I, pp. 348–51. **22** TNA C76/148 m. 7; Ballard, 'Anglo-Burgundian

Relations', p. 21.   23 *Memoires du J le Clerq*, XIV, p. 374, cit. Tucker, 'Government and Politics', p. 347; *EHD* Myers, 1042–3; Munro, *Wool, Cloth and Gold*, pp. 163–5.   24 TNA C81/1378/28; *Foedera*, XI, p. 536; Thielemans, *Bourgogne et Angleterre*, p. 414.   25 Sutton, 'Caxton was a mercer', pp. 126–32; Munro, *Wool, Cloth and Gold*, pp. 164-5; Sutton, *Mercery of London*, pp. 263–4; Ross, *Edward IV*, p. 363.   26 Sutton and Visser-Fuchs, 'A "most benevolent queen"', pp. 223–4, 232–4.   27 Hicks, 'The changing role of the Wydevilles', passim.   28 Myers, 'Household of Queen Elizabeth Woodville', passim; Given-Wilson, 'The merger of Edward III's and Queen Philippa's households', pp. 183–6.   29 Myers, 'Household of Queen Elizabeth Woodville', pp. 207–13.   30 Myers, 'Household of Queen Elizabeth Woodville', p. 476.   31 *CPR 1467–1477*, p. 33; Tucker, 'Government and Politics', pp. 320–1; Sutton, *Mercery of London*, p. 235.   32 Myers, 'Household of Queen Elizabeth Woodville', pp. 213, 216, 218; *GC*, p. 195; *John Vale's Book*, pp. 79–80, 83, 99–100; Tucker, 'Government and Politics', p. 130; Anne F. Sutton, 'Cook, Sir Thomas (c.1410–1478)', *ODNB*.   33 *Three Fifteenth-Century Chronicles*, p. 80; TNA E404/72/4/77; TNA E405/41; Scofield, *LREF*, I, pp. 364–5; Chambers, *Medieval Stage*, pp. 391–404; Kisby, 'The Royal Household Chapel', pp. 221–3.   34 *Annales*, p. 783; Lander, 'Marriage and politics', p. 111.   35 *Annales*, pp. 785–6; *Excerpta Historica*, pp. 1974–7; *PL* Gairdner, III, p. 231; C. S. L. Davies, 'Stafford, Henry, second duke of Buckingham (1455–1483)', *ODNB*; Hicks, 'Changing role of the Wydevilles', pp. 214–16.   36 *PROME*, XIII, 1463 April, item 53 (pp. 237–9).   37 Ballard, 'Anglo-Burgundian Relations', pp. 22–3; Sutton, *Mercery of London*, p. 265.   38 *PROME*, XIII, 1463 April, Introduction, pp. 89–90, item 53 (pp. 237–9).   39 *The Works of Sir John Fortescue*, I, pp. 23–5; Griffiths, 'For the might off the lande', p. 86; Kekewich, 'The Lancastrian court in exile', pp. 97–101.   40 *CSPM*, no. 142.   41 *Foedera*, XI, 28 March 1465; Ballard, 'Anglo-Burgundian Relations', pp. 21–4; Scofield, *LREF*, I, pp. 372–5.   42 Kisby, 'Royal Household Chapel', pp. 145–8; *Excerpta Historica*, p. 172.   43 *Excerpta Historica*, pp. 178, 182–3, 188–95.   44 TNA E404/73/1/124B; *Excerpta Historica*, p. 193; Ballard, 'Anglo-Burgundian Relations', p. 24; Blockmans and Prevenier, *The Promised Land*, pp. 176–7.   45 In what follows I draw on Sutton and Visser-Fuchs, 'Entry of Queen Elizabeth Woodville', pp. 6–7.   46 Smith, *Coronation of Elizabeth Wydeville*, pp. 61–8; *Annales*, p. 784; *The Register of the . . . Garter*, Appendix, passim; Pilbrow, 'Knights of the Bath', pp. 202–9; Ross, *Edward IV*, p. 95.   47 'William Gregory's Chronicle', p. 228; Fleming, 'The Hautes and their "circle"', pp. 94–5.   48 TNA E403/824; TNA E404/72/1/112, 72/4/22; E404/72/1/100, 72/2/5; *John Vale's Book*, p. 85; 'William Gregory's Chronicle', p. 222; *Calendar of Letter-Books: L*, pp. iii–iv; Tucker, 'Government and Politics', pp. 126–7, 340–41.   49 Smith, *Coronation of Elizabeth Wydeville*, passim; Hicks, *False, Fleeting Clarence* (1992 edn), pp. 24–5.   50 Smith, *Coronation of Elizabeth Wydeville*, p. 10.   51 Calmette and Périnelle, *Louis XI*, pp. 65–6, 69; Hicks, *Warwick*, p. 262.   52 *Chronicle of John Stone*, pp. 93–4; Warkworth, *Chronicle*, p. 5, 40–43; Visser-Fuchs, 'English events in Caspar Weinreich', pp. 312–13; *Annales*, p. 785; *Three Fifteenth-Century Chronicles*, p. 80; TNA E404/73/2; E404/73/3; E405/48, 13 May, 25 June; *Issues of the Exchequer*, p. 490; *CPR 1461–1467*, p. 268; Scofield, *LREF*, I, pp. 382–4; *Henry the Sixth . . . Blacman*, p. 44.   53 Jesus College, Oxford MS 114; Allan, 'Political Propaganda', pp. 285–7.

6. They Are Not to be Trusted

1 Leland, *Collectanea*, pp. 2–14; *LP WF*, II, p. 785; Woolgar, 'Fast and feast', pp. 23–5; Michael Hicks, 'George Neville (1432–1476)', *ODNB*; Pollard, *North-Eastern England*, p. 300. Scofield, *LREF*, I, p. 400.   2 *Annales*, p. 785; TNA E404/73/1/69.   3 Orme,

From Childhood to Chivalry, pp. 6–8, 16–17, 20–1, 44–8, 181–210 passim. **4** Longleat MS 257, f. 98v; Sutton and Visser-Fuchs, *Richard III's Books*, pp. 2–8, 40–1, 217–19, and Catalogue II, pp. 279–81. **5** *Issues of the Exchequer*, p. 390; Ross, 'Some "servants and lovers"', passim; Sutton, 'And to be delivered . . .', passim; Ross, *Richard III*, pp. 9–11, 24–6. **6** Wavrin, *Recueil*, V, pp. 458–9; *RP*, VI, p. 193; Hicks, *False, Fleeting Clarence* (1992 edn), pp. 20, 31; Hicks, *Warwick*, pp. 233–4. **7** *CPR 1461–1467*, pp. 198–90, 212–13, 226–7, 327–8, 331, 362, 454–5; Hicks, *False, Fleeting Clarence* (1992 edn), pp. 20, 24, 156–8; Ross, *Edward IV*, p. 117. **8** *PROME*, XIII, 1463 April, pp. 86–7; TNA C49/56–65; Hicks, *False, Fleeting Clarence* (1992 edn), p. 24 and n. 72; Wolffe, *Royal Demesne*, pp. 152–4. **9** TNA E404/73/1/124B; Meek, 'Conduct and Practice', pp. 131–2; Scofield, *LREF*, I, p. 404 n. 1. **10** Weightman, *Margaret of York*, pp. 23–4, 51–2, 65; Michael Jones, 'Margaret, duchess of Burgundy (1446–1503)', *ODNB*. **11** Commynes, *Memoirs* ed. Jones, pp. 82–3; Armstrong, 'La politique matrimoniale', pp. 260–1; Ballard, 'Anglo-Burgundian Relations', pp. 30–1. **12** Leland, *Collectanea*, IV, p. 249; Staniland, 'Royal entry into the world', passim. **13** Le Goff, *The Birth of Europe*, pp. 186–7. The following passage is based on *The Travels of Leo of Rozmital*, passim. **14** *The Travels of Leo of Rozmital*, pp. 45, 52; *Household E IV*, p. 217. **15** *The Travels of Leo of Rozmital*, p. 48; Laynesmith, *Last Medieval Queens*, p. 113. **16** *The Travels of Leo of Rozmital*, p. 47. **17** *The Travels of Leo of Rozmital*, pp. 45, 61–2; Laynesmith, *Last Medieval Queens*, pp. 250–1. **18** *Household E IV*, p. 22; Wolffe, *Royal Demesne*, pp. 175–6. **19** Grummitt, 'Public service, private interest', pp. 155–7; Scofield, *LREF*, I, pp. 397–8. **20** TNA E404 73/3/2; Clark, 'The benefits and burdens of office', passim. **21** Tucker, 'Government and Politics', App. 4B, pp. 420–1. **22** TNA E401/888 m. 13; E403/830 m. 2 [1463], cit. Grummitt, 'Public service, private interest', p. 157; Steel, *The Receipt of the Exchequer*, pp. 330–2, 356–7. **23** For Port, see Griffiths, *Henry VI*, pp. 480, 657; *CPR 1452–1461*, p. 329; *CCR 1454–1461*, p. 154; McFarlane, *England in the Fifteenth Century*, p. 137. **24** *CPR 1461–1467*, p. 476. I am grateful to Linda Clark for an advance copy of her biography of Thomas Vaughan, forthcoming in *History of Parliament: Commons 1433–1504*. **25** *Foedera*, XI, pp. 562–6; Thielemans, *Bourgogne et Angleterre*, p. 419. **26** Vaughan, *Charles the Bold*, pp. 4–5, 165; Ballard, 'Anglo-Burgundian Relations', p. 40. **27** Roover, *Rise and Decline*, pp. 338–9. **28** Roover, *Rise and Decline*, p. 88. **29** Roover, *Rise and Decline*, pp. 340–2; Walsh, *Charles the Bold and Italy*, pp. 121–3. **30** George Holmes, 'Canigiani [Caniziani], Gherardo (1424–1484)', *ODNB*; Holmes, 'Lorenzo de' Medici's London branch', passim; Mallett, 'Anglo-Florentine commercial relations', p. 254; Ruddock, *Italian Merchants*, pp. 208–11. **31** *CPR 1461–1467*, p. 518; *John Vale's Book*, p. 265; Tucker, 'Government and Politics', p. 433; TNA E404/73/1/124B; Mallett, 'Anglo-Florentine commercial relations', p. 252; Roover, *Rise and Decline*, pp. 330–1. **32** Meek, 'Conduct and Practice', pp. 131–2; Ballard, 'Anglo-Burgundian Relations', pp. 41–2; BN MS Français 20600, f. 70, quoted in Ballard, ibid., p. 42. **33** Munro, *Wool, Cloth and Gold*, pp 167–8; Thielemans, *Bourgogne et Angleterre*, pp. 420–1; Hicks, *False, Fleeting Clarence*, pp. 29–30. **34** *Lettres de Louis XI*, III, pp. 87–9; *Foedera*, XI, p. 568; Meek, 'The Practice of English diplomacy', pp. 75–6; BL Harleian MS 69, f. 19; Barber, 'Malory's "Le morte Darthur"', pp. 146–7. **35** TNA C81/1379/14; C81/1379/15; Scofield, *LREF*, I, p. 407; Lander, 'The Yorkist council', p. 38. **36** Ross, *Edward IV*, p. 110. **37** Keir, 'George Neville', pp. 195–7. **38** *Foedera*, XI, pp. 573–4. **39** ADN B330/16128; BL MS Cotton Galba B I f. 211, pr. in 'Actes concernant les rapports . . .', pp. 45–6; Ballard, 'Anglo-Burgundian Relations', p. 42; Armstrong, 'Politique matrimoniale', pp. 276–7. **40** 'Actes concernant les rapports . . .', pp. 105–6; *LP WF*, II, p. 785; Ballard, 'Anglo-Burgundian Relations', p. 142. **41** R. A. Griffiths, 'Herbert, William, first earl of Pembroke (c.1423–1469)', *ODNB*; Hicks, 'Changing role of the Wydevilles', pp. 214, 218; Scofield, *LREF*, I, p. 397. **42** *LP WF*, II, p. 785; Hicks, 'What might have been', p. 294. **43** TNA PSO 1/64/41; *Plumpton Correspondence*, no. XII; Hicks, *False, Fleeting Clarence* (1992 edn), pp. 14-15, 157-67. **44** Hicks, 'Restraint, mediation and private justice', passim and esp. p. 145, citing Birmingham Reference Library MS 437204. **45** Steel, *The Receipt of the Exchequer*, pp. 291-2, 354. **46** Holmes, 'Lorenzo de' Medici's London branch', p. 274; Mallett, 'Anglo-Florentine commercial relations', p. 252; Zippel, 'L'allume di Tolfa', pp. 430-3; Roover, *Rise and Decline*, pp. 152-3. **47** TNA E404 73/2/37; Ruddock, *Italian Merchants*, pp. 213-14. **48** *CSPM*, nos. 147, 148. **49** What follows draws on *CSPM*, no. 146; Kekewich, *The Good King*, pp. 74-5, 213-20.

7. Love Together as Brothers in Arms

1 *PL* Davis, I, nos. 116, 236, 327; II, no. 745; Castor, *Blood and Roses*, pp. 182-3, 197-8. **2** Ballard, 'Anglo-Burgundian Relations', p. 47. **3** Fox, *Cambridge University Library: The Great Collections*, pp. 65-6; Wakelin, *Humanism*, pp. 146-7; Blades, *Life and Typography of William Caxton*, pp. 96-8. **4** *CSPM*, nos. 147, 148, 149; Ballard, 'Anglo-Burgundian Relations', p. 57. **5** *PL* Davis, I, no. 237. **6** Ballard, 'Anglo-Burgundian Relations', pp. 61-2; Anglo, 'Anglo-Burgundian feats of arms', p. 275. **7** *Excerpta Historica*, p. 198. **8** TNA E404/73/3/73b. **9** *LP WF*, II, p. 786; Ballard, 'Anglo-Burgundian Relations', p. 64; Hicks, *Warwick*, p. 269. **10** Anglo, 'Anglo-Burgundian feats of arms', p. 275. **11** *PROME* XIII, 1467 June, Introduction, p. 250. *LP WF*, II, p. 786. Roskell, *The Commons and their Speakers*, p. 280. **12** *PROME*, XIII, 1467 June, item 7 (pp. 256-7), 15 (p. 354). **13** Clark, 'The benefits and burdens of office', p. 122. **14** *PROME*, XIII, 1467 June, item 8 (pp. 257-343); TNA C49/64, no. 17; *LP WF*, II, p. 786; Kleineke, *Edward IV*, p. 167; Wolffe, *Royal Demesne*, p. 153; Hicks, *Warwick*, p. 263. **15** TNA E101/474/1; E364/101 m. 71b; Anglo, 'Financial and heraldic records', p. 187. **16** Utrecht MS f. 202, cited in Anglo, 'Anglo-Burgundian feats of arms', p. 277; Anglo, 'Financial and heraldic records', pp. 183-95; Barber and Barker, *Tournaments*, pp. 107-37, esp. pp. 107, 110-12; Barber, 'Malory's "Le morte Darthur"', p. 140. **17** *Excerpta Historica*, p. 208. **18** *GC*, pp. 203-4; Anglo, 'Financial and heraldic records', p. 191. **19** Anglo, 'Anglo-Burgundian feats of arms', p. 281; Sutton, *Mercery of London*, p. 265. **20** 'Hearne's Fragment', pp. 18-19; Ballard, 'Anglo-Burgundian Relations', p. 60. **21** *Mémoires d'Olivier de la Marche*, III, p. 56. Ballard, 'Anglo-Burgundian Relations', pp. 48-50; Brown, 'Exit ceremonies in Burgundian Bruges', p. 113. **22** BN MS Français 88, ff. 228-228v; Ballard, 'Anglo-Burgundian Relations', p. 83. **23** Wavrin, *Anciennes Chroniques*, II, pp. 346-8, 353-4; *Annales*, p. 787; Calmette and Périnelle, *Louis XI*, pp. 86-8; 'Meek, The practice of English diplomacy', pp. 77-84. **24** *PROME*, XIII, 1467 June, item 16 (pp. 354-5). **25** *Foedera*, XI, pp. 580-1; *Annales*, p. 789; *Chronicles of the White Rose*, p. 22; *Three Books . . . Vergil*, p. 118; Ballard, 'Anglo-Burgundian Relations', pp. 67-8; Scofield, *LREF*, I, pp. 425-9; Hicks, *Warwick*, p. 263; Calmette and Périnelle, *Louis XI*, p. 89; Meek, 'Conduct and Practice', p. 135. **26** *Annales*, p. 789. **27** Ballard, 'Anglo-Burgundian Relations', pp. 70-1. **28** *Foedera*, XI, p. 590; Ballard, 'Du sang de Lancastre', p. 84; Scofield, *LREF*, I, pp. 430-3. **29** Carus-Wilson and Coleman, *England's Export Trade*, pp. 102-3; Tucker, 'Government and Politics', p. 363; Bolton, 'Warwick, Clarence and London', pp. 12-14; Ballard, 'An expedition of archers', passim. **30** Commynes, *Memoirs* ed. Jones, p. 181. **31** Warkworth, *Chronicle*, pp. 3-4. **32** Hicks, *False, Fleeting Clarence* (1992 edn), pp. 30-31; Wolffe, *Royal Demesne*, p. 153; Wolffe, *Crown Lands*, pp. 52-3, doc. 1. **33** *PL* Davis, I, no. 282. **34** *Annales*, pp. 788-9; *Three Books . . . Vergil*, p. 118;

Ross, *Edward IV*, p. 118. 35 Devine, 'The lordship of Richmond', passim; Hicks, *Warwick*, pp. 257, 269–70. 36 Ross, 'Treatment of traitors' children', p. 133. 37 Hicks, *False, Fleeting Clarence*, pp. 26–8. 38 *LP WF*, II, pp. 788–9. 39 *LP WF*, II, pp. 788–9; *CCR 1468–1476*, pp. 25–6; *CPR 1467–1477*, p. 55. 40 *Memoires pour server de preuves . . .*, III, pp. 159–61; Wavrin, *Anciennes Chroniques*, III, pp. 186, 191; Scofield, *LREF*, I, pp. 440– . Meek, 'The practice of English diplomacy', pp. 74–6, 129. 41 *Memoires pour server de preuves . . .*, III pp. 159–61; *GC*, p. 207. 42 *GC*, p. 207; *Calendar of Letter-Books: L*, p. 73; *Memoires pour server de preuves . . .*, III, pp. 159–61. 43 *Memoires pour server de preuves . . .*, III, pp. 159–61; Wavrin, *Anciennes Chroniques*, III, pp. 190–1. 44 Wavrin, *Anciennes Chroniques*, III, pp. 193–4; TNA E404/73/3/92; Hicks, *Warwick*, p. 265; Ross, *Edward IV*, p. 438. 45 *LP WF*, II, p. 789; *Memoires pour server de preuves . . .*, III, pp. 159–61. 46 Wavrin, *Anciennes Chroniques*, III, pp. 193–5. 47 ADN B2068, f. 43; Ballard, 'Anglo-Burgundian Relations', pp. 103–4. 48 TNA E401/893; E404/73/3/72; E404/73/3/73b. 49 TNA E73/3/72; E122/79/2; E122/162/1; Roover, *Rise and Decline*, p. 432; Holmes, 'Lorenzo de' Medici's London branch', p. 277; Ruddock, *Italian Merchants*, p. 210. 50 Wavrin, *Anciennes Chroniques*, III, pp. 194–5. 51 *Select Cases in the Exchequer Chamber*, II, p. 11; Keir, 'George Neville', pp. 199–201; Ballard, 'Anglo-Burgundian Relations', pp. 81–2; 124–5; Roover, *Rise and Decline*, pp. 157–8. 52 TNA E404/73/3/92; Keir, 'George Neville', p. 203. 53 'William Gregory's Chronicle', pp. 235–6; Keir, 'George Neville', p. 204. 54 'William Gregory's Chronicle', pp. 235–6; *Stephani Baluzii*, I, pp. 494–501; Keir, 'George Neville', pp. 213–14. 55 Ballard, 'Anglo-Burgundian Relations', pp. 116–18. 56 TNA E404/73/3/92. 57 *Foedera*, XI, pp. 605–13; 'Actes concernant les rapports . . .', pp. 110–19; Ballard, 'Anglo-Burgundian Relations', pp. 108–29. 58 *Stephani Baluzii*, I, p. 501. 59 *CSPM*, no. 158; Ballard, 'Anglo-Burgundian Relations', pp. 113–15; Scofield, *LREF*, I, pp. 446–7. 60 Walsh, *Charles the Bold and Italy*, pp. 94–5; Ballard, 'Anglo-Burgundian Relations', pp. 127–31. For the dispensation, including Trenta's seal, see ADN B429 no. 16141. 61 Ballard, 'Anglo-Burgundian Relations', pp. 127–8. 62 TNA C81/1499/4227; Ballard, 'Anglo-Burgundian Relations', p. 135. 63 *PL* Davis, II, no. 750. 64 ADN B2068, f. 124v; *PROME*, 1467 June, item 18 (pp. 355–6).

8. Robin Mend-All

1 *LP WF*, II, p. 789; *PROME*, XIII, 1467 June, items 24–9 (pp. 362–4); Michael Hicks, 'Stillington, 'Robert (d. 1491)', *ODNB*. 2 See for example Chancellor Henry Beaufort's opening sermon to Parliament on 19 November 1414: *PROME*, IX, 1414 November, item 1 (pp. 66–7). 3 *PROME*, 1467 June, items 28, 29 (pp. 363–4); *LP WF*, II, p. 789; Jurkowski, 'Parliamentary and prerogative taxation', pp. 274–5. 4 Roover, *Rise and Decline*, p. 474 n. 83; see also Scofield, *LREF*, II, pp. 446–53. 5 TNA E404/74/1/45; E403/840. 6 Ross, *Edward IV*, pp. 111–12. 7 *PROME*, XIII, 1467 June, item 41, pp. 367–8; *EHD* Williams, p. 533; Hicks, 'The 1468 Statute of Livery', pp. 22–3, 26. 8 Colvin, *History of the King's Works*, II, pp. 793–804. 9 Griffiths, 'For the myght off the lande . . .', p. 88; Hicks, 'The case of Sir Thomas Cook, 1468', p. 82; Sutton, 'Sir Thomas Cook', p. 97. 10 Paris, BN MS Français 6964, ff. 27–27v, translated by Kekewich, 'The Lancastrian court in exile', Appendix 2, p. 109; Gross, *Dissolution*, pp. 77–8; Kekewich, 'The mysterious Dr Makerell', p. 48; Griffiths, 'For the myght off the lande . . .', p. 84; Walsh, *Charles the Bold and Italy*, p. 138. 11 *LP WF*, II, p. 789; Bellamy, *Law of Treason*, p. 164. 12 *John Vale's Book*, pp. 87–92; Holland, 'Cook's case', pp. 25–6; Tucker, 'Government and Politics', pp. 351–2. 13 *GC*, p. 206; Ballard, 'Anglo-Burgundian Relations', pp. 152–4; Sutton, 'Sir Thomas Cook', pp. 89–91. 14 *Excerpta Historica*,

pp. 230–31; Weiss, *Humanism in England*, pp. 124–5; Stark, 'Anglo-Burgundian Diplomacy',pp.60–61.   15 *PL* Davis,I,no.330;ADNB2068,f.129v;Ballard,'Anglo-Burgundian Diplomacy', pp. 174–5.   16 Goossenaerts, 'Charles the Bold', pp. 97–104, at p. 100; Armstrong, 'Politique matrimoniale', p. 408.   17 *PL* Davis, I, no. 330, pp. 538–9; *Mémoires d'Olivier de la Marche*, III, pp. 101–201; *Excerpta Historica*, pp. 234–8; Goossenaerts, 'Charles the Bold', pp. 102–3; Weightman, *Margaret of York*, pp. 54–6; Ballard, 'Anglo-Burgundian Relations', pp. 162–3; Strohm, *Music in Late Medieval Bruges*, p. 99.   18 *PL* Davis, no. 330; Ballard, 'Anglo-Burgundian Relations', pp. 170–1, 179; Barber and Barker, *Tournaments*, pp. 121–5.   19 TNA E404/74/1/61A; *LP WF*, II, p. 791; 'William Gregory's Chronicle', p. 237; *CPR 1467–1477*, pp. 103, 120.   20 *GC*, pp. 204–6; TNA KB 9/319 mm. 7, 35–7, 40, 49–51; Holland, 'Cook's case', pp. 25–6; Sutton, 'Sir Thomas Cook', pp. 95–6.   21 Holland, 'Cook's case', pp. 30–1; Sutton and Visser-Fuchs, 'A "most benevolent queen"', pp. 216–18; Sutton, 'Sir Thomas Cook', pp. 96–7; Sutton and Visser-Fuchs, 'Provenance of the manuscript', pp. 89–91; Carpenter, 'The Stonor circle', p. 189.   22 TNA E403/840 m. 4, cit. McKendrick, 'An English royal collector …', Appendix, p. 524.   23 'William Gregory's Chronicle', pp. 237–8; LMA Journal 7, ff. 178–178v; Bolton, 'Warwick, Clarence and London', pp. 14–15.   24 Scofield, *LREF*, I, pp. 466–9; Postan, 'Economic and political relations of England and the Hanse', p. 133; Visser-Fuchs, 'English events in Caspar Weinreich', pp. 312–13; Tucker, 'Government and Politics', pp. 354–6; Ross, *Edward IV*, pp. 364–5; Bolton, *Medieval English Economy*, pp. 308–9; Bolton, 'Warwick, Clarence and London', p. 16.   25 LMA Journal 7, f. 179; Bolton, 'Warwick, Clarence and London', pp. 15–16.   26 'William Gregory's Chronicle', p. 237.   27 Warkworth, *Chronicle*, pp. 5–6; Kronk, *Cometography*, I, pp. 282–4; Zinner and Brown, *Regiomontanus*, pp. 93–4.   28 TNA E404/74/1/43, 65, 70, 72, 74, 83, 102; *CSPM*, no. 167; Ballard, 'Anglo-Burgundian Relations', pp. 186–8.   29 CSPM, no. 165; Scofield, *LREF*, I, p. 477.   30 *PL* Davis, no. 752.   31 TNA E403/842 m. 2; *Plumpton Correspondence*, Letter XIII; 'William Gregory's Chronicle', p. 237; 'Hearne's Fragment', p. 297; Kekewich, 'The mysterious Dr Makerell', pp. 48–50; Ross, *Edward IV*, pp. 65–6, 122–3; Bellamy, *Law of Treason*, pp. 164–5; Ross, *John de Vere*, pp. 59–61.   32 *GC*, p. 213; Ross, 'Treatment of traitors' children', passim; Steven G. Ellis, 'Fitzgerald, Thomas, seventh earl of Desmond (1426? –1468)', *ODNB*; Sutton and Visser-Fuchs, 'A "most benevolent queen"', pp. 217–18, discuss and dismiss Elizabeth Woodville's potential complicity.   33 *GC*, p. 207; *CPR 1467–1477*, p. 123.   34 Ross, *Edward IV*, p. 78 n. 2.   35 In what follows I draw on *Collection of Ordinances and Regulations*, pp. 89–105.   36 Hicks, 'The 1468 Statute of Livery', p. 17.   37 *Collection of Ordinances*, pp. 101–5; Hicks, *False, Fleeting Clarence* (1992 edn), pp. 173, 179–81.   38 Ross, *Edward IV*, pp. 122–3.   39 *CPR 1467–1477*, p. 128; TNA KB 9/320; Warkworth, *Chronicle*, p. 6; Orme, *From Childhood to Chivalry*, pp. 7–8; Palliser, 'Richard and York', p. 52; Bellamy, *Law of Treason*, p. 165.   40 *CSPM*, no. 169; Scofield, *LREF*, I, p. 482.   41 *Foedera*, XI (February 22 1469); Scofield, *LREF*, I, pp. 488–9; a point made by Ballard, 'Anglo-Burgundian Relations', pp. 193–4, 197–9; Meek, 'Conduct and Practice', pp. 138–9; Ross, *Edward IV*, p. 128.   42 *CSPM*, no. 170.   43 *PL* Gairdner, V, no. 714; *GC*, p. 208; Ballard, 'Anglo-Burgundian Relations', pp. 194–8; Scofield, *LREF*, I, pp. 489–90.   44 HMC Reports, Beverley Corporation MSS, p. 144; Summerson, 'Peacekeepers and Lawbreakers in Northumberland', p. 73; Dockray, 'The Yorkshire Rebellions of 1469', pp. 246–57; Ross, *Edward IV*, App. IV, pp. 439–40; Scofield, *LREF*, I, pp. 488–90.   45 *CPR 1467–1477*, pp. 170–71; TNA E404/74/230; *PL* Davis, I, no. 333; Ross, *Edward IV*, p. 129.   46 *Coventry Leet Book*, II, pp. 341–2; Scofield, *LREF*, I, pp. 492–3; Ross, *Edward IV*, p. 129.   47 CC, pp. 116–17.   48 Laynesmith, *Cecily Duchess of York*, p. 124.   49 Wavrin, *Anciennes Chroniques*, II, p. 403.   50 Warkworth, *Chronicle*, pp. 46–9.   51 Ross, *Edward IV*, p. 130; Bolton,

'Warwick, Clarence and London', pp. 26–7; Fleming, *Coventry and the Wars of the Roses*, pp. 19–20. 52 Horrox, *Richard III*, pp. 32–3. 53 *PL* Davis, II, nos. 762, 763.

9. The Matter Quickeneth

1 Lewis, 'The battle of Edgecote', *passim*; Ward, *Livery Collar*, pp. 149–52; 'In praise of William Herbert of Raglan', ed. Barry Lewis, accessed at http://www.gutorglyn.net/gutorglyn/poem/?poem-selection=023&first-line=001; Evans, *Wales and the Wars of the Roses*, pp. 174–85. 2 The following account is based on Warkworth, *Chronicle*, pp. 6–7; CC, pp. 114–17; GC, p. 209; Hall, *Chronicle*, pp. 273–4; see also Ross, *Edward IV*, pp. 131–2. 3 Worcester, *Itineraries*, pp. 339–41. 4 'Elegy for William Herbert of Raglan', ed. Barry Lewis, accessed at http://www.gutorglyn.net/gutorglyn/poem/?poem-selection=024; Owen and Blakeway, *A History of Shrewsbury*, I, pp. 247–8. 5 Thomas, *The Herberts of Raglan*, pp. 45–6. 6 Lewis, 'The battle of Edgecote', pp. 113–14. 7 GC, p. 209; Moreton, 'Anthony Woodville', *passim*. 8 *Coventry Leet Book*, II, p. 345; Warkworth, *Chronicle*, pp. 6–7; CC, pp. 116–17. 9 Payling, 'Widows', p. 112; Hicks, *Edward V*, pp. 34–7. 10 Laynesmith, *Last Medieval Queens*, p. 214; Leland, 'Witchcraft and the Woodvilles', pp. 267–88. 11 Hampton, 'Roger Wake of Blisworth', pp. 156–7. 12 *CPR 1467–1477*, p. 190; TNA KB 27/836, m. 61d, cit. Hicks, *False, Fleeting Clarence* (1992 edn), p. 35; Hicks, *Warwick*, p. 277. 13 *CSPM*, no. 173; Laynesmith, *Cecily Duchess of York*, pp. 125–6. 14 Calmette and Périnelle, *Louis XI et l'Angletene*, p. 108 and Pièce Justificatif no. 30. pp.116–17. 15 *PL* Davis, II, no. 786; Wavrin, *Anciennes Chroniques*, III, pp. 5–6; Warkworth, *Chronicle*, p. 7; *CSPM*, no. 173; Tucker, 'Government and Politics', p. 358; Ballard, 'Anglo-Burgundian Relations', pp. 202–5. 16 CC, pp. 116–17. 17 TNA E404/74/2/51; *PL* Davis, I, no. 245, pp. 409–10. 18 CC, pp. 116–17. 19 Ross, *Edward IV*, p. 135; Horrox, *Richard III*, p. 33; Ramsay, 'Richard III and the office of arms', pp. 146–8. 20 Ramsay, 'Richard III and the office of arms', Appendix, pp. 154–63. 21 Sutton, 'A curious searcher', pp. 61–3, 71–2. 22 TNA C81/1547; Horrox, *Richard III*, pp. 33–6 and refs; Ross, 'A governing elite?', *passim*. 23 TNA C53/195 m. 2. 24 CC, pp. 116–17; Holland, 'Lincolnshire rebellion', p. 854. 25 *Chronique Scandaleuse*, I, pp. 235–6; Ballard, 'Anglo-Burgundian Relations', pp. 208–11; Visser-Fuchs, 'English events in Caspar Weinreich', pp. 314–15. 26 'Confession of Sir Robert Welles', in *Excerpta Historica*, pp. 282–3; Warkworth, *Chronicle*, p. 8; the dating of Welles' raid is contested: see Hicks, *False, Fleeting Clarence* (1992 edn), pp. 65–9; Holland, 'Lincolnshire rebellion', pp. 853–4; Mackman, 'Lincolnshire gentry', pp. 146–59. 27 Rosemary Horrox, 'Burgh, Thomas, Baron Burgh (c.1430–1496)', *ODNB*; Emery, *Greater Medieval Houses*, II, pp. 242–50; Storey, 'Lincolnshire and the Wars of the Roses', pp. 71–2. 28 *CPR 1467–1477*, p. 224; Hicks, *False, Fleeting Clarence* (1992 edn), p. 54. 29 GC, pp. 209–10; Bolton, 'Warwick, Clarence and London', pp. 19–20. 30 *CPR 1467–1477*, p. 190. 31 *Chronicle of the Rebellion in Lincolnshire*, p. 12. 32 *PL* Davis, I, no. 248; *CCR 1468–1476*, pp. 137–8; *CPR 1467–1477*, pp. 185, 199; *Chronicle of the Rebellion in Lincolnshire*, p. 22; Hicks, *False, Fleeting Clarence*, p. 56; Mackman, 'Lincolnshire gentry', p. 153; Ross, *Edward IV*, p. 138. 33 'Confession of Sir Robert Welles', in *Excerpta Historica*, pp. 282–3. 34 *Chronicle of the Rebellion in Lincolnshire*, pp. 6, 8; GC, p. 210; *CCR 1468–1476*, pp. 129–30. 35 *CSPM*, no. 185. 36 'Confession of Sir Robert Welles', in *Excerpta Historica*, pp. 282–4. 37 Warkworth, *Chronicle*, p. 8; *Chronicle of the Rebellion in Lincolnshire*, pp. 8, 10; 'Confession of Sir Robert Welles', in *Excerpta Historica*, pp. 282–4. 38 *CCR 1468–1476*, p. 134; *Chronicles of the White Rose*, pp. 225–6; Warkworth, *Chronicle*, pp. 52–3; CC, pp. 120–1. 39 'Confession of Sir Robert Welles', in

Excerpta Historica, pp. 282–4; *Chronicle of the Rebellion in Lincolnshire*, p. 11. 40
Chronicle of the Rebellion in Lincolnshire, pp. 12–14; *CCR 1468–1476*, pp. 137–8; *PL*
Davis, II, no. 787; Pollard, *North-Eastern England*, pp. 307–9; Pollard, *Warwick*,
pp. 119–21; Ross, *Edward IV*, pp. 141–2; Holland, 'Lincolnshire rebellion', pp.
858–9. 41 Horrox, *Richard III*, pp. 36, 69; Jones, 'Richard III and the Stanleys', pp.
39–40. 42 *CCR 1468–1476*, pp. 135–6, 138; *CPR 1467–1477*, pp. 218–19; *Foedera*,
XI, pp. 173–4; Ross, *Edward IV*, p. 144. 43 Holland, 'Lincolnshire rebellion', p. 861;
Hicks, *Warwick*, pp. 286–7. 44 TNA E404/74/2/108, 111; Warkworth, *Chronicle*, p. 9;
GC, p. 210; Crawford, *Yorkist Lord*, pp. 60–1; Hicks, *Warwick*, p. 232; Richmond,
'Fauconberg's Kentish rising', p. 674. 45 Warkworth, *Chronicle*, p. 9; Keen, 'Treason
trials', pp. 88–92. 46 Commynes, *Memoires*, pp. 182–3; Ballard, 'Anglo-Burgundian
Relations', pp. 212–14; BL Additional 48976, no. 58. 47 ADN B862 no. 16197; Wavrin,
Anciennes Chroniques, III, pp. 30–1; Commynes, *Memoirs* ed. Jones, pp. 183–4; Cal-
mette and Périnelle, *Louis XI*, pp. 311–12; *Lettres de Louis XI*, IV, DII, pp. 110–14;
Visser-Fuchs, 'Warwick and Wavrin', p. 73; Ballard, 'Anglo-Burgundian Relations', pp.
213–17; Richmond, 'Fauconberg's Kentish rising', pp. 673–4; Vaughan, *Charles the Bold*,
pp. 62–3; Scofield, *LREF*, I, p. 541. 48 *CSPM*, no. 184; Hicks, *Warwick*, pp. 291–2;
Kekewich, 'The Lancastrian court in exile', pp. 105–6. 49 Hicks, *Warwick*, pp. 290–
1. 50 *John Vale's Book*, pp. 215–18. 51 *John Vale's Book*, pp. 217–18; Hicks, *False,
Fleeting Clarence*, pp. 71–2. 52 *John Vale's Book*, p. 217. 53 *PL* Davis, I, no. 256;
Pollard, 'Lord FitzHugh's Rising', p. 170. 54 *John Vale's Book*, pp. 48, 218–20; Thrupp,
Merchant Class, p. 353. 55 Medici, *Lettere*, I, pp. 191–6. 56 *CPR 1467–1477*, pp.
214–16; *Chronicles of the White Rose*, pp. 28–9; Rosemary Horrox, 'Conyers family
(per. c.1375–c.1525)', *ODNB*; Pollard, 'Lord FitzHugh's rising', passim; Pollard, *North-
Eastern England*, pp. 311–12; Storey, 'Wardens', pp. 607–8, 615; Ross, *Richard III*, p.
18. 57 *PL* Gairdner, V, no. 758; *John Vale's Book*, pp. 220–1; Ross, *Edward IV*, p.
152. 58 Ballard, 'Anglo-Burgundian Relations', p. 229. 59 *John Vale's Book*, pp. 220–
1. 60 Warkworth, *Chronicle*, p. 12; *Coventry Leet Book*, pp. 358–9; Hicks, *Warwick*,
pp. 300–1. 61 Warkworth, *Chronicle*, pp. 10–11; *Chronicles of the White Rose*, pp.
28–9; *CC*, pp. 120–3; *GC*, p. 211; Wavrin, *Anciennes Chroniques*, III, pp. 46–8; Commynes, *Memoirs* ed. Jones, p. 187; Chastellain, *Oeuvres*, V, pp. 501–3, 508; Ross, *Edward
IV*, pp. 153–4. 62 Haward, 'Economic aspects of the Wars of the Roses', p. 179.

10. They Think He Will Leave His Skin There

1 Prevenier and Blockmans, *The Burgundian Netherlands*, pp. 16–21, 390; Blockmans
and Prevenier, *The Promised Lands*, pp. 161–4; Visser-Fuchs, 'English events in Caspar
Weinreich', p. 319, n. 18. 2 Ballard, 'Anglo-Burgundian Relations', pp. 233–7; Visser-
Fuchs, 'Richard was late', pp. 616–18. 3 Visser-Fuchs, 'Richard in Holland', pp. 221–2;
Visser-Fuchs, ' "Il n'a plus lion ne lieppart" ', p. 92. 4 LMA Journal 7, ff. 221–2; LMA
Bridge House Accounts, III, ff. 182v–183; Bolton, 'Warwick, Clarence and London',
pp. 29–31. 5 LMA Journal 7, f. 223v; Bolton, 'Warwick, Clarence and London', pp.
34–6. 6 *Coventry Leet Book*, I, p. 359; *Historie of the Arrivall*, p. 17; *Political Poems
and Songs*, II, p. 281; Laynesmith, *Last Medieval Queens*, p. 173. 7 Warkworth,
Chronicle, p. 11; *Chronicles of London*, p. 182; Commynes, *Memoirs* ed. Jones, p. 190;
Knecht, 'Episcopate', p. 117; Scofield, *LREF*, I, p. 541. 8 *Chronicles of London*, p. 182;
Chastellain, *Oeuvres*, V, pp. 490, 493–4; *EHD* ed. Myers, pp. 305–7; Sharpe, *London
and the Kingdom*, III, p. 385; Hicks, *Warwick*, pp. 302–3; Ross, *John de Vere*, p. 62. 9
John Vale's Book, pp. 50–1, 217, 222–4. 10 Warkworth, *Chronicle*, pp. 11, 13; *GC*, pp.
212–13; Ross, *John de Vere*, pp. 62–3; Ashdown-Hill, 'The execution of the earl of

Desmond', p. 80; Ross, *Edward IV*, p. 155. 11 Ballard, 'Anglo-Burgundian Relations', p. 278; Visser-Fuchs, 'Edward's "memoir on paper"', p. 169; Scofield, *LREF*, I, pp. 549–51; Calmette and Périnelle, *Louis XI*, p. 122; Visser-Fuchs, '"Il n'a plus lion ne lieppart"', pp. 168–70, esp. p. 169. 12 Ballard, 'Anglo-Burgundian Relations', pp. 278–80; Ballard, 'Du sang de Lancastre', pp. 83–4, 87–8; Commynes, *Memoirs* ed. Jones, p. 190. 13 Commynes, *Memoirs* ed. Jones, Introduction, pp. 27–8. 14 Commynes, *Mémoires* eds. Calmette and Durville, I, pp. 208–9; Calmette and Périnelle, *Louis XI*, pp. 317–18; Visser-Fuchs, '"Il n'a plus lion ne lieppart"', p. 102; Scofield, *LREF*, I, p. 552. 15 Commynes, *Memoirs* ed. Jones, p. 192; ADN B577 no. 16186; Ballard, 'Anglo-Burgundian Relations', pp. 278–82; Scofield, *LREF*, I, pp. 551–3. 16 Ballard, 'Anglo-Burgundian Relations', pp. 282–3. AGR CC 1925 ff. 304v, 305, 564; for Bische's quittance for provisions for his journey, ADN B2083 no. 65949, cit. Ballard, 'Anglo-Burgundian Relations', p. 282. 17 ADN B2079, f. 53v; B862 no. 16184; B2081 no. 65757. 18 ADN B862 no. 16184; *CPR 1461–1476*, pp. 258, 260–1, 264–5, 277, 303, 336, 365; Ballard, 'Anglo-Burgundian Relations', pp. 283–4; Visser-Fuchs, '"Il n'a plus lion ne lieppart"', p. 96. 19 Warkworth, *Chronicle*, p. 12; *PROME*, XIII, 1470 November, Introduction, p. 392. 20 Wavrin, *Anciennes Chroniques*, III, pp. 196–204; Calmette and Périnelle, *Louis XI*, pp. 124–5; Hicks, *Warwick*, pp. 305–6. 21 LMA *Journal* 7, f. 227v; *John Vale's Book*, p. 222; Bolton, 'Warwick, Clarence and London', pp. 36–7; Calmette and Périnelle, *Louis XI*, p. 126; Potter, *War and Government*, p. 32. 22 Ballard, 'Anglo-Burgundian Relations', p. 287. 23 ADN B2079, ff. 40v, 64v; AGR CC 1925, f. 606v, cit. Ballard, 'Anglo-Burgundian Relations', pp. 287–8; Visser-Fuchs, '"Il n'a plus lion ne lieppart"', p. 93. 24 Commynes, *Memoirs* ed. Jones, p. 258; *Mémoires de Jean, Sire de Haynin*, II, p. 108, cit. in Visser-Fuchs, '"Il n'a plus lion ne lieppart"', p. 102. 25 Commynes, *Memoirs* ed. Jones, pp. 193–4; Ballard, 'Anglo-Burgundian Relations', pp. 289–90; Calmette and Périnelle, *Louis XI*, Piéce Justificatif no. 41; Jones and Underwood, *The King's Mother*, pp. 53–4; Hicks, *Warwick*, p. 302. 26 Commynes, *Memoirs* ed. Jones, pp. 193–4. 27 Bolton, 'Warwick, Clarence and London', pp. 39–40. 28 Warkworth, *Chronicle*, p. 11; TNA DL 37/47A/2, in Horrox, 'Preparations for Edward IV's return from exile', pp. 124–7; Edward's Christmas itinerary in Holland, in Visser-Fuchs, '"Il n'a plus lion ne lieppart"', p. 93; Ballard, 'Anglo-Burgundian Relations', p. 287. 29 Calmette and Périnelle, *Louis XI*, Piéce Justificatif no. 41. 30 Blockmans and Prevenier, *The Promised Lands*, pp. 153, 163–7, 169; Murray, *Bruges, Cradle of Capitalism*, pp. 71–3, 153, 163–7, 178–215, 222, 258. 31 Hicks, *Warwick*, p. 304; Richmond, 'Fauconberg's Kentish Rising', pp. 675–6; Visser-Fuchs, 'Edward's "memoir on paper"', pp. 169–71. 32 McKendrick, 'Edward IV: an English royal collector', p. 522. 33 McKendrick, 'The Romuléon and the manuscripts of Edward IV', passim; Kren and McKendrick, *Illuminating the Renaissance*, Introduction, pp. 3–4, nos. 58, 59, 62; Blockmans and Prevenier, *The Promised Lands*, pp. 74–5, 136–9; Armstrong, 'L'echange culturel', passim. 34 *Cely Letters*, p. 290 n. 6; Calmette and Périnelle, *Louis XI*, Piéce Justificatif no. 41; Visser-Fuchs, 'Richard in Holland', pp. 224–7; Van Praet, *Recherches sur Louis de Bruges*, pp. 10–11; Ballard, 'Anglo-Burgundian Relations', p. 291. 35 *Historie of the Arrivall*, p. 10; Hicks, *False, Fleeting Clarence*, pp. 83–7; Visser-Fuchs, 'Richard in Holland', p. 224. 36 *Historie of the Arrivall*, p. 10; Hicks, *Warwick*, pp. 306–7; Hicks, *False, Fleeting Clarence* (1992 edn), pp. 83–4; Ross, *Edward IV*, p. 157. 37 *Historie of the Arrivall*, p. 10; *Three Books . . . Vergil*, p. 135; *CPR 1467–1477*, pp. 241–3; *Foedera*, XI, p. 693; Hicks, *False, Fleeting Clarence* (1992 edn), pp. 84–5, 97–100; Jones and Underwood, *The King's Mother*, pp. 51–2. 38 *Historie of the Arrivall*, p. 10. 39 Lander, 'Attainder and forfeiture', p. 132; Laynesmith, *Cecily Duchess of York*, pp. 142–3. 40 *Chronicles of London*, p. 183; *CC*, pp. 124–5; Hicks, *False, Fleeting Clarence*, pp. 100, 105. 41 Commynes, *Memoirs* ed. Jones, p. 194; Vaughan,

Charles the Bold, p. 63. **42** *Historie of the Arrivall*, p. 2; Ballard, 'Anglo-Burgundian Relations', p. 293; Prevenier and Blockmans, *The Burgundian Netherlands*, pp. 17, 19–20; Visser-Fuchs, 'Richard in Holland', pp. 225–6; Ross, *Edward IV*, p. 160. **43** Commynes, *Memoires*, III, pp. 275–7; *CSPM*, no. 210.

11. The Knot is Knit Again

1 Warkworth, *Chronicle*, pp. 13–14; *Historie of the Arrivall*, pp. 2–3. **2** *Historie of the Arrivall*, pp. 2–6; *Three Books . . . Vergil*, pp. 137–9; Warkworth, *Chronicle*, pp. 13–14; Palliser, 'Richard and York', pp. 54–5. **3** Warkworth, *Chronicle*, p. 14; *Historie of the Arrivall*, pp. 7–8. **4** HMC, 12th report, Rutland MSS, I, pp. 2–3. **5** *Historie of the Arrivall*, pp. 7–12; *PL* Davis, II, no. 766, p. 406. Ward, *Livery Collar*, p. 61. **6** Wavrin, *Anciennes Chroniques*, III, p. 210; 'On the Recovery of the Throne by Edward IV', *Political Poems and Songs*, pp. 272–3. **7** *Historie of the Arrivall*, pp. 12–13. **8** Duffy, *Stripping of the Altars*, pp. 23–7. **9** *Historie of the Arrivall*, pp. 13–15; Warkworth, *Chronicle*, p. 17. **10** LMA Journal 7, f. 232v; LMA Journal 8, f. 4; *Historie of the Arrivall*, p. 15; *GC*, p. 214. **11** Bolton, 'Warwick, Clarence and London', p. 38. **12** *GC*, p. 215; *Historie of the Arrivall*, pp. 15–16; Kleineke, 'Gerard von Wesel's newsletter', p. 78. **13** *Historie of the Arrivall*, pp. 16–17; Warkworth, *Chronicle*, p. 15; *GC*, p. 215; Wavrin, *Anciennes Chroniques*, III, p. 211; Laynesmith, *Cecily Duchess of York*, p. 129. **14** *Political Poems and Songs*, II, pp. 271–82. **15** Laynesmith, *Cecily Duchess of York*, p. 129; Duffy, *Stripping of the Altars*, p. 29. **16** Kleineke, 'Gerard von Wesel's newsletter', p. 80; *Historie of the Arrivall*, p. 21 (but also see Warkworth, *Chronicle*, p. 15). **17** Orme, *From Childhood to Chivalry*, pp. 180–210. **18** *Historie of the Arrivall*, p. 18; Warkworth, *Chronicle*, pp. 15–17 (his account is disputed by Ross, *John de Vere*, pp. 66–7); Wavrin, *Anciennes Chroniques*, III, pp. 210–15; Commynes, *Memoirs*, ed. Jones, p. 195; Hammond, *Battles of Barnet and Tewkesbury*, pp. 72–80; Goodman, *Wars of the Roses*, pp. 159–60; Visser-Fuchs, ' "Il n'a plus lion ne lieppart" ', p. 106. **19** *Historie of the Arrivall*, p. 21; Warkworth, *Chronicle*, p. 17; *GC*, pp. 216–17; Kleineke, 'Gerard von Wesel's newsletter', pp. 81–2. **20** *Coventry Leet Book*, II, pp. 358–9; *Historie of the Arrivall*, p. 7. **21** 'The Battle of Barnet', *Historical Poems*, no. 94, pp. 226–7. **22** *PL* Davis, I, no. 261. **23** *Historie of the Arrivall*, p. 23; Warkworth, *Chronicle*, p. 16. **24** *Historie of the Arrivall*, p. 24; *CCR 1468–1476*, pp. 189–90; *CPR 1467–1477*, pp. 259, 283–5; *Coventry Leet Book*, pp. 364–6, 369; Hoare et al., *Old and New Sarum*, pp. 178–9; Ross, *Edward IV*, pp. 169–70. **25** The following passage is based on *Historie of the Arrivall*, pp. 25–30. I draw especially on Gillingham, *Wars of the Roses*, pp. 217–20, and Hammond, *Battles of Barnet and Tewkesbury*, pp. 86–92. **26** *Historie of the Arrivall*, pp. 29–31. **27** Warkworth, *Chronicle*, p. 18; *Historie of the Arrivall*, p. 30; *Six Town Chronicles*, p. 168; see also HMC 12th report, Rutland MSS, p. 4; Hammond, *Barnet and Tewkesbury*, Appendix 2, pp. 123–6. **28** 'From a Chronicle of Tewkesbury Abbey', in *EHL*, no. XIV, pp. 376–8; Hammond, *Barnet and Tewkesbury*, pp. 98–9. **29** *Historie of the Arrivall*, p. 31; 'Chronicle of Tewkesbury Abbey', p. 377; TNA SC1/44/61; Sutton and Visser-Fuchs, *Richard III's Books*, p. 102. **30** Visser-Fuchs, 'Edward's "memoir on paper" ', p. 174; *CSPM*, no. 218. **31** *Historie of the Arrivall*, p. 31; Warkworth, *Chronicle*, p. 19; *CPR 1467–1477*, p. 285; HMC 12th report, Rutland MSS, p. 5. **32** *Historie of the Arrivall*, pp. 32–3; Scofield, *LREF*, I, p. 589. **33** Scott, 'Fauconberg's Kentish Rising', pp. 361–2; *CSPM*, nos. 216, 217; LMA Journal 8, f. 7 (also see LMA Letter Book L, f. 79), pr. and trans. Sharpe, *London and the Kingdom*, III, pp. 391–2; Armstrong, 'Some examples . . .', p. 438; LMA Journal 8, f. 4v; Richmond, 'Fauconberg's Kentish rising', p. 678. **34** *Historie of the Arrivall*,

p. 34; *GC*, p. 218.   35 *GC*, pp. 218–19; *Historie of the Arrivall*, p. 36; Richmond, 'Fauconberg's Kentish rising', p. 678.   36 TNA E403/844 passim; LMA Bridge House Accounts, vol. III, ff. 182v–3 (cit. in Richmond, 'Fauconberg', p. 679); *Historie of the Arrivall*, pp. 37–8; 'On the Recovery of the Throne by Edward IV', in *Political Poems and Songs*, II, p. 279; Scofield, *LREF*, I, p. 593.   37 'On the Recovery of the Throne by Edward IV', in *Political Poems and Songs*, II, p. 273; Sutton and Visser-Fuchs, *Richard III's Books*, p. 94.   38 Duffy, *Stripping of the Altars*, pp. 136–9, 217.   39 *Issues of the Exchequer*, pp. 495–7; *Historie of the Arrivall*, p. 38; Warkworth, *Chronicle*, p. 21.   40 *GC*, p. 220; 'Yorkist Notes', in *EHL*, p. 375; Ross, *Henry VI*, p. 98.   41 CSPM, no. 220.   42 *GC*, pp. 220–1; Warkworth, *Chronicle*, pp. 21–2.

12. A New Foundation

1 *Foedera*, XI, p. 714; *CCR 1468–1476*, no. 858; Hicks, *Edward V*, pp. 55–9.   2 Grummitt, *The Calais Garrison*, pp. 68–9; Sutton and Visser-Fuchs, 'A "most benevolent queen"', p. 221; Hicks, *False, Fleeting Clarence* (1992 edn), p. 98.   3 Hicks, *False, Fleeting Clarence* (1992 edn), pp. 99–101; Hicks, 'Descent, partition and extinction', pp. 326–8.   4 Ross, 'A governing elite?', pp. 99–100.   5 Hicks, 'Richard III as duke of Gloucester', pp. 252–3; Horrox, *Richard III*, pp. 33–40.   6 Horrox, *Richard III*, pp. 45–6; Ross, *Edward IV*, pp. 198–200; Pollard, *North-Eastern England*, pp. 338–40.   7 Lander, 'Attainder and forfeiture', pp. 137–40; Ross, *Edward IV*, p. 189.   8 *PL* Davis, I, no. 263.   9 *PL* Davis, I, no. 264.   10 Britnell, 'Richard, duke of Gloucester', passim; TNA E405/54, m. 4v; *GC*, p. 221; Richmond, 'Fauconberg's Kentish rising', p. 682; *PL* Davis, I, no. 264.   11 More, *History of King Richard III*, p. 92.   12 Lander, 'Attainder and forfeiture', pp. 128–30.   13 Hicks, *False, Fleeting Clarence* (1992 edn), Chapter 3 passim.   14 Pollard, *North-Eastern England*, pp. 316–23; Laynesmith, *Last Medieval Queens*, p. 44; Ross, *Edward IV*, p. 147.   15 CC, pp. 132–3.   16 TNA C81/837; Scofield, *LREF*, II, p. 26; Kisby, 'Royal Household Chapel', pp. 164–5, 220, 224; 'The Record of Bluemantle Pursuivant'; Armstrong, 'Inauguration ceremonies', p. 72.   17 CSPM, no. 231; Commynes, *Memoirs* ed. Jones, pp. 195–6.   18 Commynes, *Memoirs* ed. Jones, pp. 201–2.   19 Weightman, *Margaret of York*, pp. 96–7.   20 TNA E101/197/15, f. 37v; E101/197/17, m. 5, cit. Meek, 'Conduct and Practice', p. 182.   21 Horrox, *Richard III*, pp. 40–54; Pollard, *North-Eastern England*, p. 327.   22 *PL* Davis, I, no. 267; Castor, *Blood and Roses*, p. 239.   23 *PL* Davis, I, no. 267; Hampson, *Medii Aevi Kalendarium*, II, p. 303; Hicks, 'Descent, partition and extinction', pp. 327–9.   24 *PL* Davis, I, no. 267; *CPR 1467–1477*, p. 330; Lander, 'Attainder and forfeiture', pp. 130–1, n. 51; CChR, pp. 239–40; Hicks, 'Descent, partition and extinction', p. 328; Hicks, *False, Fleeting Clarence* (1992 edn), p. 102; Booth, 'Landed Society in Cumberland', pp. 118–19.   25 Sutton and Visser-Fuchs, *Richard III's Books*, pp. xviii, 18, 93–4.   26 Crawford, *Yorkist Lord*, pp. 53–4; Hicks, 'Descent, partition and extinction', p. 328.   27 *Political Poems and Songs*, II, pp. 281–2; Sutton and Visser-Fuchs, 'A "most benevolent queen"', pp. 223–4, 232–4.   28 Blake, 'English Royal Marriages', pp. 1023–4 and refs; Hicks, *Anne Neville*, pp. 133–4; Ross, *Richard III*, p. 28.   29 BL Cotton MS Julius B XII, ff. 108–316v; Hicks, 'Richard III as duke of Gloucester', pp. 250–61; Hicks, 'The cartulary of Richard III', pp. 281–9.   30 *PL* Davis, I, no. 354A; Hicks, *False, Fleeting Clarence*, p. 102.   31 *PL* Davis, I, no. 268; TNA KB 9/41, no. 41; Warkworth, *Chronicle*, p. 25; Keir, 'George Neville', p. 76; Falvey, 'The More', pp. 290–302.   32 R. A. Griffiths, 'Vaughan, Sir Thomas (d. 1483)', *ODNB*; Scofield, *LREF*, II, pp. 5–6; Ross, *Foremost Man*, p. 69.   33 *PL* Davis, I, no. 268; Warkworth, *Chronicle*, pp. 24–6; *CPR 1467–1477*, p. 346; Ross, *Edward IV*, pp. 191–2; Pollard, *Wars of the Roses*, p. 141; Linda Clark, 'Thomas Vaughan',

forthcoming in *History of Parliament: Commons 1433–1504*. **34** Fortescue, *On the Laws and Governance*, pp. xxv–xxviii, 30–1. **35** Fortescue, *On the Laws and Governance*, pp. 93, 98, 103. **36** *Household EIV*, pp. 10–11. **37** *Household EIV*, pp. 18, 83–7. **38** *Household EIV*, p. 87. **39** *Household EIV*, no. 37 (p. 116); no. 27 (p. 106), nos. 42, 48 (p. 121), 'Ordinance of 1471', p. 201. **40** *Household EIV*, no. 43 (pp. 121–3); no. 44 (p. 123). **41** Rawcliffe, 'More than a bedside manner', p. 72; Rawcliffe, 'Consultants', p. 253; Rawcliffe, *Medicine and Society*, p. 164. **42** Rawcliffe, 'More than a bedside manner', p. 79. **43** *Calendar of Letter-Books: L*, p. 103; Matthews, e.g. 'Royal Apothecaries', p. 177. **44** Furnivall, 'Recipe for Edward IV's plague medicine', p. 343. **45** Rawcliffe, 'Consultants', p. 251; Rawcliffe, *Medicine and Society*, p. 149. **46** Rawcliffe, *Medicine and Society*, p. 91. **47** Scofield, *LREF*, II, pp. 19–20; Ross, *Edward IV*, pp. 205–7; Lander, 'Hundred Years War', p. 228. **48** Vaughan, *Charles the Bold*, pp. 82–3. **49** *Foedera*, XI, p. 760; *Mémoires pour server de preuves*, III, pp. 246–9; Calmette and Périnelle, *Louis XI*, pp. 152–4; Scofield, *LREF*, II, pp. 33–4. **50** The following narrative is drawn from 'The Record of Bluemantle Pursuivant', pp. 380–88. **51** 'The Record of Bluemantle Pursuivant', pp. 382–3; *PROME*, XIV, 1472 October, Introduction, p. 3.

13. Master of the Game

1 *John Vale's Book*, pp. 107–11; Christiansen, 'Evidence for London's late-medieval manuscript book trade', passim, esp. p. 99; Christiansen, *Directory*, pp. 136–7; Sutton and Visser-Fuchs, 'Choosing a book', pp. 64–8; Gross, *Dissolution*, pp. 105–23; BL Royal MS 17 D xv, ff. 302–26. For the possible dating, see Lander, 'Hundred Years War', pp. 228–9. **2** Fortescue, 'Declaration', in idem, *Works*, I, pp. 531–3. **3** *CC*, p. 132; *PROME*, XIV, 1472 October, Introduction, p. 1. **4** *Literae Cantuarienses*, III, item 1079, pp. 275–85, which dates Alcock's speech to 1474. Internal evidence suggests Alcock made it in the autumn of 1472. **5** *CC*, p. 226; Ross, *Edward IV*, pp. 344–5. **6** *PL* Davis, I, no. 269; Scofield, *LREF*, II, pp. 40–42. **7** *PROME*, XIV, 1472 October, item 10. **8** *CSPM*, no. 240. **9** Payne and Jefferson, 'Edward IV: the Garter and the Golden Fleece', pp. 194–7; Sutton, 'Chevalerie ...', pp. 112–13 and nn. 15, 16; *CSPM*, no. 240. **10** *LP HVII*, VI: 5, pp. 1–8; Stark, 'Anglo-Burgundian Diplomacy', pp. 62–5; *CSPM*, no. 245; Scofield, *LREF*, II, pp. 46–9; Ross, *Edward IV*, p. 209; Cunningham, 'The Yorkists at war', pp. 179–80. **11** *PROME*, XIV, 1472 October, Introduction, pp. 4–5; Jurkowski, 'Parliamentary and prerogative taxation', pp. 275–7. **12** *PL* Davis, I, nos. 361, 273. **13** *CSPM*, no. 246; Roover, *Rise and Decline*, pp. 296–9. **14** George Holmes, 'Canigiani [Caniziani], Gherardo (1424–1484)', *ODNB*; Steel, *Receipt of the Exchequer*, pp. 344–6, 351–3, 357; Ross, *Edward IV*, p. 379. **15** For the painting's disputed authorship, see McFarlane, *Hans Memling*, pp. 16–27. **16** *Acts of Court of the Mercers' Company*, pp. 68–76; Sutton, *Mercery of London*, p. 310. **17** *PL* Davis, I, no. 274; Hicks, *False, Fleeting Clarence*, p. 108. **18** *PL* Davis, I, no. 275. **19** *CSPM*, no. 251; Ross, *John de Vere*, pp. 70–1; Scofield, 'Early life of John de Vere'; Ross, *Edward IV*, p. 192. **20** *PL* Davis, I, nos. 275, 276. **21** Ross, *John de Vere*, p. 70. **22** *PL* Davis, no. 277, pp. 463–4; TNA E405/56 m. 3. **23** *PL* Davis, I, no. 277, pp. 463–4; Hicks, *False, Fleeting Clarence*, p. 108. **24** Hicks, 'Last days of Elizabeth, Countess of Oxford', passim. **25** Rosemary Horrox, 'Tyrell, Sir James (c.1455–1502)', *ODNB*. **26** *PL* Davis, I, no. 277; HMC, 11th Report, Appendix, Part VII, p. 95; Ross, *Edward IV*, p. 189; Hicks, 'Descent, partition and extinction', p. 329. **27** Warkworth, *Chronicle*, pp. 23–4. **28** Pollard, *North-Eastern England*, p. 327. **29** *CCR 1468–1476*, p. 315; Jones, 'Richard III and the Stanleys', pp. 39–40, cit. TNA DL 37/42/13; Ross, *Edward IV*, pp. 199, 409;

Morgan, 'The king's affinity', p. 19.   30 Hicks, *Edward V*, pp. 75-82.   31 Ross, *John de Vere*, pp. 71-3.   32 *PL* Davis, I, no. 281.   33 *PROME*, XIV, 1472 October, Introduction, pp. 6-7, Second Roll, item 6 (pp. 143-4); Lloyd, *England and the German Hanse*, p. 213.   34 *PL* Davis, I, no. 282.   35 *Ingulph's Chronicle*, p. 477.   36 *CPR 1467-1477*, p. 428; Westervelt, 'William Lord Hastings', pp. 234-6; Hicks, 'Lord Hastings' retainers', pp. 240-1.   37 Hicks, 'Lord Hastings' retainers', pp. 234-5, 241-2; Carpenter, 'The duke of Clarence and the Midlands', pp. 32-3. Westervelt, 'William Lord Hastings', pp. 244-8.   38 *Coventry Leet Book*, I, pp. 390-3; Rastall, 'Music for a royal entry', pp. 463-6.   39 *Coventry Leet Book*, I, pp. 393-4; Fleming, *Coventry and the Wars of the Roses*, pp. 21-3.   40 Hicks, 'Lord Hastings' retainers', pp. 241-2; Carpenter, 'The duke of Clarence and the Midlands', pp. 34-5.   41 Sutton, 'Caxton was a mercer', pp. 132-3; Blake, *Caxton and His World*, pp. 59-60; Blake, *Caxton's Own Prose*, pp. 85-7.   42 Blake, *Caxton's Own Prose*, p. 87; Nall, *Reading and War*, p. 50.   43 *PROME*, XIV, 1472 October, Introduction, p. 7; Second Roll, item 18 (pp. 208-9).   44 Warkworth, *Chronicle*, p. 26; Worcester, *Itineraries*, ed. Harvey, pp. 102-3; Scofield, 'Early life of John de Vere', pp. 238-43; Ross, *John de Vere*, pp. 73-5; Hicks, 'Descent, partition and extinction', pp. 329-30.   45 *PROME*, XIV, 1472 October, Second Roll, item 20 (p. 209); Ross, *Edward IV*, pp. 190-1.   46 *Foedera*, XI, pp. 814-15; Dunlop, *Anglo-Scottish Relations*, p. 161; Cunningham, 'The Yorkists at war', p. 180; Calmette and Périnelle, *Louis XI*, p. 176. Lander, 'Hundred Years War', p. 232; Jurkowski, 'Parliamentary and prerogative taxation', pp. 276-80; Ross, *Edward IV*, pp. 210-14.   47 Lander, 'Hundred Years War', p. 232.   48 *CSPM*, nos. 265, 267, 269.   49 *John Vale's Book*, p. 266; Calmette and Périnelle, *Louis XI*, p. 261, Appendix I; Scofield, *LREF*, II, p. 107; Sutton and Visser-Fuchs, 'Richard III's books: chivalric ideals', p. 191.

14. War Outward

1 Vaughan, *Charles the Bold*, pp. 312-29; Olivier de la Marche, 'L'estat de la maison du duc Charles de Bourgogne', in *Mémoires d'Olivier de la Marche*, 4, pp. 1-94.   2 Vaughan, *Charles the Bold*, p. 193.   3 *CPR 1467-1477*, pp. 395, 398, 462, 474, 479, 492; Calmette and Périnelle, *Louis XI*, Piéce Justificatif, no. 63.   4 Clough, 'The relations between the English and Urbino courts', pp. 204-5, 208-10, 216-17.   5 *PROME*, XIV, 1472 October, Introduction, p. 9, Third Roll, item 43 (pp. 309-17); Lander, 'Hundred Years War', pp. 232-3; Virgoe, 'The benevolence of 1481', p. 26.   6 *CPR 1467-1477*, p. 588; *Coventry Leet Book*, II, p. 409; Jurkowski, 'Parliamentary and prerogative taxation', pp. 280-3.   7 *CC*, pp. 134-5; *CSPM*, no. 282; *GC*, p. 223; Hall, *Union*, p. 308.   8 TNA E361/7; *GC*, p. 223; *CPR 1467-1477*, pp. 367, 591; Virgoe, 'Benevolence of 1481', p. 31; Myers, 'Household of Queen Elizabeth Woodville', p. 216.   9 *CSPM*, no. 277; *PL* Davis, I, no. 287; Scofield, *LREF*, II, pp. 106-7.   10 *PL* Gairdner, V, no. 843; *CPR 1467-1477*, p. 470.   11 *CPR 1467-1477*, pp. 494-6, 515.   12 *PL* Davis, I, no. 224.   13 *PROME*, XIV, 1472 October; Third Roll, items 16, 17 (pp. 257-60); Lander, 'Attainder and forfeiture', pp. 130-1; Hicks, 'What might have been', passim.   14 Horrox, *Richard III*, p. 70; TNA C49/53/4, cit. Cunningham, 'Yorkists at war', p. 182; Hicks, 'Dynastic change', pp. 370-2.   15 BL MS Cotton Vespasian C XVI, ff. 121-6; Dunlop, 'The Redresses and Reparations of Attemptates', pp. 340-53; Pollard, *North-Eastern England*, pp. 233-5; Scofield, *LREF*, II, p. 129.   16 *CSPM*, no. 282.   17 Lander, 'Hundred Years War', pp. 238-9; Cunningham, 'Yorkists at war', p. 183.   18 *CSPM*, no. 285.   19 McFarlane, 'William Worcester', passim; Allmand and Keen, 'History and the literature of war', passim.   20 Commynes, *Memoirs* ed. Jones, pp. 238-9;

Ross, *Edward IV*, pp. 225-6. 21 *Excerpta Historica*, pp. 366-79; Scofield, *LREF*, II, p. 125; Ross, *Edward IV*, pp. 222-3; Allen, 'Bishop Shirwood', pp. 449-50. 22 Commynes, *Memoirs* ed. Jones, pp. 237-8; Haemers and Buylaert, 'War, politics and diplomacy', p. 200. 23 BL Add. MS 10099, f. 210v, cit. Hicks, 'Edward IV's brief treatise', pp. 263-5. 24 Commynes, *Memoirs* ed. Jones, p. 261; Sutton and Visser-Fuchs, 'Richard of Gloucester and la grosse bombarde', pp. 461-5; Sutton, 'Chevalerie. . .', pp. 121-2. 25 Calmette and Périnelle, *Louis XI*, pp. 207, 209; Commynes, *Memoirs* ed. Jones, p. 262. 26 *PL Davis*, I, no. 293; Hall, *Chronicle*, p. 338. 27 Commynes, *Memoirs* ed Jones, p. 249. 28 *CSPM*, no. 313; Commynes, *Memoirs* ed. Jones. p. 251. 29 *GC*, p. 224; *CC*, pp. 136-7; Scofield, *LREF*, II, p. 150; Lander, 'Hundred Years War', pp. 234-5. 30 *Records of the Borough of Nottingham*, II, pp. 388-9; Ross, *Edward IV*, pp. 236-7; 368-70. 31 BL Cotton MS Vespasian C XIV, f. 572; TNA C81/855; *CC*, pp. 136-9; Bellamy, 'Justice', pp. 163-8; Lander, 'Edward IV', p. 44; Scofield, *LREF*, II, p. 163; Ross, *Edward IV*, p. 401. 32 *CPR 1467-1477*, p. 574. Hicks, *Edward V*, p. 118; Lowe, 'Patronage and Politics', pp. 563-4. 33 BL Harleian MS 1628, ff. 34v-35; Lang, 'Medical recipes', pp. 101-2. 34 *CPR 1467-1477*, p. 574; Hicks, *Edward V*, pp. 118-21; Horrox, *Richard III*, pp. 132-3; Lowe, 'Patronage and Politics', pp. 563-4; Evans, *Wales and the Wars of the Roses*, pp. 199-201; Griffiths, 'Wales and the Marches', pp. 75-6. 35 *Extracts from the Municipal Records of York*, pp. 50-2; Palliser, 'Richard and York', p. 55; Horrox, *Richard III*, p. 66. 36 Colvin, *History of the King's Works*, I, pp. 268-78; Ross, *Edward IV*, p. 269. 37 *Excerpta Historica*, pp. 366-79; Tatton-Brown, 'The constructional sequence and topography', pp. 6-9; Colvin, *History of the King's Works*, I, pp. 198, 246-7, 275-7, 884; II, pp. 930-7; Emery, *Greater London Houses*, III, pp. 226-30. 38 Colvin, *History of the King's Works*, III, p. 78. 39 Kekewich, *The Good King*, pp. 236-7. 40 Keir, 'George Neville', pp. 80-1, 147-53. 41 *Extracts from the Municipal Records of York*, pp. 51-5; *York Civic Records*, I, pp. 2-3, 9-11, 15-16. 42 Hammond et al., 'Reburial of Richard of York', pp. 6-7, 19. 43 Scofield, *LREF*, II, p. 170. 44 *Stonor Letters and Papers*, II, no. 169. 45 Hellinga, *William Caxton*, pp. 32-4. 46 Commynes, *Memoirs*, ed. Jones, pp. 359-61; BN MS Français 10375, ff. 18-18v, cit. Meek, *Calais Letterbook*, p. 3 n. 19. 47 *CSPM*, no. 344. 48 *CSPM*, no.331; *PL Davis*, I, no. 298, p. 494; *Dépêches . . . milanaises*, II, p. 342; Scofield, *LREF*, II, pp. 164, 171; Vaughan, *Charles the Bold*, pp. 394-8. 49 *CC*, pp. 142-3; Dugdale, *Monasticum Anglicanum*, II, pp. 64-5; Hicks, *False, Fleeting Clarence* (1992 edn), p. 116. 50 Commynes, *Memoirs* ed. Jones, pp. 305-7; Molinet, *Chroniques*, I, p. 167; Vaughan, *Charles the Bold*, pp. 421-32.

15. The Most Extreme Purposed Malice

1 *PL Davis*, I, no. 302. 2 Liot de Nortbécourt, 'La complainte d'Arras', pp. 480-4, cit. Jones, '1477 – the expedition that never was', pp. 275-6, 281; Haemers and Buylaert, 'War, politics and diplomacy', pp. 201-11. 3 *PL Davis*, I, no. 302; *Extracts from the Municipal Records of York*, p. 55. 4 *PL Davis*, I, no. 302; Jones, '1477' pp. 275-6. 5 TNA C47/30/10/20; Scofield, *LREF*, II, p. 177; Meek, *Calais Letterbook*, p. 22. 6 *CC*, p. 143; 7 Vaughan, *Charles the Bold*, pp. 152-3; Meek, *Calais Letterbook*, p. 42; Weightman, *Margaret of York*, p. 215. 8 Ross, *Edward IV*, pp. 239-40. 9 *CC*, p. 143; Commynes, *Memoirs*, ed. Jones, p. 362; Lander, 'Treason and death', p. 247. 10 BL Add. Charter 19808; TNA E159/255 (Brevia Recorda Hilary m. 21); BL Add. MS 46455 f. 69, cit. Stark, 'Anglo-Burgundian Diplomacy', p. 137. 11 Meek, *Calais Letterbook*, letters 4, 4a; *Lettres de Louis XI*, 6, p. 138; Jones, '1477' pp. 277-8; Potter, *War and Government*, pp. 37-9; Paravicini, 'Terreur royale', p. 577, cit. Meek, *Calais Letterbook*,

p. 30.   12 BN MS Français 20494, ff. 97–8, in Jones, '1477', pp. 285–9; *PL* Davis, I, no. 305.   13 Meek, *Calais Letterbook*, letter 8; Jones, '1477', p. 290; *Register of the . . . Garter*, I, pp. 200–1; Meek, *Calais Letterbook*, pp. 32–6.   14 BL Cotton MS Vespasian C xvi, f. 121, cit. Halliwell, *Letters*, I, p. 147; Macdougall, *James III*, p. 141.   15 CC, pp. 144–5.   16 CC, pp. 144–5; *RP*, VI, p. 194; Hicks, *False, Fleeting Clarence* (1992 edn), pp. 151–2.   17 Hicks, *False, Fleeting Clarence* (1992 edn), p. 120; Carpenter, *Locality and Polity*, p. 693; Bellamy, 'Justice', p. 146.   18 HMC 3rd Report, Deputy Keeper, pp. 213–14; Hicks, *False, Fleeting Clarence* (1992 edn), p. 120; Kelly, 'English kings and the fear of sorcery', passim.   19 TNA DL 37/41/4; Hicks, *False, Fleeting Clarence* (1992 edn), pp. 119–20.   20 HMC 3rd Report, Deputy Keeper, pp. 213–14; Jones, 'Information and science', p. 109.   21 CC, pp. 144–5; HMC 3rd Report, Deputy Keeper, pp. 213–14; *CPR 1467–1477*, pp. 346–7; Kelly, 'English kings', pp. 224–5; Hicks, *False, Fleeting Clarence* (1992 edn), p. 122.   22 HMC 3rd Report, Deputy Keeper, pp. 213–14; University of Michigan Library, *Middle English Dictionary*, accessed at: https://quod.lib.umich.edu/m/middle-english-dictionary/dictionary.   23 TNA E404/76/1/77; TNA DL 37/41/4, cit. Hicks, *False, Fleeting Clarence* (1992 edn), pp. 119–20.   24 Rawcliffe, 'More than a bedside manner', p. 88; Kelly, 'English kings', p. 228.   25 HMC 3rd Report, Deputy Keeper, pp. 213–14; Lander, 'Treason and death', pp. 248–9; Carpenter, 'The duke of Clarence and the Midlands', p. 40.   26 Hicks, *False, Fleeting Clarence* (1992 edn), p. 124; Fleming, 'Time, Space and Power', p. 217.   27 PROME, XIV, 1478 January, item 17, pp. 361–5; HMC 3rd Report Deputy Keeper, pp. 213–14.   28 Horrox, 'Service', p. 71; Hicks, *False, Fleeting Clarence*, p. 153; Fleming, 'Time, space and power', pp. 218–19.   29 Lander, 'Treason and death', pp. 248–9.   30 CC, pp. 144–5; for the debate over Goddard's identity, see Hicks, *False, Fleeting Clarence* (1992 edn), pp. 122–3; TNA C81/861/4452-4474.   31 CC, pp. 136–9; Lander, 'Treason and death', pp. 249–50, 264; Hicks, *False, Fleeting Clarence* (1992 edn), p. 123.   32 *Cely Letters*, no. 92.   33 *PL* Davis, II, no. 777; TNA E404 76/4/21.   34 BN MS Français 10,187, ff. 123–4, pr. in Scofield, *LREF*, II, App. XI; Calmette and Périnelle, *Louis XI*, Piéce Justificatif, nos. 72, 73; Meek, *Calais Letterbook*, pp. 14, 38–40.   35 Scofield, *LREF*, II, pp. 199–200.   36 CSPM, no. 349, 14 Sept. 1477; Lander, 'Treason and death', p. 250.   37 BL Add. MS 6113, ff. 74–5.   38 PROME, XIV, 1478 January, Introduction, pp. 345–6 and items 10–12 (pp. 351–5); Anne Crawford, 'John (VII) Mowbray, duke of Norfolk', *ODNB*; Crawford, *Yorkist Lord*, pp. 68–70, 87–8.   39 *Coventry Leet Book*, II, p. 422; Hicks, *False, Fleeting Clarence* (1992 edn), p. 126.   40 *Illustrations of Ancient State and Chivalry*, pp. 28–31; Hicks, *False, Fleeting Clarence* (1992 edn), p. 130.   41 *PL* Davis, I, no. 379.   42 *Illustrations of Ancient State and Chivalry*, pp. 28–40; Horrox, *Richard III*, pp. 132–3.   43 PROME, XIV, 1478 January, item 1 (p. 349).   44 Hicks, *False, Fleeting Clarence* (1992 edn), pp. 137–44, Appendix III. Roskell, *The Commons and their Speakers*, pp. 374–80.   45 CC, pp. 144–5.   46 *RP*, VI, p. 193; TNA C49/40/1; PROME, XIV, 1478 January, Appendix I, p. 402.   47 Hicks, *False, Fleeting Clarence* (1992 edn), pp. 151–2.   48 CC, pp. 144–7; *RP*, VI, p. 193; TNA C49/40/1; Hicks, *False, Fleeting Clarence* (1992 edn), pp. 127, 134–5. Bellamy, 'Justice', pp. 146–7; Ross, *Edward IV*, pp. 242–3.   49 SC 8/344/1281; TNA DL 29/454/7312 m. 4, cit. Hicks, *False, Fleeting Clarence* (1992 edn), p. 142.   50 CC, pp. 146–7; Mancini, *Usurpation*, p. 63; *Three Books . . . Vergil*, p. 167; Ross, *Edward IV*, p. 243.   51 Hicks, *False, Fleeting Clarence* (1992 edn), pp. 128–9.   52 More, *History of King Richard III*, p. 7; *Three Books . . . Vergil*, pp. 167–8.   53 Scofield, *LREF*, II, p. 213; Hicks, 'Richard III as duke of Gloucester', p. 262.   54 Hicks, 'Richard III as duke of Gloucester', pp. 252–4.   55 Hicks, 'What might have been', pp. 295–6.   56 Hicks, 'Richard III as Duke of Gloucester', pp. 262–3.   57 Laynesmith, *Cecily Duchess of*

York, p. 152.   58 *York Civic Records*, I, p. 24; Pollard, *North-Eastern England*, pp. 334, 338–40; Horrox, *Richard III*, pp. 56–7.

16. Diamond Cuts Diamond

1 Cobb, *Overseas Trade*, Introduction, pp. xxxiii–xxxv; *GC*, pp. 225–6.   2 Colvin, *History of the King's Works*, II, pp. 764–5 (Nottingham), 884 (Windsor), 936–7 (Eltham).   3 TNA E 404/76/4, nos. 132–5; *GC*, pp. 225–6, 352; Scofield, *LREF*, II, pp. 432–3; Backhouse, 'Founders of the royal library', pp. 27–8; McKendrick, 'A European Heritage', p. 56.   4 Ross, *Edward IV*, p. 353; Jones and Condon, *Cabot and Bristol*, pp. 12–16.   5 *CC*, pp. 136–9; Gray, 'English foreign trade', pp. 326–8; Power, 'English wool trade', pp. 20–2; Ross, *Edward IV*, pp. 352, 368–9; Bolton, *Medieval English Economy*, pp. 306–15; Mallett, 'Anglo-Florentine commercial relations', pp. 254, 256–7; Ruddock, *Italian Merchants*, pp. 211–14.   6 TNA E404/76/4/33.   7 Holmes, 'Lorenzo de' Medici's London branch', pp. 284–5; Mallett, 'Anglo-Florentine commercial relations', pp. 252, 260.   8 *GC*, p. 245; *CC*, pp. 146–7; *Acts of Court of the Mercers' Company*, pp. 118–23, 127–8 (I am grateful to Sam Harper for this reference); Lander, 'Yorkist council', p. 44.   9 Horrox, *Richard III*, p. 253.   10 Horrox, *Fifteenth-Century Attitudes*, Introduction, p. 6.   11 Gottfried, 'Population, plague and the sweating sickness', passim; Scofield, *LREF*, II, pp. 249–50.   12 BL Harleian MS 1628, cit. Lang, 'Medical recipes', pp. 98–9; Furnivall, 'Recipe for Edward IV's plague medicine', p. 343; Pollard, *Edward IV*, p. 72; Scofield, *LREF*, II, pp. 249–50.   13 Haemers and Buylaert, 'War, politics and diplomacy', pp. 204–7; Ross, *Edward IV*, pp. 251–4; Scofield, *LREF*, II, pp. 245–8.   14 Philpot, 'Maximilian I and England', pp. 35–40; Scofield, *LREF*, II, pp. 271–2.   15 *PL* Davis, I, no. 315; Castor, *Blood and Roses*, pp. 277–8.   16 *PL* Davis, I, nos. 315, 316, 383, Castor, *Blood and Roses*, p. 278.   17 *CSPM*, no. 366.   18 Pollard, *North-Eastern England*, p. 236; Macdougall, *James III*, pp. 128–9, 159–63; Grant, 'Richard III and Scotland', pp. 120–21; Cunningham, 'The Yorkists at war', pp. 181–4.   19 *Calendar of Documents Relating to Scotland*, IV, App. I, no. 28; Macdougall, *James III*, p. 174; Pollard, *North-Eastern England*, p. 236.   20 Palliser, 'Richard and York', pp. 62–7; Pollard, *North-Eastern England*, pp. 333–5.   21 Pollard, 'The crown and the county palatine of Durham', pp. 82–4.   22 Sutton and Visser-Fuchs, *Richard III's Books*, pp. 46–50; Hughes, ' "True ornaments . . ." ', p. 157; Ross, *Richard III*, pp. 131–2.   23 Ross, *Richard III*, pp. 134–5; Sutton, 'Curious searcher', pp. 68–9; Laynesmith, *Cecily Duchess of York*, p. 24.   24 Horrox, *Richard III*, pp. 65–6; Pollard, *North-Eastern England*, pp. 337–8.   25 Horrox, *Richard III*, p. 66.   26 Pollard, *North-Eastern England*, pp. 236, 242.   27 Pollard, *North-Eastern England*, pp. 236–43; Horrox, *Richard III*, p. 67.   28 Scofield, *LREF*, II, pp. 276, 278–83.   29 ADN B18823, 23691-2, cit. Haemers, *For the Common Good*, p. 24; Ballard and Davies, 'Étienne Fryon', pp. 245–6.   30 *Privy Purse Expenses of Elizabeth of York*, pp. 159–66; TNA E404/77/2/49, 77/1/33, 77/2/33; Scofield, *LREF*, II, pp. 284–5.   31 Scofield, *LREF*, II, p. 287.   32 McKendrick et al., *Royal Manuscripts*, no. 149, p. 414.   33 Here, I follow Ross, *Edward IV*, pp. 281–3.   34 Commynes, *Memoires* eds. Godefroy and Lenglet du Fresnoy, III, pp. 576–7; Meek, *Calais Letterbook*, p. 76.   35 Ballard and Davies, 'Étienne Fryon', p. 258.   36 *Cely Letters*, no. 45, pp. 47–8; Ross, *Edward IV*, p. 285.   37 *Acta Dominorum Consilii*, I, p. 78, cit. Cunningham, 'Yorkists at war', pp. 184–6; *CSPM*, no. 368, 29 Oct. 1480; Scofield, *LREF*, II, p. 306.   38 Virgoe, 'The benevolence of 1481', p. 33; Jurkowski, 'Parliamentary and prerogative taxation', p. 285.   39 *Lettres de Louis XI*, VII, p. 325; Meek, *Calais Letterbook*, pp. 79–80.   40 Ives, *Thomas Kebell*, p. 94; Roskell, 'William Catesby', pp. 153–7; Westervelt, 'William Lord Hastings', pp. 219–24, Appendix 1, pp. 287–9;

Calmette and Périnelle, *Louis XI*, pp. 248–50; Scofield, *LREF*, II, pp. 318–19. 41 Cunningham, 'Yorkists at war', p. 188; Richmond, 'English naval power', pp. 9–15; Scofield, *LREF*, II, p. 315. 42 Collier, *Household Books of John duke of Norfolk*, pp. 275–7. 43 Collier, *Household Books of John duke of Norfolk*, pp. 74–9, 274; Crawford, *Yorkist Lord*, pp. 93–4; Ross, *Edward IV*, p. 282; Richmond, 'English naval power', p. 10. 44 Cunningham, 'Yorkists at war', pp. 189–90; Macdougall, *James III*, pp. 177–8; Scofield, *LREF*, II, p. 316. 45 Pollard, *North-Eastern England*, pp. 237–8; Chandler, *Life of William Waynflete*, pp. 150–1. 46 *CSPV*, no. 483; Hoskins, 'Harvest fluctuations', pp. 95–8; Scofield, *LREF*, II, pp. 333–4. 47 *Foedera*, XII, pp. 46–50; Macdougall, *James III*, p. 182; Ross, *Edward IV*, p. 291. 48 *CC*, pp. 152–3; Commynes, *Memoirs* ed. Jones, p. 414; Mancini, *Usurpation*, p. 67; More, *History of King Richard III*, p. 5. 49 *CC*, pp. 152–153; Mancini, *Usurpation*, p. 67; Santiuste, '"Puttying down and rebuking of vices"', p. 139; Rawcliffe, 'More than a bedside manner', pp. 83–4; Rawcliffe, 'Consultants', p. 251; Pollard, *Edward IV*, p. 72. 50 Macdougall, *James III*, pp. 181–2. 51 *Calendar of Documents Relating to Scotland*, IV, no. 1472. 52 Cunningham, 'Yorkists at war', p. 190; Scofield, *LREF*, II, p. 320; Ross, *Edward IV*, p. 291. 53 Commynes, *Memoirs* ed. Jones, pp. 386, 393–4; Potter, *War and Government*, p. 40. Armstrong, 'The Burgundian Netherlands', p. 231; Philpot, 'Maximilian I and England', pp. 57–8. 54 TNA E404/77/3/46; Cunningham, 'Yorkists at war', p. 190; Scofield, *LREF*, II, p. 335. 55 *Issues of the Exchequer*, pp. 502–3; Macdougall, *James III*, p. 191. Dunlop, 'Aspects of Anglo-Scottish Relations', p. 73; Tucker, 'Government and Politics', pp. 367–83. 56 Scofield, *LREF*, II, pp. 337–8. 57 Cunningham, 'Yorkists at war', pp. 190–1. 58 Meek, *Calais Letterbook*, p. 81; Grummitt, 'William Hastings, and the Calais garrison', pp. 268–9; Macdougall, *James III*, p. 195. 59 Here I follow Macdougall's dating of the campaign: Macdougall, *James III*, pp. 191–200; Cunningham, 'Yorkists at war', p. 191; Scofield, *LREF*, II, pp. 344–5. 60 Cunningham, 'Yorkists at war', pp. 191–3; Macdougall, 'Richard III and James III', pp. 189–94; Scofield, *LREF*, II, pp. 345–9. 61 *CSPV*, no. 483; *Cely Letters*, no. 97. 62 Macdougall, 'Richard III and James III', p. 194; Cunningham, 'The establishment of the Tudor regime', pp. 140; Jones, 'Richard III and the Stanleys', p. 30.

17. They Have Taken Away the Rose of the World

1 *CC*, pp. 148–9; Calmette and Périnelle, *Louis XI*, p. 252, Piece Justificatif, no. 82, pp. 393–5. 2 *Cely Letters*, nos. 93, 96; Grummitt, 'William Hastings and the Calais garrison', pp. 268–9; Meek, *Calais Letterbook*, pp. 65–6. 3 *GC*, p. 147; *Cely Letters*, nos. 182 185. 4 TNA E315/486, 6, 12, 13; Ross, *Edward IV*, pp. 282, 288; Stark, 'Anglo-Burgundian Diplomacy', pp. 145–6. 5 Horrox, *Richard III*, p. 102; Westervelt, 'William Lord Hastings', pp. 149–50. 6 Richmond, '1485 and all that', pp. 181–2. 7 *Stonor Letters and Papers*, II, no. 288; Horrox, 'Caterpillars of the commonwealth?', p. 13. 8 *CPR 1467–1477*, p. 450; Ives, 'Andrew Dymmock', p. 221. 9 TNA E315/486, no. 24. 10 Ives, 'Andrew Dymmock', p. 221. 11 Scofield, *LREF*, II, pp. 351–3; Calmette and Périnelle, *Louis XI*, p. 252. 12 ADN B 18823, no. 23714, cit. Haemers and Buylaert, 'War, politics and diplomacy', p. 207. 13 TNA C81/1522/26, cit. Westervelt, 'William Lord Hastings', p. 149. 14 *GC*, pp. 228–9; Scofield, *LREF*, II, p. 413; Ross, *Edward IV*, p. 354; Tucker, 'Government and Politics', pp. 370–7. 15 TNA E404/77/3/44, 57, 59/60; McKendrick, 'Edward IV: An English Royal Collector', pp. 521–4. 16 *Three Books . . . Vergil*, p. 172. 17 *CC*, p. 149; Hughes, *Arthurian Myths*, p. 282. 18 *CC*, pp. 148–51; Mancini, *Usurpation*, pp. 58–9, 64–7. 19 Haemers and Buylaert, 'War, politics and diplomacy', pp. 211–12. 20 Haemers and Buylaert, 'War, politics and

diplomacy', pp. 211–12. 21 *Foedera*, VIII, pp. 124–5; *CC*, pp. 150–1; Mancini, *Usurpation*, pp. 58–9; Commynes, *Memoirs* ed. Jones, p. 396. 22 *CC*, pp. 150–1; STC 9176; Neville-Sington, 'Press, politics and religion', p. 577. 23 *PROME*, XIV, 1483 January, Introduction, pp. 403–4; Ives, 'Andrew Dymmock', pp. 226–7; Roskell, *The Commons and their Speakers*, pp. 271–93, 333–6; Jurkowski, 'Parliamentary and prerogative taxation', p. 286. 24 *PROME*, 1483 January, item 13 (p. 425). 25 Grant, 'Richard III and Scotland', p. 115; Ross, *Edward IV*, p. 293. 26 *RP*, VI, 168; Horrox, *Richard III*, pp. 70–2. 27 *PROME*, 1483 January, introduction, p. 406; Horrox, *Richard III*, pp. 123–7, 131–2, 207–8; Ives, 'Andrew Dymmock', p. 222. 28 Mancini, *Usurpation*, pp. 58–9; *CC*, pp. 148–9; Nichols, ed., *Grants &c*, p. xlvi; *Three Books ... Vergil*, p. 171; Santiuste, ' "Puttyng down and rebuking of vices" ', pp. 139–40. 29 *CC*, pp. 152–3. 30 Ross, *Edward IV*, pp. 414–15; Scofield, *LREF*, II, pp. 364–6. 31 *CC*, pp. 152–3; *Excerpta Historica*, pp. 366–79; Kleineke, *Edward IV*, p. 199. 32 *Registrum Thome Bourgchier*, p. 54; *CC*, pp. 150–1; Mancini, *Usurpation*, pp. 68–9. 33 *CC*, pp. 150–3. 34 *Issues of the Exchequer*, p. 505; LMA Journal 9, ff. 17–17v; Armstrong, 'Some examples of distribution and speed', p. 450; More, *History of King Richard III*, p. 9; Sutton and Hammond, eds., *Coronation of Richard III*, p. 13. 35 College of Arms MS I.7, f. 7, pr. in Sutton and Visser-Fuchs, 'Royal burials', p. 383; *LP RIII/HVII*, I, p. 4; Roskell, 'The office and dignity of protector', p. 196. 36 Richmond, 'Richard III, Richard Nixon', p. 95; Richmond, '1483', p. 44; Ross, *Richard III*, p. 66. 37 *CC*, pp. 152–3; Horrox, *Richard III*, pp. 93–4; Ross, *Richard III*, pp. 65–6; Roskell, 'Office and dignity', pp. 193–4; Rawcliffe, 'More than a bedside manner', pp. 86–7. 38 *CC*, pp. 152–3; Ross, *Richard III*, p. 67. 39 Ives, 'Andrew Dymmock', pp. 225, 228–9. 40 *CC*, pp. 154–5. 41 Westervelt, 'William Lord Hastings', p. 168. 42 TNA E405/71, rot. 6; Grummitt, 'William Hastings and the Calais garrison'. p. 269; Horrox, 'Financial memoranda of Edward V', pp. 223–5. 43 *CC*, pp. 154–5; Sutton and Visser-Fuchs, 'A "most benevolent queen" ', p. 223. 44 HMC 11th Report, III, p. 170. 45 Mancini, *Usurpation*, pp. 70–1; Armstrong, 'Some examples of distribution and speed', pp. 117–18. 46 Sutton and Visser-Fuchs, 'Royal burials', pp. 373, 383–5. 47 *LP RIII/HVII*, pp. 7–8; Tatton-Brown, 'The constructional sequence and topography', pp. 14–15; Colvin, *History of the King's Works*, II, pp. 884–8. 48 Sutton and Visser-Fuchs, 'Royal burials', pp. 377–8. 49 Crawford, *Yorkist Lord*, p. 99. 50 Sutton and Visser-Fuchs, 'Royal burials', p. 371. 51 Sutton and Visser-Fuchs, 'Laments for the death of Edward IV', pp. 516–18. 52 Vale, *Charles VII*, p. 215. 53 *CC*, pp. 154–5; *Three Books ... Vergil*, pp. 171–3, 176; Mancini, *Usurpation*, pp. 70–3; Sutton and Hammond, eds., *Coronation of Richard III*, pp. 14–15. 54 *PROME*, VI, 1377 October, Introduction, p. 2 and item 13 (p. 10). 55 Roskell, 'Office and dignity', pp. 214–15, 226–7. 56 See Roskell, 'Office and dignity', pp. 206–7, 210 for discussion of the terms of Henry V's will; Ross, *Richard III*, pp. 66–7. 57 *CC*, pp. 156–7; Mancini, *Usurpation*, pp. 70–1, 74–5, 80–1, 118–19; Horrox, 'Financial memoranda of Edward V', pp. 211, 220–21; Horrox, *Richard III*, p. 91. 58 *CC*, pp. 154–5. 59 Mancini, *Usurpation*, pp. 74–5; Hardyng, *Chronicle*, p. 475; Rawcliffe, *The Staffords*, pp. 28–9; Lowe, 'Patronage and politics', p. 563 60 *PL* Davis, II, no. 795; Hardyng, *Chronicle*, p. 475.

18. Old Royal Blood

1 'A Ballad made by Lydgate', in *A Chronicle of London*, I, p. 257; Mancini, *Usurpation*, p. 99; *Observations on the Popular Antiquities*, I; Hutton, *Stations of the Sun*, pp. 226–43; Bezella-Bond, 'Blood and roses', pp. 187–210; Sutton and Hammond, eds., *Coronation of Richard III*, p. 16; Edwards, *Itinerary*, p. 2; Hughes, *Arthurian Myths*,

p. 130. **2** For Hastings' influence in Northamptonshire, see Westervelt, 'William Lord Hastings', pp. 215–24. **3** Armstrong, 'Some examples of distribution and speed', *passim.* **4** CC, pp. 154–7; Mancini, *Usurpation*, pp. 74–83; Horrox, *Richard III*, p. 97. **5** CC, p. 155. **6** Richmond, '1483', p. 44; Ross, *Richard III*, p. 71. **7** *Three Books ... Vergil*, p. 174. **8** CPR 1476–1485, pp. 233, 241, 354, 567–8; Roskell, 'William Catesby', pp. 154–5. **9** *Three Books ... Vergil*, p. 174. **10** Mancini, *Usurpation*, p. 77; More, *A History of King Richard III*, p. 72; Santiuste, ' "Puttyng down and rebuking of vices" ', p. 139. **11** Rous, *Historia Regum Angliae*, p. 212; Mancini, *Usurpation*, p. 77; CC, p. 157; TNA SC1/45/236; *British Library Harleian MS 433*, II, p. 25; Pollard, *North-Eastern England*, p. 342. **12** CC, pp. 156–7; *PL* Davis, II, no. 795; Mancini, *Usurpation*, pp. 104–7; GC, p. 230. **13** Sutton and Hammond, eds., *Coronation of Richard III*, pp. 15–16; Mancini, *Usurpation*, pp. 81–3; GC, p. 230; CC, pp. 156–9; Horrox, *Richard III*, pp. 98–9. **14** Nichols, *Grants &c*, pp. 5–11; CPR 1476–1485, pp. 349–50; *Registrum Thome Bourgchier*, pp. 52–3. **15** Mancini, *Usurpation*, p. 106. **16** Horrox, 'Financial memoranda of Edward V', pp. 205–7, 211, 219–20 and n. 22; *PL* Davis, II, no. 796. **17** Mancini, *Usurpation*, pp. 81, 85; Horrox, *Richard III*, pp. 99–103; Richmond, 'English naval power', p. 11. **18** *British Library Harleian MS 433*, I, p. 101, III, p. 2; CPR 1476–1485, p. 514; Horrox, *Richard III*, p. 99. **19** See for example BL Harleian Ch. 58 F 49. **20** Mancini, *Usurpation*, pp. 90–3, 121; Horrox, *Richard III*, p. 121; Hicks, 'Richard III as duke of Gloucester', p. 31. **21** CC, pp. 156–7. **22** Wood, 'Richard III, Lord Hastings and Friday the Thirteenth', p. 168. **23** Nichols, *Grants &c*, p. xlix; Sutton, 'Curious searcher', pp. 60–2; Chrimes, *English Constitutional Ideas*, pp. 168–78 passim; Allmand and Keen, 'History and literature of war', pp. 98–9. For another interpretation of Russell's sermon, see Watts, ' "The Policie in Christen Remes" ', pp. 33–59. **24** Nichols, *Grants &c*, p. xlviii; Roskell, 'Office and dignity', pp. 226–7; Ross, *Richard III*, p. 79; Horrox, *Richard III*, pp. 113–14. **25** *Stonor Letters and Papers*, no. 330; Mancini, *Usurpation*, p. 124; LMA Journal 9, f. 23v; Rosemary Horrox, 'Ratcliffe, Sir Richard (d. 1485)', *ODNB*; Horrox, *Richard III*, p. 112. **26** *York Civic Records*, I, p. 75; More, *A History of King Richard III*, p. 57. **27** *Three Books ... Vergil*, pp. 179–80. **28** What follows is based on *Three Books ... Vergil*, p. 227; CC, pp. 158–9; More, *History of King Richard III*, pp. 46–9. **29** Appleby et al., 'The scoliosis of Richard III', passim. **30** GC, p. 231; Wood, 'Richard III, Lord Hastings and Friday the Thirteenth', pp. 156–61. Friday 13th is given as the date of Hastings' death in the Calais controller's account for 1482–3: TNA E101/200/1 f. 33v; Jones, 'Richard III and the Stanleys', p. 33; Cunningham, 'The establishment of the Tudor regime', p. 141. **31** Hicks, 'What might have been', passim. **32** More, *History of King Richard III*, pp. 45–6; Mancini, *Usurpation*, pp. 90–1; Roskell, 'William Catesby', pp. 156, 159–60; Horrox, *Richard III*, pp. 133–5. **33** BL Harleian Ch. 58 F 49; *Registra Abbatum monasterii Sancti Albani*, ed. Riley, II., pp. 113, 200, 266; *PROME*, XV, 1485 November, item 63 [68], pp. 219–22; Roskell, 'William Catesby', pp. 159–60. **34** Harper, 'London and the Crown', pp. 66–9; Sutton and Hammond, eds., *Coronation of Richard III*, p. 22. **35** CC, pp. 158–9; Ross, *Richard III*, p. 87. **36** CPR 1476–1485, p. 364; Horrox, *Richard III*, pp. 144–5. **37** Horrox, 'Financial memoranda of Edward V', *passim*. **38** Mancini, *Usurpation*, pp. 94–5; Sutton and Hammond, eds., *Coronation of Richard III*, p. 23; LMA Journal 9, ff. 26–26v; *Acts of Court of the Mercers*, p. 155. **39** *Stonor Letters and Papers*, no. 331. **40** *Three Books ... Vergil*, pp. 183–5; More, *History of King Richard III*, pp. 66–8; Laynesmith, *Cecily Duchess of York*, pp. 156–7; Sutton, 'Richard III's "Tytylle & Right" ', pp. 27–8. **41** Mancini, *Usurpation*, p. 99; Lancashire, *London Civic Theatre*, pp. 50–2, 153–70; Horrox, *Richard III*, p. 120; Ross, *Richard III*, p. 94. **42** Buckingham as Richard's alter ego: Horrox, *Richard III*, pp. 106–7. **43** GC, p. 232; Mancini, *Usurpation*, pp. 96–7. **44** Mancini, *Usurpation*, pp. 90–1; Sutton and Hammond, eds.,

Coronation of Richard III, p. 23; CC, pp. 160–1; *Excerpta Historica*, pp. 240–8; Horrox, *Richard III*, p. 129. **45** Mancini, *Usurpation*, p. 126; Rous, *Historia Regum Angliae*, p. 213; *GC*, p. 567; *Danse macabre: The Dance of Death*, ed. Warren; Harry, 'Earl Rivers' Cordyal', esp. pp. 382–3, 385; Pollard, *Richard III and the Princes in the Tower*, p. 135. **46** *British Library Harleian MS 433*, III, p. 29. **47** Sutton and Hammond, eds., *Coronation of Richard III*, p. 25. **48** Laynesmith, *Cecily Duchess of York*, pp. 157–8. **49** TNA C53/198, m. 1. I am grateful to Sean Cunningham for the reference; the translation is his. **50** Sutton, 'Curious searcher', pp. 61–2; Sutton, 'Chevalerie . . .', pp. 115–18. **51** *British Library Harleian MS 433*, III, pp. 28–91; Horrox, *Richard III*, p. 140. **52** *CPR 1476–1485*, pp. 358–9, 363, 365. **53** Roskell, 'William Catesby', p. 147. **54** TNA PSO 1/57/2901, 2904; *British Library Harleian MS 433*, I, p. 101; III, p. 150; *CPR 1476–1485*, p. 514; Payling, 'Widows', pp. 104, 108–12. **55** TNA LC 9/50, f. 45v; Sutton and Hammond, eds., *Coronation of Richard III*, pp. 67, 71, 73; Smith, 'John Caster', pp. 130–5. **56** Sutton and Hammond, eds., *Coronation of Richard III*, pp. 171–2. **57** Mancini, *Usurpation*, pp. 98–101; Sutton and Hammond, eds., *Coronation of Richard III*, p. 282; *BL Harleian MS 433*, III, pp. 29–30. **58** BL Add. MS 18669; Sutton and Hammond, eds., *Coronation of Richard III*, pp. 35–43. **59** Sutton and Hammond, eds., *Coronation of Richard III*, pp. 2–5; Sutton, 'Curious searcher', p. 37. **60** *A Relation . . .* ed. Sneyd, p. 44; Sutton and Hammond, eds., *Coronation of Richard III*, pp. 282–302; BL Add. MS 6113, f. 22v; College of Arms MS I, 18, f. 34v; LMA Journal 9, f. 43. **61** CC, pp. 158–9; Griffiths, 'Bishop Morton and the Ely Tower at Brecon', p. 20. **62** Sutton and Hammond, eds., *Coronation of Richard III*, pp. 271–3. **63** Sutton and Hammond, eds., *Coronation of Richard III*, pp. 167, 169, 279–81; Jones and Underwood, *The King's Mother*, p. 62. **64** Mancini, *Usurpation*, pp. 92–3; *Three Books . . . Vergil*, p. 189.

19. No Long Time in Rest

1 Edwards, *Itinerary*, p. 5; Jones and Underwood, *The King's Mother*, p. 62; Horrox, *Richard III*, p. 149. **2** *British Library MS Harleian 433*, III, pp. 34–5; *CPR 1476–1485*, p. 535; Jones, 'Richard III and Lady Margaret Beaufort', p. 30. **3** CC, p. 163; Crawford, *Yorkist Lord*, p. 119. **4** *British Library MS Harleian 433*, I, p. 87; II, pp. 4–5; *CPR 1476–1485*, p. 496; Collier, *Household Books of John duke of Norfolk*, p. 411; Edwards, *Itinerary*, p. 5; Ross, *Richard III*, p. 148. **5** TNA C 81/1392/1; Horrox, *Richard III*, pp. 149–52; Horrox, 'Richard III and London', pp. 325–6. **6** *LP WF*, II, p. 762; Horrox, *Richard III*, pp. 149–50; TNA E101/107/15, f. 18. **7** Jones and Underwood, *The King's Mother*, p. 62. **8** Hall, *Chronicle*, pp. 388–9; *Three Books . . . Vergil*, p. 195; Kibre, 'Lewis of Caerleon', pp. 100–8; Jones, 'Richard III and Lady Margaret Beaufort', p. 31; Horrox, *Richard III*, pp. 150–1. **9** Sutton, 'Curious searcher', pp. 75–7; Horrox, *Richard III*, pp. 147–9; Pollard, *Richard III and the Princes in the Tower*, p. 107. **10** CC, pp. 162–3. **11** *British Library Harleian MS 433*, II, pp. 7–9; *Three Books . . . Vergil*, p. 194; Horrox, *Richard III*, p. 150; Goodman, *Wars of the Roses*, p. 134. **12** Griffiths, 'Bishop Morton and the Ely Tower at Brecon', p. 15; Tudor-Craig, 'Richard III's triumphant entry', p. 109 and refs; Horrox, *Richard III*, p. 150. **13** More, *History of King Richard III*, pp. 82–7; Green, 'Historical notes of a London citizen', pp. 585–90; *Three Books . . . Vergil*, pp. 191–2; Pollard, *Richard III and the Princes in the Tower*, pp. 115–24; Edwards, *Itinerary*, p. 6. **14** *Three Books . . . Vergil*, pp. 189, 191–2; *GC*, p. 237. **15** *PL* Davis, II, nos. 800, 916. **16** *Three Books . . . Vergil*, pp. 195–6. **17** Griffiths, 'Bishop Morton and the Ely Tower at Brecon', pp. 20–1. **18** *Three Books . . . Vergil*, pp. 193–5. **19** *Three Books . . . Vergil*, pp. 194–7; More, *History of King*

Richard III, pp. 91–3; Griffiths, 'Bishop Morton and the Ely Tower at Brecon', p. 21.　20 *British Library Harleian MS 433*, II, p. 25; *Three Books . . . Vergil*, p. 188; Tudor-Craig, 'Richard III's triumphant entry', p. 109; Edwards, *Itinerary*, p. 6; Pollard, *Richard III and the Princes in the Tower*, p. 107; Ross, *Richard III*, p. 150.　21 Palliser, 'Richard and York', p. 57; Freedman and White, *Richard III and the City of York*, p. 8.　22 *Christ Church Letters*, p. 46; Hanham, *Richard III and his Early Historians*, p. 50; Sutton, 'Curious searcher', pp. 73–4.　23 York Minster Library, Bedern College Statute Book, p. 48, transcribed in Sutton and Hammond, *Richard III: The Road to Bosworth Field*, p. 140.　24 Sutton and Visser-Fuchs, *Richard III's Books*, pp. 132–3; Sutton and Hammond, *Richard III: The Road to Bosworth Field*, pp. 137–8.　25 *British Library Harleian MS 433*, II, pp. 49–50; Ross, *Richard III*, p. 194.　26 Davies, 'Richard III, Brittany and Henry Tudor', pp. 112–13.　27 Palliser, 'Richard and York', p. 58.　28 *Three Books . . . Vergil*, pp. 198–201.　29 TNA C81/1392/6; *CCR 1476–1485*, no. 1171 pp. 346–7.　30 *CPR 1476–1485*, pp. 465–6; Collier, *Household Books of John duke of Norfolk*, p. 465; Crawford, *Yorkist Lord*, pp. 121–2; Hanham, *The Celys and their World*, pp. 287–8; Horrox, *Richard III*, ch. 3 passim.　31 *Stonor Letters and Papers*, II, p. 163.　32 Horrox, *Richard III*, pp. 155, 158–9, 161–2, 167–8.　33 Horrox, *Richard III*, p. 300.　34 *Plumpton Letters and Papers*, pp. 60–1; *Plumpton Correspondence*, pp. 44–5.　35 *Three Books . . . Vergil*, p. 199; Horrox, *Richard III*, pp. 163–4.　36 *Foedera*, XII, pp. 204–5.　37 *Three Books . . . Vergil*, p. 199.　38 CC, pp. 164–5; *Three Books . . . Vergil*, p. 201; Griffiths and Thomas, *Making of the Tudor Dynasty*, pp. 108–11.　39 GC, pp. 234–5; CC, pp. 164–5; Horrox, *Richard III*, pp. 156–7.　40 *Three Books . . . Vergil*, p. 202; Griffiths and Thomas, *Making of the Tudor Dynasty*, pp. 112–13.　41 Arthurson and Kingswell, 'The proclamation of Henry Tudor', pp. 100–6.　42 Griffiths and Thomas, *Making of the Tudor Dynasty*, p. 115.　43 In what follows I draw on Horrox, *Richard III*, ch. 4 passim.　44 *British Library Harleian MS 433*, II, p. 76; CC, pp. 170–1; Horrox, *Richard III*, pp. 186–7.　45 *Cely Letters*, no. 201; GC, p. 235; Edwards, *Itinerary*, p. 10; Ross, *Richard III*, pp. 119–20.　46 Sutton, 'Richard III, the City of London and Southwark', passim; Horrox, *Richard III*, p. 313 and n. 184; Harper, 'London and the Crown', pp. 61–2.　47 *Three Books . . . Vergil*, p. 203.　48 Pollard, *Richard III and the Princes in the Tower*, p. 122.　49 TNA E159/260, various membranes.　50 *PROME*, XV, 1484 January, Introduction, pp. 2–3; Nichols, *Grants &c.*, p. lxi.　51 Helmholz, 'The sons of Edward IV', passim.　52 *PROME*, XV, 1484 January, item 1 [5], pp. 13–18.　53 *PROME*, XV, 1484 January, items 18 [22], pp. 58–9; 26 [30], 27 [31], 28 [32], 29 [33], 30 [34], 31 [35], pp. 66–78.　54 CC, pp. 170–71; *PROME*, XV, 1484 January, 3 [7], pp. 23–4; Helmholz, 'The sons of Edward IV', pp. 115–18.　55 *CPR 1476–1485*, pp. 402, 426, 465; Davies, 'Richard III, Brittany and Henry Tudor', p. 114.　56 *PROME*, XV, 1484 January, item 6, pp. 36–7; TNA PSO/1/57/2935.　57 *British Library Harleian MS 433*, III, p. 190; *Three Books . . . Vergil*, p. 210; Sutton and Hammond, *Richard III: The Road to Bosworth Field*, pp. 165–6; Horrox, *Richard III*, pp. 278–9.　58 CC, pp. 170–1; *PROME*, XV, 1484 January, Introduction, p. 5, item 1 [5], p. 17.

20. The Castle of Care

1 Edwards, *Itinerary*, pp. 15–16.　2 Hughes, ' "True ornaments . . ." ', pp. 134–5; *British Library Harleian MS 433*, III, pp. 59–61, 63–6; Sutton and Hammond, *Richard III: The Road to Bosworth Field*, pp. 169–70; Willis and Clark, *Architectural History of the University of Cambridge*, I , p. 472.　3 CC, p. 171.　4 Mancini, *Usurpation*, Appendix, pp. 136–8.　5 Mancini, *Usurpation*, p. 137 and n. 2. My adapted translation.　6 Sutton, 'Curious searcher', p. 72; Sutton and Visser-Fuchs, *Richard III's Books*, pp. 1–2.　7

British Library Harleian MS 433, II, p. 92; *Cely Letters*, no. 214; Hanham, *The Celys and their World*, p. 292; Davies, 'Richard III, Brittany and Henry Tudor', pp. 114–15; Ross, *Richard III*, p. 197.   8 Hanham, *The Celys and their World*, pp. 297–9; Horrox, *Richard III*, pp. 308–9.   9 Griffiths and Thomas, *Making of the Tudor Dynasty*, pp. 116–17, 122; Horrox, *Richard III*, pp. 298–9.   10 *CPR 1476–1485*, pp. 397–401.   11 Davies, 'Richard III, Brittany and Henry Tudor', p. 114; Grant, 'Richard III and Scotland', pp. 124, 135–6; Ross, *Richard III*, p. 199   12 *GC*, p. 236; Pollard, *North-Eastern England*, pp. 357–8; Horrox, *Richard III*, p. 276.   13 Horrox, *Richard III*, p. 330.   14 TNA KB 9/952/3, 9; C81/1531/58; *CPR 1476–1485*, pp. 519–20, cit. Horrox, *Richard III*, p. 276.   15 *British Library Harleian MS 433*, III, pp. 107–8, 114–15; Horrox, *Richard III*, pp. 214–19; Pollard, *North-Eastern England*, pp. 358–60; Ross, *Richard III*, pp. 168–9, 181–4.   16 TNA E404/78/2/27, 28; E404/78/3/43 (I am grateful to Sean Cunningham for these references); *CPR 1476–1485*, pp. 493–4; LMA Journal 9, f. 56; Harper, 'London and the Crown', p. 60; Davies, 'Richard III, Brittany and Henry Tudor', p. 115.   17 Rons, *Historia Regum Angliae*, p. 123; Hughes, *Religious Life of Richard III*, p. 103; Lovatt, 'A collector of apocryphal anecdotes', pp. 172–97; McKenna, 'Piety and propaganda', pp. 72–88.   18 Davies, 'Richard III, Brittany and Henry Tudor', pp. 116–17; Grant, 'Foreign affairs under Richard III', p. 125.   19 Griffiths and Thomas, *Making of the Tudor Dynasty*, pp. 123–4.   20 *Three Books . . . Vergil*, pp. 206–8; Gunn, *Henry VII's New Men*, p. 12.   21 Grant, 'Richard III and Scotland', pp. 137–45 and Appendix 4, pp. 193–200, 'Archibald Whitelaw's address to King Richard III'.   22 *British Library Harleian MS 433*, II, p. 175, III, pp. 116–20; Wolffe, *Crown Lands*, p. 63; Horrox, *Richard III*, p. 302.   23 *British Library Harleian MS 433*, III, pp. 108, 111; Horrox, *Richard III*, p. 332.   24 TNA PSO 1/58/2963, 2984; TNA C81/1392/15; *British Library Harleian MS 433*, I, p. 216; II, p. 260.   25 More, *History of King Richard III*, pp. 30–1; cf. Rosser, *Medieval Westminster*, p. 219.   26 TNA PSO 1/58/2963.   27 TNA C81/1392/17; *British Library Harleian MS 433*, II, pp. 164–5; Horrox, *Richard III*, pp. 277.   28 TNA PSO 1/58/3000.   29 TNA PSO 1/59/3009; TNA E159/262 recorda, m. 11–11d (I am grateful to Sean Cunningham for this reference).   30 *Three Books . . . Vergil*, p. 212.   31 TNA C81/1392/19; TNA C67/53, m. 6; *Three Books . . . Vergil*, pp. 208–9; Horrox, *Richard III*, pp. 278–9; Griffiths and Thomas, *Making of the Tudor Dynasty*, pp. 122–4; Ross, *Foremost Man*, pp. 82–3.   32 TNA KB9/953/2, 15, 17–18, cit. Horrox, *Richard III*, p. 278; Davies, 'Bishop John Morton', pp. 5–9.   33 *CFR 1471–1485*, pp. 276–7; Ross, *Richard III*, p. 120; Pollard, *North-Eastern England*, p. 348.   34 Horrox, 'Henry Tudor's letters', pp. 155–8; Griffiths and Thomas, *Making of the Tudor Dynasty*, p. 134.   35 *British Library Harleian MS 433*, III, pp. 124–8.   36 GC, p. 235.   37 GC, p. 236; *British Library Harleian MS 433*, II, p. 182.   38 TNA KB 9/951/28, cit. Horrox, *Richard III*, p. 297.   39 *Three Books . . . Vergil*, p. 205.   40 Lambeth Palace MS 474; Sutton and Visser-Fuchs, *Richard III's Books*, p. 50; Sutton and Visser-Fuchs, eds., *The Hours of Richard III*, pp. 7–38.   41 Sutton and Visser-Fuchs, eds., *The Hours of Richard III*, pp. 68–9, 72, 77–8.   42 Appleby et al., 'Multi-isotope analysis', pp. 238–53.   43 CC, pp. 174–5.   44 TNA C244/136/130, 132; *CPR 1476–1485*, pp. 511, 543; *Three Books . . . Vergil*, pp. 210, 213–14; Horrox, *Richard III*, pp. 293–4.   45 Ross, *Richard III*, p. 178 and n. 36.   46 Horrox, *Richard III*, p. 306.   47 Nichols, *Grants &c.*, p. xl; Horrox, *Richard III*, pp. 330–1.   48 *British Library Harleian MS 433*, III, p. 139.   49 CC, pp. 174–5; data from http://eclipse.gsfc.nasa.gov/SEsearch/SEsearchmap.php?Ecl=14850316.   50 *Three Books . . . Vergil*, p. 211; CC, pp. 174–5; Buck, *The History of King Richard the Third*, pp. 190–1.   51 CC, pp. 174–5; Horrox, *Richard III*, pp. 295–6.   52 CC, pp. 174–7; Horrox, *Richard III*, pp. 296–7, 316–17.   53 Halliwell, *Letters*, I, p. 159; *Acts of Court of the Mercers*, pp. 173–4; CC, pp. 174–7.   54 GC, p. 237; Horrox, *Richard III*, pp. 297–9; Harper, 'London and the Crown', pp. 66–9.   55 Langland, *Piers Plowman*, passus I, pp. 61–9; Sutton and Visser-Fuchs, *Richard III's Books*, pp. 274–5.   56 Edwards, *Itinerary*, p. 37; Bennett, *The Battle of Bosworth*, p. 70.   57 *British Library Harleian MS 433*, I, pp. 173, 186, 203, 271; Griffiths and Thomas, *Making of the Tudor Dynasty*, p. 141; Ross, *Richard III*, pp. 208–9.   58 Antonovics, 'Henry VII, king of England', passim.   59 Davies, 'Richard III, Brittany and Henry Tudor', pp. 119–20; Ross, *Richard III*, p. 203.   60 *British Library Harleian MS 433*, II, pp. 228–9; *CCR 1457*; Sutton and Hammond, *Richard III: Road to Bosworth Field*, p. 208.   61 CC, pp. 176–7; Davies, 'Richard III, Brittany and Henry Tudor', p. 120.   62 Ross, *Richard III*, p. 207 and refs; Horrox, *Richard III*, p. 297; Griffiths and Thomas, *Making of the Tudor Dynasty*, pp. 152–3.   63 CC, pp. 178–9; Jones, 'Richard III and the Stanleys', p. 34; Horrox, *Richard III*, pp. 321–3.   64 CC, pp. 178–9 dates the first outbreak of sweating sickness to before Tudor's arrival.   65 Blake, *Caxton's Own Prose*, p. 109; Blake, 'Caxton prepares his edition', p. 206; Weinberg, 'Caxton, Woodville, and the Prologue to the *Morte Darthur*', p. 60.   66 CC, pp. 175–9; HMC 12th Report, Rutland MSS, I, pp. 7–8.

21. A Beginning or End

1 *Extracts from the Municipal Records of York*, pp. 214–16; HMC 12th Report, Rutland MSS, I, pp. 7–8; Horrox, *Richard III*, pp. 318–19; Richmond, '1485', pp. 176–7.   2 CC, pp. 178–9; Edwards, *Itinerary*, p. 39.   3 Griffiths and Thomas, *Making of the Tudor Dynasty*, pp. 159–66; Guth, 'Richard III, Henry VII and the City', passim.   4 *Three Books ... Vergil*, p. 218.   5 *Three Books ... Vergil*, pp. 220–1; 'Bosworth Field', ll. 449–52.   6 BL Add. MS 12,060, f. 19v; Warnicke, 'Sir Ralph Bigod', pp. 299–303; Bennett, *The Battle of Bosworth*, Appendix III (e), pp. 140–41.   7 Hall, *Chronicle*, p. 419.   8 CC, p. 180–1.   9 *Three Books ... Vergil*, pp. 225–6; Entwistle, 'A Spanish account of the battle of Bosworth', pp. 34–7; Goodman and Mackay, 'A Castilian report on English affairs', pp. 92–9.   10 Jones, *Bosworth*, p. 194.   11 CC, p. 183.   12 GC, p. 238.   13 CC, pp. 184–5; *Three Books ... Vergil*, p. 226.   14 *PROME*, XV, 1485 November, item 18 (pp. 133–4); item 8 (pp. 107–8).   15 *PROME*, XV, 1485 November, Introduction, pp. 84–5; item 5 (p. 97).   16 *PROME*, XIV, 1485 November, item 9 (p. 112).

Epilogue

1 'John Rous's account of the reign of Richard III', in Hanham, *Richard III and his Early Historians*, pp. 120–24.   2 *PROME*, XV, 1487 November, item 12 (pp. 353–5).   3 Edwards, 'King Richard's tomb at Leicester', passim.   4 Hammond, 'The illegitimate children of Edward IV', p. 230; Sutton and Visser-Fuchs, 'A "most benevolent queen"', pp. 234–5.   5 Cunningham, *Henry VII*, p. 79; Laynesmith, *Cecily Duchess of York*, pp. 170–1.   6 'Ballard of Bosworth Field', l. 274 BL Add MS 45131, ff. 52v–53.   7 William Habington, *The historie of Edward the Fourth*, cit. Whittle, 'Historical Reputation of Edward the Fourth', pp. 277–88.

Bibliography

PRIMARY SOURCES

Manuscript sources

Archives Départmentales du Nord, Lille

Chambres des Comptes de Lille, Série B Archives

British Library, London

Additional: 6113, 10099, 18268A, 18669, 46455, 48031A, 48976, 48988, 54782, Ch. 19808; Cotton Julius B XI; Cotton Vespasian C XIV, C XVI; Harleian: 69, 543, 1628, 7353, Ch. 58 F 49; Royal MS 17 D xv

London Metropolitan Archives

CLA/007	Bridge House Accounts
COL/AD/01	Letter Book L
COL/CC/01/01	Journals of the Common Council, vols. 6–9

The National Archives, Kew

C47	Chancery Miscellanea
C49	Chancery and Exchequer: King's Remembrancer: Parliamentary and Council Proceedings
C53	Charter Rolls
C54	Chancery and Supreme Court of Judicature: Close Rolls
C67	Chancery: Supplementary Patent Rolls
C81	Chancery: Warrants for the Great Seal, Series I

C244   Chancery: Petty Bag Office: Files, Tower and Rolls Chapel Series, Corpus Cum Causa

DL37   Duchy of Lancaster and Palatinate of Lancaster: Chanceries: Enrolments

E28   Exchequer: Treasury of the Receipt: Council and Privy Seal Records

E101   Exchequer: King's Remembrancer: Accounts Various

E122   Exchequer: King's Remembrancer: Particulars of Customs Accounts

E159   Exchequer: King's Remembrancer: Memoranda Rolls and Enrolment Books

E160   Exchequer: King's Remembrancer: Memoranda Rolls, Loose Rotuli

E163   Exchequer: King's Remembrancer: Miscellanea of the Exchequer

E315   Court of Augmentations and Predecessors and Successors: Miscellaneous Books

E361   Exchequer: Pipe Office: Enrolled Wardrobe and Household Accounts

E403   Exchequer of Receipt: Issue Rolls and Registers

E404   Exchequer of Receipt: Warrants for Issues

E405   Exchequer of Receipt: Jornalia Rolls, Tellers Rolls, Certificate Books &c

E364   Exchequer: Pipe Office: Foreign Accounts Rolls

KB9   Court of King's Bench: Crown Side: Indictments Files, Oyer and Terminer Files and Informations Files

LC9   Lord Chamberlain's Department: Accounts and Miscellanea

PSO1   Privy Seal Office: Signet and Other Warrants for the Privy Seal, Series I

SC1   Special Collections: Ancient Correspondence of the Chancery and the Exchequer

Printed primary sources

Acta Dominorum Consilii: Acts of the Lords of Council in Civil Causes, ed. Thomas Thompson, 3 vols., Edinburgh, 1918–38.

'Actes concernant les rapports entre les Pays-Bas et la Grande Bretagne 1293–1468', ed. P. Bonenfant, *Bulletin de la Commission Royale d'Histoire* 109, Brussels, 1945, pp. 45–6.

Acts of Court of the Mercers' Company, 1453–1527, eds. L. Lyell and F. D. Watney, Cambridge, 1936.

The Babees Book . . . The Bokes of Nurture of Hugh Rhodes and John Russell, ed. F. J. Furnivall, EETS o.s. 32, London, 1868.

'Bale's Chronicle', in R. Flenley, ed., *Six Town Chronicles of England*, Oxford, 1911, pp. 114–52.

'A Brief Latin Chronicle', in J. Gairdner, ed. *Three Fifteenth-Century Chronicles*, London, 1880, pp. 164–85.

British Library Harleian Manuscript 433, ed. R. E. Horrox and P. W. Hammond, 4 vols., London, 1979–83.

Buck, George, *The History of King Richard the Third*, ed. A. N. Kincaid, repr. edn, Gloucester, 1982.

Calendar of the Charter Rolls preserved in the Public Record Office, 5 Henry VI–8 Henry VIII, A. D. 1427–1516, London, 1920.

Calendar of Close Rolls 1461–1485, 3 vols., London, 1949–54.

Calendar of Documents Relating to Scotland, ed. Joseph Bain, 4 vols., Edinburgh, 1881–8.

Calendar of Entries in the Papal Registers relating to Great Britain and Ireland. Papal Letters, vols. 1–12, London, 1893–1933.

Calendar of Letter-Books of the City of London: Letter-Book L, ed. R. R. Sharpe, London, 1912.

Calendar of the Patent Rolls preserved in the Public Record Office, 1461–1509, 5 vols., London, 1893–1916.

Calendar of Plea and Memoranda Rolls, 1324–1482, ed. A. H. Thomas and P. E. Jones, 6 vols., Cambridge, 1924–61.

Calendar of State Papers, Milan, vol. I, 1359–1618, ed. A. B. Hinds, London, 1912.

Calendar of State Papers and manuscripts relating to English affairs, existing in the archives and collections of Venice, vol. II, 1202–1529, ed. Rawdon Brown, London, 1864.

Caxton, William, *The Prologues and Epilogues of William Caxton*, ed. W. J. B. Crotch, EETS o.s. 176, London, 1928.

The Cely Letters 1472–1488, ed. A. Hanham, EETS o.s. 273, London, 1975.

Chastellain, Georges, *Oeuvres*, ed. M. le baron Kervyn de Lettenhove, Brussels, 1863–6.

Chrimes, S. B., *English Constitutional Ideas in The Fifteenth Century*, Cambridge, 1936.

Christ Church Letters: a volume of mediaeval letters, relating to the affairs of the Priory of Christ Church Canterbury, ed. J. B. Sheppard, London: Camden Society, n.s. 47 (1877).

The Chronicle of John Hardyng together with the continuation by Richard Grafton, London, 1812.

The Chronicle of John Stone, monk of Christ Church, 1415–1471, ed. W. G. Searle, Cambridge, 1902.

Chronicle of London, from 1089–1483 Written in the Fifteenth Century, from Manuscripts in the British Museum ..., ed. N. H. Nicolas and Edward Tyrrell, London, 1827, repr. 1995.

Chronicle of the Rebellion in Lincolnshire, 1470, ed. J. G. Nichols, London, 1847.

Chronicles of London, ed. C. L. Kingsford, Oxford, 1905.

Chronicles of the White Rose, ed. J. A. Giles, London, 1853.

Collection of Ordinances and Regulations for the Government of the Royal Household, London, 1790.

Collier, J. P., ed., *Household Books of John duke of Norfolk and Thomas earl of Surrey, 1481–1490*, Roxburghe Club, 1844.

The Commentaries of Pius II, tr. Florence Alden Gragg, introd. Leona C. Gabel., Northampton, Mass., 1937.

Commynes, Philippe de, *Memoirs: The Reign of Louis XI, 1461–83*, ed. and trans. M. C. E. Jones, Harmondsworth, 1972.

—— *Mémoires*, eds. Joseph Calmette and Georges Durville, 3 vols., Paris, 1923–5.

—— *Memoires*, eds. Denys Godefroy and P. N. Lenglet du Fresnoy, 4 vols., Paris, 1747.

The Coventry Leet Book, ed. M. D. Harris, EETS o.s. 134–5, 138, 146, London, 1907–13.

The Crowland Chronicle Continuations: 1459–1486, eds. N. Pronay and J. Cox, London, 1986.

The Declamacion of Noblesse, translated by John Tiptoft from the Controuersia de nobilitate of Buonaccorso da Montemagno, ed. R. J. Mitchell, London, 1938.

Dépêches des Ambassadeurs milanais en France sous Louis XI, ed. B. de Mandrot, 4 vols., Paris, 1916–23.

The Diary of Henry Machyn, citizen and merchant-taylor of London, from A. D. 1550 to A. D. 1563, ed. J. G. Nichols, Camden Society o. s. 42, London, 1848.

Dugdale, William, *Monasticum Anglicanum, or, The history of the ancient abbies*, new edn, London, 1848.

An English Chronicle of the Reigns of Richard II, Henry IV, Henry V, and Henry VI written before the year 1471, ed. J. S. Davies, Camden Society o. s. 64, London, 1856.

English Historical Documents 1327–1485, ed. A. R. Myers, London, 1969.

English Historical Documents 1485–1558, ed. C. H. Williams, London, 1967.

English Historical Literature in the Fifteenth Century, ed. C. L. Kingsford, Oxford, 1913.

Entwistle, W. J., 'A Spanish account of the battle of Bosworth, 1485', *Bulletin of Spanish Studies* 4 (1927), pp. 34–7.

Excerpta Historica, or, Illustrations of English History, ed. S. Bentley, London, 1833.

Extracts from the Municipal Records of the City of York during the reigns of Edward IV, Edward V and Richard III, ed. Robert Davies, London, 1843.

Fabyan, Robert, *The New Chronicles of England and France*, ed. Henry Ellis, London, 1811.

Foedera, Conventiones, Literae . . . inter Reges Angliae, ed. Thomas Rymer, 20 vols., London, 1704–35.

Fortescue, John, *De laudibus legum Anglie*, ed. and trans. S. B. Chrimes, Cambridge, 1942.

—— *On the laws and governance of England*, ed. Shelley Lockwood, Cambridge, 1997.

—— *The Works of Sir John Fortescue*, ed. Thomas Lord Clermont, 2 vols., London, 1869.

Furnivall, F. J., 'Recipe for Edward IV's plague medicine', *Notes and Queries* 9 (1878), p. 343.

George Ashby's Poems, ed. Mary Bateson, EETS e. s. 76, 1899.

Gilson, J. P., 'A defence of the proscription of the Yorkists in 1459', *English Historical Review* 26 (1911), pp. 512–25.

The Great Chronicle of London, eds. A. H. Thomas and I. D. Thornley, London, 1938, repr. Gloucester, 1983.

Green, R. Firth, 'Historical notes of a London citizen, 1483–1488', *English Historical Review* 96 (1981), pp. 585–90.

Hall, Edward, *Hall's Chronicle: containing the history of England*, ed. H. Ellis, London, 1809.

Halliwell, J. O., *Letters of the Kings of England*, 2 vols., London, 1848.

—— 'Observations upon . . . the Reign of King Edward the Fourth', *Archaeologia*, 29 (1842), pp. 128–30.

Hampson, R. T., *Medii Aevi Kalendarium, or, Dates, charters and customs of the middle ages*, 2 vols., London, 1841.

'Hearne's Fragment', in J. A. Giles, ed., *Chronicles of the White Rose*, London, 1853, pp. 5–34.

Henry the Sixth, a reprint of John Blacman's memoir, with translation and notes by M. R. James, Cambridge, 1919.

Hicks, Michael A., 'The last days of Elizabeth, Countess of Oxford', *English Historical Review* 103 (1988), pp. 76–95.

Historical Poems of the XIVth and XVth Centuries, ed. R. H. Robbins, New York, 1959.

Historie of the Arrivall of Edward IV in England, ed. J Bruce, Camden Society o. s. 1, 1838.

Horrox, R. E., 'Financial memoranda of the reign of Edward V', *Camden Miscellany* 29, (1987), pp. 199–224.

The Household of Edward IV: The Black Book and the Ordinance of 1478, ed. A. R. Myers, Manchester, 1959.

Illustrations of Ancient State and Chivalry, ed. W. H. Black, London, 1839.

Issues of the Exchequer, ed. Frederick Devon, London, 1837.

'John Benet's Chronicle for the years 1400 to 1462', eds. G. L. Harriss and M. A. Harriss, *Camden Miscellany* 9 (1972), pp. 151–233.

John Vale's Book see: *The Politics of Fifteenth Century England: John Vale's Book*.

Kleineke, Hannes, 'Gerard von Wesel's newsletter from England, 17 April 1471', *Ricardian* 16 (2006), pp. 66–83.

Knyghthode and Bataile, ed. Roman Dyboski and Z. M. Arend, EETS o. s. 201, 1936.

Langland, William, *Piers Plowman: A Parallel-text Edition of the A, B, C and Z Versions*, ed. A. V. C. Schmidt, 2nd edn, Kalamazoo, 2011.

Leland, John, *Joannis Lelandi antiquarii de rebus Britannis collectanea*, ed. Thomas Hearne, 6 vols., London, 1774.

Letters and Papers, Foreign and Domestic, of the Reign of Henry VIII, eds. J. S. Brewer, J. Gairdner and R. H. Brodie, 21 vols., with 2 vols. of addenda, London, 1862–1932.

Letters and Papers Illustrative of the Reigns of Richard III and Henry VII, ed. J. Gairdner, 2 vols., Rolls Series 24, 1861–3.

Letters and Papers Illustrative of the Wars of the English in France, ed. Joseph Stevenson, 3 vols., London, 1861–4.

Lettres de Louis XI, roi de France, eds. Joseph Vaesen and Etienne Charavay, 12 vols., Paris, 1883–1909.

Literae Cantuariensis: the letterbooks of the monastery of Christ Church, Canterbury, ed. J. B. Sheppard, 3 vols., London, 1887–9.

Malory, Thomas, *Works*, ed. Eugene Vinaver, 3 vols., Oxford, 1967.

Mancini, Dominic, *The Usurpation of Richard the Third*, ed. C. A. J. Armstrong, Oxford, 2nd edn, 1969.

Medici, Lorenzo de', *Lettere, 1460–1478*, ed. R. Fubini et al., Florence, 1977.

Meek, E. L., *The Calais Letterbook of William Lord Hastings*, Donington, 2017.

Mémoires du Jacques du Clerq, ed. M. Petitot, Paris 1826.

Mémoires de Jean, Sire de Haynin, 1465–1477, ed. D. D. Brouwers, 2 vols., Liège, 1905–6.

Mémoires d'Olivier de la Marche, maître d'hôtel et capitaine des gardes de Charles le Téméraire, eds. Henri Beaune and J. D'Arbaumont, 4 vols., Paris, 1888.

Mémoires de Philippe de Commynes, ed. L. M. E. Dupont, 3 vols., Paris, 1840–7.

Mémoires pour server de preuves . . . de Bretagne, ed. P. H. Morice, 3 vols., Paris, 1742–6.

Molinet, Jean, *Chroniques*, eds. O. Jodogne and G. Doutrepont, 3 vols., Brussels, 1935–7.

More, Thomas., *The History of King Richard III*, in *The Complete Works of St Thomas More*, vol. 2, New Haven, 1963.

Myers, A. R., 'The household of Queen Elizabeth Woodville', *Bulletin of the John Rylands Library* 50 (1967/8), pp. 207–36, 443–81.

Nichols, J. G., ed., *Grants &c from the Crown During the Reign of Edward the Fifth*, Camden Society o. s. 60, London, 1854.

Nicolas, N. H., ed., *Privy Purse Expenses of Elizabeth of York: Wardrobe accounts of Edward the Fourth*. London, 1830.

Observations on the Popular Antiquities of Great Britain, eds. John Brand, J. O. Halliwell-Phillipps and Henry Ellis, 3 vols., London, 1848.

Original Letters Illustrative of English History, ed. Sir H. Ellis, 1st series, 2 vols., London, 1824–7.

The Parliament Rolls of Medieval England, 1275–1504, vol. VII: Richard II, 1385–1397, ed. Chris Given-Wilson, Woodbridge, 2005.

The Parliament Rolls of Medieval England, 1275–1504, vol. IX: Henry V, 1413–1422, ed. Chris Given-Wilson, Woodbridge, 2005.

The Parliament Rolls of Medieval England, 1275–1504, vol. XII: Henry VI, 1447–1460, eds. Anne Curry and Rosemary Horrox, Woodbridge, 2005.

The Parliament Rolls of Medieval England, 1275–1504, vols. XIII–XVI, Edward IV, Henry VI, Richard III, Henry VII, 1461–1487, Woodbridge, 2005.

Paston Letters, ed. James Gairdner, 6 vols., London, 1904.

Paston Letters and Papers of the Fifteenth Century, ed. Norman Davis, 2 vols., Oxford, 1971, 1976.

Peter Idley's Instructions to his Son, ed. Charlotte d'Evelyn, Oxford, 1935.

The Plumpton Correspondence, ed. T. Stapleton, Gloucester, 1990.

The Plumpton Letters and Papers, ed. Joan Kirby, Camden Society, 5th series, 8, Cambridge, 1996.

Political Poems and Songs relating to English History, ed. Thomas Wright, 2 vols., London, 1859, 1861.

The Politics of Fifteenth Century England: John Vale's Book, eds. M. L. Kekewich, Colin Richmond, A. F. Sutton, Livia Visser-Fuchs and J. L. Watts, Stroud, 1995.

The Priory of Hexham, ed. J. Raine, 2 vols., Durham, 1864–5.

'Private indentures for life service in peace and war, 1278–1476', eds. Michael Jones and Simon Walker, *Camden Miscellany* 32 (1994), pp. 1–190.

Proceedings and Ordinances of the Privy Council of England, ed. N. H. Nicolas, 7 vols., 1834–7.

'The Record of Bluemantle Pursuivant', in C. L. Kingsford, ed., *English Historical Literature in the Fifteenth Century*, Oxford, 1913, pp. 379–88.

Records of the Borough of Nottingham, 9 vols., London and Nottingham, 1882–1956.

The Register of the Most Noble Order of the Garter, ed. J. Anstis, 2 vols., London, 1724.

Registrum abbatiae Johannis Whethamstede, ed. H. T. Riley, 2 vols., Cambridge, 1872.

Registrum Thome Bourgchier, Cantuarensis Archiepiscopi A. D. 1454–86, ed. F. R. H. du Boulay, Canterbury and York Society 54, 1957.

A Relation of the Island of England about the year 1500, ed. C. A. Sneyd, Camden Society, o. s. 37, London, 1947.

Reports of the Royal Commission on Historical Manuscripts.
   Third Report, London, 1872
   Fifth Report, London, 1876
   Eleventh Report, part III, London, 1887

Report on the Hastings Manuscripts I, London, 1928.

Report on the Manuscripts of the Duke of Rutland, I, London, 1888.

Rotuli Parliamentorum, ed. J. Strachey et al., 6 vols., London, 1767–77.

Rous, John, *Historia Regum Angliae*, Oxford, 1745.

Roye, Jean de, *Chronique Scandaleuse, 1460–1483*, ed. Bernard de Mandrot, 2 vols., Paris 1894–6.

Secretum Secretorum, nine English Versions, part I, texts, ed. M. A. Manzalaoui, EETS o. s. 276, London, 1977.

Select Cases in the Exchequer Chamber before all the Justices of England, ed. Mary Hemmant, 2 vols., Selden Society 51, 64, London, 1933–45.

'A Short English Chronicle', in J. Gairdner, ed., *Three Fifteenth-Century Chronicles*, London, 1880, pp. 1–80.

A Short Title Catalogue of Books Printed in England, Scotland and Ireland, and of English Books Printed Abroad, 1475–1640, ed. A. W. Pollard and F. S. Ferguson, rev. W. A. Jackson et al., 3 vols., London, 1976–91.

Six Town Chronicles of England, ed. R. Flenley, Oxford, 1911.

Smith, George, *The Coronation of Elizabeth Wydeville*, London, 1935.

Stephani Baluzii Tutelensis Miscellanea . . . Opera ac Studio J. D. Mansi Archiepiscopi Lucensis, I, Lucca, 1761.

The Stonor Letters and Papers, 1290–1483, ed. C. L. Kingsford, 2 vols., Camden Society, 3rd series, 29–30, London, 1919.

Sutton, A. F. and Hammond, P. W., eds., *The Coronation of Richard III: The Extant Documents*, Gloucester, 1983.

Sutton, A. F. and Visser-Fuchs, Livia, eds., *The Hours of Richard III*, Stroud, 1990.

—— 'The Entry of Queen Elizabeth Woodville over London Bridge, 24 May 1465', *Ricardian* 19 (2009), pp. 1–31.

Three Books of Polydore Vergil's English History, ed. Sir H. Ellis, Camden Society, 29, London, 1844.

Three Fifteenth-Century Chronicles, ed. James Gairdner, Camden Society n. s. 28, London, 1880.

The Travels of Leo von Rozmital, 1465–1467, trans. and ed. Malcolm Letts, Cambridge, 1957.

Twenty-Six Political and other Poems, ed. Josef Kail, EETS o. s. 124, London, 1904.

Virgoe, Roger, 'Some Ancient Indictments in the King's Bench referring to Kent, 1450–52', in F. R. H. DuBoulay, *Documents Illustrative of Medieval Kentish Society*, Kent Record Society 18, Ashford, 1964, pp. 214–65.

Warkworth, John, *A Chronicle of the First Thirteen Years of the Reign of King Edward IV*, ed. J. O. Halliwell, Camden Society o. s. 10, London, 1839.

Wavrin, Jean, *Anciennes Chroniques d'Angleterre*, ed. L. M. E. Dupont, 3 vols., Paris, 1858–1863.

Weiss, R., 'A letter-preface of John Free to John Tiptoft, Earl of Worcester', *Bodleian Library Record* 8 (1935), pp. 101–3.

'William Gregory's Chronicle of London', in James Gairdner, ed., *The Historical Collections of a Citizen of London in the Fifteenth Century*, Camden Society n. s. 18, London, 1876, pp. 55–239.

Worcester, William, *Itineraries [of] William Worcestre*, ed. John Harvey, Oxford, 1969.

York Civic Records, vol. I, ed. A. Raine, Yorkshire Archaeological Society, record series 98, 1938.

Secondary Sources

Allan, A. R., 'Political Propaganda Employed by the House of York in England in the Mid-fifteenth Century, 1450–1471', Ph.D. dis., University of Wales, Swansea, 1982.

—— 'Yorkist propaganda: pedigree, prophecy and the "British history" in the reign of Edward IV', in C. D. Ross, ed., *Patronage, Pedigree and Power in Later Medieval England*, Gloucester, 1979, pp. 171–92.

Allen, Martin, *Mints and Money in Medieval England*, Cambridge, 2012.

Allen, P. S., 'Bishop Shirwood of Durham and his library', *English Historical Review* 25 (1910), pp. 445–56.

Allmand, C. T. and Keen, M. H., 'History and the literature of war: the *Boke of Noblesse* of William Worcester', in C. T. Allmand, ed., *War, Government and Power in Late Medieval France*, Liverpool, 2000, pp. 92–105.

Anglo, Sydney, 'Anglo-Burgundian feats of arms (1467)', *Guildhall Miscellany* 2 (1965), pp. 271–83.

—— 'Financial and heraldic records of the English tournament', *Journal of the Society of Archivists* 2 (1960/64), pp. 183–95.

Antonovics, 'Henry VII, king of England, by the grace of Charles VIII of France', in R. A. Griffiths and J. W. Sherborne, eds., *Kings and Nobles in the Later Middle Ages*, Gloucester, 1986.

Appleby, Jo et al., 'Multi-isotope analysis demonstrates significant lifestyle changes in Richard III', *Medieval Archaeology* (2017), pp. 238–53.

—— 'Perimortem trauma in King Richard III: a skeletal analysis', *Lancet* 385 (2015), pp. 253–9.

—— 'The scoliosis of Richard III, last Plantagenet king of England: diagnosis and clinical significance', *Lancet* 383 (2014), p. 1944.

Archer, Rowena E. and Walker, Simon K., *Rulers and Ruled in Late Medieval England*, London, 1995.

Armstrong, C. A. J., 'The Burgundian Netherlands, 1477–1521', in G. R. Potter, *The Renaissance, 1493–1520*, Cambridge, 1957, pp. 224–58.

—— 'L'Échange culturel entre les cours d'Angleterre et de Bourgogne à l'époque de Charles le Téméraire', in idem, *England, France and Burgundy in the Fifteenth Century*, London, 1983, pp. 403–17.

—— 'The inauguration ceremonies of the Yorkist kings and their title to the throne', in idem, *England, France and Burgundy in the Fifteenth Century*, London, 1983, pp. 73–95.

—— 'La politique matrimoniale des ducs de Bourgogne de la maison de Valois', in ibid., pp. 237–342.

'Politics and the Battle of St Albans, 1455', *Bulletin of the Institute of Historical Research* 33 (1960), pp. 1–72.

—— 'Some examples of the distribution and speed of news in England at the time of the Wars of the Roses', in ibid, pp. 97–122.

Arthurson, Ian and Kingswell, N., 'The proclamation of Henry Tudor as king of England', *Historical Research* 83 (1990), pp. 100–6.

Ashdown-Hill, John, 'The execution of the earl of Desmond', *Ricardian* 15 (2005), pp. 70–93.

Backhouse, Janet, 'Founders of the Royal Library: Edward IV and Henry VII as collectors of illuminated manuscripts', in D. Williams, ed., *England in the Fifteenth Century. Proceedings of the 1986 Harlaxton Symposium*, Woodbridge, 1987, pp. 23–41.

Ballard, Mark H. A., 'Anglo-Burgundian Relations (1446–1472)', unpubl. dis., University of Oxford, 1992.

—— 'An expedition of archers to Liège in 1467, and the Anglo-Burgundian marriage alliance', *Nottingham Medieval Studies* 34 (1990), pp. 152–74.

—— ' "Du sang de Lancastre je suis extrait . . ." Did Charles the Bold remain a loyal Lancastrian?' in Jean-Marie Cauchies, ed., *L'Angleterre et les pays bourguignons*, Neuchâtel, 1995, pp. 83–90.

Ballard, Mark H. A. and Davies, C. S. L., 'Étienne Fryon: Burgundian agent, English royal secretary and "principal counsellor" to Perkin Warbeck', *Historical Research* 62 (1989), pp. 245–59.

Barber, Richard, 'Malory's "Le morte Darthur" and court culture under Edward IV', *Arthurian Literature* 12 (1993), pp. 133–55.

Barber, Richard and Juliet Barker, *Tournaments: Jousts, Chivalry and Pageants in the Middle Ages*, Woodbridge, 1989.

Barron, Caroline, 'Chivalry, Pageantry and Merchant Culture in Medieval London', in Peter Coss and Maurice Keen, eds., *Heraldry, Pageantry and Social Display in Medieval England*, Woodbridge, 2002, pp. 219–42.

—— 'London and the crown 1451–61', in J. R. L. Highfield and Robin Jeffs, *The Crown and Local Communities in England and France in the Fifteenth Century*, Glasgow, 1981, pp. 88–109.

Bellamy, J. G., 'Justice under the Yorkist kings', *American Journal of Legal History* 9 (1965), pp. 135–55.

—— *The Law of Treason in England in the Later Middle Ages*, London, 1973.

Bennett, J.W., 'The Medieval Loveday', *Speculum* 33 (1958), pp. 351–70.

Bennett, Michael J., *The Battle of Bosworth*, Gloucester, 1985.

—— 'Memoir of a yeoman in the service of the house of York, 1452-61', *Ricardian*, 8 (1989), pp. 259–64.

Bezella-Bond, Karen Jean, 'Blood and roses: maytime and revival in the "Morte Darthur"', in Douglas L. Biggs et al., *Reputation and Representation in Fifteenth-century Europe*, Leiden, 2004, pp. 187–210.

Bittmann, Karl, 'La campagne Lancastrienne de 1463', *Revue Belge de philologie et d'histoire* 26 (1948), pp. 1059–83.

Blades, William, *The Life and Typography of William Caxton, England's First Printer*, London, 1887.

Blake, N. F., *Caxton and His World*, London, 1969.

—— *Caxton's Own Prose*, London, 1973.

—— 'Caxton prepares his edition of the Morte Darthur', in idem, *William Caxton and English Literary Culture*, London, 1991, pp. 199–211.

Blockmans, W. P. and Prevenier, Walter, *The Promised Lands: The Low Countries under Burgundian Rule, 1369–1530*, Philadelphia, 1999.

Bolton, James L., 'The city and the crown', *London Journal* 12 (1986), pp. 11–24.

—— *The Medieval English Economy, 1150–1500*, London, 1980.

—— 'Warwick, Clarence and London', unpubl. paper.

Booth, Peter W. N., 'Landed Society in Cumberland and Westmorland c. 1440–1485', D.Phil.dis., University of Leicester, 1997.

Britnell, Richard Hugh, 'Richard, duke of Gloucester, and the death of Thomas Fauconberg', *Ricardian*, 10 (1995), pp. 174–84.

Brondarbit, Alex, 'The Allocation of Power: The Ruling Elite of Edward IV, 1461–1483', D.Phil. dis., University of Winchester, 2015.

Brown, Andrew, 'Exit ceremonies in Burgundian Bruges', in Anne van Oosterwijk et al., *Staging the Court of Burgundy*, Turnhout, 2011, pp. 113–20.

Calmette, Joseph and Périnelle, Georges, *Louis XI et l'Angleterre (1461–1483)*, Paris, 1930.

Carpenter, Christine, 'The Beauchamp affinity: a study of bastard feudalism at work', *English Historical Review* 95 (1980), pp. 514–32.

—— 'The duke of Clarence and the Midlands: a study in the interplay of local and national politics', *Midland History* 11 (1986), pp. 23–48.

—— *Locality and Polity: A Study of Warwickshire Landed Society, 1401–1499*, Cambridge, 1992.

—— 'Sir Thomas Malory and fifteenth-century local politics', *Bulletin of the Institute of Historical Research* 53 (1980), pp. 31–43.

—— 'The Stonor circle in the fifteenth century', in Rowena E. Archer and Simon K. Walker, *Rulers and Ruled in Late Medieval England*, London, 1995.

Carus-Wilson, E. M. and Coleman, O., *England's Export Trade, 1275–1547*, Oxford, 1963.

Castor, Helen, *Blood and Roses. The Paston Family in the Fifteenth Century*, London, 2004.

Challis, Christopher E., *A New History of the Royal Mint*, Cambridge, 1992.

Chamberlayne, Joanna L., 'Crowns and virgins: queenmaking during the Wars of the Roses', in Katherine J. Lewis and Kim Marie Phillips, eds., *Young Medieval Women*, Stroud, 1999, pp. 47–68.

Chambers, E. K., *The Medieval Stage*, 2 vols., Oxford, 1903.

Chandler, Richard, *The Life of William Waynflete, Bishop of Winchester*, London, 1811.

Christiansen, C. Paul, *A Directory of London Stationers and Book Artisans, 1300–1500*, New York, 1990.

—— 'Evidence for the study of London's late medieval manuscript-book trade', in Jeremy Griffiths and Derek Pearsall, eds., *Book Production and Publishing in Britain*, Cambridge, 1989, pp. 87–108.

Clark, Linda, 'The benefits and burdens of office: Henry Bourchier (1408–83), Viscount Bourgchier and earl of Essex, and the treasurership of the Exchequer', in Michael A. Hicks, ed., *Profit, Piety and the Professions in Later Medieval England*, Gloucester, 1990.

Clough, Cecil H., 'The relations between the English and Urbino courts', in idem, *The Duchy of Urbino in the Renaissance*, London, 1981, pp. 202–18.

Cobb, H. S., *The Overseas Trade of London: Exchequer Customs Accounts, 1480–1*, London, 1990.

Colvin, H. M., *The History of the King's Works. Vols. I–II: The Middle Ages*, London, 1963.

Cowley, C. J., 'Urban Capital and Urban Power Structures in the Reign of Edward IV', M.Stud. dis., University of Oxford, 2007.

Crawford, Anne, *A Yorkist Lord: John Howard, Duke of Norfolk, c.1425–1485*, London, 2010.

Cripps-Day, Francis H., *The History of the Tournament in England and in France*, New York, 1918.

Cron, B. M., 'Margaret of Anjou and the Lancastrian march on London', *Ricardian*, 11 (1999), pp. 590–615.

Cunningham, Sean, 'The Establishment of the Tudor Regime: Henry VII, Rebellion, and the Financial Control of the Aristocracy, 1485–1509', D.Phil. dis., University of Lancaster, 1995.

—— *Henry VII*, London, 2007.

—— 'The Yorkists at war: military leadership in the English war with Scotland, 1480–82', in Hannes Kleineke and Christian Steer, eds., *The Yorkist Age: Proceedings of the 2011 Harlaxton Symposium*, Donington, 2013.

Davies, C. S. L., 'Bishop John Morton, the Holy See and the Accession of Henry VII', *English Historical Review* 102 (1987), pp. 2–30.

—— 'Richard III, Brittany and Henry Tudor, 1483–1485', *Nottingham Medieval Studies* 37 (1993), pp. 110–26.

Devine, Melanie J., 'The lordship of Richmond in the later middle ages', in Michael C. Prestwich, ed., *Liberties and Identities in the Medieval British Isles*, Woodbridge, 2008, pp. 98–110.

Dillon, H. A., 'On a manuscript collection of ordinances of chivalry of the fifteenth century, belonging to Lord Hastings', *Archaeologia* 57 (1900–1), pp. 29–70.

Dockray, Keith R., 'The battle of Wakefield and the Wars of the Roses, *Ricardian* 9 (1992), pp. 238–56.

—— 'The Yorkshire rebellions of 1469', *Ricardian* 6 (1983), pp. 246–57.

—— 'Edward IV: playboy or politician?', *Ricardian* 10 (1995), pp. 306–22.

Duffy, Eamon, *The Stripping of the Altars: Traditional Religion in England, c.1400 – c.1580*, London, 1992.

Dunham, W. H., *Lord Hastings' Indentured Retainers, 1461–1483*, New Haven, 1970.

Dunlop, Annie I., *The Life and Times of James Kennedy, Bishop of St Andrews*, Edinburgh, 1950.

Dunlop David, 'Aspects of Anglo-Scottish relations from 1471 to 1513', D.Phil. dis., University of Liverpool, 1988.

—— 'The Redresses and Reparations of Attemptates: Alexander Legh's instructions from Edward IV, March–April 1475, *Historical Research* 63 (1990), pp. 340–53.

Edwards, James Frederick, 'The Transport System of Medieval England and Wales – A Geographical Synthesis', D.Phil. dis., University of Salford, 1987.

Edwards, Rhoda, *The Itinerary of Richard III, 1483–1485*, London, 1983.

—— 'King Richard's tomb at Leicester', *Ricardian* 3 (1975), pp. 8–9.

Emerson, Catherine, *Oliver de la Marche and the Rhetoric of Fifteenth-century Historiography*, Woodbridge, 2004.

Emery, Anthony, *Greater Medieval Houses of England and Wales, 1300–1500*, 3 vols., Cambridge, 2000–6.

Evans, Howell T., *Wales and the Wars of the Roses*, Cambridge, 1915.

Falvey, Conor, 'The Marriage of Edward IV and Elizabeth Woodville: A New Italian Source', English Historical Review, 76 (1961), pp. 660–72

Falvey, Heather, 'The More: Archbishop George Neville's palace in Rickmansworth, Hertfordshire', *Ricardian* 9 (1992), pp. 290–302.

Field, P. J. C., 'The last years of Sir Thomas Malory', *Bulletin of the John Rylands Library* 64 (1981/2), pp. 433–56.

—— *The Life and Times of Sir Thomas Malory*, Cambridge, 1993.

Fiorato, V. et al., *Blood Red Roses: The Archaeology of a Mass Grave from the Battle of Towton, A.D. 1461*, Oxford, 2000.

Fleming, P. W., 'The battles of Mortimer's Cross and second St Albans: the regional dimension', in Linda Clark, ed., *Essays Presented to Michael Hicks: The Fifteenth Century XIV*, Woodbridge, 2015.

—— *Coventry and the Wars of the Roses*, Coventry, 2011.

—— 'The Hautes and their "circle": culture and the English gentry', in D. Williams, ed., *England in the Fifteenth Century*, Woodbridge, 1987.

—— 'Time, space and power in later medieval Bristol', University of West of England, 2013.

Fox, Peter, ed., *Cambridge University Library: The Great Collections*, Cambridge, 1998.

Freedman, R. and White, E., *Richard III and the City of York*, York, 1983.

Getz, F. M., *Medicine in the English Middle Ages*, Princeton, 1983.

Gillingham, John, *The Wars of the Roses. Peace and Conflict in Fifteenth Century England*, London, 1981.

Given-Wilson, Chris, *Chronicles: The Writing of History in Medieval England*, London, 2007.

—— 'The chronicles of the Mortimer family, c.1250–1450', in R. Eales and S. Tyas, eds., *Family and Dynasty in Late Medieval England: Proceedings of the 1997 Harlaxton Symposium*, Donington, 2003, pp. 67–86.

—— 'The merger of Edward III's and Queen Philippa's households, 1360–69', *Bulletin of the Institute of Historical Research* 51 (1978), pp. 183–6.

Goodman, Anthony E., 'The Anglo-Scottish Marches in the fifteenth century: a frontier society', in R. A. Mason, ed., *Scotland and England, 1286–1815* (Edinburgh, 1987), pp. 18–33.

—— *The Wars of the Roses: Military Activity and English Society (1452–1497)*, London, 1981.

Goodman, Anthony E. and Mackay, Angus, 'A Castilian report on English affairs, 1486', *English Historical Review* 88 (1973), pp. 92–9.

Goodwin, George, *Fatal Colours: The Battle of Towton, 1461*, London, 2011.

Goossenaerts, Jonas, 'Charles the Bold's ten days of marriage celebration', in Anne van Oosterwijk et al., *Staging the Court of Burgundy*, Turnhout, 2011, pp. 97–104.

Gottfried, Robert S., 'Population, plague and the sweating sickness; demographic movements in late fifteenth-century England', *Journal of British Studies* 17 (1977), pp. 12–37.

Grant, Alexander, 'Foreign affairs under Richard III', in John Gillingham, ed., *Richard III: A Medieval Kingship*, London, 1993, pp. 113–32.

—— 'Richard III and Scotland', in A. J. Pollard, ed., *The North of England in the Age of Richard III*, Stroud, 1995, pp. 115–48.

Gray, Howard L., 'English foreign trade from 1446 to 1482', in Eileen E. Power and M. M. Postan, eds., *Studies in English Trade in the Fifteenth Century*, London, 1933, pp. 1–38, 361–4, 401–6.

Griffiths, R. A., 'Bishop Morton and the Ely Tower at Brecon: documenting intrigue', *Brycheiniog* 34 (2000), pp. 13–50.

—— 'Duke Richard of York's intentions in 1450 and the origins of the Wars of the Roses', in idem, *King and Country*, pp. 277–304.

—— ' "For the myght off the lande, aftire the might off the grete lords thereof, stondith most in the kynges officers", the English crown, provinces and dominions in the fifteenth century', in Anne E. Curry and E. Matthew, eds., *Concepts and Patterns of Service in the Later Middle Ages*, Stroud, 2000, pp. 80–98.

—— *King and Country: England and Wales in the Fifteenth Century*, London, 1991.

—— 'The King's council and the first protectorate of the duke of York', in idem, *King and Country*, pp. 305–20.

—— 'Local rivalries and national politics: the Percies, the Nevilles and the duke of Exeter', in idem, *King and Country*, pp. 321–64.

—— *The Reign of Henry VI: The Exercise of Royal Authority, 1422–1461*, London, 1981.

—— 'The sense of dynasty in the reign of Henry VI', in idem, *King and Country*, pp. 83–101.

—— 'Wales and the Marches in the fifteenth century', in idem, *King and Country*, pp. 55–81.

Griffiths, R. A. and Sherborne, J. W., *Kings and Nobles in the Later Middle Ages*, Gloucester, 1986.

Griffiths, R. A. and Thomas, R. S., *The Making of the Tudor Dynasty*, Gloucester, 1981.

Gross, Anthony J., *The Dissolution of the Lancastrian Kingship: Sir John Fortescue and the Crisis of Monarchy in Fifteenth Century England*, Stamford, 1996.

Grummitt, David, *The Calais Garrison: War and Military Service in England, 1436–1558*, Woodbridge, 2008.

—— 'Deconstructing Cade's Rebellion: discourse and politics in the mid fifteenth century', in Linda Clark, ed., *The Fifteenth Century VI: Identity and Insurgency in the Late Middle Ages*, Woodbridge, 2006, pp. 107–22.

—— 'Kent and national politics, 1399–1461', in Sheila Sweetinburgh, *Later Medieval Kent, 1220–1540*, Woodbridge, 2010, pp. 235–50.

——— 'Public service, private interest and patronage in the fifteenth-century exchequer', in Linda Clark, ed., *The Fifteenth Century III: Authority and Subversion*, Woodbridge, 2003, pp. 149–62.

——— 'William, Lord Hastings, the Calais garrison and the politics of Yorkist England', *Ricardian*, 12 (2001), pp. 262–74.

Gunn, Steven J., *Henry VII's New Men and the Making of Tudor England*, Oxford, 2016.

Guth, DeLloyd J., 'Richard III, Henry VII and the City: London politics and the dun cowe', in R. A. Griffiths and J. W. Sherborne, *Kings and Nobles in the Later Middle Ages*, Gloucester, 1986, pp. 185–204.

Haemers, Jelle and Frederik Buylaert, 'War, politics and diplomacy in England, France and the Low Countries, 1475–1500: an entangled history', in Hannes Kleineke and Christian Steer, eds., *The Yorkist Age*, Donington, 2013, pp. 195–200.

Haemers, Jelle, *For the Common Good: State Power and Urban Revolts in the Reign of Mary of Burgundy* (1477–1482), Turnhout, 2009.

Hammond, Peter W., *The Battles of Barnet and Tewkesbury*, Gloucester, 1990.

——— 'The illegitimate children of Edward IV', *Ricardian* 13 (2003), pp. 229–33.

——— *Richard III and the Bosworth Campaign*, Barnsley, 2010.

——— ed., *Richard III: Lordship, Loyalty and Law*, London, 1986.

Hampton, W. E., 'Roger Wake of Blisworth', in J. Petre, ed., *Richard III: Crown and People*, London, 1985, pp. 156–61.

Hanham, Alison, *The Celys and their World: An English Merchant Family of the Fifteenth Century*, Cambridge, 1985.

——— *Richard III and his Early Historians*, Oxford, 1975.

Harper, Samantha Patricia, 'London and the Crown in the Reign of Henry VII', D.Phil. dis., University of London, 2015.

Harriss, G. L., *Shaping the Nation: England 1360–1461*, Oxford, 2005.

Harry, David, 'Learning to Die in Yorkist England: Earl Rivers' Cordyal', in Hannes Kleineke and Christian Steer, eds., *The Yorkist Age*, Donington, 2013, pp. 380–98.

Harvey, I. M. W., *Jack Cade's Rebellion of 1450*, Oxford, 1991.

Harvey, Margaret M., *England, Rome and the Papacy, 1417–1464: The Study of a Relationship*, Manchester, 1993.

Haward, Winifred I., 'Economic aspects of the Wars of the Roses in East Anglia', *English Historical Review* 41 (1926), pp. 170–89.

Head, Constance, 'Pius II and the Wars of the Roses', *Archivium Historiae Pontificiae* 8 (1970), pp. 139–78.

Hellinga, Lotte, *William Caxton and Early Printing in England*, London, 2010.

Helmholz, R. H., *Marriage Litigation in Medieval England*, Cambridge, 1974.

—— 'The sons of Edward IV: a canonical assessment of the claim that they were illegitimate', in Peter W. Hammond, ed., *Richard III: Lordship, Loyalty and Law*, London, 1986, pp. 91–103.

Hepburn, Frederick, *Portraits of the Later Plantagenets*, Woodbridge, 1986.

Hicks, Michael A., *Anne Neville: Queen to Richard III*, Stroud, 2007.

—— 'The cartulary of Richard III as duke of Gloucester in British Library Manuscript Cotton Julius B XII', in idem, *Richard III and His Rivals*, pp. 281–9.

—— 'The case of Sir Thomas Cook, 1468', in idem, *Richard III and His Rivals*, pp. 419–33.

—— 'The changing role of the Wydevilles in Yorkist politics to 1483', in idem, *Richard III and His Rivals*, pp. 209–28.

—— 'Descent, partition and extinction: the Warwick inheritance', in idem, *Richard III and His Rivals*, pp. 323–35.

'Dynastic change and northern society: the career of the fourth earl of Northumberland 1470–1489', *Northern History*, 14 (1978), pp. 78–107.

—— 'Edward IV's brief treatise and the treaty of Picquigny of 1475', *Historical Research* 83 (2010), pp. 253–65.

—— 'Edward IV, the duke of Somerset and Lancastrian loyalism in the north', in idem, *Richard III and His Rivals*, pp. 149–63.

—— *Edward V: The Prince in the Tower*, London, 2003.

—— *False, Fleeting, Perjur'd Clarence: George, Duke of Clarence*, Gloucester, 1980, rev. edn 1992.

—— 'Lord Hastings' indentured retainers?' in idem, *Richard III and His Rivals*, pp. 229–46.

—— 'Restraint, mediation and private justice: George, duke of Clarence as "good lord"', in idem, *Richard III and His Rivals*, pp. 133–48.

—— *Richard III and His Rivals*, London, 1991.

—— 'Richard III as duke of Gloucester: a study in character', in idem, *Richard III and His Rivals*, pp. 247–79.

—— 'What might have been: George Neville, duke of Bedford, 1465–83', in idem, *Richard III and His Rivals*, pp. 291–6.

—— *Warwick the Kingmaker*, Oxford, 1998.

—— 'The 1468 statute of Livery', *Historical Research*, 64 (1991), pp. 15–28.

Hoare, R. C., Benson, R. and Hatcher, H., *Old and New Sarum*, London, 1843.

Holland, P., 'Cook's case in history and myth', *Historical Research* 61 (1988), pp. 21–35.

—— 'The Lincolnshire rebellion of 1470', *English Historical Review* 103 (1988), pp. 849–69.

Holmes, George A., 'The "Libel of English Policy"', *English Historical Review* 76 (1961), pp. 193–216.

—— 'Lorenzo de' Medici's London branch', in R. H. Britnell and John Hatcher, eds., *Progress and Problems in Medieval England*, Cambridge, 1996.

Horrox, Rosemary, 'Caterpillars of the commonwealth? Courtiers in late medieval England', in Rowena E. Archer and Simon K. Walker, *Rulers and Ruled in Late Medieval England*, London, 1995, pp. 1–15.

—— 'Henry Tudor's letters to England during Richard III's reign', *Ricardian* 6 (1980), pp. 155–8.

—— 'Preparations for Edward IV's return from exile', *Ricardian* 6 (1982), pp. 124–7.

—— *Richard III: A Study of Service*, Cambridge, 1989.

—— 'Service', in idem, ed., *Fifteenth Century Attitudes*, pp. 61–78.

—— ed., *Fifteenth Century Attitudes: Perceptions of Society in Late Medieval England*, Cambridge, 1994.

—— ed., *Richard III and the North*, Hull, 1986.

—— 'Richard III and London', *Ricardian* 6 (1984), pp. 322–9.

Horrox, Rosemary and Sutton, Anne F., 'Some expenses of Richard, duke of Gloucester, 1475–1477', *Ricardian* 6 (1983), pp. 266–9.

Hoskins, W. G., 'Harvest fluctuations and English economic history, 1480–1619', *Agricultural History Review* 12 (1964), pp. 28–46.

Hounslow, Oliver, 'Scattered skeletons: an introduction to the bioarchaeology of Towton', in Hannes Kleineke and Christian Steer, eds., *The Yorkist Age: Proceedings of the 2011 Harlaxton Symposium*, Donington, 2013, pp. 164–74.

Hughes, Jonathan, *Arthurian Myths and Alchemy: The Kingship of Edward IV*, Stroud, 2002.

—— *The Religious Life of Richard III: Piety and Prayer in the North of England*, Stroud, 1997.

—— ' "True ornaments to know a holy man": northern religious life and the piety of Richard III', in A. J. Pollard, ed., *The North of England in the Age of Richard III*, Stroud, 1995, pp. 149–90.

Hutton, Ronald, *Stations of the Sun: The Ritual Year in Britain*, Oxford, 1996.

Ives, E. W., 'Andrew Dymmock and the papers of Anthony, Earl Rivers, 1482–3', *Bulletin of the Institute of Historical Research* 41 (1968), pp. 216–25.

Ives, E. W., *The Common Lawyers of Pre-Reformation England: Thomas Kebell: A Case Study*, Cambridge, 1983.

Johnson, P. A., *Duke Richard of York, 1411–1460*, Oxford, 1988.

Jones, Evan T. and Condon, Margaret M., *Cabot and Bristol's Age of Discovery: The Bristol Discovery Voyages 1480–1508*, Bristol, 2016.

Jones, Michael K., *Bosworth 1485: The Psychology of a Battle*, Stroud, 2003.

—— 'Edward IV and the Beaufort family: conciliation in early Yorkist politics', *Ricardian* 6 (1983), pp. 258–66.

—— 'Edward IV, the earl of Warwick, and the Yorkist claim to the throne', *Historical Research* 70 (1997), pp. 342–52.

—— 'Richard III and Lady Margaret Beaufort: a reassessment', in P. W. Hammond, ed., *Richard III: Lordship, Loyalty and Law*, London, 1986, pp. 25–37.

—— 'Richard III and the Stanleys', in Rosemary Horrox, ed., *Richard III and the North*, Hull 1986, pp. 27–50.

—— 'Somerset, York and the Wars of the Roses', *English Historical Review* 104 (1989), pp. 285–307.

—— '1477 – the expedition that never was: chivalric expectation in Yorkist England', *Ricardian* 12 (2001), pp. 275–92.

Jones, Michael K. and Underwood, Malcolm G., *The King's Mother: Lady Margaret Beaufort, Countess of Richmond and Derby*, Cambridge, 1992.

Jones, Peter Murray, 'Information and science', in Rosemary Horrox, ed., *Fifteenth Century Attitudes*, Cambridge, 1994, pp. 97–111.

Jurkowski, Maureen, 'Parliamentary and prerogative taxation in the reign of Edward IV', *Parliamentary History* 18 (1999), pp. 291–316.

Keen, Maurice Hugh, 'The jurisdiction and origins of the constable's court', in idem, *Nobles, Knights and Men-at-Arms in the Middle Ages*, London, 1996, pp. 135–48.

—— 'Treason trials under the law of arms', in idem, *Nobles, Knights and Men-at-Arms in the Middle Ages*, pp. 149–66.

Keir, Gillian, 'The Ecclesiastical Career of George Neville, 1432–1476', B. Litt. dis., University of Oxford, 1970.

Kekewich, Margaret, *The Good King: René of Anjou and Fifteenth Century Europe*, New York, 2008.

—— 'The Lancastrian court in exile', in *The Lancastrian Court: Proceedings of the 2001 Harlaxton Symposium*, Stamford, 2003, pp. 95–110.

—— 'The mysterious Dr Makerell: his general pardon of 27 November 1469', in Margaret Aston and Rosemary Horrox, eds., *Much Heaving and Shoving: Late Medieval Gentry and their Concerns*, Chipping, 2005, pp. 45–54.

Kelly, Henry Ansgar, 'English Kings and the Fear of Sorcery', in Medieval Studies 39 (1977), pp. 206–38.

Kibre, Pearl, 'Lewis of Caerleon, doctor of medicine, astronomer and mathematician', in idem, *Studies in Medieval Science*, London, 1984, pp. 100–8.

Kisby, Fiona L., 'The Early Tudor Royal Household Chapel, 1485–1547', D.Phil. dis., University of London, 1996.

Kleineke, Hannes, *Edward IV*, London, 2009.

Kleineke, Hannes and Steer, Christian, eds., *The Yorkist Age: Proceedings of the 2011 Harlaxton Symposium*, Donington, 2013.

Knecht, Robert J., 'The episcopate and the Wars of the Roses', *University of Birmingham Historical Journal* 6 (1957/8), pp. 108–31.

Knusel, Christopher and Anthea Boylston, 'How has the Towton project contributed to our understanding of medieval culture?' in *Blood Red Roses*, ed. V. Fiorato et al., Oxford, 2000, pp. 169–88

Kren, Thomas and McKendrick, Scot, *Illuminating the Renaissance: The triumph of Flemish Manuscript Painting in Europe*, Los Angeles, 2003.

Kronk, Gary W., *Cometography: A Catalogue of Comets* vol. 1, Cambridge, 1999.

La Roncière, Charles Bourel de, *Histoire de la Marine Française*, 6 vols., Paris, 1899–1932.

Lancashire, Anne, *London Civic Theatre: City Drama and Pageantry from Roman Times to 1558*, Cambridge, 2002.

Lander, Jack R., 'Attainder and forfeiture, 1453–1509', in idem., *Crown and Nobility, 1450–1509*, pp. 127–58.

—— *Crown and Nobility, 1450–1509*, London, 1976.

—— 'Council, administration and councillors, 1461–1485', in idem, *Crown and Nobility, 1450–1509*, pp. 191–219.

—— 'Edward IV: the modern legend and a revision', in idem, *Crown and Nobility, 1450–1509*, pp. 159–70.

—— *Government and Community: England, 1450–1509*, Cambridge, Mass., 1980.

—— 'The Hundred Years War and Edward IV's 1475 campaign in France' in idem, *Crown and Nobility, 1450–1509*, pp. 220–41.

—— 'Marriage and politics in the fifteenth century: the Nevilles and the Wydevilles', in idem, *Crown and Nobility, 1450–1509*, pp. 94–126.

—— 'The Yorkist council and administration', *English Historical Review* 73 (1958), pp. 27–46.

—— 'The treason and death of the duke of Clarence: a reinterpretation', in idem, *Crown and Nobility, 1450–1509*, pp. 242–66.

Lang, Tig, 'Medical recipes from the Yorkist court', *Ricardian* 20 (2010), pp. 94–102.

Laynesmith, Joanna L., *Cecily Duchess of York*, London, 2017.

—— *The Last Medieval Queens: English Queenship 1445–1503*, Oxford, 2004.

—— 'The piety of Cecily duchess of York: a reputation reconsidered', in Hannes Kleineke and Christian Steer, eds., *The Yorkist Age*, Donington, 2013, pp. 27–43.

—— 'Telling tales of adulterous queens in medieval England: from Olympias of Macedonia to Elizabeth Woodville', in Lynette G. Mitchell, *Every Inch a King: Comparative Studies on Kings and Kingship in the Ancient and Medieval Worlds*, Leiden, 2013, pp. 195–214.

Le Goff, Jacques, *The Birth of Europe*, Malden, 2005.

Leland, John L., 'Witchcraft and the Woodvilles: a standard medieval smear?', in Douglas L. Biggs et al., *Reputation and Representation in Fifteenth-century Europe*, Leiden, 2004, pp. 267–88.

Lester, Godfrey Allen, *Sir John Paston's 'Grete Boke': A Descriptive Catalogue, with an Introduction, of British Library MS Lansdowne 285*, Sheffield, 1982.

Lewis, Barry J., 'The battle of Edgecote or Banbury (1469) through the eyes of contemporary Welsh poets', *Journal of Medieval Military History* 9 (2011), pp. 97–117.

Lewis, Katherine J., *Kingship and Masculinity in Late Medieval England*, London, 2013.

Lloyd, T. H., *England and the German Hanse, 1157–1611*, Cambridge, 1991.

—— *The English Wool Trade in the Middle Ages*, Cambridge, 1977.

Lovatt, Roger, 'A collector of apocryphal anecdotes: John Blacman revisited', in A. J. Pollard, ed., *Property and Politics: Essays in Later Medieval English History*, Gloucester, 1984, pp. 172–97.

Lowe, D. E., 'The council of the Prince of Wales and the decline of the Herbert family during the second reign of Edward IV (1471–1483)', *Bulletin of the Board of Celtic Studies* 27 (1976–8), pp. 278–97.

—— 'Patronage and politics: Edward IV, the Wydevilles and the council of the Prince of Wales, 1471–1483', *Bulletin of the Board of Celtic Studies* 29 (1981), pp. 545–73.

Lunt, W. E., *Financial Relations of the Papacy with England, 1327–1534*, Cambridge, Mass., 1962.

MacCulloch, Diarmaid, *Reformation: Europe's House Divided, 1490–1700*, London, 2004.

Macdougall, Norman, *James III: A Political Study*, Edinburgh, 1982.

—— 'Richard III and James III: contemporary monarchs, parallel mythologies', in Peter W. Hammond, ed., *Richard III: Lordship, Loyalty and Law*, London, 1986, pp. 148–71.

McFarlane, K. B., *England in the Fifteenth Century*, London, 1981.

—— *Hans Memling*, ed., Edgar Wind with the assistance of G. L. Harriss, Oxford, 1971.

—— 'The Wars of the Roses', in idem, *England in the Fifteenth Century*, pp. 231–67.

—— 'William Worcester: a preliminary survey', in idem, *England in the Fifteenth Century*, pp. 199–224.

McKendrick, Scot, 'Edward IV: an English royal collector of Netherlandish tapestry', *Burlington Magazine*, 129 (1987), pp. 521–4.

—— 'The Roméleon and the manuscripts of Edward IV', in Nicholas J. Rogers, *England in the Fifteenth Century: Proceedings of the 1992 Harlaxton Symposium*, Stamford, 1994, pp. 149–69.

McKendrick, Scot, Lowden, John and Doyle, Kathleen, *Royal Manuscripts: The Genius of Illumination*, London, 2011.

McKendrick, Scot, 'A European Heritage: Books of Continental Origin collected by the English Royal Family from Edward III to Henry VIII', in McKendrick, Scot, John Lowden and Kathleen Doyle, eds, *Royal Manuscripts: The Genius of Illumination*, London, 2011, pp. 43–65.

McKenna, John W., 'Piety and propaganda: the cult of Henry VI', in Beryl B. Rowland, *Chaucer and Middle English Studies in Honour of Rossell Hope Robbins*, London, 1974, pp. 72–88.

Mackman, Jonathan S., 'The Lincolnshire Gentry and the Wars of the Roses', D.Phil. dis., University of York, 1999.

Mallett, Michael E., 'Anglo-Florentine commercial relations, 1465–1491', *Economic History Review* 2 (1962/3), pp. 250–65.

Matthews, Leslie G., 'Royal apothecaries of the Tudor period', *Medical History* 8 (1964), pp. 170–80.

Maurer, Helen E., *Margaret of Anjou: Queenship and Power in Late Medieval England*, Woodbridge, 2003.

Meek, Edward L. 'The Conduct and Practice of Diplomacy during the Reign of Edward IV (1461–1483)', PhD thesis, University of Cambridge, 2001.

—— 'The practice of English diplomacy in France, 1461–71', in David Grummitt, ed., *The English Experience in France: War, Diplomacy and Cultural Exchange*, Aldershot, 2002, pp. 63–84.

Mercer, Malcolm, 'Kent and national politics, 1461–1509', in Sheila Sweetinburgh, *Later Medieval Kent, 1220–1540*, Woodbridge, 2010, pp. 251–71.

Moreton, Charles, 'Anthony Woodville, Norwich, and the crisis of 1469', in Margaret Aston and Rosemary Horrox, eds., *Much Heaving and Shoving: Late Medieval Gentry and their Concerns*, Chipping, 2005, pp. 62–6.

Morgan, D. A. L., 'The house of policy: the political role of the late Planta genet household, 1422–1485', in David Starkey, D. A. L. Morgan and John Murphy, eds., *The English Court: From the Wars of the Roses to the English Civil War*, London, 1987, pp. 25–70.

—— 'The king's affinity in the polity of Yorkist England', *Transactions of the Royal Historical Society* 5 (1973), pp. 1–25.

—— 'The political afterlife of Edward III: the apotheosis of a warmonger', *English Historical Review* 112 (1997), pp. 856–81.

Munro, John H. A., *Wool, Cloth and Gold: The Struggle for Bullion in Anglo-Burgundian Trade*, Toronto, 1973.

Murray, James, *Bruges, Cradle of Capitalism, 1280–1390*, Cambridge, 2005.

Nall, Catherine, *Reading and War in Fifteenth-Century England*, Cambridge, 2012.

Neville-Sington, Pamela, 'Press, politics and religion', in Lotte Hellinga and J. B. Trapp, eds., *The Cambridge History of the Book in Britain*, Cambridge, 1999, pp. 576–607.

Nightingale, Pamela, 'A crisis of credit in the fifteenth century, or of historical interpretation?', *British Numismatic Journal* 83 (2013), pp. 149–63.

Novak, Shannon, 'Battle-related Trauma', in V. Fiorato et al., *Blood Red Roses*, Oxford, 2000, pp. 90–102.

Orme, Nicholas I., *From Childhood to Chivalry. The Education of the English Kings and Aristocracy 1066–1530*, London, 1984.

Ormrod, W. Mark, *Edward III*, London, 2011.

Otway-Ruthven, Annette J., *The King's Secretary and the Signet Office in the Fifteenth Century*, Cambridge, 1939.

Owen, H. and Blakeway, J. B., *A History of Shrewsbury*, London, 1825.

Palliser, David M., 'Richard and York', in Rosemary Horrox, ed., *Richard III and the North*, Hull, 1986, pp. 51–81.

Partington, James R., *A History of Greek Fire and Gunpowder*, New York, 1960.

Payling, Simon J., 'Edward IV and the politics of conciliation in the early 1460s', in Hannes Kleineke and Christian Steer, eds., *The Yorkist Age*, Donington, 2013, pp. 81–94.

—— 'Widows and the Wars of the Roses', in Linda Clark, ed., *Essays Presented to Michael Hicks: The Fifteenth Century XIV*, Woodbridge, 2015, pp. 103–16.

Payne, Ann and Jefferson, Lisa, 'Edward IV: the Garter and the Golden Fleece', in Pierre Cockshaw and Christiane van den Bergen-Pantens, *L'Ordre de la Toison d'Or*, Brussels, 1996, pp. 194–7.

Peyronnet, Georges, 'The distant origins of the Italian wars', in David S. H. Abulafia, ed., *The French Descent into Renaissance Italy*, Aldershot, 1995, pp. 55–70.

Philpot, R., 'Maximilian I and England, 1477–1509', D.Phil. dis., University of London, 1975.

Pilbrow, Fionn, 'Knights of the Bath: dubbing to knighthood in Lancastrian and Yorkist England', in Peter R. Coss and M. H. Keen, *Heraldry, Pageantry and Social Display in Medieval England*, Woodbridge, 2002, pp. 195–218.

Pollard, Anthony J., 'The crown and the county palatine of Durham, 1437–94', in idem, *The North of England in the Age of Richard III*, Stroud, 1995, pp. 67–87.

—— 'Dominic Mancini's account of the events of 1483', *Nottingham Medieval Studies* 38 (1994), pp. 152–63.

—— *Edward IV: The Summer King*, London, 2016.

—— 'Elizabeth Woodville and her historians', in Douglas L. Biggs et al., *Traditions and Transformations in Late Medieval England*, Leiden, 2002, pp. 145–58.

—— 'Lord FitzHugh's rising in 1470', *Bulletin of the Institute of Historical Research* 52 (1979), pp. 170–74.

—— *North-Eastern England During the Wars of the Roses*, Oxford, 1990.

—— *Richard III and the Princes in the Tower*, New York, 1991.

—— 'The Richmondshire community of gentry during the Wars of the Roses', in C. D. Ross, ed., *Patronage, Pedigree and Power in Late Medieval England*, Gloucester, 1979, pp. 37–59.

—— 'The tyranny of Richard III', *Journal of Medieval History* 3 (1977), pp. 147–65.

—— *Warwick the Kingmaker: Politics, Power and Fame*, London, 2007.

—— *Wars of the Roses*, New York, 1995.

Postan, M. M., 'The economic and political relations of England and the Hanse (1400 to 1495)', in Eileen E. Power and M. M. Postan, eds., *Studies in English Trade in the Fifteenth Century*, London, 1933, pp. 91–153.

Potter, David L., *War and Government in the French Provinces: Picardy 1470–1560*, Cambridge, 1993.

Power, Eileen E., 'The English wool trade in the reign of Edward IV', *Cambridge Historical Journal* 2 (1926/8), pp. 17–35.

Powicke, Michael R., *Military Obligation in Medieval England*, Oxford, 1962.

Prevenier, Walter and Blockmans, Wim, *The Burgundian Netherlands*, Cambridge, 1986.

Pugh, Thomas B., 'Richard Plantagenet (1411–60), duke of York, as the king's lieutenant in France and Ireland', in J. G. Rowe, ed., *Aspects of Late Medieval Government and Society*, Toronto, 1986, pp. 107–41.

Radulescu, Raluca L., *The Gentry Context for Malory's Morte Darthur*, Cambridge, 2003.

Ramsay, Nigel, 'Richard III and the office of arms', in Hannes Kleineke and Christian Steer, eds., *The Yorkist Age*, Donington, 2013, pp. 142–63.

Rastall, Richard, 'Music for a royal entry, 1474', *Musical Times* 118 (1977), pp. 463–6.

Rawcliffe, Carole, 'Consultants, careerists and conspirators: royal doctors in the time of Richard III', *Ricardian* 8 (1989), pp. 250–8.

—— 'A fifteenth-century *medicus politicus*: John Somerset, physician to Henry VI', in Hannes Kleineke, ed., *Parliament, Personalities and Power: Papers Presented to Linda S. Clark*, Woodbridge, 2011, pp. 97–120.

—— *Medicine and Society in Later Medieval England*, Stroud, 1995.

—— 'More than a bedside manner: the political status of the late medieval court physician', in Colin F. Richmond and Eileen Scarff, *St George's Chapel, Windsor, in the Late Middle Ages*, Windsor, 2001, pp. 71–91.

—— 'The profits of practice: the wealth and status of medical men in later medieval England', *Social History of Medicine* 1 (1988), pp. 61–78.

—— *The Staffords, Earls of Stafford and Dukes of Buckingham*, Cambridge, 1978.

Reddaway, T. F. 'The king's mint and exchange in London, 1343–1543', *English Historical Review* 82 (1967), pp. 1–23.

Richmond, Colin F., 'The earl of Warwick's domination of the Channel and the naval dimension to the Wars of the Roses, 1456–1460', *Southern History* 20/21 (1998/9), pp. 1–19.

—— 'English naval power in the fifteenth century', *History* 52 (1967), pp. 1–15.

—— 'Fauconberg's Kentish rising of May 1471', *English Historical Review* 85 (1970), pp. 673–92.

—— 'The nobility and the Wars of the Roses: the parliamentary session of January 1461', *Parliamentary History* 18 (1999), pp. 261–70.

—— 'Richard III, Richard Nixon and the brutality of fifteenth century politics', in Sharon D. Michalove et al., *Estrangement, Enterprise and Education in Fifteenth-Century England*, Stroud, 1998, pp. 89–106.

—— '1483: the year of decision (or taking the throne)', in John Gillingham, ed., *Richard III: A Medieval Kingship*, London, 1993, pp. 39–55.

—— '1485 and all that, or what was going on at the Battle of Bosworth?', in Peter W. Hammond, ed., *Richard III: Lordship, Loyalty and Law*, London, 1986, pp. 172–211.

Roover, Raymond de, *The Rise and Decline of the Medici Bank, 1397–1494*, Cambridge, Mass., 1963.

Roskell, J. S., *The Commons and their Speakers in English Parliaments, 1376–1523*, Manchester, 1965.

—— 'The office and dignity of protector of England, with special reference to its origins', *English Historical Review* 68 (1953), pp. 193–233.

—— 'William Catesby, counsellor to Richard III', *Bulletin of the John Rylands Library* 42 (1959/60), pp. 145–74.

Ross, C. D., *Edward IV*, London, 1974.

—— *Richard III*, London, 1981.

—— 'Some "servants and lovers" of Richard III in his youth', *Ricardian* 4 (1976), pp. 2–5.

—— 'Rumour, Propaganda and Public Opinion during the Wars of the Roses', in R. A. Griffiths, ed., *Patronage, the Crown and the Provinces in Later Medieval England*, Gloucester, 1981, pp. 15–32.

Ross, James A., 'A governing elite? The higher nobility in the Yorkist and early Tudor period', in Hannes Kleineke and Christian Steer, eds., *The Yorkist Age*, Donington, 2013, pp. 95–115.

—— *John de Vere, Thirteenth Earl of Oxford (1442–1513)*, Woodbridge, 2011.

—— 'The treatment of traitors' children and Edward IV's clemency in the 1460s', in Linda Clark, ed., *Essays Presented to Michael Hicks: The Fifteenth Century XIV*, Woodbridge, 2015, pp. 131–42.

Henry VI: A Good, Simple and Innocent Man, London, 2016.

Rosser, Gervase, *Medieval Westminster, 1200–1540*, Oxford, 1989.

Ruddock, *Italian Merchants and Shipping in Southampton, 1270–1600*, Southampton, 1951.

Santiuste, David, ' "Puttyng down and rebuking of vices": Richard III and the Proclamation for the Reform of Morals', in April Harper and Caroline V. Proctor, *Medieval Sexuality: A Casebook*, New York, 2008, pp. 135–54.

Scattergood, John, *Politics and Poetry in the Fifteenth Century*, London, 1971.

Scofield, Cora L., 'The capture of Lord Rivers and Sir Antony Woodville on 19 January 1460', *English Historical Review* 38 (1922), pp. 253–5.

—— 'The early life of John de Vere, thirteenth earl of Oxford', *English Historical Review* 29 (1914), pp. 228–47.

—— *The Life and Reign of Edward the Fourth*, 2 vols., London, 1923.

—— 'Henry, duke of Somerset, and Edward IV', *English Historical Review* 21 (1906), pp. 300–1.

Scott, James B., 'Fauconberg's Kentish Rising in 1471', *Archaeologia Cantiana*, XI (1877), pp. 359–65.

Sharpe, R. R., *London and the Kingdom*, 3 vols., London, 1894.

Smith, Robert D. and DeVries, Kelly R., *The Artillery of the Dukes of Burgundy, 1363–1477*, Rochester, 2005.

Smith, Timberlake, 'John Caster, king's skinner within the Great Wardrobe', *Ricardian* 8 (1988), pp. 130–5.

Somerville, Robert, *History of the Duchy of Lancaster, vol. I (1265–1603)*, London, 1953.

Spufford, Peter, *Handbook of Medieval Exchange*, London, 1986.

—— *Money and its Use in Medieval Europe*, Cambridge, 1988.

Staniland, Kay, 'Royal entry into the world', in D. Williams, ed., *England in the Fifteenth Century. Proceedings of the 1986 Harlaxton Symposium*, Woodbridge, 1987, pp. 297–313.

Stark, Lesley, 'Anglo-Burgundian Diplomacy, 1467–1485', M.Phil. dis., University of London, 1977.

Starkey, David, 'Which age of reform?', in Christopher Coleman and David Starkey, eds., *Revolution Reassessed: Revisions in the History of Tudor Government and Administration*, Oxford, 1986.

Steel, A. B., *The Receipt of the Exchequer, 1377–1485*, Cambridge, 1954.

Storey, R. L., *The End of the House of Lancaster*, London, 1986.

—— 'Lincolnshire and the Wars of the Roses', *Nottingham Medieval Studies* 14 (1970), pp. 64–83.

—— 'The wardens of the Marches of England towards Scotland, 1377–1489', *English Historical Review* 72 (1957), pp. 593–615.

Strickland, Matthew and Hardy, Robert, *The Great Warbow: From Hastings to the* Mary Rose, Stroud, 2005.

Strohm, Reinhard, *Music in Late Medieval Bruges*, Oxford, 1990.

Summerson, Henry R.T., 'Peacekeepers and lawbreakers in medieval Northumberland, c.1200–1500' in Liberties and identities in the British Isles, ed. M. Prestwich Woodbridge, 2008, pp. 56–76,

Sutherland, Tim, 'Recording the Grave', in V. Fiorato et al., *Blood Red Roses*, Oxford, 2000, pp. 36–44.

Sutton, Anne F., 'And to be delivered to the Lord Richard duke of Gloucester, the other brother', *Ricardian* 8 (1988), pp. 20–5.

—— 'Caxton was a mercer: his social milieu and friends', in Nicholas J. Rogers, *England in the Fifteenth Century: Proceedings of the 1992 Harlaxton Symposium*, Stamford, 1994, pp. 118–48.

—— ' "Chevalerie . . . in som partie is worthi forto be comendid, and in some part to ben amendid": chivalry and the Yorkist kings', in Colin F. Richmond and Eileen Scarff, *St George's Chapel, Windsor, in the Late Middle Ages*, Windsor, 2001, pp. 107–33.

—— ' "A curious searcher for our weal public": Richard III, piety, chivalry and the concept of the "good prince" ', in Peter W. Hammond, ed., *Richard III: Lordship, Loyalty and Law*, London, 1986, pp. 58–90.

—— *The Mercery of London: Trade, Goods and People, 1130–1578*, Aldershot, 2005.

—— 'The merchant adventurers of England: their origins and the Mercers' Company of London', *Historical Research* 76 (2002), pp. 25–46.

—— 'Richard III, the City of London and Southwark', in James Petre, ed., *Richard III: Crown and People*, Gloucester, 1985, pp. 289–95.

—— 'Richard III's "Tytylle & Right": a new discovery', *Ricardian* 4 (1977), pp. 2–8.

—— 'Sir Thomas Cook and his "troubles": an investigation', *Guildhall Studies in London History* 3 (1978), pp. 85–108.

Sutton, Anne F. and Hammond, Peter W., *Richard III: The Road to Bosworth Field*, London, 1985.

Sutton, Anne F. and Visser-Fuchs, Livia, 'Choosing a book in late fifteenth-century England and Burgundy', in Caroline M. Barron and Nigel E. Saul, *England and the Low Countries in the Late Middle Ages*, Gloucester, 1995, pp. 61–98.

—— 'The device of Queen Elizabeth Woodville: a gillyflower or pink', *Ricardian* 11 (1997), pp. 17–24.

—— 'Laments for the death of Edward IV: "it was a world to see him ride about", *Ricardian* 11 (1999), pp. 506–24.

—— 'A "most benevolent queen": Queen Elizabeth Woodville's reputation, her piety and her books', *Ricardian* 10 (1995), pp. 214–45.

—— 'The provenance of the manuscript: the lives and archive of Sir Thomas Cook and his man of affairs, John Vale', in M. L. Kekewich et al., eds., *The Politics of Fifteenth Century England: John Vale's Book*, Stroud, 1995, pp. 73–123.

—— *Richard III's Books: Ideals and Reality in the Life and Library of a Medieval Prince*, Stroud, 1997.

—— 'Richard III's books, XIII: chivalric ideals and reality', *Ricardian* 9 (1992), pp. 190–205.

—— 'Richard of Gloucester and la grosse bombarde', *Ricardian* 10 (1996), pp. 461–5.

—— 'The royal burials of the house of York at Windsor', *Ricardian* 11 (1998), pp. 366–407.

—— 'The royal burials of the house of York at Windsor: II. Princess Mary, May 1482, and Queen Elizabeth Woodville, June 1492', *Ricardian* 11 (1999), pp. 446–62.

Sutton, A. F., Visser-Fuchs, Livia and Griffiths, R. A., *The Royal Funerals of the House of York at Windsor*, London, 2005.

Sutton, Anne F. and Livia Visser-Fuchs, with P. W. Hammond, *The reburial of Richard, Duke of York, 21–30 July 1476*, London, 1996.

Tatton-Brown, Tim W. T., 'The constructional sequence and topography of the chapel and college buildings at St George's', in Colin F. Richmond and Eileen Scarff, *St George's Chapel, Windsor, in the Late Middle Ages*, Windsor, 2001, pp. 3–38.

Thielemans, Marie-Rose, *Bourgogne et Angleterre*, Brussels, 1966.

Thomas, D. H., *The Herberts of Raglan and the Battle of Edgecote 1469*, Enfield, 1994.

Thrupp, Sylvia L., *The Merchant Class of Medieval London, 1300–1500*, Ann Arbor, 1948.

Tucker, Penelope, 'Government and Politics, London, 1461–1483', D.Phil. dis., University of London, 1995.

Tudor-Craig, Pamela, *Richard III*, Ipswich, 1977.

—— 'Richard III's triumphant entry into York, August 29th, 1483', in Rosemary Horrox, ed., *Richard III and the North*, Hull, 1986, pp. 108–16.

Vale, M. G. A., 'An Anglo-Burgundian nobleman and art patron: Louis de Bruges, Lord of La Gruthuyse and earl of Winchester', in Caroline M. Barron and Nigel E. Saul, *England and the Low Countries in the Late Middle Ages*, Gloucester, 1995, pp. 115–32.

—— *Charles VII*, London, 1974.

—— *War and Chivalry: Warfare and Aristocratic Culture in England, France and Burgundy at the End of the Middle Ages*, London, 1981.

Van Praet, J., *Recherches sur Louis de Bruges*, Paris, 1831.

Vaughan, Richard, *Charles the Bold: The Last Valois Duke of Burgundy*, London, 1973.

—— *Philip the Good: The Apogee of Burgundian Power*, London, 1970.

Virgoe, Roger, 'The benevolence of 1481', *English Historical Review* 104 (1989), pp. 25–45.

Visser-Fuchs, C. T. L., 'Warwick and Wavrin; Two Case Studies on the Literary Background and Propaganda of Anglo-Burgundian Relations in the Yorkist Period', D.Phil. dis., University of London, 2002.

Visser-Fuchs, Livia, 'Edward's "memoir on paper" to Charles, duke of Burgundy', *Nottingham Medieval Studies* 36 (1992), pp. 167–227.

—— 'English events in Caspar Weinreich's Danzig chronicle, 1461–1495', *Ricardian* 7 (1986), pp. 310–20.

—— ' "Il n'a plus lion ne lieppart, qui voeulle tenir de sa part": Edward in exile, October 1470 to March 1471', in Jean-Marie Cauchies, ed., *L'Angleterre et les pays bourguignons*, Neuchâtel, 1995, pp. 91–106.

—— 'Richard in Holland, 1470–1', *Ricardian* 6 (1983), pp. 220–8.

—— 'Richard was late', *Ricardian* 11 (1999), pp. 616–19.

Wakelin, Daniel, *Humanism, Reading and English Literature, 1430–1530*, Oxford, 2007.

Walsh, Richard J., *Charles the Bold and Italy (1467–1477): Politics and Personnel*, Liverpool, 2005.

Ward, Matthew, *The Livery Collar in Late Medieval England and Wales: Politics, Identity and Affinity*, Woodbridge, 2016.

—— 'The tomb of "the Butcher": the Tiptoft monument in the presbytery of Ely Cathedral', *Church Monuments* 27 (2012), pp. 22–37.

Warnicke, Retha M., 'Sir Ralph Bigod: a loyal servant to King Richard III', *Ricardian* 6 (1984), pp. 299–303.

Watts, J. L., ' "Commonweal" and "Commonwealth": England's Monarchical Republic in the making, c 1450–c. 1530', in A. Gamberini, J. P. Genet, A. Zorzi, eds, *The Language of Political Society: Western Europe ,14th–17th Centuries*, Rome, 2011, pp.147–63.

Henry VI and the Politics of Kingship, Cambridge, 1996.

—— *The Making of Polities: Europe, 1300–1550*, Cambridge, 2009.

—— 'Polemic and politics in the 1450s', in M. L. Kekewich et al., eds., *The Politics of Fifteenth Century England: John Vale's Book*, Stroud, 1995, pp. 3–42.

—— ' "The Policie in Christen Remes": Bishop Russell's parliamentary sermons of 1483–84', in G. W. Bernard and S. J. Gunn, eds., *Authority and Consent in Tudor England*, Aldershot, 2002, pp. 33–59.

—— 'The pressure of the public on later medieval politics', in Linda Clark, ed., *The Fifteenth Century IV: Political Culture in Late Medieval Britain*, Woodbridge, 2004, pp. 159–80.

Weightman, Christine, *Margaret of York, Duchess of Burgundy, 1446–1503*, New York, 1989.

Weinberg, Carole, 'Caxton, Anthony Woodville, and the Prologue to the *Morte Darthur*', *Studies in Philology* 102 (2005), pp. 42–65.

Weiss, Roberto, *Humanism in England during the 15th Century*, Oxford, 1967.

Westervelt, Theron, 'William Lord Hastings and the Governance of Edward IV, with Special Reference to the Second Reign (1471–83)', Ph.D. thesis, University of Cambridge, 2001.

Whittle, Andrew, 'The historical reputation of Edward IV, 1461–1725', Ph. D dis., University of East Anglia, 2017.

Wickham, Glynne, *Early English Stages 1300 to 1600*, London, 1981.

Willis, Robert and Clark, J. W., *The Architectural History of the University of Cambridge*, I, Cambridge, 1886.

Wise, Terence, *Medieval Heraldry*, London, 1980.

Wolffe, B. P., *The Crown Lands, 1461 to 1536: An Aspect of Yorkist and Early Tudor Government*, London, 1970.

—— 'The management of English royal estates under the Yorkist kings', *English Historical Review* 71 (1956), pp. 1–27.

—— *The Royal Demesne in English History*, London, 1971.

Wood, C. T., 'Richard III, William Lord Hastings and Friday the Thirteenth', in R. A. Griffiths and J. W. Sherborne, eds., *Kings and Nobles in the Later Middle Ages*, Gloucester, 1986, pp. 155–68.

Woolgar, Christopher M., 'Fast and feast: conspicuous consumption and the diet of the nobility in the fifteenth century', in Michael A. Hicks, ed., *Revolution and Consumption in Late Medieval England*, Woodbridge, 2001, pp. 7–25.

Zinner, E. and Brown, E., *Regiomontanus*, I, Amsterdam, 1990.

Zippel, G., 'L'allume di Tolfa e il suo commercio', *Archivio della Societa Romana di storia patria* 30 (1907), pp. 5–52.

Index

List of Illustrations

ALSO BY
THOMAS PENN